PROGRAMMING THE
WORLD WIDE WEB

SEVENTH EDITION

PROGRAMMING THE
WORLD WIDE WEB

SEVENTH EDITION

ROBERT W. SEBESTA

University of Colorado at Colorado Springs

Boston Columbus Indianapolis New York San Francisco Upper Saddle River
Amsterdam Cape Town Dubai London Madrid Milan Munich Paris Montreal Toronto
Delhi Mexico City Sao Paulo Sydney Hong Kong Seoul Singapore Taipei Tokyo

Editorial Director: Marcia Horton
Editor in Chief: Michael Hirsch
Executive Editor: Matt Goldstein
Editorial Assistant: Emma Snider
Director of Marketing: Patrice Jones
Marketing Manager: Yez Alayan
Marketing Coordinator: Kathryn Ferranti
Director of Production: Vince O'Brien
Managing Editor: Jeff Holcomb
Production Project Manager: Kayla Smith-Tarbox
Operations Supervisor: Alan Fischer
Manufacturing Buyer: Lisa McDowell
Art Director: Anthony Gemmellaro

Manager, Visual Research: Karen Sanatar
Photo Researcher: Tim Herzog
Manager, Rights and Permissions: Michael Joyce
Text Permission Coordinators: Tracy Metevier
  and Jenn Kennett
Cover Art: © Shutterstock
Lead Media Project Manager: Daniel Sandin
Project Management and Text Design: Gillian Hall
Composition: Laserwords
Printer/Binder: Courier
Cover Printer: Courier
Text Font: JansonText

Figure 2.1: © Screenshot from http://validator.w3.org/; W3C. Reprinted with permission.
Figure 2.11: © Screenshot from http://validator.w3.org/; W3C. Reprinted with permission.
Figure 3.12: © Camerapilot | Dreamstime.com
Figure 6.4: © Gl0ck | Shutterstock.com
Figure 6.9: © Nancy Nehring | ISTOCKPHOTO
Figure 6.11: © mobil11 | Shutterstock.com
Figures 8.1–8.5, 8.8–8.14, 8.16–8.34: Adobe screenshots © 2012 by Adobe Systems Incorporated. All rights reserved. Adobe and Flash is/are either [a] registered trademark[s] or a trademark[s] of Adobe Systems Incorporated in the United States and/or other countries.
Figure 10.2: © Stephen Bonk | Shutterstock.com
Figures 11.4–11.8, 11.16–11.18: © 1997, 2011, Oracle and/or its affiliates. All rights reserved.

Library of Congress Cataloging-in-Publication Data available upon request.

10 9 8 7 6 5 4 3 2—V013—14 13 12

www.pearsonhighered.com

ISBN-10:   0-13-266581-6
ISBN-13: 978-0-13-266581-0

To Aidan

New to the Seventh Edition

- **Chapter 2**   A section on the new elements of HTML5 has been added
- **Chapter 3**   All CSS font sizes from this chapter onward have been changed from points to em
- **Chapter 5**   A discussion of the HTML5 canvas element has been added
- **Chapter 8**   Includes a new section on importing graphic figures
- **Chapter 11**   Version 7 of the NetBeans development system is now covered
- **Chapter 12**   Has been revised to discuss Visual Studio 2010
- **Chapter 13**   The discussion of the PHP/MySQL functions has been revised to reflect the new versions of these functions
- **Chapter 15**   A discussion of Rails 3.1 replaces Rails 2.4

Preface

It is difficult to overestimate the effect the World Wide Web has had on the day-to-day lives of people, at least those in the developed countries. In fewer than 20 years, we have learned to use the Web for a myriad of disparate tasks, ranging from the mundane task of shopping for airline tickets to the crucial early-morning gathering of business news for a high-stakes day trader.

The speed at which millions of Web sites appeared in the last two decades would seem to indicate that the technologies used to build them were sitting on the shelf, fully developed and ready to use, even before the Web appeared. Also, one might guess that the tens of thousands of people who built those sites were sitting around unemployed, waiting for an opportunity and already possessing the knowledge and abilities required to carry out this mammoth construction task when it appeared. Neither of these was true. The need for new technologies was quickly filled by a large number of entrepreneurs, some at existing companies and some who started new companies. A large part of the programmer need was filled, at least to the extent to which it was filled, by new programmers, some straight from high school. Many, however, were previously employed by other sectors of the software development industry. All of them had to learn to use new languages and technologies.

A visit to a bookstore, either a bricks-and-mortar store or a Web site, will turn up a large variety of books on Web technologies aimed at the practicing professional. One difficulty encountered by those teaching courses in Web programming technologies in colleges is the lack of textbooks that are targeted to their needs. Most of the books that discuss Web programming were written for professionals, rather than college students. Such books are written to fulfill the needs of professionals, which are quite different from those of college students. One major difference between an academic book and a professional book lies in the assumptions made by the author about the prior knowledge and experience of the audience. On the one hand, the backgrounds of professionals vary widely, making it difficult to assume much of anything. On the other hand, a book written for junior computer science majors can make some definite assumptions about the background of the reader.

This book is aimed at college students, not necessarily only computer science majors, but anyone who has taken at least two courses in programming. Although students are the primary target, the book is also useful for professional programmers who wish to learn Web programming.

The goal of the book is to provide the reader with a comprehensive introduction to the programming tools and skills required to build and maintain server sites on the Web. A wide variety of technologies are used in the construction of a Web site. There are now many books available for professionals that focus on these technologies. For example, there are dozens of books that specifically address only HTML. The same is true for at least a half-dozen other Web technologies. This book provides an overview of how the Web works, as well as descriptions of many of the most widely used Web technologies.

The first six editions of the book were used to teach a junior-level Web programming course at the University of Colorado at Colorado Springs. The challenge for students in the course is to learn to use several different programming languages and technologies in one semester. A heavy load of programming exercises is essential to the success of the course. Students in the course build a basic, static Web site, using only HTML as the first assignment. Throughout the remainder of the semester, they add features to their site as the new technologies are discussed in the course. Our students' prior course work in Java and data structures, as well as C and assembly language, is helpful, as is the fact that many of them have learned some HTML on their own before taking the course.

The most important prerequisite to the material of this book is a solid background in programming in some language that supports object-oriented programming. It is helpful to have some knowledge of a second programming language and a bit of UNIX, particularly if a UNIX-based Web server is used for the course. Familiarity with a second language makes learning the new languages easier.

Table of Contents

The book is organized into three parts: the introduction (Chapter 1), client-side technologies (Chapters 2–8), and server-side technologies (Chapters 9–15).

Chapter 1 lays the groundwork for the rest of the book. A few fundamentals are introduced, including the history and nature of the Internet, the World Wide Web, browsers, servers, URLs, MIME types, and HTTP. Also included in Chapter 1 are brief overviews of the most important topics of the rest of the book.

Chapter 2 provides an introduction to HTML, including images, links, lists, tables, and forms. Small examples are used to illustrate many of the HTML elements that are discussed in this chapter. A discussion of the parts of HTML5 that are now widely supported is included.

The topic of Chapter 3 is cascading style sheets, which provide the standard way of imposing style on the content specified in HTML tags. Because of the size and complexity of the topic, the chapter does not cover all of the aspects of style sheets. The topics discussed are levels of style sheets, style specification formats, selector formats, property values, and color. Among the properties covered are those for fonts, lists, and margins. Small examples are used to illustrate the subjects that are discussed.

Chapter 4 introduces the core of JavaScript, a powerful language that could be used for a variety of different applications. Our interest, of course, is its use in Web programming. Although JavaScript has become a large and complex language, we use the student's knowledge of programming in other languages to leverage the discussion, thereby providing a useful introduction to the language in a manageably small number of pages. Topics covered are the object model of JavaScript, its control statements, objects, arrays, functions, constructors, and pattern matching.

Chapter 5 discusses some of the features of JavaScript that are related to HTML documents. Included is the use of the basic and DOM 2 event and event-handling model, which can be used in conjunction with some of the elements of HTML documents. The HTML5 `canvas` element is introduced.

One of the interesting applications of JavaScript is building dynamic HTML documents with the Document Object Model (DOM). Chapter 6 provides descriptions of a collection of some of the changes that can be made to documents with the use of JavaScript and the DOM. Included are positioning elements; moving elements; changing the visibility of elements; changing the color, style, and size of text; changing the content of tags; changing the stacking order of overlapped elements; moving elements slowly; and dragging and dropping elements.

Chapter 7 presents an introduction to XML, which provides the means to design topic-specific markup languages that can be shared among users with common interests. Included are the syntax and document structure used by XML, data type definitions, namespaces, XML schemas, and the display of XML documents with both cascading style sheets and XML transformations. Also included is an introduction to Web services and XML processors.

Chapter 8 introduces the Flash authoring environment, which is used to create a wide variety of visual and audio presentations—in particular, those that include animation. A series of examples is used to illustrate the development processes, including drawing figures, creating text, using color, creating motion and shape animations, adding sound tracks to presentations, and designing components that allow the user to control the Flash movie.

Chapter 9 introduces PHP, a server-side scripting language that enjoys wide popularity, especially as a database access language for Web applications. The basics of the language are discussed, as well as the use of cookies and session tracking. The use of PHP as a Web database access language is covered in Chapter 13.

Chapter 10 introduces Ajax, the relatively recent technology that is used to build Web applications with extensive user interactions that are more efficient than those same applications if they do not use Ajax. In addition to a thorough introduction to the concept and implementation of Ajax interactions, the chapter includes discussions of return document forms, Ajax toolkits, and Ajax security. Several examples are used to illustrate approaches to using Ajax.

Java Web software is discussed in Chapter 11. The chapter introduces the mechanisms for building Java servlets and gives several examples of how servlets can be used to present interactive Web documents. The NetBeans framework is introduced and used throughout the chapter. Support for cookies in servlets is presented and illustrated with an example. Then JSP is introduced through a series of examples, including the use of code-behind files. This discussion is followed by an examination of JavaBeans and JavaServer Faces, along with examples to illustrate their use.

Chapter 12 is an introduction to ASP.NET, although it begins with a brief introduction to the .NET Framework and C#. ASP.NET Web controls and some of the events they can raise and how those events can be handled are among the topics discussed in this chapter. ASP.NET AJAX is also discussed. Finally, constructing Web services with ASP.NET is introduced. Visual Studio is introduced and used to develop all ASP.NET examples.

Chapter 13 provides an introduction to database access through the Web. This chapter includes a brief discussion of the nature of relational databases, architectures for database access, the structured query language (SQL), and the free database system MySQL. Then, three approaches to Web access to databases are discussed: using PHP, using Java JDBC, and using ASP.NET. All three are illustrated with complete examples. All of the program examples in the chapter use MySQL.

Chapter 14 introduces the Ruby programming language. Included are the scalar types and their operations, control statements, arrays, hashes, methods, classes, code blocks and iterators, and pattern matching. There is, of course, much more to Ruby, but the chapter includes sufficient material to allow the student to use Ruby for building simple programs and Rails applications.

Chapter 15 introduces the Rails framework, designed to make the construction of Web applications relatively quick and easy. Covered are simple document requests, both static and dynamic, and applications that use databases, including the use of scaffolding.

Appendix A introduces Java to those who have experience with C++ and object-oriented programming, but who do not know Java. Such students can learn enough of the language from this appendix to allow them to understand the Java applets, servlets, JSP, and JDBC that appear in this book.

Appendix B is a list of 140 named colors, along with their hexadecimal codings.

Support Materials

Supplements for the book are available at the Pearson Web site www .pearsonhighered.com/sebesta. Support materials available to all readers of this book include

- A set of lecture notes in the form of PowerPoint files. The notes were developed to be the basis for class lectures on the book material.
- Source code for examples

Additional support material, including solutions to selected exercises and figures from the book, are available only to instructors adopting this textbook for classroom use. Contact your school's Pearson Education representative for information on obtaining access to this material, or visit pearsonhighered.com.

Software Availability

Most of the software systems described in this book are available free to students. These systems include browsers that provide interpreters for JavaScript and parsers for XML. Also, PHP, Ruby, and Java language processors, as well as the Rails framework, Java class libraries to support servlets, and Java JDBC, are available and free. ASP.NET is supported by the .NET software available from Microsoft. The Visual Web Developer 2010, a noncommercial version of Visual Studio, is available free from Microsoft. A free 30-day trial version of the Flash development environment is available from Adobe.

Differences between the Sixth Edition and the Seventh Edition

The seventh edition of this book differs significantly from the sixth.

The markup documents in the whole book were modified to reflect the change from XHTML 1.0 to HTML5. However, the XHTML syntax rules are used in all example documents.

Chapter 2 was revised to update the discussion for HTML, rather than XHTML 1.0. A section was added on some of the new elements in HTML5. Sections on `align`, `valign`, `cellpadding`, and `cellspacing` were removed. W3C validation was replaced by Total Validation.

Sections on contextual selectors and text spacing were removed from Chapter 3. All CSS sizes used in this chapter (and the remainder of the book) were changed from points to `em`.

A discussion of the HTML5 `canvas` element was added to Chapter 5.

Chapter 8 was revised to cover Flash 5.5, rather than Flash 4. Also, a section on importing graphic figures was added.

Chapter 11 was revised to use version 7 of the NetBeans development system, rather than 6.7. This required numerous changes.

Chapter 12 was revised to use Visual Studio 2010.

In Chapter 13, the discussion of the PHP/MySQL functions was revised to reflect the new version of these functions. The PHP/MySQL examples also were updated to use these new functions. The section on JDBC/MySQL was updated to use NetBeans 7.

Chapter 15 was revised to discuss the use of Rails 3.1 rather than Rails 2.4. This required extensive changes. Also, the discussion of Instant Rails was dropped, as was the section on Rails with Ajax.

Throughout the book, numerous small changes were made to improve the correctness and clarity of the material.

Acknowledgments

The quality of this book was significantly improved as a result of the extensive suggestions, corrections, and comments provided by its reviewers. It was reviewed by the following individuals:

Lynn Beighley

R. Blank
CTO, Almer/Blank; Training Director,
The Rich Media Institute; Faculty,
USC Viterbi School of Engineering

Stephen Brinton
Gordon College

David Brown
Pellissippi State Technical Community
College

Barry Burd
Drew University

William Cantor
Pennsylvania State University

Dunren Che
Southern Illinois University Carbondale

Brian Chess
Fortify Software

Randy Connolly
Mount Royal University

Mark DeLuca
Pennsylvania State University

Sanjay Dhamankar
President, OMNIMA Systems, Inc.

Marty Hall

Peter S. Kimble
University of Illinois

Mark Llewellyn
University of Central Florida

Chris Love
ProfessionalASPNET.com

Gabriele Meiselwitz
Towson University

Eugene A. "Mojo" Modjeski
Rose State College

Najib Nadi
Villanova University

Russ Olsen

Jamel Schiller
University of Wisconsin—Green Bay

Stephanie Smullen
University of Tennessee at
Chattanooga

Marjan Trutschl
Louisiana State
University—Shreveport

J. Reuben Wetherbee
University of Pennsylvania

Christopher C. Whitehead
Columbus State University

Matt Goldstein, Executive Editor; Emma Snider, Editorial Assistant; Kayla Smith-Tarbox, Production Project Manager; and Yez Alayan, Marketing Manager, all deserve my gratitude for their encouragement and help in completing the manuscript. Also, thanks to Gillian Hall for managing the conversion of the collection of files I provided into a bound book.

Brief Contents

Contents

13 Database Access through the Web   569

14 Introduction to Ruby   611

15 Introduction to Rails   655

Fundamentals

The lives of most inhabitants of industrialized countries, as well as many in unindustrialized countries, have been changed forever by the advent of the World Wide Web. Although this transformation has had some downsides—for example, easier access to pornography and gambling and the ease with which people with destructive ideas can propagate those ideas to others—on balance, the changes have been enormously positive. Many use the Internet and the World Wide Web daily, communicating with friends, relatives, and business associates through e-mail and social networking sites, shopping for virtually anything that can be purchased anywhere, and digging up a limitless variety and amount of information, from movie theater show times, to hotel room prices in cities halfway around the world, to the history and characteristics of the culture of some small and obscure society. In recent years, social networking has been used effectively to organize social and political demonstrations, and even revolutions. Constructing the software and data that provide all of this information requires knowledge of several different technologies, such as markup languages and meta-markup languages, as well as programming skills in a myriad of different programming languages, some specific to the World Wide Web and some designed for general-purpose computing. This book is meant to provide the required background and a basis for acquiring the knowledge and skills necessary to build the World Wide Web sites that provide both the information users want and the advertising that pays for its presentation.

This chapter lays the groundwork for the remainder of the book. It begins with introductions to, and some history of, the Internet and the World Wide Web. Then, it discusses the purposes and some of the characteristics of Web browsers and servers. Next, it describes uniform resource locators (URLs), which specify addresses of resources available on the Web. Following this, it introduces Multipurpose Internet Mail Extensions, which define types and file name extensions for files with different kinds of contents. Next, it discusses the Hypertext Transfer Protocol (HTTP), which provides the communication interface for connections between browsers and Web servers. Finally, the chapter gives brief overviews of some of the tools commonly used by Web programmers, including HTML, XML, JavaScript, Flash, Servlets, JSP, JSF, ASP.NET, PHP, Ruby, Rails, and Ajax. They are discussed in far more detail in the remainder of the book (HTML in Chapters 2 and 3; JavaScript in Chapters 4, 5, and 6; XML in Chapter 7; Flash in Chapter 8; PHP in Chapter 9; Ajax in Chapter 10; Servlets, JSP, and JSF in Chapter 11; Ruby in Chapters 14 and 15; and Rails in Chapter 15).

1.1   A Brief Introduction to the Internet

Virtually every topic discussed in this book is related to the Internet. Therefore, we begin with a quick introduction to the Internet itself.

1.1.1   Origins

In the 1960s, the U.S. Department of Defense (DoD) became interested in developing a new large-scale computer network. The purposes of this network were communications, program sharing, and remote computer access for researchers working on defense-related contracts. One fundamental requirement was that the network be sufficiently robust so that even if some network nodes were lost to sabotage, war, or some more benign cause, the network would continue to function. The DoD's Advanced Research Projects Agency (ARPA)[1] funded the construction of the first such network, which connected about a dozen ARPA-funded research laboratories and universities. The first node of this network was established at UCLA in 1969.

Because it was funded by ARPA, the network was named ARPAnet. Despite the initial intentions, the primary early use of ARPAnet was simple text-based communications through electronic mail. Because ARPAnet was available only to laboratories and universities that conducted ARPA-funded research, the great

---

1. ARPA was renamed Defense Advanced Research Projects Agency (DARPA) in 1972.

majority of educational institutions were not connected. As a result, a number of other networks were developed during the late 1970s and early 1980s, with BITNET and CSNET among them. BITNET, which is an acronym for *Because It's Time Network*, began at the City University of New York. It was built initially to provide electronic mail and file transfers. CSNET, which is an acronym for *Computer Science Network*, connected the University of Delaware, Purdue University, the University of Wisconsin, the RAND Corporation, and Bolt, Beranek, and Newman (a research company in Cambridge, Massachusetts). Its initial purpose was to provide electronic mail. For a variety of reasons, neither BITNET nor CSNET became a widely used national network.

A new national network, NSFnet, was created in 1986. It was sponsored, of course, by the National Science Foundation (NSF). NSFnet initially connected the NSF-funded supercomputer centers that were at five universities. Soon after being established, it became available to other academic institutions and research laboratories. By 1990, NSFnet had replaced ARPAnet for most nonmilitary uses, and a wide variety of organizations had established nodes on the new network—by 1992, NSFnet connected more than 1 million computers around the world. In 1995, a small part of NSFnet returned to being a research network. The rest became known as the Internet, although this term was used much earlier for both ARPAnet and NSFnet.

1.1.2   What Is the Internet?

The Internet is a huge collection of computers connected in a communications network. These computers are of every imaginable size, configuration, and manufacturer. In fact, some of the devices connected to the Internet—such as plotters and printers—are not computers at all. The innovation that allows all of these diverse devices to communicate with each other is a single, low-level protocol named Transmission Control Protocol/Internet Protocol (TCP/IP). TCP/IP became the standard for computer network connections in 1982. It can be used directly to allow a program on one computer to communicate with a program on another computer via the Internet. In most cases, however, a higher-level protocol runs on top of TCP/IP. Nevertheless, it is TCP/IP that provides the low-level interface that allows most computers (and other devices) connected to the Internet to appear exactly the same.[2]

Rather than connecting every computer on the Internet directly to every other computer on the Internet, normally the individual computers in an organization are connected to each other in a local network. One node on this local network is physically connected to the Internet. So, the Internet is actually a network of networks, rather than a network of computers.

Obviously, all devices connected to the Internet must be uniquely identifiable.

---

2. TCP/IP is not the only communication protocol used by the Internet—User Datagram Protocol/Internet Protocol (UDP/IP) is an alternative that is used in some situations.

1.1.3   Internet Protocol Addresses

For people, Internet nodes are identified by names; for computers, they are identified by numeric addresses. This relationship exactly parallels the one between a variable name in a program, which is for people, and the variable's numeric memory address, which is for the machine.

The Internet Protocol (IP) address of a machine connected to the Internet is a unique 32-bit number. IP addresses usually are written (and thought of) as four 8-bit numbers, separated by periods. The four parts are separately used by Internet-routing computers to decide where a message must go next to get to its destination.

Organizations are assigned blocks of IPs, which they in turn assign to their machines that need Internet access—which now include virtually all computers. For example, a small organization may be assigned 256 IP addresses, such as `191.57.126.0` to `191.57.126.255`. Very large organizations, such as the Department of Defense, may be assigned 16 million IP addresses, which include IP addresses with one particular first 8-bit number, such as `12.0.0.0` to `12.255.255.255`.

Although people nearly always type domain names into their browsers, the IP works just as well. For example, the IP for United Airlines (`www.ual.com`) is `209.87.113.93`. So, if a browser is pointed at `http://209.87.113.93`, it will be connected to the United Airlines Web site.

In late 1998, a new IP standard, IPv6, was approved, although it still is not widely used. The most significant change was to expand the address size from 32 bits to 128 bits. This is a change that will soon be essential because the number of remaining unused IP addresses is diminishing rapidly.

1.1.4   Domain Names

Because people have difficulty dealing with and remembering numbers, machines on the Internet also have textual names. These names begin with the name of the host machine, followed by progressively larger enclosing collections of machines, called *domains*. There may be two, three, or more domain names. The first domain name, which appears immediately to the right of the host name, is the domain of which the host is a part. The second domain name gives the domain of which the first domain is a part. The last domain name identifies the type of organization in which the host resides, which is the largest domain in the site's name. For organizations in the United States, `edu` is the extension for educational institutions, `com` specifies a company, `gov` is used for the U.S. government, and `org` is used for many other kinds of organizations. In other countries, the largest domain is often an abbreviation for the country—for example, `se` is used for Sweden, and `kz` is used for Kazakhstan.

Consider this sample address:

```
movies.marxbros.comedy.com
```

Here, `movies` is the hostname and `marxbros` is `movies`'s local domain, which is a part of `comedy`'s domain, which is a part of the `com` domain. The hostname and all of the domain names are together called a *fully qualified domain name*.

Because IP addresses are the addresses used internally by the Internet, the fully qualified domain name of the destination for a message, which is what is given by a browser user, must be converted to an IP address before the message can be transmitted over the Internet to the destination. These conversions are done by software systems called *name servers*, which implement the Domain Name System (DNS). Name servers serve a collection of machines on the Internet and are operated by organizations that are responsible for the part of the Internet to which those machines are connected. All document requests from browsers are routed to the nearest name server. If the name server can convert the fully qualified domain name to an IP address, it does so. If it cannot, the name server sends the fully qualified domain name to another name server for conversion. Like IP addresses, fully qualified domain names must be unique. Figure 1.1 shows how fully qualified domain names requested by a browser are translated into IPs before they are routed to the appropriate Web server.

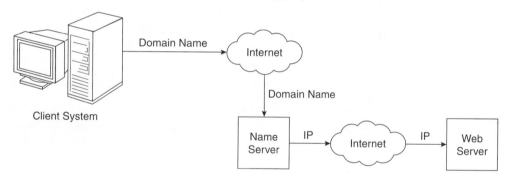

Figure 1.1 Domain name conversion

One way to determine the IP address of a Web site is by using `telnet` on the fully qualified domain name. This approach is illustrated in Section 1.7.1.

By the mid-1980s, a collection of different protocols that run on top of TCP/IP had been developed to support a variety of Internet uses. Among these protocols, the most common were `telnet`, which was developed to allow a user on one computer on the Internet to log onto and use another computer on the Internet; File Transfer Protocol (`ftp`), which was developed to transfer files among computers on the Internet; Usenet, which was developed to serve as an electronic bulletin board; and `mailto`, which was developed to allow messages to be sent from the user of one computer on the Internet to other users of other computers on the Internet.

This variety of protocols, each has its own user interface and each is useful only for the purpose for which it was designed, restricted the growth of the Internet. Users were required to learn all the different interfaces to gain all the advantages of the Internet. Before long, however, a better approach was developed: the World Wide Web.

1.2   The World Wide Web

This section provides a brief introduction to the evolution of the World Wide Web.

1.2.1   Origins

In 1989, a small group of people led by Tim Berners-Lee at CERN (Conseil Européen pour la Recherche Nucléaire, or European Organization for Particle Physics) proposed a new protocol for the Internet, as well as a system of document access to use it.[3] The intent of this new system, which the group named the World Wide Web, was to allow scientists around the world to use the Internet to exchange documents describing their work.

The proposed new system was designed to allow a user anywhere on the Internet to search for and retrieve documents from databases on any number of different document-serving computers connected to the Internet. By late 1990, the basic ideas for the new system had been fully developed and implemented on a NeXT computer at CERN. In 1991, the system was ported to other computer platforms and released to the rest of the world.

For the form of its documents, the new system used *hypertext*, which is text with embedded links to text in other documents to allow nonsequential browsing of textual material. The idea of hypertext had been developed earlier and had appeared in Xerox's NoteCards and Apple's HyperCard in the mid-1980s.

From here on, we will refer to the World Wide Web simply as "the Web." The units of information on the Web have been referred to by several different names; among them, the most common are *pages*, *documents*, and *resources*. Perhaps the best of these is *documents*, although that seems to imply only text. *Pages* is widely used, but it is misleading in that Web units of information often have more than one of the kind of pages that make up printed media. There is some merit to calling these units *resources*, because that covers the possibility of nontextual information. This book will use *documents* and *pages* more or less interchangeably, but we prefer *documents* in most situations.

Documents are sometimes just text, usually with embedded links to other documents, but they often also include images, sound recordings, or other kinds of media. When a document contains nontextual information, it is called *hypermedia*.

In an abstract sense, the Web is a vast collection of documents, some of which are connected by links. These documents are accessed by Web browsers, introduced in Section 1.3, and are provided by Web servers, introduced in Section 1.4.

---

3. Although Berners-Lee's college degree (from Oxford) was in physics, his first stint at CERN was as a consulting software engineer. Berners-Lee was born and raised in London.

1.2.2 Web or Internet?

It is important to understand that the Internet and the Web are not the same thing. The *Internet* is a collection of computers and other devices connected by equipment that allows them to communicate with each other. The *Web* is a collection of software and protocols that has been installed on most, if not all, of the computers on the Internet. Some of these computers run Web servers, which provide documents, but most run Web clients, or browsers, which request documents from servers and display them to users. The Internet was quite useful before the Web was developed, and it is still useful without it. However, most users of the Internet now use it through the Web.

1.3 Web Browsers

When two computers communicate over some network, in many cases one acts as a client and the other as a server. The client initiates the communication, which is often a request for information stored on the server, which then sends that information back to the client. The Web, as well as many other systems, operates in this client-server configuration.

Documents provided by servers on the Web are requested by *browsers*, which are programs running on client machines. They are called browsers because they allow the user to browse the resources available on servers. The first browsers were text based—they were not capable of displaying graphic information, nor did they have a graphical user interface. This limitation effectively constrained the growth of the Web. In early 1993, things changed with the release of Mosaic, the first browser with a graphical user interface. Mosaic was developed at the National Center for Supercomputer Applications (NCSA) at the University of Illinois. Mosaic's interface provided convenient access to the Web for users who were neither scientists nor software developers. The first release of Mosaic ran on UNIX systems using the X Window system. By late 1993, versions of Mosaic for Apple Macintosh and Microsoft Windows systems had been released. Finally, users of the computers connected to the Internet around the world had a powerful way to access anything on the Web anywhere in the world. The result of this power and convenience was an explosive growth in Web usage.

A browser is a client on the Web because it initiates the communication with a server, which waits for a request from the client before doing anything. In the simplest case, a browser requests a static document from a server. The server locates the document among its servable documents and sends it to the browser, which displays it for the user. However, more complicated situations are common. For example, the server may provide a document that requests input from the user through the browser. After the user supplies the requested input, it is transmitted from the browser to the server, which may use the input to perform some computation and then return a new document to the browser to inform the user of the results of the computation. Sometimes a browser directly requests the execution of a program stored on the server. The output of the program is then returned to the browser.

Although the Web supports a variety of protocols, the most common one is the Hypertext Transfer Protocol (HTTP). HTTP provides a standard form of communication between browsers and Web servers. Section 1.7 presents an introduction to HTTP.

The most commonly used browsers are Microsoft Internet Explorer (IE), which runs only on PCs that use one of the Microsoft Windows operating systems,[4] Firefox, and Chrome. The latter two are available in versions for several different computing platforms, including Windows, Mac OS, and Linux. Several other browsers are available, including Opera and Apple's Safari. However, because the great majority of browsers now in use are either IE, Firefox, or Chrome, in this book we focus on them.

1.4   Web Servers

Web servers are programs that provide documents to requesting browsers. Servers are slave programs: They act only when requests are made to them by browsers running on other computers on the Internet.

The most commonly used Web servers are Apache, which has been implemented for a variety of computer platforms, and Microsoft's Internet Information Server (IIS), which runs under Windows operating systems. As of October 2011, there were over 150 million active Web hosts in operation,[5] about 65 percent of which were Apache, about 16 percent of which were IIS, and the remainder of which were spread thinly over several others. (The third-place server was `nginx` (pronounced "engine-x"), a product produced in Russia, with about 8 percent.)[6]

1.4.1   Web Server Operation

Although having clients and servers is a natural consequence of information distribution, this configuration offers some additional benefits for the Web. On the one hand, serving information does not take a great deal of time. On the other hand, displaying information on client screens is time consuming. Because Web servers need not be involved in this display process, they can handle many clients. So, it is both a natural and efficient division of labor to have a small number of servers provide documents to a large number of clients.

Web browsers initiate network communications with servers by sending them URLs (discussed in Section 1.5). A URL can specify one of two different things: the address of a data file stored on the server that is to be sent to the client, or a program stored on the server that the client wants executed and the output of the program returned to the client.

---

4. Actually, versions 4 and 5 of IE (IE4 and IE5) were also available for Macintosh computers, and IE4 was available for UNIX systems. However, later versions are available for Windows platforms only.

5. There were more than 500 million sites on line.

6. These statistics are from `http://www.netcraft.com`.

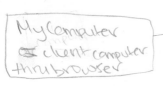

All the communications between a Web client and a Web server use the standard Web protocol, Hypertext Transfer Protocol (HTTP), which is discussed in Section 1.7.[7]

When a Web server begins execution, it informs the operating system under which it is running that it is now ready to accept incoming network connections through a specific port on the machine. While in this running state, the server runs as a background process in the operating system environment. A Web client, or browser, opens a network connection to a Web server, sends information requests and possibly data to the server, receives information from the server, and closes the connection. Of course, other machines exist between browsers and servers on the network—specifically, network routers and domain name servers. This section, however, focuses on just one part of Web communication: the server.

Simply put, the primary task of a Web server is to monitor a communications port on its host machine, accept HTTP commands through that port, and perform the operations specified by the commands. All HTTP commands include a URL, which includes the specification of a host server machine. When the URL is received, it is translated into either a file name (in which case the file is returned to the requesting client) or a program name (in which case the program is run and its output is sent to the requesting client). This process sounds pretty simple, but, as is the case in many other simple-sounding processes, there are a large number of complicating details.

All current Web servers have a common ancestry: the first two servers, developed at CERN in Europe and NCSA at the University of Illinois. Currently, the most common server configuration is Apache running on some version of UNIX.

1.4.2 General Server Characteristics

Most of the available servers share common characteristics, regardless of their origin or the platform on which they run. This section provides brief descriptions of some of these characteristics.

The file structure of a Web server has two separate directories. The root of one of these is called the *document root*. The file hierarchy that grows from the document root stores the Web documents to which the server has direct access and normally serves to clients. The root of the other directory is called the *server root*. This directory, along with its descendant directories, stores the server and its support software.

The files stored directly in the document root are those available to clients through top-level URLs. Typically, clients do not access the document root directly in URLs; rather, the server maps requested URLs to the document root, whose location is not known to clients. For example, suppose that the site name is www.tunias.com (not a real site—at least, not yet), which we will assume to be a UNIX-based system. Suppose further that the document root is named topdocs and is stored in the /admin/web directory, making its address /admin/web/topdocs. A request for a file from a client with the URL http://www.tunias.com/petunias.html will cause the server to search for the file with the file

---

7. Some of these communications use HTTPS, the secure version of HTTP.

path `/admin/web/topdocs/petunias.html`. Likewise, the URL `http://www.tunias.com/bulbs/tulips.html` will cause the server to search for the file with the address `/admin/web/topdocs/bulbs/tulips.html`.

[handwritten margin note: File address on web server]

Many servers allow part of the servable document collection to be stored outside the directory at the document root. The secondary areas from which documents can be served are called *virtual document trees.* For example, the original configuration of a server might have the server store all its servable documents from the primary system disk on the server machine. Later, the collection of servable documents might outgrow that disk, in which case part of the collection could be stored on a secondary disk. This secondary disk might reside on the server machine or on some other machine on a local area network. To support this arrangement, the server is configured to direct-request URLs with a particular file path to a storage area separate from the document-root directory. Sometimes files with different types of content, such as images, are stored outside the document root.

Early servers provided few services other than the basic process of returning requested files or the output of programs whose execution had been requested. The list of additional services has grown steadily over the years. Contemporary servers are large and complex systems that provide a wide variety of client services. Many servers can support more than one site on a computer, potentially reducing the cost of each site and making their maintenance more convenient. Such secondary hosts are called *virtual hosts*.

Some servers can serve documents that are in the document root of other machines on the Web; in this case, they are called *proxy servers*.

Although Web servers were originally designed to support only the HTTP protocol, many now support `ftp`, `gopher`, `news`, and `mailto`. In addition, nearly all Web servers can interact with database systems through server-side scripts.

1.4.3   Apache

Apache began as the NCSA server, `httpd`, with some added features. The name *Apache* has nothing to do with the Native American tribe of the same name. Rather, it came from the nature of its first version, which was *a patch*y version of the `httpd` server. As seen in the usage statistics given at the beginning of this section, Apache is the most widely used Web server. The primary reasons are as follows: It is both fast and reliable. Furthermore, it is open-source software, which means that it is free and is managed by a large team of volunteers, a process that efficiently and effectively maintains the system. Finally, it is one of the best available servers for Unix-based systems, which are the most popular for Web servers.

Apache is capable of providing a long list of services beyond the basic process of serving documents to clients. When Apache begins execution, it reads its configuration information from a file and sets its parameters to operate accordingly. A new copy of Apache includes default configuration information for a "typical" operation. The site manager modifies this configuration information to fit his or her particular needs and tastes.

For historical reasons, there are three configuration files in an Apache server: `httpd.conf`, `srm.conf`, and `access.conf`. Only one of these, `httpd.conf`, actually stores the directives that control an Apache server's behavior. The other two point to `httpd.conf`, which is the file that contains the list of directives that specify the server's operation. These directives are described at `http://httpd.apache.org/docs/2.2/mod/quickreference.html`.

1.4.4 IIS *(Internet Information Services) for use w/ MS windows*

Although Apache has been ported to the Windows platforms, it is not the most popular server on those systems. Because the Microsoft IIS server is supplied as part of Windows—and because it is a reasonably good server—most Windows-based Web servers use IIS. Apache and IIS provide similar varieties of services.

From the point of view of the site manager, the most important difference between Apache and IIS is that Apache is controlled by a configuration file that is edited by the manager to change Apache's behavior. With IIS, server behavior is modified by changes made through a window-based management program, named the IIS snap-in, which controls both IIS and `ftp`. This program allows the site manager to set parameters for the server.

This will only be available when you have installed windows server

Under Windows XP and Vista, the IIS snap-in is accessed by going to *Control Panel*, *Administrative Tools*, and *IIS Manager*. Clicking this last selection takes you to a window that allows starting, stopping, or pausing IIS. This same window allows IIS parameters to be changed when the server has been stopped.

1.5 Uniform Resource Locators

Uniform (or universal)[8] resource locators (URLs) are used to identify documents (resources) on the Internet. There are many different kinds of resources, identified by different forms of URLs.

1.5.1 URL Formats

All URLs have the same general format:

scheme:object-address

The scheme is often a communications protocol. Common schemes include `http`, `ftp`, `gopher`, `telnet`, `file`, `mailto`, and `news`. Different schemes use object addresses that have different forms. Our interest here is in the HTTP protocol, which supports the Web. This protocol is used to request and send

---

8. Fortunately, resource addresses are usually referred to as URLs, so whether it is *uniform* or *universal* is usually irrelevant.

Hypertext Markup Language (HTML) documents. In the case of HTTP, the form of the object address of a URL is as follows:

//fully-qualified-domain-name/path-to-document

Another scheme of interest to us is `file`. The `file` protocol means that the document resides on the machine running the browser. This approach is useful for testing documents to be made available on the Web without making them visible to any other browser. When `file` is the protocol, the fully qualified domain name is omitted, making the form of such URLs as follows:

`file`:*//path-to-document*

Because the focus of this book is on HTML documents, the remainder of the discussion of URLs is limited to the HTTP protocol.

The host name is the name of the server computer that stores the document (or provides access to it, although it is stored on some other computer). Messages to a host machine must be directed to the appropriate process running on the host for handling. Such processes are identified by their associated port numbers. The default port number of Web server processes is 80. If a server has been configured to use some other port number, it is necessary to attach that port number to the host name in the URL. For example, if the Web server is configured to use port 800, the host name must have `:800` attached.

URLs can never have embedded spaces.[9] Also, there is a collection of special characters, including semicolons, colons, and ampersands (`&`), that cannot appear in a URL. To include a space or one of the disallowed special characters, the character must be coded as a percent sign (`%`) followed by the two-digit hexadecimal ASCII code for the character. For example, if `San Jose` is a domain name, it must be typed as `San%20Jose` (20 is the hexadecimal ASCII code for a space). All of the details characterizing URLs can be found at `http://www.w3.org/Addressing/URL/URI_Overview.html`.

1.5.2 URL Paths

The path to the document for the HTTP protocol is similar to a path to a file or directory in the file system of an operating system and is given by a sequence of directory names and a file name, all separated by whatever separator character the operating system uses. For UNIX servers, the path is specified with forward slashes; for Windows servers, it is specified with backward slashes. Most browsers allow the user to specify the separators incorrectly—for example, using forward slashes in a path to a document file on a Windows server, as in the following:

`http://www.gumboco.com/files/f99/storefront.html`

The path in a URL can differ from a path to a file because a URL need not include all directories on the path. A path that includes all directories along the way is called a *complete path*. In most cases, the path to the document is relative

---

9. Actually, some browsers incorrectly accept spaces in URLs, although doing so is nonstandard behavior.

to some base path that is specified in the configuration files of the server. Such paths are called *partial paths*. For example, if the server's configuration specifies that the root directory for files it can serve is `files/f99`, the previous URL is specified as follows:

```
http://www.gumboco.com/storefront.html
```

If the specified document is a directory rather than a single document, the directory's name is followed immediately by a slash, as in the following:

```
http://www.gumboco.com/departments/
```

Sometimes a directory is specified (with the trailing slash) but its name is not given, as in the following example:

```
http://www.gumboco.com/
```

The server then searches at the top level of the directory in which servable documents are normally stored for something it recognizes as a home page. By convention, this page is often a file named `index.html`. The home page usually includes links that allow the user to find the other related servable files on the server.

If the directory does not have a file that the server recognizes as being a home page, a directory listing is constructed and returned to the browser.

1.6 Multipurpose Internet Mail Extensions

A browser needs some way of determining the format of a document it receives from a Web server. Without knowing the form of the document, the browser would not be able to render it, because different document formats require different rendering software. The forms of these documents are specified with Multipurpose Internet Mail Extensions (MIME).

1.6.1 Type Specifications

MIME was developed to specify the format of different kinds of documents to be sent via Internet mail. These documents could contain various kinds of text, video data, or sound data. Because the Web has needs similar to those of Internet mail, MIME was adopted as the way to specify document types transmitted over the Web. A Web server attaches a MIME format specification to the beginning of the document that it is about to provide to a browser. When the browser receives the document from a Web server, it uses the included MIME format specification to determine what to do with the document. If the content is text, for example, the MIME code tells the browser that it is text and also indicates the particular kind of text it is. If the content is sound, the MIME code tells the browser that it is sound and then gives the particular representation of sound so the browser can choose a program to which it has access to produce the transmitted sound.

MIME specifications have the following form:

type/subtype

The most common MIME types are `text`, `image`, and `video`. The most common text subtypes are `plain` and `html`. Some common image subtypes are `gif` and `jpeg`. Some common video subtypes are `mpeg` and `quicktime`. A list of MIME specifications is stored in the configuration files of every Web server. In the remainder of this book, when we say *document type*, we mean both the type and subtype of the document.

Servers determine the type of a document by using the file name's extension as the key into a table of types. For example, the extension `.html` tells the server that it should attach `text/html` to the document before sending it to the requesting browser.[10]

Browsers also maintain a conversion table for looking up the type of a document by its file name extension. However, this table is used only when the server does not specify a MIME type, which may be the case with some older servers. In all other cases, the browser gets the document type from the MIME header provided by the server.

1.6.2   Experimental Document Types

Experimental subtypes are sometimes used. The name of an experimental subtype begins with `x-`, as in `video/x-msvideo`. Any Web provider can add an experimental subtype by having its name added to the list of MIME specifications stored in the Web provider's server. For example, a Web provider might have a handcrafted database whose contents he or she wants to make available to others through the Web. Of course, this raises the issue of how the browser can display the database. As might be expected, the Web provider must supply a program that the browser can call when it needs to display the contents of the database. These programs either are external to the browser, in which case they are called *helper applications*, or are code modules that are inserted into the browser, in which case they are called *plug-ins*.

Every browser has a set of MIME specifications (file types) it can handle. All can deal with `text/plain` (unformatted text) and `text/html` (HTML files), among others. Sometimes a particular browser cannot handle a specific document type, even though the type is widely used. These cases are handled in the same way as the experimental types described previously. The browser determines the helper application or plug-in it needs by examining the browser configuration file, which provides an association between file types and their required helpers or plug-ins. If the browser does not have an application or a plug-in that it needs to render a document, an error message is displayed.

A browser can indicate to the server the document types it prefers to receive, as discussed in Section 1.7.

---

10. This is not necessarily correct. HTML documents also use the `.html` file extension, but, strictly speaking, should use a different MIME type.

1.7 **The Hypertext Transfer Protocol**

All Web communications transactions use the same protocol: the Hypertext Transfer Protocol (HTTP). The current version of HTTP is 1.1, formally defined as RFC 2616, which was approved in June 1999. RFC 2616 is available at the Web site for the World Wide Web Consortium (W3C), `http://www.w3.org`. This section provides a brief introduction to HTTP.

HTTP consists of two phases: the request and the response. Each HTTP communication (request or response) between a browser and a Web server consists of two parts: a header and a body. The header contains information about the communication; the body contains the data of the communication if there is any.

1.7.1 **The Request Phase**

The general form of an HTTP request is as follows:

1. HTTP method   Domain part of the URL   HTTP version
2. Header fields
3. Blank line
4. Message body

The following is an example of the first line of an HTTP request:

`GET /storefront.html HTTP/1.1`

Only a few request methods are defined by HTTP, and even a smaller number of these are typically used. Table 1.1 lists the most commonly used methods.

Table 1.1   HTTP request methods

Method	Description
GET	Returns the contents of the specified document
HEAD	Returns the header information for the specified document
POST	Executes the specified document, using the enclosed data
PUT	Replaces the specified document with the enclosed data
DELETE	Deletes the specified document

Among the methods given in Table 1.1, GET and POST are the most frequently used. POST was originally designed for tasks such as posting a news article to a newsgroup. Its most common use now is to send form data from a browser to a server, along with a request to execute a program on the server that will process the data.

Following the first line of an HTTP communication is any number of header fields, most of which are optional. The format of a header field is the field name followed by a colon and the value of the field. There are four categories of header fields:

1. *General:* For general information, such as the date
2. *Request:* Included in request headers
3. *Response:* For response headers
4. *Entity:* Used in both request and response headers

One common request field is the `Accept` field, which specifies a preference of the browser for the MIME type of the requested document. More than one `Accept` field can be specified if the browser is willing to accept documents in more than one format. For example; we might have any of the following:

```
Accept: text/plain
Accept: text/html
Accept: image/gif
```

A wildcard character, the asterisk (*), can be used to specify that part of a MIME type can be anything. For example, if any kind of text is acceptable, the `Accept` field could be as follows:

```
Accept: text/*
```

The `Host: host name` request field gives the name of the host. The `Host` field is required for HTTP 1.1. The `If-Modified-Since: date` request field specifies that the requested file should be sent only if it has been modified since the given date.

If the request has a body, the length of that body must be given with a `Content-length` field, which gives the length of the response body in bytes. `POST` method requests require this field because they send data to the server.

The header of a request must be followed by a blank line, which is used to separate the header from the body of the request. Requests that use the `GET`, `HEAD`, and `DELETE` methods do not have bodies. In these cases, the blank line signals the end of the request.

A browser is not necessary to communicate with a Web server; `telnet` can be used instead. Consider the following command, given at the command line of any widely used operating system:

```
>telnet blanca.uccs.edu http
```

This command creates a connection to the `http` port on the `blanca.uccs.edu` server. The server responds with the following:[11]

```
Trying 128.198.162.60 ...
Connected to blanca
Escape character is '^]'.
```

---

11. Notice that this `telnet` request returns the IP of the server.

The connection to the server is now complete, and HTTP commands such as the following can be given:

```
GET /~user1/respond.html HTTP/1.1
Host: blanca.uccs.edu
```

The header of the response to this request is given in Section 1.7.2.

1.7.2   The Response Phase

The general form of an HTTP response is as follows:

1. Status line
2. Response header fields
3. Blank line
4. Response body

The status line includes the HTTP version used, a three-digit status code for the response, and a short textual explanation of the status code. For example, most responses begin with the following:

```
HTTP/1.1  200  OK
```

The status codes begin with 1, 2, 3, 4, or 5. The general meanings of the five categories specified by these first digits are shown in Table 1.2.

Table 1.2   First digits of HTTP status codes

First Digit	Category
1	Informational
2	Success
3	Redirection
4	Client error
5	Server error

One of the more common status codes is one users never want to see: 404 Not Found, which means the requested file could not be found. Of course, 200 OK is what users want to see, because it means that the request was handled without error. The 500 code means that the server has encountered a problem and was not able to fulfill the request.

After the status line, the server sends a response header, which can contain several lines of information about the response, each in the form of a field. The only essential field of the header is Content-type.

The following is the response header for the request given near the end of Section 1.7.1:

```
HTTP/1.1 200 OK
Date: Sat, 25 July 2009 22:15:11 GMT
Server: Apache/2.2.3 (CentOS)
Last-modified: Tues, 18 May 2004 16:38:38 GMT
ETag: "1b48098-16c-3dab592dc9f80"
Accept-ranges: bytes
Content-length: 364
Connection: close
Content-type: text/html, charset=UTF-8
```

The response header must be followed by a blank line, as is the case for request headers. The response data follows the blank line. In the preceding example, the response body would be the HTML file, `respond.html`.

In HTTP versions prior to 1.1, when a server finished sending a response to the client, the communications connection was closed. However, the default operation of HTTP 1.1 is that the connection is kept open for a time so that the client can make several requests over a short span of time without needing to reestablish the communications connection with the server. This change led to significant increases in the efficiency of the Web.

1.8   Security

It does not take a great deal of contemplation to realize that the Internet and the Web are fertile grounds for security problems. On the Web server side, anyone on the planet with a computer, a browser, and an Internet connection can request the execution of software on any server computer. He or she can also access data and databases stored on the server computer. On the browser end, the problem is similar: Any server to which the browser points can download software to be executed on the browser host machine. Such software can access parts of the memory and memory devices attached to that machine that are not related to the needs of the original browser request. In effect, on both ends, it is like allowing any number of total strangers into your house and trying to prevent them from leaving anything in the house, taking anything from the house, or altering anything in the house. The larger and more complex the design of the house, the more difficult it will be to prevent any of those activities. The same is true for Web servers and browsers: The more complex they are, the more difficult it is to prevent security breaches. Today's browsers and Web servers are indeed large and complex software systems, so security is a significant problem in Web applications.

The subject of Internet and Web security is extensive and complicated, so much so that numerous books on the topic have been written. Therefore, this one section of one chapter of one book can give no more than a brief sketch of some of the subtopics of security.

One aspect of Web security is the matter of getting one's data from the browser to the server and having the server deliver data back to the browser without anyone or any device intercepting or corrupting those data along the way. Consider a simple case of transmitting a credit card number to a company from which a purchase is being made. The security issues for this transaction are as follows:

1. *Privacy*—it must not be possible for the credit card number to be stolen on its way to the company's server.
2. *Integrity*—it must not be possible for the credit card number to be modified on its way to the company's server.
3. *Authentication*—it must be possible for both the purchaser and the seller to be certain of each other's identity.
4. *Nonrepudiation*—it must be possible to prove legally that the message was actually sent and received.

The basic tool to support privacy and integrity is encryption. Data to be transmitted is converted into a different form, or encrypted, such that someone (or some computer) who is not supposed to access the data cannot decrypt it. So, if data is intercepted while en route between Internet nodes, the interceptor cannot use the data because he or she cannot decrypt it. Both encryption and decryption are done with a key and a process (applying the key to the data). Encryption was developed long before the Internet existed. Julius Caesar crudely encrypted the messages he sent to his field generals while at war. Until the middle 1970s, the same key was used for both encryption and decryption, so the initial problem was how to transmit the key from the sender to the receiver.

This problem was solved in 1976 by Whitfield Diffie and Martin Hellman of Stanford University, who developed *public-key encryption*, a process in which a public key and a private key are used, respectively, to encrypt and decrypt messages. A communicator—say, Joe—has an inversely related pair of keys, one public and one private. The public key can be distributed to all organizations that might send Joe messages. All of them can use the public key to encrypt messages to Joe, who can decrypt the messages with his matching private key. This arrangement works because the private key need never be transmitted and also because it is virtually impossible to decrypt the private key from its corresponding public key. The technical wording for this situation is that it is "computationally infeasible" to determine the private key from its public key.

The most widely used public-key algorithm is named RSA, developed in 1977 by three MIT professors—Ron Rivest, Adi Shamir, and Leonard Adleman—the first letters of whose last names were used to name the algorithm. Most large companies now use RSA for e-commerce.

Another, completely different security problem for the Web is the intentional and malicious destruction of data on computers attached to the Internet. The number of different ways this can be done has increased steadily over the life span of the Web. The sheer number of such attacks has also grown rapidly. There is now a continuous stream of new and increasingly devious denial-of-service (DoS) attacks, viruses, and worms being discovered, which have caused billions of dollars of damage, primarily to businesses that use the Web heavily. Of course, huge damage also has been done to home computer systems through Web intrusions.

DoS attacks can be created simply by flooding a Web server with requests, overwhelming its ability to operate effectively. Most DoS attacks are conducted with the use of networks of virally infected "zombie" computers, whose owners are unaware of their sinister use. So, DoS and viruses are often related.

Viruses are programs that often arrive in a system in attachments to e-mail messages or attached to free downloaded programs. Then they attach to other programs. When executed, they replicate and can overwrite memory and attached memory devices, destroying programs and data alike. Two viruses that were extensively destructive appeared in 2000 and 2001: the ILOVEYOU virus and the CodeRed virus, respectively.

Worms damage memory, like viruses, but spread on their own, rather than being attached to other files. Perhaps the most famous worm so far has been the Blaster worm, spawned in 2003.

DoS, virus, and worm attacks are created by malicious people referred to as *hackers*. The incentive for these people apparently is simply the feeling of pride and accomplishment they derive from being able to cause huge amounts of damage by outwitting the designers of Web software systems.

Protection against viruses and worms is provided by antivirus software, which must be updated frequently so that it can detect and protect against the continuous stream of new viruses and worms.

1.9   The Web Programmer's Toolbox

This section provides an overview of the most common tools used in Web programming—some are programming languages, some are not. The tools discussed are HTML, a markup language, along with a few high-level markup document-editing systems; XML, a meta-markup language; JavaScript, PHP, and Ruby, which are programming languages; JSF, ASP.NET, and Rails, which are development frameworks for Web-based systems; Flash, a technology for creating and displaying graphics and animation in HTML documents; and Ajax, a Web technology that uses JavaScript and XML.

Web programs and scripts are divided into two categories—client side and server side—according to where they are interpreted or executed. HTML and XML are client-side languages; PHP and Ruby are server-side languages; JavaScript is most often a client-side language, although it can be used for both.

We begin with the most basic tool: HTML.

1.9.1   Overview of HTML

At the onset, it is important to realize that HTML is not a programming language—it cannot be used to describe computations. Its purpose is to describe the general form and layout of documents to be displayed by a browser.

The word *markup* comes from the publishing world, where it is used to describe what production people do with a manuscript to specify to a printer how the text, graphics, and other elements in the book should appear in printed form. HTML is not the first markup language used with computers. TeX and LaTeX are older markup languages for use with text; they are now used primarily to specify how mathematical expressions and formulas should appear in print.

An HTML document is a mixture of content and controls. The controls are specified by the tags of HTML. The name of a tag specifies the category of its content. Most HTML tags consist of a pair of syntactic markers that are used to delimit particular kinds of content. The pair of tags and their content together are called an *element*. For example, a paragraph element specifies that its content, which appears between its opening tag, `<p>`, and its closing tag, `</p>`, is a paragraph. A browser has a default style (font, font style, font size, and so forth) for paragraphs, which is used to display the content of a paragraph element.

Some tags include attribute specifications that provide some additional information for the browser. In the following example, the `src` attribute specifies the location of the `img` tag's image content:

```
<img src = "redhead.jpg"/>
```

In this case, the image document stored in the file `redhead.jpg` is to be displayed at the position in the document in which the tag appears.

The history of HTML appears in Chapter 2.

1.9.2   Tools for Creating HTML Documents

HTML documents can be created with a general-purpose text editor. There are two kinds of tools that can simplify this task: HTML editors and what-you-see-is-what-you-get (WYSIWYG, pronounced *wizzy-wig*) HTML editors.

HTML editors provide shortcuts for producing repetitious tags such as those used to create the rows of a table. They also may provide a spell-checker and a syntax-checker, and they may color code the HTML in the display to make it easier to read and edit.

A more powerful tool for creating HTML documents is a WYSIWYG HTML editor. Using a WYSIWYG HTML editor, the writer can see the formatted document that the HTML describes while he or she is writing the HTML code. WYSIWYG HTML editors are very useful for beginners who want to create simple documents without learning HTML and for users who want to prototype the appearance of a document. Still, these editors sometimes produce poor-quality HTML. In some cases, they create proprietary tags that some browsers will not recognize.

Two examples of WYSIWYG HTML editors are Microsoft FrontPage and Adobe Dreamweaver. Both allow the user to create HTML-described documents without requiring the user to know HTML. They cannot handle all of the tags of HTML, but they are very useful for creating many of the common features of documents. Between the two, FrontPage is by far the most widely used. Information on Dreamweaver is available at `http://www.adobe.com/`; information on FrontPage is available at `http://www.microsoft.com/frontpage/`.

1.9.3   Plug-ins and Filters

Two different kinds of converters can be used to create HTML documents. *Plug-ins*[12] are programs that can be integrated with a word processor. Plug-ins add new capabilities to the word processor, such as toolbar buttons and menu elements that provide convenient ways to insert HTML into the document being created or edited. The plug-in makes the word processor appear to be an HTML editor that provides WYSIWYG HTML document development. The end result of this process is an HTML document. The plug-in also makes available all the tools that are inherent in the word processor during HTML document creation, such as a spell-checker and a thesaurus.

A second kind of converter is a *filter*, which converts an existing document in some form, such as LaTeX or Microsoft Word, to HTML. Filters are never part of the editor or word processor that created the document—an advantage because the filter can then be platform independent. For example, a Word-Perfect user working on a Macintosh computer can use a filter running on a UNIX platform to produce HTML documents with the same content on that machine. The disadvantage of filters is that creating HTML documents with a filter is a two-step process: First you create the document, and then you use a filter to convert it to HTML.

Neither plugs-ins nor filters produce HTML documents that, when displayed by browsers, have the identical appearance of that produced by the word processor.

The two advantages of both plug-ins and filters, however, are that existing documents produced with word processors can be easily converted to HTML and that users can use a word processor with which they are familiar to produce HTML documents. This obviates the need to learn to format text by using HTML directly. For example, once you learn to create tables with your word processor, it is easier to use that process than to learn to define tables directly in HTML.

The HTML output produced by either filters or plug-ins often must be modified, usually with a simple text editor, to perfect the appearance of the displayed document in the browser. Because this new HTML file cannot be converted to its original form (regardless of how it was created), you will have two different source files for a document, inevitably leading to version problems during maintenance of the document. This is clearly a disadvantage of using converters.

---

12. The word *plug-in* applies to many different software systems that can be added to or embedded in other software systems. For example, many different plug-ins can be added to Web browsers.

1.9.4   Overview of XML

HTML is defined with the use of the Standard Generalized Markup Language (SGML), which is a language for defining markup languages. (Such languages are called meta-markup languages.) XML (eXtensible Markup Language) is a simplified version of SGML, designed to allow users to easily create markup languages that fit their own needs. Whereas HTML users must use the predefined set of tags and attributes, when a user creates his or her own markup language with XML, the set of tags and attributes is designed for the application at hand. For example, if a group of users wants a markup language to describe data about weather phenomena, that language could have tags for cloud forms, thunderstorms, and low-pressure centers. The content of these tags would be restricted to relevant data. If such data is described with HTML, cloud forms could be put in generic tags, but then they could not be distinguished from thunderstorm elements, which would also be in the same generic tags.

Whereas HTML describes the overall layout and gives some presentation hints for general information, XML-based markup languages describe data and its meaning through their individualized tags and attributes. XML does not specify any presentation details.

The great advantage of XML is that application programs can be written to use the meanings of the tags in the given markup language to find specific kinds of data and process it accordingly. The syntax rules of XML, along with the syntax rules for a specific XML-based markup language, allow documents to be validated before any application attempts to process their data. This means that all documents that use a specific markup language can be checked to determine whether they are in the standard form for such documents. Such an approach greatly simplifies the development of application programs that process the data in XML documents.

1.9.5   Overview of JavaScript

JavaScript is a client-side scripting language whose primary uses in Web programming are to validate form data, to build Ajax-enabled HTML documents, and to create dynamic HTML documents.

The name *JavaScript* is misleading because the relationship between Java and JavaScript is tenuous, except for some of the syntax. One of the most important differences between JavaScript and most common programming languages is that JavaScript is dynamically typed. This design is virtually the opposite of that of strongly typed languages such as C++ and Java.

JavaScript "programs" are usually embedded in HTML documents,[13] which are downloaded from a Web server when they are requested by browsers. The JavaScript code in an HTML document is interpreted by an interpreter embedded in the browser on the client.

---

13. We quote the word *programs* to indicate that these are not programs in the general sense of the self-contained collections of C++ or C code we normally call programs.

One of the most important applications of JavaScript is to create and modify documents dynamically. JavaScript defines an object hierarchy that matches a hierarchical model of an HTML document. Elements of an HTML document are accessed through these objects, providing the basis for dynamic documents.

Chapter 4 provides a more detailed look at JavaScript. Chapters 5 and 6 discuss the use of JavaScript to provide access to, and dynamic modification of, HTML documents.

1.9.6   Overview of Flash

There are two components of Flash: the authoring environment, which is a development framework, and the player. Developers use the authoring environment to create static graphics, animated graphics, text, sound, and interactivity to be part of stand-alone HTML documents or to be part of other HTML documents. These documents are served by Web servers to browsers, which use the Flash player plug-in to display the documents. Much of this development is done by clicking buttons, choosing menu items, and dragging and dropping graphics.

Flash makes animation very easy. For example, for motion animation, the developer needs only to supply the beginning and ending positions of the figure to be animated—Flash builds the intervening figures. The interactivity of a Flash application is implemented with ActionScript, a dialect of JavaScript.

Flash is now the leading technology for delivering graphics and animation on the Web. It has been estimated that nearly 99 percent of the world's computers used to access the Internet have a version of the Flash player installed as a plug-in in their browsers.

1.9.7   Overview of PHP

PHP is a server-side scripting language specifically designed for Web applications. PHP code is embedded in HTML documents, as is the case with JavaScript. With PHP, however, the code is interpreted on the server before the HTML document is delivered to the requesting client. A requested document that includes PHP code is preprocessed to interpret the PHP code and insert its output into the HTML document. The browser never sees the embedded PHP code and is not aware that a requested document originally included such code.

PHP is similar to JavaScript, both in terms of its syntactic appearance and in terms of the dynamic nature of its strings and arrays. Both JavaScript and PHP use dynamic data typing, meaning that the type of a variable is controlled by the most recent assignment to it. PHP's arrays are a combination of dynamic arrays and hashes (associative arrays). The language includes a large number of predefined functions for manipulating arrays.

PHP allows simple access to HTML form data, so form processing is easy with PHP. PHP also provides support for many different database management systems. This versatility makes it an excellent language for building programs that need Web access to databases.

1.9.8   Overview of Ajax

Ajax, shorthand for *A*synchronous *Ja*vaScript + *X*ML, had been around for a few years in the early 2000s, but did not acquire its catchy name until 2005.[14] The idea of Ajax is relatively simple, but it results in a different way of viewing and building Web interactions. This new approach produces an enriched Web experience for those using a certain category of Web interactions.

In a traditional (as opposed to Ajax) Web interaction, the user sends messages to the server either by clicking a link or by clicking a form's *Submit* button. After the link has been clicked or the form has been submitted, the client waits until the server responds with a new document. The entire browser display is then replaced by that of the new document. Complicated documents take a significant amount of time to be transmitted from the server to the client and more time to be rendered by the browser. In Web applications that require frequent interactions with the client and remain active for a significant amount of time, the delay in receiving and rendering a complete response document can be disruptive to the user.

In an Ajax Web application, there are two variations from the traditional Web interaction. First, the communication from the browser to the server is asynchronous; that is, the browser need not wait for the server to respond. Instead, the browser user can continue whatever he or she was doing while the server finds and transmits the requested document and the browser renders the new document. Second, the document provided by the server usually is only a relatively small part of the displayed document, and therefore it takes less time to be transmitted and rendered. These two changes can result in much faster interactions between the browser and the server.

The *x* in *Ajax*, from *XML*, is there because in many cases the data supplied by the server is in the form of an XML document, which provides the new data to be placed in the displayed document. However, in some cases the data is plain text, which may even be JavaScript code. It can also be HTML.

The goal of Ajax is to have Web-based applications become closer to desktop (client-resident) applications, in terms of the speed of interactions and the quality of the user experience. Wouldn't we all like our Web-based applications to be as responsive as our word processors?

Ajax is discussed in more depth in Chapter 10.

1.9.9   Overview of Servlets, JavaServer Pages, and JavaServer Faces

There are many computational tasks in a Web interaction that must occur on the server, such as processing order forms and accessing server-resident databases. A Java class called a *servlet* can be used for these applications. A servlet is a compiled Java class, an object of which is executed on the server system when

---

14. Ajax was named by Jesse James Garrett, who has on numerous occasions stated that Ajax is shorthand, not an acronym. Thus, we spell it Ajax, not AJAX.

requested by the HTML document being displayed by the browser. A servlet produces an HTML document as a response, some parts of which are static and are generated by simple output statements, while other parts are created dynamically when the servlet is called.

When an HTTP request is received by a Web server, the Web server examines the request. If a servlet must be called, the Web server passes the request to the servlet processor, called a *servlet container*. The servlet container determines which servlet must be executed, makes sure that it is loaded, and calls it. As the servlet handles the request, it generates an HTML document as its response, which is returned to the server through the response object parameter.

Java can also be used as a server-side scripting language. An HTML document with embedded Java code is one form of JavaServer Pages (JSP). Built on top of servlets, JSP provides alternative ways of constructing dynamic Web documents. JSP takes an opposite approach to that of servlets: Instead of embedding HTML in Java code that provides dynamic documents, code of some form is embedded in HTML documents to provide the dynamic parts of a document. These different forms of code make up the different approaches used by JSP. The basic capabilities of servlets and JSP are the same.

When requested by a browser, a JSP document is processed by a software system called a *JSP container*. Some JSP containers compile the document when the document is loaded on the server; others compile it only when requested. The compilation process translates a JSP document into a servlet and then compiles the servlet. So, JSP is actually a simplified approach to writing servlets.

JavaServer Faces (JSF) adds another layer to the JSP technology. The most important contribution of JSF is an event-driven user interface model for Web applications. Client-generated events can be handled by server-side code with JSF.

Servlets, JSP, and JSF are discussed in Chapter 11.

1.9.10   Overview of Active Server Pages .NET

Active Server Pages .NET (ASP.NET) is a Microsoft framework for building server-side dynamic documents. ASP.NET documents are supported by programming code executed on the Web server. As we saw in Section 1.9.9, JSF uses Java to describe the dynamic generation of HTML documents, as well as to describe computations associated with user interactions with documents. ASP.NET provides an alternative to JSF, with two major differences: First, ASP.NET allows the server-side programming code to be written in any of the .NET languages.[15] Second, in ASP.NET all programming code is compiled, which allows it to execute much faster than interpreted code.

Every ASP.NET document is compiled into a class. From a programmer's point of view, developing dynamic Web documents (and the supporting code) in ASP.NET is similar to developing non-Web applications. Both involve defining classes based on library classes, implementing interfaces from a library, and calling methods defined in library classes. An application class uses, and interacts with,

---

15. In most cases, it is done in either Visual BASIC .NET or C#.

existing classes. In ASP.NET, this is exactly the same for Web applications: Web documents are designed by designing classes.

ASP.NET is discussed in Chapter 12.

1.9.11 Overview of Ruby

Ruby is an object-oriented interpreted scripting language designed by Yukihiro Matsumoto (a.k.a. Matz) in the early 1990s and released in 1996. Since then, it has continually evolved and its level of usage has grown. The original motivation for Ruby was dissatisfaction of its designer with the earlier languages Perl and Python.

The primary characterizing feature of Ruby is that it is a pure object-oriented language, just as is Smalltalk. Every data value is an object and all operations are via method calls. The operators in Ruby are only syntactic mechanisms to specify method calls for the corresponding operations. Because they are methods, many of the operators can be redefined by user programs. All classes, whether predefined or user defined, can have subclasses.

Both classes and objects in Ruby are dynamic in the sense that methods can be dynamically added to either. This means that classes and objects can have different sets of methods at different times during execution. So, different instantiations of the same class can behave differently.

The syntax of Ruby is related to that of Eiffel and Ada. There is no need to declare variables, because dynamic typing is used. In fact, all variables are references and do not have types, although the objects they reference do.

Our interest in Ruby is based on Ruby's use with the Web development framework Rails (see Section 1.9.12). Rails was designed for use with Ruby, and it is Ruby's primary use in Web programming. Programming in Ruby is introduced in Chapter 14.

Ruby is culturally interesting because it is the first programming language designed in Japan that has achieved relatively widespread use outside that country.

1.9.12 Overview of Rails

Rails is a development framework for Web-based applications that access databases. A framework is a system in which much of the more-or-less standard software parts are furnished by the framework, so they need not be written by the applications developer. ASP.NET and JSF are also development frameworks for Web-based applications. Rails, whose more official name is Ruby on Rails, was developed by David Heinemeier Hansson in the early 2000s and was released to the public in July 2004. Since then, it has rapidly gained widespread interest and usage. Rails is based on the Model–View–Controller (MVC) architecture for applications, which clearly separates applications into three parts: presentation, data model, and program logic.

Rails applications are tightly bound to relational databases. Many Web applications are closely integrated with database access, so the Rails relational database framework is a widely applicable architecture.

Rails can be, and often is, used in conjunction with Ajax. Rails uses the JavaScript framework prototype to support Ajax and interactions with the JavaScript model of the document being displayed by the browser. Rails also provides other support for developing Ajax, including producing visual effects.

Rails was designed to be used with Ruby and makes use of the strengths of that language. Furthermore, Rails is written in Ruby. Rails is discussed in Chapter 15.

Summary

The Internet began in the late 1960s as the ARPAnet, which was eventually replaced by NSFnet for nonmilitary users. NSFnet later became known as the Internet. There are now many millions of computers around the world that are connected to the Internet. Although much of the network control equipment is different and many kinds of computers are connected, all of these connections are made through the TCP/IP protocol, making them all appear, at least at the lowest level, the same to the network.

Two kinds of addresses are used on the Internet: IP addresses, which are four-part numbers, for computers; and fully qualified domain names, which are words separated by periods, for people. Fully qualified domain names are translated to IP addresses by name servers running DNS. A number of different information interchange protocols have been created, including `telnet`, `ftp`, and `mailto`.

The Web began in the late 1980s at CERN as a means for physicists to share the results of their work efficiently with colleagues at other locations. The fundamental idea of the Web is to transfer hypertext documents among computers by means of the HTTP protocol on the Internet.

Browsers request HTML documents from Web servers and display them for users. Web servers find and send requested documents to browsers. URLs are used to address all documents on the Internet; the specific protocol to be used is the first field of the URL. URLs also include the fully qualified domain name and a file path to the specific document on the server. The type of a document that is delivered by a Web server appears as a MIME specification in the first line of the document. Web sites can create their own experimental MIME types, provided that they also furnish a program that allows the browser to present the document's contents to the user.

HTTP is the standard protocol for Web communications. HTTP requests are sent over the Internet from browsers to Web servers; HTTP responses are sent from Web servers to browsers to fulfill those requests. The most commonly used HTTP requests are `GET` and `POST`.

Web programmers use several languages to create the documents that servers can provide to browsers. The most basic of these is HTML, the standard markup language for describing how Web documents should be presented by browsers. Tools that can be used without specific knowledge of HTML are available to create HTML documents. A plug-in is a program that can be integrated with a word processor to make it possible to use the word processor to create HTML. A filter converts a document written in some other format to HTML. XML is a meta-markup language that provides a standard way to define new markup languages.

JavaScript is a client-side scripting language that can be embedded in an HTML document to describe simple computations. JavaScript code is interpreted by the browser on the client machine; it provides access to the elements of an HTML document, as well as the ability to change those elements dynamically.

Flash is a framework for building animation into HTML documents. A browser must have a Flash player plug-in to be able to display the movies created with the Flash framework.

Ajax is an approach to building Web applications in which partial document requests are handled asynchronously. Ajax can significantly increase the speed of user interactions, so it is most useful for building systems that have frequent interactions.

PHP is the server-side equivalent of JavaScript. It is an interpreted language whose code is embedded in HTML documents. PHP is used primarily for form processing and database access from browsers.

Servlets are server-side Java programs that are used for form processing, database access, or building dynamic documents. JSP documents, which are translated into servlets, are an alternative approach to building these applications. JSF is a development framework for specifying forms and their processing in JSP documents.

ASP.NET is a Web development framework. The code used in ASP.NET documents, which is executed on the server, can be written in any .NET programming language.

Ruby is a relatively recent object-oriented scripting language that is introduced here primarily because of its use in Rails, a Web applications framework. Rails provides a significant part of the code required to build Web applications that access databases, allowing the developer to spend his or her time on the specifics of the application without dealing with the drudgery of the housekeeping details.

Review Questions

1.1 What was one of the fundamental requirements for the new national computer network proposed by the DoD in the 1960s?

1.2 What protocol is used by all computer connections to the Internet?

1.3 What is the form of an IP address?

1.4 Describe a fully qualified domain name.

1.5 What is the task of a DNS name server?

1.6 What is the purpose of `telnet`?

1.7 In the first proposal for the Web, what form of information was to be interchanged?

1.8   What is hypertext?

1.9   What category of browser, introduced in 1993, led to a huge expansion of Web usage?

1.10 In what common situation is the document returned by a Web server created after the request is received?

1.11 What is the document root of a Web server?

1.12 What is a virtual document tree?

1.13 What is the server root of a Web server?

1.14 What is a virtual host?

1.15 What is a proxy server?

1.16 What does the `file` protocol specify?

1.17 How do partial paths to documents work in Web servers?

1.18 When a browser requests a directory without giving its name, what is the name of the file that is normally returned by the Web server?

1.19 What is the purpose of a MIME type specification in a request–response transaction between a browser and a server?

1.20 With what must a Web server furnish the browser when it returns a document with an experimental MIME type?

1.21 Describe the purposes of the five most commonly used HTTP methods.

1.22 What is the purpose of the `Accept` field in an HTTP request?

1.23 What response header field is most often required?

1.24 Prior to HTTP 1.1, how long were connections between browsers and servers normally maintained?

1.25 What important capability is lacking in a markup language?

1.26 What problem is addressed by using a public-key approach to encryption?

1.27 Is it practically possible to compute the private key associated with a given public key?

1.28 What is the difference between a virus and a worm?

1.29 What appears to motivate a hacker to create and disseminate a virus?

1.30 What is a plug-in?

1.31 What is a filter HTML converter?

1.32 Why must code generated by a filter often be modified manually before use?

1.33   What is the great advantage of XML over HTML for describing data?

1.34   How many different tags are predefined in an XML-based markup language?

1.35   What is the relationship between Java and JavaScript?

1.36   What are the most common applications of JavaScript?

1.37   Where is JavaScript most often interpreted, on the server or on the browser?

1.38   What is the primary use of Flash?

1.39   Where are Flash movies interpreted, on the server or on the browser?

1.40   Where are servlets executed, on the server or on the browser?

1.41   In what language are servlets written?

1.42   In what way are JSP documents the opposite of servlets?

1.43   What is the purpose of JSF?

1.44   What is the purpose of ASP.NET?

1.45   In what language is the code in an ASP.NET document usually written?

1.46   Where is PHP code interpreted, on the server or on the browser?

1.47   In what ways is PHP similar to JavaScript?

1.48   In what ways is Ruby more object oriented than Java?

1.49   In what country was Ruby developed?

1.50   What is the purpose of Rails?

1.51   For what particular kind of Web application was Rails designed?

1.52   Which programming languages are used in Ajax applications?

1.53   In what fundamental way does an Ajax Web application differ from a traditional Web application?

Exercises

1.1   For the following products, to what brand do you have access, what is its version number, and what is the latest available version?

a. Browser

b. Web server

c. JavaScript

d. PHP

e. Servlets

         f. ASP.NET

         g. Ruby

         h. Rails

1.2   Search the Web for information on the history of the following technologies, and write a brief overview of those histories:

         a. TCP/IP

         b. SGML

         c. HTML

         d. ARPAnet

         e. BITnet

         f. XML

         g. JavaScript

         h. Flash

         i. Servlets

         j. JSP

         k. JSF

         l. Rails

         m. Ajax

Introduction to HTML/XHTML

This chapter introduces the most commonly used subset of the Hypertext Markup Language (HTML). Because of the simplicity of HTML, the discussion moves quickly. Although the eXtensible Hypertext Markup Language is no longer in the evolutionary line of HTML, the strictness of its syntax rules are valuable and their use is acceptable in HTML documents, so we describe and use the XHTML form of HTML. The chapter begins with a brief history of the evolution of HTML and XHTML, followed by a description of the form of tags and the structure of an HTML document. Then, tags used to specify the presentation of text are discussed, including those for line breaks, paragraph breaks, headings, and block quotations, as well as tags for specifying the style and relative size of fonts. This discussion is followed by a description of the formats and uses of images in Web documents. Next, hypertext links are introduced. Three kinds of lists—ordered, unordered, and definition—are then covered. After that, the HTML tags and attributes used to specify tables are discussed. The next section of the chapter introduces forms, which provide the means to collect information from Web clients. Following this is a section that describes and illustrates some of the most important features that are new in HTML5. Finally, the last section summarizes the syntactic differences between HTML and XHTML.

One good reference for information about HTML and XHTML is `http://www.w3schools.com`.

2.1 Origins and Evolution of HTML and XHTML

HTML is a markup language, which means it is used to mark parts of documents to indicate how they should appear, in print or on a display.[1] HTML is defined with the meta-markup language,[2] Standard Generalized Markup Language (SGML), which is an International Standards Organization (ISO) standard notation for describing information-formatting languages.[3] The original intent of HTML was different from those of other such languages, which dictate all of the presentation details of text, such as font style, size, and color. Rather, HTML was designed to specify document structure at a higher and more abstract level, necessary because HTML-specified documents had to be displayable on a variety of computer systems using different browsers.

The appearance of style sheets that could be used with HTML in the late 1990s advanced its capabilities closer to those of other information-formatting languages by providing ways to include the specification of presentation details. These specifications are introduced in Chapter 3.

2.1.1 Versions of HTML and XHTML

The original version of HTML was designed in conjunction with the structure of the Web and the first browser at Conseil Européen pour la Recherche Nucléaire (CERN), or European Laboratory for Particle Physics. Use of the Web began its meteoric rise in 1993 with the release of MOSAIC, the first graphical Web browser. Not long after MOSAIC was commercialized and marketed by Netscape, the company founded by the designers of MOSAIC, Microsoft began developing its browser, Internet Explorer (IE). The release of IE in 1995 marked the beginning of a four-year marketing competition between Netscape and Microsoft. During this time, both companies worked feverously to develop their own extensions to HTML in an attempt to gain market advantage. Naturally, this competition led to incompatible versions of HTML, both between the two developers and also between older and newer releases from the same company. These differences

---

1. The term markup comes from the publishing industry, where in the past documents were marked up by hand to indicate to a typesetter how the document should appear in print.

2. A meta-markup language is a language for defining markup languages.

3. Not all information-formatting languages are based on SGML; for example, PostScript and LaTeX are not.

made it a serious challenge to Web content providers to design single HTML documents that could be viewed by the different browsers.

In late 1994, Tim Berners-Lee, who developed the initial version of HTML, started the World Wide Web Consortium (W3C), whose primary purpose was to develop and distribute standards for Web technologies, starting with HTML. The first HTML standard, HTML 2.0, was released in late 1995. It was followed by HTML 3.2 in early 1997. Up to that point, W3C was trying to catch up with the browser makers, and HTML 3.2 was really just a reflection of the then-current features that had been developed by Netscape and Microsoft. Fortunately, since 1998 the evolution of HTML has been dominated by W3C, in part because Netscape gradually withdrew from its browser competition with Microsoft. There are now several different organizations that produce and distribute browsers, all of which except Microsoft, at least until recently, followed relatively closely the HTML standards produced by W3C. The HTML 4.0 specification was published in late 1997. The 4.01 version of HTML, which is the latest completed standard version, was approved by W3C in late 1999.

The appearance of style sheets (in 1997) that could be used with HTML made some features of earlier versions of HTML obsolete. These features, as well as some others, have been *deprecated*, meaning that they will be dropped from HTML in the future. Deprecating a feature is a warning to users to stop using it because it will not be supported forever. Although even the latest releases of browsers still support the deprecated parts of HTML, we do not include descriptions of them in this book.

There are two fundamental problems with HTML 4.01. First, it specifies loose syntax rules. These permit many variations of document forms which may be interpreted differently by different browsers. As a result of the lax syntax rules, HTML documents naturally have been haphazardly written. By some estimates, 99 percent of the HTML documents served on the Web contain errors. The second problem with HTML is that its specification does not define how a user agent (an HTML processor, most often a browser) is to recover when erroneous code is encountered. Consequently, every browser uses its own variation of error recovery.

XML[4] is an alternative to SGML. It was designed to describe data and it has strict syntax rules. The XML specification requires that XML processors not accept XML documents with any errors.

XHTML 1.0, which was approved in early 2000, is a redefinition of HTML 4.01 using XML. XHTML 1.0 is actually three standards: Strict, Transitional, and Frameset. The Strict standard requires all of the syntax rules of XHTML 1.0 be followed. The Transitional standard allows deprecated features of XHTML 1.0 to be included. The Frameset standard allows the collection of frame elements and attributes to be included, although they have been deprecated. The XHTML 1.1 standard was recommended by W3C in May 2001. This standard, primarily a modularization of XHTML 1.0, drops some of the features of its predecessor—most notably, frames.

The XHTML 1.0 specification addresses one of the problems of HTML 4.01 by providing complete rules stating what is and what is not syntactically acceptable. Furthermore, it specifies that XHTML documents must be served with the `application/xhmtl+xml` MIME type. This means that user agents were required to halt interpretation of an XHTML document when the first

---

4. XML (eXtensible Markup Language) is the topic of Chapter 7.

syntactic error was found, as is the case with XML documents. Because this was a drastic response to the error-ignoring nature of HTML 4.01, the XHTML 1.0 specification included Appendix C, which allowed XHTML documents to be served as HTML, that is, with the `text/html` MIME type, which allows the continuation of the practice of user agents ignoring syntactic errors.

The XHTML 1.1 specification, published in 2001, included only relatively minor additions to XHTML 1.0, but eliminated the Appendix C loophole. This meant that W3C officially specified that XHTML 1.1 documents had to be served as `application/xhtml+xml` MIME type and that user agents were required to reject all syntactically incorrect documents. This is an example of "draconian error handling."

Although the value of the consistent and coherent syntax rules of XHTML were widely recognized and accepted, the draconian error handling was not. It was generally agreed by developers and providers of markup documents that browser users should not be given error messages due to the syntax errors found in documents they were attempting to view. The result was that XHTML 1.1 documents were still served with the `text/html` MIME type and browsers continued to use forgiving HTML parsers.

W3C apparently ignored these issues and forged ahead with the development of the next version of XHTML, 2.0. The design of XHTML 2.0 further promoted its ultimate demise by not requiring it to be backward compatible with either HTML 4.01 or XHTML 1.1.

In reaction to the XHTML 1.1 specification and the development of XHTML 2.0, a new organization was formed in 2004 by browser vendors, Web development companies, and some W3C members. This group, which became known as the Web Hypertext Application Technology (WHAT) Working Group, began working on the next version of HTML, which was to be based on HTML 4.01, rather than XHTML 1.1. Among the goals of the new version of HTML were the following: backward compatibility with HTML 4.01, error handling that is clearly defined in the specification, and users would not be exposed to document syntax errors. Initially, W3C had no interest in being involved in this new project, which would compete with XHTML 2.0.

The first results of the WHAT Working Group were WebForm 2.0, which extended HTML forms, Web Applications 1.0, which was a new version of HTML, and an algorithm for user agent error handling.

After several years of separate work, W3C on XHTML 2.0 and the WHAT Working Group on a new version of HTML, the head of W3C, Berners-Lee, made the momentous decision in 2006 that W3C would begin working with the WHAT Working Group. In 2009, W3C decided to adopt the HTML development and drop the XHTML 2.0 development effort. The first action of W3C was to rename Web Applications 1.0 as HTML5.

2.1.2   HTML versus XHTML

Until 2010, many Web developers used XHTML to gain the advantages of stricter syntax rules, standard formats, and validation, but their documents were served as `text/html` and browsers used HTML parsers. Other developers stubbornly clung to HTML. They are now enthusiastically climbing on the HTML5 bandwagon. Meanwhile, the XHTML crowd is disappointed and confused at the realization that the W3C effort to coerce developers into using the more strict syntactic rules of XHTML to produce documents less prone to errors is over—W3C had capitulated, apparently willing to accept life in a world populated by syntactically sloppy documents.

In previous editions of this book, we followed the W3C lead in strict persuance of clear and syntactically correct documents by presenting XHTML 1.0 Strict example documents and using and encouraging validation to ensure adherence to that standard. Now, the major browser vendors have all implemented at least some of the more important new features of HTML5. This makes use of the W3C XHTML 1.0 Strict validator impossible.

There are strong reasons that one should use XHTML. One of the most compelling is that quality and consistency in any endeavor, be it electrical wiring, software development, or Web document development, rely on standards. HTML has few syntactic rules, and HTML processors (e.g., browsers) do not enforce the rules it does have. Therefore, HTML authors have a high degree of freedom to use their own syntactic preferences to create documents. Because of this freedom, HTML documents lack consistency, both in low-level syntax and in overall structure. By contrast, XHTML has strict syntactic rules that impose a consistent structure on all XHTML documents. Furthermore, the fact that there are a large number of poorly structured HTML documents on the Web is a poor excuse for generating more.

There are two issues in choosing between HTML and XHTML: First, one must decide whether the additional discipline required to use XHTML is worth the gain in document clarity and uniformity in display across a variety of browsers. Second, one must decide whether the possibility of validation afforded by authoring XHTML documents is worth the trouble.

In this edition, we follow a compromise approach. Of course we want to discuss some of the new exciting features of HTML5. At some point in the future they will be widely used. However, we also are firm believers in standards and strict syntax rules. So, our compromise is to write and promote HTML5, but also the syntax rules of XHTML 1.0 Strict, all of which are legal in HTML5. In Section 2.5.3 we describe how to validate that documents follow the XHTML 1.0 Strict syntax rules.

The remainder of this chapter provides an introduction to the most commonly used tags and attributes of HTML, as well as some of the new tags and attributes of HTML5. We present this material using the XHTML 1.0 Strict syntax, but point out the HTML form when it is different.

2.2   Basic Syntax

The fundamental syntactic units of HTML are called *tags*. In general, tags are used to specify categories of content. For each kind of tag, a browser has default presentation specifications for the specified content. The syntax of a tag is the tag's name surrounded by angle brackets (< and >). Tag names must be written in all lowercase letters.[5] Most tags appear in pairs: an opening tag and a closing tag. The name of a closing tag, when one is required, is the name of its corresponding opening tag with a slash attached to the beginning. For example, if the tag's name is p, its closing tag is `</p>`. Whatever appears between a tag and its closing tag is the *content* of the tag. A browser display of an HTML document shows the content of all of the document's tags; it is the information the document is meant to portray. Not all tags can have content.

The opening tag and its closing tag together specify a container for the content they enclose.[6] The container and its content together are called an *element*. For example, consider the following element:

```
<p> This is simple stuff. </p>
```

Attributes, which are used to specify alternative meanings of a tag, are written between an opening tag's name and its right angle bracket. They are specified in keyword form, which means that the attribute's name is followed by an equals sign and the attribute's value. Attribute names, like tag names, are written in lowercase letters. Attribute values must be delimited by double quotes.[7] There will be numerous examples of attributes in the remainder of this chapter.

Comments in programs increase the readability of those programs. Comments in HTML have the same purpose. They are written in HTML in the following form:

```
<!--   anything except two adjacent dashes -->
```

Browsers ignore HTML comments—they are for people only. Comments can be spread over as many lines as are needed. For example, you could have the following comment:

```
<!--   PetesHome.html
       This document describes the home document of
       Pete's Pickles
       -->
```

Informational comments are as important in HTML documents as they are in programs. Documents sometimes have lengthy sequences of lines of markup that together produce some part of the display. If such a sequence is not preceded by a comment that states its purpose, a document reader may have difficulty determining why the sequence is there. As is the case in programs, commenting every line is both tedious and counterproductive. However, comments that precede logical collections of lines of markup are essential to making a document (or a program) more understandable.

Besides comments, several other kinds of text that are ignored by browsers may appear in an HTML document. Browsers ignore all unrecognized tags. They also ignore line breaks. Line breaks that show up in the displayed content can

---

5. In HTML, tag names and attribute names can be written in any mixture of uppercase and lowercase letters.

6. In XHTML, the closing paragraph tag is required, although in HTML it is optional.

7. In HTML, some attribute values, for example, numbers, do not need to be quoted.

be specified, but only with tags designed for that purpose. The same is true for multiple spaces and tabs.

When introduced to HTML, programmers find it a bit frustrating. In a program, the statements specify exactly what the computer must do. HTML tags are treated more like suggestions to the browser. If a reserved word is misspelled in a program, the error is usually detected by the language implementation system and the program is not executed. However, a misspelled tag name usually results in the tag being ignored by the browser, with no indication to the user that anything has been left out. Browsers are even allowed to ignore tags that they recognize. Furthermore, the user can configure his or her browser to react to specific tags in different ways.

2.3 Standard HTML Document Structure

The first line of every HTML document is a DOCTYPE command, which specifies the particular SGML document-type definition (DTD) with which the document complies. For HTML, this declaration is simply the following:

```
<!DOCTYPE html>
```

An HTML document must include the four tags <html>, <head>, <title>, and <body>.[8] The <html> tag identifies the root element of the document. So, HTML documents always have an <html> tag following the DOCTYPE command and they always end with the closing html tag, </html>. The html element includes an attribute, lang, which specifies the language in which the document is written, as shown in the following element:

```
<html lang = "en">
```

In this example, the language is specified as "en", which means English.

An HTML document consists of two parts, named the *head* and the *body*. The head element provides information about the document but does not provide its content. The head element always contains two simple elements, a title element and a meta element. The meta element is used to provide additional information about a document. The meta element has no content; rather, all of the information provided is specified with attributes. At a minimum, the meta tag specifies the character set used to write the document. The most popular international character set used for the Web is the 8-bit Unicode Transformation Format (UTF-8). This character set uses from one to six bytes to represent a character, but is backward compatible with the ASCII character set. This compatibility is accomplished by having all of the single-byte characters in UTF-8 correspond to the ASCII characters. Following is the necessary meta element:[9]

```
<meta charset = "utf-8" />
```

---

8. This is another XHTML rule. Documents that do not include all of these are acceptable in HTML.

9. This meta element is required by HTML, but not for XHTML.

The slash at the end of this tag indicates that it has no closing tag—it is a combined opening and closing tag.

The content of the title element is displayed by the browser at the top of its display window, usually in the browser window's title bar.

The body of a document provides the content of the document.

Following is a skeletal document that illustrates the basic structure:

```
<!DOCTYPE html>
<!-- File name and document purpose -->
<html lang = "en">
  <head>
    <title> A title for the document </title>
    <meta charset = "utf-8" />
    ...
  </head>
  <body>
  ...
  </body>
</html>
```

Notice that we have used a simple formatting pattern for the document, similar to what is often used for programs. Whenever an element is nested inside a preceding element, the nested element is indented. In this book, we will indent nested elements two spaces, although there is nothing special about that number. As is the case with programs, the indentation pattern is used to enhance readability.

2.4   Basic Text Markup

This section describes how the text content of an HTML document can be formatted with HTML tags. By *formatting*, we mean layout and some presentation details. For now, we will ignore the other kinds of content that can appear in an HTML document.

2.4.1   Paragraphs

Text is normally organized into paragraphs in the body of a document.[10] The XHTML standard does not allow text to be placed directly in a document body.[11] Instead, text is often placed in the content of a paragraph element, specified with the tag <p>. In displaying text, the browser puts as many words as will fit on the

---

10. In Section 2.10, several HTML5 elements are introduced that provide more detailed ways of organizing text (and other information) in a document.

11. HTML allows text to appear virtually anywhere in a document.

lines in the browser window. The browser supplies a line break at the end of each line. As stated in Section 2.2, line breaks embedded in text are ignored by the browser. For example, the following paragraph might[12] be displayed by a browser as shown in Figure 2.1:

```
<p>
    Mary had
a
    little lamb, its fleece was white as snow. And
  everywhere that
   Mary went, the lamb
  was sure to go.
</p>
```

Mary had a little lamb, its fleece was white as snow. And everywhere that Mary went, the lamb was sure to go.

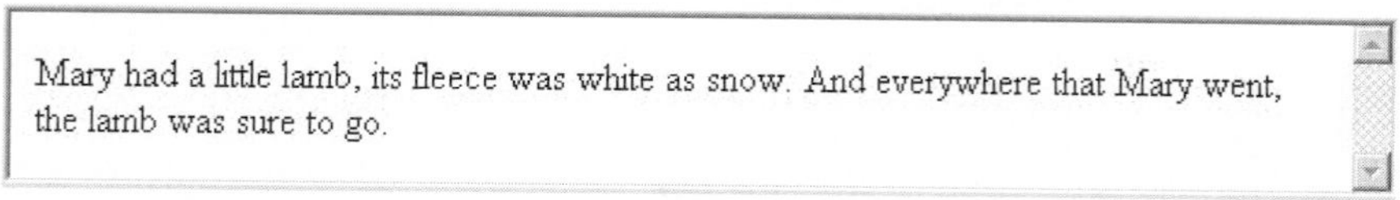

Figure 2.1 Filling lines

Notice that multiple spaces in the source paragraph element are replaced by single spaces in Figure 2.1.

The following is our first example of a complete HTML document:

```
<!DOCTYPE html>    Type of doc
<!-- greet.html
     A trivial document    comments
     -->
<html lang = "en">    html element with language attribute
  <head>    block tag
    <title> Our first document </title>
    <meta charset = "utf-8" />
  </head>
  <body>
    <p>    content (paragraph)
      Greetings from your Webmaster!
    </p>
  </body>
</html>
```

Figure 2.2 shows a browser display of `greet.html`.

---

12. We say "might" because the width of the display that the browser uses determines how many words will fit on a line.

Greetings from your Webmaster!

Figure 2.2 Display of `greet.html`

If a paragraph tag appears at a position other than the beginning of the line, the browser breaks the current line and inserts a blank line. For example, the following line would be displayed as shown in Figure 2.3:

```
<p> Mary had a little lamb, </p> <p> its fleece was white
    as snow. </p>
```

Mary had a little lamb,

its fleece was white as snow.

Figure 2.3 The paragraph element

2.4.2   Line Breaks

Sometimes text requires an explicit line break without the preceding blank line. This is exactly what the break tag does. The break tag differs syntactically from the paragraph tag in that it can have no content and therefore has no closing tag (because a closing tag would serve no purpose). In XHTML, the break tag is specified with the following:

```
<br />
```

The slash indicates that the tag is both an opening and closing tag. The space before the slash represents the absent content.[13]

Consider the following markup:

```
<p>
Mary had a little lamb, <br />
   its fleece was white as snow.
</p>
```

This markup would be displayed as shown in Figure 2.4.

Mary had a little lamb,
its fleece was white as snow.

Figure 2.4 Line breaks

---

13. Some older browsers have trouble with the tag `<br/>` but not with `<br />`. In HTML, the break tag can be written as `<br>`, without a closing tag or slash.

2.4.3   Preserving White Space

Sometimes it is desirable to preserve the white space in text—that is, to prevent the browser from eliminating multiple spaces and ignoring embedded line breaks. This can be specified with the `pre` tag—for example,

```
<pre>
Mary
     had a
          little
               lamb
</pre>
```

This markup would be displayed as shown in Figure 2.5. Notice that the content of the `pre` element is shown in monospace, rather than in the default font. The `pre` element not only keeps line breaks from the source, it also preserves the character and line spacing.

```
Mary
     had a
          little
               lamb
```

Figure 2.5 The `pre` element

A `pre` element can contain virtually any other tags, except those that cause a paragraph break, such as paragraph elements. Because other markup can appear in a `pre` element, special characters in text content, such as <, must be avoided. In Section 2.4.7, we will describe how to safely include such characters as character entities.

2.4.4   Headings

Text is often separated into sections in documents by beginning each section with a heading. Larger sections sometimes have headings that appear more prominent than headings for sections nested inside them. In HTML, there are six levels of headings, specified by the tags `<h1>`, `<h2>`, `<h3>`, `<h4>`, `<h5>`, and `<h6>`, where `<h1>` specifies the highest-level heading. Headings are usually displayed in a boldface font whose default font size depends on the number in the heading tag. On most browsers, `<h1>`, `<h2>`, and `<h3>` use font sizes that are larger than that of the default size of text, `<h4>` uses the default size, and `<h5>` and `<h6>` use smaller sizes. The heading tags always break the current line, so their content always appears on a new line. Browsers usually insert some vertical space before and after all headings.

The following example illustrates the use of headings:

```
<!DOCTYPE html>
<!-- headings.html
     An example to illustrate headings
     -->
<html lang = "en">
  <head>
    <title> Headings </title>
    <meta charset = "utf-8" />
  </head>
  <body>
    <h1> Aidan's Airplanes (h1) </h1>
    <h2> The best in used airplanes (h2) </h2>
    <h3> "We've got them by the hangarful" (h3) </h3>
    <h4> We're the guys to see for a good used airplane (h4) </h4>
    <h5> We offer great prices on great planes (h5) </h5>
    <h6> No returns, no guarantees, no refunds,
         all sales are final! (h6) </h6>
  </body>
</html>
```

Figure 2.6 shows a browser display of `headings.html`.

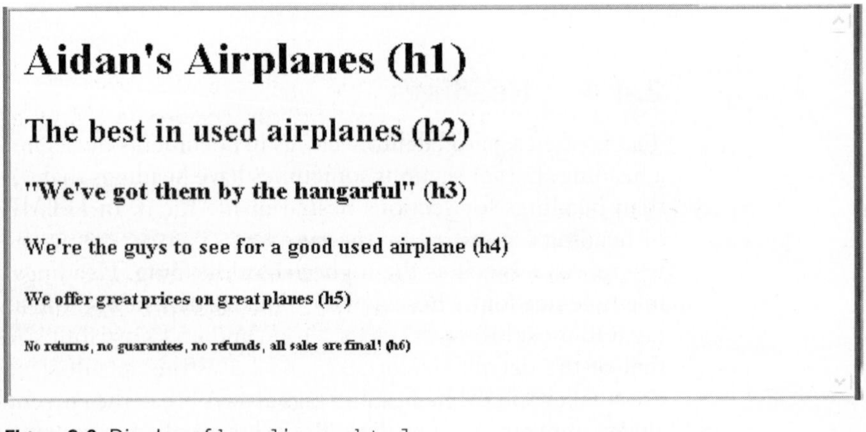

Figure 2.6 Display of `headings.html`

2.4.5   Block Quotations

Sometimes we want a block of text to be set off from the normal flow of text in a document. In many cases, such a block is a long quotation. The `<blockquote>` tag is designed for this situation. Browser designers are allowed to determine how the content of `<blockquote>` can be made to look different from the surrounding text. However, in most cases the block of text simply is indented on both sides. Consider the following example document:

```
<!DOCTYPE html>
<!-- blockquote.html
     An example to illustrate a blockquote
     -->
<html lang = "en">
  <head>
    <title> Blockquotes </title>
    <meta charset = "utf-8" />
  </head>
  <body>
    <p>
       Abraham Lincoln is generally regarded as one of the greatest
       presidents of the United States. His most famous speech was
       delivered in Gettysburg, Pennsylvania, during the Civil War.
       This speech began with
    </p>
    <blockquote>
      <p>
        "Fourscore and seven years ago our fathers brought forth on
        this continent, a new nation, conceived in Liberty, and
        dedicated to the proposition that all men are created equal.
      </p>
      <p>
        Now we are engaged in a great civil war, testing whether
        that nation or any nation so conceived and so dedicated,
        can long endure."
      </p>
    </blockquote>
    <p>
      Whatever one's opinion of Lincoln, no one can deny the
      enormous and lasting effect he had on the United States.
    </p>
  </body>
</html>
```

Figure 2.7 shows a browser display of `blockquote.html`.

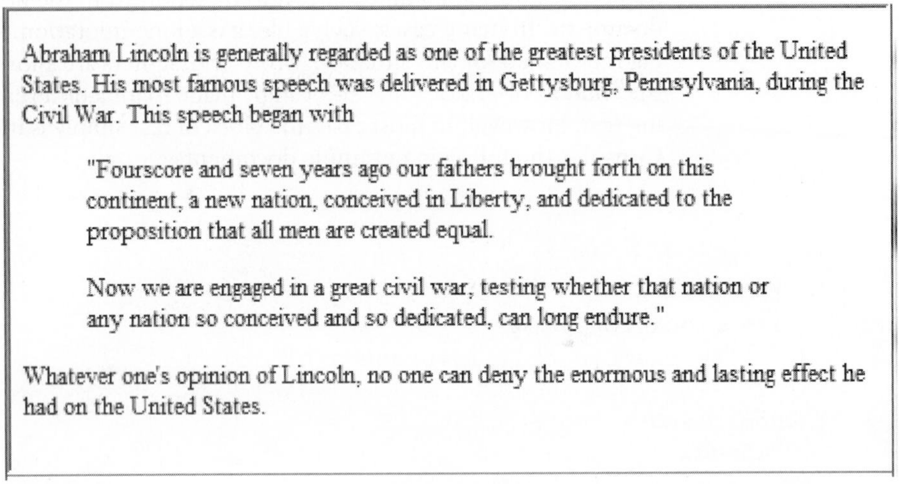

Abraham Lincoln is generally regarded as one of the greatest presidents of the United States. His most famous speech was delivered in Gettysburg, Pennsylvania, during the Civil War. This speech began with

"Fourscore and seven years ago our fathers brought forth on this continent, a new nation, conceived in Liberty, and dedicated to the proposition that all men are created equal.

Now we are engaged in a great civil war, testing whether that nation or any nation so conceived and so dedicated, can long endure."

Whatever one's opinion of Lincoln, no one can deny the enormous and lasting effect he had on the United States.

Figure 2.7 Display of `blockquote.html`.

2.4.6 Font Styles and Sizes

Early Web designers used a collection of tags to set font styles and sizes. For example, `<i>` specified italics and `<b>` specified bold. Since the advent of cascading style sheets (see Chapter 3), the use of these tags has become passé. There are a few tags for fonts that are still in widespread use, called *content-based style tags*. These tags are called content based because they indicate the particular kind of text that appears in their content. Three of the most commonly used content-based tags are the emphasis tag, the strong tag, and the code tag.

The emphasis tag, `<em>`, specifies that its textual content is special and should be displayed in some way that indicates this distinctiveness. Most browsers use italics for such content.

The strong tag, `<strong>` is like the emphasis tag, but more so. Browsers often set the content of strong elements in bold.

The code tag, `<code>`, is used to specify a monospace font, usually for program code. For example, consider the following element:

```
<code> cost = quantity * price </code>
```

This markup would be displayed as shown in Figure 2.8.

```
cost = quantity * price
```

Figure 2.8 The `<code>` element

Subscript and superscript characters can be specified by the `<sub>` and `<sup>` tags, respectively. These are not content-based tags. For example,

```
X<sub>2</sub><sup>3</sup> + y<sub>1</sub><sup>2</sup>
```

would be displayed as shown in Figure 2.9.

$$x_2^{\,3} + y_1^{\,2}$$

Figure 2.9 The `<sub>` and `<sup>` elements

Content-based style tags are not affected by `<blockquote>`, except when there is a conflict. For example, if the text content of `<blockquote>` is normally set in italics by the browser and a part of that text is made the content of an `em` element, the `em` element would have no effect.

Tags are categorized as being either block or inline. The content of an *inline* tag appears on the current line (if it fits). So, an inline tag does not implicitly include a line break. One exception is `br`, which is an inline tag, but its entire purpose is to insert a line break in the content. A *block* tag breaks the current line so that its content appears on a new line. The heading and block quote tags are block tags, whereas `<em>` and `<strong>` are inline tags. In XHTML, block tags cannot appear in the content of inline tags. Therefore, a block tag can never be nested directly in an inline tag. Also, inline tags and text cannot be directly nested in body or form elements. Only block tags can be so nested. That is why the example `greet.html` has the text content of its body nested in a paragraph element.

2.4.7   Character Entities

HTML provides a collection of special characters that are sometimes needed in a document but cannot be typed as themselves. In some cases, these characters are used in HTML in some special way—for example, > and < are used to delimit tag names. In other cases, the characters do not appear on keyboards, such as the small raised circle that represents "degrees" in a reference to temperature. Finally, there is the nonbreaking space, which browsers regard as a hard space—they do not squeeze them out, as they do other multiple spaces. These special characters are defined as *entities*, which are codes for the characters. The browser replaces an entity in a document by its associated character. Table 2.1 lists some of the most commonly used entities.

Table 2.1 Some commonly used entities

Character	Entity	Meaning
&	`&amp;`	Ampersand
<	`&lt;`	Is less than
>	`&gt;`	Is greater than
"	`&quot;`	Double quote
'	`&apos;`	Single quote (apostrophe)
$\frac{1}{4}$	`&frac14;`	One-quarter
$\frac{1}{2}$	`&frac12;`	One-half
$\frac{3}{4}$	`&frac34;`	Three-quarters
°	`&deg;`	Degree
(space)	` `	Nonbreaking space
©	`&copy;`	Copyright
€	`&euro;`	Euro

For example, the following text:

```
The price is < 10 Euros
```

could be placed in the content of a document as the following:

```
The price is &lt; 10 &euro;
```

2.4.8   Horizontal Rules

Two parts of a document can be separated from each other by placing a horizontal line between them, thereby making the document easier to read. Such lines are called *horizontal rules*, and the block tag that creates them is `<hr />`. The `<hr />` tag causes a line break (ending the current line) and places a line across the screen. The browser chooses the thickness, length, and horizontal placement of the line. Typically, browsers display lines that are three pixels thick.

Note again the slash in the `<hr />` tag, indicating that this tag has no content and no closing tag.[14]

2.4.9   Other Uses of the `meta` Element

The `meta` element, which we have been using to specify the character set used in documents, is often used to provide information about the document, primarily for search engines. The two attributes that are used for this are `name` and

---

14. The horizontal rule tag can be written in HTML as `<hr>`.

content. The user makes up a name as the value of the `name` attribute and specifies information through the `content` attribute. One commonly chosen name is `keywords`; the value of the `content` attribute associated with the keywords are those which the author of a document believes characterizes his or her document. An example is as follows:

```
<meta name = "keywords"  content = "binary trees,
linked lists, stacks" />
```

Web search engines use the information provided with the `meta` element to categorize Web documents in their indices. So, if the author of a document seeks widespread exposure for the document, one or more `meta` elements are included to ensure that it will be found by Web search engines. For example, if an entire book were published as a Web document, it might have the following `meta` elements:

[handwritten note in margin: Include many meta elements]

```
<meta name = "Title" content = "Don Quixote" />
<meta name = "Author"  content = "Miguel Cervantes" />
<meta  name = "keywords"  content = "novel,
 Spanish literature, groundbreaking work" />
```

2.5 Images

The inclusion of images in a document can dramatically enhance its appearance, although images slow the document-download process. The file in which the image is stored is specified in a tag. The image is inserted into the display of the document by the browser.

2.5.1 Image Formats

The two most common methods of representing images are the Graphic Interchange Format (GIF, pronounced like the first syllable of *jiffy*) and the Joint Photographic Experts Group (JPEG, pronounced *jay-peg*) format. Most contemporary browsers can render images in either of these two formats. Files in both formats are compressed to reduce storage needs and allow faster transfer over the Internet.

The GIF format was developed by the CompuServe network service provider for the specific purpose of transmitting images. It uses 8-bit color representations for pixels, allowing a pixel to have 256 different colors. If you are not familiar with color representations, this format may seem to be entirely adequate. However, the color displays on most contemporary computers can display a huge number of colors. Files containing GIF images use the `.gif` (or `.GIF`) extension on their names. GIF images can be made to appear transparent. *[handwritten note: ← what does this mean?]*

The JPEG format uses 24-bit color representations for pixels, which allows JPEG images to include more than 16 million different colors. Files that store JPEG images use the `.jpg` (or `.JPG` or `.jpeg`) extension on their names. The compression algorithm used by JPEG is better at shrinking an image than the one used by GIF. This compression process actually loses some of the color accuracy of the image, but because there is so much to begin with, the loss is rarely discernible by *[handwritten margin note, top right:] What does transparency mean? Make the background of the picture transparent*

[handwritten margin note, left:] Preferred Order 1. PNG 2. JPEG 3. GIF

the user. Because of this powerful compression process, even though a JPEG image has much more color information than a GIF image of the same subject, the JPEG image can be smaller than the GIF image. Hence, JPEG images are often preferred to GIF images. One disadvantage of JPEG is that it does not support transparency.

A third image format is now gaining popularity: Portable Network Graphics (PNG, pronounced *ping*). PNG was designed in 1996 as a free replacement for GIF after the patent owner for GIF, Unisys, suggested that the company might begin charging royalties for documents that included GIF images.[15] Actually, PNG is a good replacement for both GIF and JPEG because it has the best characteristics of each (the possibility of transparency, as provided by GIF, and the same large number of colors as JPEG). One drawback of PNG is that, because its compression algorithm does not sacrifice picture clarity, its images require more space than comparable JPEG images.[16] Support for PNG in the earlier IE browsers was unacceptably poor, which kept many developers from using PNG. However, IE9 has adequate support for it. Information on PNG can be found at `www.w3.org/Graphics/PNG`.

2.5.2   The Image Element

The image element, whose tag is `<img />`, is an inline element that specifies an image that is to appear in a document. In its simplest form, the image tag includes two attributes: `src`, which specifies the file containing the image; and `alt`, which specifies text to be displayed when it is not possible to display the image. If the file is in the same directory as the HTML file of the document, the value of `src` is just the image's file name. In many cases, image files are stored in a subdirectory of the directory where the HTML files are stored. For example, the image files might be stored in a subdirectory named `images`. If the image file's name is `stars.jpg` and the image file is stored in the `images` subdirectory, the value of `src` would be as follows:

```
"images/stars.jpg"
```

Some seriously aged browsers are not capable of displaying images. When such a browser finds an `<img />` tag, it simply ignores its content, possibly leaving the user confused by the text in the neighborhood of where the image was supposed to be. Also, graphical browsers, which *are* capable of displaying images, may have image downloading disabled by the browser user. This is done when the Internet connection is slow and the user chooses not to wait for images to download. It is also done by visually impaired users. In any case, it is helpful to have some text displayed in place of the ignored image. For these reasons, the `alt` attribute is required by XHTML. The value of `alt` is displayed whenever the browser cannot or has been instructed not to display the image.

Two optional attributes of `img`—`width` and `height`—can be included to specify (in pixels) the size of the rectangle for the image. These attributes

---

15. The patent expired in the United States in 2003.

16. Space is not the direct issue; download time, which depends on file size, is the real issue.

can be used to scale the size of the image (i.e., to make it larger or smaller). Care must be taken to ensure that the image is not distorted in the resizing. For example, if the image is square, the `width` and `height` attribute values must be kept equal when they are changed. For example, if the image in the file `C210.jpg` is square and we want it to fit in a 200 pixel square, we could use the following:

```
<img src = "c210.jpg"  height = "200"  width = "200"
     alt = "Picture of a Cessna 210" />
```

A percentage value can be given for the width of an image. This specifies the percentage of the width of the display that will be occupied by the image. For example, `width = "50%"` will result in the image filling half of the width of the display. If no height is given and a percentage value is given for the width, the browser will scale the height to the width, maintaining the original shape of the image.

The following example extends the airplane ad document to include information about a specific airplane and its image:

```
<!DOCTYPE html>
<!-- image.html
     An example to illustrate an image      > comment
     -->
<html lang = "en">   English
  <head>   opening head tag
    <title> Images </title>   title
    <meta charset = "utf-8" />
  </head>   closing head tag
  <body>   opening body tag
    <h1> Aidan's Airplanes </h1>
    <h2> The best in used airplanes </h2>      } h1/h2/h3 represent
    <h3> "We've got them by the hangarful" </h3>   different font sizes
    <h2> Special of the month </h2>
    <p>   paragraph opening tag
      1960 Cessna 210 <br />   linebreak
      577 hours since major engine overhaul<br />   extra line break
      1022 hours since prop overhaul <br /><br />
      <img src = "c210new.jpg"  alt = "Picture of a Cessna 210" />
      <br />
      Buy this fine airplane today at a remarkably low price
      <br />
      Call 999-555-1111 today!
    </p>   closing paragraph tag
  </body>   closing body tag
</html>   closing html tag
```

Figure 2.10 shows a browser display of `image.html`.

Figure 2.10 Display of `image.html`

2.5.3   XHTML Document Validation

For validation of the XHTML syntax of a document, we must make three temporary changes to the document. First, we replace the HTML document type with the following XHTML 1.0 Strict standard document type:

```
<!DOCTYPE html PUBLIC "-//W3C//DTD XHTML 1.0 Strict//EN"
   "http://www.w3.org/TR/xhtml11/DTD/xhtml1-strict.dtd">
```

A complete explanation of this DOCTYPE command requires more effort, both to write and to read, than is justified at this stage of our introduction to HTML. Second, we must add the following attribute to the `html` element:

```
xmlns = "http://www.w3.org/1999/xhtml"
```

This specifies the namespace used for the document, XHTML. Third, we must comment out the `meta` element, as in the following:

```
<!-- <meta charset = "utf-8" /> -->
```

The modified version of `image.html` is as follows:

```
<!DOCTYPE html PUBLIC "-//W3C//DTD XHTML 1.0 Strict//EN"
   "http://www.w3.org/TR/xhtml1/DTD/xhtml1-strict.dtd">
<!-- image.html
     An example to illustrate an image
     -->
<html lang = "en"  xmlns = "http://www.w3.org/1999/xhtml">
  <head>
    <title> Images </title>
<!--    <meta charset = "utf-8" /> -->    ← comment out
  </head>
  <body>
    <h1> Aidan's Airplanes </h1>
    <h2> The best in used airplanes </h2>
    <h3> "We've got them by the hangarful" </h3>
    <hr />
    <h2> Special of the month </h2>
    <p>
      1960 Cessna 210 <br />
      577 hours since major engine overhaul<br />
      1022 hours since prop overhaul <br /><br />
      <img src = "c210new.jpg"  alt = "Picture of a Cessna
                 210" />
      <br />
      Buy this fine airplane today at a remarkably low price
      <br />
      Call 999-555-1111 today!
    </p>
  </body>
</html>
```

After making these three temporary changes to a document, it can be validated with the Total Validator Tool, which provides a convenient way to validate documents against XHTML 1.0 Strict standard.[17] The validator program is available at `http://totalvalidator.com`. Figure 2.11 shows a browser display of the Total Validator Tool, after it has been downloaded and installed.

---

17. W3C also has an XHTML validator, available at `http://validator.w3.org`. This validator will produce errors for all HTML5 markup that is not valid in XHTML 1.0.

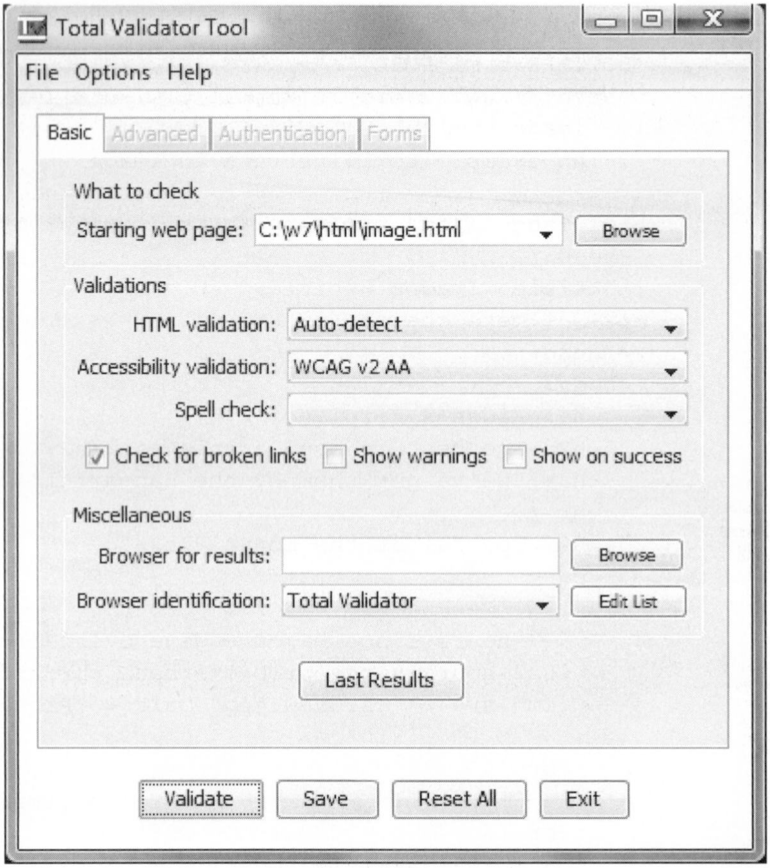

Figure 2.11 Display of the Total Validator Tool screen

The file name of the document to be validated is entered (including the path name) in the *Starting web page* text box, or found by browsing. When the *Validate* button is clicked, the validation system is run on the specified file.

Figure 2.12 shows a browser display of the document returned by the validation system for `image.html`.

One of the most common errors made in crafting HTML documents that use the XHTML syntax is putting text or elements where they do not belong. For example, putting text directly into a body element is invalid.

The Total Validator Tool is a valuable tool for producing documents that adhere to XHTML 1.0 Strict standards. Validation ensures that a document sytactically correct and more likely to display similarly on a variety of browsers. After validation, the document easily can be returned to its HTML form.

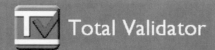

Help | Website | Feedback

Summary

Starting page: file:/C:/w7/html/image.html
Started at: 21:43:49 GMT, February 11, 2011
Time taken: 0 seconds
Validator Version: v6.10.0
Total links checked: 1
Total errors found: 0

Options:

- Accessibility: AA2
- Check for broken links: true
- Identity used: Total Validator
- (X)HTML validation: Auto Detect

⬆ top

Validation results

For websites that validate you can display an appropriate logo.

⬆ top

Figure 2.12 Total Validation Tool output for `image.html`

2.6 Hypertext Links

A hypertext link in an HTML document, which we simply call a *link* here, acts as a pointer to some particular place in some Web resource. That resource can be an HTML document anywhere on the Web, or it may be the document currently being displayed. Without links, Web documents would be boring and tedious to read. There would be no convenient way for the browser user to get from one document to a logically related document. Most Web sites consist of many different documents, all logically linked together. Therefore, links are essential to building an interesting Web site.

2.6.1   Links

A link that points to a different resource specifies the address of that resource. Such an address might be a file name, a directory path and a file name, or a complete URL. If a link points to a specific place in any document other than its beginning, that place somehow must be marked. Specifying such places is discussed in Section 2.6.2.

Links are specified in an attribute of an anchor element, a, which is an inline element. The anchor element that specifies a link is called the *source* of that link. The document whose address is specified in a link is called the *target* of that link.

As is the case with many tags, the anchor tag can include many different attributes. However, for creating links, only one attribute is required: href (an acronym for *h*ypertext *ref*erence). The value assigned to href specifies the target of the link. If the target is in another document in the same directory, the target is just the document's file name. If the target document is in some other directory, the UNIX path name conventions are used. For example, suppose we have a document in the public_html directory (which stores servable documents) that is linked to a document named C210data.html, which is stored in the airplanes subdirectory of public_html. The href value of the anchor tag would be "airplanes/c210data.html". This is the relative method of document addressing, which means the address is relative to the address of the document currently being displayed. Absolute file addresses could be used in which the entire path name for the linked-to file is given. However, relative links are easier to maintain, especially if a hierarchy of HTML files must be moved. If the document is on some other machine (not the server providing the document that includes the link), obviously relative addressing cannot be used.

The content of an anchor element, which becomes the clickable link the user sees, is usually text or an image, and cannot be another anchor element. Links are usually implicitly rendered in a different color than that of the surrounding text. Sometimes they are also underlined. When the mouse cursor is placed over the anchor-tag content and the left mouse button is pressed, the link is taken by the browser. If the target is in a different document, that document is loaded and displayed, replacing the currently displayed document. If the target is in the current document, the document is scrolled by the browser to display the part of the document in which the target of the link is defined.

As an example of a link to the top of a different document, consider the following document, which adds a link to the document displayed in Figure 2.10:

```
<!DOCTYPE html>
<!-- link.html
     An example to illustrate a link
     -->
<html lang = "en">
  <head>
    <title> A link </title>
    <meta charset = "utf-8" />
  </head>
```

```
<body>
  <h1> Aidan's Airplanes </h1>
  <h2> The best in used airplanes </h2>
  <h3> "We've got them by the hangarful" </h3>
  <h2> Special of the month </h2>
  <p>
    1960 Cessna 210 <br />
    <a href = "C210data.html"> Information on the Cessna 210 </a>
  </p>
</body>
</html>
```

In this case, the target is a complete document that is stored in the same directory as the HTML document. Figure 2.13 shows a browser display of `link.html`. When the link shown in Figure 2.13 is clicked, the browser displays the screen shown in Figure 2.14.

Aidan's Airplanes

The best in used airplanes

"We've got them by the hangarful"

Special of the month

1960 Cessna 210
Information on the Cessna 210

Figure 2.13 Display of `link.html`

Links can include images in their content, in which case the browser displays the image together with the textual link:

```
<a href = "c210data.html" >
  <img src = "small-airplane.jpg"
      alt = "An image of a small airplane" />
    Information on the Cessna 210
</a>
```

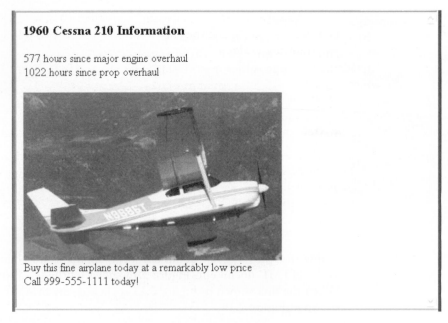

1960 Cessna 210 Information

577 hours since major engine overhaul
1022 hours since prop overhaul

Buy this fine airplane today at a remarkably low price
Call 999-555-1111 today!

Figure 2.14 Following the link from `link.html`

An image itself can be an effective link (the content of the anchor element). For example, an image of a small house can be used for the link to the home document of a site. The content of an anchor element for such a link is just the image element.

2.6.2 Targets within Documents

If the target of a link is not at the beginning of a document, it must be some element within the document, in which case there must be some means of specifying that target element. If the target element has an `id` attribute, that value can be used to specify the target. Consider the following example:

```
<h2 id = "avionics"> Avionics </h2>
```

Nearly all elements can include an `id` attribute. The value of an `id` attribute must be unique within the document.

If the target is in the same document as the link, the target is specified in the `href` attribute value by preceding the `id` value with a pound sign (#), as in the following example:

```
<a href = "#avionics"> What about avionics? </a>
```

When the `What about avionics?` link is taken, the browser moves the display so that the element whose `id` is `avionics` is at the top.

When the target is an element in another document, the value of that element's id is specified at the end of the URL, separated by a pound sign (#), as in the following example:

```
<a href = "aidan1.html#avionics"> Avionics </a>
```

2.6.3 Using Links

One common use of links to parts of the same document is to provide a table of contents in which each entry has a link. This technique provides a convenient way for the user to get to the various parts of the document simply and quickly. Such a table of contents is implemented as a stylized list of links by using the list specification capabilities of HTML, which are discussed in Section 2.7.

Links exemplify the true spirit of hypertext. The reader can click on links to learn more about a particular subtopic of interest and then return to the location of the link. Designing links requires some care because they can be annoying if the designer tries too hard to convince the user to take them. For example, making them stand out too much from the surrounding text can be distracting. A link should blend into the surrounding text as much as possible so that reading the document without clicking any of the links is easy and natural.

2.7 Lists

We frequently make and use lists in daily life—for example, to-do lists and grocery lists. Likewise, both printed and displayed information is littered with lists. HTML provides simple and effective ways to specify lists in documents. The primary list types supported are those with which most people are already familiar: unordered lists such as grocery lists and ordered lists such as the assembly instructions for a new desktop computer. Definition lists can also be defined. The tags used to specify unordered, ordered, and definition lists are described in this section.

2.7.1 Unordered Lists

The `<ul>` tag, which is a block tag, creates an unordered list. Each item in a list is specified with an `<li>` tag (li is an acronym for *list item*). Any tags can appear in a list item, including nested lists. When displayed, each list item is implicitly preceded by a bullet. The following document, `unordered.html`, illustrates an unordered element:

```
<!DOCTYPE html>
<!-- unordered.html
     An example to illustrate an unordered list
     -->
<html lang = "en">
```

```
<head>
  <title> Definition lists </title>
  <meta charset = "utf-8" />
</head>
<body>
  <h3> Single-Engine Cessna Airplanes </h3>
  <dl>
    <dt> 152 </dt>
    <dd> Two-place trainer </dd>
    <dt> 172 </dt>
    <dd> Smaller four-place airplane </dd>
    <dt> 182 </dt>
    <dd> Larger four-place airplane </dd>
    <dt> 210 </dt>
    <dd> Six-place airplane - high performance </dd>
  </dl>
</body>
</html>
```

Figure 2.18 shows a browser display of definition.html.

Single-Engine Cessna Airplanes

152
    Two-place trainer
172
    Smaller four-place airplane
182
    Larger four-place airplane
210
    Six-place airplane - high performance

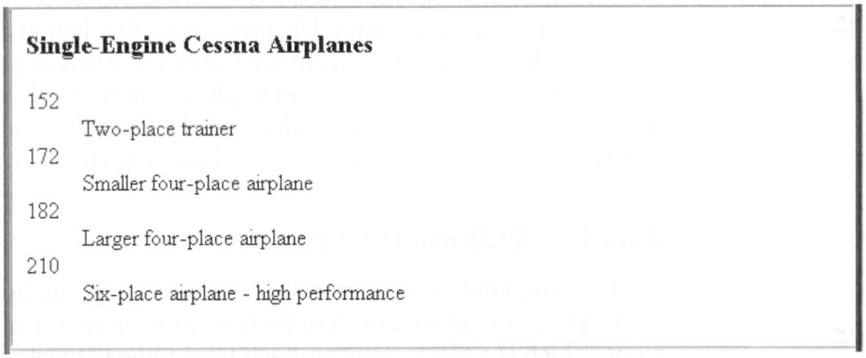

Figure 2.18 Display of definition.html

2.8 Tables

Tables are common fixtures in printed documents, books, and, of course, Web documents. Tables provide a highly effective way of presenting many kinds of information.

A table is a matrix of cells. The cells in the top row often contain column labels, those in the leftmost column often contain row labels, and most of the rest of the cells contain the data of the table. The content of a cell can be almost any document element, including text, a heading, a horizontal rule, an image, or a nested table.

2.8.1   Basic Table Tags

In HTML 4.01 and XHTML 1.0, the `table` element has an attribute, `border`, that specifies the styles of the border around the outside of the table and that of the rules, or lines that separate the cells of a table. This attribute is not included in HTML5. The styles of the border and rules in a table are specified in HTML5 with style sheets, as we will describe in Chapter 3. So, the tables in this chapter will have neither borders nor rules.

In most cases, a displayed table is preceded by a title, given as the content of a `caption` element, which can immediately follow the opening `<table>` tag. The cells of a table are specified one row at a time. Each row of a table is specified with a row tag, `<tr>`. Within each row, the row label is specified by the table heading tag, `<th>`. Although the `<th>` tag has *heading* in its name, we call these tags *labels* to avoid confusion with headings created with the `<hx>` tags. Each data cell of a row is specified with a table data tag, `<td>`. The first row of a table usually has the table's column labels. For example, if a table has three data columns and their column labels are, respectively, `Apple`, `Orange`, and `Screwdriver`, the first row can be specified by the following:

```
<tr>
  <th> Apple </th>
  <th> Orange </th>
  <th> Screwdriver </th>
</tr>
```

Each data row of a table is specified with a heading tag and one data tag for each data column. For example, the first data row for our work-in-progress table might be as follows:

```
<tr>
  <th> Breakfast </th>
  <td> 0 </td>
  <td> 1 </td>
  <td> 0 </td>
</tr>
```

In tables that have both row and column labels, the upper-left corner cell is often empty. This empty cell is specified with a table header tag that includes no content (either `<th></th>` or just `<th />`).

The following document describes the whole table:

```
<!DOCTYPE html>
<!-- table.html
     An example of a simple table
     -->
<html lang = "en">
```

```
<head>
   <title> A simple table </title>
   <meta charset = "utf-8" />
</head>
<body>
   <table>
      <caption> Fruit Juice Drinks </caption>
      <tr>
         <th> </th>
         <th> Apple </th>
         <th> Orange </th>
         <th> Screwdriver </th>
      </tr>
      <tr>
         <th> Breakfast </th>
         <td> 0 </td>
         <td> 1 </td>
         <td> 0 </td>
      </tr>
      <tr>
         <th> Lunch </th>
         <td> 1 </td>
         <td> 0 </td>
         <td> 0 </td>
      </tr>
      <tr>
         <th> Dinner </th>
         <td> 0 </td>
         <td> 0 </td>
         <td> 1 </td>
      </tr>
   </table>
</body>
</html>
```

Figure 2.19 shows a browser display of this table.

Fruit Juice Drinks			
	Apple	**Orange**	**Screwdriver**
Breakfast	0	1	0
Lunch	1	0	0
Dinner	0	0	1

Figure 2.19 Display of `table.html`

2.8.2 The `rowspan` and `colspan` Attributes

In many cases, tables have multiple levels of row or column labels in which one label covers two or more secondary labels. For example, consider the display of a partial table shown in Figure 2.20. In this table, the upper-level label **Fruit Juice Drinks** spans the three lower-level label cells. Multiple-level labels can be specified with the `rowspan` and `colspan` attributes.

Fruit Juice Drinks
Apple Orange Screwdriver

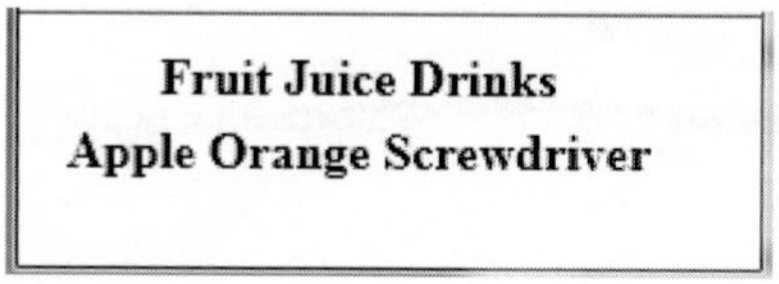

Figure 2.20 Two levels of column labels

The `colspan` attribute specification in a table header or table data tag tells the browser to make the cell as wide as the specified number of rows below it in the table. For the previous example, the following markup could be used:

```
<tr>
  <th colspan = "3"> Fruit Juice Drinks </th>
</tr>
<tr>
  <th> Apple </th>
  <th> Orange </th>
  <th> Screwdriver </th>
</tr>
```

If there are fewer cells in the rows above or below the spanning cell than the `colspan` attribute specifies, the browser stretches the spanning cell over the number of cells that populate the column in the table.[18] The `rowspan` attribute of the table heading and table data tags does for rows what `colspan` does for columns.

A table that has two levels of column labels and also has row labels must have an empty upper-left corner cell that spans both the multiple rows of column labels and the multiple columns. Such a cell is specified by including both `rowspan` and `colspan` attributes. Consider the following table specification, which is a minor modification of the previous table:

```
<!DOCTYPE html>
<!-- cell_span.html
     An example to illustrate rowspan and colspan
     -->
<html lang = "en">
```

---

18. Some browsers add empty row cells to allow the specified span to occur.

```
<head>
  <title> Rowspan and colspan </title>
  <meta charset = "utf-8" />
</head>
<body>
  <table>
    <caption> Fruit Juice Drinks and Meals </caption>
    <tr>
      <td rowspan = "2"> </td>
      <th colspan = "3"> Fruit Juice Drinks </th>
    </tr>
    <tr>
      <th> Apple </th>
      <th> Orange </th>
      <th> Screwdriver </th>
    </tr>
    <tr>
      <th> Breakfast </th>
      <td> 0 </td>
      <td> 1 </td>
      <td> 0 </td>
    </tr>
    <tr>
      <th> Lunch </th>
      <td> 1 </td>
      <td> 0 </td>
      <td> 0 </td>
    </tr>
    <tr>
      <th> Dinner </th>
      <td> 0 </td>
      <td> 0 </td>
      <td> 1 </td>
    </tr>
  </table>
</body>
</html>
```

Figure 2.21 shows a browser display of cell_span.html.

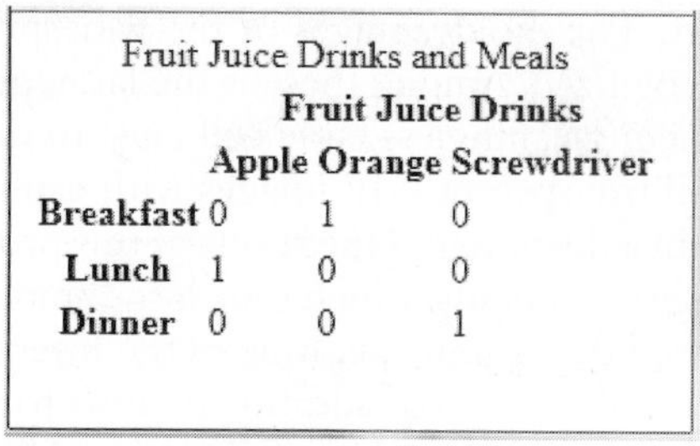

Fruit Juice Drinks and Meals			
	Fruit Juice Drinks		
	Apple	**Orange**	**Screwdriver**
Breakfast	0	1	0
Lunch	1	0	0
Dinner	0	0	1

Figure 2.21 Display of `cell_span.html`: multiple-labeled columns and labeled rows

2.8.3   Table Sections

Tables naturally occur in two and sometimes three parts: header, body, and footer. (Not all tables have a natural footer.) These three parts can be respectively denoted in HTML with the `thead`, `tbody`, and `tfoot` elements. The header includes the column labels, regardless of the number of levels in those labels. The body includes the data of the table, including the row labels. The footer, when it appears, sometimes has the column labels repeated after the body. In some tables, the footer contains totals for the columns of data above. A table can have multiple body sections, in which case the browser may separate them with horizontal lines that are thicker than the rule lines within a body section.

2.8.4   Uses of Tables

During the late 1990s a widespread trend evolved among Web document developers to use tables for whole document layout. There were several reasons behind this trend, including the following: At that time, CSS was not uniformly supported by the major browsers. Web document developers were not yet familiar with CSS. There was no widespread understanding of the advantages of the division of document design into the use of HTML for semantics and CSS for presentation. There was an explosion of demand for Web document designers during the dotcom boom of the late 1990s that led to a significant infusion of designers with little background in Web design. Many of these found it easier to use tables than CSS for document layout. Finally, Web design tools of the time encouraged the use of tables for general layout (by using tables themselves).

When the dotcom expansion collapsed in 2001, many of those drawn into the business of Web document design in the late 1990s departed for other areas of endeavor. One result of this was a rise in the average skill level of those who remained in the business of developing Web documents. Also, knowledge of CSS and its advantages grew. This environment produced a new trend in the use of tables—tableless layout. The disadvantages of the widespread use of tables for general layout were recognized. Among these is the large proliferation of tags in documents, many of them meaningless table cell tags. In many cases, table cells consisted of single pixel transparent GIF images with explicit width and height used to align elements in a document. One result of this proliferation of tags was many unnecessarily large documents, which took large amounts of time to download, which in turn slowed the overall operation of the Internet. This unnecessary complexity of documents also required additional effort to maintain them.

Using CSS, rather than tables, to design document layout results in smaller and less complex documents. The smaller size of documents speeds their downloads and raises the overall performance of the Internet. The use of CSS also lowers the cost of maintaining documents.

Even when tableless design is embraced, there are still many situations that can make good use of tables. Any time a natural table of information must be part of a document, an HTML table should be used for it. However, the use of tables for general layout of elements in a document should be avoided.

2.9   Forms

The most common way for a user to communicate information from a Web browser to the server is through a form. Modeled on the paper forms that people frequently are required to fill out, forms can be described in HTML and displayed by the browser. HTML provides tags to generate the commonly used objects on a screen form. These objects are called *controls* or *widgets* or *components*. There are controls for single-line and multiple-line text collection, checkboxes, radio buttons, and menus, among others. All control tags are inline tags. Most controls are used to gather information from the user in the form of either text or button selections. Each control can have a value, usually given through user input. Together, the values of all of the controls (that have values) in a form are called the *form data*. Every form whose data is to be processed on the server requires a *Submit* button (see Section 2.9.5). When the user clicks the *Submit* button, the form data is encoded and sent to the Web server. Form processing is discussed in three subsequent chapters (Chapters 9, 11, and 12).

2.9.1   The `form` Element

All of the controls of a form appear in the content of a `form` element. `<form>`, which is a block tag, can have several different attributes, only one of which, `action`, is required.[19] The `action` attribute specifies the URL of the application on the Web server that is to be called when the user clicks the *Submit* button. In this chapter, our examples of form elements will not have corresponding application programs, so the value of their `action` attributes will be the empty string (`" "`).

---

19. Actually, the action attribute is not required by HTML. However, it is required by XHTML, so we will include it in our examples.

The method attribute of `<form>` specifies which technique, get or post, will be used to pass the form data to the server. The default is get, so if no method attribute is given in the `<form>` tag, get will be used. The alternative technique is post. In both techniques, the form data is coded into a text string when the user clicks the *Submit* button. This text string is often called the **query string**.[20]

When the get method is used, the browser attaches the query string to the URL of the HTTP request, so the form data is transmitted to the server together with the URL. The browser inserts a question mark at the end of the actual URL just before the first character of the query string so that the server can easily find the beginning of the query string. The get method can also be used to pass parameters to the server when forms are not involved. (This cannot be done with post.) One last advantage of get is that a site bookmark can include specific form values, which makes it more specific than one with only the URL. One disadvantage of the get method is that some servers place a limit on the length of the URL string and truncate any characters past the limit. So, if the form has more than a few controls, get is not a good choice. Because the form values are displayed by the browser, get should not be used if sensitive information such as passwords or credit card numbers are included in the form data.

When the post method is used, the query string is passed by some other method to the form-processing program. There is no length limitation for the query string with the post method, so, obviously, it is the better choice when there are more than a few controls in the form. There are also some security concerns with get that are not a problem with post.

2.9.2   The input Element

Many of the commonly used controls are specified with the inline tag `<input>`, including those for text, passwords, checkboxes, radio buttons, and the action buttons reset, submit, image, and button. There is also a hidden control, which is used in Chapter 12. The text, password, checkboxes, and radio controls are discussed in this section. The action buttons are discussed in Section 2.9.5.

The type attribute, which specifies the particular kind of control, is required in the input tag. All of the previously listed controls except reset and submit also require a name attribute. The values of the name attributes are included in the form data that is sent to the server. They are used by the server form processing software to find the specific component values in the form data. The controls for checkboxes and radio buttons require a value attribute, which initializes the value of the control. The values of these controls are placed in the form data that is sent to the server when the *Submit* button is clicked.

Because most forms are processed on the server, we will always include name attributes in the controls in our examples. In many cases, controls are also referenced in code on the client, primarily for client-side validation. Client code often

---

20. The query string has an assignment statement for each control that has a data value, with the name of the control as its left side and its value as its right side. These assignment statements are separated by ampersands (&).

references controls through their `id` attribute values. Therefore, it is common to include both name and `id` attributes on form control elements.

A text control, which we usually refer to as a text box, creates a horizontal box into which the user can type text. Text boxes usually are used to gather information from the user, such as the user's name and address. The default size of a text box is often 20 characters. Because the default size can vary among browsers, it is a good idea to include a size on each text box. This is done with the `size` attribute of `<input>`. If the user types more characters than will fit in the box, the box is scrolled. If you do not want the box to be scrolled, you can include the `maxlength` attribute to specify the maximum number of characters that the browser will accept in the box. Any additional characters are ignored. As an example of a text box, consider the following:

```
<form action = "">          URL for application would
                                       go here
  <p>
    <input type = "text"  name = "theName"  size = "25" />
    . . .
  </p>
</form>
```

Suppose the user typed the following line:

```
Alfred Paul von Frickenburger
```

The text box would collect the whole string, but the string would be scrolled to the right, leaving the following shown in the box:

```
ed Paul von Frickenburger
```

The left end of the line would be part of the value of `theName`, even though it does not appear in the box. The ends of the line can be viewed in the box by moving the cursor off the ends of the box.

Notice that controls cannot appear directly in the form content—they must be placed in some block container, such as a paragraph. This is because neither text nor inline tags can appear directly in a form element and `<input>` is an inline tag.[21]

Now consider a similar text box that includes a `maxlength` attribute:

```
<form action = "">
  <p>
    <input type = "text"  name = "theName"  size = "25"
           maxlength = "25" />
    . . .
  </p>
</form>
```

---

21. This restriction is for XHTML, not HTML.

If the user typed the same name as in the previous example, the resulting value of the theName text box would be as follows:

```
Alfred Paul von Frickenbu
```

No matter what was typed after the u in that person's last name, the value of theName would be as shown.

   If the contents of a text box should not be displayed when they are entered by the user, a password control can be used as follows:

```
<input type = "password"  name = "myPassword"
       size = "10" maxlength = "10" />
```

In this case, regardless of what characters are typed into the password control, only bullets or asterisks are displayed by the browser.

   There are no restrictions on the characters that can be typed into a text box. So, the string "?!34,:" could be entered into a text box meant for names. Therefore, the entered contents of text boxes nearly always must be validated, either on the browser or on the server to which the form data is passed for processing, or on both. Validation is done on the client to avoid wasting time by sending invalid data to the server. It is also done on the server because client-side validation can be subverted by unscrupulous users.

   Text boxes, as well as most other control elements, should be labeled. Labeling could be done simply by inserting text into the appropriate places in the form:

```
Phone: <input type = "text"  name = "thePhone" />
```

This markup effectively labels the text box, but there are several ways the labeling could be better. For one thing, there is no connection between the label and the control. Therefore, they could become separated in maintenance changes to the document. A control and its label can be connected by putting the control and its label in the content of a label element, as in the following:

```
<label> Phone: <input type = "text"  name = "thePhone" />
</label>
```

Now the text box and its label are encapsulated together. There are several other benefits of this approach to labeling controls. First, browsers often render the text content of a label element differently to make it stand out. Second, if the text content of a label element is selected, the cursor is implicitly moved to the control in the content of the label. This feature is an aid to new Web users. Third, the text content of a label element can be rendered by a speech synthesizer on the client machine when the content of the label element is selected. This feature can be a great aid to a user with a visual disability.

   Checkbox and radio controls are used to collect multiple-choice input from the user. A checkbox control is a single button that is either on or off (checked or not). If a checkbox button is on, the value associated with the name of the button is the string assigned to its value attribute. A checkbox button does not contribute to the form data if it is not checked. Every checkbox button requires a name attribute and a `value` attribute in its `<input>` tag. For form processing on the server, the name identifies the button and the value is its value (if the button is checked). The attribute `checked`, which is assigned the value `checked`, specifies that the checkbox button is initially on. In many cases, checkboxes appear in lists, with each one in the list having the same name, thereby forming a checkbox group. Checkbox elements should appear in label elements, for the same reasons that text boxes should. The following example illustrates a checkbox:

```
<!DOCTYPE html>
<!-- checkbox.html
     An example to illustrate a checkbox
     -->
<html lang = "en">
  <head>
    <title> Checkboxes </title>
    <meta charset = "utf-8" />
  </head>
  <body>
    <p>
      Grocery Checklist
    </p>
    <form action = "">
      <p>
        <label> <input type = "checkbox"  name = "groceries"
              value = "milk"  checked = "checked" /> Milk </label>
        <label> <input type = "checkbox"  name = "groceries"
              value = "bread" /> Bread </label>
        <label> <input type = "checkbox"  name = "groceries"
              value = "eggs" /> Eggs </label>
      </p>
    </form>
  </body>
</html>
```

[handwritten annotations: "Milk is automatically checked", "label content"]

Figure 2.22 shows a browser display of `checkbox.html`.

Grocery Checklist

☑ Milk ☐ Bread ☐ Eggs

Figure 2.22 Display of `checkbox.html`

If the user does not turn on any of the checkbox buttons in our example, `milk` will be the value for `groceries` in the form data. If the `milk` checkbox is left on and the `eggs` checkbox is also turned on by the user, the values of `groceries` in the form data would be `milk` and `eggs`.

Radio buttons are closely related to checkbox buttons. The difference between a group of radio buttons and a group of checkboxes is that only one radio button can be on or pressed at any time. Every time a radio button is pressed, the button in the group that was previously on is turned off. Radio buttons are named after the mechanical push buttons on the radios of cars of the 1950s—when you pushed one button on such a radio, the previously pushed button was mechanically forced out. The `type` value for radio buttons is `radio`. All radio buttons in a group must have the `name` attribute set in the `<input>` tag, and all radio buttons in a group must have the same name value. A radio button definition may specify which button is to be initially in the pressed, or on, state. This specification is indicated by including the `checked` attribute, set to the value `checked`, in the `<input>` tag of the button's definition. The following example illustrates radio buttons:

```
<!DOCTYPE html>
<!-- radio.html
     An example to illustrate radio buttons
     -->
<html lang = "en">
  <head>
    <title> Radio </title>
    <meta charset = "utf-8" />
  </head>
  <body>
    <p>
      Age Category
    </p>
    <form action = "">
      <p>
        <label><input type = "radio"  name = "age"
              value = "under20" checked = "checked" />
              0-19 </label>
        <label><input type = "radio"  name = "age"
              value = "20-35" /> 20-35 </label>
        <label><input type = "radio"  name = "age"
              value = "36-50" /> 36-50 </label>
        <label><input type = "radio"  name = "age"
              value = "over50" /> Over 50 </label>
      </p>
    </form>
  </body>
</html>
```

Figure 2.23 shows a browser display of `radio.html`.

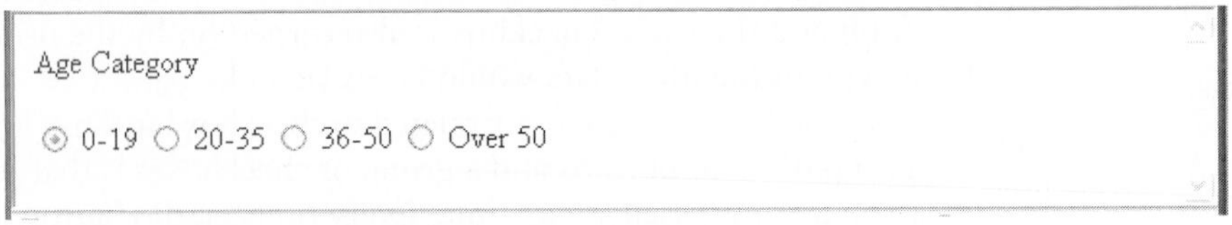

Figure 2.23 Display of `radio.html`

2.9.3   The `select` Element

Checkboxes and radio buttons are effective methods for collecting multiple-choice data from a user. However, if the number of choices is large, the form may become too long to display. In these cases, a menu should be used. A menu is specified with a `<select>` tag (rather than with the `<input>` tag). There are two kinds of menus: those in which only one menu item can be selected at a time (which are related to radio buttons) and those in which multiple menu items can be selected at a time (which are related to checkboxes). The default option is the one related to radio buttons. The other option can be specified by adding the `multiple` attribute, set to the value `"multiple"`.[22] When only one menu item is selected, the value sent in the form data is the value of the `name` attribute of the `<select>` tag and the chosen menu item. When multiple menu items are selected, the value for the menu in the form data includes all selected menu items. If no menu item is selected, no value for the menu is included in the form data. The `name` attribute, of course, is required in the `<select>` tag.

The `size` attribute, specifying the number of menu items that initially are to be displayed for the user, can be included in the `<select>` tag. If no `size` attribute is specified, the value 1 is used. If the value for the `size` attribute is 1 and `multiple` is not specified, just one menu item is displayed, with a downward scroll arrow. If the scroll arrow is clicked, the menu is displayed as a popup menu. If either `multiple` is specified or the `size` attribute is set to a number larger than 1, the menu is usually displayed as a scrolled list.

Each of the items in a menu is specified with an `<option>` tag, nested in the select element. The content of an `<option>` tag is the value of the menu item, which is just text. (No tags may be included.) The `<option>` tag can include the `selected` attribute, which specifies that the item is preselected. The value assigned to `selected` is `"selected"`, which can be overridden by the user. The following document describes a menu with the default value (1) for `size`:

```
<!DOCTYPE html>
<!-- menu.html
     An example to illustrate menus
     -->
<html lang = "en">
```

---

22. HTML does require a value for the `multiple` attribute; XHTML does.

```
    <head>
      <title> Menu </title>
      <meta charset = "utf-8" />
    </head>
    <body>
      <p>
        Grocery Menu - milk, bread, eggs, cheese
      </p>
      <form action = "">
        <p>
          With size = 1 (the default)
          <select name = "groceries">
            <option> milk </option>
            <option> bread </option>
            <option> eggs </option>
            <option> cheese </option>
          </select>
        </p>
      </form>
    </body>
</html>
```

Figure 2.24 shows a browser display of menu.html. Figure 2.25 shows a browser display of menu.html after clicking the scroll arrow. Figure 2.26 shows a browser display of menu.html after modification to set size to "2."

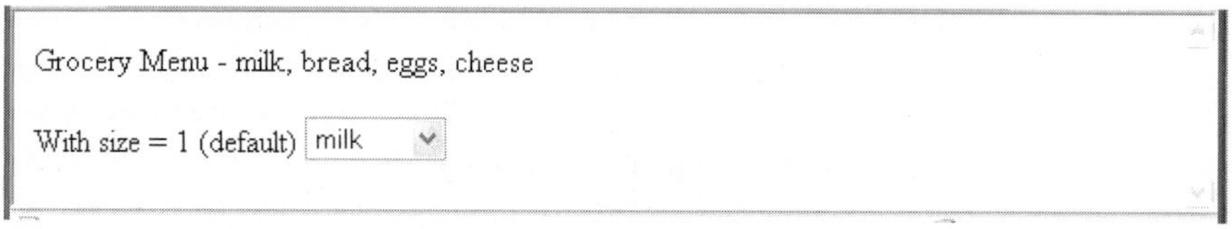

Figure 2.24 Display of menu.html (default size of 1)

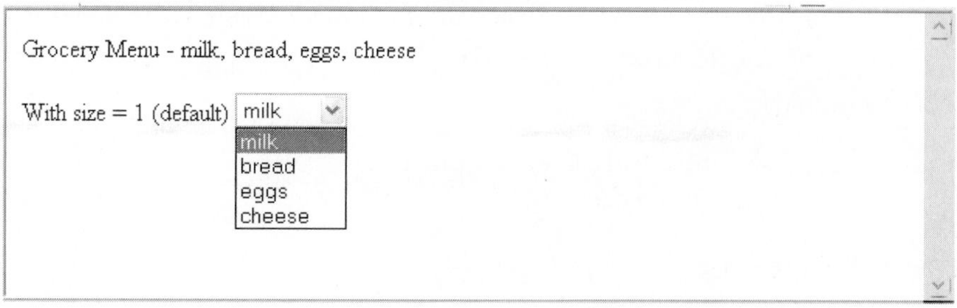

Figure 2.25 Display of menu.html after the scroll arrow is clicked

Figure 2.26 Display of `menu.html` with `size` set to 2

When the `multiple` attribute of the `<select>` tag is set, adjacent options can be chosen by dragging the mouse cursor over them while the left mouse button is held down. Nonadjacent options can be selected by clicking them while holding down the keyboard *Control* key.

2.9.4   The `textarea` Element

In some situations, a multiline text area is needed. The `textarea` element is used to create such a control. The text typed into the area created by `textarea` is not limited in length, and there is implicit scrolling when needed, both vertically and horizontally. The default size of the visible part of the text in a text area is often quite small, so the `rows` and `cols` attributes should usually be included and set to reasonable sizes. If some default text is to be included in the text area, it can be included as the content of the text area element. The following document describes a text area whose window is 40 columns wide and three lines tall:

```
<!DOCTYPE html>
<!-- textarea.html
     An example to illustrate a textarea
     -->
<html lang = "en" >
  <head>
    <title> Textarea </title>
    <meta charset = "utf-8" />
  </head>
  <body>
    <p>
      Please provide your employment aspirations
    </p>
    <form action = "handler">
      <p>
        <textarea name = "aspirations"  rows = "3"  cols = "40">
          (Be brief and concise)
        </textarea>
      </p>
    </form>
  </body>
</html>
```

Figure 2.27 shows a browser display of `textarea.html` after some text has been typed into the area.

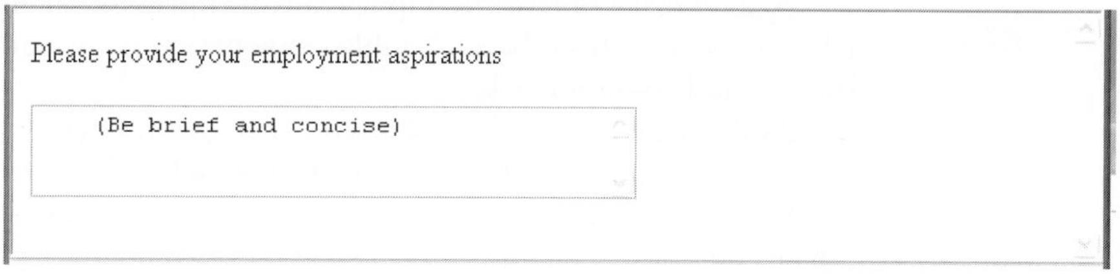

Figure 2.27 Display of `textarea.html` after some text entry

2.9.5   The Action Buttons

The *Reset* button clears all of the controls in the form to their initial states. The *Submit* button has two actions: First, the form data is encoded and sent to the server; second, the server is requested to execute the server-resident program specified in the `action` attribute of the `<form>` tag. The purpose of such a server-resident program is to process the form data and return some response to the user. Neither *Submit* nor *Reset* buttons require name or `id` attributes. The *Submit* and *Reset* buttons are created with `<input>` tags, as shown in the following example:

```
<form action = "">
  <p>
    <input type = "submit"  value = "Submit Form" />
    <input type = "reset"  value = "Reset Form" />
  </p>
</form>
```

Figure 2.28 shows a browser display of *Submit* and *Reset* buttons.

Figure 2.28 *Submit* and *Reset* buttons

The image button is an alternative *Submit* button. The difference is that an image is the clickable area, rather than a button. A plain button has the type `button`. Plain buttons are used to cause an action, which is written in JavaScript, similar to an event handler, as described in Chapter 5.

2.9.6   Example of a Complete Form

The document that follows describes a form for taking sales orders for popcorn. Three text boxes are used at the top of the form to collect the buyer's name and address. A table is used to collect the actual order. Each row of this table names a product with the content of a `<td>` tag, displays the price with another `<td>` tag, and uses a text box with `size` set to 2 to collect the quantity ordered. The payment method is input by the user through one of four radio buttons.

Notice that none of the input controls in the order table are embedded in label elements. This is because table elements cannot be labeled, except by using the row and column labels.

Tables present special problems for the visually impaired. The best solution is to use style sheets (see Chapter 3) instead of tables to lay out tabular information.

```
<!DOCTYPE html>
<!-- popcorn.html
     This describes a popcorn sales form document>
     -->
<html lang = "en">
  <head>
    <title> Popcorn Sales Form </title>
    <meta charset = "utf-8" />
  </head>
  <body>
    <h2> Welcome to Millennium Gymnastics Booster Club Popcorn
         Sales
    </h2>
    <form action = "">
      <p>

<!-- Text boxes for name and address -->
        <label> Buyer's Name:
          <input type = "text"  name = "name"
                 size = "30" /> </label>
        <br />
        <label> Street Address:
          <input type = "text"  name = "street"
                 size = "30" /> </label>
         <br />
        <label> City, State, Zip:
          <input type = "text"  name = "city"
                 size = "30" /> </label>
      <p />

<!-- A table for item orders -->
      <table>

<!-- First, the column headings -->
        <tr>
          <th> Product Name </th>
          <th> Price </th>
```

```
                         <th> Quantity </th>
                    </tr>

<!-- Now, the table data entries -->
                    <tr>
                         <td> Unpopped Popcorn (1 lb.) </td>
                         <td> $3.00 </td>
                         <td> <input type = "text"  name = "unpop"
                                    size = "2" />
                         </td>
                    </tr>
                    <tr>
                         <td> Caramel Popcorn (2 lb. canister) </td>
                         <td> $3.50 </td>
                         <td> <input type = "text"  name = "caramel"
                                    size = "2" />
                         </td>
                    </tr>
                    <tr>
                         <td> Caramel Nut Popcorn (2 lb. canister) </td>
                         <td> $4.50 </td>
                         <td> <input type = "text"  name = "caramelnut"
                                    size = "2" />
                         </td>
                    </tr>
                    <tr>
                         <td> Toffey Nut Popcorn (2 lb. canister) </td>
                         <td> $5.00 </td>
                         <td> <input type = "text"  name = "toffeynut"
                                    size = "2" />
                         </td>
                    </tr>

               </table>
               <p />

<!-- The radio buttons for the payment method -->
               <h3> Payment Method: </h3>
               <p>
                    <label> <input type = "radio"  name = "payment"
                                   value = "visa"  checked = "checked" />
                                   Visa
                    </label>
                    <br />
                    <label> <input type = "radio"  name = "payment"
                                   value = "mc" /> Master Card
                    </label>
```

```
            <br />
            <label> <input type = "radio"  name = "payment"
                          value = "discover" /> Discover
            </label>
            <br />
            <label> <input type = "radio"  name = "payment"
                          value = "check" /> Check
            </label>
            <br />
        </p>
<!-- The submit and reset buttons -->
        <p>
            <input type = "submit"  value = "Submit Order" />
            <input type = "reset"  value = "Clear Order Form" />
        </p>
    </form>
  </body>
</html>
```

Figure 2.29 shows a browser display of `popcorn.html`.

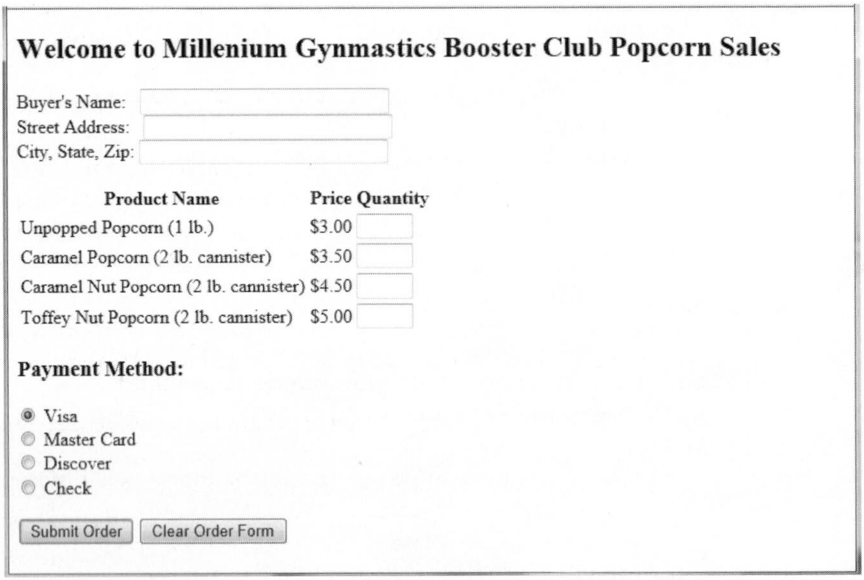

Figure 2.29 Display of `popcorn.html`

Chapter 9 has a PHP script for processing the data from the form in `popcorn.html`.

2.10 **HTML5**

This section introduces a few of the more important parts of HTML5 that are currently implemented by the three major browsers, IE9, FireFox 3.6, and Chrome 9. The first issue with using HTML5 elements in a document is that there are a large number of browsers in use that will not recognize these new elements. Eventually, all or least nearly all browsers in use will support HTML5, but that day is some time off. Until then, we need to provide documents that allow browsers that do not support HTML5 to inform users of that fact. Browsers usually simply ignore tags they do not recognize, which can lead to confusing displays. One way to avoid this is by providing code to detect support for an element that is new in HTML5 and produce a message to the user. One approach to doing this is to include and use a free JavaScript program, `modernizr-1.5.min.js`. To do this, the JavaScript code must be downloaded and stored in the directory where servable HTML documents reside on the Web server machine. This process will be discussed in Chapter 4.

2.10.1 **The** `audio` **Element**

Although it has been long recognized that the inclusion of sound during the display of a Web document can enhance its effect, until the arrival of HTML5 there was no standard way of doing that without a plug-in, such as Flash or Microsoft's Media Player. The audio element of HTML5 changes that.

Audio information is coded into digital streams with encoding algorithms called *audio codecs*. There are a large number of different audio codecs. Among these the most commonly used on the Web are MPEG-3 (MP3), Vorbis, and Wav.

Coded audio data is packaged in containers. A container can be thought of as a zip file; it is a way to pack data into a file, but the encoding of the data in the file is irrelevant to the container. A zip file may contain textual data coded in ASCII or it might contain floating-point numbers coded in binary. Likewise, an audio container may contain MP3 or Vorbis coded audio. There are three different audio container types, Ogg, MP3, and Wav. The type of container is indicated by the extension on the file's name. For example, an Ogg container file has the `.ogg` file name extension; Vorbis codec audio data is stored in Ogg containers; MP3 codec audio data is stored in MP3 containers; Wav codec audio data is stored in Wav containers.

The only commonly used attribute of the audio element is `controls`, which we always set to `"controls"`. This attribute, when present, creates a display of a start/stop button, a clock, a slider of the progress of the play, the total time of the file, and a slider for volume control. The general syntax of an audio element is as follows:

```
<audio attributes>
  <source src = "filename₁">
  ...
  <source src = "filenameₙ">
  Your browser does not support the audio element
</audio>
```

A browser chooses the first audio file it can play and skips the content of the audio element. If it cannot play any of the audio files that appear in the source elements, it does nothing other than displaying its content. Unfortunately, different browsers are capable of playing different audio container/codec combinations. The Firefox 3.5+ browsers support the Ogg/Vorbis and Wav/Wav container/codec audio files. The Chrome 3.0+ browsers support the Ogg/Vorbis and MP3/MP3 container/codec audio files. IE9 browsers support the MP3/MP3 container/codec audio files. Safari 3.0+ browsers support the Wav/Wav container/codec audio files.

Following is a simple document that illustrates the use of the audio element:

```
<!DOCTYPE html>
<!-- audio.html
     test the audio element
     -->
<html lang = "en">
  <head>
    <title> test audio element </title>
    <meta charset = "utf-8" />
  </head>
  <body>
    This is a test of the audio element      — Does not display
    <audio controls = "controls" >
      <source src = "nineoneone.ogg" />
      <source src = "nineoneone.wav" />
      <source src = "nineoneone.mp3" />
      Your browser does not support the audio element
    </audio>                                  \ does not display
  </body>
</html>
```

Note that `audio.html` includes three elements that specify three different audio container files. This allows IE9, Firefox 3.5+, Chrome 3.0+, and Safari 3.0+ browsers to play the sound clip. A chosen sound file can be converted to the other audio container/codec combinations with software available on the Web.

2.10.2   The `video` Element

Prior to HTML5, there was no standard way of including video clips in a Web document. The most common approach to video on the Web was the use of the Flash plug-in. The appearance of the video element in HTML5 changes that.

Video information, like audio information, must be digitized into data files before it can be played by a browser, this time by algorithms called *video codecs*. As is the case with audio, video data is stored in containers. There are many different video containers and many different video codecs. Further complicating the situation is the fact that not all video codecs can be stored in all video containers. The most common video containers used on the Web are MPEG-4 (`.mp4` files), Flash Video (`.flv` files), Ogg (`.ogv` files), WebM (`.webm` files), and Audio Video Interleave (`.avi` files).

As of the fall of 2011, the most common video codecs used on the Web are H.264 (also known as MPEG-4 Advance Video Coding, or MPEG-4 AVC), which can be embedded in MP4 containers, Theora, which can be embedded in any container, and VP8, which can be embedded in WebM containers. In addition to video data, video containers also store audio data, because most video is accompanied by audio. The three most common container/video codec/audio codec combinations used on the Web are the Ogg container with Theora video codec and Vorbis audio codec, MPEG-4 container with H.264 video codec and AAC audio codec, and WebM container with VP8 video codec and Vorbis audio codec.

IE9 browsers support the MPEG-4 video containers, Firefox 3.5+ browsers support the Ogg video containers, Firefox 4.0+ browsers support Ogg and WebM video containers, Chrome 6.0+ browsers support all three of the most common video containers, and Safari 3.0+ browsers support the MPEG-4 video containers.

The video element can have several attributes and, like the audio element, can include several nested source elements. The width and height attributes set the size of the screen for the video in pixels. The `autoplay` attribute specifies that the video plays automatically as soon as it is ready. The preload attribute tells the browser to load the video file or files as soon as the document is loaded. This is not a good thing if not all users will play the video. The controls attribute specifies that play, pause, and volume controls be included in the display. The loop attribute specifies that the video is to be played continuously.

The syntax of a video element is similar to that of the audio element. The general form is as follows:

```
<video attributes>
  <source src = "filename₁">
  ...
  <source src = "filenameₙ">
  Your browser does not support the video element
</video>
```

The semantics of the video element is similar to that of the audio element.
Following is an example of a document that includes a video element:

```
<!DOCTYPE html>
<!-- testvideo.html
     test the video element
     -->
<html lang = "en">
  <head>
    <meta charset = "utf-8" />
    <title> test video element </title>
  </head>
  <body>
    This is a test of the video element.....
    <video width = "600" height = "500" autoplay = "autoplay"
           controls = "controls"  preload = "preload">
```

```
            <source src = "NorskTippingKebab.mp4" />
            <source src = "NorskTippingKebab.ogv" />
            <source src = "NorskTippingKebab.webm" />
            Your browser does not support the video element
        </video>
    </body>
</html>
```

Older browsers, probably most common among those is IE8, do not recognize the video element. One way to allow such browsers is to nest an object element in the video element that plays the video with Flash. This process is described in Pilgrim.[23]

2.10.3   Organization Elements

One of the deficiencies of HTML 4.01 (and XHTML 1.0) is that it is difficult to organize displayed information in meaningful ways. The primary elements for this in those languages were division (div) and paragraph (p). Headers were the only way to implement an outline, but it was logical to use just one h1 header in a document. Furthermore, the h2, h3, and other header elements had to be nested according to their numbers (for example, h3 headers inside h2 headers). HTML5 has a collection of new elements that assist in organizing documents and outlines of documents.

The first part of many documents is a header. If the header consists of just a single phrase, it can be an h1 element. However, headers of documents often include more information, in many cases a second phrase or sentence called a *tagline*. The new HTML5 header element was designed to encapsulate the whole header of a document. This makes clear what is in the header. For example, one might have the following header:

```
<header>
  <h1> The Podunk Press </h1>
  <h2> "All the news we can fit" </h2>
</header>
```

The beginning part of a document may contain further information that precedes the body of the document, for example, a table of contents. For situations such as this, the hgroup element can be used to enclose the header and the other information that precedes the body. Following is an example of this:

```
<hgroup>
  <header>
    <h1> The Podunk Press </h1>
    <h2> "All the news we can fit" </h2>
  </header>
  -- table of contents --
</hgroup>
```

---

23. Mark Pilgrim, *HTML5 Up and Running*, O'Reilly (2010): pp.114-115.

The `footer` element is designed to enclose footer content in a document, such as author and copyright data. For example, consider the following footer element:

```
<footer>
  &copy; The Podunk Press, 2012
  <br />
  Editor in Chief: Squeak Martin
</footer>
```

The following document, `organized.html`, illustrates the `header`, `hgroup`, and `footer` elements:

```
<!DOCTYPE html>
<!-- organized.html
     An example to illustrate organization elements of HTML5
     -->
<html lang = "en">
  <head>
    <title> Organization elements </title>
    <meta charset = "utf-8" />
  </head>
  <body>
    <hgroup>
      <header>
        <h1> The Podunk Press </h1>
        <h3> "All the news we can fit" </h2>
      </header>
       <ol>
        <li> Local news </li>
        <li> National news </li>
        <li> Sports </li>
        <li> Entertainment </li>
       </ol>
    </hgroup>
    <p>
      -- Put the paper's content here --
    </p>
    <footer>
      &copy; The Podunk Press, 2012
      <br />
      Editor in Chief: Squeak Martin
    </footer>
  </body>
</html>
```

Figure 2.30 shows a display of `organized.html`.

The Podunk Press

"All the news we can fit"

1. Local news
2. National news
3. Sports
4. Entertainment

-- Put the paper's content here --

© The Podunk Press, 2012
Editor in Chief: Squeak Martin

Figure 2.30 Display of `organized.html`

The `section` element is for encapsulating the sections of a document, for example the chapters of a book or separate parts of a paper. A `footer` element may include one or more sections.

The `article` element is used to encapsulate a self-contained part of a document that comes from some external source, such as a post from a forum or a newspaper article. An `article` element can include a header, a footer, and sections. `article` elements are convenient when a document is put together from several separately written parts.

The `aside` element is for content that is tangential to the main information of the document. In print, such content is often placed in a sidebar.

The `nav` element is for encapsulating navigation sections; that is, lists of links to different parts of the document. The `nav` elements clearly mark the parts of a document that are used to get to other documents. They are especially useful for visually impaired users who use text-to-speech readers to "view" documents.

2.10.4   The `time` Element

The time element is used to time stamp an article or document. This element includes both a textual part, in which the time and/or date information can be in any format, and a machine-readable part, which of course has a strict format. The machine-readable part is given as the value of the `datetime` attribute of the time element, which is optional. The date part of `datetime` is given as a four-digit year, a dash, the two-digit month, a dash, and the two-digit day of the month, for example, `"2011-02-14"`. If a time is included with the machine-readable data, it is added to the date with an uppercase `T`, followed by the hour, a colon, the minute, a colon, and the second. The second is optional if its value is zero. The hour, minute, and second values must be in two-digit form. For example, we could have `"2010-02-14T08:00"`. There is another optional attribute of the time element, pubdate. If the time element is not nested in an article element, the `pubdate` attribute specifies that the time stamp is the publication date of the document. If the time element is nested inside an article element, it is the publication date of the article. An example of a complete time element is as follows:

```
<time datetime = "2011-02-14T08:00" pubdate = "pubdate">
  February 14, 2011 8:00am MDT
</time>
```

Note that the information in the content of a time element is not necessarily related to the information in the `datetime` attribute.

The time part of the value of `datetime` can have a time zone offset attached. The time zone value is an offset in the range of −12:00 to +14:00 (from Coordinated Universal Time). The sign on the time zone value separates it from the time value. For example, we could have the following `datetime` value:

```
"2011-02-14T08:00-06:00"
```

There are two deficiencies with the time element. First, no years before the beginning of the Christian era can be represented, because negative years are not acceptable. The second problem is that no approximations are possible—you cannot specify "circa 1900."

There are two other new features of HTML5 that involve the use of Java-Script, so their description is delayed until Chapter 5. These are the canvas element and local storage.

Also included in HTML5 are a collection of new form elements. However, because these are not yet implemented by the most popular browsers, they are not described here. HTML5 also includes a few other new elements and attributes that are not yet implemented by current browsers.

2.11 Syntactic Differences between HTML and XHTML

The discussion that follows points out some significant differences between the syntactic rules of HTML (or lack thereof) and those of XHTML.

Case sensitivity. In HTML, tag and attribute names are case insensitive, meaning that <FORM>, <form>, and <Form> are equivalent. In XHTML, tag and attribute names must be all lowercase.

Closing tags. In HTML, closing tags may be omitted if the processing agent (usually a browser) can infer their presence. For example, in HTML, paragraph elements often do not have closing tags. The appearance of another opening paragraph tag is used to infer the closing tag on the previous paragraph. Thus, in HTML we could have

```
<p>
During Spring, flowers are born. ...
<p>
During Fall, flowers die. ...
```

In XHTML, all elements must have closing tags. For elements that do not include content, in which the closing tag appears to serve no purpose, a slash can be included at the end of the opening tag as an abbreviation for the closing tag. For example, the following two lines are equivalent in XHTML:

```
<input type = "text"  name = "address" > </input>
```

and

```
<input type = "text"  name = "address" />
```

Recall that some browsers can become confused if the slash at the end is not preceded by a space.

Quoted attribute values. In HTML, attribute values must be quoted only if there are embedded special characters or white-space characters. Numeric attribute values are rarely quoted in HTML. In XHTML, all attribute values must be double quoted, regardless of what characters are included in the value.

Explicit attribute values. In HTML, some attribute values are implicit; that is, they need not be explicitly stated. For example, if the multiple attribute appears in a select tag without a value, it specifies that multiple items can be selected. The following is valid in HTML:

```
<select multiple>
```

This select tag is invalid in XHTML, in which such an attribute must be assigned a string of the name of the attribute. For example, the following is valid in XHTML:

```
<select multiple = "multiple">
```

Other such attributes are checked and selected.

id *and* name *attributes.* HTML markup often uses the name attribute for elements. This attribute was deprecated for some elements in HTML 4.0, which added the id attribute to nearly all elements. In XHTML, the use of id is encouraged and the use of name is discouraged. However, form elements must still use the name attribute because it is employed in processing form data on the server.

Element nesting. Although HTML has rules against improper nesting of elements, they are not enforced. Examples of nesting rules are (1) an anchor element cannot contain another anchor element, and a form element cannot contain another form element; (2) if an element appears inside another element, the closing tag of the inner element must appear before the closing tag of the outer element; (3) block elements cannot be nested in inline elements; (4) text cannot be directly nested in body or form elements; and (5) list elements cannot be directly nested in list elements. In XHTML, these nesting rules are strictly enforced.

All of the XHTML syntactic rules are checked by the Total Validator Tool software.

Summary

Without the style sheets to be described in Chapter 3, HTML is capable of specifying only the general layout of documents, with few presentation details. The current version of HTML is still 4.01, although the HTML5 specification has been distributed via the Web. Although the XHTML development process has stopped, the strict syntactic rules of XHTML are still valuable and can be used with both HTML 4.01 and HTML5.

The tags of HTML specify how content is to be arranged in a display by a browser (or some other HTML processor). Most tags consist of opening and closing tags to encapsulate the content that is to be affected by the tag. HTML documents have two parts: the head and the body. The head describes some things about the document, but does not include any content. The body has the content, as well as the tags and attributes that describe the layout of that content.

Line breaks in text are ignored by browsers. The browser fills lines in its display window and provides line breaks when needed. Line breaks can be specified with the `<br />` tag. Paragraph breaks can be specified with `<p>`. Headings can be created with the `<hx>` tags, where x can be any number from 1 to 6. The `<blockquote>` tag is used to set off a section of text. The `<sub>` and `<sup>` tags are used to create subscripts and superscripts, respectively. Horizontal lines can be specified with the `<hr />` tag.

Images in GIF, JPEG, or PNG format can be inserted into documents with the `<img />` tag. The `alt` attribute of `<img />` is used to present a message to the user when his or her browser is unable (or unwilling) to present the associated image.

Links support hypertext by allowing a document to define links that reference positions in either the current document or other documents. These links can be taken by the user viewing the document on a browser.

HTML supports unordered lists, using the `<ul>` tag, and ordered lists, using the `<ol>` tag. Both of these kinds of lists use the `<li>` tag to define list elements. The `<dl>` tag is used to describe definition lists. The `<dt>` and `<dd>` tags are used to specify the terms and their definitions, respectively.

Tables are easy to create with HTML, through a collection of tags designed for that purpose. The `<table>` tag is used to create a table, `<tr>` to create table rows, `<th>` to create label cells, and `<td>` to create data cells in the table. The `colspan` and `rowspan` attributes, which can appear in both `<th>` and `<td>` tags, provide the means of creating multiple levels of column and row labels, respectively.

HTML forms are sections of documents that contain controls used to collect input from the user. The data specified in a form can be sent to a server-resident program in either of two methods: `get` or `post`. The most commonly used controls (text boxes, checkboxes, passwords, radio buttons, and the action buttons submit, reset, and button) are specified with the `<input>` tag. The *Submit* button is used to indicate that the form data is to be sent to the server for processing. The *Reset* button is used to clear all of the controls in a form. The text box control is used to collect one line of input from the user. Checkboxes are one or more buttons used to select one or more elements of a list. Radio buttons are like checkboxes, except that, within a group, only one button can be on at a time. A password is a text box whose content is never displayed by the browser.

Menus allow the user to select items from a list when the list is too long to use checkboxes or radio buttons. Menu controls are created with the `<select>` tag. A text area control, which is created with the `<textarea>` tag, creates a multiple-line text-gathering box with implicit scrolling in both directions.

HTML5 includes a long list of new elements and capabilities. Among the most important of these are the audio element, which allows a document to specify the playing of audio files, the video element, which allows a document to specify the playing of video files, the time element, which provides a way to specify a date and time stamp in machine-readable form in a document, and some new semantic structuring elements.

Review Questions

2.1   What does it mean for a tag or attribute of HTML to be deprecated?

2.2   What is the form of an HTML comment?

2.3   How does a browser treat line breaks in text that is to be displayed?

2.4   What is the difference in the effect of a paragraph tag and a break tag?

2.5   Which heading elements use fonts that are smaller than the normal text font size?

2.6   How do browsers usually set block quotations differently from normal text?

2.7   What does the `<code>` tag specify for its content?

2.8   What are the differences between the JPEG and GIF image formats?

2.9   What are the two required attributes of an `<img />` tag?

2.10   What is the purpose of the `alt` attribute of `<img />`?

2.11   What tag is used to define a link?

2.12   What attribute is required in all anchor tags?

2.13   Does HTML allow nested links?

2.14   How is the target of a link usually identified in a case where the target is in the currently displayed document but not at its beginning?

2.15 What is the form of the value of the `href` attribute in an anchor tag when the target is a fragment of a document other than the one in which the link appears?

2.16 What is the default bullet form for the items in an unordered list?

2.17 What are the default sequence values for the items in an ordered list?

2.18 What tags are used to define the terms and their definitions in a definition list?

2.19 What is the purpose of the `colspan` attribute of the `<th>` tag?

2.20 What is the purpose of the `rowspan` attribute of the `<td>` tag?

2.21 What are controls?

2.22 Which controls discussed in this chapter are created with the `<input>` tag?

2.23 What is the default size of a text control's text box?

2.24 What is the difference between the `size` and `maxlength` attributes of `<input>` for text controls?

2.25 What is the difference in behavior between a group of checkbox buttons and a group of radio buttons?

2.26 Under what circumstances is a menu used instead of a radio button group?

2.27 How are scroll bars specified for text-area controls?

2.28 Before HTML5, how were sound clips played while a browser displayed a Web document?

2.29 What is an audio codec?

2.30 What is an audio container?

2.31 Why would an audio element include more than one source element?

2.32 Before HTML5, what was the most common way to play video clips when a Web document was displayed?

2.33 What does the `autoplay` attribute of the video element do?

2.34 Before HTML5, what HTML elements were used to organize documents?

2.35 What is the purpose of the article element?

2.36 What is the format of the date part of the value of the `datetime` attribute?

Exercises

2.1 Create, test, and validate an HTML document for yourself, including your name, address, and e-mail address. If you are a student, you must include your major and your grade level. If you work, you must include your employer, your employer's address, and your job title. This document must use several headings and `<em>`, `<strong>`, `<hr />`, `<p>`, and `<br />` tags.

2.2 Add pictures of yourself and at least one other image (of your friend, spouse, or pet) to the document created for Exercise 2.1.

2.3 Add a second document to the document created for Exercise 2.1 that describes part of your background, using `background` as the link content. This document should have a few paragraphs of your personal or professional history.

2.4 Create, test, and validate an HTML document that describes an unordered list equivalent to your typical grocery shopping list. (If you've never written a grocery list, use your imagination.)

2.5 Create, test, and validate an HTML document that describes an unordered list of at least four states. Each element of the list must have a nested list of at least three cities in the state.

2.6 Create, test, and validate an HTML document that describes an ordered list of your five favorite movies.

2.7 Modify the list of Exercise 2.6 to add nested, unordered lists of at least two actors and/or actresses in your favorite movies.

2.8 Create, test, and validate an HTML document that describes an ordered list with the following contents: The highest level should be the names of your parents, with your mother first. Under each parent, you must have a nested, ordered list of the brothers and sisters of your parents (your aunts and uncles) in order by age, eldest first. Each of the nested lists in turn must have nested lists of the children of your aunts and uncles (your cousins)—under the proper parents, of course. Regardless of how many aunts, uncles, and cousins you actually have, there must be at least three list items in each sublist below each of your parents and below each of your aunts and uncles.

2.9 Create, test, and validate an HTML document that describes a table with the following contents: The columns of the table must have the headings "Pine," "Maple," "Oak," and "Fir." The rows must have the labels "Average Height," "Average Width," "Typical Life Span," and "Leaf Type." You can make up the data cell values.

2.10 Modify, test, and validate an HTML document from Exercise 2.9 that adds a second-level column label, "Tree," and a second-level row label, "Characteristics."

2.11   Create, test, and validate an HTML document that defines a table with columns for state, state bird, state flower, and state tree. There must be at least five rows for states in the table.

2.12   Create, test, and validate an HTML document that defines a table with two levels of column labels: an overall label, "Meals," and three secondary labels, "Breakfast," "Lunch," and "Dinner." There must be two levels of row labels: an overall label, "Foods," and four secondary labels, "Bread," "Main Course," "Vegetable," and "Dessert." The cells of the table must contain a number of grams for each of the food categories.

2.13   Create, test, and validate an HTML document that is the home page of a business, Tree Branches, Unlimited, that sells tree branches. This document must include images and descriptions of at least three different kinds of tree branches. There must be at least one unordered list, one ordered list, and one table. Detailed descriptions of the different branches must be stored in separate documents that are accessible through links from the home document. You must invent several practical uses for tree branches and include sales pitches for them.

2.14   Create, test, and validate an HTML document that has a form with the following controls:
   a. A text box to collect the user's name
   b. Four checkboxes, one each for the following items:
      i.   Four 25-watt light bulbs for $2.39
      ii. Eight 25-watt light bulbs for $4.29
      iii. Four 25-watt long-life light bulbs for $3.95
      iv. Eight 25-watt long-life light bulbs for $7.49
   c. A collection of three radio buttons that are labeled as follows:
      i.   Visa
      ii. Master Card
      iii. Discover

2.15   Modify the document from one of the earlier exercises to add a sound track that plays continuously while the document is displayed. The audio must be in all three of the common container/codec forms.

2.16   Modify the document from one of the earlier exercises to add a video that plays continuously while the document is displayed. The video should be related to the information displayed by the document. The video must be in all three of the common container/codec forms.

2.17   Modify the document from one of the earlier exercises to add both header and footer elements. An article element that contains information relevant to that of the document but which is from some external source must also be included.

3

Cascading Style Sheets

This chapter introduces the concept of style sheets and describes how they are used to override the default styles of the elements of HTML documents. To begin, the three levels of style sheets and the format of style specifications are introduced. Then, the many varieties of property-value forms are described. Next, specific properties for fonts and lists are introduced and illustrated. A discussion of the properties for specifying colors, background images, and text alignment follows. The box model of document elements is then discussed, along with borders and the associated padding and margin properties. The chapter's next section describes two tags, `<span>` and `<div>`, that are used to delimit the scope of style sheet specifications. Finally, the last section of the chapter provides an overview of the resolution process for conflicting style specifications.

There are several CSS properties that are used to specify the position of elements in the display of a document. Because these are used to build dynamic documents, they are discussed in Chapter 6, rather than in this chapter.

3.1   Introduction

We have said that HTML is concerned primarily with content rather than the details of how that content is presented by browsers. That is not entirely true, however, even with the tags discussed in Chapter 2. Some of those tags—for example, `<code>`—specify presentation details, or style. However, these presentation specifications can be more precisely and more consistently described with style sheets. Furthermore, many of the tags and attributes that can be used for describing presentation details have been deprecated in favor of style sheets.

Most HTML tags have associated properties that store presentation information for browsers. Browsers use default values for these properties when the document does not specify values. For example, the `<h2>` tag has the `font-size` property, for which a browser would have the default value of a particular size. A document could specify that the `font-size` property for `<h2>` be set to a larger size, which would override the default value. The new value could apply to one occurrence of an `<h2>` element, some subset of the occurrences, or all such occurrences in the document, depending on how the property value is set.

A style sheet is a syntactic mechanism for specifying style information. The idea of a style sheet is not new: Word processors and desktop publishing systems have long used style sheets to impose a particular style on documents. The first style-sheet specification for use in HTML documents, dubbed Cascading Style Sheets (CSS1), was developed in 1996 by the W3C. In mid-1998, the second standard, CSS2, was released. CSS2 added many properties and property values to CSS1. It also extended presentation control to media other than Web browsers, such as printers. As a result of the incomplete implementation of (and perhaps a lack of interest in) parts of CSS2 by browser implementors, W3C developed a new standard, CSS2.1, which reflected the level of acceptance of CSS2. Internet Explorer 8 and later (IE8+), Chrome 5 and later (C5+), and Firefox 3 and later (FX3+) fully support CSS2.1, which was at the "working draft" stage as of spring 2011. CSS3 has been in development since the late 1990s. Current versions of browsers already have implemented some parts of CSS3. This chapter covers most of CSS2.1.

Perhaps the most important benefit of style sheets is their capability of imposing consistency on the style of Web documents. For example, they allow the author to specify that all paragraphs of a document have the same presentation style and therefore the same appearance.

CSS style sheets are called *cascading* style sheets because they can be defined at three different levels to specify the style of a document. Lower-level style sheets can override higher level style sheets, so the style of the content of an element is determined, in effect, through a cascade of style-sheet applications.

3.2 Levels of Style Sheets

The three levels of style sheets, in order from lowest level to highest level, are *inline*, *document level*, and *external*. Inline style sheets apply to the content of a single HTML element, document-level style sheets apply to the whole body of a document, and external style sheets can apply to the bodies of any number of documents. Inline style sheets have precedence over document style sheets, which have precedence over external style sheets. For example, if an external style sheet specifies a value for a particular property of a particular element, that value is used until a different value is specified in either a document style sheet or an inline style sheet. Likewise, document style sheet property values can be overridden by different property values in an inline style sheet. In effect, the properties of a specific element are those that result from a merge of all applicable style sheets, with lower-level style sheets having precedence in cases of conflicting specifications. There are other ways style specification conflicts can occur. These ways and their resolution are discussed in Section 3.13.

If no style sheet provides a value for a particular style property, the browser default property value is used. Because none of the example HTML documents in Chapter 2 includes style sheets, every element in those documents uses the browser default value for its properties.[1]

As is the case with tags and tag attributes, a particular browser may not be capable of using the property values specified in a style sheet. For example, if the value of the font-size property of a paragraph is set to a particular size, but the browser cannot display the particular font being used in that size, the browser obviously cannot fulfill the property specification. In this case, the browser either would substitute an alternative value or would simply ignore the given font-size value and use its default font size.

Inline style specifications appear within the opening tag and apply only to the content of that element. This fine-grain application of style defeats one of the primary advantages of style sheets—that of imposing a uniform style on the elements of at least one whole document. Another disadvantage of inline style sheets is that they result in style information, which is expressed in a language distinct from HTML markup, being embedded in various places in documents. It is better to keep style specifications separate from HTML markup. For this reason, among others, W3C deprecated inline style sheets in XHTML 1.1.[2] Therefore, inline style specifications should be used sparingly. This chapter discusses inline style sheets, but we follow our own advice and make little use of them in our examples.

Doesn't do this. This is a disadvantage

because style sheets were deprecated by XHTML.

---

1. This is not precisely true; some property values could come from browser user overrides of the browser default values.

2. A feature's being placed on the list of deprecated features is a warning to users to restrict their use of that feature, because sometime in the future it will be discontinued.

Document-level style specifications appear in the document head section and apply to the entire body of the document. This is obviously an effective way to impose a uniform style on the presentation of all of the content of a single document.

In many cases, it is desirable to have a style sheet apply to more than one document. That is the purpose of external style sheets, which are not part of any of the documents to which they apply. They are stored separately and are referenced in all documents that use them. Another advantage of external style sheets is that their use cleanly separates CSS from HTML. External style sheets are written as text files with the MIME type `text/css`. They can be stored on any computer on the Web. The browser fetches external style sheets just as it fetches HTML documents. The `<link>` tag is used to specify external style sheets.[3] Within `<link>`, the `rel` attribute is used to specify the relationship of the linked-to document to the document in which the link appears. The `href` attribute of `<link>` is used to specify the URL of the style sheet document, as in the following example:

```
<link rel = "stylesheet"  type = "text/css"
      href = "http://www.cs.usc.edu/styles/wbook.css" />
```

The link to an external style sheet must appear in the head of the document. If the external style sheet resides on the Web server computer, only its path address must be given as the value of `href`. An example of an external style sheet appears in Section 3.6.

Because it is good to separate CSS from markup, it is preferable to use external style sheets. However, because the example documents in this book are all relatively small and we want to keep the CSS near where it is used so it is easy to reference, we nearly always use document-level style sheets in our examples.

External style sheets can be validated with the service provided at `http://jigsaw.w3.org/css-validator/`.

3.3 Style Specification Formats

The format of a style specification depends on the level of style sheet. Inline style specifications appear as values of the `style` attribute of a tag,[4] the general form of which is as follows:

```
style = "property_1 : value_1; property_2 : value_2; ...;
         property_n : value_n;"
```

Although it is not required, it is recommended that the last property-value pair be followed by a semicolon.

---

3. There is an alternative to using the `<link>` tag, `@import`. However, `@import` is slower so there is no good reason to use it.

4. The `style` attribute is deprecated in the XHTML 1.1 recommendation. However, it is still part of HTML5.

Document style specifications appear as the content of a `style` element within the header of a document, although the format of the specification is quite different from that of inline style sheets. The general form of the content of a style element is as follows:[5]

```
<style type = "text/css">
    rule_list
</style>
```

The `type` attribute of the `<style>` tag tells the browser the type of style specification, which is `text/css` for CSS.

Each style rule in a rule list has two parts: a selector, which indicates the element or elements affected by the rule, and a list of property-value pairs. The list has the same form as the quoted list for inline style sheets, except that it is delimited by braces rather than double quotes. So, the form of a style rule is as follows:

selector {property_1 : value_1; property_2 : value_2; ...;
        property_n : value_n; }

If a property is given more than one value, those values usually are separated with spaces. For some properties, however, multiple values are separated with commas.

Like all other kinds of coding, complicated CSS rule lists should be documented with comments. Of course, HTML comments cannot be used here, because CSS is not HTML. Therefore, a different form of comment is needed. CSS comments are introduced with /* and terminated with */,[6] as in the following element:

```
<style type = "text/css">
    /* Styles for the initial paragraph */
    ...
    /* Styles for other paragraphs */
    ...
</style>
```

An external style sheet consists of a list of style rules of the same form as in document style sheets. The `<style>` tag is not included. An example of an external style sheet appears in Section 3.6.

3.4 Selector Forms

A selector specifies the elements to which the following style information applies. The selector can have a variety of forms.

---

5. Browsers so old that they do not recognize the `<style>` tag may display the content of the style element at the top of the document. There are now so few such browsers in use that we ignore the issue here. Those who are concerned put the rule list in an HTML comment.

6. This form of comment is adopted from the C programming language and some of its descendants.

3.4.1 Simple Selector Forms

The simplest selector form is a single element name, such as h1. In this case, the property values in the rule apply to all occurrences of the named element. The selector could be a list of element names separated by commas, in which case the property values apply to all occurrences of all of the named elements. Consider the following examples:

```
h1 {property-value list}
h2, h3 {property-value list}
```

The first of these selector forms specifies that the following property-value list applies to all h1 elements. The second specifies that the following property-value list applies to all h2 and h3 elements.

3.4.2 Class Selectors

Class selectors are used to allow different occurrences of the same tag to use different style specifications. A style class is defined in a style element by giving the style class a name, which is attached to the tag's name with a period. For example, if you want two paragraph styles in a document—say, normal and warning—you could define these two classes in the content of a style element as follows:

```
p.normal {property-value list}
p.warning {property-value list}
```

Within the document body, the particular style class that you want is specified with the class attribute of the affected tag—in the preceding example, the paragraph tag. For example, you might have the following markup:

```
<p class = "normal">
A paragraph of text that we want to be presented in
'normal' presentation style
</p>
<p class = "warning">
A paragraph of text that is a warning to the reader, which
should be presented in an especially noticeable style
</p>
```

3.4.3 Generic Selectors

Sometimes it is convenient to have a class of style specifications that applies to the content of more than one kind of tag. This is done by using a generic class, which is defined without a tag name in its selector. Without the tag name, the name of the generic class begins with a period, as in the following generic style class:

```
.sale {property-value list}
```

Now, in the body of a document, you could have the following markup:

```
<h3 class = "sale"> Weekend Sale </h3>
. . .
<p class = "sale">
. . .
</p>
```

3.4.4   `id` Selectors

An `id` selector allows the application of a style to one specific element. The general form of an `id` selector is as follows:[7]

#specific-id {property-value list}

As you would probably guess, the style specified in the `id` selector applies to the element with the given `id`. For example, consider the following selector:

`#section14` *{property-value list}*

Following is the h2 element to which this style applies:

```
<h2 id = "section14"> 1.4 Calico Cats </h2>
```

3.4.5   Contextual Selectors

Selectors can specify, in several different ways, that the style should apply only to elements in certain positions in the document. The simplest form of contextual selector is the descendant selector. Element B is a *descendant* of element A if it appears in the content of A. In this situation, A is the *ancestor* of B. A particular element can be selected by listing one or more of the ancestors of the element in the selector, with only white space separating the element names. For example, the following rule applies its style only to the content of ordered list elements that are descendants of unordered list elements in the document:

`ul ol` *{property-value list}*

An element is a *child* of another element if it is a descendant and it is nested directly in that element. Element B is directly nested in element A if there are no opening tags between the opening tag of A and that of B that do not have corresponding closing tags. Also, if B is the child of A, we call A the *parent* of B. For example, in the following, the first and third li elements are children of the ol element. The second li element is a descendant of the ol element, but is not a child of it, because its parent is the ul element.

---

7. For the oddly curious reader, the Bell Labs name for the # symbol is *octothorpe*. It was named that when it was first put on the telephone dial. The name comes from the eight points of intersection of the figure with the circumference of its circumscribed circle.

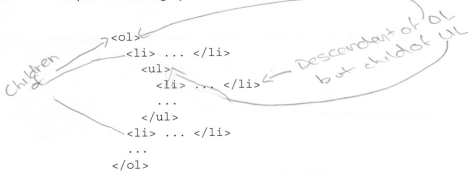

```
<ol>
    <li> ... </li>
        <ul>
            <li> ... </li>
            ...
        </ul>
        <li> ... </li>
    ...
</ol>
```

CSS includes a child selector. For example, the following selector applies to `li` elements only if they are children of `ol` elements:

`ol > li` *{property-value list}*

Child selectors can be specified over any number of elements in a family hierarchy (not just one generation). For example, the following selector selects em elements that are children of `h1` elements that are children of paragraph elements:

`p > h1 > em` *{property-value list}*

3.4.6   Pseudo Classes

Pseudo classes specify that certain styles apply when something happens, rather than because the target element simply exists. In this section, we describe and illustrate four pseudo classes, two that are used exclusively to style hypertext links, and two that can be used to style any element.

The two pseudo classes for styling links are `link` and `visited`. The `link` pseudo class is used to style a link that has not been selected; `visited` is used to style a link that previously has been selected.

The style of the `hover` pseudo class applies when its associated element has the mouse cursor over it. The style of the `focus` pseudo class applies when its associated element has focus.[8]

Browsers often use blue as the default color for unvisited links and red or purple for visited links. They usually also underline links. If the background color is white, this is fine. However, if the background color is not white, it is better to make the unvisited links some bright color that contrasts with the background color of the document. Contrasting colors can be found with a color sphere, such as can be found at `http://www.colorjack.com/sphere`. In such a sphere, contrasting colors are 180 degrees apart on the sphere. Visited links can then be a muted version of the chosen contrasting color.

When using the `hover` pseudo class, changing the size of an element from its initial size, for example by enlarging or shrinking the font size, can lead to problems. For example, if the font size is made larger, the larger size could cause the element to overflow the area reserved for it in the display, causing the whole document to be rearranged. That would likely annoy the user.

---

8. One way an element acquires focus is when the user places the mouse cursor over it and clicks the left mouse button.

Whereas the names of style classes and generic classes begin with a period, the names of pseudo classes begin with a colon. For example, the selector for the hover pseudo class applied to an h2 element is as follows:

h2:hover *{property-value list}*

Any time the mouse cursor is positioned over an h2 element, the styles defined in the given property-value list are applied to the content of the h2 element.

3.4.7 The Universal Selector

The universal selector, denoted by an asterisk (*), applies its style to all elements in a document. For example, if we wanted every element in a document to have a particular set of properties, we could include the following:

* *{property-value list}*

3.5 Property-Value Forms

CSS includes a large number of different properties, arranged in categories. The most commonly used categories are: fonts, lists, alignment of text, margins, colors, backgrounds, and borders. As you probably would guess, only a fraction of the properties are discussed here. The complete details of all properties and property values can be found at http://www.w3.org/TR/2011/REC-CSS2-20110607/propidx.html.

Property values can appear in a variety of forms. Keyword property values are used when there are only a few possible values and they are predefined—for example, large, medium, and small. Keyword values are not case sensitive, so Small, SmAlL, and SMALL are all the same as small.

Number values are used when no meaningful units can be attached to a numeric property value. A number value can be either an integer or a sequence of digits with a decimal point and can be preceded by a sign (+ or -).

Length values are specified as number values that are followed immediately by a two-character abbreviation of a unit name. There can be no space between the number and the unit name. The possible unit names are px, for pixels; in, for inches; cm, for centimeters; mm, for millimeters; pt, for points (a point is 1/72 inch); and pc, for picas, which are 12 points. Note that on a display, in, cm, mm, pt, and pc are approximate measures. Their actual values depend on the screen resolution. There are also two relative length values: em, which is the value of the current font size in pixels, and ex, which is the height of the letter *x*.

Percentage values are used to provide a measure that is relative to the previously used measure for a property value. Percentage values are numbers that are followed immediately by a percent sign (%). For example, if the font size were set to 75% with a style sheet, it would make the new current size for the font 75 percent of its previous value. Font size would stay at the new value until changed again. Percentage values can be signed. If preceded by a plus sign, the percentage is added to the previous value; if negative, the percentage is subtracted.

URL property values use a form that is slightly different from references to URLs in links. The actual URL, which can be either absolute or relative, is placed in parentheses and preceded by `url`, as in the following property:

```
url(tetons.jpg)
```

There can be no space between `url` and the left parenthesis. If there is one, the property and its value will be ignored by the browser.

Color property values can be specified as color names, as six-digit hexadecimal numbers, or in RGB form. RGB form is just the word `rgb` followed by a parenthesized list of three decimal numbers in the range of 0 to 255 or three percentage values. These numbers or percentages specify the levels of red, green, and blue, respectively. For example, a value of 0 or 0% as the first of the three values would specify that no red be included in the color. A value of 255 or 100% would specify the maximum amount of red. Hexadecimal numbers must be preceded with pound signs (#), as in `#43AF00`. For example, fuchsia (a mixture of red and blue) could be specified with

```
fuchsia
```

or

```
rgb(255, 0, 255)
```

or

```
#FF00FF
```

As is the case with `url`, there can be no space between `rgb` and the left parenthesis. If there is, the value will be ignored by the browser.

CSS also includes properties for counters and strings, but they are not covered here.

As has been hinted previously, many property values are inherited by descendent elements. For example, because `font-size` is an inherited property, setting it to a value on the `<body>` tag effectively sets that value as the new default property value all of the elements for the whole body of the document (because all elements in the body of a document are descendants of the body element).

Not all properties are inherited, although those cases are somewhat intuitive. For example, `background-color` and the margin properties are not inherited.[9]

Color values in hexadecimal and rgb can be converted between the two forms with calculators at `http://www.javascripter.net/faz/hextorgb.htm`.

---

9. `inherit` is CSS keyword. By default, most properties are set to `inherit`. If a property is set to `inherit`, its value will be inherited. Some of the properties that are not `inherit` by default can be set to `inherit`, as in the following: `div {background-color: inherit;}`

3.6 **Font Properties**

The font properties are among the most commonly used of the style-sheet properties. Virtually all HTML documents include text, which is often used in a variety of different situations. This creates a need for text in many different fonts, font styles, and sizes. The font properties allow us to specify these different forms.

3.6.1   **Font Families**

The `font-family` property is used to specify a list of font names. The browser uses the first font in the list that it supports.[10] For example, the following property:

```
font-family: Arial, Helvetica, Futura
```

tells the browser to use Arial if it supports that font. If it does not support Ariel, it should use Helvetica if it supports it. If the browser supports neither Arial nor Helvetica, it should use Futura if it supports it. If the browser does not support any of the specified fonts, it will use an alternative of its choosing.

A generic font can be specified as a `font-family` value. The possible generic fonts and examples of each are shown in Table 3.1. Every browser has a font defined for each of these generic names. A good approach to specifying fonts is to use a generic font as the last font in the value of a `font-family` property. For example, because Arial, Helvetica, and Futura are sans-serif fonts,[11] the previous example would be better as follows:

Table 3.1   Generic fonts

Generic Name	Examples
serif	Times New Roman, Garamond
sans-serif	Arial, Helvetica
cursive	Caflisch Script, Zapf-Chancery
fantasy	Critter, Cottonwood
monospace	Courier, Prestige

```
font-family: Arial, Helvetica, Futura, sans-serif
```

Now, if the browser does not support any of the named fonts, it will use a font from the same category, in this case, sans serif.

---

10. Typically, browsers support all fonts that are installed on the browser's host computer.

11. Serifs are nonstructural decorations that may appear at the ends of strokes in a character. Sans-serif fonts do not have serifs.

If a font name has more than one word, the whole name should be delimited by single quotes,[12] as in the following example:

```
font-family: 'Times New Roman'
```

[handwritten note: use '' because of spaces between name]

In practice, the quotes may not be required, but their use is recommended because they may be necessary in the future.

3.6.2 Font Sizes

The `font-size` property does what its name implies its value specifies the size of the font. Unfortunately, it is not as simple as we wish it were.

There are two categories of `font-size` values, absolute and relative. In the absolute category, the size value could be given as a length value in points, picas, or pixels, or as a keyword from the list: `xx-small`, `x-small`, `small`, `medium`, `large`, `x-large`, and `xx-large`. One problem with the keyword sizes is that the size relationship between adjacent keywords is not exactly the same on different browsers.

The relative size values are `smaller` and `larger`, which adjust the font size relative to the font size of the parent element. Once again, however, the amount of change that results from these is not the same among browsers. Percent values can also be used to adjust the font size relative to the font size of the parent element. But in this case, the property value is a uniform size adjustment. Finally, a number with the unit em can be used. For example,

```
font-size: 1.2em
```

[handwritten note: 'em' represents the value of the current font size n pixels]

This sets the font size to 1.2 times the font size of the parent element. So, percentages and the use of em are equivalent. `1.2em` and `120%` are exactly the same.

One problem with using points and picas for font sizes is that they do not display in the same size on different computers. Points and picas were designed for printed media—that is where they should be used. Furthermore, if the user changes the default font size, on some browsers these will not change. If a relative size is given, the font size will be scaled relative to a new default set by the user. Although the keywords are in the absolute category, they are set relative to the default font size of the browser.

Considering all of these issues, percentages and em are good choices for setting font sizes. We use em in the example documents in the remainder of the book.

[handwritten note: Impt Best Practices!!!]

3.6.3 Font Variants

The default value of the `font-variant` property is `normal`, which specifies the usual character font. This property can be set to `small-caps` to specify small capital letters. These are all uppercase, but the letters that are normally uppercase are a bit larger than those that are normally lowercase.

---

12. Single quotes are used here, because in the case of inline style sheets, the whole property list is delimited by double quotes.

3.6.4   Font Styles

The `font-style` property is usually used to specify italic, as in

```
font-style: italic
```

An alternative to `italic` is `oblique`, but when displayed, the two are nearly identical,[13] so `oblique` is not a terribly useful font style.

There is one other possible value for font-style, `normal`, which specifies that the font be the normal style. This tells the browser to stop using whatever non-normal style it had been using until instructed otherwise.

3.6.5   Font Weights

The `font-weight` property is used to specify the degree of boldness, as in

```
font-weight: bold
```

Besides `bold`, the possible values `normal` (the default), `bolder`, and `lighter` can be specified. The `bolder` and `lighter` values are taken as relative to the level of boldness of the parent element. Specific numbers also can be given in multiples of `100` from `100` to `900`, where `400` is the same as `normal` and `700` is the same as `bold`. Because many fonts are available only in normal and bold, the use of these numbers often just causes the browser to choose either `normal` or `bold`.

3.6.6   Font Shorthands

If more than one font property must be specified, the values can be stated in a list as the value of the `font` property. The browser then determines which properties to assign from the forms of the values. For example, the property

```
font: bold 1.1em 'Times New Roman' Palatino
```

specifies that the font weight should be `bold`, the font size should be 1.1 times that of its parent element, and either Times New Roman or Palatino font should be used, with precedence given to Times New Roman.

The order in which the property values are given in a `font` value list is important. The order must be as follows: The font names must be last, the font size must be second to last, and the font style, font variant, and font weight, when they are included, can be in any order but must precede the font size. Only the font size and the font family are required in the `font` value list.

---

13. Actually, italic fonts have slightly extended serifs, whereas oblique fonts have normal serifs. Both are slanted to the right.

The document `fonts.html` illustrates some aspects of style-sheet specifications of the font properties in headings and paragraphs:

```
<!DOCTYPE html>
<!-- fonts.html
     An example to illustrate font properties
     -->
<html lang = "en">
  <head>
    <title> Font properties </title>
    <meta charset = "utf-8" />
    <style type = "text/css">
      p.major {font-size: 1.1em;
               font-style: italic;
               font-family: 'Times New Roman';
              }
      p.minor {font: 0.9em bold 'Courier New';}
      h2 {font-family: 'Times New Roman';
          font-size: 2em; font-weight: bold;}
      h3 {font-family: 'Courier New'; font-size: 1.5em;}
    </style>
  </head>
  <body>
    <p class = "major">
      If a job is worth doing, it's worth doing right.
    </p>
    <p class = "minor">
      Two wrongs don't make a right, but they certainly
      can get you in a lot of trouble.
    </p>
    <h2> Chapter 1 Introduction </h2>
    <h3> 1.1 The Basics of Computer Networks </h3>
  </body>
</html>
```

[handwritten annotation: Note: Different formatting — font shorthand used]

Figure 3.1 shows a browser display of `fonts.html`.

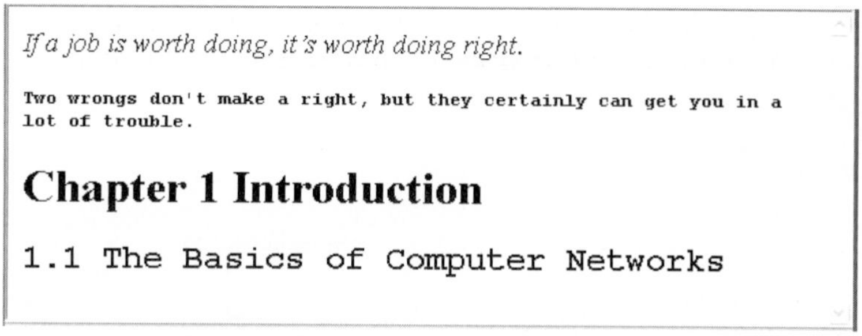

> *If a job is worth doing, it's worth doing right.*
>
> `Two wrongs don't make a right, but they certainly can get you in a lot of trouble.`
>
> # Chapter 1 Introduction
>
> ## 1.1 The Basics of Computer Networks

Figure 3.1 Display of `fonts.html`

The following document, called `fonts2.html`, is a revision of `fonts.html` that uses an external style sheet in place of the document style sheet used in `fonts.html` (the external style sheet, `styles.css`, follows the revised document):

```
<!DOCTYPE html>
<!-- fonts2.html
     An example to test external style sheets
     -->
<html lang = "en">
  <head>
    <title> External style sheets </title>
    <meta charset = "utf-8" />
    <link rel = "stylesheet"  type = "text/css"
          href = "styles.css" />
  </head>
  <body>
    <p class = "major">
      If a job is worth doing, it's worth doing right.
    </p>
    <p class = "minor">
      Two wrongs don't make a right, but they certainly
      can get you in a lot of trouble.
    </p>
    <h2> Chapter 1 Introduction </h2>
    <h3> 1.1 The Basics of Computer Networks </h3>
  </body>
</html>
```

```
/* styles.css - an external style sheet
      for use with fonts2.html
   */
p.major {font-size: 1.1em;
           font-style: italic;
           font-family: 'Times New Roman';
         }
p.minor {font: bold 0.9em 'Courier New';}
h2 {font-family: 'Times New Roman';
     font-size: 2em; font-weight: bold;}
h3 {font-family: 'Courier New';
     font-size: 1.5em;}
```

3.6.7   Text Decoration

The text-decoration property is used to specify some special features of text. The available values are line-through, overline, underline, and none, which is the default. Many browsers implicitly underline links. The none value can be used to avoid this underlining.[14] Note that text-decoration is _not_ inherited. The following document, decoration.html, illustrates the line-through, overline, and underline values:

```
<!DOCTYPE html>
<!-- decoration.html
      An example that illustrates several of the
      possible text decoration values
      -->
<html lang = "en">
  <head>
    <title> Text decoration </title>
    <meta charset = "utf-8" />
    <style type = "text/css">
      p.delete {text-decoration: line-through;}
      p.cap {text-decoration: overline;}
      p.attention {text-decoration: underline;}
    </style>
  </head>
```

---

14. Setting text-decoration to none for a link is a bad idea, because it makes it less likely the link will be noticed.

```
<body>
  <p class = "delete">
    This illustrates line-through
  </p>
  <p class= "cap">
    This illustrates overline
  </p>
  <p class = "attention">
    This illustrates underline
  </p>
</body>
</html>
```

Figure 3.2 shows a browser display of `decoration.html`.

Figure 3.2 Display of `decoration.html`

3.6.8   Text Spacing

The `letter-spacing` property controls the amount of space between the letters in words. This spacing is called *tracking*. The possible values of `letter-spacing` are `normal` or any length property value. Positive values increase the letter spacing; negative values decrease it. For example, `letter-spacing: 1px` spreads the letters of words. Likewise, `letter-spacing: -1px` squeezes the letters of words together. The value `normal` resets `letter-spacing` back to that of the parent element.

The space between words in text can be controlled with the `word-spacing` property, whose values are `normal` or any length value. Once again, a positive value increases the space between words and negative values decrease that space and `normal` resets word-spacing back to that of the parent element.

The space between lines of text can be controlled with the `line-height` property. This spacing is called *leading*. The value of `line-height` can be a number, in which case a positive number sets the line spacing to that number times the font size (`2.0` means double spacing). The value could be a length, such as `24px`. If the font size is 12 pixels, this would specify double spacing. The value could be a percentage, which is relative to the spacing of the parent element.

Finally, `normal`, which overrides the current value, is used to set line spacing back to that of the parent element.

The following document, `text_space.html`, illustrates the text spacing properties:

```
<!DOCTYPE html>
<!-- text_space.html
     An example to illustrate text spacing properties
     -->
<html lang = "en">
  <head>
    <title> Text spacing properties </title>
    <meta charset = "utf-8" />
    <style type = "text/css">
      p.big_tracking {letter-spacing: 0.4em;}
      p.small_tracking {letter-spacing: -0.08em;}
      p.big_between_words {word-spacing: 0.4em;}
      p.small_between_words {word-spacing: -0.1em;}
      p.big_leading {line-height: 2.5;}
      p.small_leading {line-height: 1.0;}
    </style>
  </head>
  <body>
    <p class = "big_tracking">
      On the plains of hesitation [letter-spacing: 0.4em]
    </p> <p />
    <p class = "small_tracking">
      Bleach the bones of countless millions [letter-
      spacing: -0.08em]
    </p> <br />
    <p class = "big_between_words">
      Who at the dawn of victory [word-spacing: 0.4em]
    </p> <p />
    <p class = "small_between_words">
      Sat down to wait and waiting died [word-spacing:
      -0.1em]
    </p> <br />
    <p class = "big_leading">
      If you think CSS is simple, [line-height: 2.5] <br />
      You are quite mistaken
    </p> <br />
    <p class = "small_leading">
      If you think HTML5 is all old stuff, [line-height:
      1.0] <br />
      You are quite mistaken
    </p>
  </body>
</html>
```

Figure 3.3 shows a display of `text_space.html`.

```
O n   t h e   p l a i n s   o f   h e s i t a t i o n   [ l e t t e r - s p a c i n g :   0 . 4 e m ]

Bleach the bones of countless millions [letter-spacing: -0.08em]



Who  at  the  dawn  of  victory  [word-spacing:  0.4em]

Sat down to wait and waiting died [word-spacing: -0.1em]



If you think CSS is simple, [line-height: 2.5]

You are quite mistaken



If you think HTML5 is all old stuff, [line-height: 1.0]
You are quite mistaken
```

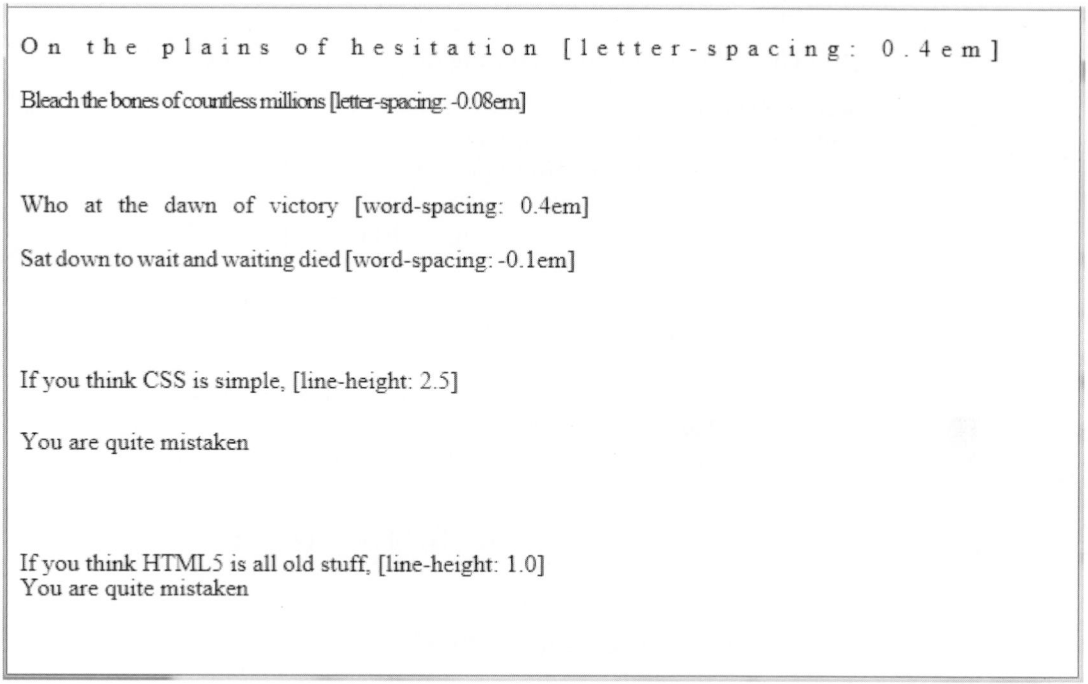

Figure 3.3 A display of `text_space.html`

3.7 List Properties

Two presentation details of lists can be specified in HTML documents: the shape of the bullets that precede the items in an unordered list and the sequencing values that precede the items in an ordered list. The `list-style-type` property is used to specify both of these. If `list-style-type` is set for a `ul` or an `ol` tag, it applies to all of the list items in the list. If a `list-style-type` is set for an `li` tag, it only applies to that list item.

The `list-style-type` property of an unordered list can be set to `disc` (the default), `circle`, `square`, or `none`. A `disc` is a small filled circle, a `circle` is an unfilled circle, and a `square` is a filled square. For example, the following markup illustrates a document style sheet that sets the bullet type in all items in unordered lists to `square`:

```
<!-- bullets1 -->
<style type = "text/css">
  ul {list-style-type: square;}
</style>
...
<h3> Some Common Single-Engine Aircraft </h3>
  <ul>
    <li> Cessna Skyhawk </li>
```

```
    <li> Beechcraft Bonanza </li>
    <li> Piper Cherokee </li>
  </ul>
```

The following illustrates setting the style for individual list items:

```
<!-- bullets2 -->
<style type = "text/css">
  li.disc {list-style-type: disc;}
  li.square {list-style-type: square;}
  li.circle {list-style-type: circle;}
</style>
...
<h3> Some Common Single-Engine Aircraft </h3>
  <ul>
    <li class = "disc"> Cessna Skyhawk </li>
    <li class = "square"> Beechcraft Bonanza </li>
    <li class = "circle"> Piper Cherokee </li>
  </ul>
```

Figure 3.4 shows a browser display of these two lists.

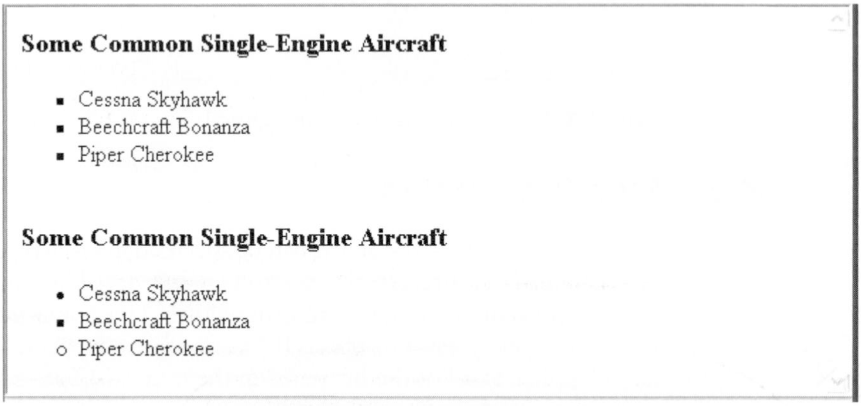

Figure 3.4 Examples of unordered lists

Bullets in unordered lists are not limited to discs, squares, and circles. An image can be used in a list item bullet. Such a bullet is specified with the `list-style-image` property, whose value is specified with the `url` form. For example, if `small_plane.gif` is a small image of an airplane that is stored in the same directory as the HTML document, it could be used as follows:

```
<style type = "text/css">
  li.image {list-style-image: url(small_airplane.gif);}
</style>
  ...
  <li class = "image"> Beechcraft Bonanza </li>
```

When ordered lists are nested, it is best to use different kinds of sequence values for the different levels of nesting. The `list-style-type` property can be used to specify the types of sequence values. Table 3.2 lists the different possibilities defined by CSS2.1.

Table 3.2 Possible sequencing value types for ordered lists in CSS2.1

Property Values	Sequence Type
decimal	Arabic numerals starting with 1
decimal-leading-zero	Arabic numerals starting with 0
lower-alpha	Lowercase letters
upper-alpha	Uppercase letters
lower-roman	Lowercase Roman numerals
upper-roman	Uppercase Roman numerals
lower-greek	Lowercase Greek letters
lower-latin	Same as lower-alpha
upper-latin	Same as upper-alpha
armenian	Traditional Armenian numbering
georgian	Traditional Georgian numbering
none	No bullet

The following example illustrates the use of different sequence value types in nested lists:

```
<!DOCTYPE html>
<!-- sequence_types.html
     An example to illustrate sequence type styles
     -->
<html lang = "en">
  <head>
    <title> Sequence types </title>
    <meta charset = "utf-8" />
    <style type = "text/css">
      ol {list-style-type: upper-roman;}
      ol ol {list-style-type: upper-alpha;}
      ol ol ol {list-style-type: decimal;}
    </style>
  </head>
```

```
<body>
  <h3> Aircraft Types </h3>
  <ol>
    <li> General Aviation (piston-driven engines)
      <ol>
        <li> Single-Engine Aircraft
          <ol>
            <li> Tail wheel </li>
            <li> Tricycle </li>
          </ol>
        </li>
        <li> Dual-Engine Aircraft
          <ol>
            <li> Wing-mounted engines </li>
            <li> Push-pull fuselage-mounted engines </li>
          </ol>
        </li>
      </ol>
    </li>
    <li> Commercial Aviation (jet engines)
      <ol>
        <li> Dual-Engine
          <ol>
            <li> Wing-mounted engines </li>
            <li> Fuselage-mounted engines </li>
          </ol>
        </li>
        <li> Tri-Engine
          <ol>
            <li> Third engine in vertical stabilizer </li>
            <li> Third engine in fuselage </li>
          </ol>
        </li>
      </ol>
    </li>
  </ol>
</body>
</html>
```

Figure 3.5 shows a browser display of sequence_types.html.

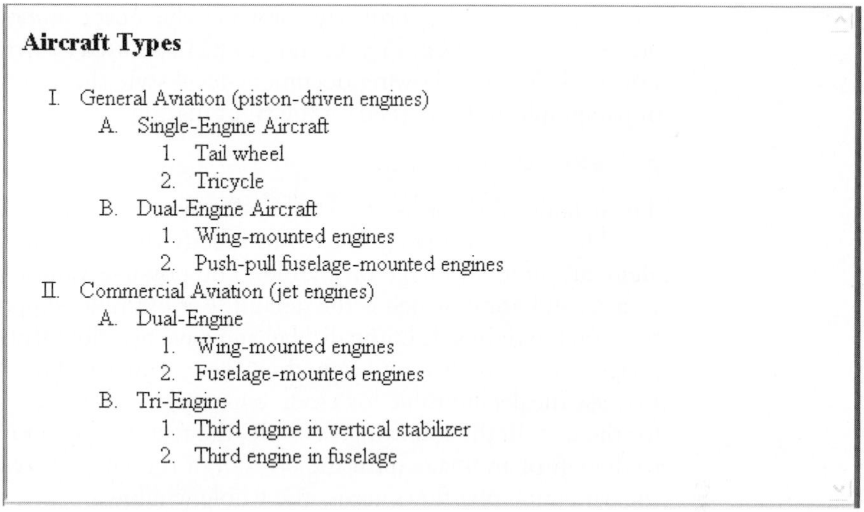

Aircraft Types

    I. General Aviation (piston-driven engines)
        A. Single-Engine Aircraft
           1. Tail wheel
           2. Tricycle
        B. Dual-Engine Aircraft
           1. Wing-mounted engines
           2. Push-pull fuselage-mounted engines
   II. Commercial Aviation (jet engines)
        A. Dual-Engine
           1. Wing-mounted engines
           2. Fuselage-mounted engines
        B. Tri-Engine
           1. Third engine in vertical stabilizer
           2. Third engine in fuselage

Figure 3.5 Display of `sequence_types.html`

3.8 Alignment of Text

The `text-indent` property can be used to indent the first line of a paragraph. This property takes either a length or a percentage value, as in the following markup:

```
<style type = "text/css">
  p.indent {text-indent: 2em}
</style>
...
<p class = "indent">
  Now is the time for all good Web developers to begin
  using cascading style sheets for all presentation
  details in their documents. No more deprecated tags
  and attributes, just nice, precise style sheets.
</p>
```

This paragraph would be displayed as shown in Figure 3.6.

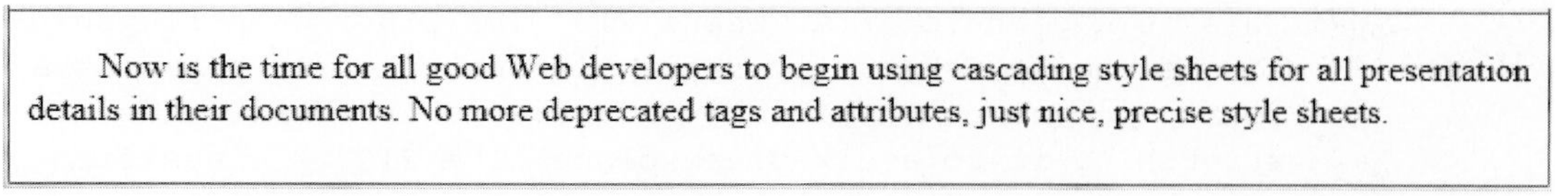

    Now is the time for all good Web developers to begin using cascading style sheets for all presentation details in their documents. No more deprecated tags and attributes, just nice, precise style sheets.

Figure 3.6 Indenting text

The text-align property, for which the most commonly used keyword values are left, center, right, and justify, is used to arrange text horizontally. For example, the following document-level style sheet entry causes the content of paragraphs to be aligned on the right margin:

```
p {text-align: right}
```

The default value for text-align is left.

The float property is used to specify that text should flow around some element, often an image or a table. The possible values for float are left, right, and none, which is the default. For example, suppose we want an image to be on the right side of the display and have text flow around the left side of the image. To specify this condition, the float property of the image is set to right. Because the default value for text-align is left, text-align need not be set for the text. In the following example, the text of a paragraph is specified to flow to the left of an image until the bottom of the image is reached, at which point the paragraph text flows across the whole window:

```
<!DOCTYPE html>
<!-- float.html
     An example to illustrate the float property
     -->
<html lang = "en">
  <head>
    <title> The float property </title>
    <meta charset = "utf-8" />
    <style type = "text/css">
      img {float: right;}
    </style>
  </head>
  <body>
    <p>
      <img src = "c210new.jpg"  alt = "Picture of a Cessna 210" />
    </p>
    <p>
      This is a picture of a Cessna 210. The 210 is the flagship
      single-engine Cessna aircraft. Although the 210 began as a
      four-place aircraft, it soon acquired a third row of seats,
      stretching it to a six-place plane. The 210 is classified
      as a high-performance airplane, which means its landing
      gear is retractable and its engine has more than 200
      horsepower. In its first model year, which was 1960,
      the 210 was powered by a 260-horsepower fuel-injected
      six-cylinder engine that displaced 471 cubic inches.
```

```
        The 210 is the fastest single-engine airplane ever
      built by Cessna.
    </p>
  </body>
</html>
```

When rendered by a browser, `float.html` might appear as shown in Figure 3.7, depending on the width of the browser display window.

This is a picture of a Cessna 210. The 210 is the flagship single-engine Cessna aircraft. Although the 210 began as a four-place aircraft, it soon acquired a third row of seats, stretching it to a six-place plane. The 210 is classified as a high-performance airplane, which means its landing gear is retractable and its engine has more than 200 horsepower. In its first model year, which was 1960, the 210 was powered by a 260-horsepower fuel-injected six-cylinder engine that displaced 471 cubic inches. The 210 is the fastest single-engine airplane ever built by Cessna.

Figure 3.7 Display of `float.html`

3.9   Color

Over the last decade the issue of color in Web documents has become much more settled. In the past, one had to worry about the range of colors client machine monitors could display, as well as the range of colors browsers could handle. Now, however, there are few color limitations with the great majority of client machine monitors and browsers.

3.9.1   Color Groups

There are three groups of predefined colors that were designed for Web documents, the original group of seventeen named colors, which included far too few colors to be useful, a group of 147 named colors that are widely supported by browsers (see Appendix B), and the so-called Web palette (see `http://www .web-source.net/216_color_chart.htm`), which includes 216 named colors, which at one time were the only predefined colors that were widely supported by browsers. Rather than being restricted to the use of only predefined named colors, contemporary professional Web designers are more likely to define their own colors.

3.9.2   Color Properties

The `color` property is used to specify the foreground color[15] of HTML elements. For example, consider the following description of a small table:

```
<style type = "text/css">
  th.red {color: red;}
  th.orange {color: orange;}
</style>
  ...
<table>
  <tr>
    <th class = "red"> Apple </th>
    <th class = "orange"> Orange </th>
    <th class = "orange"> Screwdriver </th>
  </tr>
</table>
```

The `background-color` property is used to set the background color of an element, where the element could be the whole body of the document. For example, consider the following paragraph element:

```
<style type = "text/css">
  p.standout {font-size: 2em; color: blue;
              background-color: magenta";}
</style>
...
<p class = "standout">
  To really make it stand out, use a magenta background!
</p>
```

When displayed by a browser, this might appear as shown in Figure 3.8.

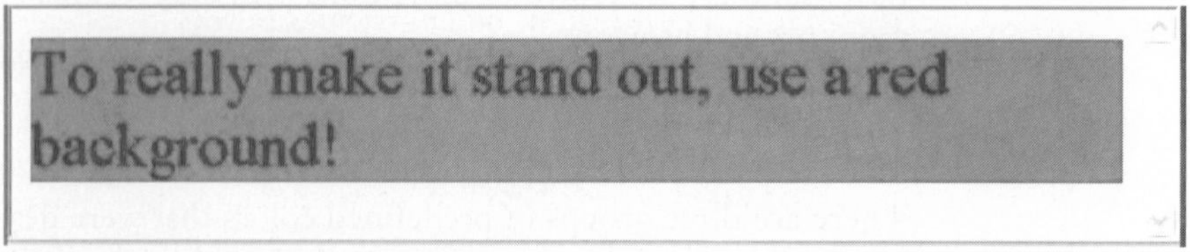

Figure 3.8 The `background-color` property

---

15. The foreground color of an element is the color in which it is displayed.

3.10   The Box Model

Virtually all document elements can have borders with various styles, such as color and width. Furthermore, the amount of space between the content of an element and its border, known as *padding*, can be specified, as well as the space between the border and an adjacent element, known as the *margin*. This model, called the *box model*, is shown in Figure 3.9.

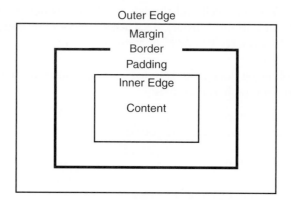

Figure 3.9 The box model

3.10.1   Borders

Every element has a property, `border-style`, that controls whether the element's content has a border, and also specifies the style of the border. CSS provides several different border styles, among them `dotted`, `dashed`, `solid`, and `double`. The default value for `border-style` is `none`, which is why the contents of elements normally do not have borders. The styles of one particular side of an element can be set with `border-top-style`, `border-bottom-style`, `border-left-style`, or `border-right-style`.

The `border-width` property is used to specify the thickness of a border. Its possible values are `thin`, `medium` (the default), `thick`, or a length value, which is in pixels. Setting `border-width` sets the thickness of all four sides of an element. The width of one particular border of an element can be specified with `border-top-width`, `border-bottom-width`, `border-left-width`, or `border-right-width`.

The color of a border is controlled by the `border-color` property. Once again, the individual borders of an element can be colored differently through the properties `border-top-color`, `border-bottom-color`, `border-left-color`, or `border-right-color`.

There is a shorthand for setting the style properties of all four borders of an element, `border`. For example, we could have the following:

```
border: 5px solid blue;
```

This is equivalent to the following:

```
border_width: 5px; border-style: solid; border-color: blue;
```

The cells of a table can have borders, like any other element. We could specify borders on the cells with the following:

```
td, th {border: thin solid black;}
```

In many cases, we want just one border between table cells, rather than the default double borders that result from this specification (for example, the right border of a cell and the left border of its neighbor cell to the right together form a double border). To get just one border between table cells, we set the table property `border-collapse` to `collapse` (its default value is `separate`).

The following document, `borders.html`, illustrates borders, using a table and a short paragraph as examples:

```
<!-- borders.html
     Examples of various borders
     -->
<html lang = "en">
  <head>
    <title> Borders </title>
    <meta charset = "utf-8" />
    <style type = "text/css">
      td, th {border: thin solid black;}
      table {border: thin solid black;
             border-collapse: collapse;
             border-top-width: medium;
             border-bottom-width: thick;
             border-top-color: red;
             border-bottom-color: blue;
             border-top-style: dotted;
             border-bottom-style: dashed;
             }
      p {border: thin dashed green;}
    </style>
  </head>
  <body>
    <table>
      <caption> Fruit Juice Drinks </caption>
      <tr>
        <th> </th>
        <th> Apple </th>
        <th> Orange </th>
        <th> Screwdriver </th>
      </tr>
```

```
        <tr>
          <th> Breakfast </th>
          <td> 0 </td>
          <td> 1 </td>
          <td> 0 </td>
        </tr>
        <tr>
          <th> Lunch </th>
          <td> 1 </td>
          <td> 0 </td>
          <td> 0 </td>
        </tr>
        <tr>
          <th> Dinner </th>
          <td> 0 </td>
          <td> 0 </td>
          <td> 1 </td>
        </tr>
      </table>
      <p>
        Now is the time for all good Web developers to
        learn to use style sheets.
      </p>
    </body>
</html>
```

Notice that if a table has borders that were specified with its `border` or `border-style` attribute, as well as border properties that are specified for one particular border, as in `borders.html`, those for the particular border override those of the original border. In `borders.html`, the table element uses its `border` attribute to set the border to `thin`, but the top and bottom borders are replaced by those specified with the `border-top` and `border-bottom` properties.

The display of `borders.html` is shown in Figure 3.10.

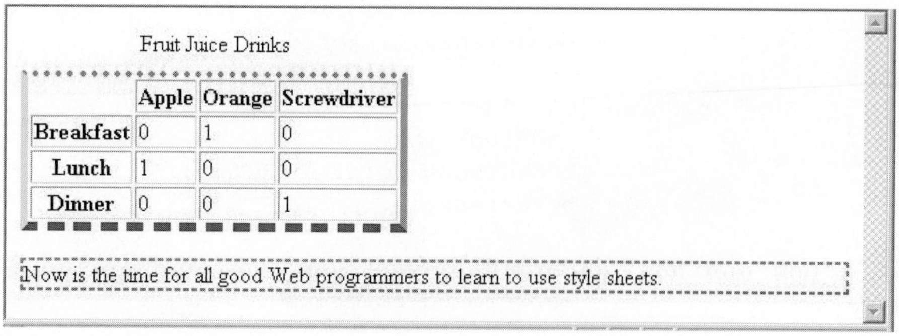

Figure 3.10 Borders

3.10.2   Margins and Padding

Recall from the box model that padding is the space between the content of an element and its border. The margin is the space between the border of an element and the element's neighbors. When there is no border, the margin plus the padding is the space between the content of an element and its neighbors. In this scenario, it may appear that there is no difference between padding and margins. However, there is a difference when the element has a background: The background extends into the padding, but not into the margin.

The margin properties are named `margin`, which applies to all four sides of an element, `margin-left`, `margin-right`, `margin-top`, and `margin-bottom`. The padding properties are named `padding`, which applies to all four sides, `padding-left`, `padding-right`, `padding-top`, and `padding-bottom`.

The following example, `marpads.html`, illustrates several combinations of margins and padding, both with and without borders:

```
<!DOCTYPE html>
<!-- marpads.html
     An example to illustrate margins and padding
     -->
<html lang = "en">
  <head>
    <title> Margins and Padding </title>
    <meta charset = "utf-8" />
    <style type = "text/css">
      p.one   {margin: 15px;
               padding: 15px;
               background-color: #C0C0C0;
               border-style: solid;
              }
      p.two   {margin: 5px;
               padding: 25px;
               background-color: #C0C0C0;
               border-style: solid;
              }
      p.three {margin: 25px;
               padding: 5px;
               background-color: #C0C0C0;
               border-style: solid;
              }
      p.four  {margin: 25px;
               background-color: #C0C0C0;}
```

```
          p.five   {padding: 25px;
                    background-color: #C0C0C0;
                   }
      </style>
   </head>
   <body>
    <p>
      Here is the first line.
    </p>
    <p class = "one">
      Now is the time for all good Web programmers to
      learn to use style sheets. <br /> [margin = 15px,
      padding = 15px]
    </p>
    <p class = "two">
      Now is the time for all good Web programmers to
      learn to use style sheets. <br /> [margin = 5px,
      padding = 25px]
    </p>
    <p class = "three">
      Now is the time for all good Web programmers to
      learn to use style sheets. <br /> [margin = 25px,
      padding = 5px]
    </p>
    <p class = "four">
      Now is the time for all good Web programmers to
      learn to use style sheets. <br /> [margin = 25px,
      no padding, no border]
    </p>
    <p class = "five">
      Now is the time for all good Web programmers to
      learn to use style sheets. <br /> [padding = 25px,
      no margin, no border]
    </p>
    <p>
      Here is the last line.
    </p>
   </body>
</html>
```

Figure 3.11 shows a browser display of marpads.html.

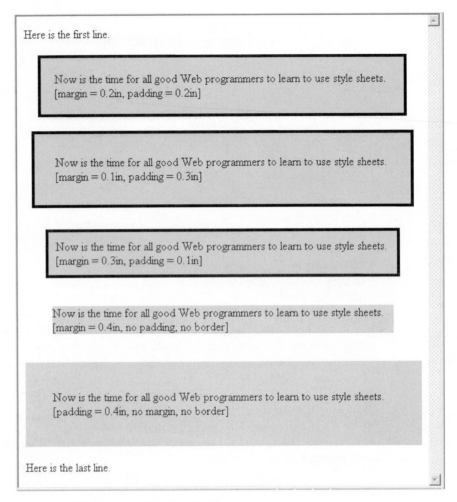

Here is the first line.

Now is the time for all good Web programmers to learn to use style sheets. [margin = 0.2in, padding = 0.2in]

Now is the time for all good Web programmers to learn to use style sheets. [margin = 0.1in, padding = 0.3in]

Now is the time for all good Web programmers to learn to use style sheets. [margin = 0.3in, padding = 0.1in]

Now is the time for all good Web programmers to learn to use style sheets. [margin = 0.4in, no padding, no border]

Now is the time for all good Web programmers to learn to use style sheets. [padding = 0.4in, no margin, no border]

Here is the last line.

Figure 3.11 Display of `marpads.html`

3.11 Background Images

The `background-image` property is used to place an image in the background of an element. For example, an image of an airplane might be an effective background for text about the airplane. The following example, `back_image.html`, illustrates background images:

```
<!DOCTYPE html>
<!-- back_image.html
     An example to illustrate background images
     -->
<html lang = "en">
```

```
<head>
  <title> Background images </title>
  <meta charset = "utf-8" />
  <style type = "text/css">
    body {background-image: url(../images/airplane2sx.png);
         background-size: 375px 300px;}
    p {margin-left: 30px; margin-right: 30px;
       margin-top: 50px; font-size: 1.1em;}
  </style>
</head>
<body>
  <p>
    The Cessna 172 is the most common general aviation airplane
    in the world. It is an all-metal, single-engine piston,
    high-wing, four-place monoplane. It has fixed gear and is
    categorized as a non-high-performance aircraft. The current
    model is the 172R.
    The wingspan of the 172R is 36'1". Its fuel capacity is 56
    gallons in two tanks, one in each wing. The takeoff weight
    is 2,450 pounds. Its maximum useful load is 837 pounds.
    The maximum speed of the 172R at sea level is 142 mph.
    The plane is powered by a 360-cubic-inch gasoline engine
    that develops 160 horsepower. The climb rate of the 172R
    at sea level is 720 feet per minute.
  </p>
</body>
</html>
```

Figure 3.12 shows a browser display of back_image.html.

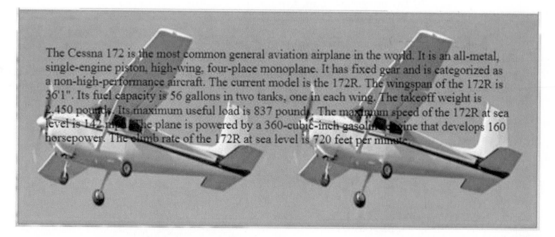

Figure 3.12 Display of back_image.html

Text over a background image can be difficult or even impossible to read if the image has areas that are nearly the same color as the text. Therefore, care must be taken in selecting the color of background images. In many cases, images with various textures in light-gray colors are best, assuming the text is in black.

In the example, notice that the background image is replicated as necessary to fill the area of the element. This replication is called *tiling*. Tiling can be controlled with the `background-repeat` property, which can take the value `repeat` (the default), `no-repeat`, `repeat-x`, or `repeat-y`. The `no-repeat` value specifies that just one copy of the image is to be displayed. The `repeat-x` value means that the image is to be repeated horizontally; `repeat-y` means that the image is to be repeated vertically. In addition, the position of a nonrepeated background image can be specified with the `background-position` property, which can take a large number of different values. The keyword values are `top`, `center`, `bottom`, `left`, and `right`, all of which can be used in combinations. It is easiest to use one keyword to specify the horizontal placement and one to specify the vertical placement, such as `top left`, `bottom right`, and `top center`. If only one keyword is given, the other is assumed to be `center`. So, `top` is equivalent to `top center` (or `center top`), and `left` is the same as `center left` (or `left center`).

3.12   The `<span>` and `<div>` Tags

In many situations, we want to apply special font properties to less than a whole paragraph of text. For example, it is often useful to have a word or phrase in a line appear in a different font size or color. The `<span>` tag is designed for just this purpose. Unlike most other tags, there is no default layout for the content of `<span>`. So, in the following example, the word `total` is not displayed differently from the rest of the paragraph:

```
<p>
   It sure is fun to be in <span> total </span>
   control of text
</p>
```

The purpose of `<span>` is to change property values of part of a line of content, as in the following example:

```
<style type = "text/css" >
  .spanred {font-size: 2em;
            font-family: Ariel; color: red;}
</style>
...
<p>
   It sure is fun to be in
   <span class = "spanred"> total </span>
   control of text
</p>
```

The display of this paragraph is shown in Figure 3.13.

It sure is fun to be in total control of text

Figure 3.13 The `<span>` tag

It is common for documents to have sections, each consisting of some number of paragraphs that have their own presentation styles. Using style classes on paragraphs, you can do this with what has already been discussed. It is more convenient, however, to be able to apply a style to a section of a document rather than to each paragraph. This can be done with the `<div>` tag. As with `<span>`, there is no implied layout for the content of the `<div>` tag, so its primary use is to specify presentation details for a section or division of a document.

Consider the following example, in which a division of a document is to use a specific paragraph style:

```
<div class = "primary">
  <p>
  . . .
  </p>
  <p>
  . . .
  </p>
  <p>
  . . .
  </p>
</div>
```

The `span` and `div` elements are used in examples in Chapter 6.

Recall that HTML5 has several new elements that provide more sophisticated sectioning of a document than is possible with `div`.

3.13 Conflict Resolution

When there are two different values for the same property on the same element in a document, there is an obvious conflict that the browser (or other HTML processor) must resolve. So far, we have considered only one way this conflict can occur: when style sheets at two or more levels specify different values for the same property on the same element. This particular kind of conflict is resolved by the precedence of the three different levels of style sheets. Inline style sheets have precedence over document and external style sheets, and document style sheets have precedence over external style sheets. The following shows an external style sheet and an HTML document that has three paragraph elements. The first

If there are conflicts after this first sorting takes place, the next step in their resolution is a sort by specificity. This sort is based on the following rules, in which the first has the highest precedence:

1. id selectors
2. Class and pseudo class selectors
3. Contextual selectors (more element type names means that they are more specific)
4. Universal selectors

If there are still conflicts, they are resolved by giving precedence to the most recently seen specification. For this process, the specifications in an external style sheet are considered to occur at the point in the document where the link element or @import rule that references the external style sheet appears. For example, if a style sheet specifies the following, and there are no further conflicting specifications before the element is displayed, the value used will be the last (in this case, 0.9em):

```
p {font-size: 1em}
p {font-size: 0.9em}
```

The whole sorting process that is used to resolve style specification conflicts is called *the cascade*. The name is apropos because the rules apply the lowest priority styles first and then cascade progressively to those with higher priorities.

Summary

Cascading style sheets were introduced to provide a consistent way to specify presentation details in HTML documents. Many of the style tags and attributes designed for specifying styles that had crept into HTML were deprecated in HTML 4.0 in favor of style sheets, which can appear at three levels: inline, which apply only to the content of one specific tag; document, which can apply to all appearances of specific tags in the body of a document; and external, which are stored in files by themselves and can apply to any number of documents. The property values in inline style sheets are specified in the string value of the style attribute. Document style sheets are specified in the content of a <style> element in the head of the document. External style sheets appear in separate files. Both document-level and external style specifications have the form of a list of style rules. Each style rule has a selector and a list of property-value pairs. The latter apply to all occurrences of the selected tags. There are a variety of selectors, such as simple, child, descendant, and id.

A style class, which is defined in the content of a <style> element, allows different occurrences of the same tag to have different property values. A generic style-class specification allows tags with different names to use the same presentation style. A pseudo class takes effect when a particular event occurs. There are many different property-value forms, including lengths, percentage values, URLs, and colors. Several different properties are related to fonts. The `font-family` property specifies one or more font names. Because different browsers support different sets of fonts, there are five generic font names. Each browser supports at least one font in each generic category. The `font-size` property can specify a length value or one of a number of different named size categories. The `font-style` property can be set to `italic` or `normal`. The `font-weight` property is used to specify the degree of boldness of text. The `font` property provides an abbreviated form for font-related properties. The `text-decoration` property is used to specify underlining, overlining, and line-through text.

The `letter-spacing` property is used to set the space between letters in words. The `word-spacing` property is used to set the space between words in text. The `line-height` property is used to set the amount of vertical space between lines of text.

The `list-style-type` property is used to specify the bullet form for items in unordered lists. It is also used to specify the sequence type for the items in ordered lists.

The foreground and background colors of the content of a document are specified by the `color` and `background-color` properties, respectively. Colors can be specified by name, by hex number, or by `rgb`.

The first line of a paragraph can be indented with `text-indent`. Text can be aligned with the `text-align` property, whose values are `left`, `right`, and `justify`, which means both left and right alignment. When the `float` property is set to `left` or `right` on an element, text can be made to flow around that element on the right or left, respectively, in the display window.

Borders can be specified to appear around any element, in any color and any of the forms—dotted, solid, dashed, or double. The margin, which is the space between the border (or the content of the element if it has no border) and the element's neighbors, can be set with the margin properties. The padding, which is the space between the content of an element and its border (or neighbors if it has no border) can be set with the padding properties.

When the cells of a table have borders, the double borders between cells can be eliminated with the `border-collapse` property.

The `background-image` property is used to place an image in the background of an element.

The `<span>` tag provides a way to include an inline style sheet that applies to a range of text that is smaller than a line or a paragraph. The `<div>` tag provides a way to define a section of a document that has its own style properties.

Conflict resolution for property values is a complicated process, using the origin of specifications, their specificity, inheritance, and the relative position of specifications.

Review Questions

3.1   What is the advantage of document-level style sheets over inline style sheets?

3.2   What is the purpose of external style sheets?

3.3   What attributes are required in a link to an external style sheet?

3.4   What is the format of an inline style sheet?

3.5   What is the format of a document-level style sheet, and where does the sheet appear?

3.6   What is the format of an external style sheet?

3.7   What is the form of comments within the rule list of a document-level style sheet?

3.8   What is the purpose of a style class selector?

3.9   What is the purpose of a generic class?

3.10 What is the difference between the two selectors `ol ul` and `ol > ul`?

3.11 Describe the two pseudo classes that are used exclusively for links.

3.12 Are keyword property values case sensitive or case insensitive?

3.13 Why is a list of font names given as the value of a `font-family` property?

3.14 What are the five generic fonts?

3.15 Why is it better to use `em` than `pt` for font sizes?

3.16 In what order must property values appear in the list of a `font` property?

3.17 In what ways can text be modified with `text-decoration`?

3.18 What are tracking and leading?

3.19 How is the `list-style-type` property used with unordered lists?

3.20 What are the possible values of the `list-style-type` property when it is used with ordered lists?

3.21 If you want text to flow around the right side of an image, which value, `right` or `left`, must be assigned to the `float` property of the image?

3.22 Why must background images be chosen with care?

3.23 What are the possible values for the `text-align` property?

3.24 What purpose does the `text-indent` property serve?

3.25   What properties are used to set margins around elements?

3.26   What are the three ways color property values can be specified?

3.27   If you want a background image to be repeated vertically but not horizontally, what value must be set to what property?

3.28   What properties and what values must be used to put a dotted border around a text box if the border is red and thin on the left and blue and thick on the right?

3.29   What is the shorthand property for border styles?

3.30   What is the purpose of the `border-collapse` property?

3.31   What layout information does a `<span>` tag by itself indicate to the browser?

3.32   What is the purpose of the `<div>` tag?

3.33   Which has higher precedence, an `id` selector or a universal selector?

3.34   Which has higher precedence, a user-origin specification or a browser specification?

3.35   If there are two conflicting specifications in a document-level style sheet, which of the two has precedence?

Exercises

3.1   Create an external style sheet for the chapters of this book.

3.2   Create and test an HTML document that displays a table of football scores from a collegiate football conference in which the team names have one of the primary colors of their respective schools. The winning scores must appear larger and in a different font than the losing scores. The team names must be in a script font.

3.3   Create and test an HTML document that includes at least two images and enough text to precede the images, flow around them (one on the left and one on the right), and continue after the last image.

3.4   Create and test an HTML document that has at least a half page of text and that has a small box of text embedded on the left margin, with the main text flowing around the small box. The embedded text must appear in a smaller font and also must be set in italic.

3.5   Create and test an HTML document that has six short paragraphs of text that describe various aspects of the state in which you live. You must define three different paragraph styles, p1, p2, and p3. The p1 style must use left and right margins of 20 pixels, a background color of pink, and a foreground color of blue. The p2 style must use left and right margins of 30 pixels, a background color of black, and a foreground color of yellow. The p3 style must use a text indent of 1 centimeter, a background color of green, and a foreground color of white. The first and fourth paragraph must use p1, the second and fifth must use p2, and the third and sixth must use p3.

3.6   Create and test an HTML document that describes nested ordered lists of cars. The outer list must have three entries: compact, midsize, and sports. Inside each of these three lists there must be two sublists of body styles. The compact- and midsize-car sublists are two door and four door; the sports-car sublists are coupe and convertible. Each body-style sublist must have at least three entries, each of which is the make and model of a particular car that fits the category. The outer list must use uppercase Roman numerals, the middle lists must use uppercase letters, and the inner lists must use Arabic numerals. The background color for the compact-car list must be pink; for the midsize-car list, it must be blue; for the sports-car list, it must be red. All of the styles must be in a document style sheet.

3.7   Rewrite the document of Exercise 3.6 to put all style-sheet information in an external style sheet. Validate your external style sheet with the W3C CSS validation service.

3.8   Rewrite the document of Exercise 3.6 to use inline style sheets only.

3.9   Create and test an HTML document that contains at least five lines of text from a newspaper story. Every verb in the text must be green, every noun must be blue, and every preposition must be yellow.

3.10   Create and test an HTML document that describes an unordered list of at least five popular books. The bullet for each book must be a small image of the book's cover. Find the images on the Web.

3.11   Use a document style sheet to modify the HTML document, nested_lists.html in Section 2.7.2 to make the different levels of lists different colors.

3.12   Using a document style sheet, modify the HTML document definition.html in Section 2.7.3 to set the font in the dt elements to Courier 1em font and the dd elements to Times Roman 1.1em italic font.

The Basics of JavaScript

This chapter takes the reader on a quick tour of the basics of JavaScript, introducing its most important concepts and constructs, but, for the sake of brevity, leaves out many of the details of the language. Topics discussed include the following: primitive data types and their operators and expressions, screen output and keyboard input, control statements, objects and constructors, arrays, functions, and pattern matching. An experienced programmer should be able to learn how to be an effective JavaScript programmer by studying this brief chapter, along with Chapters 5 and 6. More comprehensive descriptions of JavaScript can be found in the numerous books devoted solely to the language.

4.1   Overview of JavaScript

This section discusses the origins of JavaScript, a few of its characteristics, and some of its uses. Included are a comparison of JavaScript and Java and a brief introduction to event-driven programming.

4.1.1   Origins

JavaScript, which was originally developed at Netscape by Brendan Eich, was initially named Mocha but soon after was renamed LiveScript. In late 1995 LiveScript became a joint venture of Netscape and Sun Microsystems, and its name again was changed, this time to JavaScript. A language standard for JavaScript was developed in the late 1990s by the European Computer Manufacturers Association (ECMA) as ECMA-262. This standard has also been approved by the International Standards Organization (ISO) as ISO-16262. The ECMA-262 standard is now in version 5. Most contemporary browsers implement languages that conform to ECMA-262 version 3 (at least). The current standard specification can be found at

```
http://www.ecma-international.org/publications/standards/Ecma-262.htm
```

The official name of the standard language is ECMAScript. Because it is nearly always called JavaScript elsewhere, we will use that term exclusively in this book. Microsoft's JavaScript is named JScript.

JavaScript can be divided into three parts: the core, client side, and server side. The *core* is the heart of the language, including its operators, expressions, statements, and subprograms. *Client-side* JavaScript is a collection of objects that support the control of a browser and interactions with users. For example, with JavaScript, an HTML document can be made to respond to user inputs such as mouse clicks and keyboard use. *Server-side* JavaScript is a collection of objects that make the language useful on a Web server—for example, to support communication with a database management system. Server-side JavaScript is used far less frequently than client-side JavaScript. Therefore, this book does not cover server-side JavaScript.

This chapter introduces core JavaScript from the client-side perspective. Client-side JavaScript programming is covered in Chapters 5 and 6.

Client-side JavaScript is an HTML-embedded scripting language. We refer to every collection of JavaScript code as a *script*. An HTML document can include any number of embedded scripts.

4.1.2 JavaScript and Java

Although JavaScript's name appears to connote a close relationship with Java, JavaScript and Java are actually very different. One important difference is support for object-oriented programming. Although JavaScript is sometimes said to be an object-oriented language, its object model is quite different from that of Java and C++, as you will see in Section 4.2. In fact, JavaScript does not support the object-oriented software development paradigm.[1]

Java is a strongly typed language. Types are all known at compile time, and operand types are checked for compatibility. Variables in JavaScript need not be declared and are dynamically typed,[2] making compile-time type checking impossible. Another important difference between Java and JavaScript is that objects in Java are static in the sense that their collection of data members and methods is fixed at compile time. JavaScript objects are dynamic: The number of data members and methods of an object can change during execution.

The main similarity between Java and JavaScript is the syntax of their expressions, assignment statements, and control statements.

4.1.3 Uses of JavaScript

The original goal of JavaScript was to provide programming capability at both the server and the client ends of a Web connection. Since then, JavaScript has grown into a full-fledged programming language that can be used in a variety of application areas. As stated, this book focuses on client-side JavaScript.

Client-side JavaScript can serve as an alternative for some of what is done with server-side programming, in which computational capability resides on the server and is requested by the client. Because client-side JavaScript is embedded in HTML documents (either physically or logically) and is interpreted by the browser, this transfer of load from the often overloaded server to the often underloaded client can obviously benefit other clients. Client-side JavaScript cannot replace all server-side computing, however. In particular, although server-side software supports file operations, database access, and networking, client-side JavaScript supports none of these.

Interactions with users through form elements, such as buttons and menus, can be conveniently described in JavaScript. Because button clicks and mouse movements are easily detected with JavaScript, they can be used to trigger computations and provide feedback to the user. For example, when a user moves the mouse cursor from a text box, JavaScript can detect that movement and check the appropriateness of the text box's value (which presumably was just filled by the user). Even without forms, user interactions are both possible and simple to program in JavaScript. These interactions, which take place in dialog windows, include getting input from the user and allowing the user to make choices

---

1. Microsoft's Jscript .NET is an extended dialect of JavaScript that does support object-oriented programming.

2. The type of dynamically typed variables cannot be determined before the script is executed.

through buttons. It is also easy to generate new content in the browser display dynamically with JavaScript.

Another interesting capability of JavaScript was made possible by the development of the Document Object Model (DOM), which allows JavaScript scripts to access and modify the style properties and content of the elements of a displayed HTML document, making formally static documents highly dynamic. Various techniques for designing dynamic HTML documents with JavaScript are discussed in Chapter 6.

Much of what JavaScript scripts typically do is event driven, meaning that the actions often are executed in response to the browser user's actions, among them mouse clicks and form submissions. This sort of computation supports user interactions through the HTML form elements on the client display. The mechanics of event-driven computation in JavaScript are discussed in detail in Chapter 5.

4.1.4   Browsers and HTML-JavaScript Documents

If an HTML document does not include embedded scripts, the browser reads the lines of the document and renders its window according to the tags, attributes, and content it finds. When a JavaScript script is encountered in the document, the browser uses its JavaScript interpreter to "execute" the script. Output from the script becomes the next markup to be rendered. When the end of the script is reached, the browser goes back to reading the HTML document and displaying its content.

There are two different ways to embed JavaScript in an HTML document: implicitly and explicitly. In *explicit embedding*, the JavaScript code physically resides in the HTML document. This approach has several disadvantages. First, mixing two completely different kinds of notation in the same document makes the document difficult to read. Second, in some cases, the person who creates and maintains the HTML is distinct from the person who creates and maintains the JavaScript. Having two different people doing two different jobs working on the same document can lead to many problems. To avoid these problems, the JavaScript can be placed in its own file, separate from the HTML document. This approach, called *implicit embedding*, has the advantage of hiding the script from the browser user. It also avoids the problem of hiding scripts from older browsers, a problem that is discussed later in this section. Except for the chapter's first simple example, which illustrates explicit embedding of JavaScript in an HTML document, all of the JavaScript example scripts in this chapter are implicitly embedded.

When JavaScript scripts are explicitly embedded, they can appear in either part of an HTML document—the head or the body—depending on the purpose of the script. On the one hand, scripts that produce content only when requested or that react to user interactions are placed in the head of the document. Generally, these scripts contain function definitions and code associated with form elements such as buttons. On the other hand, scripts that are to be interpreted just once, when the interpreter finds them, are placed in the document body. Accordingly, the interpreter notes the existence of scripts that appear in the head of a document, but it does not interpret them while processing the head. Scripts that are found in the body of a document are interpreted as they are found. When implicit embedding is used, these same guidelines apply to the markup code that references the external JavaScript files.

4.2 Object Orientation and JavaScript

As stated previously, JavaScript is not an object-oriented programming language. Rather, it is an object-based language. JavaScript does not have classes. Its objects serve both as objects and as models of objects. Without classes, JavaScript cannot have class-based inheritance, which is supported in object-oriented languages such as C++ and Java. It does, however, support a technique that can be used to simulate some of the aspects of inheritance. This is done with the prototype object; thus, this form of inheritance is called *prototype-based inheritance* (not discussed in this book).

Without class-based inheritance, JavaScript cannot support polymorphism. A polymorphic variable can reference related methods of objects of different classes within the same class hierarchy. A method call through such a polymorphic variable can be dynamically bound to the method in the object's class.[3]

Despite the fact that JavaScript is not an object-oriented language, much of its design is rooted in the concepts and approaches used in object-oriented programming. Specifically, client-side JavaScript deals in large part with documents and document elements, which are modeled with objects.

4.2.1 JavaScript Objects

In JavaScript, objects are collections of properties, which correspond to the members of classes in Java and C++. Each property is either a data property or a function or method property. Data properties appear in two categories: primitive values and references to other objects. (In JavaScript, variables that refer to objects are often called *objects* rather than *references*.) Sometimes we will refer to the data properties simply as *properties*; we often refer to the method properties simply as *methods* or *functions*. We prefer to call subprograms that are called through objects methods and subprograms that are not called through objects functions.

JavaScript uses nonobject types for some of its simplest types; these nonobject types are called *primitives*. Primitives are used because they often can be implemented directly in hardware, resulting in faster operations on their values (faster than if they were treated as objects). Primitives are like the simple scalar variables of non-object-oriented languages such as C. C++, Java, and JavaScript all have both primitives and objects; JavaScript's primitives are described in Section 4.4.

All objects in a JavaScript program are indirectly accessed through variables. Such variables are like references in Java. All primitive values in JavaScript are

---

3. This technique is often called *dynamic binding*. It is an essential part of full support for object-oriented programming in a language.

accessed directly—these are like the scalar types in Java and C++. These are often called *value types*. The properties of an object are referenced by attaching the name of the property to the variable that references the object. For example, if `myCar` is a variable referencing an object that has the property `engine`, the `engine` property can be referenced with `myCar.engine`.

The root object in JavaScript is `Object`. It is the ancestor, through prototype inheritance, of all objects. `Object` is the most generic of all objects, having some methods but no data properties. All other objects are specializations of `Object`, and all inherit its methods (although they are often overridden).[4]

A JavaScript object appears, both internally and externally, as a list of property–value pairs. The properties are names; the values are data values or functions. All functions are objects and are referenced through variables. The collection of properties of a JavaScript object is dynamic: Properties can be added or deleted at any time during execution.

Every object is characterized by its collection of properties, although objects do not have types in any formal sense. Recall that `Object` is characterized by having no properties. Further discussions of objects appear in Sections 4.7 and 4.11.

4.3 General Syntactic Characteristics

In this book all JavaScript scripts are embedded, either directly or indirectly, in HTML documents. Scripts can appear directly as the content of a `<script>` tag. The `type` attribute of `<script>` must be set to `"text/javascript"`.[5] The JavaScript script can be indirectly embedded in an HTML document with the `src` attribute of a `<script>` tag, whose value is the name of a file that contains the script—for example,

```
<script type = "text/javascript" src = "tst_number.js" >
</script>
```

Notice that the `script` element requires the closing tag, even though it has no content when the `src` attribute is included.

There are some situations when a small amount of JavaScript code is embedded in an HTML document. Furthermore, some documents have more than a few places where JavaScript code is embedded. Therefore, it is sometimes inconvenient and cumbersome to place all JavaScript code in a separate file.

In JavaScript, identifiers, or names, are similar to those of other common programming languages. They must begin with a letter, an underscore (_), or a dollar sign ($).[6] Subsequent characters may be letters, underscores, dollar signs, or digits.

---

4. It sounds like a contradiction when we say that all objects inherit methods from `Object`, because we said earlier that `Object` has no properties. The resolution of this paradox lies in the design of prototype inheritance in JavaScript. Every object has a prototype object associated with it. It is `Object`'s prototype object that defines the methods that are inherited by all other objects.

5. With HTML5, the default value of the `type` attribute is `"text/javascript"`, so it need not be included in the script tag. However, we keep it in our documents in case some older browser might require it.

6. Dollar signs are not intended to be used by user-written scripts, although using them is valid.

There is no length limitation for identifiers. As with most C-based languages, the letters in a variable name in JavaScript are case sensitive, meaning that FRIZZY, Frizzy, FrIzZy, frizzy, and friZZy are all distinct names. However, by convention, programmer-defined variable names do not include uppercase letters.

JavaScript has 25 reserved words, which are listed in Table 4.1.

Table 4.1 JavaScript reserved words

Break	delete	function	return	typeof
case	Do	if	switch	var
catch	Else	in	this	void
continue	Finally	instanceof	throw	while
default	For	new	try	with

Besides its reserved words, another collection of words is reserved for future use in JavaScript—these can be found at the ECMA Web site. In addition, JavaScript has a large collection of predefined words, including alert, open, java, and self.

JavaScript has two forms of comments, both of which are used in other languages. First, whenever two adjacent slashes (//) appear on a line, the rest of the line is considered a comment. Second, /* may be used to introduce a comment, and */ to terminate it, in both single- and multiple-line comments.

Two issues arise regarding embedding JavaScript in HTML documents. First, some browsers that are still in use recognize the <script> tag but do not have JavaScript interpreters. Fortunately, these browsers simply ignore the contents of the script element and cause no problems. Second, a few browsers that are still in use are so old that they do not recognize the <script> tag. Such browsers would display the contents of the script element as if it were just text. It has been customary to enclose the contents of all script elements in HTML comments to avoid this problem. Because there are so few browsers that do not recognize the <script> tag, we believe that the issue no longer exists. However, the HTML validator can have problems with embedded JavaScript. When the embedded JavaScript happens to include recognizable tags—for example <br /> tags in the output of the JavaScript—these tags can cause validation errors. Therefore, we still enclose embedded JavaScript in HTML comments when we explicitly embed JavaScript.

The HTML comment used to hide JavaScript uses the normal beginning syntax, <!--. However, the syntax for closing such a comment is special. It is the usual HTML comment closer, but it must be on its own line and must be preceded by two slashes (which makes it a JavaScript comment). The following HTML comment form hides the enclosed script from browsers that do not have JavaScript interpreters, as well as the validator, but makes it visible to browsers that do support JavaScript:

```
<!--
-- JavaScript script --
// -->
```

There are other problems with putting embedded JavaScript in comments in HTML documents. These problems are discussed in Chapter 6. The best solution to all of these problems is to put all JavaScript scripts that are of significant size in separate files and embed them implicitly.

The use of semicolons in JavaScript is unusual. The JavaScript interpreter tries to make semicolons unnecessary, but it does not always work. When the end of a line coincides with what could be the end of a statement, the interpreter effectively inserts a semicolon there. But this implicit insertion can lead to problems. For example, consider the following lines of code:

```
return                ← interpreter will put a semi-colon after Return
x;                       so return;
                         should have it all on one line return x;
```

The interpreter will insert a semicolon after `return`, because `return` need not be followed by an expression, making `x` an invalid orphan. The safest way to organize JavaScript statements is to put each on its own line whenever possible and terminate each statement with a semicolon. If a statement does not fit on a line, be careful to break the statement at a place that will ensure that the first line does not have the form of a complete statement.

In the following complete, but trivial, HTML document that simply greets the client who requests it, there is but one line of JavaScript—the call to `write` through the `document` object to display the message:[7]

```
<!DOCTYPE.html>
<!-- hello.html
     A trivial hello world example of HTML/JavaScript
     -->
<html lang = "en">
  <head>
    <title> Hello world </title>
    <meta charset = "utf-8" />
  </head>
  <body>
    <script type = "text/javascript">
      <!--
      document.write("Hello, fellow Web programmers!");
      // -->
    </script>
  </body>
</html>
```

---

7. The `document` object and its `write` method are described in Section 4.5.

4.4   **Primitives, Operations, and Expressions**

The primitive data types, operations, and expressions of JavaScript are similar to those of other common programming languages. Therefore, our discussion of them is brief.

4.4.1   **Primitive Types**

JavaScript has five primitive types: Number, String, Boolean, Undefined, and Null.[8] Each primitive value has one of these types. JavaScript includes predefined objects that are closely related to the Number, String, and Boolean types, named `Number`, `String`, and `Boolean`, respectively. (Is this confusing yet?) These objects are called *wrapper objects*. Each contains a property that stores a value of the corresponding primitive type. The purpose of the wrapper objects is to provide properties and methods that are convenient for use with values of the primitive types. In the case of `Number`, the properties are more useful; in the case of `String`, the methods are more useful. Because JavaScript coerces values between the Number type primitive values and `Number` objects and between the String type primitive values and `String` objects, the methods of `Number` and `String` can be used on variables of the corresponding primitive types. In fact, in most cases you can simply treat **Number and String** type values as if they were objects.

The difference between primitives and objects is shown in the following example. Suppose that `prim` is a primitive variable with the value `17` and `obj` is a `Number` object whose property value is `17`. Figure 4.1 shows how `prim` and `obj` are stored.

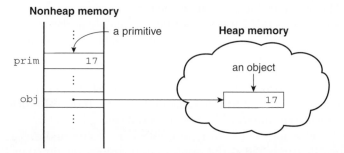

Figure 4.1 Primitives and objects

4.4.2   **Numeric and String Literals**

All numeric literals are primitive values of type Number. The Number type values are represented internally in double-precision floating-point form. Because there is only a single numeric data type, numeric values in JavaScript are often called *numbers*. Literal numbers in a script can have the forms of either integer

---

8. Undefined and Null are often called *trivial* types, for reasons that will be obvious when these types are discussed in Section 4.4.3.

or floating-point values. Integer literals are strings of digits. Floating-point literals can have decimal points, exponents, or both. Exponents are specified with an uppercase or lowercase e and a possibly signed integer literal. The following are valid numeric literals:

```
72    7.2    .72    72.    7E2    7e2    .7e2    7.e2    7.2E-2
```

Integer literals can be written in hexadecimal form by preceding their first digit with either 0x or 0X. (The first character is zero, not "oh.")

A string literal is a sequence of zero or more characters delimited by either single quotes (') or double quotes ("). String literals can include characters specified with escape sequences, such as \n and \t. If you want an actual single-quote character in a string literal that is delimited by single quotes, the embedded single quote must be preceded by a backslash:

```
'You\'re the most freckly person I\'ve ever seen'
```

A double quote can be embedded in a double-quoted string literal by preceding it with a backslash. An actual backslash character in any string literal must be itself backslashed, as in the following example:

```
"D:\\bookfiles"
```

There is no difference between single-quoted and double-quoted literal strings. The null string (a string with no characters) can be denoted with either '' or "". All string literals are primitive values.

4.4.3   Other Primitive Types

The only value of type Null is the reserved word null, which indicates no value. A variable is null if it has not been explicitly declared or assigned a value. If an attempt is made to use the value of a variable whose value is null, that will cause a runtime error.

The only value of type Undefined is undefined. Unlike null, there is no reserved word undefined. If a variable has been explicitly declared, but not assigned a value, it has the value undefined. If the value of an undefined variable is displayed, the word undefined is displayed.

The only values of type Boolean are true and false. These values are usually computed as the result of evaluating a relational or Boolean expression. (See Section 4.6.1.) The existence of both the Boolean primitive type and the Boolean object can lead to some confusion (also discussed in Section 4.6.1).

4.4.4   Declaring Variables

One of the characteristics of JavaScript that sets it apart from most common non-scripting programming languages is that it is dynamically typed. This means that a variable can be used for anything. Variables are not typed; values are. A variable can have the value of any primitive type, or it can be a reference to any object. The type of the value of a particular appearance of a variable in a program can be determined by the interpreter. In many cases, the interpreter converts the type of a value to whatever is needed for the context in which it appears.

A variable can be declared either by assigning it a value, in which case the interpreter implicitly declares it to be a variable, or by listing it in a declaration statement that begins with the reserved word `var`. Initial values can be included in a `var` declaration, as with some of the variables in the following declaration:

```
var counter,
    index,
    pi = 3.14159265,
    quarterback = "Elway",
    stop_flag = true;
```

We recommend that all variables be explicitly declared.

As stated previously, a variable that has been declared but not assigned a value has the value `undefined`.

4.4.5 Numeric Operators

JavaScript has the typical collection of numeric operators: the binary operators + for addition, - for subtraction, * for multiplication, / for division, and % for modulus. The unary operators are plus (+), negate (-), decrement (--), and increment (++). The increment and decrement operators can be either prefix or postfix.[9] As with other languages that have the increment and decrement unary operators, the prefix and postfix uses are not always equivalent. Consider an expression consisting of a single variable and one of these operators. If the operator precedes the variable, the value of the variable is changed and the expression evaluates to the new value. If the operator follows the variable, the expression evaluates to the current value of the variable and then the value of the variable is changed. For example, if the variable `a` has the value 7, the value of the following expression is 24:

```
(++a) * 3
```

But the value of the following expression is 21:

```
(a++) * 3
```

In both cases, `a` is set to 8.

All numeric operations are done in double-precision floating point.

The *precedence rules* of a language specify which operator is evaluated first when two operators with different precedence are adjacent in an expression. Adjacent operators are separated by a single operand. For example, in the following code, * and + are adjacent:

```
a * b + 1
```

---

9. *Prefix* means that the operator precedes its operand; *postfix* means that the operator follows its operand.

The *associativity rules* of a language specify which operator is evaluated first when two operators with the same precedence are adjacent in an expression. The precedence and associativity of the numeric operators of JavaScript are given in Table 4.2.

Table 4.2   Precedence and associativity of the numeric operators

Operator*	Associativity
`++`, `--`, unary `-`, unary `+`	Right (though it is irrelevant)
`*`, `/`, `%`	Left
Binary `+`, binary `-`	Left

*The first operators listed have the highest precedence.

As examples of operator precedence and associativity, consider the following code:

```
var a = 2,
    b = 4,
    c,
    d;
c = 3 + a * b;
// * is first, so c is now 11 (not 24)
d = b / a / 2;
// / associates left, so d is now 1 (not 4)
```

Parentheses can be used to force any desired precedence. For example, the addition will be done before the multiplication in the following expression:

```
(a + b) * c
```

4.4.6   The `Math` Object

The `Math` object provides a collection of properties of `Number` objects and methods that operate on `Number` objects. The `Math` object has methods for the trigonometric functions, such as `sin` (for sine) and `cos` (for cosine), as well as for other commonly used mathematical operations. Among these are `floor`, to truncate a number; `round`, to round a number; and `max`, to return the largest of two given numbers. The `floor` and `round` methods are used in the example script in Section 4.10. All of the `Math` methods are referenced through the `Math` object, as in `Math.sin(x)`.

Table 4.3 Properties of `Number`

Property	Meaning
MAX_VALUE	Largest representable number on the computer being used
MIN_VALUE	Smallest representable number on the computer being used
NaN	Not a number
POSITIVE_INFINITY	Special value to represent infinity
NEGATIVE_INFINITY	Special value to represent negative infinity
PI	The value of π

4.4.7   The `Number` Object

The `Number` object includes a collection of useful properties that have constant values. Table 4.3 lists the properties of `Number`. These properties are referenced through `Number`. For example,

```
Number.MIN_VALUE
```

references the smallest representable number on the computer being used.

Any arithmetic operation that results in an error (e.g., division by zero) or that produces a value that cannot be represented as a double-precision floating-point number, such as a number that is too large (an overflow), returns the value "not a number," which is displayed as NaN. If NaN is compared for equality against any number, the comparison fails. Surprisingly, in a comparison, NaN is not equal to itself. To determine whether a variable has the NaN value, the predefined predicate function `isNaN()` must be used. For example, if the variable `a` has the NaN value, `isNaN(a)` returns `true`.

The `Number` object has a method, `toString`, which it inherits from `Object` but overrides. The `toString` method converts the number through which it is called to a string. Because numeric primitives and `Number` objects are always coerced to the other when necessary, `toString` can be called through a numeric primitive, as in the following code:

```
var price = 427,
    str_price;
. . .
str_price = price.toString();
```

4.4.8   The String Catenation Operator

JavaScript strings are not stored or treated as arrays of characters; rather, they are unit scalar values. String catenation is specified with the operator denoted by a plus sign (+). For example, if the value of `first` is `"Freddie"`, the value of the following expression is `"Freddie Freeloader"`:

```
first + " Freeloader"
```

4.4.9   Implicit Type Conversions

The JavaScript interpreter performs several different implicit type conversions. Such conversions are called *coercions*. In general, when a value of one type is used in a position that requires a value of a different type, JavaScript attempts to convert the value to the type that is required. The most common examples of these conversions involve primitive string and number values.

If either operand of a + operator is a string, the operator is interpreted as a string catenation operator. If the other operand is not a string, it is coerced to a string. For example, consider the following expression:

```
"August " + 1977     ← gets converted
                        to string
```

In this expression, because the left operand is a string, the operator is considered to be a catenation operator. This forces string context on the right operand, so the right operand is implicitly converted to a string. Therefore, the expression evaluates to

```
"August 1997"
```

The number 1977 in the following expression is also coerced to a string:

```
1977 + "August"     ← converted to string
                       because of + "concatenation"
```

Now consider the following expression:

```
7 * "3"     ← gets converted
               to a number
```

In this expression, the operator is one that is used only with numbers. This forces a numeric context on the right operand. Therefore, JavaScript attempts to convert it to a number. In this example, the conversion succeeds, and the value of the expression is 21. If the second operand were a string that could not be converted to a number, such as "August", the conversion would produce NaN, which would then be the value of the expression.

When used as a number, null is 0. Unlike its usage in C and C++, however, null is not the same as 0. When used as a number, undefined is interpreted as NaN. (See Section 4.4.7.)

Not a number —

4.4.10   Explicit Type Conversions

There are several different ways to force type conversions, primarily between strings and numbers. Strings that contain numbers can be converted to numbers with the String constructor, as in the following statement:

```
                    ✓ Force conversion
var str_value = String(value);
```

This conversion can also be done with the toString method, which has the advantage that it can be given a parameter to specify the base of the resulting number (although the base of the number to be converted is taken to be decimal). An example of such a conversion is

```
var num = 6;
var str_value = num.toString();
var str_value_binary = num.toString(2);
```

[handwritten annotations: using toString method on object; 2 value for toString method equals a binary value return; 8 = octal value; 16 = hexadecimal value]

In the first conversion, the result is `"6"`; in the second, it is `"110"`.

A number also can be converted to a string by catenating it with the empty string.

Strings can be explicitly converted to numbers in several different ways. One way is with the `Number` constructor, as in the following statement:

```
var number = Number(aString);
```

The same conversion could be specified by subtracting zero from the string, as in the following statement:

```
var number = aString - 0;
```

Both of these conversions have the following restriction: The number in the string cannot be followed by any character except a space. For example, if the number happens to be followed by a comma, the conversion will not work. JavaScript has two predefined string functions that do not have this problem. The two, `parseInt` and `parseFloat`, are not `String` methods, so they are not called through `String` objects. They operate on the strings given as parameters. The `parseInt` function searches its string parameter for an integer literal. If one is found at the beginning of the string, it is converted to a number and returned. If the string does not begin with a valid integer literal, `NaN` is returned. The `parseFloat` function is similar to `parseInt`, but it searches for a floating-point literal, which could have a decimal point, an exponent, or both. In both `parseInt` and `parseFloat`, the numeric literal could be followed by any nondigit character.

Because of the coercions JavaScript normally does, as discussed in Section 4.4.9, `parseInt` and `parseFloat` are not often needed.

4.4.11 `String` Properties and Methods

Because JavaScript coerces primitive string values to and from `String` objects when necessary, the differences between the `String` object and the String type have little effect on scripts. `String` methods can always be used through String primitive values, as if the values were objects. The `String` object includes one property, `length`, and a large collection of methods.

The number of characters in a string is stored in the `length` property as follows:

```
var str = "George";
var len = str.length;
```

[handwritten annotation: length property of variable str which is 6]

In this code, `len` is set to the number of characters in `str`, namely, 6. In the expression `str.length`, `str` is a primitive variable, but we treated it as if it were an object (referencing one of its properties). In fact, when `str` is used with the `length` property, JavaScript implicitly builds a temporary `String` object with a property whose value is that of the primitive variable. After the second statement is executed, the temporary `String` object is discarded.

A few of the most commonly used `String` methods are shown in Table 4.4.

Table 4.4   `String` methods

Method	Parameters	Result
charAt	A number	Returns the character in the `String` object that is at the specified position
indexOf	One-character string	Returns the position in the `String` object of the parameter
substring	Two numbers	Returns the substring of the `String` object from the first parameter position to the second
toLowerCase	None	Converts any uppercase letters in the string to lowercase
toUpperCase	None	Converts any lowercase letters in the string to uppercase

Note that, for the `String` methods, character positions start at zero. For example, suppose `str` has been defined as follows:

```
                  0 1 2 3 4 5
var str = "George";
```

Then the following expressions have the values shown:

```
str.charAt(2)   is 'o'
str.indexOf('r')   is 3
str.substring(2, 4)   is 'org'
str.toLowerCase()   is 'george'
```

Several `String` methods associated with pattern matching are described in Section 4.12.

4.4.12   The `typeof` Operator

The `typeof` operator returns the type of its single operand. This operation is quite useful in some circumstances in a script. `typeof` produces `"number"`, `"string"`, or `"boolean"` if the operand is of primitive type Number, String, or Boolean, respectively. If the operand is an object or `null`, `typeof` produces `"object"`. This illustrates a fundamental characteristic of JavaScript: Objects do not have types. If the operand is a variable that has not been assigned a value, `typeof` produces `"undefined"`, reflecting the fact that variables themselves are not typed. Notice that the `typeof` operator always returns a string. The operand for `typeof` can be placed in parentheses, making it appear to be a function. Therefore, `typeof x` and `typeof(x)` are equivalent.

4.4.13   Assignment Statements

The assignment statement in JavaScript is exactly like the assignment statement in other common C-based programming languages. There is a simple assignment operator, denoted by `=`, and a host of compound assignment operators, such as `+=` and `/=`. For example, the statement

```
a += 7;
```

means the same as

```
a = a + 7;
```

In considering assignment statements, it is important to remember that JavaScript has two kinds of values: primitives and objects. A variable can refer to a primitive value, such as the number `17`, or an object, as shown in Figure 4.1. Objects are allocated on the heap, and variables that refer to them are reference variables. When used to refer to an object, a variable stores an address only. Therefore, assigning the address of an object to a variable is fundamentally different from assigning a primitive value to a variable.

[handwritten margin note: Impt regarding what is stored the value or a reference]

4.4.14   The `Date` Object

There are occasions when information about the current date and time is useful in a program. Likewise, sometimes it is convenient to be able to create objects that represent a specific date and time and then manipulate them. These capabilities are available in JavaScript through the `Date` object and its rich collection of methods. In what follows, we describe this object and some of its methods.

A `Date` object is created with the `new` operator and the `Date` constructor, which has several forms. Because we focus on uses of the current date and time, we use only the simplest `Date` constructor, which takes no parameters and builds an object with the current date and time for its properties. For example, we might have

```
var today = new Date();
```

The date and time properties of a `Date` object are in two forms: local and Coordinated Universal Time (UTC), which was formerly named Greenwich Mean Time. We deal only with local time in this section.

Table 4.5 shows the methods, along with the descriptions, that retrieve information from a `Date` object.

Table 4.5   Methods for the `Date` object

Method	Returns
`toLocaleString`	A string of the `Date` information
`getDate`	The day of the month
`getMonth`	The month of the year, as a number in the range from 0 to 11
`getDay`	The day of the week, as a number in the range from 0 to 6
`getFullYear`	The year
`getTime`	The number of milliseconds since January 1, 1970
`getHours`	The hour, as a number in the range from 0 to 23
`getMinutes`	The minute, as a number in the range from 0 to 59
`getSeconds`	The second, as a number in the range from 0 to 59
`getMilliseconds`	The millisecond, as a number in the range from 0 to 999

The use of the `Date` object is illustrated in Section 4.6.

4.5   Screen Output and Keyboard Input

A JavaScript script is interpreted when the browser finds the script or a reference to a separate script file in the body of the HTML document. Thus, the normal output screen for JavaScript is the same as the screen in which the content of the host HTML document is displayed. JavaScript models the HTML document with the `Document` object. The window in which the browser displays an HTML document is modeled with the `Window` object. The `Window` object includes two properties, `document` and `window`. The `document` property refers to the `Document` object. The `window` property is self-referential; it refers to the `Window` object.

The `Document` object has several properties and methods. The most interesting and useful of its methods, at least for now, is `write`, which is used to create output, which is dynamically created HTML document content. This content is specified in the parameter of `write`. For example, if the value of the variable `result` is 42, the following statement produces the screen shown in Figure 4.2:

Parameters seperated by commas

```
document.write("The result is: ", result, "<br />");
```

Could you use concatenation here instead of commas

```
The result is: 42
```

Figure 4.2 An example of the output of `document.write`

← inpt

Because `write` is used to create markup, the only useful punctuation in its parameter is in the form of HTML tags. Therefore, the parameter of `write` often includes `<br />`. The `writeln` method implicitly adds `"\n"` to its parameter, but since browsers ignore line breaks when displaying HTML, it has no effect on the output.[10]

The parameter of `write` can include any HTML tags and content. The parameter is simply given to the browser, which treats it exactly like any other part of the HTML document. The `write` method actually can take any number of parameters. Multiple parameters are catenated and placed in the output.

As stated previously, the `Window` object is the JavaScript model for the browser window. `Window` includes three methods that create dialog boxes for three specific kinds of user interactions. The default object for JavaScript is the `Window` object currently being displayed, so calls to these methods need not include an object reference. The three methods—`alert`, `confirm`, and `prompt`—which are described in the following paragraphs, often are used for debugging rather than as part of a servable document.

The `alert` method opens a dialog window and displays its parameter in that window. It also displays an *OK* button. The string parameter of `alert` is not HTML code; it is plain text. Therefore, the string parameter of `alert` may include `\n` but never should include `<br />`. As an example of an `alert`, consider the following code, in which we assume that the value of `sum` is `42`.

```
alert("The sum is:" + sum + "\n");
```
← not `<br />` since not HTML

This call to `alert` produces the dialog window shown in Figure 4.3.

Figure 4.3 An example of the output of `alert`

The `confirm` method opens a dialog window in which the method displays its string parameter, along with two buttons: *OK* and *Cancel*. `confirm` returns a Boolean value that indicates the user's button input: `true` for *OK* and `false` for *Cancel*. This method is often used to offer the user the choice of continuing

---

10. The `writeln` method is useful only if the browser is used to view a non-HTML document, which is rarely done.

some process. For example, the following statement produces the screen shown in Figure 4.4:

```
var question =
    confirm("Do you want to continue this download?");
```

After the user presses one of the buttons in the `confirm` dialog window, the script can test the variable, `question`, and react accordingly.

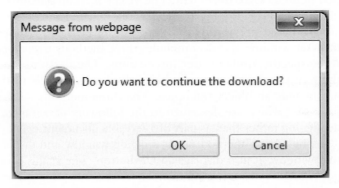

Figure 4.4 An example of the output of `confirm`

The `prompt` method creates a dialog window that contains a text box used to collect a string of input from the user, which `prompt` returns as its value. As with `confirm`, this window also includes two buttons: *OK* and *Cancel*. `prompt` takes two parameters: the string that prompts the user for input and a default string in case the user does not type a string before pressing one of the two buttons. In many cases, an empty string is used for the default input. Consider the following example: *2 parameters*

```
name = prompt("What is your name?", "");
```

Figure 4.5 shows the screen created by this call to `prompt`.

Explorer User Prompt	X
Script Prompt:	OK
What is your name?	Cancel

Figure 4.5 An example of the output of `prompt`

`alert`, `prompt`, and `confirm` cause the browser to wait for a user response. In the case of `alert`, the *OK* button must be pressed for the JavaScript interpreter to continue. The `prompt` and `confirm` methods wait for either *OK* or *Cancel* to be pressed.

The next two example HTML and JavaScript files—roots.html and roots.js—illustrate some of the JavaScript features described so far. The JavaScript script gets the coefficients of a quadratic equation from the user with prompt and computes and displays the real roots of the given equation. If the roots of the equation are not real, the value NaN is displayed. This value comes from the sqrt function, which returns NaN when the function is given a negative parameter. This result corresponds mathematically to the equation not having real roots.

```
<!DOCTYPE html>
<!-- roots.html
     A document for roots.js
     -->
<html lang = "en">
  <head>
    <title> roots.html </title>
    <meta charset = "utf-8" />
  </head>
  <body>
    <script type = "text/javascript"  src = "roots.js" >
    </script>
  </body>
</html>
```

HTML document that uses the roots.js file

```
// roots.js
//   Compute the real roots of a given quadratic
//   equation. If the roots are imaginary, this script
//   displays NaN, because that is what results from
//   taking the square root of a negative number

// Get the coefficients of the equation from the user
var a = prompt("What is the value of 'a'? \n", "");
var b = prompt("What is the value of 'b'? \n", "");
var c = prompt("What is the value of 'c'? \n", "");

// Compute the square root and denominator of the result
var root_part = Math.sqrt(b * b - 4.0 * a * c);
var denom = 2.0 * a;

// Compute and display the two roots
var root1 = (-b + root_part) / denom;
var root2 = (-b - root_part) / denom;
document.write("The first root is: ", root1, "<br />");
document.write("The second root is: ", root2, "<br />");
```

In the examples in the remainder of this chapter, the HTML document that uses the associated JavaScript file is not shown.

4.6   Control Statements

This section introduces the flow-control statements of JavaScript. Before discussing the control statements, we must describe control expressions, which provide the basis for controlling the order of execution of statements. Once again, the similarity of these JavaScript constructs to their counterparts in Java and C++ makes them easy to learn for those who are familiar with one of those languages.

Control statements often require some syntactic container for sequences of statements whose execution they are meant to control. In JavaScript, that container is the compound statement. A *compound statement* in JavaScript is a sequence of statements delimited by braces. A *control construct* is a control statement together with the statement or compound statement whose execution it controls.

Unlike several related languages, JavaScript does not allow compound statements to create local variables. If a variable is declared in a compound statement, access to it is not confined to that compound statement. Such a variable is visible in the whole HTML document.[11] Local variables are discussed in Section 4.9.2.

4.6.1   Control Expressions

The expressions upon which statement flow control can be based include primitive values, relational expressions, and compound expressions. The result of evaluating a control expression is one of the Boolean values `true` and `false`. If the value of a control expression is a string, it is interpreted as `true` unless it is either the empty string (`""`) or a zero string (`"0"`). If the value is a number, it is `true` unless it is zero (`0`). If the special value, `NaN`, is interpreted as a Boolean, it is false. If `undefined` is used as a Boolean, it is false. When interpreted as a Boolean, `null` is false. When interpreted as a number, `true` has the value `1` and `false` has the value `0`.

A relational expression has two operands and one relational operator. Table 4.6 lists the relational operators.

Table 4.6   Relational operators

Operation	Operator
Is equal to	==
Is not equal to	!=
Is less than	<
Is greater than	>
Is less than or equal to	<=
Is greater than or equal to	>=
Is strictly equal to	===
Is strictly not equal to	!==

---

11. The only exception to this rule is if the variable is declared in a function.

If the two operands are not of the same type and the operator is neither === nor !==, JavaScript will attempt to convert the operands to a single type. In the case in which one operand is a string and the other is a number, JavaScript attempts to convert the string to a number. If one operand is Boolean and the other is not, the Boolean value is converted to a number (1 for true, 0 for false).

The last two operators in Table 4.6 disallow type conversion of either operand. Thus, the expression "3" === 3 evaluates to false, while "3" == 3 evaluates to true.

Comparisons of variables that reference objects are rarely useful. If a and b reference different objects, a == b is never true, even if the objects have identical properties. a == b is true only if a and b reference the same object.

JavaScript has operators for the AND, OR, and NOT Boolean operations. These are && (AND), || (OR), and ! (NOT). Both && and || are short-circuit operators, as they are in Java and C++. This means that if the value of the first operand of either || or && determines the value of the expression, the second operand is not evaluated and the Boolean operator does nothing. JavaScript also has bitwise operators, but they are not discussed in this book.

The properties of the object Boolean must not be confused with the primitive values true and false. If a Boolean object is used as a conditional expression, it evaluates to true if it has any value other than null or undefined. The Boolean object has a method, toString, which it inherits from Object, that converts the value of the object through which it is called to one of the strings "true" and "false".

The precedence and associativity of all operators discussed so far in this chapter are shown in Table 4.7.

Table 4.7 Operator precedence and associativity

Operators*	Associativity
++, --, unary -	Right
*, /, %	Left
+, -	Left
>, <, >= ,<=	Left
==, !=	Left
===,!==	Left
&&	Left
||	Left
=, +=, -=, *=, /=, &&=, ||=, %=	Right

*Highest-precedence operators are listed first.

4.6.2   Selection Statements

The selection statements (`if-then` and `if-then-else`) of JavaScript are similar to those of the common programming languages. Either single statements or compound statements can be selected—for example,

```
if (a > b)
    document.write("a is greater than b <br />");
else {
    a = b;
    document.write("a was not greater than b <br />",
                   "Now they are equal <br />");
}
```

4.6.3   The `switch` Statement

JavaScript has a `switch` statement that is similar to that of Java. The form of this construct is as follows:

```
switch (expression) {
    case value_1:
        // statement(s)
    case value_2:
        // statement(s)

    . . .
    [default:
        // statement(s)]
}
```

In any `case` segment, the statement(s) can be either a sequence of statements or a compound statement.

The semantics of a `switch` construct is as follows: The expression is evaluated when the `switch` statement is reached in execution. The value is compared with the values in the cases in the construct (those values that immediately follow the `case` reserved words). If one matches, control is transferred to the statement immediately following that case value. Execution then continues through the remainder of the construct. In the great majority of situations, it is intended that only the statements in one case be executed in each execution of the construct. To implement this option, a `break` statement appears as the last statement in each sequence of statements following a case. The `break` statement is exactly like the `break` statement in Java and C++: It transfers control out of the compound statement in which it appears.

The control expression of a `switch` statement could evaluate to a number, a string, or a Boolean value. Case labels also can be numbers, strings, or Booleans, and different case values can be of different types. Consider the following script, which includes a `switch` construct (the HTML file that includes this script is very simple and thus is not shown):

[Handwritten note, top]: Note: HTML file is not shown. It would simply reference this JS file

```javascript
// borders2.js
//    An example of a switch statement for table border
//    size selection

var bordersize;
var err = 0;
bordersize = prompt("Select a table border size: " +
                    "0 (no border), " +
                    "1 (1 pixel border), " +
                    "4 (4 pixel border), " +
                    "8 (8 pixel border), ");

switch (bordersize) {
  case "0": document.write("<table>");
            break;
  case "1": document.write("<table border = '1'>");
            break;
  case "4": document.write("<table border = '4'>");
            break;
  case "8": document.write("<table border = '8'>");
            break;
  default: {
            document.write("Error - invalid choice: ",
                            bordersize, "<br />");
            err = 1;
            }
}

If (err == 0) {
  document.write("<caption> 2010 NFL Divisional",
                 " Winners </caption>");
  document.write("<tr>",
                 "<th />",
                 "<th> American Conference </th>",
                 "<th> National Conference </th>",
                 "</tr>",
                 "<tr>",
                 "<th> East </th>",
                 "<td> New England Patriots </td>",
                 "<td> Philadelphia Eagles </td>",
                 "</tr>",
                 "<tr>",
                 "<th> North </th>",
                 "<td> Pittsburgh Steelers </td>",
                 "<td> Chicago Bears </td>",
```

[Handwritten notes]: inside parameters when using document, write is written in HTML; transfers control out of the compound statement; Note: in HTML format; err = 0 unless a wrong choice is entered; again, all text in HTML formatting

```
                                   "</tr>",
                                   "<tr>",
                                   "<th> West </th>",
                                   "<td> Kansas City Chiefs </td>",
                                   "<td> Seattle Seahawks </td>",
                                   "</tr>",
                                   "<tr>",
                                   "<th> South </th>",
                                   "<td> Indianapolis Colts </td>",
                                   "<td> Atlanta Falcons </td>",
                                   "</tr>",
                                   "</table>");
}
```

The entire table element is produced with calls to `write`. Alternatively, we could have given all of the elements of the table, except the `<table>` and `</table>` tags, directly as HTML in the HTML document. Because `<table>` is in the content of the script element, the validator would not see it. Therefore, the `</table>` tag would also need to be hidden.

Browser displays of the prompt dialog box and the output of `borders2.js` are shown in Figures 4.6 and 4.7, respectively.

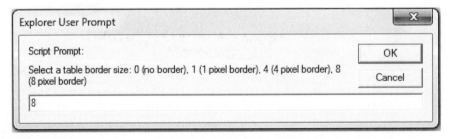

Figure 4.6 Dialog box from `borders2.js`

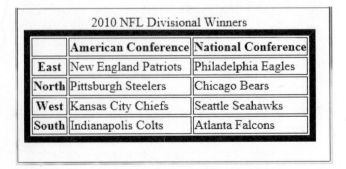

Figure 4.7 Display produced by `borders2.js`

4.6.4   Loop Statements

The JavaScript `while` and `for` statements are similar to those of Java and C++. The general form of the `while` statement is as follows:

`while` (*control expression*)
  statement or compound statement

The general form of the `for` statement is as follows:

`for` (*initial expression*; *control expression*; *increment expression*)
  statement or compound statement

Both the initial expression and the increment expression of the `for` statement can be multiple expressions separated by commas. The initial expression of a `for` statement can include variable declarations. Such variables are visible in the entire script unless the `for` statement is in a function definition, in which case the variable is visible in the whole function. The following code illustrates a simple `for` construct:

```
var sum = 0,
    count;
for (count = 0; count <= 10; count++)
    sum += count;
```

The following example illustrates the `Date` object and a simple `for` loop:

```
// date.js
//   Illustrates the use of the Date object by
//   displaying the parts of a current date and
//   using two Date objects to time a calculation

// Get the current date
var today = new Date();

// Fetch the various parts of the date
var dateString = today.toLocaleString();
var day = today.getDay();
var month = today.getMonth();
var year = today.getFullYear();
var timeMilliseconds = today.getTime();
var hour = today.getHours();
var minute = today.getMinutes();
var second = today.getSeconds();
var millisecond = today.getMilliseconds();

// Display the parts
document.write(
  "Date: " + dateString + "<br />",
  "Day: " + day + "<br />",
```

```
        "Month: " + month + "<br />",
        "Year: " + year + "<br />",
        "Time in milliseconds: " + timeMilliseconds + "<br />",
        "Hour: " + hour + "<br />",
        "Minute: " + minute + "<br />",
        "Second: " + second + "<br />",
        "Millisecond: " + millisecond + "<br />");

// Time a loop
var dum1 = 1.00149265, product = 1;
var start = new Date();

for (var count = 0; count < 10000; count++)
  product = product + 1.000002 * dum1 / 1.00001;

var end = new Date();
var diff = end.getTime() - start.getTime();
document.write("<br />The loop took " + diff +
            " milliseconds <br />");
```

A display of `date.js` is shown in Figure 4.8.

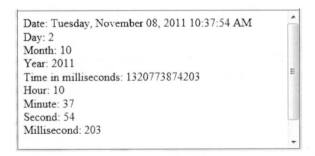

Date: Tuesday, November 08, 2011 10:37:54 AM
Day: 2
Month: 10
Year: 2011
Time in milliseconds: 1320773874203
Hour: 10
Minute: 37
Second: 54
Millisecond: 203

Figure 4.8 Display produced by `date.js`

In addition to the `while` and `for` loop statements, JavaScript has a `do-while` statement, whose form is as follows:

`do` *statement or compound statement*
`while` (*control expression*)

The `do-while` statement is related to the `while` statement, but the test for completion is logically (and physically) at the end, rather than at the beginning, of the loop construct. The body of a `do-while` construct is always executed at least once. The following is an example of a `do-while` construct:

```
do {
    count++;
    sum = sum + (sum * count);
} while (count <= 50);
```

JavaScript includes one more loop statement, the `for-in` statement, which is most often used with objects. The `for-in` statement is discussed in Section 4.7.

4.7 Object Creation and Modification

Objects are often created with a `new` expression, which must include a call to a constructor method. The constructor that is called in the `new` expression creates the properties that characterize the new object. In an object-oriented language such as Java, the `new` operator creates a particular object, meaning an object with a type and a specific collection of members. Thus, in Java, the constructor initializes members but does not create them. In JavaScript, however, the `new` operator creates a blank object—that is, one with no properties. Furthermore, JavaScript objects do not have types. The constructor both creates and initializes the properties.

The following statement creates an object that has no properties:

```
var my_object = new Object();
```

In this case, the constructor called is that of `Object`, which endows the new object with no properties, although it does have access to some inherited methods. The variable `my_object` references the new object. Calls to constructors must include parentheses, even if there are no parameters. Constructors are discussed in detail in Section 4.11.

The properties of an object can be accessed with dot notation, in which the first word is the object name and the second is the property name. Properties are not actually variables—they are just the names of values. They are used with object variables to access property values. Because properties are not variables, they are never declared.

The number of members of a class in Java or C++ is fixed at compile time. The number of properties in a JavaScript object is dynamic. At any time during interpretation, properties can be added to or deleted from an object. A property for an object is created by assigning a value to that property's name. Consider the following example:

```
// Create an Object object
var my_car = new Object();
// Create and initialize the make property
my_car.make = "Ford";
// Create and initialize model
my_car.model = "Fusion";
```

This code creates a new object, `my_car`, with two properties: `make` and `model`.

There is an abbreviated way to create an object and its properties. For example, the object referenced with `my_car` in the previous example could be created with the following statement:

```
var my_car = {make: "Ford", model: "Fusion"};
```

Notice that this statement includes neither the `new` operator nor the call to the `Object` constructor.

Because objects can be nested, you can create a new object that is a property of my_car with properties of its own, as in the following statements:

```
my_car.engine = new Object();
my_car.engine.config = "V6";
my_car.engine.hp = 263;
```

Properties can be accessed in two ways. First, any property can be accessed in the same way it is assigned a value, namely, with the object-dot-property notation. Second, the property names of an object can be accessed as if they were elements of an array. To do so, the property name (as a string literal) is used as a subscript. For example, after execution of the statements

```
var prop1 = my_car.make;
var prop2 = my_car["make"];
```

the variables prop1 and prop2 both have the value "Ford".

If an attempt is made to access a property of an object that does not exist, the value undefined is used. A property can be deleted with delete, as in the following example:

```
delete my_car.model;
```

JavaScript has a loop statement, for-in, that is perfect for listing the properties of an object. The form of for-in is

```
for (identifier in object)
  statement or compound statement
```

Consider the following example:

```
for (var prop in my_car)
  document.write("Name: ", prop, "; Value: ",
                 my_car[prop], "<br />");
```

In this example, the variable, prop, takes on the values of the properties of the my_car object, one for each iteration. So, this code lists all of the values of the properties of my_car.

4.8 Arrays

In JavaScript, arrays are objects that have some special functionality. Array elements can be primitive values or references to other objects, including other arrays. JavaScript arrays have dynamic lengths.

4.8.1 Array Object Creation

Array objects, unlike most other JavaScript objects, can be created in two distinct ways. The usual way to create any object is with the new operator and a call to a constructor. In the case of arrays, the constructor is named Array:

```
var my_list = new Array(1, 2, "three", "four");
var your_list = new Array(100);
```

In the first declaration, an `Array` object of length 4 is created and initialized. Notice that the elements of an array need not have the same type. In the second declaration, a new `Array` object of length 100 is created, without actually creating any elements. Whenever a call to the `Array` constructor has a single parameter, that parameter is taken to be the number of elements, not the initial value of a one-element array.

The second way to create an `Array` object is with a literal array value, which is a list of values enclosed in brackets:

```
var my_list_2 = [1, 2, "three", "four"];
```

The array `my_list_2` has the same values as the `Array` object `my_list` created previously with `new`.

4.8.2   Characteristics of Array Objects

The lowest index of every JavaScript array is zero. Access to the elements of an array is specified with numeric subscript expressions placed in brackets. The length of an array is the highest subscript to which a value has been assigned, plus 1. For example, if `my_list` is an array with four elements and the following statement is executed, the new length of `my_list` will be 48.

```
my_list[47] = 2222;
```

The length of an array is both read and write accessible through the `length` property, which is created for every array object by the `Array` constructor. Consequently, the length of an array can be set to whatever you like by assigning the `length` property, as in the following example:

```
my_list.length = 1002;
```

Now, the length of `my_list` is 1002, regardless of what it was previously. Assigning a value to the `length` property can lengthen, shorten, or not affect the array's length (if the value assigned happens to be the same as the previous length of the array).

Only the assigned elements of an array actually occupy space. For example, if it is convenient to use the subscript range of 100 to 150 (rather than 0 to 99), an array of length 151 can be created. But if only the elements indexed 100 to 150 are assigned values, the array will require the space of 51 elements, not 151. The `length` property of an array is not necessarily the number of elements allocated. For example, the following statement sets the `length` property of `new_list` to `1002`, but `new_list` may have no elements that have values or occupy space:

```
new_list.length = 1002;
```

To support JavaScript's dynamic arrays, all array elements are allocated dynamically from the heap. Assigning a value to an array element that did not previously exist creates that element.

The next example, `insert_names.js`, illustrates JavaScript arrays. This script has an array of names, which are in alphabetical order. It uses `prompt` to get new names, one at a time, and inserts them into the existing array while maintaining its alphabetical order. Our approach is to move elements down one at a time, starting at the end of the array, until the correct position for the new name is found. Then the new name is inserted, and the new array is displayed. Each new name causes the array to grow by one element. This is achieved by assigning a value to the element following what was the last allocated element. Here is the code:

```javascript
// insert_names.js
//    This script has an array of names, name_list,
//    whose values are in alphabetical order. New
//    names are input through a prompt. Each new
//    name is inserted into the name_list array,
//    after which the new list is displayed.


// The original list of names
var name_list = new Array("Al", "Betty", "Kasper",
                          "Michael", "Roberto", "Zimbo");
var new_name, index, last;


// Loop to get a new name and insert it
while (new_name =
       prompt("Please type a new name", "")) {
  last = name_list.length - 1;


// Loop to find the place for the new name
  while (last >= 0 && name_list[last] > new_name) {
    name_list[last + 1] = name_list[last];
    last--;
  }


// Insert the new name into its spot in the array
  name_list[last + 1] = new_name;


// Display the new array
  document.write("<p><strong>The new name list is:</strong> ",
                 "<br />");
  for (index = 0; index < name_list.length; index++)
    document.write(name_list[index], "<br />");
  document.write("</p>");
} //** end of the outer while loop
```

4.8.3   Array **Methods**

Array objects have a collection of useful methods, most of which are described in this section. The join method converts all of the elements of an array to strings and catenates them into a single string. If no parameter is provided to join, the values in the new string are separated by commas. If a string parameter is provided, it is used as the element separator. Consider the following example:

```
var names = new Array["Mary", "Murray", "Murphy", "Max"];
. . .
var name_string = names.join(" : ");
```

The value of name_string is now "Mary : Murray : Murphy : Max".

The reverse method does what you would expect: It reverses the order of the elements of the Array object through which it is called.

The sort method coerces the elements of the array to become strings if they are not already strings and sorts them alphabetically. For example, consider the following statement:

```
names.sort();
```

The value of names is now ["Mary", "Max", "Murphy", "Murray"]. Section 4.9.4 discusses the use of sort for different orders and for nonstring elements.

The concat method catenates its actual parameters to the end of the Array object on which it is called. Consider the following statements:

```
var names = new Array["Mary", "Murray", "Murphy", "Max"];
. . .
var new_names = names.concat("Moo", "Meow");
```

The new_names array now has length 6, with the elements of names, along with "Moo" and "Meow", as its fifth and sixth elements.

The slice method does for arrays what the substring method does for strings, returning the part of the Array object specified by its parameters, which are used as subscripts. The array returned has the elements of the Array object through which it is called, from the first parameter up to, but not including, the second parameter. For example, consider the following statements:

```
var list = [2, 4, 6, 8, 10];
. . .
var list2 = list.slice(1, 3);
```

The value of list2 is now [4, 6]. If slice is given just one parameter, the array that is returned has all of the elements of the object, starting with the specified index. In the following statements

```
var list = ["Bill", "Will", "Jill", "dill"];
. . .
var listette = list.slice(2);
```

the value of listette is set to ["Jill", "dill"].

4.9.2   Local Variables

The *scope* of a variable is the range of statements over which it is visible. When JavaScript is embedded in an HTML document, the scope of a variable is the range of lines of the document over which the variable is visible.

A variable that is not declared with a `var` statement is implicitly declared by the JavaScript interpreter at the time it is first encountered in the script. Variables that are implicitly declared have *global scope*—that is, they are visible in the entire HTML document (or entire file if the script is in its own file)—even if the implicit declaration occurs within a function definition. Variables that are explicitly declared outside function definitions also have global scope. As stated earlier, we recommend that all variables be explicitly declared.

It is usually best for variables that are used only within a function to have *local scope*, meaning that they are visible and can be used only within the body of the function. Any variable explicitly declared with `var` in the body of a function has local scope.

If a variable that is defined both as a local variable and as a global variable appears in a function, the local variable has precedence, effectively hiding the global variable with the same name. This is the advantage of local variables: When you make up their names, you need not be concerned that a global variable with the same name may exist somewhere in the collection of scripts in the HTML document.

Although JavaScript function definitions can be nested, the need for nested functions in client-side JavaScript is minimal. Furthermore, they can greatly complicate scripts. Therefore, we do not recommend the use of nested functions and do not discuss them.

4.9.3   Parameters

The parameter values that appear in a call to a function are called *actual parameters*. The parameter names that appear in the header of a function definition, which correspond to the actual parameters in calls to the function, are called *formal parameters*. Like C, C++, and Java, JavaScript uses the pass-by-value parameter-passing method. When a function is called, the values of the actual parameters specified in the call are, in effect, copied into their corresponding formal parameters, which behave exactly like local variables. Because references are passed as the actual parameters of objects, the called function has access to the objects and can change them, thereby providing the semantics of pass-by-reference parameters. However, if a reference to an object is passed to a function and the function changes its corresponding formal parameter (rather than the object to which it points), then the change has no effect on the actual parameter. For example, suppose an array is passed as a parameter to a function, as in the following code:

```
function fun1(my_list) {
  var list2 = new Array(1, 3, 5);
  my_list[3] = 14;
  . . .
  my_list = list2;
  . . .
```

```
}
. . .
var list = new Array(2, 4, 6, 8)
fun1(list);
```

The first assignment to `my_list` in `fun1` changes the object to which `my_list` refers, which was created in the calling code. However, the second assignment to `my_list` changes it to refer to a different array object. This does not change the actual parameter in the caller.

Because of JavaScript's dynamic typing, there is no type checking of parameters. The called function itself can check the types of parameters with the `typeof` operator. However, recall that `typeof` cannot distinguish between different objects. The number of parameters in a function call is not checked against the number of formal parameters in the called function. In the function, excess actual parameters that are passed are ignored; excess formal parameters are set to `undefined`.

All parameters are communicated through a property array, `arguments`, that, like other array objects, has a property named `length`. By accessing `arguments.length`, a function can determine the number of actual parameters that were passed. Because the `arguments` array is directly accessible, all actual parameters specified in the call are available, including actual parameters that do not correspond to any formal parameters (because there were more actual parameters than formal parameters). The following example illustrates a variable number of function parameters:

```
// params.js
//    The params function and a test driver for it.
//    This example illustrates a variable number of
//    function parameters

// Function params
// Parameters: A variable number of parameters
// Returns: nothing
// Displays its parameters
function params(a, b) {
  document.write("Function params was passed ",
      arguments.length, " parameter(s) <br />");
  document.write("Parameter values are: <br />");

  for (var arg = 0; arg < arguments.length; arg++)
    document.write(arguments[arg], "<br />");

  document.write("<br />");
}

// A test driver for function params
params("Mozart");
params("Mozart", "Beethoven");
params("Mozart", "Beethoven", "Tchaikowsky");
```

Figure 4.10 shows a browser display of `params.js`.

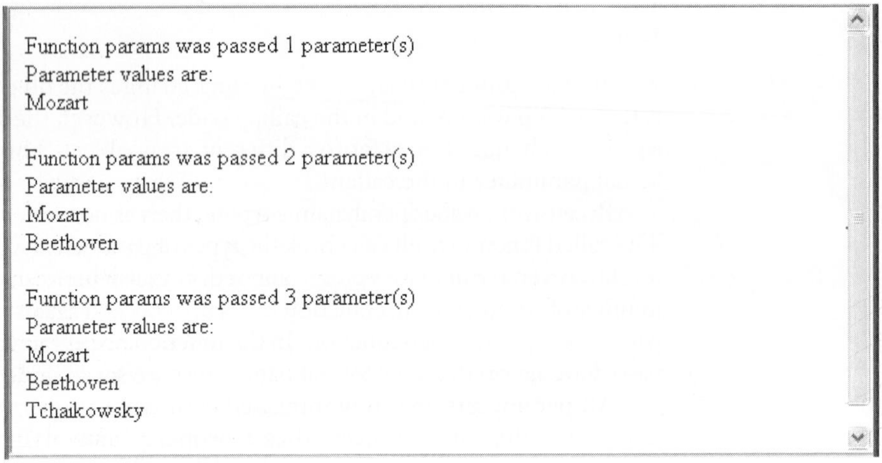

Function params was passed 1 parameter(s)
Parameter values are:
Mozart

Function params was passed 2 parameter(s)
Parameter values are:
Mozart
Beethoven

Function params was passed 3 parameter(s)
Parameter values are:
Mozart
Beethoven
Tchaikowsky

Figure 4.10 Display of `params.js`

There is no elegant way in JavaScript to pass a primitive value by reference. One inelegant way is to put the value in an array and pass the array, as in the following script:

```
// Function by10
//    Parameter: a number, passed as the first element
//               of an array
//  Returns: nothing
//  Effect: multiplies the parameter by 10
function by10(a) {
    a[0] *= 10;
}
 . . .
var x;
var listx = new Array(1);
 . . .
listx[0] = x;
by10(listx);
x = listx[0];
```

This approach works because arrays are objects.

Another way to have a function change the value of a primitive-type actual parameter is to have the function return the new value as follows:

```
function by10_2(a) {
    return 10 * a;
}
```

```
. . .
var x;
. . .
x = by10_2(x);
```

4.9.4   The `sort` Method, Revisited

Recall that the `sort` method for array objects converts the array's elements to strings, if necessary, and then sorts them alphabetically. If you need to sort something other than strings, or if you want an array to be sorted in some order other than alphabetically as strings, the comparison operation must be supplied to the `sort` method by the caller. Such a comparison operation is passed as a parameter to `sort`. The comparison function must return a negative number if the two elements being compared are in the desired order, zero if they are equal, and a number greater than zero if they must be interchanged. For numbers, simply subtracting the second from the first produces the required result. For example, if you want to use the `sort` method to sort the array of numbers `num_list` into descending order, you could do so with the following code:

```
// Function num_order
// Parameter: Two numbers
// Returns: If the first parameter belongs before the
//             second in descending order, a negative number
//          If the two parameters are equal, 0
//          If the two parameters must be
//             interchanged, a positive number
function num_order(a, b) {return b - a;}
// Sort the array of numbers, list, into
// ascending order
  num_list.sort(num_order);
```

Rather than defining a comparison function elsewhere and passing its name, the function definition can appear as the actual parameter in the call to `sort`. Such a function is nameless and can be used only where its definition appears. A nameless function is illustrated in the sample script in Section 4.10.

4.10   An Example

The following example of an HTML document contains a JavaScript function to compute the median of an array of numbers. The function first uses the `sort` method to sort the array. If the length of the given array is odd, the median is the middle element and is determined by dividing the length by 2 and truncating the result with the use of `floor`. If the length is even, the median is the average of the two middle elements. Note that `round` is used to compute the result of the average computation. Here is the code:

```
// medians.js
//    A function and a function tester
//    Illustrates array operations


// Function median
//    Parameter: An array of numbers
//    Result: The median of the array
//    Return value: none
function median(list) {
  list.sort(function (a, b) {return a - b;});
  var list_len = list.length;


// Use the modulus operator to determine whether
//    the array's length is odd or even
// Use Math.floor to truncate numbers
// Use Math.round to round numbers
  if ((list_len % 2) == 1)
    return list[Math.floor(list_len / 2)];
  else
    return Math.round((list[list_len / 2 - 1] +
                       list[list_len / 2]) / 2);
}   // end of function median


// Test driver
var my_list_1 = [8, 3, 9, 1, 4, 7];
var my_list_2 = [10, -2, 0, 5, 3, 1, 7];
var med = median(my_list_1);
document.write("Median of [", my_list_1, "] is: ",
               med, "<br />");
med = median(my_list_2);
document.write("Median of [", my_list_2, "] is: ",
               med, "<br />");
```

Figure 4.11 shows a browser display of `medians.js`.

```
Median of [1,3,4,7,8,9] is: 6
Median of [-2,0,1,3,5,7,10] is: 3
```

Figure 4.11 Display of `medians.js`

One significant side effect of the `median` function is that it leaves the given array in ascending order, which may not always be acceptable. If it is not, the array could be moved to a local array in `median` before the sorting operation.

Notice that this script depends on the fact that the array subscripts begin with 0.

4.11 Constructors

JavaScript constructors are special functions that create and initialize the properties of newly created objects. Every `new` expression must include a call to a constructor whose name is the same as that of the object being created. As you saw in Section 4.8, for example, the constructor for arrays is named `Array`. Constructors are actually called by the `new` operator, which immediately precedes them in the `new` expression.

Obviously, a constructor must be able to reference the object on which it is to operate. JavaScript has a predefined reference variable for this purpose, named `this`. When the constructor is called, `this` is a reference to the newly created object. The `this` variable is used to construct and initialize the properties of the object. For example, the following constructor:

```
function car(new_make, new_model, new_year) {
    this.make = new_make;
    this.model = new_model;
    this.year = new_year;
}
```

could be used as in the following statement:

```
my_car = new car("Ford", "Fusion", "2012");
```

So far, we have considered only data properties. If a method is to be included in the object, it is initialized the same way as if it were a data property. For example, suppose you wanted a method for `car` objects that listed the property values. A function that could serve as such a method could be written as follows:

```
function display_car() {
    document.write("Car make: ", this.make, "<br/>");
    document.write("Car model: ", this.model, "<br/>");
    document.write("Car year: ", this.year, "<br/>");
}
```

The following line must then be added to the `car` constructor:

```
this.display = display_car;
```

Now the call `my_car.display()` will produce the following output:

```
Car make: Ford
Car model: Fusion
Car year: 2012
```

The collection of objects created by using the same constructor is related to the concept of class in an object-oriented programming language. All such objects have the same set of properties and methods, at least initially. These objects can diverge from each other through user code changes. Furthermore, there is no convenient way to determine in the script whether two objects have the same set of properties and methods.

4.12   Pattern Matching by Using Regular Expressions

JavaScript has powerful pattern-matching capabilities based on regular expressions. There are two approaches to pattern matching in JavaScript: one that is based on the methods of the `RegExp` object and one that is based on methods of the `String` object. The regular expressions used by these two approaches are the same and are based on the regular expressions of the Perl programing language. This book covers only the `String` methods for pattern matching.

As stated previously, patterns are specified in a form that is based on regular expressions, which were developed to define members of a simple class of formal languages. Elaborate and complex patterns can be used to describe specific strings or categories of strings. Patterns, which are sent as parameters to the pattern-matching methods, are delimited with slashes.

The simplest pattern-matching method is `search`, which takes a pattern as a parameter. The `search` method returns the position in the `String` object (through which it is called) at which the pattern matched. If there is no match, `search` returns –1. Most characters are normal, which means that, in a pattern, they match themselves. The position of the first character in the string is 0. As an example, consider the following statements:

```
var str = "Rabbits are furry";
var position = str.search(/bits/);
if (position >= 0)
    document.write("'bits' appears in position", position,
                "<br />");
else
    document.write("'bits' does not appear in str <br />");
```

These statements produce the following output:

```
'bits' appears in position 3
```

4.12.1   Character and Character-Class Patterns

The "normal" characters are those that are not metacharacters. Metacharacters are characters that have special meanings in some contexts in patterns. The following are the pattern metacharacters:

```
\ | ( ) [ ] { } ^ $ * + ? .
```

Metacharacters can themselves be matched by being immediately preceded by a backslash.

A period matches any character except newline. So, the following pattern matches "snowy", "snowe", and "snowd", among others:

```
/snow./
```

To match a period in a string, the period must be preceded by a backslash in the pattern. For example, the pattern /3\.4/ matches 3.4. The pattern /3.4/ matches 3.4 and 374, among others.

It is often convenient to be able to specify classes of characters rather than individual characters. Such classes are defined by placing the desired characters in brackets. Dashes can appear in character class definitions, making it easy to specify sequences of characters. For example, the following character class matches 'a', 'b', or 'c':

```
[abc]
```

The following character class matches any lowercase letter from 'a' to 'h':

```
[a-h]
```

If a circumflex character (^) is the first character in a class, it inverts the specified set. For example, the following character class matches any character except the letters 'a', 'e', 'i', 'o', and 'u':

```
[^aeiou]
```

Because they are frequently used, some character classes are predefined and named and can be specified by their names. These are shown in Table 4.8, which gives the names of the classes, their literal definitions as character classes, and descriptions of what they match.

Table 4.8 Predefined character classes

Name	Equivalent Pattern	Matches
\d	[0-9]	A digit
\D	[^0-9]	Not a digit
\w	[A-Za-z_0-9]	A word character (alphanumeric)
\W	[^A-Za-z_0-9]	Not a word character
\s	[\r\t\n\f]	A white-space character
\S	[^ \r\t\n\f]	Not a white-space character

The following examples show patterns that use predefined character classes:

```
/\d\.\d\d/    // Matches a digit, followed by a period,
              // followed by two digits
/\D\d\D/      // Matches a single digit
/\w\w\w/      // Matches three adjacent word characters
```

In many cases, it is convenient to be able to repeat a part of a pattern, often a character or character class. To repeat a pattern, a numeric quantifier, delimited by braces, is attached. For example, the following pattern matches xyyyyz:

```
/xy{4}z/
```

There are also three symbolic quantifiers: asterisk (*), plus (+), and question mark (?). An asterisk means zero or more repetitions, a plus sign means one or more repetitions, and a question mark means one or none. For example, the following pattern matches strings that begin with any number of x's (including zero), followed by one or more y's, possibly followed by z:

```
/x*y+z?/
```

The quantifiers are often used with the predefined character-class names, as in the following pattern, which matches a string of one or more digits followed by a decimal point and possibly more digits:

```
/\d+\.\d*/
```

As another example, the pattern

```
/[A-Za-z]\w*/
```

matches the identifiers (a letter, followed by zero or more letters, digits, or underscores) in some programming languages.

There is one additional named pattern that is often useful: \b (boundary), which matches the boundary position between a word character (\w) and a non-word character (\W), in either order. For example, the following pattern matches "A tulip is a flower" but not "A frog isn't":

```
/\bis\b/
```

The pattern does not match the second string because the "is" is followed by another word character (n).

The boundary pattern is different from the named character classes in that it does not match a character; instead, it matches a position between two characters.

4.12.2   Anchors

Frequently, it is useful to be able to specify that a pattern must match at a particular position in a string. The most common example of this type of specification is requiring a pattern to match at one specific end of the string. A pattern is tied to a string position with an anchor. A pattern can be specified to match only at the beginning of the string by preceding it with a circumflex (^) anchor. For example, the following pattern matches "pearls are pretty" but does not match "My pearls are pretty":

```
/^pearl/
```

A pattern can be specified to match at the end of a string only by following the pattern with a dollar sign anchor. For example, the following pattern matches "I like gold" but does not match "golden":

```
/gold$/
```

Anchor characters are like boundary-named patterns: They do not match specific characters in the string; rather, they match positions before, between, or after characters. When a circumflex appears in a pattern at a position other than the beginning of the pattern or at the beginning of a character class, it has no special meaning. (It matches itself.) Likewise, if a dollar sign appears in a pattern at a position other than the end of the pattern, it has no special meaning.

4.12.3   Pattern Modifiers

Modifiers can be attached to patterns to change how they are used, thereby increasing their flexibility. The modifiers are specified as letters just after the right delimiter of the pattern. The i modifier makes the letters in the pattern match either uppercase or lowercase letters in the string. For example, the pattern /Apple/i matches 'APPLE', 'apple', 'APPle', and any other combination of uppercase and lowercase spellings of the word "apple."

The x modifier allows white space to appear in the pattern. Because comments are considered white space, this provides a way to include explanatory comments in the pattern. For example, the pattern

```
/\d+         # The street number
\s           # The space before the street name
[A-Z][a-z]+  # The street name
/x
```

is equivalent to

```
/\d+\s[A-Z][a-z]+/
```

4.12.4   Other Pattern-Matching Methods of String

The replace method is used to replace substrings of the String object that match the given pattern. The replace method takes two parameters: the pattern and the replacement string. The g modifier can be attached to the pattern if the replacement is to be global in the string, in which case the replacement is done for every match in the string. The matched substrings of the string are made available through the predefined variables $1, $2, and so on. For example, consider the following statements:

```
var str = "Fred, Freddie, and Frederica were siblings";
str.replace(/Fre/g, "Boy");
```

In this example, str is set to "Boyd, Boyddie, and Boyderica were siblings", and $1, $2, and $3 are all set to "Fre".

The `match` method is the most general of the `String` pattern-matching methods. The `match` method takes a single parameter: a pattern. It returns an array of the results of the pattern-matching operation. If the pattern has the `g` modifier, the returned array has all of the substrings of the string that matched. If the pattern does not include the `g` modifier, the returned array has the match as its first element, and the remainder of the array has the matches of parenthesized parts of the pattern if there are any:

```
var str =
  "Having 4 apples is better than having 3 oranges";
var matches = str.match(/\d/g);
```

In this example, `matches` is set to `[4, 3]`.

Now consider a pattern that has parenthesized subexpressions:

```
var str = "I have 428 dollars, but I need 500";
var matches = str.match(/(\d+)([^\d]+)(\d+)/);
document.write(matches, "<br />");
```

The following is the value of the `matches` array after this code is interpreted:

```
["428 dollars, but I need 500", "428",
 " dollars, but I need ", "500"]
```

In this result array, the first element, `"428 dollars, but I need 500"`, is the match; the second, third, and fourth elements are the parts of the string that matched the parenthesized parts of the pattern, `(\d+)`, `([^\d]+)`, and `(\d+)`.

The `split` method of `String` splits its object string into substrings on the basis of a given string or pattern. The substrings are returned in an array. For example, consider the following code:

```
var str = "grapes:apples:oranges";
var fruit = str.split(":");
```

In this example, `fruit` is set to `[grapes, apples, oranges]`.

4.13 Another Example

One of the common uses for JavaScript is to check the format of input from HTML forms, which is discussed in detail in Chapter 5. The following example presents a simple function that uses pattern matching to check a given string that is supposed to contain a phone number, in order to determine whether the format of the phone number is correct:

```
// forms_check.js
//   A function tst_phone_num is defined and tested.
//   This function checks the validity of phone
//   number input from a form
```

```
// Function tst_phone_num
//    Parameter: A string
//    Result: Returns true if the parameter has the form of a valid
//            seven-digit phone number (3 digits, a dash, 4 digits)

function tst_phone_num(num) {

// Use a simple pattern to check the number of digits and the dash
  var ok = num.search(/^\d{3}-\d{4}$/);

  if (ok == 0)
    return true;
  else
    return false;

}  // end of function tst_phone_num

// A script to test tst_phone_num
var tst = tst_phone_num("444-5432");
if (tst)
  document.write("444-5432 is a valid phone number <br />");
else
  document.write("Error in tst_phone_num <br />");

tst = tst_phone_num("444-r432");
if (tst)
  document.write("Program error <br />");
else
  document.write(
          "444-r432 is not a valid phone number <br />");

tst = tst_phone_num("44-1234");
if (tst)
  document.write("Program error <br />");
else
  document.write("44-1234 is not a valid phone number <br /");
```

Handwritten annotations:
- Above the pattern: nothing before / 3 digs / - / 4 digs / nothing after
- "if num.search parameter matches, then 0 is returned. If not, -1 is returned."
- Next to `if (tst)` (first): (tst = true)
- Next to `if (tst)` (second): (tst = false)
- Next to `if (tst)` (third): (tst = false)

Figure 4.12 shows a browser display of `forms_check.js`.

```
444-5432 is a valid phone number
444-r432 is not a valid phone number
44-1234 is not a valid phone number
```

Figure 4.12 Display of `forms_check.js`

4.14   **Errors in Scripts**

The JavaScript interpreter is capable of detecting various errors in scripts. These are primarily syntax errors, although uses of undefined variables are also detected. Debugging a script is a bit different from debugging a program in a more typical programming language, mostly because errors that are detected by the JavaScript interpreter are found while the browser is attempting to display a document. In some cases, a script error causes the browser not to display the document and does not produce an error message. Without a diagnostic message, you must simply examine the code to find the problem. This is, of course, unacceptable for all but the smallest and simplest scripts. Fortunately, there are ways to get some debugging assistance.

Although the default settings for IE8 provide JavaScript syntax error detection and debugging, IE9 has these features turned off by default. To turn them on, select *Tools/Internet Options* and the *Advanced* tab. Under *Browsing* remove the check on *Disable script debugging (Internet Explorer)* and set the check on *Display a notification about every script error*. Then you will get syntax error detection and the display of error messages, along with the offending line and character position in the line with the error. These messages are shown in a small window. For example, consider the following sample script:

```
// debugdemo.js
//    An example to illustrate debugging help

var row;
row = 0;

while(row != 4 {
  document.write("row is ", row, "<br />");
  row++;
}
```

Notice the syntax error in the `while` statement (a missing right parenthesis). Figure 4.13 shows the browser display of what happens when an attempt is made to run `debugdemo.js`.

The FX3 browser has a special console window that displays script errors. Select *Tools/Web Developer/Error Console* to open the window. When you use this browser to display documents that include JavaScript, the window should be opened. After an error message has appeared and has been used to fix a script, press the *Clear* button on the console. Otherwise, the old error message will remain there and possibly cause confusion about subsequent problems. An example of the FX3 JavaScript Console window is shown in Figure 4.14.

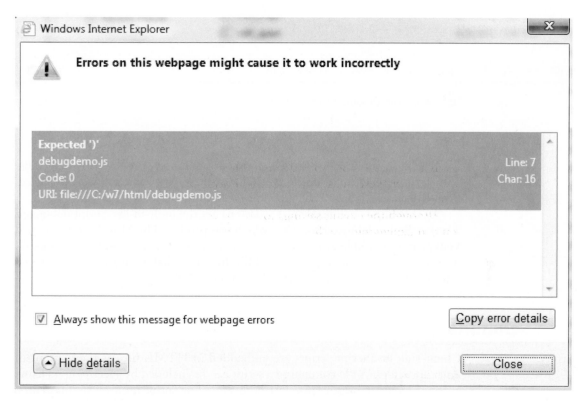

Figure 4.13 Result of running `debugdemo.js` with IE9

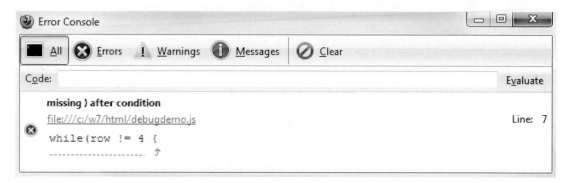

Figure 4.14 Display of the FX3 error console after attempting to run `debugdemo.js`

In C12, the JavaScript error console is accessed by selecting the wrench icon, *Tools, JavaScript console*. An example of this console is shown in Figure 4.15.

Uncaught SyntaxError: Unexpected token {   debugdemo.js:7

Figure 4.15 The Chrome error console

The more interesting and challenging programming problems are detectable only during execution or interpretation. For these problems, a debugger is used. Both IE9 and FX3 have debuggers for JavaScript.

In IE9, click on *Tools/Developer Tools* to get the built-in JavaScript debugger. The JavaScript debugger for FX3, which was produced by Mozilla and is named Venkman, is available at http://www.mozilla.org/projects/venkman/. Another JavaScript debugger, named Firebug, is available for FX3 at https://addons.mozilla.org/en-US/firefox/addon/1843.

Summary

Client-side JavaScript scripts are embedded in HTML files as the content of <script> tags. A file containing a script can be included by specifying its name as the value of the <script> attribute src. The script itself must appear in a special HTML comment.

Values in JavaScript are either primitives or objects. The primitive types are Number, String, Boolean, Undefined, and Null. Numbers are represented in double-precision floating-point format. The Number, String, and Boolean types have corresponding objects named Number, String, and Boolean, which act as wrapper objects. String literals can use either single or double quotes as delimiters.

JavaScript is dynamically typed, which is not the same as being a typeless language. Variables are typeless, but the values they reference are typed. The type of the value referenced by a variable can change every time a new value is assigned to the variable. It is best to declare all variables explicitly.

The Number object includes a collection of useful properties such as MIN_VALUE and PI. The Math object has many methods for commonly used operations on numbers, such as round and cos. The catenation operator, +, creates a new string by putting two operand strings together. The String property length stores the number of characters in a string. There are String methods to return the character at a specified position in the string, the position of a specified character in the string, and a specified substring of the string. There are a large number of other String methods as well.

The typeof operator returns the type name of its operand if the operand is a primitive type; otherwise, it returns "object".

The `Date` object provides the current time and date. It includes a large number of methods to produce various parts of the time and date, such as the day of the week and the hour of the day.

The `alert` method of `Window` produces output in a dialog box. The `confirm` method of `Window` asks the user to select either an *OK* button or a *Cancel* button. The `prompt` method of `Window` asks the user for textual input. The `document.write` method dynamically produces HTML content. The control statements of JavaScript are closely related to those of other common programming languages. Included is a `switch` statement.

Arrays in JavaScript are objects, as they are in Java. They have dynamic length. An `Array` object can be created in a `new` expression, which includes a call to the `Array` constructor, or simply by assigning an `Array` literal to a variable. `Array` literals are lists of values enclosed in brackets. Every `Array` object has a `length` property, which is both readable and writable. The `length` property stores the number of elements in the array. `Array` objects have a collection of useful methods, among which are `join`, which joins the elements of an array in a string; `reverse`, which reverses the order of elements in an array; `sort`, which converts the elements of the array to strings and sorts them alphabetically; and `slice`, which returns a specified part of the array. The array methods `pop`, `push`, `shift`, and `unshift` were designed to implement stacks and queues in arrays.

Function definitions name their formal parameters, but do not include type names. All functions return values, but the type of the value is not specified in the function's definition. Variables declared in a function with `var` are local to that function. Parameters are passed by value, resulting in pass-by-value semantics for primitives and pass-by-reference semantics for objects. The `arguments` property stores the values of the parameters that are passed. Neither the types of the parameters nor the number of parameters is checked by the JavaScript interpreter.

The regular expressions used in the pattern-matching facilities of JavaScript are like the regular expressions of Perl. Pattern matches are specified by one of the three methods—`search`, `replace`, or `match`—of the `String` object. The regular expressions, or patterns, comprise special characters, normal characters, character classes, and operators. Patterns are delimited with slashes. Character classes are delimited with brackets. If a circumflex appears at the left end of a character class, it inverts the meaning of the characters in the class. Several of the most common character classes are predefined. Subpatterns can be followed by numeric or symbolic quantifiers. Patterns can be anchored at the left or right end of the string against which the pattern is being matched. The `search` method searches its object string for the pattern given as its parameter. The `replace` method replaces matches in its object string with its second parameter. The `match` method searches its object string for the given pattern and returns an array of all matches.

JavaScript syntax error messages are produced by both IE9 and FX3. IE9 and FX3 have JavaScript debuggers available, although with FX3 it must be downloaded and installed.

Review Questions

4.1   Describe briefly three major differences between Java and JavaScript.

4.2   Describe briefly three major uses of JavaScript on the client side.

4.3   Describe briefly the basic process of event-driven computation.

4.4   What are the two categories of properties in JavaScript?

4.5   Why does JavaScript have two categories of data variables, namely, primitives and objects?

4.6   Describe the two ways to embed a JavaScript script in an HTML document.

4.7   What are the two forms of JavaScript comments?

4.8   Why are JavaScript scripts sometimes hidden in HTML documents by putting them into HTML comments?

4.9   What are the five primitive data types in JavaScript?

4.10 Do single-quoted string literals have any characteristics different from those of double-quoted string literals?

4.11 In what circumstances would a variable have the value `undefined`?

4.12 If the value `undefined` is used as a Boolean expression, is it interpreted as `true` or `false`?

4.13 What purpose do rules of operator precedence serve in a programming language?

4.14 What purpose do rules of operator associativity serve in a programming language?

4.15 Describe the purpose and characteristics of `NaN`.

4.16 Why is `parseInt` not used more often?

4.17 What value does `typeof` return for an object operand?

4.18 What is the usual end-of-line punctuation for the string operand passed to `document.write`?

4.19 What is the usual end-of-line punctuation for the string operand passed to `alert`?

4.20 Describe the operation of the `prompt` method.

4.21 What is a control construct?

4.22 What are the three possible forms of control expressions in JavaScript?

4.23 What is the difference between `==` and `===`?

4.24 What does short-circuit evaluation of an expression mean?

4.25 What is the semantics of a `break` statement?

4.26 What is the difference between a `while` statement and a `do-while` statement?

4.27 When is a JavaScript constructor called?

4.28 What is the difference between a constructor in Java and one in JavaScript?

4.29 What are the properties of an object created with a `new` operator and the `Object` constructor?

4.30 Describe the two ways the properties of an object can be referenced.

4.31 How is a new property of an object created?

4.32 Describe the semantics of the `for-in` statement.

4.33 Describe the two ways an `Array` object can be created.

4.34 What is the relationship between the value of the `length` property of an `Array` object and the actual number of existing elements in the object?

4.35 Describe the semantics of the `join` method of `Array`.

4.36 Describe the semantics of the `slice` method when it is given just one parameter.

4.37 What is the form of a nested array literal?

4.38 What value is returned by a function that contains no `return` statement?

4.39 Define the scope of a variable in a JavaScript script embedded in an HTML document when the variable is not declared in a function.

4.40 Is it possible to reference global variables in a JavaScript function?

4.41 What is the advantage of using local variables in functions?

4.42 What parameter-passing method does JavaScript use?

4.43 Does JavaScript check the types of actual parameters against the types of their corresponding formal parameters?

4.44 How can a function access actual parameter values for those actual parameters that do not correspond to any formal parameter?

4.45 What is one way in which primitive variables can be passed by reference to a function?

4.46 In JavaScript, what exactly does a constructor do?

4.47 What is a character class in a pattern?

4.48 What are the predefined character classes, and what do they mean?

4.49   What are the symbolic quantifiers, and what do they mean?

4.50   Describe the two end-of-line anchors.

4.51   What does the `i` pattern modifier do?

4.52   What exactly does the `String` method `replace` do?

4.53   What exactly does the `String` method `match` do?

Exercises

Write, test, and debug (if necessary) JavaScript scripts for the problems that follow. When required to write a function, you must include a script to test the function with at least two different data sets. In all cases, for testing, you must write an HTML file that references the JavaScript file.

4.1   *Output*: A table of the numbers from 5 to 15 and their squares and cubes, using `alert`.

4.2   *Output*: The first 20 Fibonacci numbers, which are defined as in the sequence

$$1, 1, 2, 3, \ldots$$

where each number in the sequence after the second is the sum of the two previous numbers. You must use `document.write` to produce the output.

4.3   *Input*: Three numbers, using `prompt` to get each.

Output: The largest of the three input numbers.

Hint: Use the predefined function `Math.max`.

4.4   Modify the script of Exercise 4.2 to use `prompt` to input a number n that is the number of the Fibonacci number required as output.

4.5   *Input*: A text string, using `prompt`.

Output: Either `"Valid name"` or `"Invalid name"`, depending on whether the input names fit the required format, which is

```
Last name, first name, middle initial
```

where neither of the names can have more than 15 characters.

4.6   *Input*: A line of text, using `prompt`.

Output: The words of the input text, in alphabetical order.

4.7   Modify the script of Exercise 4.6 to get a second input from the user, which is either `"ascending"` or `"descending"`. Use this input to determine how to sort the input words.

4.8 *Function*: `no_zeros`

Parameter: An array of numbers.

Result: The given array must be modified to remove all zero values.

Returns: `true` if the given array included zero values; `false` otherwise.

4.9 *Function*: `e_names`

Parameter: An array of names, represented as strings.

Returns: The number of names in the given array that end in either `"ie"` or `"y"`.

4.10 *Function*: `first_vowel`

Parameter: A string.

Returns: The position in the string of the leftmost vowel.

4.11 *Function*: `counter`

Parameter: An array of numbers.

Returns: The numbers of negative elements, zeros, and values greater than zero in the given array.

Note: You must use a `switch` statement in the function.

4.12 *Function*: `tst_name`

Parameter: A string.

Returns: `true` if the given string has the form

```
string1, string2 letter
```

where both strings must be all lowercase letters except for the first letter and `letter` must be uppercase; `false` otherwise.

4.13 *Function*: `row_averages`

Parameter: An array of arrays of numbers.

Returns: An array of the averages of each of the rows of the given matrix.

4.14 *Function*: `reverser`

Parameter: A number.

Returns: The number with its digits in reverse order.

JavaScript and HTML Documents

Client-side JavaScript does not include language constructs that are not in core JavaScript. Rather, it defines the collection of objects, methods, and properties that allow scripts to interact with HTML documents on the browser. This chapter describes some of these features and illustrates their use with examples.

The chapter begins with a description of the execution environment of client-side JavaScript: the object hierarchy that corresponds to the structure of documents. Then it gives a brief overview of the Document Object Model (DOM), noting that you need not know the details of this model to be able to use client-side JavaScript. Next, the techniques for accessing HTML document elements in JavaScript are discussed. The fundamental concepts of events and event handling are then introduced, using the DOM 0 event model. Although the event-driven model of computation is not a new idea in programming, it has become more important to programmers with the advent of Web programming. Next, the chapter describes the relationships among event objects, HTML tag attributes, and tags, primarily by means of two tables.

Applications of basic event handling are introduced through a sequence of complete HTML-JavaScript examples. The first of these illustrates handling the `load` event from a body element. The next two examples demonstrate the use of the `click` event created when radio buttons are pressed. This discussion is followed by an example that uses the `blur` event to compare passwords that are input twice. The next example demonstrates the use of the `change` event to validate the format of input to a text box. The last example shows the use of the `blur` event to prevent user changes to the values of text box elements.

Next, the event model of DOM 2 is discussed, using a revision of an earlier example to illustrate the new features of this model. The chapter then introduces the use of the `navigator` object to determine which browser is being used. Finally, a few of the methods and properties used to traverse and modify DOM structures are briefly introduced.

Nearly all of the JavaScript in the examples in this chapter is in separate files. Therefore, each of the examples consists of an HTML document and one or two JavaScript files.

5.1 The JavaScript Execution Environment

A browser displays an HTML document in a window on the screen of the client. The JavaScript `Window` object represents the window that displays the document.

All JavaScript variables are properties of some object. The properties of the `Window` object are visible to all JavaScript scripts that appear either implicitly or explicitly in the window's HTML document, so they include all of the global variables. When a global variable is created in a client-side script, it is created as a new property of the `Window` object, which provides the largest enclosing referencing environment for JavaScript scripts.

There can be more than one `Window` object. In this book, however, we deal only with scripts with a single `Window` object.

The JavaScript `Document` object represents the displayed HTML document. Every `Window` object has a property named `document`, which is a reference to the `Document` object that the window displays. The `Document` object is used more often than any other object in client-side JavaScript. Its `write` method was used extensively in Chapter 4.

Every `Document` object has a `forms` array, each element of which represents a form in the document. Each `forms` array element has an `elements` array as a property, which contains the objects that represent the HTML form elements, such as buttons and menus. The JavaScript objects associated with the elements in a document can be addressed in a script in several ways, discussed in Section 5.3.

`Document` objects also have property arrays for anchors, links, images, and applets. There are many other objects in the object hierarchy below a `Window` object, but in this chapter we are interested primarily in documents, forms, and form elements.

5.2 The Document Object Model

The Document Object Model (DOM) has been under development by the W3C since the mid-1990s. DOM Level 3 (usually referred to as DOM 3) is the current approved version. The original motivation for the standard DOM was to provide a specification that would allow Java programs and JavaScript scripts that deal with HTML documents to be portable among various browsers.

Although the W3C never produced such a specification, DOM 0 is the name often applied to describe the document model used by the early browsers that supported JavaScript. Specifically, DOM 0 is the version of the document model implemented in the Netscape 3.0 and Internet Explorer 3.0 browsers. The DOM 0 model was partially documented in the HTML 4 specification.

DOM 1, the first W3C DOM specification, issued in October 1998, focused on the HTML and XML (see Chapter 7) document model. DOM 2, issued in November 2000, specified a style-sheet object model and defined how style information attached to a document can be manipulated. It also included document traversals and provided a complete and comprehensive event model. DOM 3, issued in 2004, dealt with content models for XML (DTDs and schemas), document validation, and document views and formatting, as well as key events and event groups. As stated previously, DOM 0 is supported by all JavaScript-enabled browsers. DOM 2 is nearly completely supported by FX3, but IE9 leaves some parts unimplemented. No part of DOM 3 is covered in this book.

The DOM is an application programming interface (API) that defines an interface between HTML documents and application programs. It is an abstract model because it must apply to a variety of application programming languages. Each language that interfaces with the DOM must define a binding to that interface. The actual DOM specification consists of a collection of interfaces, including one for each document tree node type. These interfaces are similar to Java interfaces and C++ abstract classes. They define the objects, methods, and properties that are associated with their respective node types. With the DOM, users can write code in programming languages to create documents, move around in their structures, and change, add, or delete elements and their content.

Documents in the DOM have a treelike structure, but there can be more than one tree in a document (although that is unusual). Because the DOM is an abstract interface, it does not dictate that documents be implemented as trees or collections of trees. Therefore, in an implementation, the relationships among the elements of a document could be represented in any number of different ways.

A language that is designed to support the DOM must have a binding to the DOM constructs. This binding amounts to a correspondence between constructs in the language and elements in the DOM. In the JavaScript binding to the DOM, the elements of a document are objects, with both data and operations. The data are called *properties*, and the operations are, naturally, called *methods*. For example, the following HTML element would be represented as an object with two properties, type and name, with the values "text" and "address", respectively:

```
<input type = "text"  name = "address">
```

In most cases, the property names in JavaScript are the same as their corresponding attribute names in HTML.

IE8+, FX3, and C10+ provide a way of viewing the DOM structure of a displayed document. After displaying a document with IE9, select *Tools/Developer Tools*. The lower-left area of the resulting display will show an elided version of the DOM structure.[1] By clicking all of the eliding icons (square boxes that have plus signs in them), the whole structure will be displayed. Consider the following simple document:

```html
<!DOCTYPE html>
<!-- table2.html
     A simple table to demonstrate DOM trees
     -->
<html lang = "en">
  <head>
    <title> A simple table </title>
    <meta charset = "utf-8" />
  </head>
  <body>
    <table>
      <tr>
        <th> </th>
        <th> Apple </th>
        <th> Orange </th>
      </tr>
      <tr>
        <th> Breakfast </th>
        <td> 0 </td>
        <td> 1 </td>
      </tr>
    </table>
  </body>
</html>
```

The display of this document and its complete DOM structure are shown in Figure 5.1.

---

1. Eliding abstracts away parts of the structure. An elided part can be restored to the display.

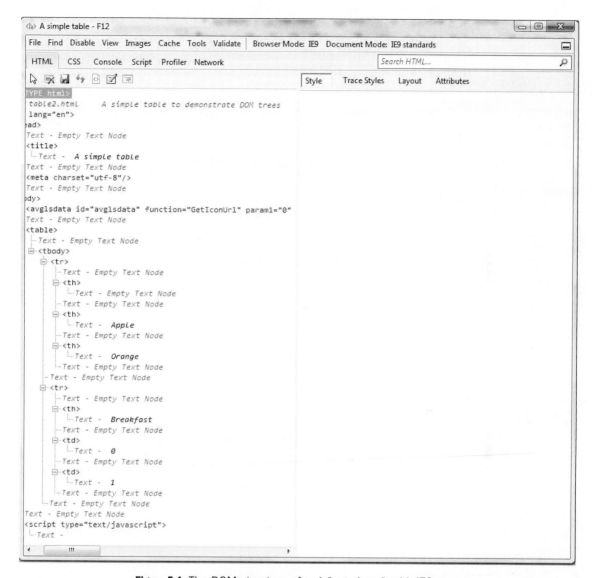

Figure 5.1 The DOM structure of `table2.html` with IE9

The IE9 Developer Tools are helpful for developing and analyzing HTML documents. However, our interest here is in the DOM structure it produces.

To be able to display the DOM structure of a document with FX3, an add-on must be downloaded. The source of the download is `https://addons .mozilla.org/en-US/firefox/addon/6622`. After the DOM Inspector add-on has been downloaded and installed, the DOM of a document can be displayed by selecting *Tools/DOM Inspector*. If this selection is made while a document is being displayed, FX3 opens a new window that is similar to the IE9 window for DOM viewing. As with IE9, the elements are initially elided. The upper-right area is for displaying information about the DOM structure. As was the case with the IE9 Developer Tools, the DOM Inspector of FX3 has far more uses than simply viewing the DOM structure of a document but they are not discussed here. The FX3 DOM Inspector display of `table2.html` is shown in Figure 5.2.

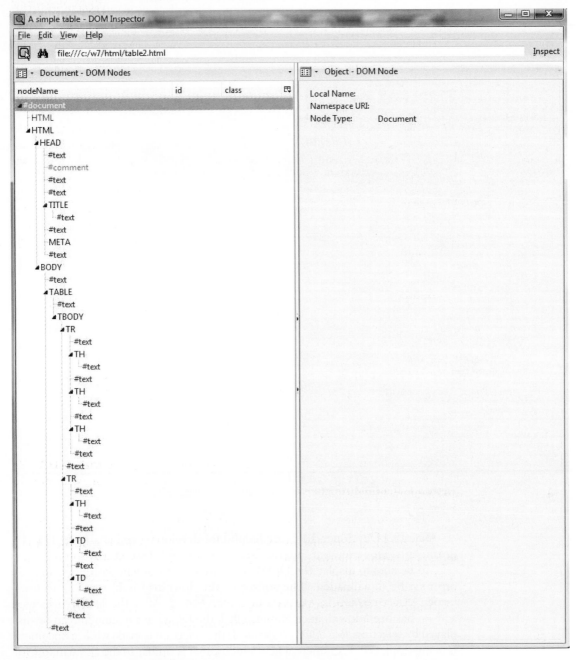

Figure 5.2 The DOM Inspector display of `table2.html` with FX3

With Chrome, to get the DOM one selects the wrench icon, *Tools*, and *Developer Tools*.

Anything resembling a complete explanation of the DOM is far beyond the scope of this book. Our introduction to the DOM here is intended only to provide the basis for our discussion of how JavaScript can be used to respond to document-related events and to modify element attributes, styles, and content dynamically.[2] A detailed description of the DOM can be found at the W3C Web site.

5.3 Element Access in JavaScript

The elements of an HTML document have corresponding objects that are visible to an embedded JavaScript script. The addresses of these objects are required, both by the event handling discussed in this chapter and by the code for making dynamic changes to documents, which is discussed in Chapter 6.

There are several ways the object associated with a form element can be addressed in JavaScript. The original (DOM 0) way is to use the `forms` and `elements` arrays of the `Document` object, which is referenced through the `document` property of the Window object. As an example, consider the following document:

```
<html lang = "en">
  <head>
    <title> Access to form elements </title>
    <meta charset = "utf-8" />
  </head>
  <body>
    <form action = "">
      <input type = "button"  name = "turnItOn" />
    </form>
  </body>
</html>
```

We refer to the address of the JavaScript object that is associated with an HTML element as the *DOM address* of the element. The DOM address of the button in this example, using the `forms` and `elements` arrays, is as follows:

```
var dom = document.forms[0].elements[0];
```

The problem with this approach to element addressing is that the DOM address is defined by the position of elements in the document, which could change. For example, if a new button were added before the `turnItOn` button in the form, the DOM address shown would be wrong.

Another approach to DOM addressing is to use element names. For this, the element and its enclosing elements, up to but not including the body

---

2. We will discuss modifications of style properties in Chapter 6.

element, must include `name` attributes. For example, consider the following document:

```
<html lang = "en">
  <head>
    <title> Access to form elements </title>
    <meta charset = "utf-8" />
  </head>
  <body>
    <form name = "myForm"  action = "">
      <input type = "button"  name = "turnItOn" />
    </form>
  </body>
</html>
```

Using the `name` attributes, the button's DOM address is as follows:

```
var dom = document.myForm.turnItOn;
```

One minor drawback of this approach is that the XHTML 1.1 standard does not allow the `name` attribute in the form element, even though the attribute is now valid for form elements. This is a validation problem, but it causes no difficulty for browsers. Furthermore, the `name` attribute is valid in form tags in HTML5.

Yet another approach to element addressing is to use the JavaScript method `getElementById`, which is defined in DOM 1. Because an element's identifier (`id`) is unique in the document, this approach works, regardless of how deeply the element is nested in other elements in the document. For example, if the `id` attribute of our button is set to `"turnItOn"`, the following could be used to get the DOM address of that button element:

```
var dom = document.getElementById("turnItOn");
```

The parameter of `getElementById` can be any expression that evaluates to a string. In many cases, it is a variable.

Because ids are useful for DOM addressing and names are required for form-processing code, form elements often have both ids and names, set to the same value.

Buttons in a group of checkboxes often share the same name. The buttons in a radio button group *always* have the same name. In these cases, the names of the individual buttons obviously cannot be used in their DOM addresses. Of course, each radio button and checkbox can have an id, which would make them easy to address by using `getElementById`. However, this approach does not provide a convenient way to search a group of radio buttons or checkboxes to determine which is checked.

An alternative to both names and ids is provided by the implicit arrays associated with each checkbox and radio button group. Every such group has an array, which has the same name as the group name, that stores the DOM addresses of the individual buttons in the group. These arrays are properties of the form in which the buttons appear. To access the arrays, the DOM address of the form object must first be obtained, as in the following example:

```
<form id = "vehicleGroup">
  <input type = "checkbox"  name = "vehicles"
        value = "car" />  Car
  <input type = "checkbox"  name = "vehicles"
        value = "truck" />  Truck
  <input type = "checkbox"  name = "vehicles"
        value = "bike" />  Bike
</form>
```

The implicit array, `vehicles`, has three elements, which reference the three objects associated with the three checkbox elements in the group. This array provides a convenient way to search the list of checkboxes in a group. The `checked` property of a checkbox object is set to `true` if the button is checked. For the preceding sample checkbox group, the following code counts the number of checkboxes that were checked:

```
var numChecked = 0;
var dom = document.getElementById("vehicleGroup");
for (index = 0; index < dom.vehicles.length; index++)
  if (dom.vehicles[index].checked)
    numChecked++;
```

Radio buttons can be addressed and handled exactly as are the checkboxes in the foregoing code.

5.4   Events and Event Handling

The HTML 4.0 standard provided the first specification of an event model for markup documents. This model is sometimes referred to as the DOM 0 event model. Although the DOM 0 event model is limited in scope, it is the only event model supported by all browsers that support JavaScript. A complete and comprehensive event model was specified by DOM 2. The DOM 2 model is supported by the FX3 and Chrome browsers. However, although IE9 supports it, earlier versions of IE do not. Our discussion of events and event handling is divided into two parts, one for the DOM 0 model and one for the DOM 2 model.

5.4.1   Basic Concepts of Event Handling

One important use of JavaScript for Web programming is to detect certain activities of the browser and the browser user and provide computation when those activities occur. These computations are specified with a special form of programming called *event-driven programming*. In conventional (non-event-driven) programming, the code itself specifies the order in which it is executed, although the order is usually affected by the program's input data. In event-driven programming, parts of the program are executed at completely unpredictable times, often triggered by user interactions with the program that is executing.

An *event* is a notification that something specific has occurred, either in the browser, such as the completion of the loading of a document, or a browser user action, such as a mouse click on a form button. Strictly speaking, an event is an object that is implicitly created by the browser and the JavaScript system in response to something having happened.

An *event handler* is a script that is implicitly executed in response to the appearance of an event. Event handlers enable a Web document to be responsive to browser and user activities. One of the most common uses of event handlers is to check for simple errors and omissions in user input to the elements of a form, either when they are changed or when the form is submitted. This kind of checking saves the time of sending incorrect form data to the server.

If you are familiar with the exceptions and exception-handling capabilities of a programming language such as C++ or Java, you should see the close relationship between events and exceptions. Events and exceptions occur at unpredictable times, and both often require some special program actions.

Because events are JavaScript objects, their names are case sensitive. The names of all event objects have only lowercase letters. For example, `click` is an event, but `Click` is not.

Events are created by activities associated with specific HTML elements. For example, the `click` event can be caused by the browser user clicking a radio button or the link of an anchor tag, among other things. Thus, an event's name is only part of the information pertinent to handling the event. In most cases, the specific HTML element that caused the event is also needed.

The process of connecting an event handler to an event is called *registration*. There are two distinct approaches to event handler registration, one that assigns tag attributes and one that assigns handler addresses to object properties. These are further discussed in Sections 5.5 and 5.6.

The `write` method of `document` should never be used in an event handler. Remember that a document is displayed as its markup is parsed by the browser. Events usually occur after the whole document is displayed. If `write` appears in an event handler, the content produced by it might be placed over the top of the currently displayed document.

The remainder of this section and Sections 5.5 through 5.7 describe the DOM 0 event model and some of its uses.

5.4.2   Events, Attributes, and Tags

HTML4 defined a collection of events that browsers implement and with which JavaScript can deal. These events are associated with HTML tag attributes, which can be used to connect the events to handlers. The attributes have names that are closely related to their associated events. Table 5.1 lists the most commonly used events and their associated tag attributes.

Table 5.1 Events and their tag attributes

Events	Tag Attribute
`blur`	`onblur`
`change`	`onchange`
`click`	`onclick`
`dblclick`	`ondblclick`
`focus`	`onfocus`
`keydown`	`onkeydown`
`keypress`	`onkeypress`
`keyup`	`onkeyup`
`load`	`onload`
`mousedown`	`onmousedown`
`mousemove`	`onmousemove`
`mouseout`	`onmouseout`
`mouseover`	`onmouseover`
`mouseup`	`onmouseup`
`reset`	`onreset`
`select`	`onselect`
`submit`	`onsubmit`
`unload`	`onunload`

In many cases, the same attribute can appear in several different tags. The circumstances under which an event is created are related to a tag and an attribute, and they can be different for the same attribute when it appears in different tags.

An HTML element is said to *get focus* when the user puts the mouse cursor over it and clicks the left mouse button. An element can also get focus when the user tabs to the element. When a text element has focus, any keyboard input goes into that element. Obviously, only one text element can have focus at one time. An element becomes blurred when the user moves the cursor away from the element and clicks the left mouse button or when the user tabs away from the element. An element obviously becomes blurred when another element gets focus. Several nontext elements can also have focus, but the condition is less useful in those cases.

Table 5.2 shows (1) the most commonly used attributes related to events, (2) tags that can include the attributes, and (3) the circumstances under which the associated events are created. Only a few of the situations shown in the table are discussed in this chapter.

Table 5.2 Event attributes and their tags

Attributes	Tag	Description
onblur	`<a>`	The link loses focus.
	`<button>`	The button loses focus.
	`<input>`	The input element loses focus.
	`<textarea>`	The text area loses focus.
	`<select>`	The selection element loses focus.
onchange	`<input>`	The input element is changed and loses focus.
	`<textarea>`	The text area is changed and loses focus.
	`<select>`	The selection element is changed and loses focus.
onclick	`<a>`	The user clicks the link.
	`<input>`	The input element is clicked.
ondblclick	Most elements	The user double-clicks the left mouse button.
onfocus	`<a>`	The link acquires focus.
	`<input>`	The input element acquires focus.
	`<textarea>`	A text area acquires focus.
	`<select>`	A selection element acquires focus.
onkeydown	`<body>`, form elements	A key is pressed.
onkeypress	`<body>`, form elements	A key is pressed and released.
onkeyup	`<body>`, form elements	A key is released.
onload	`<body>`	The document is finished loading.
onmousedown	Most elements	The user clicks the left mouse button.
onmousemove	Most elements	The user moves the mouse cursor within the element.
onmouseout	Most elements	The mouse cursor is moved away from being over the element.

Table 5.2 Event attributes and their tags   (*continued*)

Attributes	Tag	Description
onmouseover	Most elements	The mouse cursor is moved over the element.
onmouseup	Most elements	The left mouse button is unclicked.
onreset	<form>	The reset button is clicked.
onselect	<input>	Any text in the content of the element is selected.
	<textarea>	Any text in the content of the element is selected.
onsubmit	<form>	The *Submit* button is pressed.
onunload	<body>	The user exits the document.

As mentioned previously, there are two ways to register an event handler in the DOM 0 event model. One of these is by assigning the event handler script to an event tag attribute, as in the following example:

```
<input type = "button" id = "myButton"
        onclick = "alert('You clicked my button!');" />
```

In many cases, the handler consists of more than a single statement. In these cases, often a function is used and the literal string value of the attribute is the call to the function. Consider the following example of a button element:

```
<input type = "button" id = "myButton"
        onclick = "myButtonHandler();" />
```

An event handler function could also be registered by assigning its name to the associated event property on the button object, as in the following example:

```
document.getElementById("myButton").onclick =
                                    myButtonHandler;
```

This statement must follow both the handler function and the form element so that JavaScript has seen both before assigning the property. Notice that only the name of the handler function is assigned to the property—it is neither a string nor a call to the function.

5.5 Handling Events from Body Elements

The events most often created by body elements are `load` and `unload`. As our first example of event handling, we consider the simple case of producing an alert message when the body of the document has been loaded. In this case, we use the `onload` attribute of <body> to specify the event handler:

```
<!DOCTYPE html>
<!-- load.html
     A document for load.js
     -->
<html lang = "en">
  <head>
    <title> load.html </title>
    <meta charset = "utf-8" />
    <script type = "text/javascript"  src = "load.js" >
    </script>
  </head>
  <body onload="load_greeting();">
    <p />
  </body>
</html>
```

```
// load.js
//   An example to illustrate the load event

// The onload event handler
function load_greeting () {
  alert("You are visiting the home page of \n" +
        "Pete's Pickled Peppers \n" + "WELCOME!!!");
}
```

Figure 5.3 shows a browser display of load.html.

Figure 5.3 Display of load.html

The `unload` event is probably more useful than the `load` event. It is used to do some cleanup before a document is unloaded, as when the browser user goes on to some new document. For example, if the document opened a second browser window, that window could be closed by an `unload` event handler.

5.6 Handling Events from Button Elements

Buttons in a Web document provide an effective way to collect simple input from the browser user. The most commonly used event created by button actions is `click`. Section 5.4.2 includes an example of a plain button.

The next example presents a set of radio buttons that enables the user to select information about a specific airplane. The `click` event is used in this example to trigger a call to `alert`, which presents a brief description of the selected airplane. The calls to the event handlers send the value of the pressed radio button to the handler. This is another way the handler can determine which of a group of radio buttons is pressed. Here is the document and the JavaScript file:

```
<!DOCTYPE html>
<!-- radio_click.hmtl
     A document for radio_click.js
     Creates four radio buttons that call the planeChoice
     event handler to display descriptions
     -->
<html lang = "en">
  <head>
    <title> radio_click.html </title>
    <meta charset = "utf-8" />
    <script type = "text/javascript"  src = "radio_click.js" >
    </script>
  </head>
  <body>
    <h4> Cessna single-engine airplane descriptions </h4>
    <form id = "myForm"  action = "">
      <p>
      <label> <input type = "radio"  name = "planeButton"
                     value = "152"
                     onclick = "planeChoice(152)" />
      Model 152 </label>
      <br />
      <label> <input type = "radio"  name = "planeButton"
                     value = "172"
                     onclick = "planeChoice(172)" />
      Model 172 (Skyhawk) </label>
```

```
            <br />
            <label> <input type = "radio"  name = "planeButton"
                           value = "182"
                           onclick = "planeChoice(182)" />
            Model 182 (Skylane) </label>
            <br />
            <label> <input type = "radio"  name = "planeButton"
                           value = "210"
                           onclick = "planeChoice(210)" />
            Model 210 (Centurian) </label>
          </p>
        </form>
      </body>
    </html>
```

```
// radio_click.js
//   An example of the use of the click event with radio buttons,
//   registering the event handler by assignment to the button
//   attributes


// The event handler for a radio button collection
function planeChoice (plane) {


// Produce an alert message about the chosen airplane
  switch (plane) {
    case 152:
      alert("A small two-place airplane for flight training");
      break;
    case 172:
      alert("The smaller of two four-place airplanes");
      break;
    case 182:
      alert("The larger of two four-place airplanes");
      break;
    case 210:
      alert("A six-place high-performance airplane");
      break;
    default:
      alert("Error in JavaScript function planeChoice");
      break;
  }
}
```

Figure 5.4 shows a browser display of `radio_click.html`. Figure 5.5 shows the `alert` window that results from choosing the Model 182 radio button in `radio_click.html`.

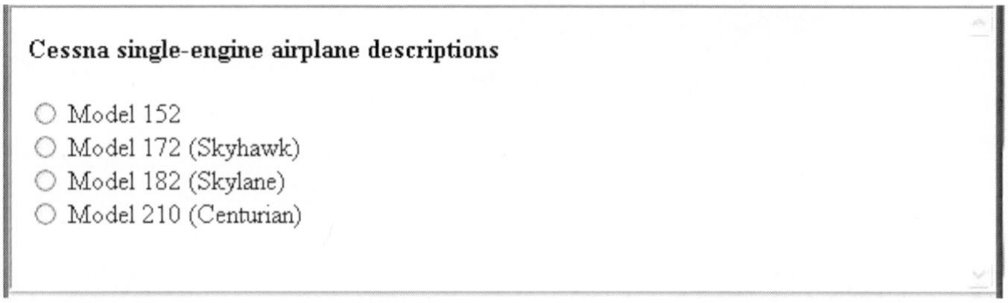

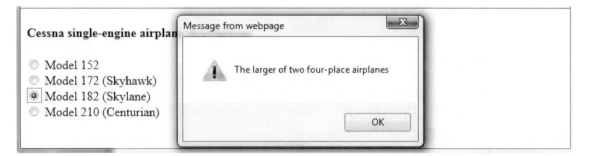

Figure 5.4 Display of `radio_click.html`

Figure 5.5 The result of pressing the Model 182 button in `radio_click.html`

In `radio_click.html`, the event handler is registered by assigning its call to the `onclick` attribute of the radio buttons. The specific button that was clicked is identified by the parameter sent in the handler call in the button element. An alternative to using the parameter would be to include code in the handler to determine which radio button was pressed.

The next example, `radio_click2.html`, whose purpose is the same as that of `radio_click.html`, registers the event handler by assigning the name of the handler to the event properties of the radio button objects. For example, the following line of code registers the handler on the first radio button:

```
document.getElementById("myForm").elements[0].onclick =

        planeChoice;
```

Recall that this statement must follow both the handler function and the HTML form specification so that JavaScript sees both before assigning the property. The following example uses three files—one for the HTML, one for the script for the event handlers, and one for the script to register the handlers:

```html
<!DOCTYPE html>
<!-- radio_click2.hmtl
     A document for radio_click2.js
     -->
<html lang = "en">
  <head>
    <title> radio_click2.html </title>
    <meta charset = "utf-8" />
    <script type = "text/javascript"  src = "radio_click2.js" >
    </script>

  </head>
  <body>
    <h4> Cessna single-engine airplane descriptions </h4>
    <form id = "myForm"  action = "">
      <p>
        <label> <input type = "radio"  name = "planeButton"
                    value = "152" />
        Model 152 </label>
        <br />
        <label> <input type = "radio"  name = "planeButton"
                    value = "172" />
        Model 172 (Skyhawk) </label>
        <br />
        <label> <input type = "radio"  name = "planeButton"
                    value = "182" />
        Model 182 (Skylane) </label>
        <br />
        <label> <input type = "radio"  name = "planeButton"
                    value = "210" />
        Model 210 (Centurian) </label>
      </p>
    </form>

<!-- Script for registering the event handlers -->
    <script type = "text/javascript"  src = "radio_click2r.js" >
    </script>

  </body>
</html>
```

```js
// radio_click2.js
//   An example of the use of the click event with radio buttons,
//   registering the event handler by assigning an event property


// The event handler for a radio button collection
function planeChoice (plane) {


// Put the DOM address of the elements array in a local variable
  var dom = document.getElementById("myForm");


// Determine which button was pressed
  for (var index = 0; index < dom.planeButton.length;
       index++) {
    if (dom.planeButton[index].checked) {
      plane = dom.planeButton[index].value;
      break;
    }
  }


// Produce an alert message about the chosen airplane
  switch (plane) {
    case "152":
      alert("A small two-place airplane for flight training");
      break;
    case "172":
      alert("The smaller of two four-place airplanes");
      break;
    case "182":
      alert("The larger of two four-place airplanes");
      break;
    case "210":
      alert("A six-place high-performance airplane");
      break;
    default:
      alert("Error in JavaScript function planeChoice");
      break;
  }
}
```

[handwritten margin note: event handlers registered outside of HTML]

```
// radio_click2r.js
//   The event registering code for radio_click2
var dom = document.getElementById("myForm");
dom.elements[0].onclick = planeChoice;
dom.elements[1].onclick = planeChoice;
dom.elements[2].onclick = planeChoice;
dom.elements[3].onclick = planeChoice;
```

[handwritten margin note: Calls the planechoice function]

In `radio_click2r.js` (the JavaScript file that registers the event handlers), the form elements (radio buttons in this case) are addressed as elements of the `elements` array. An alternative would be to give each radio button an `id` attribute and use the id to register the handler. For example, the first radio button could be defined as follows:

```
<input type = "radio"  name = "planeButton" value = "152"
    id = "152" />
```

Then the event handler registration would be as follows:

```
document.getElementById("152").onclick = planeChoice;
document.getElementById("172").onclick = planeChoice;
document.getElementById("182").onclick = planeChoice;
document.getElementById("210").onclick = planeChoice;
```

There is no way to specify parameters on the handler function when it is registered by assigning its name to the event property. Therefore, event handlers that are registered this way cannot use parameters—clearly a disadvantage of this approach. In `radio_click2.js`, the handler includes a loop to determine which radio button created the `click` event.

There are two advantages to registering handlers as properties over registering them in HTML attributes. First, it is good to keep HTML and JavaScript separated in the document. This allows a kind of modularization of HTML documents, resulting in a cleaner design that will be easier to maintain. Second, having the handler function registered as the value of a property allows for the possibility of changing the function during use. This could be done by registering a different handler for the event when some other event occurred—an approach that would be impossible if the handler were registered with HTML.

5.7 Handling Events from Text Box and Password Elements

Text boxes and passwords can create four different events: `blur`, `focus`, `change`, and `select`.

5.7.1   The Focus Event

Suppose JavaScript is used to compute the total cost of an order and display it to the customer before the order is submitted to the server for processing. An unscrupulous user may be tempted to change the total cost before submission, thinking that somehow an altered (and lower) price would not be noticed at the server end. Such a change to a text box can be prevented by an event handler that blurs the text box every time the user attempts to put it in focus. Blur can be forced on an element with the `blur` method. The following example illustrates this method:

```html
<!DOCTYPE html>
<!-- nochange.html
     A document for nochange.js
     -->
<html lang = "en">
  <head>
    <title> nochange.html </title>
    <meta charset = "utf-8" />
    <script type = "text/javascript"  src = "nochange.js" >
    </script>
    <style type = "text/css">
      td, th, table {border: thin solid black}
    </style>


  </head>
  <body>
    <form action = "">
      <h3> Coffee Order Form </h3>

<!-- A bordered table for item orders -->
      <table>

<!-- First, the column headings -->
        <tr>
          <th> Product Name </th>
          <th> Price </th>
          <th> Quantity </th>
        </tr>

<!-- Now, the table data entries -->
        <tr>
          <th> French Vanilla (1 lb.) </th>
          <td> $3.49 </td>
```

```
            <td> <input type = "text"  id = "french"
                       size ="2" /> </td>
        </tr>
        <tr>
          <th> Hazlenut Cream (1 lb.) </th>
          <td> $3.95 </td>
          <td> <input type = "text"  id = "hazlenut"
                size = "2" /> </td>
        </tr>
        <tr>
          <th> Colombian (1 lb.) </th>
          <td> $4.59 </td>
          <td> <input type = "text"  id = "colombian"
                size = "2" /></td>
        </tr>
      </table>


<!-- Button for precomputation of the total cost -->
      <p>
        <input type = "button"  value = "Total Cost"
              onclick = "computeCost();" />
        <input type = "text"  size = "5"  id = "cost"
              onfocus = "this.blur();" />
      </p>


<!-- The submit and reset buttons -->
      <p>
        <input type = "submit"  value = "Submit Order" />
        <input type = "reset"  value = "Clear Order Form" />
      </p>
    </form>
  </body>
</html>
```

```
// nochange.js
//   This script illustrates using the focus event
//   to prevent the user from changing a text field


// The event handler function to compute the cost
function computeCost() {
  var french = document.getElementById("french").value;
```

```
    var hazlenut = document.getElementById("hazlenut").value;
    var colombian = document.getElementById("colombian").value;


// Compute the cost
  document.getElementById("cost").value =
  totalCost = french * 3.49 + hazlenut * 3.95 +
          colombian * 4.59;
} //* end of computeCost
```

In this example, the button labeled `Total Cost` allows the user to compute the total cost of the order before submitting the form. The event handler for this button gets the values (input quantities) of the three kinds of coffee and computes the total cost. The cost value is placed in the text box's value property, and it is then displayed for the user. Whenever this text box acquires focus, it is forced to blur with the `blur` method, which prevents the user from changing the value.

5.7.2 Validating Form Input

One of the common uses of JavaScript is to check the values provided in forms by users to determine whether the values are sensible. Without client-side checks of such values, form values must be transmitted to the server for processing in the absence of any prior reality checks. The program or script on the server that processes the form data checks for invalid input data. When invalid data is found, the server must transmit that information back to the browser, which then must ask the user to resubmit corrected input. It is obviously more efficient to perform input data checks and carry on the user dialog concerning invalid input data entirely on the client. This approach shifts the task from the usually busy server to the client, which in most cases is only lightly used. It also results in less network traffic, because it avoids sending bad data to the server, only to have it returned without being processed. Furthermore, detecting incorrect form data on the client produces quicker responses to users. Validity checking of form data is often performed on the server as well, in part because client-side validity checking can be subverted by an unscrupulous user. Also, for some data, validity is crucial. For example, if the data is to be put in a database, invalid data could corrupt the database. Even though form data is checked on the server, any errors that can be detected and corrected on the client save server and network time.

When a user fills in a form input element incorrectly and a JavaScript event handler function detects the error, the function should produce an `alert` message indicating the error to the user and inform the user of the correct format for the input. Next, it would be good to put the element in focus, which would position the cursor in the element. This could be done with the `focus` method, but unfortunately, many recent versions of browsers do not implement that method in a way that it consistently operates correctly. Therefore, we will not use it.

If an event handler returns `false`, that tells the browser not to perform any default actions of the event. For example, if the event is a click on the *Submit* button, the default action is to submit the form data to the server for processing. If user input is being validated in an event handler that is called when the `sub-mit` event occurs and some of the input is incorrect, the handler should return `false` to avoid sending the bad data to the server. We use the convention that event handlers that check form data always return `false` if they detect an error and `true` otherwise.

When a form requests a password from the user and that password will be used in future sessions, the user is often asked to enter the password a second time for verification. A JavaScript function can be used to determine whether the entered passwords are the same.

The form in the next example includes the two password input elements, along with *Reset* and *Submit* buttons. The JavaScript function that checks the passwords is called either when the *Submit* button is clicked, using the `onsubmit` event to trigger the call, or when the second text box loses focus, using the `blur` event. The function performs two different tests. First, it determines whether the user typed the initial password (in the first input box) by testing the value of the element against the empty string. If no password has been typed into the first field, the function calls `alert` to produce an error message and returns `false`. The second test determines whether the two typed passwords are the same. If they are different, once again the function calls `alert` to generate an error message and returns `false`. If they are the same, it returns `true`. Following is the HTML document that creates the text boxes for the passwords, as well as the *Reset* and *Submit* buttons, and the two scripts for the event handlers and the event handler registrations for the example:

```
<!DOCTYPE html>
<!-- pswd_chk.html
     A document for pswd_chk.ps
     Creates two text boxes for passwords
     -->
<html lang = "en">
  <head>
    <title> Illustrate password checking> </title>
    <meta charset = "utf-8" />
    <script type = "text/javascript"  src = "pswd_chk.js" >
    </script>
  </head>
  <body>
    <h3> Password Input </h3>
    <form id = "myForm"  action = "" >
```

```html
          <p>

        <label> Your password
          <input type = "password" id = "initial"
                 size = "10" />
        </label>
        <br /><br />


        <label> Verify password
          <input type = "password"  id = "second"
                 size = "10" />
        </label>
        <br /><br />


        <input type = "reset"  name = "reset" />
        <input type = "submit"  name = "submit" />
        </p>
      </form>


  <!-- Script for registering the event handlers  -->
      <script type = "text/javascript"  src = "pswd_chkr.js">
      </script>


    </body>
  </html>
```

```javascript
// pswd_chk.js
//   An example of input password checking using the submit
//   event
// The event handler function for password checking
function chkPasswords() {
  var init = document.getElementById("initial");
  var sec = document.getElementById("second");
  if (init.value == "") {
    alert("You did not enter a password \n" +
          "Please enter one now");
    return false;
  }
```

```
    if (init.value != sec.value) {
      alert("The two passwords you entered are not the same \n" +
            "Please re-enter both now");
      return false;
    } else
      return true;
}
```

```
// pswd_chkr.js
//   Register the event handlers for pswd_chk.html

document.getElementById("second").onblur = chkPasswords;
document.getElementById("myForm").onsubmit = chkPasswords;
```

Figure 5.6 shows a browser display of `pswd_chk.html` after the two password elements have been input but before *Submit Query* has been clicked.

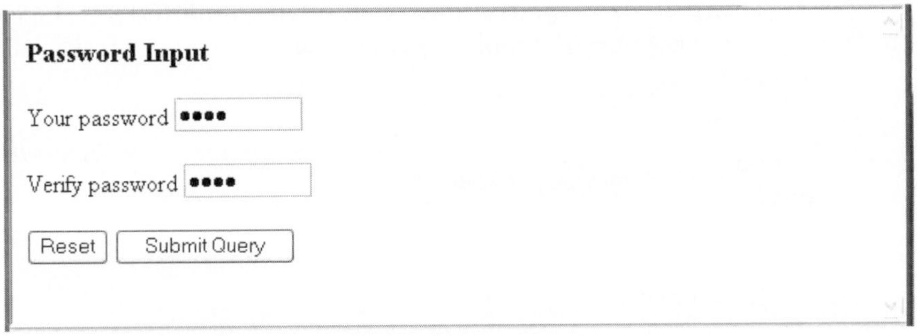

Figure 5.6 Display of `pswd_chk.html` after it has been filled out

Figure 5.7 shows a browser display that results from pressing the *Submit Query* button on `pswd_chk.html` after different passwords have been entered.

Figure 5.7 Display of `pswd_chk.html` after *Submit Query* has been clicked

We now consider an example that checks the validity of the form values for a name and phone number obtained from text boxes. Functions are used to check the form of each input when the values of the text boxes are changed—an event that is detected by the appearance of a `change` event.

In both cases, if an error is detected, an `alert` message is generated to prompt the user to fix the input. The `alert` message includes the correct format, which, for the name, is last-name, first-name, middle-initial, where the first and last names must begin with uppercase letters and have at least one lowercase letter. Both must be followed immediately by a comma and, possibly, one space. The middle initial must be uppercase and may or may not be followed by a period. There can be no characters before or after the whole name. The pattern for matching such names is as follows:

```
/^[A-Z][a-z]+, ?[A-Z][a-z]+, ?[A-Z]\.?$/
```

Note the use of the anchors ^ and $ on the ends of the pattern. This precludes any leading or trailing characters. Note also the question marks after the spaces (following the first and last names) and after the period. Recall that the question mark qualifier means zero or one of the qualified subpatterns. The period is back-slashed, so it matches only a period.

The correct format of the phone number is three digits and a dash, followed by three digits and a dash, followed by four digits. As with names, no characters can precede or follow the phone number. The pattern for phone numbers is as follows:

```
/^\d{3}-\d{3}-\d{4}$/
```

The following is the HTML document, `validator.html`, that displays the text boxes for a customer's name and phone number:

```html
<!DOCTYPE html>
<!-- validator.html
     A document for validator.js
     Creates text boxes for a name and a phone number
     -->
<html lang = "en">
  <head>
    <title> Illustrate form input validation> </title>
    <meta charset = "utf-8" />
    <script type = "text/javascript"  src = "validator.js" >
    </script>
  </head>
  <body>
    <h3> Customer Information </h3>
    <form action = "">
      <p>
        <label>
```

the natural central place for event handling is at the document or window level, so that is the direction of bubbling.

Many events cause the browser to perform some action; for example, a mouse click on a link causes the document referenced in the link to replace the current document. In some cases, we want to prevent this action from taking place. For example, if a value in a form is found to be invalid by a *Submit* button event handler, we do not want the form to be submitted to the server. In the DOM 0 event model, the action is prevented by having the handler return `false`. The DOM 2 event interface provides a method, `preventDefault`, that accomplishes the same thing. Every event object implements `preventDefault`.

5.8.2   Event Handler Registration

The DOM 0 event model uses two different ways of registering event handlers. First, the handler code can be assigned as a string literal to the event's associated attribute in the element. Second, the name of the handler function can be assigned to the property associated with the event. Handler registration in the DOM 2 event model is performed by the method `addEventListener`, which is defined in the `EventTarget` interface, which is implemented by all objects that descend from `Document`.[3]

The `addEventListener` method takes three parameters, the first of which is the name of the event as a string literal. For example, `"mouseup"` and `"submit"` would be legitimate first parameters. The second parameter is the handler function, which could be specified as the function code itself or as the name of a function that is defined elsewhere. Note that this parameter is not a string type, so it is not quoted. The third parameter is a Boolean value that specifies whether the handler is enabled for calling during the capturing phase. If the value `true` is specified, the handler is enabled for the capturing phase. In fact, an enabled handler can be called *only* during capturing. If the value is `false`, the handler is not enabled and can be called either at the target node or on any node reached during bubbling.

When a handler is called, it is passed a single parameter, the `event` object. For example, suppose we want to register the event handler `chkName` on the text element whose `id` is `custName` for the `change` event. The following call accomplishes the task:

```
document.custName.addEventListener(
                "change", chkName, false);
```

In this case, we want the handler to be called at the target node, which is `custName` in this example, so we passed `false` as the third parameter.

Sometimes it is convenient to have a temporary event handler. This can be done by registering the handler for the time when it is to be used and then deleting that registration. The `removeEventListener` method deletes the

---

3. The name of this method includes "listener" rather than "handler" because handlers are called *listeners* in the DOM 2 specification. This is also the term used in Java for widget event handlers.

registration of an event handler. This method takes the same parameters as `addEventListener`.

With the DOM 0 event model, when an event handler is registered to a node, the handler becomes a method of the object that represents that node. This approach makes every use of `this` in the handler a reference to the target node. FX3 browsers implement event handlers for the DOM 2 model in the same way. However, this is not required by the DOM 2 model, so some other browsers may not use such an approach, making the use of `this` in a handler potentially non-portable. The safe alternative is to use the `currentTarget` property of `Event`, which will always reference the object on which the handler is being executed. If the handler is called through the object of the target node, `currentTarget` is the target node. However, if the handler is called during capturing or bubbling, `currentTarget` is the object through which the handler is called, which is not the target node object. Another property of `Event`, `target`, is a reference to the target node.

The `MouseEvent` interface inherits from the `Event` interface. It adds a collection of properties related to mouse events. The most useful of these are `clientX` and `clientY`, which have the *x*- and *y*-coordinates of the mouse cursor, relative to the upper-left corner of the client area of the browser window. The whole browser window is taken into account, so if the user has scrolled down the document, the `clientY` value is measured from the top of the document, not the top of the current display.

5.8.3   An Example of the DOM 2 Event Model

The next example is a revision of the `validator.html` document and `validator.js` script from Section 5.7, which used the DOM 0 event model. Because this version uses the DOM 2 event model, it does not work with IE8. Notice that no call to `preventDefault` appears in the document. The only event handled here is `change`, which has no default actions, so there is nothing to prevent. Here is the document and the JavaScript file:

```
<!DOCTYPE html>
<!-- validator2.html
     A document for validator2.js
     Creates text boxes for a name and a phone number
     Note: This document does not work with IE browsers before IE9
     -->
<html lang = "en">
  <head>
    <title> Illustrate form input validation with DOM 2> </title>
    <meta charset = "utf-8" />
    <script type = "text/javascript"  src = "validator2.js" >
    </script>
  </head>
```

```
<body>
  <h3> Customer Information </h3>
  <form action = "">
    <p>
      <label>
        <input type = "text"  id = "custName" />
        Name (last name, first name, middle initial)
      </label>
      <br /><br />

      <label>
        <input type = "text"  id = "phone" />
        Phone number (ddd-ddd-dddd)
      </label>
      <br /><br />

      <input type = "reset" />
      <input type = "submit"  id = "submitButton" />
    </p>
  </form>
<!-- Script for registering event handlers -->
  <script type = "text/javascript"  src = "validator2r.js" />
  </body>
</html>
```

```
// validator2.js
//   An example of input validation using the change and submit
//   events using the DOM 2 event model
//   Note: This document does not work with IE8


// ************************************************************ //
// The event handler function for the name text box
function chkName(event) {

// Get the target node of the event
  var myName = event.currentTarget;


// Test the format of the input name
//  Allow the spaces after the commas to be optional
//  Allow the period after the initial to be optional
  var pos = myName.value.search(
                  /^[A-Z][a-z]+, ?[A-Z][a-z]+, ?[A-Z]\.?$/);
```

```
      if (pos != 0) {
        alert("The name you entered (" + myName.value +
              ") is not in the correct form. \n" +
              "The correct form is: " +
              "last-name, first-name, middle-initial \n" +
              "Please go back and fix your name");
      }
}
// ***************************************************** //
// The event handler function for the phone number text box
function chkPhone(event) {

// Get the target node of the event
  var myPhone = event.currentTarget;

// Test the format of the input phone number
  var pos = myPhone.value.search(/^\d{3}-\d{3}-\d{4}$/);

  if (pos != 0) {
    alert("The phone number you entered (" + myPhone.value +
          ") is not in the correct form. \n" +
          "The correct form is: ddd-ddd-dddd \n" +
          "Please go back and fix your phone number");
  }
}
```

```
// validator2r.js
//    The last part of validator2. Registers the
//    event handlers
//    Note: This script does not work with IE8

// Get the DOM addresses of the elements and register
//   the event handlers
      var customerNode = document.getElementById("custName");
      var phoneNode = document.getElementById("phone");
      customerNode.addEventListener("change", chkName, false);
      phoneNode.addEventListener("change", chkPhone, false);
```

Note that the two event models can be mixed in a document. If a DOM 0 feature happens to be more convenient than the corresponding DOM 2 feature, there is no reason it cannot be used. Chapter 6 includes an example of the use of the DOM 2 event model for something that is more difficult to do with the DOM 0 event model.

5.9 The `canvas` Element

A canvas element creates a rectangle into which can be drawn bit-mapped graphics using JavaScript. The canvas element usually includes three attributes, `height`, `width`, and `id`, although all three are optional. The attributes for height and width are given as non-negative integers, which specify the dimensions of the canvas rectangle in pixels.[4] The default values for `height` and `width` are `150` and `300`, respectively. The `id` attribute is required to allow anything to be drawn on the canvas rectangle. The content of a canvas element is displayed when the browser does not support canvas. Following is an example of a canvas element:

```
<canvas  id = "myCanvas"  height = "200"  width = "400">
Your browser does not support the canvas element
</canvas>
```

The content of the `canvas` element is displayed if the browser does not support the element.

HTML5 defines a JavaScript API for a set of drawing subprograms. Among these are subprograms to draw lines, arcs, rectangles, and text.

5.10 The `navigator` Object

The navigator object indicates which browser is being used to view the HTML document. The browser's name is stored in the `appName` property of the object. The version of the browser is stored in the `appVersion` property of the object. These properties allow the script to determine which browser is being used and to use processes appropriate to that browser. The following example illustrates the use of `navigator`, in this case just to display the browser name and version number:

```
<!DOCTYPE html>
<!-- navigate.html
     A document for navigate.js
     Calls the event handler on load
     -->
<html lang = "en">
  <head>
    <title> navigate.html </title>
    <meta charset = "utf-8" />
    <script type = "text/javascript"  src = "navigate.js" >
    </script>
  </head>
  <body onload = "navProperties()">
  </body>
</html>
```

---

4. The dimensions are not always interpreted as pixels. On a high-resolution display, two actual pixels may represent each specified pixel.

```
// navigate.js
//  An example of using the navigator object


// The event handler function to display the browser name
//  and its version number
function navProperties() {
  alert("The browser is: " + navigator.appName + "\n" +
    "The version number is: " + navigator.appVersion + "\n");
}
```

Figure 5.10 shows the result of displaying `navigate.html` with FX3. Figure 5.11 shows the result of displaying `navigate.html` with IE9. Notice that the version number of IE9 is 5. Microsoft intentionally set the version number to 5 because of some compatibility issues with earlier browsers. Firefox is not any better in this regard: Using FX3, it displays `version 5.0`. The C12 browser says it is Netscape version 5.0, as with FX3.

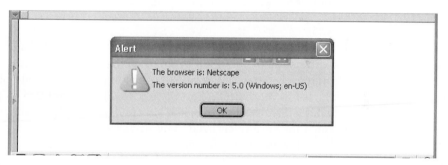

Figure 5.10 The `navigator` properties `appName` and `appVersion` for FX3

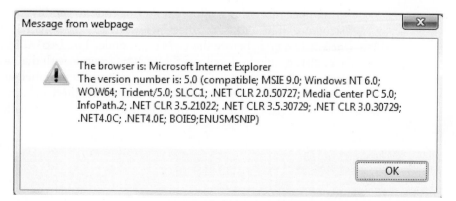

Figure 5.11 The `navigator` properties `appName` and `appVersion` for IE9

5.11   DOM Tree Traversal and Modification

There are many objects, properties, and methods associated with DOM 2 document representations that we have not discussed. One collection of these is defined in the Node interface, which is implemented by all node objects in the DOM structure. Some can be used to traverse and modify the DOM tree structure of the document being displayed. In this section, a few of the most useful ones are briefly described. All of the properties and methods mentioned here are supported by both IE9 and FX3.

5.11.1   DOM Tree Traversal

The parentNode property has the DOM address of the parent node of the node through which it is referenced. The childNodes property is an array of the child nodes of the node through which it is referenced. For example, if the document has an unordered list with the id mylist, the number of items in the list can be displayed with the following code:

```
var nod = document.getElementById("mylist");
var listitems = nod.childNodes.length;
document.write("Number of list items is: " +
               listitems + "<br />");
```

The previousSibling property has the DOM address of the previous sibling node of the node through which it is referenced. The nextSibling property has the DOM address of the next sibling node of the node through which it is referenced. The firstChild and lastChild properties have the DOM addresses of the first and last child nodes, respectively, of the node through which they are referenced. The nodeType property has the type of the node through which it is referenced.

5.11.2   DOM Tree Modification

A number of methods allow JavaScript code to modify an existing DOM tree structure. The insertBefore(newChild, refChild) method places the newChild node before the refChild node. The replaceChild(newChild, oldChild) method replaces the oldChild node with the newChild node. The removeChild(oldChild) method removes the specified node from the DOM structure. The appendChild(newChild) method adds the given node to the end of the list of siblings of the node through which it is called.

Summary

The highest levels of the execution environment of client-side JavaScript are represented with the `Window` and `Document` objects. The `Document` object includes a `forms` array property, which contains references to all forms in the document. Each element of the `forms` array has an `elements` array, which contains references to all elements in the form.

The DOM is an abstract interface whose purpose is to provide a language-independent way to access the elements of an HTML document. Also included are the means to navigate around the structure in which the HTML elements appear. HTML tags are represented in JavaScript as objects; tag attributes are represented as properties.

There are three different ways to access HTML elements in JavaScript: through the `forms` and `elements` arrays, through the names of the element and its enclosing elements, and through the `getElementById` method.

Events are simply notifications that something specific has happened that may require some special processing. Event-handling code provides that special processing. There are two distinct event models currently in use. The first is the model implemented by all browsers that support JavaScript: the DOM 0 model. The second is the more elaborate and powerful model defined in DOM 2.

With the DOM 0 model, there are two ways to register an event handler. First, an attribute of the tag that defines the HTML element can be assigned the handler code. Second, the property associated with the event of the object that represents the HTML element can be assigned the name of a function that implements the handler. The `write` method of `document` should not be used in event handlers.

With the DOM 0 model, each event has an associated tag attribute. A particular attribute may appear in several different tags. Each of these appearances is identified as a different occurrence of the same event. The `load` and `unload` events are often used with the `<body>` tag to perform some operation when a document has been loaded and unloaded, respectively. The `click` event is used for all of the different HTML buttons, as well as for the link of an anchor tag. Form input can be conveniently checked by using the `change` event. The `submit` event can also be used to check form data just before the form is submitted.

The DOM 2 event model defines three phases of event processing: capturing, target node, and bubbling. During the capturing phase, the event object travels from the document root to the target node, where the event was created. During the bubbling phase, the event travels back up the document tree to the root, triggering any handlers registered on nodes that are encountered. Event handlers can be set to allow them to be triggered during the capturing phase. Event handler registration is done with the `addEventListener` method, which sets whether capturing-phase triggering will take place. Events can be unregistered with the `removeEventListener` method. The `currentTarget` property of `Event` has the object through which the handler was called. The `target` property has the target node object. The `mouseEvent` object has two properties—`clientX` and `clientY`—which have the coordinates of the position of the mouse cursor in the browser display window when a mouse event occurs.

The `navigator` object has information about which browser is being used, as well as its version number and other related information.

There are many objects, methods, and properties defined in DOM 2 that are used to traverse and modify the DOM tree structure of a document.

Review Questions

5.1   Global variables in JavaScript are properties of what object?

5.2   How are HTML elements and attributes represented in the JavaScript binding to DOM?

5.3   What is an event?

5.4   What is an event handler?

5.5   What is the origin of the DOM 0 event model?

5.6   What are the two ways in which an event handler can be associated with an event generated by a specific HTML element in the DOM 0 event model?

5.7   Why should `document.write` not be used in an event handler?

5.8   In what ways can an HTML element acquire focus?

5.9   Describe the approach to addressing HTML elements using `forms` and `elements`.

5.10   Describe the approach to addressing HTML elements using `name` attributes.

5.11   Describe the approach to addressing HTML elements using `getElementById`.

5.12   What is the disadvantage of assigning event handlers to event properties?

5.13   What are the advantages of assigning event handlers to event properties?

5.14   Why is it good to use JavaScript to check the validity of form inputs before the form data is sent to the server?

5.15 What three things should be done when a form input element is found to have incorrectly formatted data?

5.16 What happens when an event handler for the `onsubmit` event returns `false`?

5.17 What event is used to trigger an event handler that checks the validity of input for a text button in a form?

5.18 What event propagation takes place in the DOM 0 event model?

5.19 Explain the three phases of event processing in the DOM 2 event model.

5.20 Give two examples of default actions of events.

5.21 Explain the first two parameters of the `addEventListener` method.

5.22 How is an event handler registered so that it will be called during the capturing phase?

5.23 How can an event handler be unregistered?

5.24 What exactly do the `clientX` and `clientY` properties store?

5.25 What purpose does the `navigator` object have?

Exercises

5.1 Modify the `radio_click.html` example to have five buttons, labeled *red*, *blue*, *green*, *yellow*, and *orange*. The event handlers for these buttons must produce messages stating the chosen favorite color. The event handler must be implemented as a function whose name must be assigned to the `onclick` attribute of the radio button elements. The chosen color must be sent to the event handler as a parameter.

5.2 Rewrite the document for Exercise 5.1 to assign the event handler to the event property of the button element. This requires the chosen color to be obtained from the `value` property of the button element rather than through the parameter.

5.3 Develop, test, and validate an HTML document that has checkboxes for apple (59 cents each), orange (49 cents each), and banana (39 cents each), along with a *Submit* button. Each of the checkboxes should have its own `onclick` event handler. These handlers must add the cost of their fruit to a total cost. An event handler for the *Submit* button must produce an `alert` window with the message *Your total cost is $xxx*, where *xxx* is the total cost of the chosen fruit, including 5 percent sales tax. This handler must return `false` (to avoid actual submission of the form data).

5.4 Develop, test, and validate an HTML document that is similar to that of Exercise 5.3. In this case, use text boxes rather than checkboxes. These text boxes take a number, which is the purchased number of the particular fruit. The rest of the document should behave exactly like that of Exercise 5.3.

5.5 Add reality checks to the text boxes of the document in Exercise 5.4. The checks on the text box inputs should ensure that the input values are numbers in the range from 0 to 99.

5.6 Range checks for element inputs can be represented as new properties of the object that represents the element. Modify the document in Exercise 5.5 to add a `max` property value of 99 and a `min` property value of 0. Your event handler must use the properties for the range checks on values input through the text boxes.

5.7 Develop, test, and validate an HTML document that collects the following information from the user: last name, first name, middle initial, age (restricted to be greater than 17), and weight (restricted to the range from 80 to 300). You must have event handlers for the form elements that collect this information. These handlers must check the input data for correctness. Messages in `alert` windows must be produced when errors are detected.

5.8 Revise the document of Exercise 5.1 to use the DOM 2 event model.

5.9 Revise the document of Exercise 5.3 to use the DOM 2 event model.

Dynamic Documents with JavaScript

Informally, a dynamic HTML document is an HTML document that, in some way, can be changed while it is being displayed by a browser. The most common client-side approach to providing dynamic documents is to use JavaScript to manipulate the objects of the Document Object Model (DOM) of the displayed document. Changes to documents can occur when they are explicitly requested by user interactions, at regular timed intervals, or when browser events occur.

HTML elements can be initially positioned at any given location on the browser display. If they're positioned in a specific way, elements can be dynamically moved to new positions on the display. Elements can be made to disappear and reappear. The colors of the background and the foreground (the elements) of a document can be changed. The font, font size, and font style of displayed text can be changed. Even the content of an element can be changed. Overlapping elements in a document can be positioned in a specific top-to-bottom stacking order, and their stacking arrangement can be dynamically changed. The position of the mouse cursor on the browser display can be determined when a mouse button is clicked. Elements can be made to move around the display screen. Finally, elements can be defined to allow the user to drag and drop them anywhere in the display window. This chapter discusses the JavaScript code that can create all of these effects.

6.1 Introduction

Dynamic HTML is not a new markup language. It is a collection of technologies that allows dynamic changes to documents defined with HTML. Specifically, a *dynamic HTML document* is an HTML document whose tag attributes, tag contents, or element style properties can be changed by user interaction or the occurrence of a browser event after the document has been, and is still being, displayed. Such changes can be made with an embedded script that accesses the elements of the document as objects in the associated DOM structure.

Support for dynamic HTML is not uniform across the various browsers. As in Chapter 5, the discussion here is restricted to W3C-standard approaches rather than including features defined by a particular browser vendor. All of the examples in this chapter, except the document in Section 6.11, use the DOM 0 event model and work on both Internet Explorer 8 (IE8) and Firefox 3 (FX3) browsers. The example in Section 6.11 uses the DOM 2 event model because it cannot be designed in a standard way with the DOM 0 event model. Because IE8 (and earlier versions of IE) does not support the DOM 2 event model, that example does not work with IE8. However, IE9 supports the DOM 2 event model, so that example works with IE9.

This chapter discusses user interactions through HTML documents using client-side JavaScript. Chapters 8 through 10 discuss user interactions through HTML documents using server-side technologies.

6.2 Positioning Elements

Before the browsers that implemented HTML 4.0 appeared, Web site authors had little control over how HTML elements were arranged in documents. In many cases, the elements found in the HTML file were simply placed in the document the way text is placed in a document with a word processor: Fill a row, start a new row, fill it, and so forth. HTML tables provide a framework of columns for arranging elements, but they lack flexibility and also take a considerable time to display.[1] This lack of powerful and efficient element placement

---

1. Frames provide another way to arrange elements, but they were deprecated in XHTML 1.0 and eliminated in XHTML 1.1 and HTML5.

control ended when Cascading Style Sheets–Positioning (CSS-P) was released by the W3C in 1997.

CSS-P is completely supported by IE8, IE9, FX3, and C12. It provides the means not only to position any element anywhere in the display of a document, but also to move an element to a new position in the display dynamically, using JavaScript to change the positioning style properties of the element. These style properties, which are appropriately named `left` and `top`, dictate the distance from the left and top of some reference point to where the element is to appear. Another style property, `position`, interacts with `left` and `top` to provide a higher level of control of placement and movement of elements. The `position` property has three possible values: `absolute`, `relative`, and `static`.

6.2.1   Absolute Positioning

The `absolute` value for `position` is specified when the element is to be placed at a specific location in the document display without regard to the positions of other elements. For example, if a paragraph of text is to appear 100 pixels from the left edge and 200 pixels from the top of the display window, the following element could be used:

```
<p style = "position: absolute; left: 100px; top: 200px">
    -- text --
</p>
```

One use of absolute positioning is to superimpose special text over a paragraph of ordinary text to create an effect similar to a watermark on paper. A larger italicized font, in a light-gray color and with space between the letters, could be used for the special text, allowing both the ordinary text and the special text to be legible. Remember that em is a relative size, so the text size of embedded elements is relative to their parents. The HTML document that follows provides an example that implements this effect. In this example, a paragraph of normal text that describes apples is displayed. Superimposed on this paragraph is the somewhat subliminal message "APPLES ARE GOOD FOR YOU". Here is the document:

```
<!DOCTYPE html>
<!-- absPos.html
     Illustrates absolute positioning of elements
     -->
<html lang = "en">
  <head>
    <title> Absolute positioning </title>
    <meta charset = "utf-8" />
    <style type = "text/css">

/* A style for a paragraph of text */
    .regtext {font-family: Times; font-size: 1.2em; width: 500px}
```

```
/* A style for the text to be absolutely positioned */
    .abstext {position: absolute; top: 25px; left: 25px;
            font-family: Times; font-size: 1.9em;
            font-style: italic; letter-spacing: 1em;
            color: rgb(160,160,160); width: 450px}
  </style>
</head>
<body>
  <p class = "regtext">
    Apple is the common name for any tree of the genus Malus,
    of the family Rosaceae. Apple trees grow in any of the
    temperate areas of the world. Some apple blossoms are white,
    but most have stripes or tints of rose. Some apple blossoms
    are bright red. Apples have a firm and fleshy structure that
    grows from the blossom. The colors of apples range from
    green to very dark red. The wood of apple trees is fine
    grained and hard. It is, therefore, good for furniture
    construction. Apple trees have been grown for many
    centuries. They are propagated by grafting because they
    do not reproduce themselves.
    <span class = "abstext">
      APPLES ARE GOOD FOR YOU
    </span>
  </p>
</body>
</html>
```

Figure 6.1 shows a display of absPos.html.

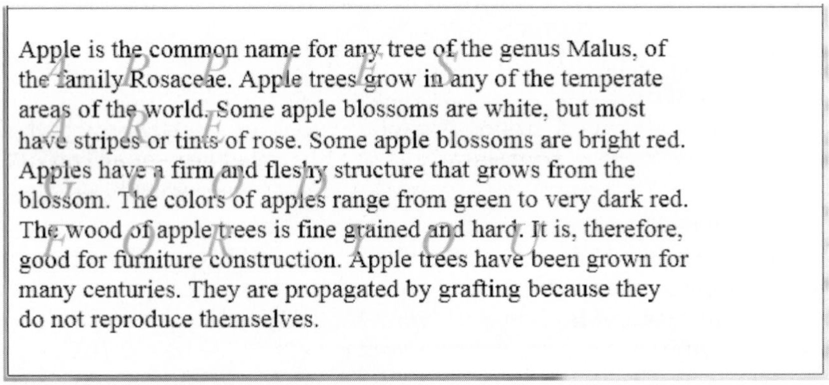

Figure 6.1 Display of absPos.html

Notice that a `width` property value is included in the style for both the regular and the special text. This property is used here to ensure that the special text is uniformly embedded in the regular text. Without it, the text would extend to the right end of the browser display window—and, of course, the width of the window could vary widely from client to client and even from minute to minute on the same client because the user can resize the browser window at any time.

When an element is absolutely positioned inside another positioned element (one that has the `position` property specified), the `top` and `left` property values are measured from the upper-left corner of the enclosing element (rather than the upper-left corner of the browser window).

To illustrate the placement of nested elements, the document `absPos.html` is modified to place the regular text 100 pixels from the top and 100 pixels from the left. The special text is nested inside the regular text by using `<div>` and `<span>` tags. The modified document, which is named `absPos2.html`, is as follows:

```
<!DOCTYPE html>
<!-- absPos2.html
     Illustrates nested absolute positioning of elements
     -->
<html lang = "en">
  <head>
    <title> Nested absolute positioning </title>
    <meta charset = "utf-8" />
    <style type = "text/css">

/* A style for a paragraph of text */
    .regtext {font-family: Times; font-size: 1.2em; width: 500px;
              position: absolute; top: 100px; left: 100px;}

/* A style for the text to be absolutely positioned */
    .abstext {position: absolute; top: 25px; left: 25px;
              font-family: Times; font-size: 1.9em;
              font-style: italic; letter-spacing: 1em;
              color: rgb(160,160,160); width: 450px;}
    </style>
  </head>
  <body>
    <p class = "regtext">
      Apple is the common name for any tree of the genus Malus,
      of the family Rosaceae. Apple trees grow in any of the
      temperate areas of the world. Some apple blossoms are white,
```

```
        but most have stripes or tints of rose. Some apple blossoms
        are bright red. Apples have a firm and fleshy structure that
        grows from the blossom. The colors of apples range from
        green to very dark red. The wood of apple trees is fine
        grained and hard. It is, therefore, good for furniture
        construction. Apple trees have been grown for many
        centuries. They are propagated by grafting because they
        do not reproduce themselves.
        <span class = "abstext">
           APPLES ARE GOOD FOR YOU
        </span>
      </p>
    </body>
  </html>
```

Figure 6.2 shows a display of `absPos2.html`.

Apple is the common name for any tree of the genus Malus, of the family Rosaceae. Apple trees grow in any of the temperate areas of the world. Some apple blossoms are white, but most have stripes or tints of rose. Some apple blossoms are bright red. Apples have a firm and fleshy structure that grows from the blossom. The colors of apples range from green to very dark red. The wood of apple trees is fine grained and hard. It is, therefore, good for furniture construction. Apple trees have been grown for many centuries. They are propagated by grafting because they do not reproduce themselves.

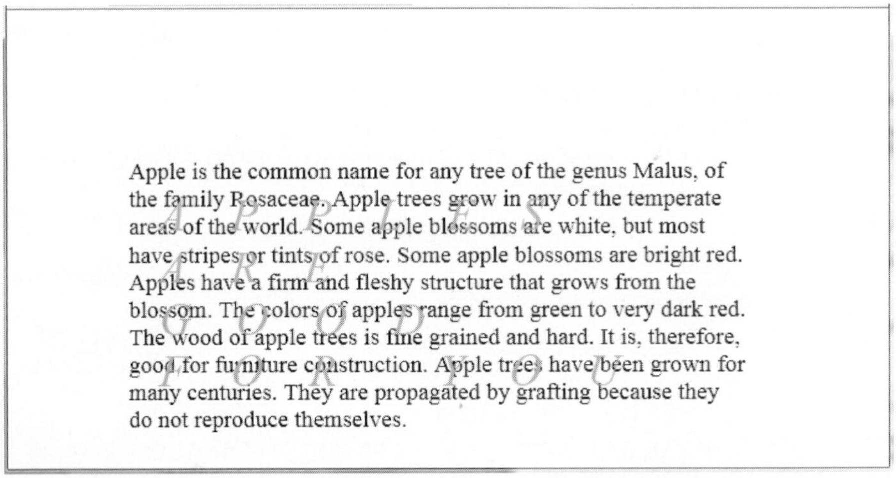

Figure 6.2 Display of `absPos2.html`

6.2.2 Relative Positioning

An element that has the `position` property set to `relative`, but does not specify `top` and `left` property values, is placed in the document as if the `position` attribute were not set at all. However, such an element can be moved later. If the `top` and `left` properties are given values, they displace the element by the specified amount from the position where it would have been placed (if `top` and `left` had not been set). For example, suppose that two buttons are placed in a document and the `position` attribute has its default value, which is static. Then the buttons would appear next to each other in a row, assuming that the current row has sufficient horizontal space for them. If position has been set to relative and the second button has its left property set to 50px, the effect would be to move the second button 50 pixels farther to the right than it otherwise would have appeared.

In both the case of an absolutely positioned element inside another element and the case of a relatively positioned element, negative values of top and left displace the element upward and to the left, respectively.[2]

Relative positioning can be used for a variety of special effects in placing elements. For example, it can be used to create superscripts and subscripts by placing the values to be raised or lowered in <span> tags and displacing them from their regular positions. In the next example, a line of text is set in a normal font style in 2em size. Embedded in the line is one word that is set in italic, 2em, red font. Its size is also set to 2em, but because its parent is the paragraph in which it is embedded, the 2em means it will be twice as large as the paragraph text. Normally, the bottom of the special word would align with the bottom of the rest of the line. In this case, the special word is to be vertically centered in the line, so its position property is set to relative and its top property is set to 15 pixels, which lowers it by that amount relative to the surrounding text. The HTML document to specify this, which is named relPos.html, is as follows:

```
<!DOCTYPE html>
<!-- relPos.html
     Illustrates relative positioning of elements
     -->
<html lang = "en">
  <head>
    <title> Relative positioning </title>
    <meta charset = "utf-8" />
    <style type = "text/css">
      .regtext {font: 2em Times}
      .spectext {font: 2em Times; color: red; position: relative;
                 top: 15px;}
    </style>
  </head>
  <body>
    <p class = "regtext">
      Apples are
      <span class = "spectext"> GOOD </span> for you.
    </p>
  </body>
</html>
```

---

2. Of course, if the left or top property is set to a negative value for an absolutely positioned element, only part of the element (or possibly none of the element) will be visibly displayed.

Figure 6.3 shows a display of `relPos.html`.

Apples are GOOD for you.

Figure 6.3 Display of `relPos.html`

6.2.3 Static Positioning

The default value for the `position` property is `static`. A statically positioned element is placed in the document as if it had the `position` value of `relative` but no values for `top` or `left` were given. The difference is that a statically positioned element cannot have its `top` or `left` properties initially set or changed later. Therefore, a statically placed element initially cannot be displaced from its normal position and cannot be moved from that position later.

6.3 Moving Elements

As stated previously, an HTML element whose `position` property is set to either `absolute` or `relative` can be moved. Moving an element is simple: Changing the `top` or `left` property values causes the element to move on the display. If its `position` is set to `absolute`, the element moves to the new values of `top` and `left`; if its `position` is set to `relative`, it moves from its original position by distances given by the new values of `top` and `left`.

In the next example, an image is absolutely positioned in the display. The document includes two text boxes, labeled `x coordinate` and `y coordinate`, respectively. The user can enter new values for the `left` and `top` properties of the image in these boxes. When the *Move It* button is pressed, the values of the `left` and `top` properties of the image are changed to the given values, and the element is moved to its new position.

A JavaScript function, stored in a separate file, is used to change the values of `left` and `top` in this example. Although it is not necessary here, the id of the element to be moved is sent to the function that does the moving, just to illustrate that the function could be used on any number of different elements. The values of the two text boxes are also sent to the function as parameters. The actual parameter values are the DOM addresses of the text boxes, with the `value` attribute attached, which provides the complete DOM addresses of the text box values. Notice that `style` is attached to the DOM address of the image to be moved because `top` and `left` are style properties. Because the input `top` and `left` values from the text boxes are just string representations of numbers, but the `top` and `left` properties must end with some unit abbreviation, the event handler catenates `"px"` to each value before assigning it to the `top` and `left` properties. This document, called `mover.html`, and the associated JavaScript file, `mover.js`, are as follows:

```
<!DOCTYPE html>
<!-- mover.html
     Uses mover.js to move an image within a document
     -->
<html lang = "en">
  <head>
    <title> Moving elements </title>
    <meta charset = "utf-8" />
    <script type = "text/javascript"  src = "mover.js" >
    </script>
  </head>
  <body>
    <form action = "">
      <p>
        <label>
          x coordinate:
          <input type = "text"  id = "leftCoord" size = "3" />
        </label>
        <br />
        <label>
          y coordinate:
          <input type = "text"  id = "topCoord" size = "3" />
        </label>
        <br />
        <input type = "button"  value = "Move it"
              onclick =
                "moveIt('saturn',
                document.getElementById('topCoord').value,
                document.getElementById('leftCoord').value)" />
      </p>
    </form>
    <div id = "saturn"  style = "position: absolute;
        top: 115px; left: 0;">
      <img src = "../images/saturn.png"
          alt = "(Picture of Saturn)" />
    </div>
  </body>
</html>
```

```
// mover.js
//   Illustrates moving an element within a document


// The event handler function to move an element
function moveIt(movee, newTop, newLeft) {
  dom = document.getElementById(movee).style;


// Change the top and left properties to perform the move
//   Note the addition of units to the input values
  dom.top = newTop + "px";
  dom.left = newLeft + "px";
}
```

← because top & left
are style properties

Figures 6.4 and 6.5 respectively show the initial and new positions of an image in mover.html.

Figure 6.4 Display of mover.html (before pressing the *Move It* button)

Figure 6.5 Display of `mover.html` (after pressing the *Move It* button)

6.4 Element Visibility

Document elements can be specified to be visible or hidden with the value of their `visibility` property. The two possible values for `visibility` are, quite naturally, `visible` and `hidden`. The appearance or disappearance of an element can be controlled by the user through a widget.

The following example displays an image and allows the user to toggle a button, causing the image to appear and not appear in the document display (once again, the event handler is in a separate file):

```
<!DOCTYPE html>
<!-- showHide.html
     Uses showHide.js
     Illustrates visibility control of elements
     -->
```

```html
<html lang = "en">
  <head>
    <title> Visibility control </title>
    <meta charset = "utf-8" />
    <script type = "text/javascript"  src = "showHide.js" >
    </script>
  </head>
  <body>
    <form action = "">
      <div id = "saturn"  style = "position: relative;
          visibility: visible;">
        <img src = "../images/saturn.png"
            alt = "(Picture of Saturn)" />
      </div>
      <p>
        <br />
        <input type = "button"  value = "Toggle Saturn"
            onclick = "flipImag()" />
      </p>
    </form>
  </body>
</html>
```

```javascript
// showHide.js
//    Illustrates visibility control of elements


// The event handler function to toggle the visibility
//   of the images of Saturn
function flipImag() {
  dom = document.getElementById("saturn").style;
// Flip the visibility adjective to whatever it is not now
  if (dom.visibility == "visible")
    dom.visibility = "hidden";
  else
    dom.visibility = "visible";
}
```

6.5   Changing Colors and Fonts

The background and foreground colors of the document display can be dynamically changed, as can the font properties of the text.

6.5.1   Changing Colors

Dynamic changes to colors are relatively simple. In the next example, the user is presented with two text boxes into which color specifications can be typed—one for the document background color and one for the foreground color. The colors can be specified in any of the three ways that color properties can be given in CSS. A JavaScript function that is called whenever one of the text boxes is changed makes the change in the document's appropriate color property: `backgroundColor` or `color`. The first of the two parameters to the function specifies whether the new color is for the background or foreground; the second specifies the new color. The new color is the `value` property of the text box that was changed by the user.

In this example, the calls to the handler functions are in the HTML text box elements. This approach allows a simple way to reference the element's DOM address. The JavaScript `this` variable in this situation is a reference to the object that represents the element in which it is referenced. A reference to such an object is its DOM address. Therefore, in a text element, the value of `this` is the DOM address of the text element. So, in the example, `this.value` is used as an actual parameter to the handler function. Because the call is in an input element, `this.value` is the DOM address of the value of the input element. This document, called `dynColors.html`, and the associated JavaScript file are as follows:

```
<!DOCTYPE html>
<!-- dynColors.html
     Uses dynColors.js
     Illustrates dynamic foreground and background colors
     -->
<html lang = "en">
  <head>
    <title> Dynamic colors </title>
    <meta charset = "utf-8" />
    <script type = "text/javascript"  src = "dynColors.js" >
    </script>
  </head>
  <body>
    <p style = "font-family: Times; font-style: italic;
                font-size: 2em;" >
      This small page illustrates dynamic setting of the
      foreground and background colors for a document
    </p>
    <form action = "">
      <p>
```

```
        <label>
          Background color:
          <input type = "text"  name = "background" size = "10"
                 onchange = "setColor('background', this.value)" />
        </label>
        <br />
        <label>
          Foreground color:
          <input type = "text"  name = "foreground" size = "10"
                 onchange = "setColor('foreground', this.value)" />
        </label>
        <br />
      </p>
    </form>
  </body>
</html>
```

```
// dynColors.js
//    Illustrates dynamic foreground and background colors

// The event handler function to dynamically set the
// color of background or foreground
function setColor(where, newColor) {
  if (where == "background")
    document.body.style.backgroundColor = newColor;
  else
    document.body.style.color = newColor;
}
```

6.5.2   Changing Fonts

Web users are accustomed to having links in documents change color when the cursor is placed over them. Use of the mouseover event to trigger a JavaScript event handler allows us to change any property of any element in a document, including text, when the mouse cursor is placed over it. Thus, the font style and font size, as well as the color and background color of text, can be changed when the cursor is placed over the text. The text can be changed back to its original form when an event handler is triggered with the mouseout event.

For CSS attribute names that are single words without hyphens, the associated JavaScript property names are the same as the attribute names. But when an attribute name includes a hyphen, as in font-size, the associated property name must be different (because a property name cannot include a hyphen). The convention is that when an attribute name has a hyphen, the hyphen is deleted and the letter that follows is capitalized in its associated property name. So, the property name associated with the attribute `font-size` is `fontSize`.

In the next example, the only element is a one-line paragraph with an embedded special word. The special word is the content of a span element, so its attributes can be changed. The foreground color for the document is the default black. The word is presented in blue. When the mouse cursor is placed over the word, its color changes to red, its font style changes to italic, and its size changes from 16 point to 24 point. When the cursor is moved off the word, it reverts to its original style. Here is this document, called `dynFont.html`:

```
<!DOCTYPE html>
<!-- dynFont.html
     Illustrates dynamic font styles and colors
     -->
<html lang = "en">
  <head>
    <title> Dynamic fonts </title>
    <meta charset = "utf-8" />
    <style type = "text/css">
      .regText {font: 1.1em 'Times New Roman';}
      .wordText {color: blue;}
    </style>
  </head>
  <body>
    <p class = "regText">
      The state of
      <span class = "wordText";
        onmouseover = "this.style.color = 'red';
                       this.style.fontStyle = 'italic';
                       this.style.fontSize = '2em';";
        onmouseout = "this.style.color = 'blue';
                      this.style.fontStyle = 'normal';
                      this.style.fontSize = '1.1em';";>
        Washington
      </span>
      produces many of our nation's apples.
    </p>
  </body>
</html>
```

Notice that the event handlers in this example are embedded in the markup. This is one of those cases where the small amount of JavaScript needed does not justify putting it in a separate file.

Figures 6.6 and 6.7 show browser displays of the `dynFont.html` document with the mouse cursor not over, and then over, the link.

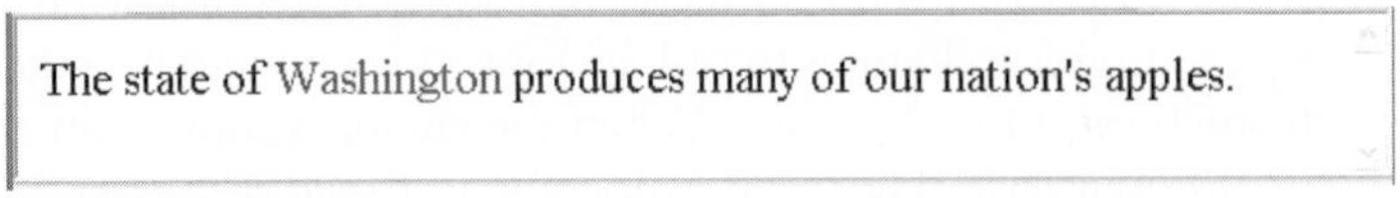

The state of Washington produces many of our nation's apples.

Figure 6.6 Display of `dynFont.html` with the mouse cursor not over the word

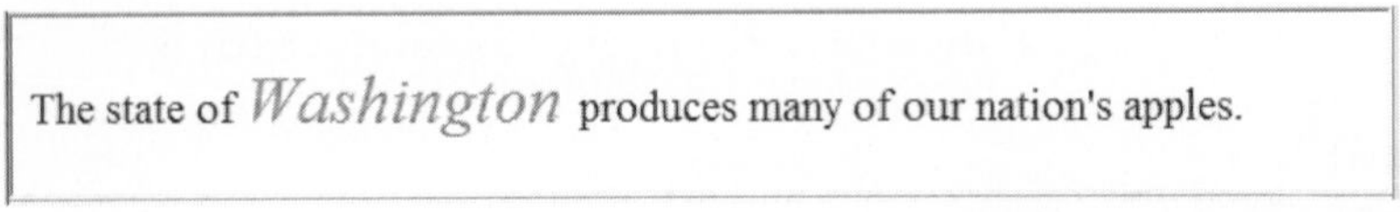

The state of *Washington* produces many of our nation's apples.

Figure 6.7 Display of `dynFont.html` with the mouse cursor over the word

6.6   Dynamic Content

We have explored the options of dynamically changing the positions of elements, their visibility, colors, background colors, and the styles of text fonts. This section investigates changing the content of HTML elements. The content of an element is accessed through the `value` property of its associated JavaScript object. So, changing the content of an element is not essentially different from changing the style properties of the element. We now develop an example that illustrates one use of dynamic content.

Assistance to a browser user filling out a form can be provided with an associated text area, often called a *help box*. The content of the help box can change, depending on the placement of the mouse cursor. When the cursor is placed over a particular input field, the help box can display advice on how the field is to be filled in. When the cursor is moved away from all input fields, the help box content can be changed to simply indicate that assistance is available.

In the next example, an array of messages that can be displayed in the help box is defined in JavaScript. When the mouse cursor is placed over an input field, the `mouseover` event is used to call a handler function that changes the help box content to the appropriate value (the one associated with the input field). The appropriate value is specified with a parameter sent to the handler function. The `mouseout` event is used to trigger the change of the content of the help box back to the "standard" value. Following is the markup document and associated JavaScript file:

```html
<!DOCTYPE html>
<!-- dynValue.html
     Illustrates dynamic values
     -->
<html lang = "en">
  <head>
    <title> Dynamic values </title>
    <meta charset = "utf-8" />
    <script type = "text/javascript"  src = "dynValue.js" >
    </script>
    <style type = "text/css">
      textarea {position: absolute; left: 250px; top: 0px;}
      span {font-style: italic;}
      p {font-weight: bold;}
    </style>
  </head>
  <body>
    <form action = "">
      <p>
        <span>
          Customer information
        </span>
        <br /><br />
        <label>
          Name:
          <input type = "text"  onmouseover = "messages(0)"
                 onmouseout = "messages(4)" />
        </label>
        <br />
        <label>
          Email:
          <input type = "text"  onmouseover = "messages(1)"
                 onmouseout = "messages(4)" />
        </label>
        <br /> <br />
        <span>
          To create an account, provide the following:
        </span>
        <br /> <br />
        <label>
          User ID:
          <input type = "text"  onmouseover = "messages(2)"
                 onmouseout = "messages(4)" />
        </label>
        <br />
```

```
            <label>
              Password:
              <input type = "password"
                       onmouseover = "messages(3)"
                       onmouseout = "messages(4)" />
            </label>
            <br />
          </p>
          <textarea id = "adviceBox"  rows = "3"  cols = "50">
            This box provides advice on filling out the form
            on this page. Put the mouse cursor over any input
            field to get advice.
          </textarea>
          <br /><br />
          <input type = "submit"  value = "Submit" />
          <input type = "reset"  value = "Reset" />
        </form>
    </body>
</html>
```

```
// dynValue.js
//    Illustrates dynamic values

var helpers = ["Your name must be in the form: \n \
 first name, middle initial., last name",
  "Your email address must have the form: \
user@domain",
  "Your user ID must have at least six characters",
  "Your password must have at least six \
characters and it must include one digit",
  "This box provides advice on filling out\
the form on this page. Put the mouse cursor over any \
 input field to get advice"]


// ****************************************************************
// The event handler function to change the value of the
// textarea

function messages(adviceNumber) {
  document.getElementById("adviceBox").value =
                                     helpers[adviceNumber];
}
```

Note that the backslash characters that terminate some of the lines of the literal array of messages specify that the string literal is continued on the next line.

Figure 6.8 shows a browser display of the document defined in `dynValue.html`.

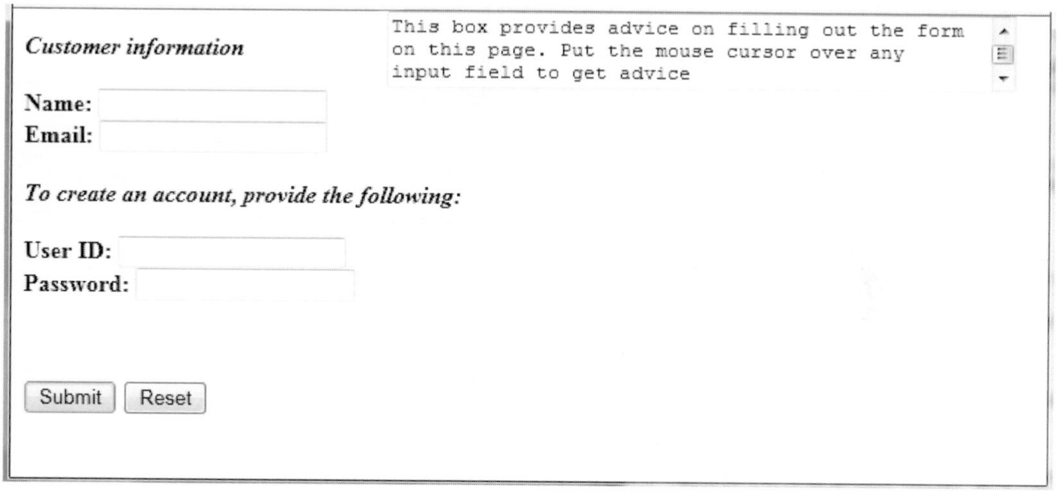

Figure 6.8 Display of `dynValue.html`

6.7 Stacking Elements

The `top` and `left` properties allow the placement of an element anywhere in the two dimensions of the display of a document. Although the display is restricted to two physical dimensions, the effect of a third dimension is possible through the simple concept of stacked elements, such as that used to stack windows in graphical user interfaces. Although multiple elements can occupy the same space in the document, one is considered to be on top and is displayed. The top element hides the parts of the lower elements on which it is superimposed. The placement of elements in this third dimension is controlled by the `z-index` attribute of the element. An element whose `z-index` is greater than that of an element in the same space will be displayed over the other element, effectively hiding the element with the smaller `z-index` value. The JavaScript style property associated with the `z-index` attribute is `zIndex`.

In the next example, three images are placed on the display so that they overlap. In the HTML description of this situation, each image tag includes an `onclick` attribute, which is used to trigger the execution of a JavaScript handler function. First, the function defines DOM addresses for the last top element and the new top element. Then, the function sets the `zIndex` value of the two elements so that the old top element has a value of `0` and the new top element has the value `10`, effectively putting it at the top. The script keeps track of which image is currently on top with the global variable topp,[3] which is changed every time a new element is moved to the top with the toTop function. Note that the zIndex value, as is the case with other properties, is a string. This document, called stacking.html, and the associated JavaScript file are as follows:

```
<!DOCTYPE html>
<!-- stacking.html
     Uses stacking.js
     Illustrates dynamic stacking of images.
         -->
<html lang = "en">
  <head>
    <title> Dynamic stacking of images </title>
    <meta charset = "utf-8" />
    <script type = "text/javascript"  src = "stacking.js" >
    </script>
    <style type = "text/css">
      .plane1 {position: absolute; top: 0; left: 0;
               z-index: 0;}
      .plane2 {position: absolute; top: 50px; left: 110px;
               z-index: 0;}
      .plane3 {position: absolute; top: 100px; left: 220px;
               z-index: 0;}
    </style>
  </head>
  <body>
    <p>
      <img class = "plane1"  id = "airplane1"
           src = "../images/airplane1.png"
           alt = "(Picture of an airplane)"
           onclick = "toTop('airplane1')" />
      <img class = "plane2"  id = "airplane2"
           src = "../images/airplane2.png"
           alt = "(Picture of an airplane)"
           onclick = "toTop('airplane2')" />
      <img class = "plane3"  id = "airplane3"
           src = "../images/airplane3.png"
           alt = "(Picture of an airplane)"
           onclick = "toTop('airplane3')" />
    </p>
  </body>
</html>
```

3. We use topp, rather than top, because there is a JavaScript keyword top, which is a property of window. Using top confuses Chrome browsers, although it does not affect IE or FX browsers.

```
// stacking.js
//   Illustrates dynamic stacking of images
var topp = "airplane1";
// The event handler function to move the given element
// to the top of the display stack
function toTop(newTop) {


// Set the two dom addresses, one for the old top
// element and one for the new top element
  domTop = document.getElementById(topp).style;
  domNew = document.getElementById(newTop).style;


// Set the zIndex properties of the two elements, and
// reset topp to the new top
  domTop.zIndex = "0";
  domNew.zIndex = "10";
  topp = newTop;
}
```

Figures 6.9, 6.10, and 6.11 show the document described by stacking .html in three of its possible configurations.

Figure 6.9 The initial display of stacking.html (photographs courtesy of Cessna Aircraft Company)

Figure 6.10 The display of stacking.html after clicking the second image (photographs courtesy of Cessna Aircraft Company)

Figure 6.11 The display of stacking.html after clicking the bottom image (photographs courtesy of Cessna Aircraft Company)

6.8 Locating the Mouse Cursor

Recall from Chapter 5 that every event that occurs while an HTML document is being displayed creates an event object. This object includes some information about the event. A mouse-click event is an implementation of the Mouse-Event interface, which defines two pairs of properties that provide geometric coordinates of the position of the element in the display that created the event. One of these pairs, clientX and clientY, gives the coordinates of the element relative to the upper-left corner of the browser display window, in pixels. The other pair, screenX and screenY, also gives coordinates of the element, but relative to the client computer's screen. Obviously, the former pair is usually more useful than the latter.

In the next example, where.html, two pairs of text boxes are used to display these four properties every time the mouse button is clicked. The handler is triggered by the onclick attribute of the body element. An image is displayed just below the display of the coordinates, but only to make the screen more interesting.

The call to the handler in this example sends event, which is a reference to the event object just created in the element, as a parameter. This is a bit of magic, because the event object is implicitly created. In the handler, the formal parameter is used to access the properties of the coordinates. Note that the handling of the event object is not implemented the same way in the popular browsers. The Firefox browsers send it as a parameter to event handlers, whereas Internet Explorer and Chrome browsers make it available as a global property. The code in where.html works for both of these approaches by sending the event object in the call to the handler. It is available in the call with IE and Chrome browsers because it is visible there as a global variable. Of course, for these browsers, it need not be sent at all. The where.html document and its associated JavaScript file are as follows:

```
<!DOCTYPE html>
<!-- where.html
     Uses where.js
     Illustrates x- and y-coordinates of the mouse cursor
     -->
<html lang = "en">
  <head>
    <title> Where is the cursor? </title>
    <meta charset = "utf-8" />
    <script type = "text/javascript"  src = "where.js" >
    </script>
  </head>
```

```
<body onclick = "findIt(event)">
  <form action = "">
    <p>
      Within the client area: <br />
      x:
      <input type = "text"  id = "xcoor1"  size = "4" />
      y:
      <input type = "text"  id = "ycoor1"  size = "4" />
      <br /><br />
      Relative to the origin of the screen coordinate system:
      <br />
      x:
      <input type = "text"  id = "xcoor2"  size = "4" />
      y:
      <input type = "text"  id = "ycoor2"  size = "4" />
    </p>
  </form>
  <p>
    <img src = "../images/airplane1.png"  alt = "(Picture of an
              airplane)" />
  </p>
</body>
</html>
```

```
// where.js
//   Show the coordinates of the mouse cursor position
//   in an image and anywhere on the screen when the mouse
//   is clicked

// The event handler function to get and display the
//   coordinates of the cursor, both in an element and
//   on the screen
function findIt(evt) {
  document.getElementById("xcoor1").value = evt.clientX;
  document.getElementById("ycoor1").value = evt.clientY;
  document.getElementById("xcoor2").value = evt.screenX;
  document.getElementById("ycoor2").value = evt.screenY;
}
```

Figure 6.12 shows a browser display of where.html.

Within the client area:
x: 556   y: 277

Relative to the origin of the screen coordinate system:
x: 1217   y: 532

Figure 6.12 Display of `where.html` (the cursor was in the tail section of the plane)

One interesting note about the preceding cursor-finding example is that, with IE9 and C12, the mouse clicks are ignored if the mouse cursor is below the last element on the display. The FX3 browser always responds the same way, regardless of where the cursor is on the display.

6.9 Reacting to a Mouse Click

The next example is another one related to reacting to mouse clicks. In this case, the mousedown and mouseup events are used, respectively, to show and hide the message "Please don't click here!" on the display under the mouse cursor whenever the mouse button is clicked, regardless of where the cursor is at the time. The offsets (-130 for left and -25 for top) modify the actual cursor position so that the message is approximately centered over it. Here is the document and its associated JavaScript file:

```html
<!DOCTYPE html>
<!-- anywhere.html
     Uses anywhere.js
     Display a message when the mouse button is pressed,
     no matter where it is on the screen
     -->
<html lang = "en">
  <head>
    <title> Sense events anywhere </title>
    <meta charset = "utf-8" />
    <script type = "text/javascript"  src = "anywhere.js" >
    </script>
  </head>
  <body onmousedown = "displayIt(event);"
        onmouseup = "hideIt();">
    <p>
      <span id= "message"
            style = "color: red; visibility: hidden;
                     position: relative;
                     font-size: 1.7em; font-style: italic;
                     font-weight: bold;">
          Please don't click here!
      </span>
      <br /><br /><br /><br /><br /><br /><br /><br />
      <br /><br /><br /><br /><br /><br /><br /><br />
    </p>
  </body>
    </html>
```

```javascript
// anywhere.js
//   Display a message when the mouse button is pressed,
//   no matter where it is on the screen


// The event handler function to display the message
function displayIt(evt) {
  var dom = document.getElementById("message");
  dom.style.left = (evt.clientX - 130) + "px";
  dom.style.top = (evt.clientY - 25) + "px";
  dom.style.visibility = "visible";
}
```

```
// ***************************************************
// The event handler function to hide the message
function hideIt() {
  document.getElementById("message").style.visibility =
      "hidden";
}
```

As was the case with `where.html`, with IE and Chrome browsers, the only clicks that cause the text to be displayed are those that occur in the area of the display defined by the `br` elements. With Firefox, a click anywhere on the screen works.

6.10 Slow Movement of Elements

So far, only element movements that happen instantly have been considered. These movements are controlled by changing the `top` and `left` properties of the element to be moved. The only way to move an element slowly is to move it by small amounts many times, with the moves separated by small amounts of time. JavaScript has two `Window` methods that are capable of this task: `setTimeout` and `setInterval`.

The `setTimeout` method takes two parameters: a string of JavaScript code to be executed and a number of milliseconds of delay before executing the given code. For example, the call

```
setTimeout("mover()", 20);
```

causes a 20-millisecond delay, after which the function `mover` is called.

The `setInterval` method has two forms. One form takes two parameters, exactly as does `setTimeout`. It executes the given code repeatedly, using the second parameter as the interval, in milliseconds, between executions. The second form of `setInterval` takes a variable number of parameters. The first parameter is the name of a function to be called, the second is the interval in milliseconds between the calls to the function, and the remaining parameters are used as actual parameters to the function being called.

The example presented here, `moveText.html`, moves a string of text from one position (100, 100) to a new position (300, 300). The move is accomplished by using `setTimeout` to call a mover function every millisecond until the final position (300, 300) is reached. The initial position of the text is set in the span element that specifies the text. The `onload` attribute of the body element is used to call a function, `initText`, to initialize the *x*- and *y*-coordinates of the initial position with the `left` and `top` properties of the element and call the mover function.

The mover function, named `moveText`, takes the current coordinates of the text as parameters, moves them one pixel toward the final position, and then, using `setTimeout`, calls itself with the new coordinates. The recomputation of the coordinates is complicated by the fact that we want the code to work regardless of the direction of the move (even though in our example the move is always down and to the right).

One consideration with this script is that the properties of the coordinates are stored as strings with units attached. For example, if the initial position of an element is (100, 100), its `left` and `top` property values both have the string value `"100px"`. To change the properties arithmetically, they must be numbers. Therefore, the property values are converted to strings with just numeric digit characters in the `initText` function by stripping the nondigit unit parts. This conversion allows them to be coerced to numbers when they are used as operands in arithmetic expressions. Before the `left` and `top` properties are set to the new coordinates, the units abbreviation (in this case, `"px"`) is catenated back onto the coordinates.

It is interesting that, in this example, placing the event handler in a separate file avoids a problem that would occur if the JavaScript were embedded in the markup. The problem is the use of HTML comments to hide JavaScript and having possible parts of HTML comments embedded in the JavaScript. For example, if the JavaScript statement x--; is embedded in an HTML comment, the validator complains that the -- in the statement is an invalid comment declaration.[4]

In the code file, `moveText.js`, note the complexity of the call to the `moveText` function in the call to `setTimeout`. This level of complexity is required because the call to `moveText` must be built from static strings with the values of the variables x and y catenated in.

The `moveText.html` document and the associated JavaScript file, `moveText.js`, are as follows:

```
<!DOCTYPE html>
<!-- moveText.html
     Uses moveText.js
     Illustrates a moving text element
     -->
<html lang = "en">
  <head>
    <title> Moving text </title>
    <meta charset = "utf-8" />
    <script type = "text/javascript"
            src = "moveText.js">
    </script>
  </head>
<!-- Call the initializing function on load, giving the
     destination coordinates for the text to be moved
     -->
  <body onload = "initText()">
```

---

4. In the JavaScript code of our example, the statement x--; is used to move the x-coordinate of the text being moved.

```
<!-- The text to be moved, including its initial position -->
  <p>
    <span id = 'theText' style =
              "position: absolute; left: 100px; top: 100px;
               font: bold 1.7em 'Times Roman';
               color: blue;"> Jump in the lake!
    </span>
  </p>
 </body>
</html>
```

```
//*********************************************************
// This is moveText.js - used with moveText.html
   var dom, x, y, finalx = 300, finaly = 300;


// ************************************************** //
// A function to initialize the x- and y-coordinates
//  of the current position of the text to be moved
//  and then call the mover function
   function initText() {
       dom = document.getElementById('theText').style;

   /* Get the current position of the text */
      var x = dom.left;
      var y = dom.top;


   /* Convert the string values of left and top to
      numbers by stripping off the units */
      x = x.match(/\d+/);
      y = y.match(/\d+/);


   /* Call the function that moves it */
      moveText(x, y);
   } /*** end of function initText */


// ************************************************** //
// A function to move the text from its original
//  position to (finalx, finaly)
   function moveText(x, y) {
```

```
/* If the x-coordinates are not equal, move
   x toward finalx */
   if (x != finalx)
      if (x > finalx) x--;
      else if (x < finalx) x++;


/* If the y-coordinates are not equal, move
   y toward finaly */
   if (y != finaly)
      if (y > finaly) y--;
      else if (y < finaly) y++;


/* As long as the text is not at the destination,
   call the mover with the current position */
   if ((x != finalx) || (y != finaly)) {


/* Put the units back on the coordinates before
   assigning them to the properties to cause the
   move */
      dom.left = x + "px";
      dom.top = y + "px";


/* Recursive call, after a 1-millisecond delay */
      setTimeout("moveText(" + x + "," + y + ")", 1);
   }


} /*** end of function moveText */
```

The speed of the animation in moveText.html varies considerably among browsers. On our system, it took about two seconds with C12, about three seconds with FX3, and more than five seconds with IE9.

6.11 Dragging and Dropping Elements

One of the more powerful effects of event handling is allowing the user to drag and drop elements around the display screen. The mouseup, mousedown, and mouse-move events can be used to implement this feature. Changing the top and left properties of an element, as seen earlier in the chapter, causes the element to move. To illustrate drag and drop, an HTML document and a JavaScript file that creates a magnetic poetry system is developed, showing two static lines of a poem and allowing the user to create the last two lines from a collection of movable words.

This example uses a mixture of the DOM 0 and DOM 2 event models. The DOM 0 model is used for the call to the handler for the mousedown event. The rest of the process is designed with the DOM 2 model. The mousedown event handler, grabber, takes the Event object as its parameter. It gets the element to be moved from the currentTarget property of the Event object and puts it in a global variable so that it is available to the other handlers. Then it determines the coordinates of the current position of the element to be moved and computes the difference between each of them and the corresponding coordinates of the position of the mouse cursor. These two differences, which are used by the handler for mousemove to actually move the element, are also placed in global variables. The grabber handler also registers the event handlers for mousemove and mouseup. These two handlers are named mover and dropper, respectively. The dropper handler disconnects mouse movements from the element-moving process by unregistering the handlers mover and dropper. The following is the document we have just described, called dragNDrop.html. Following it is the associated JavaScript file.

```
<!DOCTYPE html>
<!-- dragNDrop.html
     An example to illustrate the DOM 2 Event model
     Allows the user to drag and drop words to complete
     a short poem.
     Does not work with IE browsers before IE9
     -->
<html lang = "en">
  <head>
    <title> Drag and drop </title>
    <meta charset = "utf-8" />
    <script type = "text/javascript"  src = "dragNdrop.js" >
    </script>
  </head>
  <body style = "font-size: 20;">
    <p>
      Roses are red <br />
      Violets are blue <br />


      <span style = "position: absolute; top: 200px; left: 0px;
                  background-color: lightgrey;"
          onmousedown = "grabber(event);"> candy </span>
      <span style = "position: absolute; top: 200px; left: 75px;
                  background-color: lightgrey;"
          onmousedown = "grabber(event);"> cats </span>
      <span style = "position: absolute; top: 200px; left: 150px;
                  background-color: lightgrey;"
          onmousedown = "grabber(event);"> cows </span>
```

```
      <span style = "position: absolute; top: 200px; left: 225px;
                background-color: lightgrey;"
         onmousedown = "grabber(event);"> glue </span>
      <span style = "position: absolute; top: 200px; left: 300px;
                background-color: lightgrey;"
         onmousedown = "grabber(event);"> is </span>
      <span style = "position: absolute; top: 200px; left: 375px;
                background-color: lightgrey;"
         onmousedown = "grabber(event);"> is </span>
      <span style = "position: absolute; top: 200px; left: 450px;
                background-color: lightgrey;"
         onmousedown = "grabber(event);"> meow </span>
      <span style = "position: absolute; top: 250px; left: 0px;
                background-color: lightgrey;"
         onmousedown = "grabber(event);"> mine </span>
      <span style = "position: absolute; top: 250px; left: 75px;
                background-color: lightgrey;"
         onmousedown = "grabber(event);"> moo </span>
      <span style = "position: absolute; top: 250px; left: 150px;
                background-color: lightgrey;"
         onmousedown = "grabber(event);"> new </span>
      <span style = "position: absolute; top: 250px; left: 225px;
                background-color: lightgrey;"
         onmousedown = "grabber(event);"> old </span>
      <span style = "position: absolute; top: 250px; left: 300px;
                background-color: lightgrey;"
         onmousedown = "grabber(event);"> say </span>
      <span style = "position: absolute; top: 250px; left: 375px;
                background-color: lightgrey;"
         onmousedown = "grabber(event);"> say </span>
      <span style = "position: absolute; top: 250px; left: 450px;
                background-color: lightgrey;"
         onmousedown = "grabber(event);"> so </span>
      <span style = "position: absolute; top: 300px; left: 0px;
                background-color: lightgrey;"
         onmousedown = "grabber(event);"> sticky </span>
      <span style = "position: absolute; top: 300px; left: 75px;
                background-color: lightgrey;"
         onmousedown = "grabber(event);"> sweet </span>
      <span style = "position: absolute; top: 300px; left: 150px;
                background-color: lightgrey;"
         onmousedown = "grabber(event);"> syrup </span>
      <span style = "position: absolute; top: 300px; left: 225px;
                background-color: lightgrey;"
         onmousedown = "grabber(event);"> too </span>
```

```
            <span style = "position: absolute; top: 300px; left: 300px;
                           background-color: lightgrey;"
                  onmousedown = "grabber(event);"> yours </span>
        </p>
      </body>
</html>
```

```
// dragNDrop.js
//    An example to illustrate the DOM 2 Event model
//    Allows the user to drag and drop words to complete
//    a short poem.
//    Does not work with IE browsers before IE9


// Define variables for the values computed by
// the grabber event handler but needed by mover
// event handler
     var diffX, diffY, theElement;


// *********************************************************
// The event handler function for grabbing the word
function grabber(event) {


// Set the global variable for the element to be moved
  theElement = event.currentTarget;


// Determine the position of the word to be grabbed,
// first removing the units from left and top
  var posX = parseInt(theElement.style.left);
  var posY = parseInt(theElement.style.top);


// Compute the difference between where it is and
// where the mouse click occurred
  diffX = event.clientX - posX;
  diffY = event.clientY - posY;


// Now register the event handlers for moving and
// dropping the word
  document.addEventListener("mousemove", mover, true);
  document.addEventListener("mouseup", dropper, true);
```

```
// Stop propagation of the event and stop any default
// browser action
   event.stopPropagation();
   event.preventDefault();


}  //** end of grabber


// ***********************************************************
// The event handler function for moving the word
function mover(event) {


// Compute the new position, add the units, and move the word
   theElement.style.left = (event.clientX - diffX) + "px";
   theElement.style.top = (event.clientY - diffY) + "px";


// Prevent propagation of the event
   event.stopPropagation();
}  //** end of mover


// ***********************************************************
// The event handler function for dropping the word
function dropper(event) {


// Unregister the event handlers for mouseup and mousemove
   document.removeEventListener("mouseup", dropper, true);
   document.removeEventListener("mousemove", mover, true);


// Prevent propagation of the event
   event.stopPropagation();
}  //** end of dropper
```

Figure 6.13 shows a browser display of `dragNDrop.html`, after some interaction.

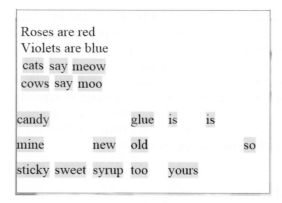

Figure 6.13 Display of `dragNDrop.html`

Note that the drag-and-drop process can be written with the DOM 0 event model. However, it can be made portable only by having the script detect which browser is being used and using different code for the different browsers. We have chosen to write it with the DOM 2 event model rather than deal with that untidy situation.

Summary

The CSS-P standard enables us initially to place HTML elements wherever we want in a document and then move them later. Elements can be positioned at any given location in the display of the document if their `position` property is set to `absolute` or `relative`. Absolute positioning uses the `left` and `top` properties of an element to place the element at a position relative to the upper-left corner of the display of the document. Relative positioning is used to place an element at a specified offset from the `top` and `left` coordinates of where it would have gone with the default static positioning. Relative positioning also allows an element to be moved later. Static positioning, which is the default, disallows both specific initial placement and dynamic moving of the element.

An HTML element can be made to disappear and reappear by changing its `visibility` property.

The color of the background of a document is stored in its `background-Color` property; the color of an element is stored in its `color` property. Both of these can be dynamically changed. The font, font size, and font style of text also can be changed.

The content of an element can be changed by changing its `value` property. An element in a document can be set to appear to be in front of other elements, and this top-to-bottom stacking order can be dynamically changed. The coordinates of the mouse cursor can be found by means of properties of the event object every time a mouse button is pressed. An element can be animated, at least in a crude way, by changing its `top` and `left` properties repeatedly by small amounts. Such an operation can be controlled by the `Window` method `setTimeout`. Event handlers for the mouse events can be written to allow the user to drag and drop elements anywhere on the display screen.

Review Questions

6.1   Define a dynamic HTML document.

6.2   If you know the id of an HTML element, how can you get the DOM address of that element in JavaScript?

6.3   If you have a variable that has the id of an HTML element, how can you get the DOM address of that element in JavaScript?

6.4   In what additional way can you obtain the DOM addresses of radio buttons and checkboxes?

6.5   What is CSS-P?

6.6   Describe all of the differences between the three possible values of the `position` property.

6.7   What are the standard values for the `visibility` property?

6.8   What properties control the foreground and background colors of a document?

6.9   What events can be used to change a font when the mouse cursor is moved over and away from an element?

6.10 What property has the content of an element?

6.11 What JavaScript variable is associated with the `z-index` property?

6.12 To move an element to the top of the display, do you set its `z-index` property to a large number or a small number?

6.13 What exactly is stored in the `clientX` and `clientY` properties after a mouse click?

6.14 What exactly is stored in the `screenX` and `screenY` properties after a mouse click?

6.15 Describe the parameters and actions of the `setTimeout` function.

Exercises

Write, test, validate, and debug (if necessary) the following documents:

6.1   The document must have a paragraph of at least 10 lines of text that describe you. This paragraph must be centered on the page and have space for 20 characters per line only. A light-gray image of yourself must be superimposed over the center of the text as a nested element.

6.2   Modify the document described in Exercise 6.1 to add four buttons labeled, respectively, *Northwest*, *Northeast*, *Southwest*, and *Southeast*. When they're pressed, the buttons must move your image to the specified corner of the text. Initially, your image must appear in the northwest (upper-left) corner of the text.

6.3   Modify the document described in Exercise 6.2 to make the buttons toggle their respective copies of your image on and off so that, at any time, the document may include none, one, two, three, or four copies of your image. The initial document should have no images shown.

6.4   The document must have a paragraph of text that describes your home. Choose at least three different phrases (three to six words each) of this paragraph, and make them change font, font style, color, and font size when the mouse cursor is placed over them. Each of the different phrases must change to a different font, font style, color, and font size.

6.5   The document must display an image and three buttons. The buttons should be labeled simply *1*, *2*, and *3*. When pressed, each button should change the content of the image to that of a different image.

6.6   The document must contain four short paragraphs of text, stacked on top of each other, with only enough of each showing so that the mouse cursor can always be placed over some part of them. When the cursor is placed over the exposed part of any paragraph, it should rise to the top to become completely visible.

6.7   Modify the document of Exercise 6.6 so that when a paragraph is moved from the top stacking position, it returns to its original position rather than to the bottom.

6.8   The document must have a small image of yourself, which must appear at the position of the mouse cursor when the mouse button is clicked, regardless of the position of the cursor at the time.

6.9   The document must contain the statement "Save time with TIME-SAVER 2.2," which continuously moves back and forth across the top of the display.

6.10   Modify the document of Exercise 6.9 to make the statement change color between red and blue every fifth step of its movement (assuming that each move is 1 pixel long).

6.11   Modify the `mover` example in Section 6.10 to input the starting and ending position of the element to be moved.

Introduction to XML

Some people consider the eXtensible Markup Language (XML) to be one of the most important among the parade of technologies developed to support the World Wide Web. Clearly, it has already had far-reaching effects on the storage and processing of data. XML consists of a collection of related technologies specified by recommendations developed by the W3C. This chapter provides introductions to the most important of these.

The chapter begins with a brief discussion of the origins of XML, followed by a description of some of its characteristics. Then the general syntactic structure of XML documents is described. Next, the chapter details the purpose and form of document type definitions (DTDs), including the declarations of elements, attributes, and entities. A DTD provides the elements and attributes for a markup language, as well as the rules for how the elements can appear in documents. This discussion is followed by a description of XML namespaces.

Next, XML Schema is introduced. XML Schema provides a more elaborate way to describe the structure of XML documents than DTDs. Two different approaches to formatting XML documents—CSS and XSLT style sheets—are then discussed and illustrated with examples. Actually, XSLT style sheets are used to transform XML documents. The targets of the transformations we describe are HTML documents, which can include CSS style specifications for display. Finally, we discuss the issues associated with reading and processing XML documents. Keep in mind that this chapter describes only a small part of XML and its associated technologies.

7.1   Introduction

A meta-markup language is a language for defining markup languages. The Standard Generalized Markup Language (SGML) is a meta-markup language for defining markup languages that can describe a wide variety of document types. In 1986, SGML was approved as an International Standards Organization (ISO) standard. In 1990, SGML was used as the basis for the development of HTML as the standard markup language for Web documents. In 1996, the World Wide Web Consortium (W3C) began work on XML, another meta-markup language. The first XML standard, 1.0, was published in February 1998. The second, 1.1, was published in 2004. Because this newer version is not widely supported, only version 1.0 is described in this chapter.

Part of the motivation for the development of XML was the deficiencies of HTML. The purpose of HTML is to describe the layout of information in Web documents. For this purpose, HTML defines a collection of tags and attributes. An HTML user is restricted to use that set of tags and attributes. One problem with HTML is that it was defined to describe the layout of information without considering the meaning of that information. So, regardless of the kind of information being described with HTML, only its general form and layout can be described in a document. For example, suppose that a document stores a list of used cars for sale and the color and price are included for each car. With HTML, those two pieces of information about a car could be stored as the content of paragraph elements, but there would be no way to find them in the document because paragraph tags could have been used for many different kinds of information. To describe a particular kind of information, it would be necessary to have tags indicating the meaning of the element's content. That would allow the processing of specific categories of information in a document. For example, if the price of a used car is stored as the content of an element named `price`, an application could find all cars in the document that cost less than $20,000. Of course, no markup language could include meaningful tags for all of the different kinds of information that might be stored in documents.

Another potential problem with HTML is that it enforces few restrictions on the arrangement or order of tags in a document. For example, an opening tag can appear in the content of an element, but its corresponding closing tag can appear after the end of the element in which its opening tag is nested. An example of this situation is as follows:

```
<strong> Now <em> is </strong> the time </em>
```

Note that although this problem was evident in HTML 4, which was in use when XML was developed, it is not a problem with XHTML

One solution that addresses the deficiencies of HTML is for each group of users with common document needs to develop its own set of tags and attributes and then use the SGML standard to define a new markup language to meet those needs. Each application area would have its own markup language. The problem with this solution, however, is that SGML is too large and complex to make this approach feasible. SGML includes a large number of capabilities that are only rarely used. A program capable of parsing SGML documents would be very large and costly to develop. In addition, SGML requires that a formal definition be provided with each new markup language. So, although having area-specific markup languages is a good idea, basing them on SGML is not.

An alternative solution to the problems of HTML is to define a simplified version of SGML and allow users to define their own markup languages based on it. XML was designed to be that simplified version of SGML. In this context, "users" refers to organizations of people with common data description and processing needs (rather than individual users). For example, chemists need to store chemical data in a standard format, providing a way to share data with other chemists and allowing all to use data-processing tools that work on chemical data stored in the same standard format, regardless of the origin of the data. Likewise, this is the case for many other groups with their own kinds of data to represent and process.

It is important to understand that XML was not meant to be a replacement for HTML. In fact, the two languages have different goals: Whereas HTML is a markup language that is meant to describe the layout of general information, as well as provide some guidance as to how it should be displayed, XML is a meta-markup language that provides a framework for defining specialized markup languages. HTML itself can be defined as an XML markup language. In fact, XHTML is an XML-based version of HTML.

XML is far more than a solution to the deficiencies of HTML: It provides a simple and universal way of storing any textual data. Data stored in XML documents can be electronically distributed and processed by any number of different applications. These applications are relatively easy to write because of the standard way in which the data is stored. Therefore, XML is a universal data interchange language.

XML is not a markup language; it is a meta-markup language that specifies rules for creating markup languages. As a result, XML includes no tags. When designing a markup language using XML, the designer must define a collection of tags that are useful in the intended area. As with XHTML, an XML tag and its content, together with the closing tag, are called an *element*.

Strictly speaking, a markup language designed with XML is called an *XML application*. However, a program that processes information stored in a document formatted with an XML application is also called an application. To avoid confusion, we refer to an XML-based markup language as a *tag set*. We call documents that use an XML-based markup language *XML documents*.

XML documents can be written by hand with a simple text editor. This approach is, of course, impractical for large data collections, documents for which are likely to be written by programs. There are many XML-oriented text editors that assist with the creation and maintenance of XML documents. Among these are the Altova XMLSpy, the graphical editor for Windows, the PSGML plug-in for the Emacs editor, XMLFox, and the Morphon XML-Editor.

A browser has a default presentation style for every HTML element, which makes it possible for the browser to display any HTML document, whether CSS information is included or not. However, a browser cannot be expected to have default presentation styles for elements it has never seen. Therefore, the data in an XML document can be displayed by browsers only if the presentation styles are provided by style sheets of some kind.

Application programs that process the data in XML documents must analyze the documents before they gain access to the data. This analysis is performed by an XML processor, which has several tasks, one of which is to parse XML documents, a process that isolates the constituent parts (such as tags, attributes, and data strings) and provides them to an application. XML processors are described in Section 7.10.

Unlike most documents produced by word-processing systems, XML documents have no hidden specifications. Therefore, XML documents are plain text, which is easily readable by both people and application programs (although there are no compelling reasons for people to read them).

All contemporary browsers support XML.

7.2 The Syntax of XML

The syntax of XML can be thought of at two distinct levels. First, there is the general low-level syntax of XML, which imposes its rules on all XML documents. The other syntactic level is specified by either document type definitions (DTDs) or XML schemas. DTDs and XML schemas specify the set of tags and attributes that can appear in a particular document or collection of documents and also the orders and arrangements in which they can appear. So, either a DTD or an XML schema can be used to define an XML-based markup language. DTDs are described in Section 7.4. XML schemas are discussed in Section 7.6. This section describes the low-level XML syntax, which applies to all XML documents.

An XML document can include several different kinds of statements. The most common are the data elements of the document. XML documents may also include markup declarations, which are instructions to the XML parser, and processing instructions, which are instructions for an application program that will process the data described in the document.

All XML documents begin with an XML declaration, which looks like a processing instruction but technically is not one. The XML declaration identifies the document as XML and provides the version number of the XML standard used. It may also specify an encoding standard.

Comments in XML are the same as in HTML. They cannot contain two adjacent dashes, for obvious reasons.

XML names are used to name elements and attributes. An XML name must begin with a letter or an underscore and can include digits, hyphens, and periods. XML names are case sensitive, so `Body`, `body`, and `BODY` are all distinct names. There is no length limitation for XML names.

A small set of syntax rules applies to all XML documents. XHTML uses the same rules, and the HTML markup in this book complies with them.

Every XML document defines a single root element, whose opening tag must appear on the first line of XML code. All other elements of an XML document must be nested inside the root element. The root element of every HTML document is `html`, but in XML it has whatever name the author chooses. XML tags, like those of HTML, are surrounded by angle brackets.

Every XML element that can have content must have a closing tag. Elements that do not include content must use a tag with the following form:

<element_name />

As is the case with HTML, XML tags can have attributes, which are specified with name–value assignments. All attribute values must be enclosed by either single or double quotation marks.

An XML document that strictly adheres to these syntax rules is considered *well formed*. The following is a simple, but complete, example:

```
<?xml version = "1.0" encoding = "utf-8"?>
<ad>
  <year> 1960 </year>
  <make> Cessna </make>
  <model> Centurian </model>
  <color> Yellow with white trim </color>
  <location>
    <city> Gulfport </city>
    <state> Mississippi </state>
  </location>
</ad>
```

Notice that none of the tags in this document is defined in HTML—all are designed for the specific content of the document. This document defines an XML tag set, illustrating that an XML-based markup language can be defined without a DTD or an XML schema, although it is an informal definition of a tag set (in this case, no attributes were defined) with no structure rules.

When designing an XML document, the designer is often faced with the choice between adding a new attribute to an element or defining a nested element.

In some cases, there is no choice. For example, if the data in question is an image, a reference to it can only be an attribute because such a reference cannot be the content of an element (since images are binary data and XML documents can contain text only). In other cases, it may not matter whether an attribute or a nested element is used. However, there are some situations in which there is a choice and one is clearly preferable.

In some cases, nested tags are better than attributes. A document or category of documents for which tags are being defined might need to grow in structural complexity in the future. Nested tags can be added to any existing tag to describe its growing size and complexity. Nothing can be added to an attribute, however. Attributes cannot describe structure at all, so a nested element should be used if the data in question has some substructure of its own. A nested element should be used if the data is subdata of the parent element's content rather than information about the data of the parent element.

There is one situation in which an attribute should always be used: to identify numbers or names of elements, exactly as the id and name attributes are used in HTML. An attribute also should be used if the data in question is one value from a given set of possibilities. Finally, attributes should be used if there is no substructure or if it is really just information about the element.

The following versions of an element named patient illustrate three possible choices between tags and attributes:

```
<!-- A tag with one attribute -->
<patient name = "Maggie Dee Magpie">
  ...
</patient>


<!-- A tag with one nested tag -->
<patient>
  <name> Maggie Dee Magpie </name>
  ...
</patient>


<!-- A tag with one nested tag, which contains
     three nested tags -->
<patient>
  <name>
    <first> Maggie </first>
    <middle> Dee </middle>
    <last> Magpie </last>
  </name>
  ...
</patient>
```

In this example, the third choice is probably the best because it provides easy access to all of the parts of the data, which may be needed. Also, there is no compelling reason to use attributes in this structure.

7.3 XML Document Structure

An XML document often uses two auxiliary files: one that defines its tag set and structural syntactic rules and one that contains a style sheet to describe how the content of the document is to be printed or displayed. The structural syntactic rules are given as either a DTD or an XML schema. Two approaches to style specification are discussed in Sections 7.8 and 7.9.

An XML document consists of one or more entities, which are logically related collections of information, ranging in size from a single character to a chapter of a book. One of these entities, called the *document entity*, is always physically in the file that represents the document. The document entity can be the entire document, but in many cases, it includes references to the names of entities that are stored elsewhere. For example, the document entity for a technical article might contain the beginning material and ending material but have references to the article body sections, which are entities stored in separate files. Every entity except the document entity must have a name.

There are several reasons to break a document into multiple entities. First, it is good to define a large document as a number of smaller parts to make it more manageable. Also, if the same data appears in more than one place in the document, defining that data as an entity allows any number of references to a single copy of it. This approach avoids the problem of inconsistency among the occurrences. Finally, many documents include information that cannot be represented as text, such as images. Such information units are usually stored as binary data. If a binary data unit is logically part of a document, it must be a separate entity because XML documents cannot include binary data. These entities are called *binary entities*. The use of binary entities is discussed in Section 7.4.5.

When an XML processor encounters the name of a nonbinary entity in a document it replaces the name with the value it references. Binary entities can be handled only by applications that deal with the document, such as browsers. XML processors deal with text only.

Entity names can be any length. They must begin with a letter, a dash, or a colon. After the first character, a name can have letters, digits, periods, dashes, underscores, or colons. A reference to an entity is its name together with a prepended ampersand and an appended semicolon. For example, if `apple_image` is the name of an entity, `&apple_image;` is a reference to it.

One of the common uses of entities is to allow characters that are normally used as markup delimiters to appear as themselves in a document. Because this is a common need, XML includes the entities that are predefined for HTML, the most common of which are shown in Table 2.1 (in Chapter 2). User-defined entities can be defined only in DTDs, which are discussed in Section 7.4.

When several predefined entities must appear near each other in an XML document, their references clutter the content and make it difficult to read. In such cases, a character data section can be used. The content of a character data section is not parsed by the XML parser, so any tags it may include are not recognized as tags. This makes it possible to include special markup delimiter characters directly in the section without using their entity references. The form of a character data section is as follows:

```
<![CDATA[ content ]]>
```

For example, instead of

```
The last word of the line is &gt;&gt;&gt; here &it;&it;&it;.
```

the following could be used:

```
<![CDATA[The last word of the line is >>> here <<<]]>
```

The opening keyword of a character data section is not just CDATA; it is, in effect, [CDATA[. An important consequence of this rule is that there cannot be any spaces between the [and the C or between the A (the last character of CDATA) and the second [. The only thing that cannot appear in the content of a CDATA section is the closing delimiter,]]>.

Because the content of a character data section is not parsed by the XML parser, any entity references that are included are not expanded. For example, the content of the line

```
<![CDATA[The form of a tag is &it;tag name&gt;]]>
```

is as follows:

```
The form of a tag is &it;tag name&gt;
```

7.4 Document Type Definitions

A document type definition (DTD) is a set of structural rules called *declarations*, which specify a set of elements and attributes that can appear in a document, as well as how and where these elements and attributes may appear. DTDs also provide entity definitions. Not all XML documents need a DTD. The use of a DTD is related to the use of an external style sheet for HTML documents. External style sheets are used to impose a uniform style over a collection of documents. DTDs are used when the same tag set definition is used by a collection of documents—perhaps a collection of users—and the documents must have a consistent and uniform structure, as well as the same set of elements and attributes.

A document can be tested against the DTD to determine whether it conforms to the rules the DTD describes. Application programs that process the data in the collection of XML documents can be written so that they assume the particular document form. Without the set of structural restrictions provided by a single DTD, developing such applications would be difficult if not impossible.

A DTD can be embedded in the XML document whose syntax rules it describes, in which case it is called an *internal DTD*. The alternative is to have the DTD stored in a separate file, in which case it is called an *external DTD*. Because external DTDs allow use with more than one XML document, they are preferable. A group of users defines a DTD for its particular kind of data and uses that DTD, which imposes structural uniformity across all of the group's documents. Another reason to put a DTD in a different file is to separate the DTD, which is not XML, from the XML code of the document—that is, to avoid two different notations from appearing in the same document.

It is common knowledge that the earlier errors in software systems are found, the less expensive it is to correct them. The situation is similar in the case of DTDs. A DTD with an incorrect or inappropriate declaration can have widespread consequences. Fixing the DTD and all copies of it is the first and simplest step. After the correction of the DTD is completed, all documents that use the DTD must be tested against it and often modified to conform to the changed DTD. Changes to associated style sheets also might be necessary.

Syntactically, a DTD is a sequence of declarations, each of which has the form of a markup declaration:

```
<!keyword ... >
```

Four possible keywords can be used in a declaration: ELEMENT, used to define tags; ATTLIST, used to define tag attributes; ENTITY, used to define entities; and NOTATION, used to define data type notations. The first three of these kinds of declarations are respectively described in the three subsections that follow. Because of their infrequent use, NOTATION declarations are not discussed.

7.4.1 Declaring Elements

The element declarations of a DTD have a form that is related to that of the rules of context-free grammars, also known as Backus–Naur form (BNF).[1] BNF is used to define the syntactic structure of programming languages. A DTD describes the syntactic structure of a particular set of documents, so it is natural for its rules to be similar to those of BNF.

Each element declaration in a DTD specifies the structure of one category of elements. The declaration provides the name of the element whose structure is being defined, along with the specification of the structure of that element. Although an XML document actually is a string of characters, it is often convenient to think of it in terms of a general tree. An element is a node in such a tree, either a leaf node or an internal node. If the element is a leaf node, its syntactic description is its character pattern. If the element is an internal node, its syntactic

---

1. BNF is named after its primary designer, John Backus, and Peter Naur, who helped by providing some small modifications.

description is a list of its child elements, each of which can be a leaf node or an internal node.

The form of an element declaration for elements that contain elements is as follows:

<!ELEMENT *element_name* (*list of names of child elements*)>

For example, consider the following declaration:

```
<!ELEMENT memo (from, to, date, re, body)>
```

This element declaration would describe the document tree structure shown in Figure 7.1.

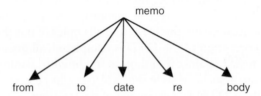

Figure 7.1 An example of the document tree structure for an element definition

In many cases, it is necessary to specify the number of times that a child element may appear. This can be done in a DTD declaration by adding a modifier to the child element specification. These modifiers, described in Table 7.1, are borrowed from regular expressions. Any child element specification can be followed by one of the modifiers.

Table 7.1   Child element specification modifiers

Modifier	Meaning
+	One or more occurrences
*	Zero or more occurrences
?	Zero or one occurrence

Consider the following DTD declaration:

```
<!ELEMENT person (parent+, age, spouse?, sibling*)>
```

In this example, a person element is specified to have the following child elements: one or more parent elements, one age element, possibly a spouse element, and zero or more sibling elements.

The leaf nodes of a DTD specify the data types of the content of their parent nodes, which are elements. In most cases, the content of an element is type PCDATA, for *parsable* character *data*. Parsable character data is a string of any printable characters except "less than" (<), "greater than" (>), and the ampersand (&). Two other content types can be specified: EMPTY and ANY. The EMPTY type specifies that the element has no content; it is used for elements similar to the HTML img element. The ANY type is used when the element may contain literally any content. The form of a leaf element declaration is as follows:

```
<!ELEMENT element_name (#PCDATA)>
```

7.4.2 Declaring Attributes

The attributes of an element are declared separately from the element declaration in a DTD. An attribute declaration must include the name of the element to which the attribute belongs, the attribute's name, its type, and a default option. The general form of an attribute declaration is as follows:

```
<!ATTLIST element_name attribute_name attribute type default_option>
```

If more than one attribute is declared for a given element, the declarations can be combined, as in the following element:

```
<!ATTLIST element_name
          attribute name_1 attribute type default_option_1
          attribute_name_2 attribute_type default_option_2
          ...
          attribute_name_n attribute_type default_option_n
>
```

There are 10 different attribute types. For this chapter, only two, CDATA and ENTITY, will be used. CDATA type is just any string of characters that does not include >, <, or &. ENTITY type is for declaring an entity attribute for a binary entity (see Section 7.4.3).

The default option in an attribute declaration can specify either an actual value or a requirement for the value of the attribute in the XML document. Table 7.2 lists the possible default options.

Table 7.2 Possible default options for attributes

Options	Meaning
A value	The quoted value, which is used if none is specified in an element
#FIXED value	The quoted value, which every element will have and which cannot be changed
#REQUIRED	No default value is given; every instance of the element must specify a value
#IMPLIED	No default value is given (the browser chooses the default value); the value may or may not be specified in an element

For example, suppose the DTD included the following attribute specifications:

```
<!ATTLIST airplane places CDATA "4">
<!ATTLIST airplane engine_type CDATA #REQUIRED>
<!ATTLIST airplane price CDATA #IMPLIED>
<!ATTLIST airplane manufacturer CDATA #FIXED "Cessna">
```

Then the following XML element would be valid for this DTD:

```
<airplane places = "10" engine_type = "jet"> </airplane>
```

Attributes that include #FIXED in the DTD may or may not be specified in particular instances of elements.

7.4.3   Declaring Entities

Entities can be defined so that they can be referenced anywhere in the content of an XML document, in which case they are called *general entities*. The predefined entities are all general entities. Entities can also be defined so that they can be referenced only in DTDs, in which case they are called *parameter entities*. Only general entities are discussed in this chapter.

The form of an entity declaration is

```
<!ENTITY [%] entity_name "entity_value">
```

When the optional percent sign (%) is present in an entity declaration, it specifies that the entity is a parameter entity rather than a general entity.

Consider the following example of an entity: Suppose that a document includes a large number of references to the full name of President Kennedy. Then you can define an entity to represent his complete name as follows:

```
<!ENTITY jfk "John Fitzgerald Kennedy">
```

Any XML document that uses a DTD that includes this declaration can specify the complete name with just the reference &jfk;.

When an entity is longer than a few words, such as a section of a technical article, its text is defined outside the DTD. In such cases, the entity is called an *external text entity*. The form of the declaration of an external text entity is

```
<!ENTITY entity_name SYSTEM "file_location">
```

The keyword SYSTEM specifies that the definition of the entity is in a different file, which is specified as the string following SYSTEM.

As stated in Section 7.3, binary data (not text) can be included in an XML document as an entity. Such an entity has a special form of declaration that includes two additional keywords. The first of these, NDATA, specifies that the entity value is not to be parsed. The second is a notation identifier that specifies the encoding of the entity value, for example, JPEG, GIF, MPEG, or WAV. For example, we could have the following:

```
<!ENTITY JFKPhoto SYSTEM "myEntities/JFKPhoto.jpg"
        NDATA JPEG>
```

Binary entities also require special references. For example,

```
This is a photograph of Kennedy: <photo ent = "JFKPhoto" />
```

Of course, this requires that the photo element and its attribute ent have been previously declared, as in the following:

```
<!ELEMENT photo EMPTY>
...
<!ATTLIST photo ent ENTITY #REQUIRED>
```

7.4.4 A Sample DTD

As an example of a DTD, consider a booklet of ads for used airplanes. In this case, the DTD describes the form of the booklet and each of its ads:

```
<?xml version = "1.0" encoding = "utf-8"?>


<!-- planes.dtd - a document type definition for
                  the planes.xml document, which specifies
                  a list of used airplanes for sale   -->


<!ELEMENT planes_for_sale (ad+)>
<!ELEMENT ad (year, make, model, color, description,
              price?, seller, location)>
<!ELEMENT year (#PCDATA)>
<!ELEMENT make (#PCDATA)>
<!ELEMENT model (#PCDATA)>
<!ELEMENT color (#PCDATA)>
<!ELEMENT description (#PCDATA)>
<!ELEMENT price (#PCDATA)>
<!ELEMENT seller (#PCDATA)>
<!ELEMENT location (city, state)>
<!ELEMENT city (#PCDATA)>
<!ELEMENT state (#PCDATA)>


<!ATTLIST seller phone CDATA #REQUIRED>
<!ATTLIST seller email CDATA #IMPLIED>


<!ENTITY c "Cessna">
<!ENTITY p "Piper">
<!ENTITY b "Beechcraft">
```

Some XML parsers check documents that have DTDs in order to ensure that the documents conform to the structure specified in the DTDs. These parsers are called *validating parsers*. Not all XML parsers are validating parsers. If an XML document specifies a DTD and is parsed by a validating XML parser, and the parser determines that the document conforms to the DTD, the document is called *valid*.

Handwritten XML documents often are not well formed, which means that they do not follow XML's syntactic rules. Any errors they contain are detected by all XML parsers, which must report them. Because errors are common, it is important to check that XML documents are well formed before making them available to site visitors. XML parsers are not allowed to either repair or ignore errors. Validating XML parsers detect and report all inconsistencies in documents relative to their DTDs. XML parsers are discussed in Section 7.10.

7.4.5   Internal and External DTDs

Recall that a DTD can appear inside an XML document or in an external file, as is the case with the DTD planes.dtd. If the DTD is included in the XML code, it must be introduced with <!DOCTYPE *root_name* [and terminated with]>. For example, the structure of the planes XML document, with its DTD included, is as follows:

```
<?xml version = "1.0" encoding = "utf-8"?>
    <!DOCTYPE planes [
        <!-- The DTD for planes -->
    ]>
<!-- The planes XML document -->
```

An internal DTD can be used just to define entities when there is no external DTD.

When the DTD is in a separate file, the XML document refers to it with a DOCTYPE declaration as its second line. This declaration then has the following form:

<!DOCTYPE *XML_document_root_name* SYSTEM "*DTD_file_name*">

For the planes example, assuming that the DTD is stored in the file named planes.dtd, this declaration would be

<!DOCTYPE planes_for_sale SYSTEM "planes.dtd">

The following is an example of an XML document that is valid for the planes DTD:

```
<?xml version = "1.0" encoding = "utf-8"?>

<!-- planes.xml - A document that lists ads for
                  used airplanes -->
```

```
<!DOCTYPE planes_for_sale SYSTEM "planes.dtd">
<planes_for_sale>
  <ad>
    <year> 1977 </year>
    <make> &c; </make>
    <model> Skyhawk </model>
    <color> Light blue and white </color>
    <description> New paint, nearly new interior,
        685 hours SMOH, full IFR King avionics </description>
    <price> 23,495 </price>
    <seller phone = "555-222-3333"> Skyway Aircraft </seller>
    <location>
      <city> Rapid City, </city>
      <state> South Dakota </state>
    </location>
  </ad>
  <ad>
    <year> 1965 </year>
    <make> &p; </make>
    <model> Cherokee </model>
    <color> Gold </color>
    <description> 240 hours SMOH, dual NAVCOMs, DME,
        new Cleveland brakes, great shape </description>
    <seller phone = "555-333-2222"
        email = "jseller@www.axl.com">
        John Seller </seller>
    <location>
      <city> St. Joseph, </city>
      <state> Missouri </state>
    </location>
  </ad>
</planes_for_sale>
```

7.5 Namespaces

It is often convenient to construct XML documents that use tag sets that are defined for and used by other documents. When a tag set is available and appropriate for a particular XML document or class of documents, it is better to use it than to invent a new collection of element types. For example, suppose you must define an XML markup language for a furniture catalog with `<chair>`, `<sofa>`, and `<table>` tags. Suppose also that the catalog document must include several different tables of specific furniture pieces, wood types, finishes, and prices. Then it obviously would be convenient to use HTML table tags to define these tables rather than invent a new vocabulary for them.

One problem with using different markup vocabularies in the same document is that collisions between names that are defined in two or more of those tag sets could result. An example of this situation is having a `<table>` tag for a category of furniture and a `<table>` tag from HTML for information tables. Clearly, software systems that process XML documents must be capable of unambiguously recognizing the element names in those documents. To deal with this problem, the W3C has developed a standard for XML namespaces (at `http://www.w3.org/TR/REC-xml-names`).

An *XML namespace* is a collection of element and attribute names used in XML documents. The name of a namespace usually has the form of a URL, although XML processors never reference the site whose URL is used as the name of a namespace. The name of a namespace for the elements and attributes of the hierarchy rooted at a particular element is declared as the value of the attribute `xmlns`. A namespace declaration for an element is given as the value of the `xmlns` attribute, as in the following:

<element_name `xmlns[`:*prefix]` `=` URL*>*

The square brackets here indicate that what is within them is optional. The prefix, if included, is the name that must be attached to the names in the declared namespace. If the prefix is not included, the namespace is the default for the document.

A prefix is used for two reasons. First, most URLs are too long to be typed on every occurrence of every name from the namespace. Second, a URL includes characters that are invalid in XML. Note that the element for which a namespace is declared is usually the root of a document.

As an example of a prefixed namespace declaration, consider the following:

```
<birds xmlns:bd = "http://www.audubon.org/names/species">
```

Within the `birds` element, including all of its children elements, the names from the given namespace must be prefixed with `bd`, as in the following element:

```
<bd:lark>
```

If an element has more than one namespace declaration, they are declared as in the following example:

```
<birds  xmlns:bd = "http://www.audubon.org/names/species"
        xmlns:html = "http://www.w3.org/1999/xhtml" >
```

In this tag, the standard HTML and XHTML namespace has been added to the `birds` element. One of the namespaces can be specified as the default by omitting the prefix in any namespace declaration.

The next example declares two namespaces. The first is declared to be the default namespace; the second defines the prefix, `cap`:

```
<states>
  xmlns = "http://www.states-info.org/states"
  xmlns:cap = "http://www.states-info.org/state-capitals"
  <state>
```

```
      <name> South Dakota </name>
      <population> 754844 </population>
      <capital>
        <cap:name> Pierre </cap:name>
        <cap:population> 12429 </cap:population>
      </capital>
    </state>
    <!-- More states -->
</states>
```

Each state element has name and population child elements from both namespaces.

Attribute names are not included in namespaces because attribute names are local to elements, so a tag set may use the same attribute name in more than one element without causing ambiguity.

If an XML document uses a DTD and a prefixed name, the DTD must define an element with exactly the same prefix and name.

Because of their form, it is tempting to think that a namespace is a Web resource that lists element names. But that is never the case. The standard namespaces (e.g., `http://www.w3.org/1999/xhtml`) often are valid URLs, but they are documents that describe far more than a set of element names. User-defined namespace names do not need to use the URL form, although that is a good way to prevent conflicts with namespace names.

7.6 XML Schemas

DTDs have several disadvantages. One is that DTDs are written in a syntax unrelated to XML, so they cannot be analyzed with an XML processor. Also, it can be confusing for people to deal with two different syntactic forms, one that defines a document and one that defines its structure. A second disadvantage is that DTDs do not allow restrictions on the form of data that can be the content of a particular tag. For example, if the content of an element represents time, then, regardless of the form of the time data, a DTD can only specify that it is text, which could be anything. In fact, the content of an element could be an integer number, a floating-point number, or a range of numbers. All of these would be specified as text. With DTDs, there are only 10 data types, none of which is numeric. A third disadvantage of DTDs is that the child elements of an element must be in a specific order, even if the order is not important to the application. This is a case or requiring overspecification. Finally, all elements that are used in a DTD must be declared there; no externally defined elements can be used. This prevents a DTD from using names from the HTML namespace, for example, which is often useful. So, while XML naturally allows the use of external namespaces, DTDs do not.

Several alternatives to DTDs have been developed to overcome their weaknesses. The XML Schema standard, which was designed by the W3C, is one of these alternatives.[2] We have chosen to discuss it because of its W3C support and

---

2. Two others are RELAX NG and Schematron.

the likelihood that it will become the primary successor to DTD. An XML schema is an XML document, so it can be parsed with an XML parser. It also provides far more control over data types than do DTDs. The content of a specific element can be required to be any one of 44 different data types. Furthermore, the user can define new types with constraints on existing data types. For example, a numeric data value can be required to have exactly seven digits.

To promote the transition from DTDs to XML schemas, XML Schema was designed to allow any DTD to be automatically converted to an equivalent XML schema. For the remainder of this chapter, we will sometimes refer to an XML schema simply as a schema.

7.6.1   Schema Fundamentals

Schemas can conveniently be related to the idea of a class and an object in an object-oriented programming language. A schema is similar to a class definition; an XML document that conforms to the structure defined in the schema is similar to an object of the schema's class. In fact, XML documents that conform to a specific schema are considered instances of that schema.

Schemas have three primary purposes. First, a schema specifies the elements and attributes of an XML language. Second, a schema defines the structure of the instance XML documents of the language, including where and how often the elements may appear. Third, a schema specifies the data type of every element in its instance XML documents. This is the area in which schemas far outshine DTDs.

It has been said that XML schemas are "namespace centric." There is some truth to that depiction. In XML schemas, as in XML, namespaces are represented by names that have the form of URLs. Because they must be unique, it is customary to use URLs that start with the author's Web site address for namespaces. For example, for namespaces that appear in this section, we use the prefix `"http://cs.uccs.edu/"`, to which we add whatever name connotes the specific application.

7.6.2   Defining a Schema

Schemas themselves are written with the use of a collection of tags, or a vocabulary, from a namespace that is, in effect, a schema of schemas. The name of this namespace is `http://www.w3.org/2001/XMLSchema`. Some of the elements in the namespace are `element`, `schema`, `sequence`, and `string`.

Every schema has `schema` as its root element. The `schema` element specifies the namespace for the schema of schemas from which the schema's elements and attributes will be drawn. It often also specifies a prefix that will be used for the names in the schema. This namespace specification appears as follows:

```
xmlns:xsd = "http://www.w3.org/2001/XMLSchema"
```

Note that the specification provides the prefix xsd for the names from the namespace for the schema of schemas.

A schema defines a namespace in the same sense as a DTD defines a tag set. The name of the namespace defined by a schema must be specified with the targetNamespace attribute of the schema element. The name of every top-level (not nested) element that appears in a schema is placed in the target namespace, which is specified by assigning a namespace to the target namespace attribute:

```
targetNamespace = "http://cs.uccs.edu/planeSchema"
```

If the names of the elements and attributes that are not defined directly in the schema element (because they are nested inside top-level elements) are to be included in the target namespace, schema's elementFormDefault must be set to qualified, as follows:

```
elementFormDefault = "qualified"
```

The default namespace, which is the source of the unprefixed names in the schema, is given with another xmlns specification, but this time without the prefix:

```
xmlns = "http://cs.uccs.edu/planeSchema"
```

An example of a complete opening tag for a schema is as follows:

```
<xsd:schema
<!-- The namespace for the schema itself (prefix is xsd) -->
  xmlns:xsd = http://www.w3.org/2001/XMLSchema
<!-- The namespace where elements defined here will be
placed -->
  targetNamespace = http://cs.uccs.edu/planeSchema
<!-- The default namespace for this document (no prefix) -->
  xmlns = http://cs.uccs.edu/planeSchema
<!-- We want to put non-top-level elements in the target
namespace -->
  elementFormDefault = "qualified">
```

In this example, the target namespace and the default namespace are the same.

One alternative to the preceding opening tag would be to make the XMLSchema names the default so that they do not need to be prefixed in the schema. Then the names in the target namespace would need to be prefixed. The following schema tag illustrates this approach:

```
<schema
  xmlns = "http://www.w3.org/2001/XMLSchema"
  targetNamespace = "http://cs.uccs.edu/planeSchema"
  xmlns:plane = "http://cs.uccs.edu/planeSchema"
  elementFormDefault = "qualified">
```

7.6.5   Simple Types

Elements are defined in an XML schema with the element tag, which is from the XMLSchema namespace. Recall that the prefix xsd is normally used for names from this namespace. An element that is named includes the name attribute for that purpose. The other attribute that is necessary in a simple element declaration is type, which is used to specify the type of content allowed in the element. Here is an example:

```
<xsd:element name = "engine"  type = "xsd:string" />
```

An instance of the schema in which the engine element is defined could have the following element:

```
<engine> inline six cylinder fuel injected </engine>
```

An element can be given a default value with the default attribute:

```
<xsd:element name = "engine"   type = "xsd:string"
            default = "fuel injected V-6"  />
```

Elements can have constant values, meaning that the content of the defined element in every instance document has the same value. Constant values are given with the fixed attribute, as in the following example:

```
<xsd:element name = "plane"   type = "xsd:string"
            fixed = "single wing"  />
```

We now turn our attention to user-defined data types, which are constrained predefined types. A simple user-defined data type is described in a simpleType element with the use of facets. Facets must be specified in the content of a restriction element, which gives the base type name. The facets themselves are given in elements named for the facets: the value attribute specifies the value of the facet. For example, the following element declares a user-defined type, firstName, for strings of fewer than 11 characters:

```
<xsd:simpleType name = "firstName">
  <xsd:restriction base = "xsd:string">
    <xsd:maxLength value = "10" />
  </xsd:restriction>
</xsd:simpleType>
```

The length facet is used to restrict the string to an exact number of characters. The minLength facet is used to specify a minimum length. The number of digits of a decimal number can be restricted with the value attribute of the precision facet, as in the following example:

```
<xsd:simpleType name = "phoneNumber">
  <xsd:restriction base = "xsd:decimal">
    <xsd:precision value = "7" />
  </xsd:restriction>
</xsd:simpleType>
```

7.6.6   Complex Types

Most XML documents include nested elements, so few XML schemas do not have complex types. Although there are several categories of complex element types, the discussion here is restricted to those called *element-only elements*, which can have elements in their content, but no text. All complex types can have attributes.

Complex types are defined with the `complexType` tag. The elements that are the content of an element-only element must be contained in an ordered group, an unordered group, a choice, or a named group. Ordered and unordered groups are discussed here.

The `sequence` element is used to contain an ordered group of elements, as in the following type definition:

```
<xsd:complexType name = "sports_car">
  <xsd:sequence>
    <xsd:element name = "make"  type = "xsd:string" />
    <xsd:element name = "model"  type = "xsd:string" />
    <xsd:element name = "engine"  type = "xsd:string" />
    <xsd:element name = "year"  type = "xsd:decimal" />
  </xsd:sequence>
</xsd:complexType>
```

A complex type whose elements are an unordered group is defined in an `all` element.

Elements in `all` and `sequence` groups can include the `minOccurs` and `maxOccurs` attributes to specify the numbers of occurrences. The possible values of `minOccurs` are the nonnegative integers (including zero). The possible values for `maxOccurs` are the nonnegative integers plus the value `unbounded`, which has the obvious meaning.

Consider the following complete example of a schema:

```
<?xml version = "1.0" encoding = "utf-8"?>

<!-- planes.xsd
     A simple schema for planes.xml
     -->
<xsd:schema
  xmlns:xsd = "http://www.w3.org/2001/XMLSchema"
  targetNamespace = "http://cs.uccs.edu/planeSchema"
  xmlns = "http://cs.uccs.edu/planeSchema"
  elementFormDefault = "qualified">

  <xsd:element name = "planes">
    <xsd:complexType>
      <xsd:all>
```

```
            <xsd:element name = "make"
                         type = "xsd:string"
                         minOccurs = "1"
                         maxOccurs = "unbounded" />
        </xsd:all>
      </xsd:complexType>
    </xsd:element>
</xsd:schema>
```

Notice that we use the `all` element to contain the single element of the complex type `planes`, although `sequence` could have been used instead. Because there is only one contained element, the two are not different.

The `choice` element can contain any number of elements, only one of which can appear in any XML document that complies with the schema.

An XML instance that conforms to the `planes.xsd` schema is as follows:

```
<?xml version = "1.0" encoding = "utf-8"?>

<!-- planes1.xml
     A simple XML document for illustrating a schema
     The schema is in planes.xsd
     -->
<planes
  xmlns = "http://cs.uccs.edu/planeSchema"
  xmlns:xsi = "http://www.w3.org/2001/XMLSchema-instance"
  xsi:schemaLocation = "http://cs.uccs.edu/planeSchema
                        planes.xsd">
    <make> Cessna </make>
    <make> Piper </make>
    <make> Beechcraft </make>
</planes>
```

If we want the `year` element in the `sports_car` element that was defined earlier to be a derived type, the derived type could be defined as another global element and we could refer to it in the `sports_car` element. For example, the `year` element could be defined as follows:

```
<xsd:element name = "year">
  <xsd:simpleType>
    <xsd:restriction base = "xsd:decimal">
      <xsd:minInclusive value = "1900" />
```

```
        <xsd:maxInclusive value = "2012" />
      </xsd:restriction>
    </xsd:simpleType>
</xsd:element>
```

With the `year` element defined globally, the `sports_car` element can be defined with a reference to the `year` with the `ref` attribute:

```
<xsd:complexType name = "sports_car">
  <xsd:sequence>
    <xsd:element name = "make"  type = "xsd:string" />
    <xsd:element name = "model"  type = "xsd:string" />
    <xsd:element name = "engine"  type = "xsd:string" />
    <xsd:element ref = "year" />
  </xsd:sequence>
</xsd:complexType>
```

The reader may have noticed that while DTDs can define elements, attributes, and entities, so far we have not mentioned defining entities in schemas. There are two ways to do this. If an entity is only needed in one instance document whose structure is defined in a schema, an internal DTD declaration can be used. For example, consider the following document:

```
<?xml version = "1.0" ?>
<!DOCTYPE planes [
   <!ENTITY c "Cessna">
]>
<planes ...>
...
</planes>
```

If the entity is used by more than one instance document, it could be defined in the schema as an element, as in the following example:

```
<xsd:element-name = "c" type = "xsd:token" fixed = "Cessna"
/>
```

In an instance document, this can be used as follows:

```
<make> <c> </make>
```

7.6.7   Validating Instances of Schemas

An XML schema provides a definition of a category of XML documents. However, developing a schema is of limited value unless there is some mechanical way to determine whether a given XML instance document conforms to the schema. Fortunately, several XML schema validation tools are available. One of them is named `xsv`, an abbreviation for XML Schema Validator. It was developed by Henry S. Thompson and Richard Tobin at the University of Edinburgh in Scotland. If the schema and the instance document are available on the Web, `xsv` can be used online, like the XHTML validation tool at the W3C Web site. This tool can also be downloaded and run on any computer. The Web site for `xsv` is `http://www.w3.org/XML/Schema#XSV`.

The output of `xsv` is an XML document. When the tool is run from the command line, the output document appears on the screen with no formatting, so it is a bit difficult to read. The following is the output of `xsv` run on `planes.xml`:

```
<?XML version='1.0' encoding = 'utf-8'?>
<xsv docElt='{http://cs.uccs.edu/planeSchema}planes'
     instanceAssessed='true'
     instanceErrors = '0'
     rootType='[Anonymous]'
     schemaErrors='0'
     schemaLocs='http://cs.uccs.edu/planeSchema ->
planes.xsd'
     target='file:/c:/wbook2/xml/planes.xml'
     validation='strict'
     version='XSV 1.197/1.101 of 2001/07/07 12:10:19'
     xmlns='http://www.w3.org/2000/05/xsv' >

  <importAttempt URI='file:/c:wbook2/xml/planes.xsd'
                 namespace='http://cs.uccs.edu/planeSchema'
                 outcome='success' />
</xsv>
```

The actual output from `xsv` is displayed with no formatting: Each line is filled to the right end of the screen, and attribute values are broken across line boundaries in several places.

One useful thing to know about validation with `xsv` is that if the schema is not in the correct format, the validator will report that it could not find the specified schema.

7.7 Displaying Raw XML Documents

An XML-enabled browser—or any other system that can deal with XML documents—cannot know how to format the tags defined in any given document. (After all, someone just made them up.) Therefore, if an XML document is displayed without a style sheet that defines presentation styles for the document's tags, the displayed document will not have formatted content. Most contemporary browsers include default style sheets that are used when no style sheet is specified in the XML document. The display of such an XML document is only a somewhat stylized listing of the XML markup. The FX3 browser display of the `planes.xml` document is shown in Figure 7.2.

This XML file does not appear to have any style information associated with it. The document tree is shown below.

```
- <!--
     planes.xml - A document that lists ads for
          used airplanes
  -->
- <planes_for_sale>
  - <ad>
      <year> 1977 </year>
      <make> Cessna </make>
      <model> Skyhawk </model>
      <color> Light blue and white </color>
    - <description>
        New paint, nearly new interior, 685 hours SMOH, full IFR King avionics
      </description>
      <seller phone="555-222-3333"> Skyway Aircraft </seller>
    - <location>
        <city> Rapid City, </city>
        <state> South Dakota </state>
      </location>
    </ad>
  - <ad>
      <year> 1965 </year>
      <make> Piper </make>
      <model> Cherokee </model>
      <color> Gold </color>
    - <description>
        240 hours SMOH, dual NAVCOMs, DME, new Cleveland brakes, great shape
      </description>
      <seller phone="555-333-2222"> John Seller </seller>
    - <location>
        <city> St. Joseph, </city>
        <state> Missouri </state>
      </location>
    </ad>
  </planes_for_sale>
```

Figure 7.2 A display of the XML document planes.xml with the FX3 default style sheet

Some of the elements in the display shown in Figure 7.2 are preceded by dashes. These elements can be elided (temporarily suppressed) by placing the mouse cursor over the dash and clicking the left mouse button. For example, if the mouse cursor is placed over the dash to the left of the first <ad> tag and the left mouse button is clicked, the result is as shown in Figure 7.3.

It is unusual to display a raw XML document. This is usually done only to review and check the structure and content of the document during its development.

```
– <!--
     planes.xml - A document that lists ads for
          used airplanes
   -->
– <planes_for_sale>
   + <ad></ad>
   – <ad>
        <year> 1965 </year>
        <make> Piper </make>
        <model> Cherokee </model>
        <color> Gold </color>
      – <description>
          240 hours SMOH, dual NAVCOMs, DME, new Cleveland brakes, great shape
        </description>
        <seller phone="555-333-2222"> John Seller </seller>
      – <location>
          <city> St. Joseph, </city>
          <state> Missouri </state>
        </location>
     </ad>
   </planes_for_sale>
```

This XML file does not appear to have any style information associated with it. The document tree is shown below.

Figure 7.3 The document of Figure 7.2 with the first ad element elided

By default, IE browsers prior to IE9 restrict the eliding process. By clicking the information bar (which appears at the top of the display when eliding is attempted) and then clicking *Allow Blocked Content*, eliding is allowed. The Chrome browsers do not use a default style sheet. However, an XML file can be viewed by clicking *Tools/View Source*.

7.8 Displaying XML Documents with CSS

Style-sheet information can be provided to the browser for an XML document in two ways. First, a Cascading Style Sheet (CSS) file that has style information for the elements in the XML document can be developed. Second, the XSLT style-sheet technology, which was developed by the W3C, can be used. Although using CSS is effective, XSLT provides far more power over the appearance of the document's display. XSLT is discussed in Section 7.9.

The form of a CSS style sheet for an XML document is simple: It is just a list of element names, each followed by a brace-delimited set of the element's CSS attributes. This is the form of the rules in a CSS document style sheet. The following shows a CSS style sheet for the `planes` XML document:

```
<!-- planes.css - a style sheet for the planes.xml document -->
ad { display: block; margin-top: 15px; color: blue;}
year, make, model { color: red; font-size: 16pt;}
color {display: block; margin-left: 20px; font-size: 12pt;}
description {display: block; margin-left: 20px; font-size: 12pt;}
seller { display: block; margin-left: 15px; font-size: 14pt;}
location {display: block; margin-left: 40px; }
city {font-size: 12pt;}
state {font-size: 12pt;}
```

The only style property in this style sheet that has not been discussed previously is `display`, which is used to specify whether an element is to be displayed inline or in a separate block. These two options are specified with the values `inline` and `block`. The `inline` value is the default. When `display` is set to `block`, the content of the element is usually separated from its sibling elements by line breaks.

The connection of an XML document to a CSS style sheet is established with the processing instruction `xml-stylesheet`, which specifies the particular type of the style sheet via its `type` attribute and the name of the file that stores the style sheet via its `href` attribute. For the `planes` example, this processing instruction is as follows:

```
<?xml-stylesheet type = "text/css" href = "planes.css" ?>
```

Figure 7.4 shows the display of `planes.xml`, in which the `planes.css` style sheet is used to format the document.

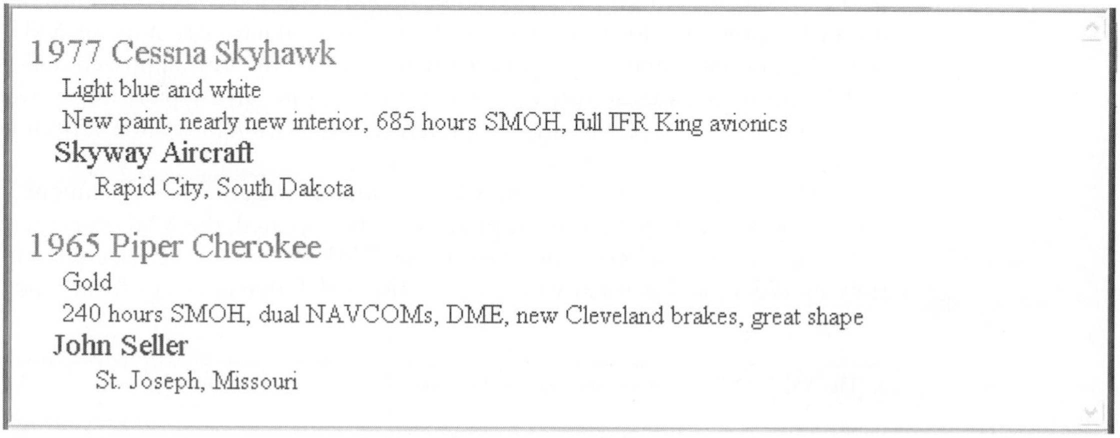

1977 Cessna Skyhawk
  Light blue and white
  New paint, nearly new interior, 685 hours SMOH, full IFR King avionics
  Skyway Aircraft
    Rapid City, South Dakota

1965 Piper Cherokee
  Gold
  240 hours SMOH, dual NAVCOMs, DME, new Cleveland brakes, great shape
  John Seller
    St. Joseph, Missouri

Figure 7.4 The result of using a CSS style sheet to format `planes.xml`

7.9   **XSLT Style Sheets**

The eXtensible Stylesheet Language (XSL) is a family of recommendations for defining the presentation and transformations of XML documents. It consists of three related standards: XSL Transformations (XSLT), XML Path Language (XPath), and XSL Formatting Objects (XSL-FO). Each of these has an importance and use of its own. Together, they provide a powerful means of formatting XML documents. Because the primary use of XSL-FO is to generate high-quality printable documents in formats such as PDF and PostScript, it is not discussed in this chapter.

XSLT style sheets are used to transform XML documents into different forms or formats, including XSL-FO, HTML and plain text. When the output is HTML, it is used primarily for display. In the transformation of an XML document, the content of elements can be moved, modified, sorted, and converted to attribute values, among other things. XSLT style sheets are XML documents, so they can be validated against XML schemas. They can even be transformed with the use of other XSLT style sheets. The XSLT 1.0 standard[3] is given at `http://www.w3.org/TR/xslt`. XSLT style sheets and their uses are the primary topics of this section.

XPath is a language for expressions used to identify parts of XML documents, such as specific elements that are in specific positions in the document or elements that have particular attribute values. XSLT requires such expressions to specify transformations. XPath is also used for XML document querying languages, such as XQL, and to build new XML document structures with XPointer. The XPath standard is given at `http://www.w3.org/TR/xpath`. This chapter uses simple XPath expressions in the discussion of XSLT and does not explore them further.

7.9.1   **Overview of XSLT**

XSLT is actually a simple declarative programming language, somewhat related to the logic programming language Prolog. Included in XSLT are functions, parameters, names to which values can be bound, selection constructs, and conditional expressions for multiple selection. The syntactic structure of XSLT is XML, so each statement is specified with an element. This approach makes XSLT documents appear very different from programs in a typical imperative programming language, but not completely different from programs written in Prolog.

XSLT processors take both an XML document and an XSLT document as input. The XSLT document is the program to be executed; the XML document is the input data to the program. Parts of the XML document are selected, possibly modified, and merged with parts of the XSLT document to form a new

3. The XSLT 2.0 standard was approved in 2007, but thus far it is not widely supported.

document, which is sometimes called an *XSL document*. Note that the XSL document is also an XML document, which could be again the input to an XSLT processor. The output document can be stored for future use by applications, or it may be immediately displayed by an application, often a browser. Neither the XSLT document nor the input XML document is changed by the XSLT processor.

The transformation process used by an XSLT processor is shown in Figure 7.5.

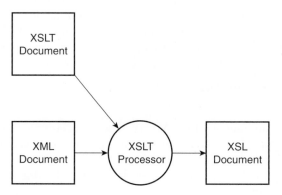

Figure 7.5 XSLT processing

An XSLT document consists primarily of one or more templates, which use XPath-like expressions to describe element–attribute patterns in the input XML document. Each template has associated with it a section of XSLT "code," which is "executed" when a match to the template is found in the XML document. So, each template describes a function that is executed whenever the XSLT processor finds a match to the template's pattern.

An XSLT processor sequentially examines the input XML document, searching for parts that match one of the templates in the XSLT document. XML documents consist of nodes—elements, attributes, comments, text, and processing instructions. If a template matches an element, the element is not processed until the closing tag is found. When a template matches an element, the child elements of that element may or may not be processed.

One XSLT model of processing XML data is called the *template-driven model*, which works well when the data consists of multiple instances of highly regular data collections, as with files containing records. XSLT can also deal with irregular and recursive data, using template fragments in what is called the *data-driven model*. A single XSLT style sheet can include the mechanisms for both the template- and data-driven models. The discussion of XSLT in this chapter is restricted to the template-driven model.

To keep the complexity of the discussion manageable, the focus is on transformations that are related to presentation. The examples in this section were processed with the XSLT processor that is part of IE9.

7.9.2   XSL Transformations for Presentation

Although XSLT style sheets can be used to control page layout, including orientation, writing direction, margins, and page numbering, this chapter discusses only the simplest of formatting specifications for the smallest units of information. XSLT includes more than 50 formatting object (element) types and more than 230 attributes, so it is a large and complex tag set.

In this section, we assume that the XSLT processor processes an XML document with its associated XSLT style-sheet document and produces as its output an XSL document that is an HTML document to be displayed.

An XML document that is to be used as data to an XSLT style sheet must include a processing instruction to inform the XSLT processor that the style sheet is to be used. The form of this instruction is as follows:

```
<?xml-stylesheet type = "text/xsl" href =
                               "XSL_stylesheet_name" ?>
```

There is an issue with the MIME type in this instruction: text/xsl is not a standard type. However, at this time it is the only one that works on most contemporary browsers.

The following is a simple example of an XML document that illustrates XSLT formatting:

```
<?xml version = "1.0" encoding = "utf-8"?>
<!-- xslplane.xml -->
<?xml-stylesheet type = "text/xsl"  href = "xslplane1.xsl" ?>
<plane>
   <year> 1977 </year>
   <make> Cessna </make>
   <model> Skyhawk </model>
   <color> Light blue and white </color>
</plane>
```

Notice that this document specifies xslplane1.xsl as its XSLT style sheet.

An XSLT style sheet is an XML document whose root element is the special-purpose element stylesheet. The stylesheet tag defines namespaces as its attributes and encloses the collection of elements that defines its transformations. It also identifies the document as an XSLT document. The namespace for all XSLT elements is specified with a W3C URI. If the style sheet includes XHTML elements, the style sheet tag also specifies the XHTML namespace, which is also the namespace for HTML. In the style sheet tag

```
<xsl:stylesheet xmlns:xsl =
            "http://www.w3.org/1999/XSL/Transform"
            xmlns = "http://www.w3.org/1999/xhtml">
```

notice that this tag specifies that the prefix for XSLT elements is `xsl` and the default namespace is that for XHTML.

An XSLT style-sheet document contains one or more `template` elements. The template opening tag includes a `match` attribute to specify an XPath-like expression that selects a node in the XML document.[4] The content of a template element specifies what is to be placed in the output document.

The XSLT processor examines the nodes, or elements, of the XML document, comparing each with the templates in the XSLT style sheet. When a node matches a template, the template is added to a list of templates that could be applied. In simple situations, there will be either none or just one such template. In the more general case, a complicated set of rules determines which template will be applied. We only consider the simple situation here.

Applying a template causes its body to be placed in the XSL document.

In many XSLT documents, a template is included to match the root node of the XML document. This can be done in two ways. One way is to use the XPath expression `"/"`, as in

```
<xsl:template match = "/">
```

This causes the XSLT processor to process the entire XML document. Note the notation similar to that used to specify UNIX directory addresses. The alternative to using `"/"` is to use the actual root of the document. In the example `xslplane.xml`, the document root is `plane`. If the output of the XSLT processor is an HTML document, the template that matches the root node can be used to create the HTML header of the output document. The header code appears as the content of the template element. An example of a skeletal template element is

```
<xsl:template match = "plane">
<html><head><title> Example </title></head><body>
...
</body></html>
</xsl:template>
```

Style sheets nearly always have templates for specific nodes of the XML document, as in the following example:

```
<xsl:template match = "year">
```

Values of the `match` attribute that begin with the slash are absolute addresses within the document. Those that do not begin with a slash are relative addresses. The value `"year"` in the preceding example is obviously a relative address. Relative addresses are relative to the "current" node of the XML document, which is the last node found by the XSLT processor in the document.

The template for the root node is implicitly applied. However, all other templates in an XSLT document must be explicitly applied to the XML document. This can be done in several ways. The `apply-templates` element applies

---

4. It may also include a `priority` attribute, but they are not discussed here.

appropriate templates to the descendant nodes of the current node. If only some of the descendent nodes are to be processed, they can be specified by including a `select` attribute, such as the following:

```
select = "make"
```

This would cause all of the other descendent nodes, other than `make`, to be skipped. Also, the `select` could specify all except one descendent node, as in the following:

```
select = "not(year)"
```

If no `select` attribute is included in the `apply-templates` element, the XSLT processor will attempt to apply templates to every descendent node. For those nodes for which the XSLT document has not defined a template, a default template is used. For example, both text and attributes have default templates that output them as text.

Template elements are of two distinct kinds: those that literally contain content and those that specify content to be copied from the associated XML document. XSLT elements that represent HTML elements often are used to specify content. XSLT elements have the appearance of their associated HTML elements, like the following HTML element:

```
<span style = "font-size: 14pt"> Happy Holidays! </span>
```

All XSLT elements that represent HTML elements are copied by the XSLT processor to the XSL document being generated.

In many cases, the content of an element of the XML document is to be copied to the XSL document. This is done with the `value-of` element, which uses a `select` attribute to specify the element of the XML document whose contents are to be copied. For example, the element

```
<xsl:value-of select = "AUTHOR" />
```

specifies that the content of the AUTHOR element of the XML document is to be copied to the output document. Because the `value-of` element cannot have content, it is terminated with a slash and a right angle bracket.

The `select` attribute can specify any node of the XML document. This is an advantage of XSLT formatting over CSS, in which the order of data as stored is the only possible order of display.

The attribute value `"."` for the `select` attribute of `value-of` denotes the selection of all elements within the current element—just the current node if it contains no nested elements.[5]

The following is a complete XSLT style sheet for the XML document `xslplane.xml` shown previously:

---

5. If `select = "."` is included in an `<xsl:apply-templates>` tag, it does nothing, because `apply-templates` implicitly specifies all immediate child nodes.

```
<?xml version = "1.0" encoding = "utf-8"?>
<!-- xslplane1.xsl
     An XSLT stylesheet for xslplane.xml using child templates
     -->
<xsl:stylesheet version = "1.0"
                 xmlns:xsl = "http://www.w3.org/1999/XSL/Transform"
                 xmlns = "http://www.w3.org/1999/xhtml">

<!-- The template for the whole document (the plane element) -->
  <xsl:template match = "plane">
    <html><head><title> Style sheet for xslplane.xml </title>
    </head><body>
    <h2> Airplane Description </h2>

<!-- Apply the matching templates to the elements in plane -->
    <xsl:apply-templates />
    </body></html>
  </xsl:template>

<!-- The templates to be applied (by apply-templates) to the
     elements nested in the plane element -->
  <xsl:template match = "year">
    <span style = "font-style: italic; color: blue;"> Year:
    </span>
    <xsl:value-of select = "." /> <br />
  </xsl:template>
  <xsl:template match = "make">
    <span style = "font-style: italic; color: blue;"> Make:
    </span>
    <xsl:value-of select = "." /> <br />
  </xsl:template>
  <xsl:template match = "model">
    <span style = "font-style: italic; color: blue;"> Model:
    </span>
    <xsl:value-of select = "." /> <br />
  </xsl:template>
  <xsl:template match = "color">
    <span style = "font-style: italic; color: blue;"> Color:
    </span>
    <xsl:value-of select = "." /> <br />
  </xsl:template>
</xsl:stylesheet>
```

Figure 7.6 shows an IE9 display of the output document created by the XSLT processor from `xslplane.xml` with `xslplane1.xsl`.[6]

Airplane Description

Year: 1977
Make: Cessna
Model: Skyhawk
Color: Light blue and white

Figure 7.6 An output document from the XSLT processor

The XSLT document, `xslplane1.xsl`, is more general and complex than necessary for the simple use for which it was written. There is actually no need to include templates for all of the child nodes of `plane`, because the `select` clause of the `value-of` element finds them. The following XSLT document, `xslplane2.xsl`, produces the same output as `xslplane1.xsl`.

```
<?xml version = "1.0" encoding = "utf-8"?>
<!-- xslplane2.xsl
     An XSLT Stylesheet for xslplane.xml using implicit templates
     -->
<xsl:stylesheet version = "1.0"
                xmlns:xsl = "http://www.w3.org/1999/XSL/Transform"
                xmlns = "http://www.w3.org/1999/xhtml">

<!-- The template for the whole document (the plane element) -->
  <xsl:template match = "plane" >
    <html><head><title> Style sheet for xslplane.xml </title>
    </head><body>
    <h2> Airplane Description </h2>
    <span style = "font-style: italic; color: blue;"> Year:
    </span>
    <xsl:value-of select = "year" /> <br />
    <span style = "font-style: italic; color: blue;"> Make:
    </span>
    <xsl:value-of select = "make" /> <br />
    <span style = "font-style: italic; color: blue;"> Model:
    </span>
```

---

6. For unknown reasons, it works with IE9 and FX3, but it does not work with Chrome.

```
          <xsl:value-of select = "model" /> <br />
          <span style = "font-style: italic; color: blue;"> Color:
          </span>
          <xsl:value-of select = "color" /> <br />
          </body></html>
      </xsl:template>
</xsl:stylesheet>
```

Now we consider an XML document that includes a collection of data elements, all with the same structure. For example, a document named `airplanes.xml` could have a list of airplane descriptions. The XSLT template used for one plane can be used repeatedly with the `for-each` element, which employs a `select` attribute to specify an element in the XML data. The value of the `select` attribute is a pattern, which is a path expression that specifies an element. Any child elements of the specified element are included.

Consider the following XML document:

```
<?xml version = "1.0" encoding = "utf-8"?>
<!-- xslplanes.xml -->
<?xml-stylesheet type = "text/xsl" href = "xslplanes.xsl" ?>
<planes>
  <plane>
    <year> 1977 </year>
    <make> Cessna </make>
    <model> Skyhawk </model>
    <color> Light blue and white </color>
  </plane>
  <plane>
    <year> 1975 </year>
    <make> Piper </make>
    <model> Apache </model>
    <color> White </color>
  </plane>
  <plane>
    <year> 1960 </year>
    <make> Cessna </make>
    <model> Centurian </model>
    <color> Yellow and white </color>
  </plane>
```

```
    <plane>
      <year> 1956 </year>
      <make> Piper </make>
      <model> Tripacer </model>
      <color> Blue </color>
    </plane>
  </planes>
```

The following XSLT style sheet processes the previous XML document:

```
<?xml version = "1.0" encoding = "utf-8"?>
<!-- xslplanes.xsl -->
<xsl:stylesheet version = "1.0"
                xmlns:xsl = "http://www.w3.org/1999/XSL/Transform"
                xmlns = "http://www.w3.org/1999/xhtml" >


<!-- The template for the whole document (the planes element) -->
  <xsl:template match = "planes">
    <h2> Airplane Descriptions </h2>


<!-- Apply the following to all occurrences of the plane element -->
  <xsl:for-each select = "plane">
      <span style = "font-style: italic; color: blue;"> Year: </span>
      <xsl:value-of select = "year" /> <br />
      <span style = "font-style: italic; color: blue;"> Make: </span>
      <xsl:value-of select = "make" /> <br />
      <span style = "font-style: italic; color: blue;"> Model: </span>
      <xsl:value-of select = "model" /> <br />
      <span style = "font-style: italic; color: blue;"> Color: </span>
      <xsl:value-of select = "color" /> <br /> <br />
  </xsl:for-each>

  </xsl:template>
</xsl:stylesheet>
```

Figure 7.7 shows an IE9 display of the document produced by an XSLT processor on `xslplanes.xml`, which uses the `xslplanes.xsl` style sheet.[7]

---

7. As with `xslplane.xml`, this does not work with Chrome.

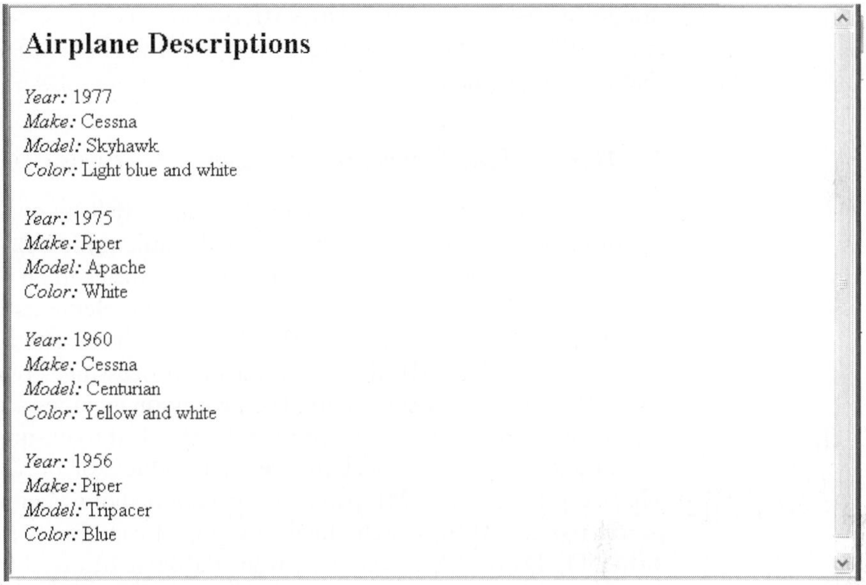

Airplane Descriptions

Year: 1977
Make: Cessna
Model: Skyhawk
Color: Light blue and white

Year: 1975
Make: Piper
Model: Apache
Color: White

Year: 1960
Make: Cessna
Model: Centurian
Color: Yellow and white

Year: 1956
Make: Piper
Model: Tripacer
Color: Blue

Figure 7.7 Using the `for-each` element for lists of elements

There are characteristics of templates that make them even more like the subprograms of programming languages. For example, templates can be named and explicitly called by name. Furthermore, parameters can be passed to named templates.

XSLT provides a simple way to sort the elements of the XML document before sending them or their content to the output document. This is done with the `sort` element, which can take several attributes. The `select` attribute specifies the node that is used for the key of the sort. The `data-type` attribute is used to specify whether the elements are to be sorted as text (`"text"`) or numerically (`"number"`). Ascending order is the default. The `order` attribute can be set to `"descending"` to produce the reverse order. By inserting the following single line into the `xslplanes.xsl` document, the output will appear in ascending numeric order of the year of the airplane:

```
<xsl:sort  select = "year"  data-type = "number" />
```

7.10 XML Processors

So far in this chapter, we have discussed the structure of XML documents, the rules for writing them, the DTD and XML Schema approaches to specifying the particular tag sets and structure of collections of XML documents, and the CSS and XSLT methods of displaying the contents of XML documents. That is tantamount to telling a long story about how data can be stored and displayed, without providing any hint on how it may be processed. Although we do not discuss processing data stored in XML documents in this section, we do introduce approaches to making that data conveniently available to application programs that process the data.

7.10.1   The Purposes of XML Processors

Several purposes of XML processors have already been discussed. First, the processor must check the basic syntax of the document for well-formedness. Second, the processor must replace all references to entities in an XML document with their definitions. Third, attributes in DTDs and elements in XML schemas can specify that their values in an XML document have default values, which must be copied into the XML document during processing. Fourth, when a DTD or an XML schema is specified and the processor includes a validating parser, the structure of the XML document must be checked to ensure that it is legitimate.

One simple way to check the well-formedness of an XML document is with a browser that has an XML parser. Information about Microsoft's MSXML XML parser (part of IE9), which checks for well-formedness and validation against either DTDs or XML schemas, is available at `http://msdn2.microsoft.com/en-US/xml/bb291077.aspx`. Information on the XML parsers in other browsers can be found at `http://www.w3.org/XML/Schema`.

Although an XML document exhibits a regular and elegant structure, that structure does not provide applications with convenient access to the document's data. It was recognized early on that, because the process of the initial syntactic analysis required to expose the embedded data must be repeated for every application that processes XML documents, standard syntax analyzers for XML documents were needed. Actually, the syntax analyzers themselves need not be standard; rather, they should expose the data of XML documents in a standard application programmer interface (API). This need led to the development of two different standard APIs for XML processors. Because there are different needs and uses of XML applications, having two standards is not a negative. The two APIs parallel the two kinds of output that are produced by the syntax analyzers of compilers for programming languages. Some of these syntax analyzers produce a stream of the syntactic structures of an input program. Others produce a parse tree of the input program that shows the hierarchical structure of the program in terms of its syntactic structures.

7.10.2   The SAX Approach

The Simple API for XML (SAX) standard, which was released in May 1998, was developed by an XML users group, XML-DEV. Although not developed or supported by any standards organization, SAX has been widely accepted as a de facto standard and is now widely supported by XML processors.

The SAX approach to processing is called *event processing*. The processor scans the XML document from beginning to end. Every time a syntactic structure of the document is recognized, the processor signals an event to the application by calling an event handler for the particular structure that was found. The syntactic structures of interest naturally include opening tags, attributes, text, and closing tags. The interfaces that describe the event handlers form the SAX API.

7.10.3   The DOM Approach

The natural alternative to the SAX approach to XML document parsing is to build a hierarchical syntactic structure of the document. Given the use of DOM representations of HTML documents to create dynamic documents in Chapter 6, this is a familiar idea. In the case of HTML, the browser parses the document and builds the DOM tree. In the case of XML, the parser part of the XML processor builds the DOM tree. In both cases, the nodes of the tree are represented as objects that can be accessed and processed or modified by the application. When parsing is complete, the complete DOM representation of the document is in memory and can be accessed in a number of different ways, including tree traversals of various kinds as well as random accesses.

The DOM representation of an XML document has several advantages over the sequential listing provided by SAX parsers. First, it has an obvious advantage if any part of the document must be accessed more than once by the application. Second, if the application must perform any rearrangement of the elements of the document, it can most easily be done if the whole document is accessible at the same time. Third, accesses to random parts of the document are possible. Finally, because the parser sees the whole document before any processing takes place, this approach avoids any processing of a document that is later found to be invalid (according to a DTD or XML schema).

In some situations, the SAX approach has advantages over the DOM method. The DOM structure is stored entirely in memory, so large documents require a great deal of memory. In fact, because there is no limit on the size of an XML document, some documents cannot be parsed with the DOM method. This is not a problem with the SAX approach. Another advantage of the SAX method is speed: It is faster than the DOM approach.

The process of building the DOM structure of an XML document requires some syntactic analysis of the document, similar to that done by SAX parsers. In fact, most DOM parsers include a SAX parser as a front end.

7.11   Web Services

The movement toward Web services began in earnest when Bill Gates, who was Microsoft chairman at the time, introduced a concept he called BizTalk in 1999. BizTalk later was renamed .NET. The idea was to provide the technologies to allow software in different places, written in different languages and resident on different platforms, to connect and interoperate.

The Web began as a Web service focused on information and is still primarily just that. Through two fundamental HTTP methods, GET and POST, and a vast collection of public markup documents, information is provided to anyone with an Internet connection and a computer running a browser. The more general concept of a Web service is a similar technology for services. Rather than deploying documents through a Web server, services are deployed (through the same Web server). Rather than documents, access to software components is provided. Components are not downloaded, but are run on the Web server as a remote service. In most cases, the components are remotely callable methods.

Web services are, of course, not a completely new idea: Remote Procedure Call (RPC) is an earlier and closely related concept. RPC was invented to allow distributed components to communicate. There were two successful (widely used) RPC technologies: DCOM and CORBA. Both, however, are too complex to provide a simple and convenient way to support interoperability among the components of different systems. DCOM is proprietary, supported only by Microsoft software systems. CORBA is designed to be a cross-platform technology, but it requires a great deal of manual integration work. DCOM uses the Object Remote Procedure Call (ORPC) protocol to interface components. CORBA uses Object Management Group's Internet Inter-ORB Protocol (IIOP). Needless to say, these two protocols are not compatible. Therefore, neither DCOM nor CORBA supports the goal of Web services: universal component interoperability.

The dream of Web services is that there will be protocols that allow all components to interoperate entirely under the control of the computers, without human intervention. This means that when a software system needs a service, it can implicitly find one on the Web and use it. Standard nonproprietary protocols and languages to support this dream have been developed, although they are not yet widely used. Web services are now being offered by a number of large software companies, including Microsoft, Amazon, IBM, and Google.

Three roles are required to provide and use Web services: service providers, service requestors, often called consumers, and a service registry. A service provider must develop and deploy software that provides a service. This service must have a standard description. The W3C language designed for writing such descriptions is Web Services Definition Language (WSDL, pronounced "wiz -dul"), which is an XML-based format. The WSDL description is published on a Web server, just as is a Web-accessible document. It is used to describe the specific operations provided by the Web service, as well as the protocols for the messages the Web service can send and receive. The descriptions of data, both input and output, in a WSDL description are often written in XML Schema.

A Web services registry is created with another standard protocol: Universal Description, Discovery, and Integration Service (UDDI). UDDI also provides ways to query a Web services registry to determine what specific services are available. So, a requestor queries a registry with a WSDL query, to which the registry responds with the protocol of how the requestor may interact with the requested Web service. UDDI has two kinds of clients: service providers and those who want to find and use Web services.

SOAP is an XML tag set that defines the forms of messages and RPCs. SOAP was originally an acronym for Standard Object Access Protocol, designed to describe data objects. However, it is now a name for the XML tag set with wider use in Web services communications. The root element of a SOAP document is `Envelope`, so SOAP documents are often called envelopes. The body of a SOAP message is either a request, which is an RPC, or a response, which contains values returned from the called method, or service. SOAP messages are sent with the HTTP POST method.

Most Web services are developed with the use of powerful tools, such as Microsoft's Visual Studio and Sun's NetBeans.

Web services consumers are clients of the service. Such a client could be a Web application, a non-Web application, or another Web service. The architecture of a Web service client includes a proxy running on the client machine. The proxy is a local substitute for the remote Web service. Once the proxy has been constructed, compiled, and referenced in the client, the client can call the methods of the remote Web service, although the calls will actually be received locally by the proxy. So the client interacts with the proxy, and the proxy interacts through the Internet with the remote Web service. The client acts as if it is calling the remote Web service, but in fact is calling the proxy.

Chapter 12 discusses ASP.NET approaches to defining and using Web services.

Summary

XML is a simplified version of SGML, which is a meta-markup language. XML provides a standard way for a group of users to define the structure of their data documents, using a subject-specific markup language.

XML documents can include elements, markup declarations, and processing instructions. Every XML document has the form of a single document tree, so there can be just one root element.

An XML document is a document entity that can include any number of references to other entities defined elsewhere. An entity can be several different things, including plain text and references to images.

A DTD is a document that describes the syntactic structure of an XML document or collection of documents that uses a particular tag set. A validating XML parser compares a document it is analyzing with its DTD if one is specified. If no DTD is specified for an XML document, only well-formedness can be checked during parsing. A DTD has declarations for elements, attributes, entities, and notations. An element declaration specifies the name of the element and its structure. If an element represents an internal node in the document tree, its structure is a list of the children nodes. Any internal node can include a modifier that specifies the number of times that its children nodes can or must appear. A leaf node's structure is usually either empty or plain text.

A DTD attribute declaration specifies the attribute's name, the name of its associated element, the type of its values, and, optionally, a default value. In many cases, the type of an attribute value is simply text. The default value can be an actual value, but it may also specify something about the value. There are several predefined entities that represent the special characters used as markup delimiters. A character data section allows these special characters to appear as themselves, without using entities. Binary entities can be included in XML documents, though they require a different form of declaration. A DTD specification could appear embedded in an XML document, but that arrangement makes it inconvenient to use for other documents.

An XML document can include the predefined element names for some other application, such as the names of the elements of HTML. To avoid name clashes between these different sources of names, XML uses the concepts of namespaces and name prefixes, which indicate the namespace of a name in a document. Namespaces are specified in declarations as URIs. A default namespace can be declared for a document. Names from the default namespace can be used without being prefixed.

XML schemas provide an alternative to DTDs. XML schemas allow much stricter control over the structure, and especially the data types, of an XML document. A schema defines the structure of a class of XML documents. The documents that conform to a specific schema are considered instances of that schema. A schema, which is an XML document, is an instance of XMLSchema. A schema specifies a target namespace with the targetNamespace attribute. The target namespace is also often designated the default namespace. Schemas can define simple and complex data types. Simple data types cannot contain other elements or attributes. One common category of complex types is those that can contain other elements but no text. There are many predefined types. Users are allowed to define new simple types as constrained versions of existing simple types, using facets. Users can also define new complex types. Instances of schemas can be validated with several different validation programs that are now available, among them xsv.

An XML parser includes a default style sheet, which is used when no other style sheet is specified in the document being parsed. The default style sheet simply produces a somewhat stylized listing of the XML. CSS style sheets can be used with XML documents to provide formatting information. Such a CSS style sheet has the form of an external CSS style sheet for HTML.

XML documents can also be formatted with XSLT style sheets, which specify document transformations and can include HTML and CSS presentation information. XSLT style sheets define templates into which XML document elements are mapped. An XSLT processor creates an output document from the XML document and the XSLT style sheet. If the style sheet includes HTML style specifications, the document will have style information embedded in its elements. XSLT style sheets actually are XML applications. An XSLT style sheet can have a template that is reused for any number of occurrences of a document branch in the associated XML document.

XML applications require that the nodes (tags, attributes, text, and so forth) of the XML document be provided in some standard way by the XML parser. The two ways in which this is done are the SAX approach, which calls an event handler for each node it finds, and the DOM approach, which provides a complete tree structure of the whole document.

A Web service is a method that resides and is executed on a Web server, but that can be called from any computer on the Web. The standard technologies to support Web services are WSDL, UDDI, SOAP, and XML.

Review Questions

7.1 Is XML more closely related to SGML or HTML?

7.2 What is the main deficiency of HTML?

7.3 What is the goal of HTML?

7.4 What is the goal of XML?

7.5 What are the two primary tasks of a validating XML parser?

7.6 Under what circumstances are nested tags better than attributes?

7.7 Under what circumstances are attributes better than nested tags?

7.8 What is a document entity?

7.9 Why should a document be broken into multiple entities?

7.10 What is a binary entity?

7.11 How does an XML parser handle binary entities?

7.12 What is the purpose of a DTD?

7.13 Why is it better to find an error in a DTD before the DTD is used?

7.14 What are the four possible keywords in a DTD declaration?

7.15 What are the meanings of the modifiers (+, *, and ?) that can be used in element declarations?

7.16 Explain the three types that can be used to describe data in an element declaration.

7.17 What are the four possible parts of an attribute declaration in a DTD?

7.18 Describe the meanings of the default attribute values `#REQUIRED` and `#IMPLIED`.

7.19 What is the difference between general and parameter entities?

7.20 Why do some special characters have predefined entity references?

7.21 What is the purpose of a character data section?

7.22 How does the XML parser distinguish between a general entity and a parameter entity?

7.23 What does the key word `SYSTEM` specify in an entity declaration?

7.24 What is the purpose of an `NDATA` entity declaration?

7.25 What is the syntactic form of an internal DTD?

7.26 What is the markup vocabulary of a markup language?

7.27 What is an XML namespace?

7.28   What are the two primary advantages of XML schemas over DTDs?

7.29   From where do the names used in defining an XML schema come?

7.30   What three namespaces are normally named in an XML schema?

7.31   What are the two ways to define entities when using an XML schema?

7.32   What is the form of the assignment to the `schemaLocation` attribute?

7.33   What are the differences between simple and complex XML schema types?

7.34   Define local and global declarations in an XML schema.

7.35   What is a facet?

7.36   What are the four categories of complex types in an XML schema?

7.37   What is the difference between the `sequence` and `all` schema elements?

7.38   Why would you use a CSS style sheet for an XML document?

7.39   How does an XSLT processor use an XSLT style sheet with an XML document?

7.40   What is a `template` element of an XSLT style sheet?

7.41   What two kinds of elements are included in XSLT style sheets?

7.42   What does the `value-of` XSLT element do?

7.43   What does the `select` attribute of the `value-of` element do?

7.44   What does the `for-each` element of an XSLT style sheet do?

7.45   What is produced by a SAX parser?

7.46   What is produced by a DOM parser?

7.47   What advantages does a SAX parser have over a DOM parser?

7.48   What advantages does a DOM parser have over a SAX parser?

7.49   Explain the ultimate goal of Web services.

7.50   Describe the three roles required to provide and use Web services.

7.51   What is UDDI?

7.52   What is SOAP?

Exercises

Write, test, and debug (if necessary) each of the documents described:

7.1 Create a DTD for a catalog of cars, where each `car` has the child elements `make`, `model`, `year`, `color`, `engine`, `number_of_doors`, `transmission_type`, and `accessories`. The `engine` element has the child elements `number_of_cylinders` and `fuel_system` (carbureted or fuel injected). The `accessories` element has the attributes `radio`, `air_conditioning`, `power_windows`, `power_steering`, and `power_brakes`, each of which is required and has the possible values `yes` and `no`. Entities must be declared for the names of popular car models.

7.2 Create an XML document with at least three instances of the `car` element defined in the DTD of Exercise 7.1. Process this document by using the DTD of Exercise 7.1, and produce a display of the raw XML document.

7.3 Create an XML schema for the XML document described in Exercises 7.1 and 7.2.

7.4 Create a CSS style sheet for the XML document of Exercise 7.2, and use it to create a display of that document.

7.5 Create an XSLT style sheet for one `car` element of the XML document of Exercise 7.2, and use it to create a display of that element.

7.6 Modify the XSLT style sheet of Exercise 7.5 to format all the `car` elements in the XML document of Exercise 7.2, and use the style sheet to create a display of the whole document.

7.7 Design an XML document that stores information about patients in a hospital. Information about patients must include their name (in three parts), Social Security number, age, room number, primary insurance company—including member identification number, group number, phone number, and address—secondary insurance company (with the same parts as the primary insurance company has), known medical problems, and known drug allergies. Both attributes and nested tags must be included. Make up sample data for at least four patients.

7.8 Write a DTD for the document described in Exercise 7.7, but with the following restrictions: name, Social Security number, age, room number, and primary insurance company are required. All the other elements are optional, as are middle names.

7.9   Create a CSS style sheet for the XML document of Exercise 7.7, and use it to create a display of that document.

7.10 Create an XSLT style sheet for one `patient` element of the XML document of Exercise 7.7, and use it to create a display of that element.

7.11 Modify the XSLT style sheet of Exercise 7.6 so that it formats all the `patient` elements in the XML document of Exercise 7.7, and use the style sheet to create a display of the whole document.

Introduction to Flash

This chapter introduces the Flash authoring environment. Flash is a complex and powerful tool for creating rich interactive and animated content for a wide variety of applications, including Web sites. There are two fundamental parts to Flash: the Flash authoring environment, used to create Flash applications, which are called movies; and the Flash player, a program that can be embedded in various software systems, including its use as a plug-in in Web browsers. The Flash player displays movies, much as a Web browser displays HTML documents. When the target of a Flash movie is the Web, it is embedded as an `object` element in an HTML document. Although there are other uses of Flash movies, this chapter deals only with Flash on the Web. Because of the complexity of the Flash authoring environment, we only provide a brief introduction to some of its most commonly used features. The structure of this chapter is similar to that of a tutorial: After an overview of the Flash authoring environment, the reader is led through several sequences of steps that produce simple Flash movies.

The chapter begins with a brief discussion of the origins of Flash. Next, the primary parts of the Flash authoring environment are introduced. Then, the most commonly used Flash drawing tools, including those for producing geometric figures, lines, hand-drawn figures, and text, are described. The remainder of the chapter presents examples to illustrate some of the elementary uses of Flash and its authoring environment.

The first example illustrates text and static figures. The next is a movie that demonstrates two kinds of motion animation. Then a sound clip is added to this movie. Next, shape animation is illustrated with a simple example that morphs a circle into a square and then into a triangle. Finally, two buttons are added to a movie with motion animation to allow the user to control that animation.

8.1   Origins and Uses of Flash

In the mid-1990s, a product named FutureSplash Animator was created by adding animation capabilities to an earlier drawing program named SmartSketch. The first copy of FutureSplash Animator was shipped in the summer of 1996. At the same time, Macromedia was developing and selling a multimedia player named ShockWave. In late 1996, Macromedia bought FutureSplash Animator, which then became Flash 1.0. In 2005, Adobe bought Macromedia. Flash has evolved and grown steadily since the appearance of its initial version.

Flash is now used to create movies, television commercials, games, instructional media, presentations, and Web content, including that for mobile devices.

The interactivity of a Flash application is implemented with a programming language called ActionScript, which is now in version 3.0. ActionScript is compliant with ECMA-262 Third Edition, which is the ISO name for its standard version of JavaScript. Although the syntax and basic constructs of ActionScript are like those of JavaScript, there are also some differences. ActionScript is interpreted by the ActionScript Virtual Machine, which is built into the Flash player.

Flash is now the leading technology for delivering graphics, animation, and video on the Web, although the HTML5 capability of embedding audio and video is expected to diminish this dominance, especially for embedded video clips. It has been estimated that nearly 99 percent of the world's computers used to access the Internet have a version of the Flash player installed as a plug-in in their browsers. It is preinstalled in most new browsers.

The current version of the Flash authoring environment is Flash CS5.5, which is the version described in this chapter. The current version of the Flash player is 11. The Flash player is free—it can be downloaded from `http://www.adobe.com/downloads`. The Flash player is included in the Flash authoring environment. A copy of the latest version of the Flash authoring environment can be obtained as a 30-day trial from `http://www.adobe.com/products/flash`. There are Flash tutorials available, both in the Flash environment and at other sites on the Web.

8.2   A First Look at the Flash Authoring Environment

Given that the Flash authoring environment has been installed, starting it is a simple matter of double-clicking the desktop icon for Flash. This produces the welcome screen shown in Figure 8.1. Note that the welcome screen is embedded in the initial workspace screen, although the workspace is not shown in the figure.

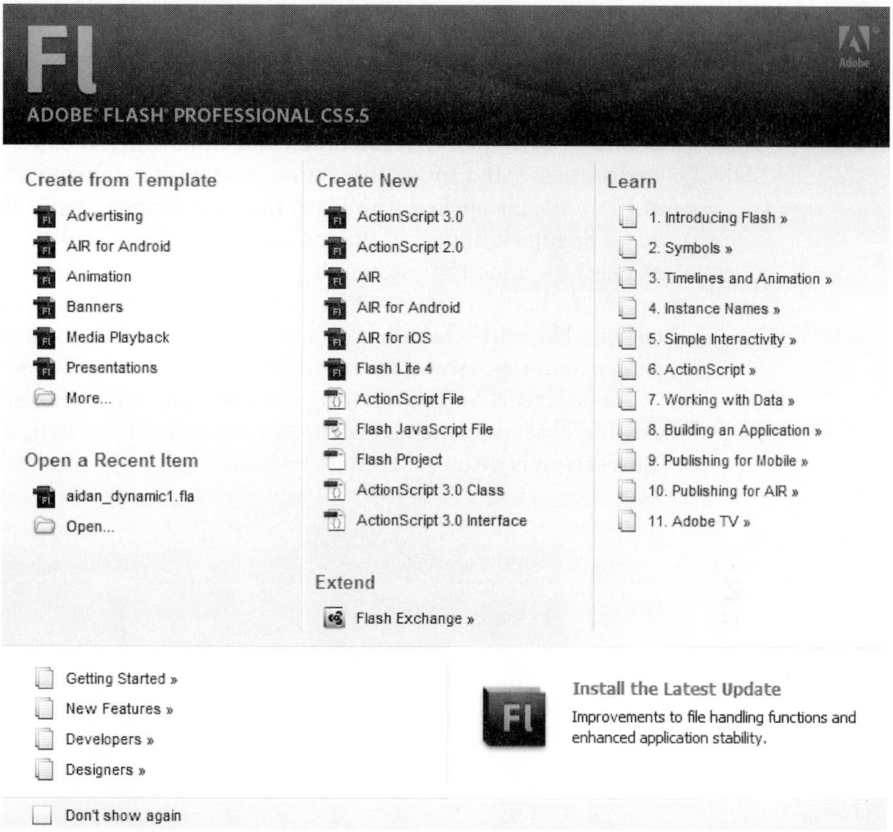

Figure 8.1 The Flash welcome screen

The top part of the welcome screen has five lists: *Create from Template*, *Create New*, *Learn*, *Open a Recent Item*, and *Extend*.

The left top list of the welcome screen, titled *Create from Template*, allows a Flash movie to be made according to a predefined pattern for movies that advertise. This chapter does not discuss templates.

The middle top list of the welcome screen, titled *Create New*, has creatable file types. To create a new Flash file, the first of these is usually chosen. It creates a Flash file that uses the current version of the scripting language, ActionScript 3.0. Note that ActionScript 3.0 is incompatible with earlier versions of Action-Script and cannot be interpreted by Flash players prior to version 9. This chapter uses only the *Flash File (ActionScript 3.0)* entry.

On the lower left is a list titled *Open a Recent Item*. On the initial use of Flash, there are no recent items, so there is no list beneath the *Open a Recent Item* title. After one or more Flash documents have been created, the most recently used of those will appear in this list. Following the list is the *Open* button. Clicking *Open* opens a dialog box (provided by the operating system) for the directory where Flash files are stored, which shows both recent and older files. Most of the files in the *Recent Item* list and in the dialog box fall into three categories: Flash movies, with the file name extension .swf (an abbreviation for *small Web files*[1], swf is pronounced "swiff."); Flash documents with the file name extension .fla; and files that contain ActionScript code, which have the file name extension .as. Clicking any one of the recent Flash document files or a Flash document file chosen from the dialog box displayed when *Open* is clicked will open that document for modification or testing in the authoring environment. If a movie file name (one with extension .swf) in the directory of Flash files is clicked, the Flash player is launched and the movie is played.

The top right part of the screen is titled *Learn*. It lists eleven different topics of Flash for which the system has lessons.

At the bottom center part of the screen is the title *Extend* (over the *Flash Exchange* button). When this button is clicked, the browser opens a document that lists third-party extensions, as well as contributed files and code for Flash development.

The screen of the authoring environment, which is displayed when either an existing Flash document is opened or a new one is created, is shown in Figure 8.2. This screen is often called the *workspace*.

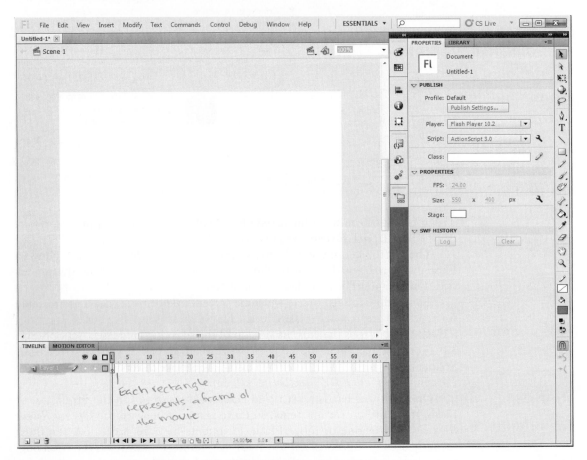

Figure 8.2 The default Flash development environment

---

1. Originally, swf was an abbreviation for *Shockwave Flash*.

At this point, only the general areas of the workspace will be discussed. If your display does not match what appears in Figure 8.2, select *Window/Workspace/Essentials*.

Across the top of the workspace is a menu bar of the kind found at the top of many applications that have graphical user interfaces, with menu titles such as *File*, *Edit*, and *View*.

The large white rectangle at the left center of the workspace is the *stage*, which is where the frames of a movie are displayed. Attached (or docked) to the right side and bottom of the stage are panels that are often used in the development of a Flash movie. These panels can be closed, opened, resized, and moved to customize the workspace.

Panels that are not displayed can be made visible by selecting *Window* and checking the name of the panel. Panels can be moved around the workspace by dragging them with the mouse cursor held down over the panel's header bar. A panel can be removed from the workspace by selecting *Window* and unchecking the panel's name. The workspace can be returned to its default configuration by selecting *Window/Workspace/Essentials*.

Immediately below the stage is a tabbed panel with the two tabs *TIMELINE* and *MOTION EDITOR*. In this book, we describe only the *TIMELINE* panel, the primary part of which is the timeline. The timeline initially consists of a row of white rectangles with numbers above every fifth rectangle. Each one of the rectangles represents a frame of the movie. To the left of both the numbers and the frame rectangles are some icons, which will be described as needed later. Notice that also to the left of the row of frames is the label *Layer 1*. There can be any number of layers of frames. When the movie is played, the contents of the layers are displayed, layer on top of layer. Multiple layers allow the various parts of the movie to be treated separately. For example, a figure in one layer could be animated while the figures in other layers are left stationary.

The rectangle covering the number of the first frame (frame 1) is red and has a red line protruding downward. This line indicates the position of the *playhead*—the frame that is currently being displayed on the stage in the authoring environment. The playhead can be dragged with the mouse cursor to display any frame in the movie. Initially, a movie has just frame 1.

Attached to the right side of the stage is a tabbed panel with the tabs *PROPERTIES* and *LIBRARY*. When the *PROPERTIES* tab of the *PROPERTIES/LIBRARY* panel is selected, we will call the panel the *properties panel*. We discuss only the *PROPERTIES* panel in this section. The three sections of the *PROPERTIES* panel are labeled *PUBLISH*, *PROPERTIES*, and *SWF HISTORY*. Only the *PROPERTIES* part is discussed here. When an empty area of the stage is selected, the stage properties panel is displayed. It can be used to change the default values of the size of the stage, the background color of the stage, and the frame rate, which is the speed at which the document's movie will be played, in frames per second (fps). The size of the stage can be changed by clicking the *Edit* button in the properties panel when an empty spot on the stage has been clicked and then making changes in the dialog box that appears. The background color of the stage can be changed by placing the cursor in the empty box to the right of the label *Stage:* in the properties panel.

When any text or other object on the stage is selected, its properties are shown in the properties panel. Different kinds of objects have different forms of properties panels.

Attached to the right side of the *PROPERTIES/LIBRARY* panel is the tools panel, with its group of tool icons. The tools panel is shown in Figure 8.3, which includes the names of the tools. If the *Show Tooltips* option is set, as it is by default, the name of each tool in the tools panel is displayed next to the tool's icon when the cursor is placed over the icon.[2]

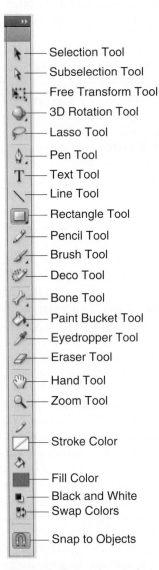

— Selection Tool
— Subselection Tool
— Free Transform Tool
— 3D Rotation Tool
— Lasso Tool
— Pen Tool
— Text Tool
— Line Tool
— Rectangle Tool
— Pencil Tool
— Brush Tool
— Deco Tool
— Bone Tool
— Paint Bucket Tool
— Eyedropper Tool
— Eraser Tool
— Hand Tool
— Zoom Tool
— Stroke Color
— Fill Color
— Black and White
— Swap Colors
— Snap to Objects

Figure 8.3 The tools panel

2. If no name appears when the cursor is placed over one of the tools, *Show Tooltips* is not set. Set it by selecting *Edit* (or *Flash* on a Mac) and *Preferences* and then clicking the *Selection/Show Tooltips* checkbox.

The *COLOR* panel can be displayed by selecting *Window/Color*. The *COLOR* panel is shown in Figure 8.4.

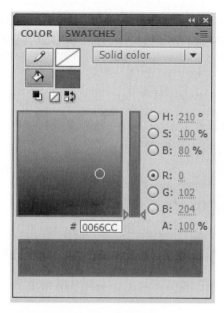

Figure 8.4 The *COLOR* panel

The *stroke* of a figure is its border; the *fill* of a figure is the area enclosed by its border. The *COLOR* panel can be used to set the colors for both stroke and fill. The *stroke color* is the color that will be used for the lines drawn on the stage, including the outlines of graphical figures. In HTML, this is called the *foreground color*. The *fill color* is the color that will be used to fill graphical figures on the stage. The choice between stroke and fill before choosing a color is made by clicking the appropriate button in the upper-left corner of the *COLOR* panel (a pencil for stroke and a paint bucket below the pencil for fill). There are several ways of choosing a color, ranging from simple to complicated. One of the simplest ways is to place the cursor in the square rainbow box in the right center of the panel and the mouse button is held down, placing the cursor over a particular color and releasing the button chooses that color. Another simple option for specifying a color is to enter the numeric values for red, green, and blue in the spaces to the right of the *R*, *G*, and *B* radio buttons. A color can also be specified by entering the hexadecimal number of the color in the text box below the color panel. A color for either stroke or fill also can be chosen from the color swatches panel, which opens when the *SWATCHES* tab on the *COLOR* window is clicked, or when either the stroke or fill buttons are clicked on the tools panel. The same panel, except for the panel label (*SWATCHES*) can be opened by selecting *Window/Swatches*. The radio buttons in the *COLOR* window provide a more complicated way to choose a color. From top to bottom, the buttons are for hue (*H*), with values ranging from 0 to 360; saturation (*S*), with values ranging from 0 to 100 percent; brightness (*B*), with values ranging from 0 to 100 percent; and *R*, *G*, and *B*, for red, green, and blue, with values ranging from 0 to 255. If any of these radio buttons is clicked, that color characteristic is held constant while the cursor is dragged around the rainbow.

The transparency of a color can be selected in the *COLOR* panel. A text box labeled *Alpha* below the column of radio buttons accepts a percentage, which will become the amount of transparency, with 0% being completely transparent and 100% being completely opaque.

8.3   Drawing Tools

Flash includes a variety of tools for drawing graphic figures on the stage. Some of the most commonly used ones are described briefly in this section.

8.3.1   Predefined Figures

Predefined geometric figures are placed on the stage with the rectangle tool in the tools panel. If the mouse cursor is placed over the icon for the *Rectangle Tool* (a rectangle with a small triangle off its lower-right corner) and the mouse button is held down, a menu of shapes is displayed, as shown in Figure 8.5.

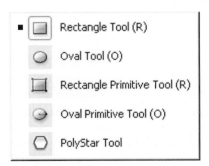

Figure 8.5 The *Rectangle Tool* menu

In the rest of this section, we briefly describe the five tools in the *Rectangle Tool* menu.

Rectangles can be created, modified, and moved about on the stage. After displaying the *Rectangle Tool* menu and selecting the *Rectangle Tool* from it, we can select the stroke style, stroke color, and fill color. Note that the square with the red diagonal line in the *COLOR* panel indicates no color. If this icon is chosen for the stroke color, the figure will have no border; if it is chosen for the fill color, the figure will be filled with the stage color. Of course, if a rectangle has neither stroke color nor fill color, it will be invisible on the stage. The fill and stroke buttons in the properties panel are exactly like the corresponding buttons in the tools menu. The stroke style can be selected only in the properties panel: We can select any of seven different styles, including plain lines, dashed lines, and dotted lines.

After choosing the stroke style, stroke color, and fill color, we place the cursor in the stage area. Pressing and holding down the mouse button starts the drawing; releasing the button stops it. If we want a square (all sides of equal length), the *Shift* key can be held down as we draw a rectangle.

Drawing ovals is similar to drawing rectangles. Circles are drawn with the *Shift* key held down. Drawing a polygon or star is a bit different, because these figures have more options, which are chosen in the *TOOL SETTINGS* section of the properties panel. To begin, the *Polystar Tool* must be chosen from the rectangle tool menu. Then the parameters of the figure are chosen in the window that appears when the *Options* button, which is in the *TOOL SETTINGS* section of the properties panel, is clicked. This action opens a *Tool Settings* dialog box with one menu and two text boxes. The menu lets you choose between a polygon (the default) and a star. The first text box, labeled *Number of Sides*, lets you choose the number of sides, although the term "side" applies only to polygons, in which the number of sides and the number of points are equal. For a star, the value of *Number of Sides* really means the number of points. The default value of the *Number of Sides* text box is 5. The second text box is labeled *Star point size*, which has a default value of 0.5. The star point size is a measure of the width of the points on stars. The first row of Figure 8.6 shows a polygon and three stars, all with five sides or points. The second row shows the same figures as the first, except that the polygon has seven sides and the stars have seven points.

Figure 8.6 Polygons and stars

The leftmost stars in Figure 8.6 have a point width of 0.25, the middle stars have a point width of 0.5, and the rightmost stars have a point width of 0.75.

A figure that has already been drawn on the stage can be modified by selecting it and changing its properties in the properties panel. Its stroke color, fill color, stroke style, size, and position can be changed. When the parameters of the figure are changed in the properties panel, the figure changes immediately. The stroke, or border, of a figure is selected by choosing the *Select Tool* in the tools menu and then clicking the mouse button with the cursor on the stroke of the figure. One of the strokes of a figure can be selected with a single click with the select cursor on that stroke. The whole stroke of a figure is selected by double-clicking any of the figure's strokes. Any stroke of a figure can be moved by selecting it, holding down the mouse key, and moving the cursor. Figure 8.7 shows two modified figures. In the first, the two vertical sides have been pulled to the right. In the second, three of the points of a six-point star have been extended. A point is stretched by selecting the *Selection Tool*, pressing the mouse button with the mouse cursor over the point of the star, and dragging the point away from the star's center. If the star is selected (by clicking anywhere in its fill area), clicking anywhere on its stroke allows the figure to be moved. So, do not select the star before trying to stretch its points. Also, do not try to click on the point of a star, as this will select one of the two strokes of the point.

Figure 8.7 Modified figures

A single click with the select cursor inside a figure selects its fill. A complete figure—stroke and fill—is selected by double-clicking with the select cursor inside the figure.[3]

Like the *Rectangle Tool*, the *Rectangle Primitive Tool* is used to draw rectangles, but the drawn figures are of a different kind. Both primitive and nonprimitive rectangles are created from a master template, which has a set of parameters that determine its characteristics. The difference between primitive and nonprimitive rectangles is that the nonprimitive ones are disconnected from the master template as soon as they are created. This has two effects. First, a rectangle that has been disconnected can be changed with the *Selection Tool*—the sides can be moved, removed, or bent in any direction, as shown in Figure 8.7. Second, because the rectangle is no longer connected to the master template, the master template parameters cannot be changed. The parameters of the master template for rectangles control the radius of the corners. So, the corners of a primitive rectangle can be changed by changing these parameters in the properties panel, but the rectangle's sides cannot be bent with the *Selection Tool*. The properties panel for a primitive rectangle is shown in Figure 8.8.

---

3. Figures that are instances of symbols have special selection behavior. (See Section 8.3.4.)

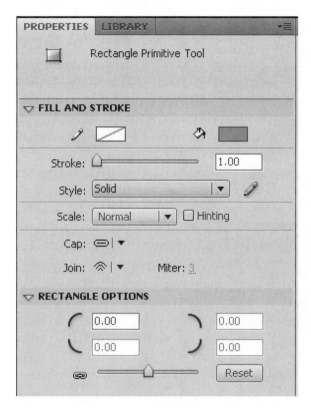

Figure 8.8 The properties panel for a primitive rectangle

The radius of any corner of a rectangle can be changed in either direction, positive or negative. The corner radius is initially set to zero, which specifies a right-angle corner. Changing it to positive values rounds the corner in the usual way. Changing it to negative values rounds the corner to the inside. Figure 8.9 shows a primitive rectangle with the upper-left corner set to a radius of 30 and the upper-right corner set to a radius of –30.

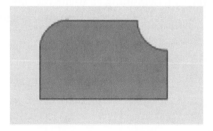

Figure 8.9 A primitive rectangle with positive and negative corner radii

The *Oval Primitive Tool* is similar to the *Rectangle Primitive Tool*—it creates ovals that remain connected to the master template for ovals. The properties panel for primitive ovals is shown in Figure 8.10.

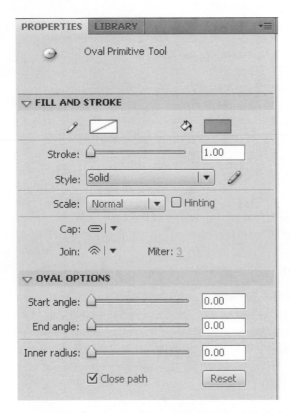

Figure 8.10 The properties panel for a primitive oval

The difference in the properties panel between a primitive oval and a nonprimitive oval is shown in the controls in the lower center of the panel. The *Start angle* and *End angle* sliders control where the drawing of the outline of the oval begin and end. Setting the *Start angle* at 30 leaves a pie-shaped piece out of the oval starting at 0 degrees, which is straight to the right on the screen, and ending at 30 degrees clockwise from there. Setting the *End angle* to 330 leaves a pie-shaped piece out of the oval beginning at 30 degrees above straight right and ending at 30 degrees below straight right. Such an oval is shown in Figure 8.11.

Figure 8.11 A primitive oval with *Start angle* at 30 and *End angle* at 330

The inner radius of an oval is its inside border, which is initially set to zero, which means that there is no visible inner border. Setting the *Inner radius* parameter to a positive number increases the radius of the inner border. Figure 8.12 shows the same oval as is shown in Figure 8.11, except that the *Inner radius* has been set to 40.

Figure 8.12 A primitive oval with *Inner radius* set to 40, *Start angle* to 30, and *End angle* to 330

Many different figures can be created with the primitive and nonprimitive tools from the *Rectangle Tool* set.

A *keyframe* is a frame in which there is something new or changed. (Frame 1 is implicitly a keyframe.) When a figure is placed on the stage, a black dot appears in the first frame of the timeline. The dot indicates that this frame is now a *populated keyframe*, which means that it has user-defined content.

8.3.2　Lines and Hand Drawings

Lines are drawn on the stage with the *Line Tool* from the tools menu. The *Line Tool* icon is a diagonal line from upper left to lower right. This tool simply draws straight lines. The parameters of the line are specified in the properties panel. The style of the line is chosen from the menu of solid lines, dashed lines, dotted lines, and so forth. The thickness of the line can be specified with the slide just left of the line style menu.

Freehand drawing can be done with the *Pencil Tool*, the *Pen Tool*, or the *Brush Tool*. Only the *Pencil Tool* will be discussed here. There are three optional modes for this tool. When the *Pencil Tool* is selected, a small icon appears at the bottom of the tools panel. This icon consists of two vertical lines, with the bottom of the upper line connected to the top of the lower line by a horizontal line. When this icon is clicked, a menu with three items appears: *Straighten*, *Smooth*, and *Ink*. Each item has an icon, which is also displayed. The *Straighten* option fits straight and curved line segments to whatever is drawn, allowing the designer to draw rough circles, ellipses, rectangles, and squares and have the system convert them to perfect figures. The *Smooth* option smooths whatever is drawn after the mouse button is released. This option is useful for removing jitters from a hand-drawn figure. The *Ink* option, which is the default, leaves exactly what is drawn on the stage.

We will refer to any figures drawn with the drawing tools, as well as imported images, as *graphic figures*.

8.3.3   Text

Flash has two different approaches to creating and manipulating text, classic text and TLF text. In this chapter, we only discuss classic text.

Placing text on the stage is straightforward. By selecting the *Text Tool*, moving the cursor over the stage, and clicking the mouse button, we create a narrow text box under the cursor. As text is entered into the box, the box extends in width to accommodate the entered text, but the text will not wrap to an additional line. Each corner of the box can be dragged left or right to lengthen it in that direction. When the box is lengthened, the upper-right corner mark changes from a small circle to a small square and the mode changes to wrap mode. In wrap mode, if the text that is entered will not fit into the box, the excess characters are wrapped onto an additional line, expanding the box on its bottom side. If the square at the upper-right corner of a text box that has been lengthened is double-clicked, the box reverts to the width it had before being lengthened. The default parameters of the entered text can be changed in the properties panel: When the *Text Tool* is clicked, a special version of that panel that handles text appears. This special panel is shown in Figure 8.13.

Figure 8.13 The properties panel for the *Text Tool*, after expanding *PARAGRAPH*

The top menu in the properties panel allows the user to choose between the default *Classic Text* and the option *TLF Text*. The second menu displays the default value *Static Text*. The other options in this menu are *Dynamic Text* and *Input Text*. *Dynamic Text* is for text fields that can be changed during display. *Input Text* is for text fields that will accept user input. *Static Text* is for text that cannot be changed while it is displayed. Only *Static Text* is discussed and used in this chapter.

The *CHARACTER* part of the properties panel allows changes in the font characteristics, among which are the font family, style, size, and color. The *PARAGRAPH* section, which is elided by default, allows changes in the paragraph parameters.

8.3.4 Imported Graphic Figures

Graphic figures, or images, are often imported to Flash movies. There are two distinct approaches to representing images: bitmap, sometimes called raster graphics, and vector graphics. A *bitmap image* consists of pixels, each of which contains color information and represents a small rectangular area of the image. Bitmaps are ideal for photographic images that include complex fills, shadowing, and gradient effects. Because the size of pixels is static, when a bitmap image is enlarged, the program that performs the enlargement must create new pixels based on the surrounding pixels. Because the properties of the new pixels are only guesses of what they should be, the more new pixels the enlargement needs, the less accurate the image becomes, leading to blurriness. Furthermore, bitmap images lose quality when they are rotated or skewed. Most images that are embedded in Web documents, including all GIF, JPEG, and PNG images, are bitmap images. Many of the Microsoft clip art figures are Windows MetaFiles (WMF), which have both bitmap and vector components.

A *vector graphic image* consists of lines and curves. It is stored as a set of mathematical instructions for how to draw the image. Vector images can be drawn to any size without any loss of quality. They also have the advantage of requiring less storage than comparable bitmap images. However, at least in the case of photographic images, the quality of vector images can be lower than that of bitmap images.

Flash supports both bitmap and vector figures. Vector figures can be created and edited in Flash, but bitmap figures must be imported. Editing a bitmap figure in Flash is limited to trimming edges and erasing portions of the figure. Anything more must be done outside Flash, after which the figure is reimported. The alternative to this approach is to convert the image from a bitmap image to a vector image. However, this process is nontrivial and, as a result, is not covered in this chapter.

8.3.5 Symbols and Libraries

A Flash symbol is related to a class in a programming language—it is a description of an object. Instances of a symbol can be created and placed on the stage. Regardless of the number of instances of a symbol that are used in a movie, the symbol must be stored only once.[4]

---

4. Although each instance of a symbol requires some memory, the amount required is much less than that needed to store the figure represented by the symbol.

The most commonly used symbols are of graphic figures, which are the only kind discussed in this section.

Anytime a graphic figure appears more than once in a movie, it should be a symbol, because that results in a reduction in the movie's file size.

The color, size, and shape of a symbol can be edited. To edit a symbol, select a symbol instance by double-clicking the instance on the stage. Then the properties panel can be used to make the changes, which modify the symbol and all of its instances. To modify a single instance, select the instance with a single click.

All figures drawn on the stage with the Flash drawing tools are vector graphic figures. To convert a vector graphic figure to a symbol and place it in the library, first select the figure on the stage. Then select *Modify/Convert to Symbol* from the menu at the top of the workspace. This opens a dialog box, shown in Figure 8.14.

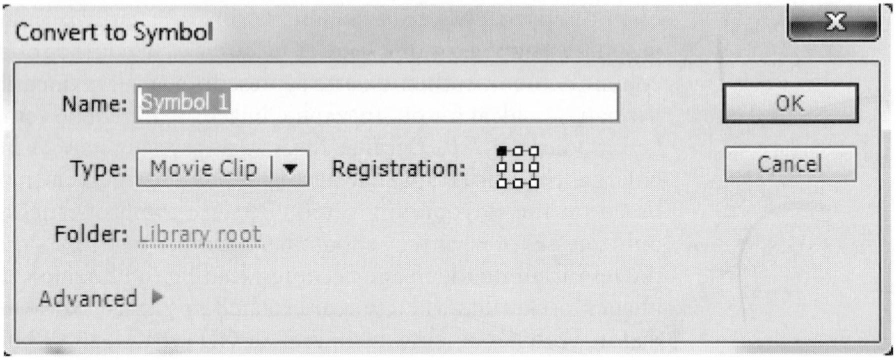

Figure 8.14 The *Convert to Symbol* dialog box

In this dialog box, the symbol is renamed by replacing the default name, which is *Symbol 1*. The dialog box has two modes: basic and advanced. Basic mode is the default and is the only one described here.

The *Convert to Symbol* dialog box includes a menu that specifies the symbol's type: *Movie Clip*, *Button*, or *Graphic*. The difference between the movie clip and graphic types is complex and mostly beyond the scope of this book. Briefly, a movie clip runs continuously in its own timeline, independently of the main timeline. Movie clips are movies within movies. Movie clip type symbols provide some interesting animation possibilities. However, they are not discussed any further in this book. For now, we deal only with graphic symbols, which run in the main timeline.

When a graphic figure on the stage is converted to a symbol, a box appears around the figure on the stage to indicate that it is now an instance of a symbol.

Every Flash document has a library. The library stores symbols, bitmap graphics, sound clips, video clips, and fonts, all of which are called *assets*. An instance of any symbol in the library can be dragged to the stage to become part of the movie.

The contents of the library of a document are displayed in the *LIBRARY* panel. The specific library that is being displayed is shown in the menu at the top of the *LIBRARY* panel. Initially, the displayed library is that of the currently open active document. The library of any open, but inactive, document can be displayed, and any symbol from any of these libraries can be placed in the current movie. The contents of a library can be organized into folders and subfolders, but that topic is not covered in this book.

If an instance of a symbol is deleted from the stage, it has no effect on the symbol in the library.

8.4 Static Graphics

This section demonstrates the use of Flash to build a static movie with graphic figures and text. Without animation, a movie occupies a single frame. A movie usually has multiple layers, each with a different part of the scene being depicted. However, when there is no animation, a movie often has just a single layer. Because this movie is static, it will have a single frame with a single layer.

The example of this section, which we name `aidan_static2`, is a banner for an ad document for used airplanes. To begin, we open a new Flash document and resize the stage to 700 by 350 pixels. To resize the stage, we change the *Size* values in the properties panel after the stage has been selected. We also set the background color of the stage to a light blue. To do this, we click the *Stage:* box and choose a light blue from the swatches panel that appears.

Next, we add a text box with the company's name and slogan to the upper center of the stage. The company title font is Times New Roman, 50 points; the slogan is also Times New Roman, but 28 points. These features are shown in Figure 8.15.

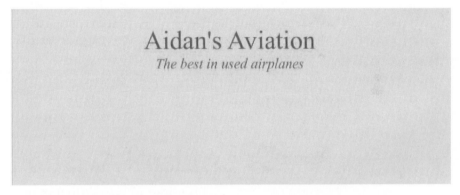

Figure 8.15 The text of the movie `aidan_static2`

The next things we add to the movie are two small airplane figures, one to be placed on each side of the text. These figures are obtained from a free clip-art Web site—in this case, `http://office.microsoft.com/en-us/clipart/default.aspx`. External clip art can be placed in a movie by selecting *File/Import*, which provides four options. The easiest way to place external bitmap graphic figures into a movie is to import them directly to the stage. This places the figure both on the stage and in the library. If the figure is not to be animated, that is all there is to it. If the external figure is a vector graphic figure—for example, a WMF figure—it is better to import it into the library and then drag one or more instances of it to the stage.[5] For our example, we import one bitmap airplane figure to the stage (and library) and one vector graphic airplane figure to the library. Then we rename the figures (in the library) `airplane1` and `airplane2`. To rename a library entry, right click it and select *Rename* from the resulting menu. The *LIBRARY* panel now appears as in Figure 8.16.

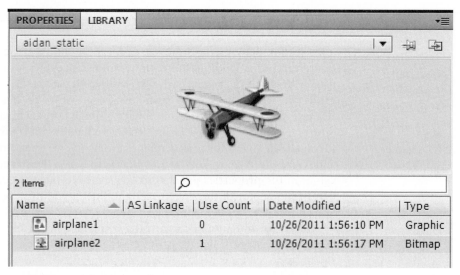

Figure 8.16 The library after two figures are imported into it

Notice that one of the figures (`airplane1`) appears as a graphic—it is actually a WMF file—and the other (`airplane2`) appears as a bitmap—it is actually a PNG file.

At this point, `airplane2` is already on the stage, since we imported it there. To get the other airplane image (`airplane1`) to the stage, we drag an instance of it there. The new stage is as shown in Figure 8.17.

Figure 8.17 The stage after the clip-art airplanes are added to it

5. Importing a vector graphic figure to the stage causes some problems for Flash, so we avoid doing it.

One of the motivations for our example movie is to announce a sale at Aidan's Aviation. To make this known, we add another figure to the movie—in this case, a star with the word *SALE* inside. We begin by drawing an eight-pointed star, using a point size of 0.25, on the stage. We use a blue solid 3-pixel-thick stroke and a white fill. We then stretch all of the star's points except the one pointing up and the one pointing down. This flattens the star's appearance.

Next, we convert the star to a symbol and use the *Text Tool* to put the word SALE inside it. We use Times Roman 18-point bold font in red for the text. We convert the star to a symbol by selecting the whole star by double-clicking inside it, selecting *Modify*, and clicking *Convert to Symbol*, once again choosing *Graphic* as the type. The resulting stage is shown in Figure 8.18.

The next step is to save and test the movie. Flash allows movies to be tested within the authoring environment, without requiring that the movie be loaded into a browser. This is done by selecting *Control/Test Movie*. The resulting display window, whose content is the same as that of Figure 8.18, is shown in Figure 8.19.

Figure 8.18 The stage with the complete sale announcement

Figure 8.19 The test of the movie, `aidan_static2`

There are a variety of ways to publish a movie. All are accessed by selecting *File/Publish Settings*. The dialog box that results is shown in Figure 8.20.

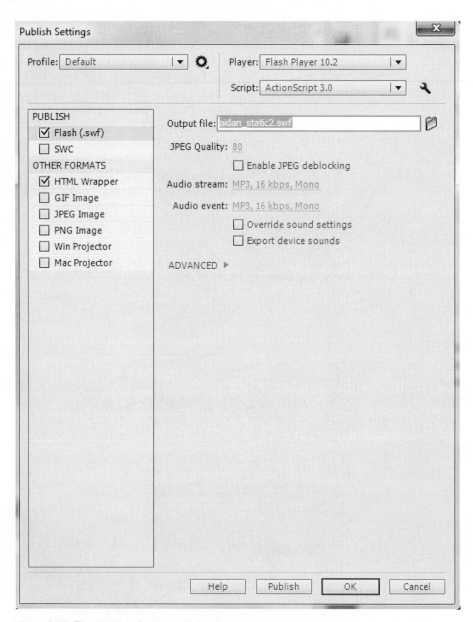

Figure 8.20 The *Publish Settings* dialog box

If the movie is to be placed on a Web site, it needs to be published as a Flash file and as HTML. Because this is the usual choice, these two check-boxes are checked by default. The *GIF*, *JPEG*, and *PNG* checkboxes are used to produce images of the movie. The *Windows Projector* checkbox creates a file that can be executed under Windows. This file, when executed, plays the movie without a Flash player being installed on the computer on which it is executed. The *Macintosh Projector* button creates a similar file for Macintosh computers.

If only the *Flash* and *HTML* checkboxes are checked, several files are created in the directory in which the Flash document resides. The Flash movie is in the file `aidan_static2.swf`. The HTML file is implicitly named `aidan_static2.html`, although that could be changed to whatever the author likes. The other created file contains a JavaScript script that allows Flash movies to be played in Microsoft browsers without requiring interaction by the user. The name of this file is `AC_RunActiveContent.js`.

If the browser of the system on which the Flash movie was built is pointed to the HTML document, the movie will be played on that browser.

A movie can be published just as a `swf` file and inserted into an HTML document. To do this, the HTML object element is used.

In many cases, a markup document consists of the HTML produced by Flash, as well as HTML written by a Web designer. The handwritten HTML can be added to the HTML document created by Flash. As an example, we next modify the HTML document from the `aidan_static2` movie by adding a small amount of text. The style element for this addition is as follows:

```
<style type = "text/css">
  p.special {text-indent: "2.5in"; font-family: 'Times New Roman';
            font-size: 24pt; font-style: italic; color: "red";
            text-decoration: "underline";}
  p.list {text-indent: "1in"; font-family: 'Times New Roman';
          font-size: 16pt; color: "blue";}
</html>
```

The content for the addition is as follows:

```
<!-- Content added to the Flash-produced file for the
     aidan_static3 movie -->
<p></p><p></p>
<p class = "special">
  Specials of the Week
</p>
<p></p>
```

```
<p class = "list">
1. 1960 Cessna 210 <span style = "position: absolute; left: 3in">
   $49,000 </span>
</p>
<p class = "list">
2. 1977 Piper Commanche <span style = "position: absolute; left:
   3in">  $72,000 </span>
</p>
<p class = "list">
3. 1980 Cessna 182RG <span style = "position: absolute; left: 3in">
   $81,000 </span>
</html>
```

The display of the new version of `aidan_static2`, named `aidan_static3`.`html`, is shown in Figure 8.21.

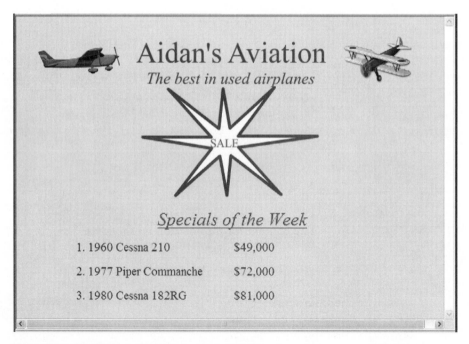

Figure 8.21 The display of `aidan_static3.html`

The markup that is added to the markup file produced by Flash must be saved separately, because every time a Flash movie is changed and republished, the previous markup file is replaced.

8.5   Animation and Sound

The sample movie of this section is similar to the static movie of Section 8.4, but with modifications to animate part of it and to add sound to it.

8.5.1   Introduction to Animation

When a movie has multiple frames, those frames are displayed by the Flash player in sequence, repeatedly, from first to last. Flash animation is created by the player showing sequences of frames, each with a slightly changed appearance. Early animated movies, which were mostly cartoons, were made by hand painting long sequences of slightly different scenes and photographing each in its own frame on film. To create object movement with Flash, the author only needs to create the initial and final frames, showing the initial and final positions of the object to be moved. Flash creates the intervening frames that morph the first frame into the last. These intervening frames are created through a process called *tweening*.

In the example (static) movie of Section 8.4, all of the parts in the movie are in the same layer. This is unusual, because most movies have multiple layers. In fact, it is normal to place each object in its own layer, because each can then be treated separately and differently, especially with regard to animation. Placing different objects in different layers allows some objects to be animated while others are static over the playing time of the movie.

8.5.2   Moving a Figure

Flash CS5.5 provides two approaches to moving stage objects: *classic tweening* and *motion tweening*. Motion tweening is slightly easier to develop, but has some restrictions. For example, code cannot be attached to frames of the animated object. Because we need to attach code to frames of an animated object in the example of Section 8.6.3, which begins as a copy of the example of this section, we describe classic tweening here.

The example of this section is similar to the example in Section 8.4: a banner that provides the name of a company and its slogan. Instead of two stationary airplane figures, this movie will have just one airplane figure, but it will move across the stage from left to right. The motion is created by placing one instance of the airplane figure in frame 1 at the left end of the stage and copying it to frame 100 at the right end of the stage. Then classic tweening is used to create the airplane figure in frames 2 through 99, each succeeding figure moved slightly to the right.

We begin by creating a new Flash document named `aidan_dynamic1` and setting its size to 800 by 400 pixels and its background color to a light blue. Then we change the name of the initial layer to *name*. This is done by double-clicking the layer name, typing in the new name, and pressing *Enter* (or *Return* on a Mac). After frame 1 is selected, the company name and slogan are placed on the stage, with sufficient space left above for the animated airplane figure. To ensure that the text will not accidentally be deleted, and to disallow any other objects from being placed in the *name* layer, we lock the layer by clicking the second dot to the right of the layer's name that is below the small lock icon, which is on the same row as the frame numbers. When this dot is clicked, it turns into an image of a small padlock.

The next step is to create a new layer for the animated airplane figure. Upper layers have precedence over lower layers. In effect, the bottom layer is displayed first, then the upper layers are progressively revealed. So, graphic figures in a layer above can hide a figure in a lower layer. If no two layers have overlapping objects, which is the case in the example here, then the order of display of the layers is irrelevant. We create a new layer by selecting *Insert/Timeline/Layer* or by clicking the *Insert Layer* button at the bottom left of the layers panel. (The name *Insert Layer* appears when the cursor is over the button.) This creates a new layer directly above the selected layer. If you want the new layer to be below the current bottom layer, drag it there with the mouse cursor after it has been created. In the example, we create the new layer and drag it to the bottom. Then we rename the layer *animate1*.

Next, we need a figure of a small airplane. We import a WMF vector graphic figure of an airplane to the library with *File/Import/Import to Library*. After importing the figure and renaming it `airplane` in the library, we select frame 1 of the *animate1* layer and drag an instance of it from the library onto the stage. (If the *LIBRARY* panel is not displayed, select *Window/Library* to make it appear.) Then, we convert it to a graphic type symbol with *Modify/Convert to Symbol*.

The Flash player always begins by displaying the contents of the first frame of the movie. If the movie has but one frame, as is the case with the `aidan_static2` example of Section 8.4, that is all that is ever displayed. To make the movie change, objects must be placed in other frames. When the Flash player plays a movie with multiple frames, it displays them in sequence, repeatedly.

Figure 8.22 shows the stage at this point in its development, with the airplane figure in the upper-left corner.

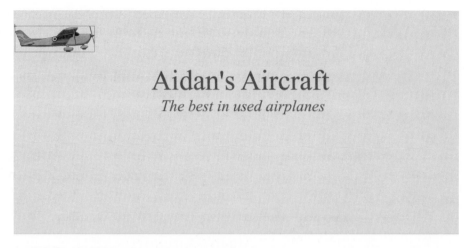

Aidan's Aircraft

The best in used airplanes

Figure 8.22 The workspace before adding animation

To create the airplane animation for our movie, we must create a new keyframe. A keyframe with content is indicated by a dot in its frame in the timeline. A keyframe without graphical content is indicated by a small circle in its timeline frame. Such a keyframe is called a *blank keyframe*. A blank keyframe can contain sound and actions, but no graphical figures. For our example, we create a new keyframe at frame 100 by right-clicking (Control-click on a Mac) frame 100 of the *animate1* layer and selecting *Insert Keyframe* from the menu that appears. This creates a new keyframe in frame 100 and copies the contents of the previous keyframe (frame 1 in this case) into the new keyframe. Then, with frame 100 of the *animate1* layer selected, we drag the airplane figure instance from the upper-left corner of the stage to the upper-right corner of the stage. If frame 1 is selected, the airplane is where we initially put it, in the upper-left corner of the stage. If we drag the playhead from frame 1 to frame 99, the airplane remains displayed in the upper-left corner, because it was implicitly copied to frames 2 to 99. So, at this point, we have the airplane figure displayed in the upper-left corner in frames 1 to 99. Then it jumps to the upper-right corner when the playhead is moved to frame 100.

To create reasonable animation, the frames between 1 and 100 must be filled with copies of the airplane figure at positions between the first and 100th frames. We could do this manually, but it would be very tedious. Classic tweening creates the in-between, or tweening, frames for animation. To create the tweening frame contents, we select a frame between the two ends—say, frame 50—in the *animate1* layer. We then select *Insert/Classic Tween*. This causes Flash to create copies of the airplane figure in frames between frame 1 and frame 100, each with the airplane moved slightly to the right of its position in the preceding frame. It also changes the `animate1` layer of the timeline by placing an arrow in it from frame 1 to frame 100 and coloring it pale purple. The animation can be checked by selecting the playhead on the top of the timeline and moving it between frames 1 and 100.

Figure 8.23 shows the workspace with the airplane figure in its final position in the upper-right corner of the stage.

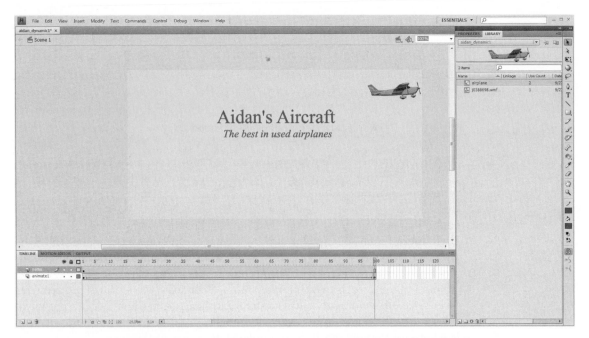

Figure 8.23 The workspace with the airplane figure in its final position

One remaining issue for the airplane image animation is that the rest of the parts of the movie—in this case, just the text—are shown only when the playhead is over frame 1. To make the text remain throughout the movie, it must be placed in all of the frames from 2 to 100. This is done by clicking the *name* layer in frame 100 and selecting *Insert/Timeline/Frame*. Now if the playhead is dragged from frame 1 to frame 100, the airplane image moves and the text remains while all of the frames are shown.

To run the movie from the first frame to the last—here, from frame 1 to frame 100—simply click the *Enter* button (*Return* on a Mac). To run the movie repeatedly, select *Control/Loop Playback* and click *Enter* (or *Return*).[6] The movie can be stopped by clicking *Enter* (or *Return*) again. Of course, you can also run the movie by selecting *Control/Test Movie*.

---

6. If the *Loop Playback* checkbox of the *Control* menu is already checked, this step is unnecessary.

8.5.3   More Animation

We now create a new movie by adding another animated figure to the movie `aidan_dynamic1` of Section 8.5.2. We will add the star from the example `aidan_static2` (Section 8.4). The star will be made to grow and shrink as the movie is played. We begin by opening the `aidan_dynamic1` movie and saving it as `aidan_dynamic2`. Next, we add a new layer for the star by selecting *Insert/Timeline/Layer* or by clicking the *New Layer* button at the bottom left of the *TIMELINE* panel. We then change the name of this layer to *animate2*. While frame 1 in the new layer is selected, we draw a 12-pointed star with a dark-blue three-pixel stroke and a white fill onto the stage. We then stretch the six points on the left and right sides to make the star slightly flat, rather than circular, as was done with the star figure in Section 8.4. Next, we select the star and convert it to a symbol by selecting *Modify/Convert to Symbol*. We name the symbol *star* and set its type to *Graphic*. Then we add the text, SALE, in a red, bold, 18-point font to the center of the star. The text is added in the *name* layer, where the company name and slogan text appear (if the *name* layer is locked, it must be unlocked before placing the new text in it). The stage is now displayed as shown in Figure 8.24.

Figure 8.24 The initial star in `aidan_dynamic2`

The next step in creating the animated star is to create two new keyframes in the *animate2* layer, one at frame 50 and one at frame 100. We create these keyframes by selecting the frame number and the desired layer (*animate2*) and then selecting *Insert/Timeline/Keyframe*. Both keyframes implicitly get copies of the star in frame 1. (If a keyframe is accidentally created in the wrong frame, it can be removed by selecting the keyframe and then selecting *Modify/Timeline/Clear Keyframe*.) Next, we modify the star in frame 50. We want the star to start (in frame 1) large, then shrink to a smaller size by frame 50, and then grow back to its original size by frame 100. To build the smaller star, we select frame 50 and select the star figure on the stage. Be careful to select the star with a single click.

If you double-click the star, any changes you make will be to the symbol and all of its instances.[7] Next, we select the *Free Transform Tool*, which is just below the *Selection Tool* (if the tools are displayed in one column). Its icon is a black dashed square with a triangular tool on the left side. The dashed square turns red when the cursor is placed over it, at which time its name also appears. Selecting this tool displays a rectangle with black squares on the corners and embedded in the sides. These squares can be dragged to change the size of the figure. Dragging a corner toward the center with the *Shift* key held down changes the figure proportionally, so it retains its original shape. If the *Alt* button is also held down, the figure changes size proportionally relative to the center of the figure. This is how we make a smaller version of the star. We now have a large star in frames 1 and 100 and a smaller star in frame 50. Figure 8.25 shows the stage at frame 50 after the star has been made smaller.

Figure 8.25 The stage at frame 50 after the star has been shrunk

Next, we create the tween frames between 1 and 50. First, we select frame 25 in the *animate2* layer. Then we select *Insert/Classic Tween*. This creates all of the figures in the frames from 2 to 49. After that, we select frame 75 and select *Insert/Classic Tween*, which creates the figures in the frames from 51 to 99. Classic tweening (rather than shape tweening) is chosen because the shape of the star need not be changed (and because symbols cannot be shape tweened).

The next step is to save the document and test its movie by dragging the playhead from frame 1 to frame 100. The small airplane should still fly across the top of the stage from left to right. Also, the star at the bottom should shrink and grow as the airplane moves across the stage. Then we use *Control/Test Movie* to again test the movie. Finally, we publish the movie as HTML and as a Flash document. As one more test, we point the browser at the HTML file, which produces the same movie as *Test Movie*.

---

7. Of course, in this case there is only one instance.

8.5.4   Shape Animation

In Sections 8.5.2 and 8.5.3, motion-tweened animation was illustrated. Shape animation is the process of morphing one shape into another. In Flash, this process is closely related to classic tweening and is called *shape tweening*. As in classic tweening, the developer creates the beginning and ending keyframes and their shapes and Flash creates the intervening shapes. Only vector figures can be shape tweened.[8] We demonstrate shape-tweened animation in this section. The example will be simple: A red circle will be morphed into a blue square, which will then be morphed into a green triangle.

We begin by creating a new movie named shape_morph. For this example, the default stage size of 550 by 400 pixels is acceptable, so we do not change it. The initial layer is renamed *morph*. In frame 1, we draw a circle with a dark-red stroke color and a light-red fill on the stage. Then, we create a blank keyframe in frame 50 by right-clicking (Control-click on a Mac) frame 50 of the morph layer and selecting *Insert Blank Keyframe* from the menu that appears. We use a blank keyframe because we do not want the new keyframe to inherit the objects of any other keyframe—in this case, the circle figure we drew in the first keyframe. After selecting frame 50, we draw a square about the same size as the circle, this time with a dark-blue stroke color and a light-blue fill. At this time, we need not worry about it being in exactly the same position as the circle. Next, we create the frames to transform the circle to the square. We select frame 25 and then select *Insert/Shape Tween*.

Next, we create a new blank keyframe in frame 100 and draw a triangle (a three-sided polygon) in that frame. We use a dark-green stroke color and a light-green fill for the triangle. We then select frame 75 to create the tweening figures between the square and the triangle by selecting *Insert/Shape Tween*.

After the frames have been filled, the figures may need to be aligned with each other. To do this, first we click the *Edit Multiple Frames* button, whose icon is two small filled squares, one overlaying the other—appears below the timeline. This places two square brackets on the timeline. Next, we drag the left bracket to frame 1 and the right bracket to frame 100. Then, we click Control-A (command-A on a Mac) to select all elements on the stage. Finally, we select *Modify/Align*. From the resulting menu, we select *Horizontal Center*. Then, we select *Modify/Align* again and select *Vertical Center*. Now, all three figures are centered on the stage.

Next, we click *Edit Multiple Frames* to turn it off. Now we can test the movie to be sure the shape tweening works.

In some movies, it is desirable to have an animation sequence reversed as another part of the movie. For example, if you want to animate a ball moving back and forth across the stage and you have already created the forward animation, the reverse animation is easy to implement with Flash. The first step is to copy the sequence of frames that moves the ball across the stage. This is done by selecting the layer of those frames. Then, click and drag the frames to the first frame after the existing movie, but do not release the mouse button. Hold down the *Alt* key (the *Opt* key on a Mac) and release the mouse button. Now there is a

---

8. You can determine whether a figure on the stage is an instance of a symbol by selecting it. If selecting it places a boundary box around it, it is an instance of a symbol.

copy of the original frames on the timeline. Next, select the new frames and select *Modify/Timeline/Reverse Frames*. This reverses the order of the selected frames. You now have both forward and backward animation of the ball.

Text as initially created by the *Text Tool* is in an editable format (not a symbol). If the text is double-clicked, it can be changed. Editable text cannot be shape tweened. However, text can be shape tweened if it is first broken apart, by selecting the text and then selecting *Modify/Break Apart*.

Both shape and motion animation can be made smoother by placing the animated objects farther apart on the timeline. For instance, in the shape-morphing example, the square could have been placed in frame 100 and the triangle in frame 200. This would have resulted in many more frames in the movie, thereby smoothing the transitions.

Animation created from discrete pictures, like that of movie films and Flash movies, is effective because, if the pictures change fast enough, the human brain fills in between them. If the actual pictures change too slowly, the animation appears jerky, because the brain no longer fills in between them. If the pictures change too quickly, the picture becomes blurred. The speed of the Flash player is controlled by the movie being played. The frame rate, which is the number of frames displayed per second, has a default value of 12 frames per second (fps). The frame rate can be changed in the properties panel when the stage has been selected.

The standard frame rate for film is 24 fps, but older versions of the Flash player were not able to play movies that fast. Starting with Version 9, the Flash player can display movies far faster than 24 fps. For example, the movie `aidan_dynamic2` can be played at 100 fps, but at that speed, the animated airplane is a blur. It would take many more frames in the movie to make it appear realistic at that frame rate. However, Flash movies with a large number of frames require larger files for storage and longer times to download. Furthermore, if a movie has complex animation and the frame rate is high, the CPU of the viewer's computer can become overwhelmed. The range of frame rates that can be downloaded and played by most computers and their Internet connections is 15 to 20.

There are two ways to slow the animation of a Flash movie. The simplest way is to lower the frame rate. This approach is limited, however, because slow frame rates result in jerky animation. The alternative is to insert ordinary frames (not keyframes) between the frames of the movie. This extends the timeline and extends the time between keyframes. A new frame inserted after an existing frame inherits the contents of that frame. A frame is inserted by selecting an existing frame and selecting *Insert/Timeline/Frame*. To double the length of a movie, one frame could be inserted after each existing frame of the movie. More than one frame could be inserted after each existing frame to slow it even more. A part of a movie can be slowed by adding frames only in that part.

8.5.5   Sound

Sound clips can be added to a Flash movie. The first step in adding sound is to import the sound file to the library of the movie. Sound clips are widely available on the Web. The clip used in this example was downloaded from `http://avanimation.avsupport.com/Sound.htm`. To import a sound file, select *File/Import/Import to Library*[9] and then select the sound file. The sound file will then appear in the *LIBRARY* panel as a new item. If the new item is clicked, the waveform of the sound file will appear in the window above the library's list of assets. When adding sounds to the timeline, it is best to place the soutnds in their own layer in a movie.

As an example, we will add a sound clip to the example movie of Section 8.5.3. We begin by opening that movie, *aidan_dynamic1*, and saving it in *aidan_dynamic2*. We then add a new layer (*Insert/Timeline/Layer*) and name it *sound*. We place the new layer at the bottom of the list of layers, just to make it easy to find.

At this point, the sound clip is in the library, but not in the movie, and we have an empty layer named *sound*. We insert the sound clip in the movie by selecting the first frame of the *sound* layer and dragging the sound clip from the library to the stage. (It does not matter what spot on the stage is chosen.)

In the case of this example, the chosen sound clip was too long. Sound clips can be shortened by removing parts of either or both ends. This is done in the properties panel displayed when the keyframe of the beginning of the clip is clicked. The panel is shown in Figure 8.26.

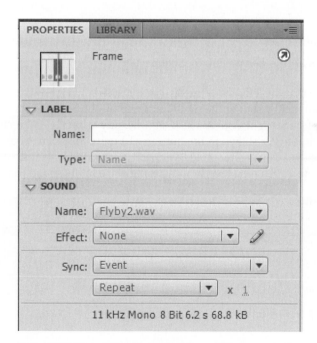

Figure 8.26 The properties panel for editing sound clips

---

9. You can also select *File/Import/Import to Stage*, but it has the same effect as *Input to Library*. Neither places the sound clip on the stage.

Included in the properties panel shown in Figure 8.26 is an edit button, which, when clicked, displays the window shown in Figure 8.27. The edit button icon is a pencil, located just to the right of the *Effect* menu.

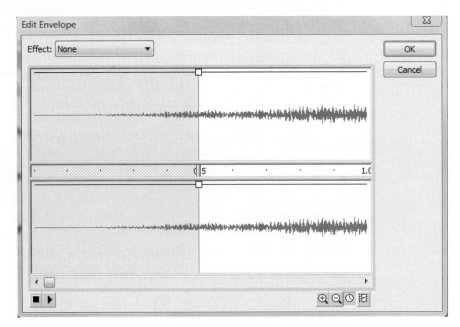

Figure 8.27 The *Edit* window for sound clips

Notice that the left half of the display is shaded. This shows the part of the clip that we trimmed by sliding the small rectangle on the center scale to the right. For this example, the right end was also significantly trimmed. The clip was actually 6.2 seconds long, as shown in the bottom of Figure 8.26. Since our animation is about 4 seconds, we made the sound layer similarly short. The length of the sound is shown in Figure 8.28 by the length of the soundwave in the sound layer of the timeline.

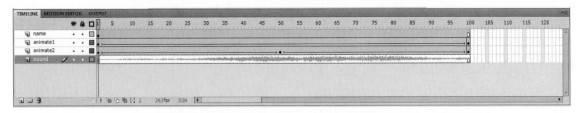

Figure 8.28 The timeline showing the sound layer

When the movie `aidan_dynamic2` is played, the sound clip, which is the sound of a small airplane flying past, is heard.

Notice in Figure 8.26 that the size of the sound file we imported is 68.8 kB. This size can be made smaller by compressing it. Select the library entry for the sound clip, and click the third icon from the left at the bottom of the library panel. The icon's name is *Properties*, which is displayed when the cursor is placed over the icon. This produces the window shown in Figure 8.29.

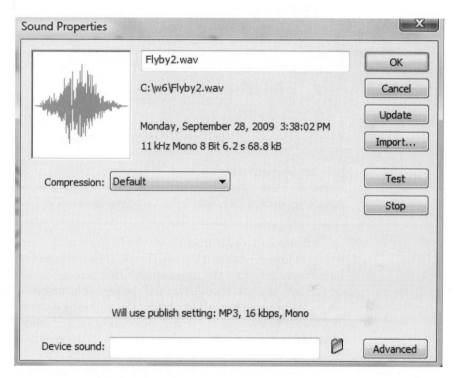

Figure 8.29 The *Sound Properties* window

Now choose the *MP3* entry in the *Compression* menu, which produces the change in the *Sound Properties* window, shown in Figure 8.30.

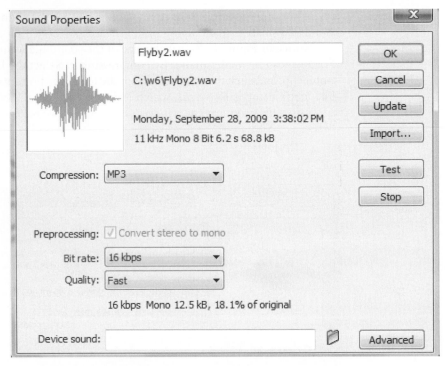

Figure 8.30 The *Sound Properties* window after *MP3* has been selected

There are two adjustments that can be made in two menus of the *Sound Properties* window: *Bit rate* and *Quality*. The *Bit rate* menu includes a list of possible bit rates, ranging from 8 kbs (thousand bits per second) to 160 kbs. The higher the bit rate, the larger is the file size and the higher is the quality of the sound clip. It is easy to experiment with the bit rate by choosing a value and then clicking the *Test* button to listen to the sound. Selecting an appropriate bit rate is a matter of choosing the slowest bit rate that produces an acceptable level of sound quality. After choosing a bit rate, you can select *Quality*. The possible values are *Fast*, *Medium*, and *Best*, names that are based on whether you want a fast conversion time, a medium time of conversion, or the slowest conversion time, respectively. The *Best* option results in the best quality sound at the chosen bit rate. The file size is determined entirely by the bit rate. For our airplane sound, which is simple, we chose a bit rate of 24 bps and the *Best* quality. This selection results in a file size of 18.7 kB, which is less than 28 percent of the size of the original file and which exemplifies the importance of sound file compression.

8.6 User Interactions

In Chapters 5 and 6, JavaScript is used to allow the user to interact with HTML documents through graphical elements to control the presentation details of how they are displayed, among other things. The Flash dialect of JavaScript, ActionScript, can be used to control the content of a Flash movie, also through graphical elements, or components. Most commonly, in Flash these components are buttons. However, a variety of components can be placed in a Flash movie, to deal with virtually any user interaction. In this section, simple buttons and their associated ActionScript code are illustrated with an example that allows the user to control the animation of a movie through buttons.

8.6.1   Actions

Actions associated with user interactions through components are programmed in ActionScript. There are two ways to add ActionScript to a Flash movie: as frame actions, which is code associated with particular keyframes of the movie, and as custom classes, which is code that resides in an external file. In this book, we deal only with frame actions. Actions are similar to those written in Chapter 5 to implement user interactions with components. Flash component interactions create events, and the associated actions are programmed as event handler functions. The DOM 2 event model method `addEventListener` is used to register event handlers on the components.

Because the user interactions implemented in Flash usually control the player, methods for player control are predefined in ActionScript. Among these methods are `nextFrame()`, which instructs the player to play the next frame, `gotoAndStop(frame number)`, `gotoAndPlay(frame number)`, `play()`, and `stop()`, which do what their names imply. The parameter of `gotoAndStop` and `gotoAndPlay` can be a frame label, which can be created in another layer.

Actions are usually added to a new layer of the movie—often named *actions*. When such a layer has ActionScript associated with it in a keyframe, that keyframe is displayed in the timeline with a lowercase 'a'. Action layers are usually locked to prevent the accidental placement of graphic figures or other assets in them. Being locked does not prevent the placement of ActionScript in the layer.

ActionScript is written in a workspace window named *Actions*, which is accessed by selecting *Window/Actions*. The upper-left panel of this window, titled *ActionScript 3.0* (assuming that the movie was created for ActionScript 3.0), is a menu of buttons that create skeletal ActionScript constructs. This menu is part of a tool named *Script Assist*, which helps create ActionScript code. Because we assume that the reader is already versed in JavaScript, we do not describe how to use Script Assist in this book. The main panel of the *Actions* window is where ActionScript code is typed. Above this panel is a row of buttons, only one of which—*Check syntax*, whose symbol is a check mark (✓)—is of interest at this stage. This tool is used to check the correctness of the syntax of the code in the panel before the author uses the player to test it.

8.6.2   Flash Components

In Flash, components can be designed by the programmer. For example, a button can be designed by choosing a graphic figure such as a circle, an ellipse, or a square to represent the button. Also a collection of predefined components is available in the workspace. Among these are simple buttons, checkboxes, sliders, and radio buttons. We deal only with predesigned components here.

8.6.3 An Example

Our example to illustrate user interactions will be simple: We begin with just the animated airplane figure and the business title from the previous examples. To this we will add two buttons, one to stop the airplane and one to restart its motion.

We begin by opening `aidan_dynamic1` and saving it as `interact`. Recall that in the `aidan_dynamic1` movie the animation runs in the main timeline. The first step is to add a layer for the buttons and another one for actions. We do so by selecting *Insert/Timeline/Layer*. The names we choose for these layers are *buttons* and *actions*.

Next, we create the two buttons in the button layer by dragging the *Button* component to the lower-left corner of the stage. The components are found in the window that is opened by selecting *Window/Components* and expanding the *User Interface* section. This window is shown in Figure 8.31.

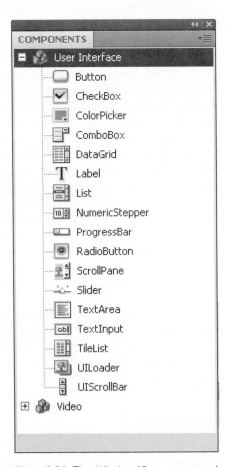

Figure 8.31 The *Window/Components* window

If you look at the properties panel for either of the two buttons, you will see that they are movie clip type objects. In fact, all button components are a special kind of movie clip. Being movie clips allows buttons to have instance names (graphic type symbols cannot have instance names), which are essential to writing event handlers for them.

After creating the two buttons, we change their labels to *start airplane* and *stop airplane*, respectively. The label of a button is changed by selecting the button and then making the change in the property panel. This panel is shown in Figure 8.32.

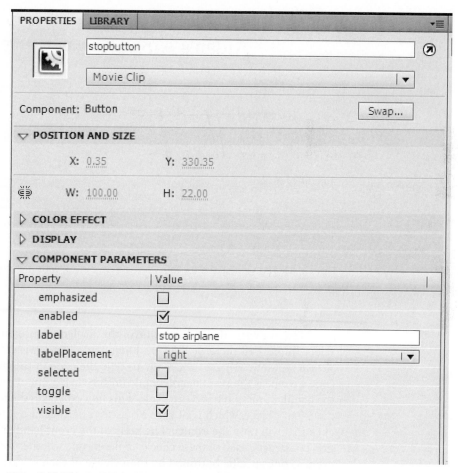

Figure 8.32 The *Window/Component Inspector* window

The labels are changed by typing the new labels in the *label* entry's *Value* box.

The instances of the buttons must have their *Instance Name* changed in their property panels. The *Instance Name* box is at the top of the panel. For this example, they are named *stopButton* and *startButton*.

The workspace, minus the *PROPERTIES/LIBRARY*, with the *stop airplane* button selected is shown in Figure 8.33.

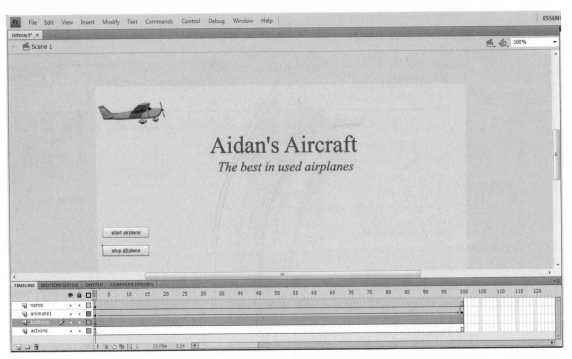

Figure 8.33 The workspace for the `interact` movie, with the *stop airplane* button selected

Next, we write the code to control the airplane figure on the stage. First, we select frame 1 of the *actions* layer. Then, we select *Window/Actions* to open the *Actions* window. We are now ready to type the code in the code panel. The first code we type is the event handler code for the click event of the buttons. We name the handler function `handleClick`. This function takes the formal parameter for the event object, which is of type `MouseEvent` (because it is the mouse button click that will raise the event). The body of the event handler contains two selection constructs, each of these checks to determine whether the target of the raised event is one specific button. The then clause of each selection is a call either to the `stop` method or the `play` method. The whole handler function follows:

```
function handleClick(bEvent: MouseEvent) {
    if (bEvent.target == stopButton)
        stop();
    if (bEvent.target == startButton)
        play();
}
```

Next, we must add the code for the registrations of the handler for the two buttons. This code is as follows:

```
stopButton.addEventListener(MouseEvent.CLICK,
                            handleClick);
startButton.addEventListener(MouseEvent.CLICK,
                            handleClick);
```

Finally, we must add a call to `stop` at the beginning of the code. Without this, the animation will always start automatically. The *Actions* window is now as appears in Figure 8.34.

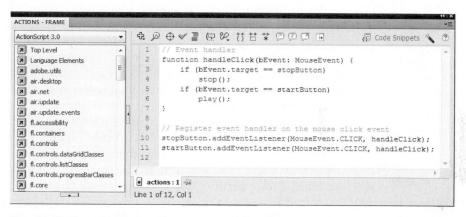

Figure 8.34 The *Actions* window with the button code

The `interact` movie can be tested, as usual, with *Control/Test Movie*.

We remind the reader at this point that there is far more to Flash components and interactivity. What we present here is a small and exceedingly simple example of these facilities.

Summary

The Flash system consists of two fundamental parts: an environment for constructing documents, called movies, that can include both static and animated parts; and a player, which resides as a plug-in in browsers.

The Flash authoring environment, or workspace, is a complex and powerful tool for creating Flash movies. It allows the author to specify the content of the movie in terms of a sequence of frames. This content is usually separated into several layers, which are displayed on top of one another. The author can create or edit one layer at a time. This layering simplifies the creation and editing processes and allows parts of a frame to be animated while other parts remain static.

If the *Rectangle Tool* button is held down for a few seconds, a menu appears for drawing rectangles, ovals, and stars on the stage. Straight lines and freehand figures can be drawn with the *Pencil Tool*.

Every figure on the stage has a properties panel, which can be displayed on the right side of the stage, on which the author can modify the characteristics of the figure, such as its size, location, stroke color, thickness, and fill color.

All figures should be converted to symbols, an action that also stores them in the library of the movie. Any number of instances of a symbol can be placed on the stage, but only one copy must be stored in the movie's file. Figures that are instances of a symbol can be modified as a group or individually. The contents of a movie's library are displayed in the *Library* panel.

Graphic images can be represented as bitmap or vector graphics. Bitmap graphics are ideal for photographic images, but degrade when enlarged significantly. Vector graphics can be enlarged to any degree without loss of quality, but are not as detailed as bitmap graphics. Flash supports both bitmap and vector graphics, although all figures drawn in Flash are vector graphics figures.

A Flash movie without animation can be represented in a single frame in a single layer. When a movie is completed, Flash can produce a number of different versions of it, among them Flash movies, which can be played by the Flash player, and HTML documents that include the Flash movie, which can be displayed by any browser that has the Flash player plug-in installed.

Animation is supported by creating a sequence of versions of the display stage in a sequence of frames. This is made simple by the capability of Flash to create frames between the actual frames. For example, motion animation is created by placing the figure to be moved at the two endpoints of the motion and then letting Flash create all of the frames in between, with the figure in a slightly different location in each frame. As the Flash player plays the sequence of frames, the animation is realized. Shape animation does something similar with the shapes of figures.

Sound clips can be added to a movie. The length of such clips can be shortened to make the sound fit the animation of the movie. Sound clip files can be compressed to make the movie in which they are embedded require less storage.

Flash movies support user interactions through components. A collection of predefined components can be dragged from a menu onto the stage. The actions of components are defined in ActionScript, which is based on JavaScript. The code is written as event handlers. The event model used is that of DOM 2, so event handlers are registered with `addEventListener`. User interactions often are employed in Flash to allow the user to control various aspects of the movie.

Review Questions

8.1   What are the two parts of Flash?

8.2   What does a row of the timeline represent?

8.3   What does a column of the timeline represent?

8.4   Why are different parts of movies placed in different layers?

8.5   What is the playhead?

8.6   What are the differences between the rectangles produced by the *Rectangle Tool* and the *Rectangle Primitive Tool*?

8.7   Describe the stroke and fill of a figure.

8.8   What figures can be created with the *Polystar Tool*?

8.9   What is a star point size?

8.10 How is the transparency of a color selected?

8.11 Explain what the *Straighten*, *Smooth*, and *Ink* menu items for freehand drawing do.

8.12 How does one specify that a text box is to wrap its contents?

8.13 What is the library of a movie?

8.14 What is the advantage of representing graphic figures as symbols?

8.15 What is the relationship between a symbol and an instance of a symbol?

8.16 What is an asset?

8.17 For what kind of images do bitmap representations have an advantage over vector graphics?

8.18 By what are vector graphic figures represented internally?

8.19 What advantage do vector graphic figures have over bitmap graphic figures?

8.20 What actions convert a drawn figure on the stage into a symbol?

8.21 What is in a file with the `.swf` extension?

8.22 What is in a file with the `.fla` extension?

8.23 What is the purpose of the predefined JavaScript code in the HTML file that embeds a Flash movie?

8.24 What is the basic process of animation in a movie?

8.25 How is a layer renamed?

8.26 What is tweening?

8.27 What is a keyframe?

8.28 What is a blank keyframe?

8.29 What are the ways in which a movie can be tested without a browser?

8.30 What is the purpose of the *Free Transform Tool*?

8.31 How can two figures on the stage be aligned with each other?

8.32 How can a sequence of frames be reversed?

8.33 What must be done to text before it can be animated?

8.34   What aspect of a sound clip can be modified?

8.35   How does one choose the best bit rate for a sound clip?

8.36   What are the two categories of Flash components?

8.37   Which event model does Flash use?

8.38   What method is used to register event handlers for a Flash movie?

Exercises

8.1   Create a static Flash movie that displays your name and address and includes at least four different figures of things you like and at least four different figures that use different stroke colors, thicknesses, styles, and fill colors.

8.2   Create a Flash movie that animates two figures, one from the top to the bottom of the left side of the stage and the other on the right side of the stage.

8.3   Create a Flash movie that uses motion animation to change a figure from a large size to a small size and back as it moves from the top to the bottom of the right side of the stage.

8.4   Create a Flash movie that uses motion animation to show a ball bouncing continuously between the top and bottom of the right side of the stage.

8.5   Create a Flash movie that plays a sound clip of some music continuously while the movie plays.

8.6   Create a Flash movie that shows some text, has a mostly transparent ball that moves from the upper-left corner of the stage to the lower-right corner of the stage, and includes start and stop buttons that control the animation.

8.7   Explain the two kinds of tweening and their uses.

8.8   Explain two different ways of changing the speed of a movie.

Introduction to PHP

This chapter is the first of the second part of the book, the topic of which is server-side software. In the first part, all of the software discussed was executed or interpreted on the client. Although some tasks that are done on the server could be done on the browser, most cannot.

The topic of this chapter is PHP and its use as a server-side scripting language. The chapter begins with a brief look at the origins of PHP, followed by an overview of its primary characteristics and some of its general syntactic conventions. Next, the core language is introduced. Because PHP is similar to JavaScript, the discussion of its expressions and statements is brief. PHP's arrays, which are different from those of any other language, are then introduced, followed by a description of PHP's functions and their parameter-passing mechanisms. Because

PHP uses the same regular expressions for pattern matching as JavaScript,[1] regular expressions are not described in this chapter. The form-handling techniques of PHP are discussed next, including a complete example. Finally, both cookies and session tracking in PHP are introduced.

Significant parts of PHP are not covered in this chapter. Among these are references and support for object-oriented programming. PHP access to databases is discussed in Chapter 13.

9.1   Origins and Uses of PHP

PHP was developed by Rasmus Lerdorf, a member of the Apache Group,[2] in 1994. Its initial purpose was to provide a tool to help Lerdorf track visitors to his personal Web site. In 1995 he developed a package called Personal Home Page Tools, which became the first publicly distributed version of PHP. Originally, PHP was an acronym for Personal Home Page. Later, its user community began using the recursive name PHP: Hypertext Preprocessor, which subsequently forced the original name into obscurity.

Within two years of its release, PHP was being used at a large number of Web sites. By then, the job of managing its development had grown beyond the abilities of a single person, and that task was transferred to a small group of devoted volunteers. Today, PHP is developed, distributed, and supported as an open-source product. A PHP processor is now resident on most Web servers.

As a server-side scripting language, PHP is naturally used for form handling and database access. Because database access has been a prime focus of PHP development, it has driver support for 15 different database systems. PHP supports the common electronic mail protocols POP3 and IMAP. It also supports the distributed object architectures COM and CORBA.

9.2   Overview of PHP

PHP is a server-side HTML-embedded scripting language. As such, it is an alternative to Microsoft's Active Server Pages (see Chapter 12) and Sun's Java Server Pages (see Chapter 11).

The way its scripts are interpreted, PHP is related to client-side JavaScript. When a browser finds JavaScript code embedded in an HTML document it is displaying, it calls its JavaScript interpreter to interpret the script. When a browser requests a document that includes PHP script, the Web server that provides the document calls its PHP processor. The server determines that a document includes PHP script by the file-name extension. If it is `.php`, `.php3`, or `.phtml`, the document has embedded PHP.

---

1. Actually, PHP can use two different kinds of regular expressions: POSIX and Perl style (as is used in JavaScript).

2. The Apache Group develops and distributes the Apache Web server, among other things.

The PHP processor has two modes of operation: copy mode and interpret mode. It takes a PHP document file as input and produces an HTML document file. When the PHP processor finds markup code (which may include embedded client-side script) in the input file, it simply copies it to the output file. When the processor encounters PHP script in the input file, it interprets it and sends any output of the script to the output file. This implies that the output from a PHP script must be HTML, either of which could include embedded client-side script. The new file (the output file) is sent to the requesting browser. The client never sees the PHP script. If the user clicks *View Source* while the browser is displaying the document, only the markup (and embedded client-side script) will be shown, because that is all that ever arrives at the client.

PHP is usually purely interpreted, as is the case with JavaScript. However, recent PHP implementations perform some precompilation, at least on complex scripts, which increases the speed of interpretation.

The syntax and semantics of PHP are closely related to the syntax and semantics of JavaScript. Thus, PHP should be relatively easy to learn, assuming that the reader knows JavaScript.

PHP uses dynamic typing, as does JavaScript. Variables are not type declared, and they have no intrinsic type. The type of a variable is set every time it is assigned a value; the assigned variable takes the type of that value. Like JavaScript, PHP is far more forgiving than most common programming languages. Dynamic typing is largely responsible for this feature, but the dynamic nature of PHP's strings and arrays also contributes. PHP's arrays are a merge of the arrays of common programming languages and associative arrays, having the characteristics of both. There is a large collection of functions for creating and manipulating PHP's arrays. PHP supports both procedural and object-oriented programming.

PHP has an extensive library of functions, making it a flexible and powerful tool for server-side software development. Many of the predefined functions are used to provide interfaces to other software systems, such as mail and database systems.

As is the case with JavaScript, processors for PHP are free and easily obtainable. In addition, the PHP processor is an open-source system. It is available on all common computing platforms. The Web site for official information on PHP is http://www.php.net.

9.3 General Syntactic Characteristics

PHP scripts either are embedded in markup documents or are in files that are referenced by such documents. PHP code is embedded in documents by enclosing it between the `<?php` and `?>` tags.

If a PHP script is stored in a different file, it can be brought into a document with the `include` construct, which takes the file name as its string parameter—for example,

```
include("table2.inc");
```

This construct causes the contents of the file `table2.inc` to be copied into the document in which the `include` appears. The included file can contain markup or client-side script, as well as PHP code, but any PHP script it includes must be the content of a `<?php` tag, even if the `include` itself appears in the content of a `<?php` tag. The PHP interpreter changes from interpret to copy mode when an `include` is encountered.

Every variable name in PHP begins with a dollar sign ($). The part of the name after the dollar sign is like the names of variables in many common programming languages: a letter or an underscore followed by any number (including zero) of letters, digits, or underscores. PHP variable names are case sensitive.

Table 9.1 lists the PHP reserved words. Although variable names in PHP are case sensitive, neither reserved words nor function names are. For example, there is no difference between `while`, `WHILE`, `While`, and `wHiLe`.

Table 9.1   The reserved words of PHP

and	else	global	require	virtual
break	elseif	if	return	xor
case	extends	include	static	while
class	false	list	switch	
continue	for	new	this	
default	foreach	not	true	
do	function	or	var	

PHP allows comments to be specified in three different ways. Single-line comments can be specified either with # or with //, as in JavaScript. Multiple-line comments are delimited with /* and */, as in many other programming languages.

PHP statements are terminated with semicolons. Braces are used to form compound statements for control structures. Unless used as the body of a function definition, a compound statement cannot be a block. (A compound statement cannot define locally scoped variables.)

9.4   Primitives, Operations, and Expressions

PHP has four scalar types—Boolean, integer, double, and string; two compound types—array and object; and two special types—resource and NULL. In this section, only the scalar types and NULL are discussed. Arrays are discussed in Section 9.7; objects and resource types are not covered in this book.

9.4.1   Variables

Because PHP is dynamically typed, it has no type declarations. In fact, there is no way or need to ever declare the type of a variable.[3] The type of a variable is set every time the variable is assigned a value. An unassigned variable, sometimes called an *unbound variable*, has the value NULL, which is the only value of the NULL type. If an unbound variable is used in an expression, NULL is coerced to a value that is dictated by the context of the use. If the context specifies a number, NULL is coerced to 0; if the context specifies a string, NULL is coerced to the empty string.

A variable can be tested to determine whether it currently has a value. The test is carried out with the IsSet function, which takes the variable's name as its parameter and returns a Boolean value. For example, IsSet($fruit) returns TRUE if $fruit currently has a non-NULL value, FALSE otherwise. A variable that has been assigned a value retains that value until either it is assigned a new value or it is set back to the unassigned state, which is done with the unset function.

If you want to be informed when an unbound variable is referenced, include a call to the error_reporting function with the parameter value 15. This call is placed at the beginning of the script in the document file. The default error-reporting level is 7, which does not require the interpreter to report the use of an unbound variable.

9.4.2   Integer Type

PHP has a single integer type, named integer. This type corresponds to the long type of C and its successors, which means its size is that of a word in the machine on which the program is run. In most cases, this is 32 bits, or a bit less (not fewer) than 10 decimal digits.

9.4.3   Double Type

PHP's double type corresponds to the double type of C and its successors. Double literals can include a decimal point, an exponent, or both. The exponent has the usual form of an E or an e, followed by a possibly signed integer literal. There need not be any digits before or after the decimal point, so both .345 and 345. are legal double literals.

9.4.4   String Type

Characters in PHP are single bytes; Unicode is not supported. There is no character type. A single character data value is represented as a string of length 1.

String literals are defined with either single-quote (') or double-quote (") delimiters. In single-quoted string literals, escape sequences, such as \n, are not recognized as anything special and the values of embedded variables are not

---

3. Variables are sometimes declared to have nondefault scopes or lifetimes, as discussed in Section 9.8.

substituted for their names. (Such substitution is called *interpolation*.) In double-quoted string literals, escape sequences are recognized and embedded variables are replaced by their current values. For example, the value of

```
'The sum is: $sum'
```

is exactly as it is typed. However, if the current value of $sum is 10.2, then the value of

```
"The sum is: $sum"
```

is

```
The sum is: 10.2
```

If a double-quoted string literal includes a variable name, but you do not want it interpolated, precede the first character of the name (the dollar sign) with a backslash (\). If the name of a variable that is not set to a value is embedded in a double-quoted string literal, the name is replaced by the empty string.

Double-quoted strings can include embedded newline characters that are created with the *Enter* key. Such characters are exactly like those that result from typing \n in the string.

The length of a string is limited only by the memory available on the computer.

9.4.5   Boolean Type

The only two possible values for the Boolean type are TRUE and FALSE, both of which are case insensitive. Although Boolean is a data type in the same sense as integer, expressions of other types can be used in a Boolean context. If a non-Boolean expression appears in a Boolean context, the programmer obviously must know how it will be interpreted. If an integer expression is used in a Boolean context, it evaluates to FALSE if it is zero; otherwise, it is TRUE. If a string expression is used in a Boolean context, it evalutes to FALSE if it is either the empty string or the string "0"; otherwise, it is TRUE. This implies that the string "0.0" evaluates to TRUE.

The only double value that is interpreted as FALSE is exactly 0.0. Because of rounding errors, as well as the fact that the string "0.0" evaluates to TRUE, it is not a good idea to use expressions of type double in a Boolean context. A value can be very close to zero, but because it is not exactly zero, it will evaluate to TRUE.

9.4.6   Arithmetic Operators and Expressions

PHP has the usual (for C-based programming languages) collection of arithmetic operators (+, -, *, /, %, ++, and --) with the usual meanings. In the cases of +, -, and *, if both operands are integers, the operation is integer and an integer result is produced. If either operand is a double, the operation is double and a double result is produced. Division is treated the same way, except that if integer division is done and the result is not an integral value, the result is returned as a double. Any operation on integers that results in integer overflow also produces a double. The operands of the modulus operator (%) are expected to be integers. If one or both are not, they are coerced to integers.

PHP has a large number of predefined functions that operate on numeric values. Some of the most useful of these are shown in Table 9.2. In this table, "number" means either integer or double.

Table 9.2 Some useful predefined functions

Function	Parameter Type	Returns
floor	Double	Largest integer less than or equal to the parameter
ceil	Double	Smallest integer greater than or equal to the parameter
round	Double	Nearest integer
srand	Integer	Initializes a random-number generator with the parameter
rand	Two numbers	A pseudorandom number greater than the first parameter and smaller than the second
abs	Number	Absolute value of the parameter
min	One or more numbers	Smallest
max	One or more numbers	Largest

The other predefined functions for number values are for doing number base conversion and computing exponents, logarithms, and trigonometric functions.

9.4.7 String Operations

The only string operator is the catenation operator, specified with a period (.).

String variables can be treated somewhat like arrays for access to individual characters. The position of a character in a string, relative to zero, can be specified in braces immediately after the variable's name. For example, if $str has the value "apple", $str{3} is "l".

PHP includes many functions that operate on strings. Some of the most commonly used are described in Table 9.3.

Table 9.3 Some commonly used string functions

Function	Parameter Type	Returns
strlen	A string	The number of characters in the string
strcmp	Two strings	Zero if the two strings are identical, a negative number if the first string belongs before the second (in the ASCII sequence), or a positive number if the second string belongs before the first
strpos	Two strings	The character position in the first string of the first character of the second string if the second string is in the first string; false if it is not there
substr	A string and an integer	The substring of the string parameter, starting from the position indicated by the second parameter; if a third parameter (an integer) is given, it specifies the length of the returned substring
chop	A string	The parameter with all white-space characters removed from its end
trim	A string	The parameter with all white-space characters removed from both ends
ltrim	A string	The parameter with all white-space characters removed from its beginning
strtolower	A string	The parameter with all uppercase letters converted to lowercase
strtoupper	A string	The parameter with all lowercase letters converted to uppercase

Note re strpos: Because false is interpreted as zero in a numeric context, this can be a problem. To avoid it, use the === operator (see Section 9.6.1) to compare the returned value with zero to determine whether the match was at the beginning of the first string parameter (or whether there was no match).

Consider the following example of the use of a string function:

```
$str = "Apples are good";
$sub = substr($str, 7, 1);
```

The value of $sub is now 'a'.

9.4.8 Scalar Type Conversions

PHP, like most other programming languages, includes both implicit and explicit type conversions. Implicit type conversions are called *coercions*. In most cases, the context of an expression determines the type that is expected or required. The context can cause a coercion of the type of the value of the expression. Some of the coercions that take place between the integer and double types and between Boolean and other scalar types have already been discussed. There are also frequent coercions between numeric and string types. Whenever a numeric value appears in a string context, the numeric value is coerced to a string. Likewise, whenever a string value appears in a numeric context, the string value is coerced to a numeric value. If the string contains a period, an e, or an E, it is converted to double; otherwise, it is converted to an integer. If the string does not begin with a sign or a digit, the conversion fails and zero is used. Nonnumeric characters following the number in the string are ignored.

When a double is converted to an integer, the fractional part is dropped; rounding is not done.

Explicit type conversions can be specified in three different ways. Using the syntax of C, one can cast an expression to a different type. The cast is a type name in parentheses preceding the expression. For example, if the value of $sum is 4.777, the following line of code produces 4:

```
(int) $sum
```

Another way to specify explicit type conversion is to use one of the functions intval, doubleval, or strval. For example, if $sum is still 4.777, the following call returns 4:

```
intval($sum)
```

The third way to specify an explicit type conversion is with the settype function, which takes two parameters: a variable and a string that specifies a type name. For example, if $sum is still 4.777, the following statement converts the value of $sum to 4 and its type to integer:

```
settype($sum, "integer");
```

The type of the value of a variable can be determined in two different ways. The first is the gettype function, which takes a variable as its parameter and returns a string that has the name of the type of the current value of the variable. One possible return value of gettype is "unknown". The other way to determine the type of the value of a variable is to use one or more of the type-testing functions, each of which takes a variable name as a parameter and returns a Boolean value. These functions are is_int, is_integer, and is_long, which test for integer type; is_double, is_float, and is_real, which test for double type; is_bool, which tests for Boolean type; and is_string, which tests for string type.[4]

9.4.9 Assignment Operators

PHP has the same set of assignment operators as its predecessor language, C, including the compound assignment operators such as += and /=.

---

4. PHP also has the is_array function to test for arrays and the is_object function to test for objects.

9.5 Output

Any output from a PHP script becomes part of the document the PHP processor is building. Therefore, all output must be in the form of HTML or XHTML, which may include embedded client-side script.

The print function[5] is used to create simple unformatted output. It can be called with or without parentheses around its parameter. For example, the following statement is valid:

```
print "Apples are red <br /> Kumquats aren't <br />";
```

Although print expects a string parameter, if some other type value is given, the PHP interpreter will coerce it to a string without complaint. For example, the following statement will produce 47:

```
print(47);
```

Because variables that appear in double-quoted strings are interpolated, it is easy to label output. The following print statement is illustrative:

```
print "The result is: $result <br />";
```

PHP borrows the printf function from C. It is used when control over the format of displayed data is required. The general form of a call to printf is as follows:

printf (*literal_string*, *param1*, *param2*, . . .)

The literal string can include labeling information about the parameters whose values are to be displayed. It also contains format codes for those values. The form of the format codes is a percent sign (%) followed by a field width and a type specifier. The most common type specifiers are s for strings, d for integers, and f for floats and doubles. The field width is either an integer literal (for integers) or two integer literals separated by a decimal point (for floats and doubles). The integer literal to the right of the decimal point specifies the number of digits to be displayed to the right of the decimal point. The following examples illustrate how to specify formatting information:

> %10s—a character string field of 10 characters
>
> %6d—an integer field of six digits
>
> %5.2f—a float or double field of eight spaces, with two digits to the right of the decimal point, the decimal point, and five digits to the left

The position of the format code in the first parameter of printf indicates the place in the output where the associated value should appear, as in the following code:

```
$day = "Tuesday";
$high = 79;
printf("The high on %7s was %3d", $day, $high);
```

---

5. PHP also has the echo function, which is similar to print.

Note that `printf` requires parentheses around its parameters.

The following simple example displays a welcome message and the current day of the week, month, and day of the month:

```
<!DOCTYPE html>
<!-- today.php - A trivial example to illustrate a php document -->
<html lang = "en">
  <head>
    <title> today.php </title>
    <meta charset = "utf-8" />
  </head>
  <body>
      <p>
      <?php
        print "<b>Welcome to my home page <br /> <br />";
        print "Today is:</b> ";
        print date("l, F jS");
        print "<br />";
      ?>
      </p>
  </body>
</html>
```

Note that the date information is generated with the `date` function, whose first parameter is a string that specifies the parts of the date you want to see. In this example, `l` requests the day of the week, `F` requests the month, `j` requests the day of the week, and an `S` next to the `j` gets the correct suffix for the day (e.g., `st` or `nd`). The details of `date` can be found at `http://www.php.net`. Figure 9.1 displays the output of `today.php`.

Welcome to my home page

Today is: Saturday, June 1st

Figure 9.1 Display of the output of `today.php`

9.6 Control Statements

The control statements of PHP are not remarkable—in fact, they are similar to those of C and its descendants. The control expression used in PHP's control statements can be of any type. The interpreter evaluates the control expression and, in the cases of `if` and loop statements, coerces the resulting value, if necessary, to Boolean.

9.6.1   Relational Operators

PHP uses the eight relational operators of JavaScript. The usual six (>, <, >=, <=, !=, and ==) have the usual meanings. PHP also has ===, which produces TRUE only if both operands are the same type and have the same value, and !==, the opposite of ===. If the types of the operands of the other six relational operators are not the same, one is coerced to the type of the other. If a string is compared with a number and the string can be converted to a number (if it is in fact a string version of a number—for example, "42"), the string will be converted and a numeric comparison will be done. If the string cannot be converted to a number, the numeric operand will be converted to a string and a string comparison will be done. If both operands are strings that can be converted to numbers, both will be converted and a numeric comparison will be done. This is often not what is desired. To avoid it and similar problems associated with string-to-number coercions, if either or both operands are strings that could be converted to numbers, the strcmp function should be used rather than one of the comparison operators.

9.6.2   Boolean Operators

There are six Boolean operators: and, or, xor, !, &&, and ||. The and and && operators perform the same operation, as do or and ||. The difference between them is that the precedence of and and or is lower than that of && and ||. All of PHP's binary Boolean operators are evaluated as short-circuit operators.

9.6.3   Selection Statements

PHP's if statement is like that of C. The control expression can be an expression of any type, but its value is coerced to Boolean. The controlled statement segment can be either a single statement or a compound statement. An if statement can include any number of elseif clauses. Following is a simple example of an if construct:

```
if ($num > 0)
  $pos_count++;
elseif ($num < 0)
  $neg_count++;
else {
  $zero_count++;
  Print "Another zero! <b />";
}
```

The switch statement has the form and semantics of that of JavaScript. The type of the control expression and of the case expressions is either integer, double, or string. If necessary, the values of the case expressions are coerced to the type of the control expression for the comparisons. A default case can be included. As with its ancestor in C and Java, a break statement must follow each selectable segment if control is not to flow to the next segment. Following is a simple example of a `switch` construct:

```
switch ($bordersize) {
  case "0": print "<table>";
            break;
  case "1": print "<table border = '1'>";
            break;
  case "4": print "<table border = '4'>";
            break;
  case "8": print "<table border = '8'>";
            break;
  default: print "Error-invalid value: $bordersize <br />";
}
```

9.6.4   Loop Statements

The `while`, `for`, and `do-while` statements of PHP are exactly like those of JavaScript. PHP also has a `foreach` statement, which is discussed in Section 9.7.4. The following example computes the factorial of $n:

```
$fact = 1;
$count = 1;
while ($count < $n) {
  $count++;
  $fact *= $count;
}
```

This example computes the sum of the positive integers up to `100`:

```
$count = 1;
$sum = 0;
do {
  $sum += $count;
  $count++;
} while ($count <= 100);
```

The following example computes the factorial of $n:

```
for ($count = 1, $fact = 1; $count < $n;) {
  $count++;
  $fact *= $count;
}
```

The `break` statement can be used to terminate the execution of a `for`, `foreach`, `while`, or `do-while` construct. The `continue` statement is used in loop constructs to skip the remainder of the current iteration but continue execution at the beginning of the next.

9.6.5 An Example

The next example is meant to illustrate the form of an HTML-PHP document, as well as some simple mathematical functions and the intermingling of HTML and PHP in a document. The `sqrt` function returns the square root of its parameter; the `pow` function raises its first parameter to the power of its second parameter. Here is the document:

```
<!DOCTYPE html>
<!-- powers.php
     An example to illustrate loops and arithmetic
     -->
<html lang = "en">
  <head>
    <title> powers.php </title>
    <meta charset = "utf-8" />
    <style type = "text/css">
      td, th, table {border: thin solid black;}
    </style>
  </head>
  <body>
    <table>
      <caption> Powers table </caption>
      <tr>
        <th> Number </th>
        <th> Square Root </th>
        <th> Square </th>
        <th> Cube </th>
        <th> Quad </th>
      </tr>
      <?php
        for ($number = 1; $number <=10; $number++) {
          $root = sqrt($number);
          $square = pow($number, 2);
          $cube = pow($number, 3);
          $quad = pow($number, 4);
          print("<tr align = 'center'> <td> $number </td>");
          print("<td> $root </td> <td> $square </td>");
          print("<td> $cube </td> <td> $quad </td> </tr>");
        }
      ?>
    </table>
  </body>
</html>
```

Figure 9.2 displays the output of `powers.php`.

Powers table				
Number	**Square Root**	**Square**	**Cube**	**Quad**
1	1	1	1	1
2	1.4142135623731	4	8	16
3	1.7320508075689	9	27	81
4	2	16	64	256
5	2.2360679774998	25	125	625
6	2.4494897427832	36	216	1296
7	2.6457513110646	49	343	2401
8	2.8284271247462	64	512	4096
9	3	81	729	6561
10	3.1622776601684	100	1000	10000

Figure 9.2 Display of the output of `powers.php`.

9.7 Arrays

Arrays in PHP are unlike those of any other common programming language. They are best described as a combination of the arrays of a typical language and associative arrays, or hashes, found in some other languages, such as Ruby and Python. This feature makes PHP arrays the ultimate in flexible built-in data structures. Each array element consists of two parts: a key and a value. If the array has a logical structure that is similar to an array in another language, the keys just happen to be nonnegative integers and are always in ascending order. If the array has a logical structure that is similar to a hash, its keys are strings and the order of its elements is determined with a system-designed hashing function. The string keys of a PHP array are sometimes people's names, sometimes the names of the days of the week. They are always a collection of strings of some significance. One interesting thing about PHP arrays is that they can have some elements with integer keys and some with string keys.

9.7.1 Array Creation

There are two ways to create an array in PHP. The assignment operation creates scalar variables. The same operation works for arrays: Assigning a value to a subscripted variable that previously was not an array creates the array. For example, if no array named `$list` currently exists, the following statement creates one:

```
$list[0] = 17;
```

Even if the script has a scalar variable named `$list` prior to this assignment, `$list` is now an array. If empty brackets are used in an assignment to an array, a numeric key is implicitly furnished. The furnished subscript is 1 greater than the largest numeric key used so far in the array (if the array already has elements with numeric keys). If the array currently has no elements with numeric keys, the value `0` is used. For example, in the following statements, the second element's key will be `2`:

```
$list[1] = "Today is my birthday!";
$list[] = 42;
```

This example also demonstrates that the elements of an array need not be of the same type.

The second way to create an array is with the `array` construct. We call it a construct because, although the syntax of using it is the same as that of a function call, it is not a function. The parameters of `array` specify the values to be placed in a new array and sometimes also the keys. If the array is like a traditional array, only the values need to be specified; the PHP interpreter will furnish the numeric keys. For example, the assignment

```
$list = array(17, 24, 45, 91);
```

creates a traditional array of four elements, with the keys `0`, `1`, `2`, and `3`. If you would rather have different keys, you can specify them in the array construct, as follows:

```
$list = array(1 => 17, 2 => 24, 3 => 42, 4 => 91);
```

An array construct with empty parentheses creates an empty array. For example, in the following statement, `$list` becomes a variable whose value is an array with no elements:

```
$list = array();
```

The following statement creates an array that has the form of a hash:

```
$ages = array("Joe" => 42, "Mary" => 41, "Bif" => 17);
```

Some built-in functions—for example, some of the functions that access databases—return arrays.

PHP arrays do not need to be purely in the form of traditional arrays or hashes; they can be mixtures of both. For example, we could have the following statement:

```
$stuff = array("make" => "Cessna", "model" => "C210",
               "year" => 1960, 3 => "sold");
```

9.7.2 Accessing Array Elements

Individual array elements can be accessed by subscripting, as in other programming languages. The value in the subscript, which is enclosed in brackets, is the key of the value being referenced. The same brackets are used regardless of whether the key is a number or a string. For example, the value of the element whose key is "Mary" in the $ages array can be set to 29 with the following statement:

```
$ages['Mary'] = 29;
```

The list construct can be used to assign multiple elements of an array to scalar variables in one statement. For example, in the statements

```
$trees = array("oak", "pine", "binary");
list($hardwood, $softwood, $data_structure) = $trees;
```

$hardwood, $softwood, and $data_structure are set to "oak", "pine", and "binary", respectively.

9.7.3   Functions for Dealing with Arrays

A whole array can be deleted with unset, as with a scalar variable. Individual elements of an array also can be removed with unset, as in the following code:

```
$list = array(2, 4, 6, 8);
unset($list[2]);
```

After executing these statements, $list has three remaining elements with keys 0, 1, and 3 and elements 2, 4, and 8.

The collection of keys and the collection of values of an array can be extracted with built-in functions. The array_keys function takes an array as its parameter and returns an array of the keys of the given array. The returned array uses 0, 1, and so forth as its keys. The array_values function does for values what array_keys does for keys. For example, consider the following statements:

```
$highs = array("Mon" => 74, "Tue" => 70, "Wed" => 67,
               "Thu" => 62, "Fri" => 65);
$days = array_keys($highs);
$temps = array_values($highs);
```

These statements set the value of $days to ("Mon", "Tue", "Wed", "Thu", "Fri") and the value of $temps to (74, 70, 67, 62, 65). In both cases, the keys are (0, 1, 2, 3, 4).

The existence of an element of a specific key can be determined with the array_key_exists function, which returns a Boolean value. The following code is illustrative:

```
$highs = array("Mon" => 74, "Tue" => 70, "Wed" => 67,
               "Thu" => 62, "Fri" => 65);
if (array_key_exists("Tue", $highs)) {
  $tues_high = $highs["Tue"];
  print "The high on Tuesday was $tues_high <br />";
} else
  print
    "There is data for Tuesday in the \$highs array <br />";
```

Note that PHP does not interpolate array elements embedded in double-quoted strings. That is the reason for the assignment statement in the preceding `if` construct. An array name embedded in a double-quoted string results in the word `Array` being inserted into the string in place of the array's name.

The `is_array` function is similar to the `is_int` function: It takes a variable as its parameter and returns `TRUE` if the variable is an array, `FALSE` otherwise. The `in_array` function takes two parameters—an expression and an array—and returns `TRUE` if the value of the expression is a value in the array; otherwise, it returns `FALSE`.

The number of elements in an array can be determined with the `sizeof` function. For example, after the following statements are interpreted, `$len` will be 4 .

```
$list = array("Bob", "Fred", "Alan", "Bozo");
$len = sizeof($list);
```

It is often useful to be able to convert between strings and arrays. These conversions can be done with the `implode` and `explode` functions. The `explode` function explodes a string into substrings and returns them in an array. The delimiters of the substrings are defined by the first parameter of `explode`, which is a string; the second parameter is the string to be converted. For example, consider the following:

```
$str = "April in Paris, Texas is nice";
$words = explode(" ", $str);
```

Now `$words` contains (`"April"`, `"in"`, `"Paris,"`, `"Texas"`, `"is"`, `"nice"`).

The `implode` function does the inverse of `explode`. Given a separator character (or a string) and an array, it catenates the elements of the array together, placing the given separator string between the elements, and returns the result as a string. Consider, for example,

```
$words = array("Are", "you", "lonesome", "tonight");
$str = implode(" ", $words);
```

Now `$str` has `"Are you lonesome tonight"` (which is obviously a rhetorical question).

Internally, the elements of an array are stored in a linked list of cells, where each cell includes both the key and the value of the element. The cells themselves are stored in memory through a key-hashing function so that they are randomly distributed in a reserved block of storage. Accesses to elements through string keys are implemented through the hashing function. However, the elements all have links that connect them in the order in which they were created, allowing them to be accessed in that order if the keys are strings and in the order of their keys if the keys are numbers. Section 9.7.4 discusses the ways array elements can be accessed in order.

Figure 9.3 shows the internal logical structure of an array. Although arrays may not be implemented in this exact way, it shows how the two different access methods could be supported.

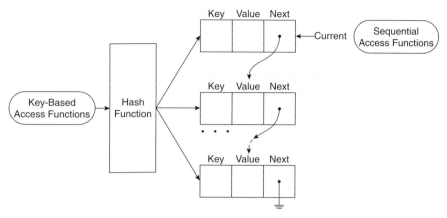

Figure 9.3 Logical internal structure of an array

9.7.4   Sequential Access to Array Elements

PHP includes several different ways to access array elements in sequential order. Every array has an internal pointer that references one element of the array. We call this the "current" pointer. This pointer is initialized to reference the first element of the array at the time the array is created. The element being referenced by the pointer can be obtained with the current function. For example, consider the following statements:

```
$cities = array("Hoboken", "Chicago", "Moab", "Atlantis");
$city = current($cities);
print("The first city is $city <br />");
```

When interpreted, the following output is produced:

```
The first city is Hoboken
```

The "current" pointer can be moved with the next function, which both moves the pointer to the next array element and returns the value of that element. If the "current" pointer is already pointing at the last element of the array, next returns FALSE. For example, if the "current" pointer is referencing the first element of the $cities array, the following code produces a list of all of the elements of that array:

```
$city = current($cities);
print("$city <br />");
while ($city = next($cities))
  print("$city <br />");
```

One problem with using the next function for loop control, as shown in the preceding example, occurs when the array includes an element with the value FALSE. The loop ends, but not because the "current" pointer ran off the end of the array. The each function, which returns a two-element array consisting of the key and the value of the "current" element, avoids this problem. It returns FALSE only if the "current" pointer has gone past the last element of the array. The keys of the two elements of the return value from each are the strings `"key"` and `"value"`. Another difference between each and next is that each returns the element being referenced by the "current" pointer and then moves that pointer. The next function first moves the "current" pointer and then returns the value being referenced by the "current" pointer. As an example of the use of each, consider the following statements:

```php
$salaries = array("Mike" => 42500, "Jerry" => 51250,
                  "Fred" => 37920);
while ($employee = each($salaries)) {
  $name = $employee["key"];
  $salary = $employee["value"];
  print("The salary of $name is $salary <br />");
}
```

The output produced by this code is as follows:

```
The salary of Mike is 42500
The salary of Jerry is 51250
The salary of Fred is 37920
```

The "current" pointer can be moved backward (i.e., to the element before the "current" element) with the prev function. Like the next function, the prev function returns the value of the element referenced by the "current" pointer after the pointer has been moved. The "current" pointer can be set to the first element with the reset function, which also returns the value of the first element. It can be set to the last element of the array with the end function, which also returns the value of the last element.

The key function, when given the name of an array, returns the key of the "current" element of the array.

The array_push and array_pop functions provide a simple way to implement a stack in an array. The array_push function takes an array as its first parameter. After this first parameter, there can be any number of additional parameters. The values of all subsequent parameters are placed at the end of the array. The array_push function returns the new number of elements in the array. The array_pop function takes a single parameter: the name of an array. It removes the last element from the array and returns it. The value NULL is returned if the array is empty.

The foreach statement is designed to build loops that process all of the elements of an array. This statement has two forms:

```
foreach (array as scalar_variable)  loop body
foreach (array as key => value)  loop body
```

In the first form, one of the array's values is set to the scalar variable for each iteration of the loop body. The "current" pointer is implicitly initialized, as with reset, before the first iteration. For example, consider the following statements:

```php
foreach ($list as $temp)
  print("$temp <br />");
```

When interpreted, these statements produce the values of all of the elements of $list.

The second form of foreach provides both the key and the value of each element of the array:

```
$lows = array("Mon" => 23, "Tue" => 18, "Wed" => 27);
foreach ($lows as $day => $temp)
   print("The low temperature on $day was $temp <br />");
```

9.7.5   Sorting Arrays

The sort function, which takes an array as a parameter, sorts the values in the array, replacing the keys with the numeric keys, 0, 1, 2, ... The array can have both string and numeric values. The string values migrate to the beginning of the array in alphabetical order. The numeric values follow in ascending order. Regardless of the types of the keys in the original array, the sorted array has 0, 1, 2, and so forth as keys. This function is obviously meant for sorting traditional arrays of either strings or numbers. Although it causes no errors, it seems to be a rare situation in which one would want to sort an array with both strings and numbers as values.

The asort function is used to sort arrays that correspond to hashes. It sorts the elements of a given array by their values, but keeps the original key–value associations. As with sort, string values all appear before the numeric values in alphabetical order. The numeric values follow in ascending order.

The ksort function sorts its given array by keys, rather than values. The key–value associations are maintained by the process.

The rsort, arsort, and krsort functions behave like the sort, asort, and ksort functions, respectively, except that they sort into the reverse orders of their counterparts.

The following example illustrates sort, asort, and ksort:

```
<!DOCTYPE html>
<!-- sorting.php - An example to illustrate several of the
     sorting functions -->
<html lang = "en">
  <head>
    <title> Sorting </title>
    <meta charset = "utf-8" />
  </head>
  <body>
    <?php
      $original = array("Fred" => 31, "Al" => 27,
                        "Gandalf" => "wizard",
```

```
                                "Betty" => 42, "Frodo" => "hobbit");
        ?>
        <h4> Original Array </h4>
        <?php
          foreach ($original as $key => $value)
            print("[$key] => $value <br />");

          $new = $original;
          sort($new);
        ?>
        <h4> Array sorted with sort </h4>
        <?php
          foreach ($new as $key => $value)
            print("[$key] = $value <br />");

          $new = $original;
          asort($new);
        ?>
        <h4> Array sorted with asort </h4>
        <?php
          foreach ($new as $key => $value)
            print("[$key] = $value <br />");

          $new = $original;
          ksort($new);
        ?>
        <h4> Array sorted with ksort </h4>
        <?php
          foreach ($new as $key => $value)
            print("[$key] = $value <br />");
        ?>
      </body>
  </html>
```

Figure 9.4 displays the output of sorting.php.

We have now discussed just a few of the most useful built-in functions for arrays. PHP has 57 such functions, so most remain unmentioned here.

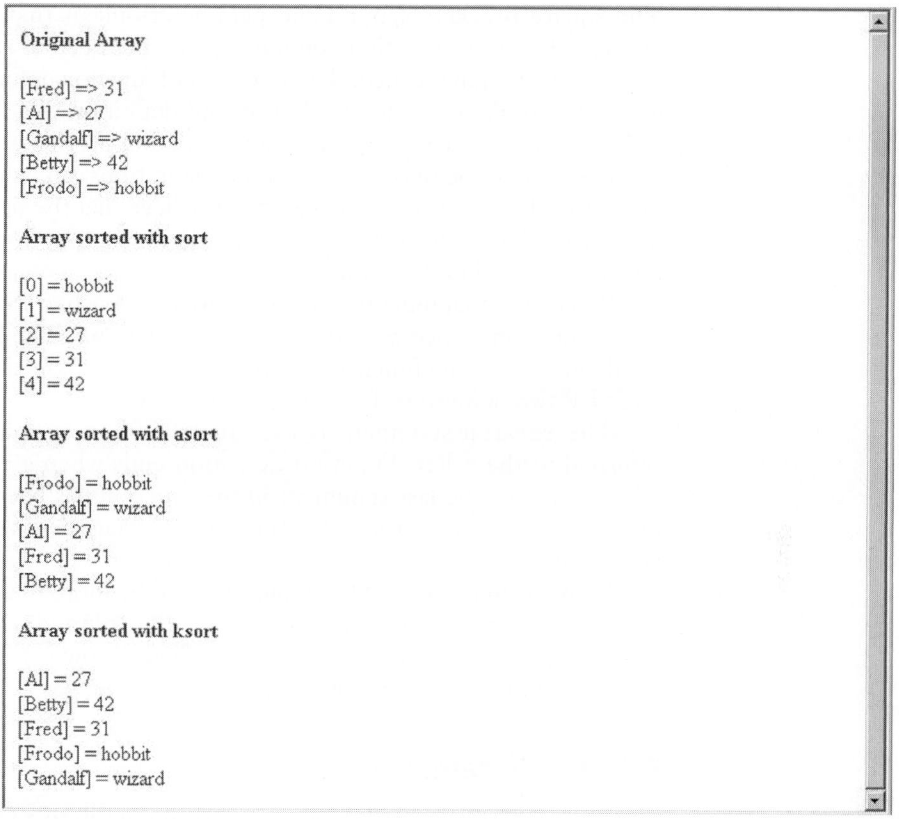

```
Original Array

[Fred] => 31
[Al] => 27
[Gandalf] => wizard
[Betty] => 42
[Frodo] => hobbit

Array sorted with sort

[0] = hobbit
[1] = wizard
[2] = 27
[3] = 31
[4] = 42

Array sorted with asort

[Frodo] = hobbit
[Gandalf] = wizard
[Al] = 27
[Fred] = 31
[Betty] = 42

Array sorted with ksort

[Al] = 27
[Betty] = 42
[Fred] = 31
[Frodo] = hobbit
[Gandalf] = wizard
```

Figure 9.4 Display of the output of `sorting.php`

9.8　Functions

PHP supports user-defined functions that are typical of C-based programming languages.

9.8.1　General Characteristics of Functions

The general form of a PHP function definition is as follows:

```
function name([parameters]) {
  ...
}
```

The square brackets around the parameters mean that the parameters are optional. Because a function's definition does not need to appear in a document before the function is called, the placement of function definitions in a document is, strictly speaking, irrelevant. If a second definition of a function appears in a script, it is reported as an error because function overloading is not allowed and functions cannot be redefined. Function definitions can be nested, as they can in JavaScript. However, because we do not believe that the benefit of nested functions is worth the additional complexity they bring to scripts that use them, they are not discussed in this book.

Remember that function names are not case sensitive. So, a document cannot have a function named `sum` and another named `Sum`. The PHP interpreter will see them as the same function and issue an error message stating that the document has two definitions for the same function.

The `return` statement is used in a function to specify the value to be returned to the caller. Function execution ends when a `return` statement is encountered or the last statement in the function has been executed. In either case, control returns to the caller. If no `return` statement was executed, no value is returned.

If one or more related functions are used by more than one document, it is convenient to store their definitions in a separate file and copy that file into those documents when they are requested by a client (browser). This is done with the `include` function, which was described in Section 9.3.

9.8.2   Parameters

As with JavaScript, we call the parameters in the call to a function *actual parameters*. We call the parameters that are listed in the function definition *formal parameters*. An actual parameter can be any expression. A formal parameter must be a variable name.

The number of actual parameters in a call to a function need not match the number of formal parameters defined in that function. If there are too few actual parameters in a call, the corresponding formal parameters will be unbound variables. If there are too many actual parameters, the excess actual parameters will be ignored. The absence of a requirement for matching numbers of parameters allows the language to support functions with a variable number of parameters.

The default parameter-passing mechanism of PHP is pass by value. This means that, in effect, the values of actual parameters are copied into the memory locations associated with the corresponding formal parameters in the called function. The values of the formal parameters are never copied back to the caller, so passing by value implements one-way communication to the function. This is the most commonly needed mechanism for parameter passing. Consider the following function definition:

```
function max_abs($first, $second) {
  $first = abs($first);
  $second = abs($second);
```

```
    if ($first >= $second)
      return $first;
    else
      return $second;
}
```

This function returns the larger of the absolute values of the two given numbers. Although it potentially changes both of its formal parameters, the actual parameters in the caller are unchanged (because they were passed by value).

Sometimes, parameters that provide two-way communication between the caller and the function are needed—for example, so a function can return more than one value. One common way to provide two-way communication is to pass the address of the actual parameter, rather than its value, to the function. Then, when the formal parameter is changed (in the function), it also changes the corresponding actual parameter. Such parameters are said to be passed by reference.

Pass-by-reference parameters can be specified in PHP in two ways. One way is to add an ampersand (&) to the beginning of the name of the formal parameter that you want to be passed by reference. Of course, passing by reference makes sense only if the actual parameter is a variable. The other way to specify pass-by-reference is to add an ampersand to the actual parameter in the function call. These two techniques have identical semantics. Consider the following example:

```
function set_max(&$;max, $first, $second) {
  If ($first >= $second)
    $max = $first;
  else
    $max = $second;
}
```

In this example, the first actual parameter in the caller is set to the larger of the second and third parameters.

9.8.3   The Scope of Variables

The default scope of a variable defined in a function is local. If a variable defined in a function has the same name as a variable used outside the function, there is no interference between the two. A nonlocal variable is hidden by a local variable with the same name. A local variable is visible only in the function in which it is used. For example, the code

```
function summer($list) {
  $sum = 0;
  foreach ($list as $value)
    $sum += $value;
  return $sum;
}
```

```
$sum = 10;
$nums = array(2, 4, 6, 8);
$ans = summer($nums);
print "The sum of the values in \$nums is: $ans <br />";
print "The value of \$sum is still: $sum <br />";
```

produces the following output:

```
The sum of the values in $nums is: 20
The value of $sum is still: 10
```

This output shows that the value of `$sum` in the calling code is not affected by the use of the local variable `$sum` in the function. The purpose of the design of local variables is simple: A function should behave the same way, regardless of the context of its use. Furthermore, when naming a variable while designing a function, the author should not need to worry about conflicts with the names of variables used outside the function.

In some cases, it is convenient for the code in a function to be able to access a variable that is defined outside the function. For this situation, PHP has the `global` declaration. When a variable is listed in a `global` declaration in a function, that variable is expected to be defined outside the function. So, such a variable has the same meaning inside the function as outside. For example, consider the following code:

```
$big_sum = 0;
...
/* Function summer
    Parameter: An array of integers
    Returns: The sum of the elements of the parameter
             array
    Side effect: Add the computed sum to the global,
                 $big_sum
*/
function summer ($list) {
  global $big_sum;    //** Get access to $big_sum
  $sum = 0;
  foreach ($list as $value)
    $sum += $value;
  $big_sum += $sum;
  return $sum;
} //** end of summer
...
$ans1 = summer($list1);
$ans2 = summer($list2);
...
print "The sum of all array elements is: $big_sum <br />";
```

If the `global` declaration were not included in the function, the script would have two variables named `$big_sum`: the global one and the one that is local to the function. Without the declaration, this script cannot do what it is meant to do. The global variable `$big_sum` would not be visible in the function.

9.8.4   The Lifetime of Variables

In some situations, a function must be history sensitive; that is, it must retain information about previous activations. The default lifetime of local variables in a PHP function is from the time the variable is first used (i.e., when storage for it is allocated) until the function's execution terminates. To support history sensitivity, a function must have static local variables. The lifetime of a static variable in a function begins when the variable is first used in the first execution of the function. Its lifetime ends when the script execution ends. In the case of PHP, this is when the browser leaves the document in which the PHP script is embedded.

In PHP, a local variable in a function can be specified to be static by declaring it with the reserved word `static`. Such a declaration can include an initial value, which is only assigned the first time the declaration is reached. For example, consider the following function definition:

```
function do_it ($param) {
  static $count = 0;
  count++;
  print "do_it has now been called $count times <br />";
  ...
}
```

When called, this function displays the number of times it has been called, even if it is called from several different places. The fact that its local variable `$count` is static allows this to be done.

9.9   Pattern Matching

PHP includes two different kinds of string pattern matching using regular expressions: one that is based on POSIX regular expressions and one that is based on Perl regular expressions, like those of JavaScript. The POSIX regular expressions are compiled into PHP, but the Perl-Compatible Regular Expression (PCRE) library must be compiled before Perl regular expressions can be used. A detailed discussion of PHP pattern matching is beyond the scope of this chapter. Furthermore, Perl-style regular expressions are described in Sections 4.12.1 to 4.12.3. Therefore, in this section we provide only a brief description of a single PHP function for pattern matching.

The preg_match[6] function takes two parameters, the first of which is the Perl-style regular expression as a string. The second parameter is the string to be searched. The following code is illustrative:

```
if (preg_match("/^PHP/", $str))
  print "\$str begins with PHP <br />";
else
    print "\$str does not begin with PHP <br />";
```

The preg_split function operates on strings but returns an array and uses patterns, so it is discussed here rather than with the other string functions in Section 9.4.7. The function takes two parameters, the first of which is a Perl-style pattern as a string. The second parameter is the string to be split. For example, consider the following sample code:

```
$fruit_string = "apple : orange : banana";
$fruits = preg_split("/ : /", $fruit_string);
```

The array $fruits now has ("apple", "orange", "banana").

The following example illustrates the use of preg_split on text to parse out the words and produce a frequency-of-occurrence table:

```
<!DOCTYPE html>
<!-- word_table.php
        Uses a function to split a given string of text into
        its constituent words. It also determines the frequency of
        occurrence of each word. The words are separated by
        white space or punctuation, possibly followed by white space.
        The punctuation can be a period, a comma, a semicolon, a
        colon, an exclamation point, or a question mark.
        -->

<html lang = "en">
  <head>
    <title> word_table.php </title>
    <meta charset = "utf-8" />
  </head>
  <body>
    <?php

// Function splitter
//    Parameter: a string of text containing words and punctuation
//    Returns: an array in which the unique words of the string are
//             the keys and their frequencies are the values.
```

---

6. The first part of the name, preg, is an acronym for *Perl regular*, which indicates the style of regular expression used.

```
function splitter($str) {

// Create the empty word frequency array
   $freq = array();

// Split the parameter string into words
   $words = preg_split("/[ \.,;:!\?]\s*/", $str);

// Loop to count the words (either increment or initialize to 1)
   foreach ($words as $word) {
     $keys = array_keys($freq);
     if(in_array($word, $keys))
       $freq[$word]++;
     else
       $freq[$word] = 1;
   }
   return $freq;
} #** End of splitter

// Main test driver
   $str = "apples are good for you, or don't you like apples?
          or maybe you like oranges better than apples";

// Call splitter
   $tbl = splitter($str);

// Display the words and their frequencies
   print "<br /> Word Frequency <br /><br />";
   $sorted_keys = array_keys($tbl);
   sort($sorted_keys);
   foreach ($sorted_keys as $word)
     print "$word $tbl[$word] <br />";
   ?>
   </body>
</html>
```

The output of this script is as follows:

```
Word Frequency
apples 3
are 1
better 1
don't 1
for 1
good 1
```

```
like 2
maybe 1
or 2
oranges 1
than 1
you 3
```

9.10 Form Handling

One common way for a browser user to interact with a Web server is through forms. A form is presented to the user, who is invited to fill in the text boxes and click the buttons of the form. The user submits the form to the server by clicking the form's *Submit* button. The contents of the form are encoded and transmitted to the server, which must use a program to decode the contents, perform whatever computation is necessary on the data, and produce output in the form of a markup document that is returned to the client. When PHP is used to process form data, it implicitly decodes the data.

It may seem strange, but when PHP is used for form handling, the PHP script is embedded in an HTML document, as it is with other uses of PHP. Although it is possible to have a PHP script handle form data in the same HTML document that defines the form, it is perhaps clearer to use two separate documents. For this latter case, the document that defines the form specifies the document that handles the form data in the action attribute of its <form> tag.

PHP can be configured so that form data values are directly available as implicit variables whose names match the names of the corresponding form elements. However, this implicit access is not allowed in many Web servers (through the configuration of PHP), because it creates a security risk. The recommended approach is to use the implicit arrays $_POST and $_GET for form values. These arrays have keys that match the form element names and values that were input by the client. For example, if a form has a text box named phone and the form method is POST, the value of that element is available in the PHP script as follows:

```
$_POST["phone"]
```

The following is an HTML document that presents a form for popcorn sales:

```
<!DOCTYPE html>
<!-- popcorn3.html - This describes the popcorn sales form -->
<html lang = "en">
  <head>
    <title> Popcorn Sales - for PHP handling </title>
    <meta charset = "utf-8" />
    <style type = "text/css">
```

```
              td, th, table {border: thin solid black;}
          </style>
        </head>
        <body>
          <form action = "http://localhost/popcorn3.php"
                method = "post">
          <h2> Welcome to Millennium Gymnastics Booster Club Popcorn
                Sales </h2>
          <table>

<!-- Text widgets for the customer's name and address -->
              <tr>
                <td> Buyer's Name: </td>
                <td> <input type = "text" name = "name"
                            size = "30" /></td>
              </tr>
              <tr>
                <td> Street Address: </td>
                <td> <input type = "text" name = "street"
                            size = "30" /></td>
              </tr>
              <tr>
                <td> City, State, Zip: </td>
                <td> <input type = "text" name = "city"
                            size = "30" /></td>
              </tr>
          </table>
          <p />
          <table>

<!-- First, the column headings -->
              <tr>
                <th> Product </th>
                <th> Price </th>
                <th> Quantity </th>
              </tr>

<!-- Now, the table data entries -->
              <tr>
                <td> Unpopped Popcorn (1 lb.) </td>
                <td> $3.00 </td>
                <td>
                  <input type = "text" name = "unpop"
                          size = "3" /></td>
              </tr>
```

```
            <tr>
              <td> Caramel Popcorn (2 lb. canister) </td>
              <td> $3.50 </td>
              <td>
                <input type = "text" name = "caramel"
                       size = "3" /> </td>
            </tr>
            <tr>
              <td> Caramel Nut Popcorn (2 lb. canister) </td>
              <td> $4.50 </td>
              <td>
                <input type = "text" name = "caramelnut"
                       size = "3" /> </td>
            </tr>
            <tr>
              <td> Toffey Nut Popcorn (2 lb. canister) </td>
              <td> $5.00 </td>
              <td>
                <input type = "text" name = "toffeynut"
                       size = "3" /> </td>
            </tr>
          </table>
          <p />

<!-- The radio buttons for the payment method -->
        <h3> Payment Method </h3>
        <p>
          <input type = "radio" name = "payment" value = "visa"
                 checked = "checked" />
            Visa <br />
          <input type = "radio" name = "payment" value = "mc" />
            Master Card <br />
          <input type = "radio" name = "payment"
                 value = "discover" />
            Discover <br />
          <input type = "radio" name = "payment" value = "check" />
            Check <br /> <br />

<!-- The submit and reset buttons -->
          <input type = "submit" value = "Submit Order" />
          <input type = "reset" value = "Clear Order Form" />
        </p>
      </form>
    </body>
</html>
```

Figure 9.5 displays the output of `popcorn3.html`, after it has been filled out.

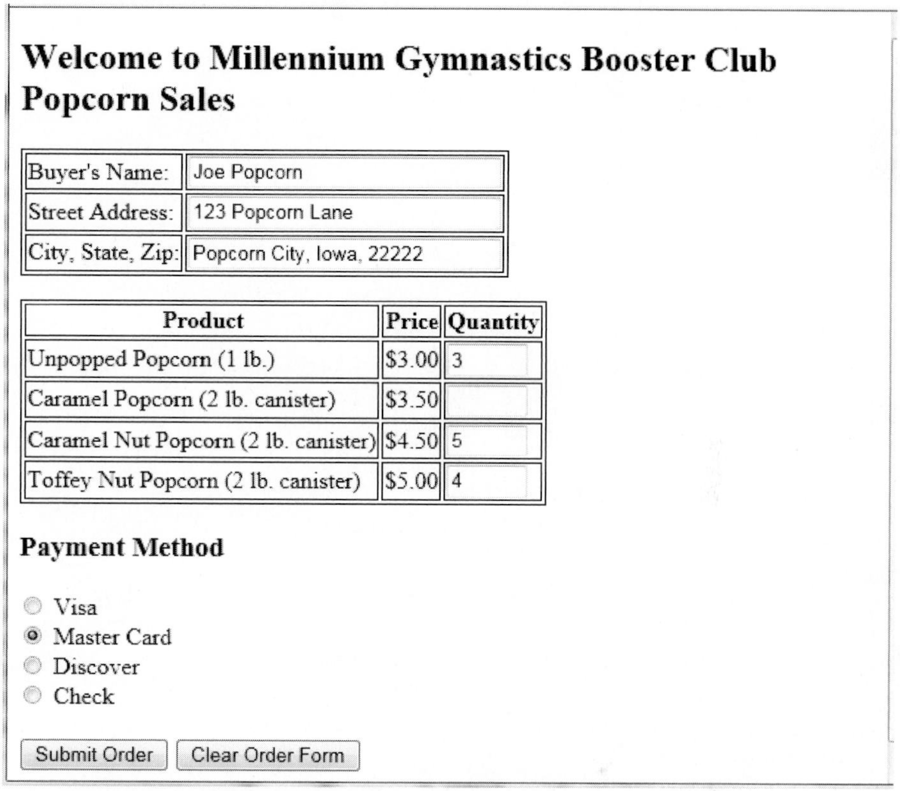

Welcome to Millennium Gymnastics Booster Club Popcorn Sales

Buyer's Name:	Joe Popcorn
Street Address:	123 Popcorn Lane
City, State, Zip:	Popcorn City, Iowa, 22222

Product	Price	Quantity
Unpopped Popcorn (1 lb.)	$3.00	3
Caramel Popcorn (2 lb. canister)	$3.50	
Caramel Nut Popcorn (2 lb. canister)	$4.50	5
Toffey Nut Popcorn (2 lb. canister)	$5.00	4

Payment Method

- ○ Visa
- ◉ Master Card
- ○ Discover
- ○ Check

[Submit Order] [Clear Order Form]

Figure 9.5 Display of the output of `popcorn3.html`

The PHP script that handles the data from the form described in `popcorn3.html` follows. It uses the form data to compute the cost of each product, the total cost of the order, and the total number of items ordered. The name, unit price, number ordered, and total cost for each product are presented to the client in a table defined with interwoven HTML markup and PHP script. The table structure is described with HTML, but the contents of some of the data cells are defined with PHP. Here is the document:

```
<!DOCTYPE html>
<!-- popcorn3.php - Processes the form described in
     popcorn3.html
     -->
<html lang = "en">
  <head>
    <title> Process the popcorn3.html form </title>
```

```
    <meta charset = "utf-8" />
    <style type = "text/css">
      td, th, table {border: thin solid black;}
    </style>

  </head>

  <body>
    <?php

// Get form data values
      $unpop = $_POST["unpop"];
      $caramel = $_POST["caramel"];
      $caramelnut = $_POST["caramelnut"];
      $toffeynut = $_POST["toffeynut"];
      $name = $_POST["name"];
      $street = $_POST["street"];
      $city = $_POST["city"];
      $payment = $_POST["payment"];

// If any of the quantities are blank, set them to zero
      if ($unpop == "") $unpop = 0;
      if ($caramel == "") $caramel = 0;
      if ($caramelnut == "") $caramelnut = 0;
      if ($toffeynut == "") $toffeynut = 0;

// Compute the item costs and total cost
      $unpop_cost = 3.0 * $unpop;
      $caramel_cost = 3.5 * $caramel;
      $caramelnut_cost = 4.5 * $caramelnut;
      $toffeynut_cost = 5.0 * $toffeynut;
      $total_price = $unpop_cost + $caramel_cost +
                     $caramelnut_cost + $toffeynut_cost;
      $total_items = $unpop + $caramel + $caramelnut + $toffeynut;

// Return the results to the browser in a table
    ?>
    <h4> Customer: </h4>
    <?php
      print ("$name <br /> $street <br /> $city <br />");
    ?>
    <p /> <p />
    <table>
      <caption> Order Information </caption>
```

```
        <tr>
          <th> Product </th>
          <th> Unit Price </th>
          <th> Quantity Ordered </th>
          <th> Item Cost </th>
        </tr>
        <tr>
          <td> Unpopped Popcorn </td>
          <td> $3.00 </td>
          <td> <?php print ("$unpop"); ?> </td>
          <td> <?php printf ("$ %4.2f", $unpop_cost); ?>
          </td>
        </tr>
        <tr>
          <td> Caramel Popcorn </td>
          <td> $3.50 </td>
          <td> <?php print ("$caramel"); ?> </td>
          <td> <?php printf ("$ %4.2f", $caramel_cost); ?>
          </td>
          </tr>
        <tr>
          <td> Caramel Nut Popcorn </td>
          <td> $4.50 </td>
          <td> <?php print ("$caramelnut"); ?> </td>
          <td> <?php printf ("$ %4.2f", $caramelnut_cost); ?>
          </td>
        </tr>
        <tr>
          <td> Toffey Nut Popcorn </td>
          <td> $5.00 </td>
          <td> <?php print ("$toffeynut"); ?> </td>
          <td> <?php printf ("$ %4.2f", $toffeynut_cost); ?>
          </td>
        </tr>
      </table>
      <p /> <p />

      <?php
        print "You ordered $total_items popcorn items <br />";
        printf ("Your total bill is: $ %5.2f <br />", $total_price);
        print "Your chosen method of payment is: $payment <br />";
      ?>
  </body>
</html>
```

Notice that the `printf` function is used to implement the numbers that represent money, so exactly two digits appear to the right of the decimal points. Figure 9.6 displays the output of `popcorn3.php`.

Customer:

Joe Popcorn
123 Popcorn Lane
Popcorn City, Iowa, 22222

Order Information

Product	Unit Price	Quantity Ordered	Item Cost
Unpopped Popcorn	$3.00	3	$ 9.00
Caramel Popcorn	$3.50	0	$ 0.00
Caramel Nut Popcorn	$4.50	5	$ 22.50
Toffey Nut Popcorn	$5.00	4	$ 20.00

You ordered 12 popcorn items
Your total bill is: $ 51.50
Your chosen method of payment is: mc

Figure 9.6 Display of the output of `popcorn3.php`

9.11   Cookies

PHP includes convenient support for creating and using cookies.

9.11.1   Introduction to Cookies

A *session* is the time span during which a browser interacts with a particular server. A session begins when a browser connects to the server. That session ends either when the browser is terminated or because the server terminated the session because of client inactivity. The length of time a server uses as the maximum time of inactivity is set in the configuration of the server. For example, the default maximum for some servers is 30 minutes.

The HTTP protocol is essentially stateless: It includes no means to store information about a session that is available to a subsequent session. However, there are a number of different reasons that it is useful for the server to be capable of connecting a request made during a session to the other requests made by the same client during that session, as well as to requests made during previous and subsequent sessions.

One of the most common needs for information about a session is to implement shopping carts on Web sites. An e-commerce site can have any number of simultaneous online customers. At any time, any customer can add an item to or remove an item from his or her cart. Each user's shopping cart is identified by a session identifier, which could be implemented as a cookie. So, cookies can be used to identify each of the customers visiting the site at a given time.

Besides identifying customers, another common use of cookies is for a Web site to create profiles of visitors by remembering which parts of the site are perused by that visitor. Sometimes this is called *personalization*. Later sessions can use such profiles to target advertising to the client in line with the client's past interests. Also, if the server recognizes a request as being from a client who has made an earlier request from the same site, it is possible to present a customized interface to that client. These situations require that information about clients be accumulated and stored. Storing session information is becoming increasingly important as more and more Web sites make use of shopping carts, targeted advertising, and personalization.

Cookies provide a general approach to storing information about sessions on the browser system itself. The server is given this information when the browser makes subsequent requests for resources from the server. Note that many of the uses of cookies require them to be stored after the session in which they were created ends.

A *cookie* is a small object of information that includes a name and a textual value. A cookie is created by some software system on the server. Every HTTP communication between a browser and a server includes a header, which stores information about the message. The header part of an HTTP communication can include cookies. So, every request sent from a browser to a server, and every response from a server to a browser, can include one or more cookies.

At the time it is created, a cookie is assigned a lifetime. When the time a cookie has existed reaches its associated lifetime, the cookie is deleted from the browser's host machine.

Every browser request includes all of the cookies its host machine has stored that are associated with the Web server to which the request is directed. Only the server that created a cookie can ever receive the cookie from the browser, so a particular cookie is information that is exchanged exclusively between one specific browser and one specific server.

Because cookies allow servers to record browser activities, some consider them to involve privacy concerns. Accordingly, browsers allow the client to change a browser setting to refuse to accept cookies from servers. This is clearly a drawback of using cookies—they are useless when clients reject them.

Cookies also can be deleted by the browser user, although the deletion process is different for different browsers. The help facility of a browser can be consulted to determine the cookie deletion process on any given browser.

9.11.2 PHP Support for Cookies

A cookie is set in PHP with the `setcookie` function. This function takes one or more parameters. The first parameter, which is mandatory, is the cookie's name given as a string. The second, if present, is the new value for the cookie, also a string. If the value is absent, `setcookie` undefines the cookie. The third parameter, when present, is the expiration time in seconds for the cookie, given as an integer. The default value for the expiration time is zero, which specifies that the cookie is destroyed at the end of the current session. When specified, the expiration time is often given as the number of seconds in the UNIX epoch, which began on January 1, 1970. The `time` function returns the current time in seconds. So, the cookie expiration time is given as the value returned from `time` plus some number. For example, consider the following call to `setcookie`:

```
setcookie("voted", "true", time() + 86400);
```

This call creates a cookie named `"voted"` whose value is `"true"` and whose lifetime is one day (86,400 is the number of seconds in a day).

The `setcookie` function has three more optional parameters, the details of which can found in the PHP manual.

The most important thing to remember about creating a cookie or setting a cookie to a new value is that it must be done before any other HTML is created by the PHP document. Recall that cookies are stored in the HTTP header of the document returned to the requesting browser. The HTTP header is sent before the body of the document is sent. The server sends the header when it receives the first character of the body of the document. So, if any part of the body is created, it is too late to add a cookie to the header. If you create a cookie or change the value of a cookie after even a single character of document body has been generated, the cookie operation will not be successful. (The cookie or the cookie's new value will not be sent to the browser.)

The other cookie operation is getting the cookies and their values from subsequent browser requests. In PHP, cookie values are treated much as are form values. All cookies that arrive with a request are placed in the implicit `$_COOKIES` array, which has the cookie names as keys and the cookie values as values. A PHP script can test whether a cookie came with a request by using the `IsSet` predicate function on the associated variable.

As is the case with using cookies with other technologies, remember that cookies cannot be depended upon because some users set their browsers to reject all cookies. Furthermore, most browsers have a limit on the number of cookies that will be accepted from a particular server site.

9.12 Session Tracking

In some cases, information about a session is needed only during the session. Also, the needed information about a client is nothing more than a unique identifier for the session—commonly used in shopping cart applications. For these cases, a different process, named *session tracking*, can be used. Rather than using one or more cookies, a single session array can be used to store information about the previous requests of a client during a session. In particular, session arrays often store a unique session ID for a session. One significant way that session arrays differ from cookies is that they can be stored on the server, whereas cookies are stored on the client.

In PHP, a session ID is an internal value that identifies the session. Session IDs need not be known or handled in any way by PHP scripts. PHP is made aware that a script is interested in session tracking by calling the `session_start` function, which takes no parameters. The first call to `session_start` in a session causes a session ID to be created and recorded. On subsequent calls to `session_start` in the same session, the function retrieves the `$_SESSION` array, which stores any session variables and their values that were registered in previously executed scripts in that session.

Session key-value pairs are created or changed by assignments to the `$_SESSION` array. They can be destroyed with the `unset` operator, as in the following example:

```
session_start();
if (!IsSet($_SESSION["page_number"]))
  $_SESSION["page_number"] = 1;
$page_num = $_SESSION["page_number"];
print("You have now visited $page_num page(s) <br />");
$_SESSION["page_number"]++;
```

If this is not the first document visited that calls `session_start` and sets the `page_number` session variable, the script that it executes will produce the specified line with the last set value of `$_SESSION["page_number"]`. If no document that was previously visited in this session set `page_number`, the script sets `page_number` to 1, produces the line,

```
You have now visited 1 page(s)
```

and increments `page_number`.

Summary

PHP is a server-side, HTML-embedded scripting language that is similar to JavaScript. The PHP processor takes as input a file of markup with embedded PHP code, copies the markup to an output file, and interprets the PHP script in the input file. The output of any PHP script is written into the output file. PHP scripts either are directly embedded in markup files or are referenced in the markup files and subsequently copied into them.

PHP has four scalar types: integer, Boolean, double, and string. PHP variable names all begin with dollar signs. The language is dynamically typed. Arithmetic and Boolean expressions in PHP are similar to those in other common languages. PHP includes a large number of functions for arithmetic and string operations. The current type of a variable is maintained internally and can be determined by a script through several different built-in functions. The `print` and `printf` functions are used to produce output, which becomes part of the PHP processor output file. The control statements of PHP are similar to those of other common programming languages.

PHP's arrays are a combination of the traditional arrays of C and its descendant languages and hashes. Arrays can be created by assigning values to their elements. They also can be created with the `array` construct, which allows the specification of values and, optionally, the keys for one or more elements of an array. PHP has predefined functions for many array operations. Among these functions are `explode` and `implode`, for converting between strings and arrays; `current`, `next`, and `prev`, for fetching elements in sequential order; `each`, for obtaining both the keys and values of the elements of an array in sequential order; and `array_keys` and `array_values`, which return an array of the keys and values of the array, respectively. There are also functions for stack operations on arrays. The `foreach` statement provides sequential access to the elements of an array. Finally, PHP has a collection of functions for sorting the elements of arrays in various ways.

User-defined functions in PHP are similar to those of other languages, except for parameter passing. Pass-by-reference parameters can be specified in either the function call or the function definition. Variables used only in a function are local to that function. Access to variables used outside a function is specified with a `global` declaration. Static variables can be declared with a `static` declaration.

PHP's pattern matching can use either POSIX-style or Perl-style regular expressions. Form data is placed in user-accessible variables implicitly by the PHP system, making form handling very simple.

Cookies are created and set to values with the `setcookie` function, which has parameters for the cookie name, its value, and a lifetime in seconds. Cookies created or set in a previous script are available to a current script directly through the `$_COOKIES` array. A script can use `IsSet` to test whether a cookie exists and is set to a value. Session tracking is relatively simple in PHP. The `session_start` function creates a session ID. Session variables are stored in the `$_SESSION` array.

Review Questions

9.1   How does a Web server determine whether a requested document includes PHP code?

9.2   What are the two modes of the PHP processor?

9.3   What are the syntax and semantics of the `include` construct?

9.4   Which parts of PHP are case sensitive and which are not?

9.5   What are the four scalar types of PHP?

9.6   How can a variable be tested to determine whether it is bound?

9.7   How can you specify to the PHP processor that you want uses of unbound variables to be reported?

9.8   How many bytes are used to store a character in PHP?

9.9   What are the differences between single- and double-quoted literal strings?

9.10 If an integer expression appears in a Boolean context, how is its Boolean value determined?

9.11 What happens when an integer arithmetic operation results in a value that cannot be represented as an integer?

9.12 If a variable stores a string, how can the character at a specific position in that string be referenced?

9.13 What does the `chop` function do?

9.14 What is a coercion?

9.15 What are the three ways the value of a variable can be explicitly converted to a specific type?

9.16 How can the type of a variable be determined?

9.17 If a string is compared with a number, what happens?

9.18 What is the advantage of using unique closing reserved words such as `endwhile`?

9.19 In what two ways can arrays in PHP be created?

9.20 What keys are used when an array is created but no keys are specified?

9.21 Must all of the values of an array be of the same type?

9.22 Must all of the keys of an array be of the same type?

9.23 What exactly do the `array_keys` and `array_values` functions do?

9.24 What exactly does the `in_array` function do?

9.25 Explain the actions of the `implode` and `explode` functions.

9.26 Describe the actions of the `next`, `reset`, and `prev` functions.

9.27 What are the syntax and semantics of the two forms of the `foreach` statement?

9.28 Describe the result of using the `sort` function on an array that has both string and numeric values.

9.29 What is the difference betweeen the `sort` and `asort` functions?

9.30 What happens if a script defines the same function more than once?

9.31 Are function names case sensitive?

9.32 What value is returned by a function if its execution does not end by executing a `return` statement?

9.33   What are the two ways you can specify that a parameter is to be passed by reference?

9.34   How can a variable used outside a function be accessed by the function?

9.35   How can you define a variable in a function so that its lifetime extends beyond the time the function is in its first execution?

9.36   How can the value of a form element be accessed by a PHP script?

9.37   How can a cookie be created in a PHP script?

9.38   How can a script determine whether a particular cookie exists?

9.39   How can a variable be saved in a session?

Exercises

Write, test, and debug (if necessary) PHP scripts for the specifications that follow. For Exercises 9.1 to 9.7, write functions and the code to test them.

9.1   *Parameter*: An array of strings.

   Return value: A list of the unique strings in the parameter array.

9.2   *Parameter*: An array of numbers.

   Return value: The average and median of the parameter array.

9.3   *Parameter*: An array of strings.

   Return value: A list of the three strings that occur most frequently in the parameter array.

9.4   *Parameters*: An array of numbers (pass by value) and two arrays (pass by reference).

   Return value: None.

   Result: The first pass-by-reference parameter must have the values of the given array that are greater than zero; the second must have the values that are less than zero.

9.5   *Parameter*: A string of numbers separated by spaces.

   Return value: The first four-digit number in the string; `false` if none.

9.6   *Parameter*: A string containing words that are delimited on the left with spaces and on the right with spaces, commas, periods, or question marks.

   Return value: The three most common words in the string that have more than three letters.

9.7   Modify the sample script in Section 9.9, `word_table.php`, to place the output table in an HTML table.

9.8 Write an HTML document that includes an anchor tag that calls a PHP document. Also, write the called PHP document, which returns a randomly chosen greeting from a list of five different greetings. The greetings must be stored as constant strings in the script. A random number between 0 and 4 can be computed with these lines:

```
# Set the seed for mtrand with the number of microseconds
#  since the last full second of the clock
mt_srand((double)microtime() * 1000000);
$number = mtrand(0, 4);  # Computes a random integer 0-4
```

9.9 Write the HTML markup to create a form with the following capabilities:
   a. A text widget to collect the user's name
   b. Four checkboxes, one each for the following items:
      i. Four 25-watt light bulbs for $2.39
      ii. Eight 25-watt light bulbs for $4.29
      iii. Four 25-watt long-life light bulbs for $3.95
      iv. Eight 25-watt long-life light bulbs for $7.49
   c. A collection of three radio buttons that are labeled as follows:
      i. Visa
      ii. MasterCard
      iii. Discover

9.10 Write a PHP script that computes the total cost of the ordered light bulbs from Exercise 9.9 after adding 6.2 percent sales tax. The program must inform the buyer of exactly what was ordered, in a table.

9.11 Write the HTML markup to create a form that collects favorite popular songs, including the name of the song, the composer, and the performing artist or group. This document must call one PHP script when the form is submitted and another to request a current list of survey results.

9.12 Write the PHP script that collects the data from the form of Exercise 9.11 and writes it to a file.

9.13 Write the PHP script that produces the current results of the survey of Exercise 9.11.

9.14 Write the HTML markup to provide a form that collects names and telephone numbers. The phone numbers must be in the format ddd-ddd-dddd. Write a PHP script that checks the submitted telephone number to be sure that it conforms to the required format and then returns a response indicating whether the number was correct.

Introduction to Ajax

This chapter provides an introduction to Ajax. As described in Chapter 1, Ajax is a process of using asynchronous requests from the browser to the server to fetch data, which is used to update a part of the browser-displayed document. The first section is an overview of the concepts and processes of Ajax. This is followed by an introduction to the basics of Ajax, including a simple, but complete, example of Ajax being used to help a user fill out a form. Next, the issues associated with the cross-browser implementation of Ajax are discussed. Following that, several different forms of return data are described and evaluated. In the next section of the chapter, two Ajax toolkits, Dojo and Prototype, are introduced. A complete example application using Dojo is developed in this section. The last section discusses security issues concerning Ajax.

10.1   Overview of Ajax

The goal of Ajax technology is to provide Web-based applications with rich user interfaces and responsiveness similar to those of desktop applications. The motivation for this goal is the great increase in the demand for Rich Internet Applications (RIAs). These applications present the user with an elaborate interface that invites and, in many cases, requires frequent interactions between the user and the server. The speed of these interactions determines the usability of the application.

10.1.1   History of Ajax

The first possibility of the Ajax approach arrived with the introduction of the HTML `iframe` element in the fourth versions of the browsers from Netscape and Microsoft. Web programmers discovered that an `iframe` element could be made to be invisible simply by setting its width and height to zero pixels. Furthermore, it could be used to send asynchronous requests to the server. Although this approach worked, it was far from elegant.

Microsoft introduced two nonstandard extensions to the DOM and its Java-Script binding with the `XmlDocument` and `XMLHTML` objects, which began as ActiveX components in IE5. These objects were designed to support asynchronous requests to the server, thereby allowing data to be fetched from the server in the background. A similar object is now supported by most commonly used browsers, although the object is now named `XMLHttpRequest` in most browsers, including IE9.

Before 2005 some developers were using Ajax technology, but there was no widespread interest in it or enthusiasm for it. Two events were the catalysts that began the rush of Web developers to Ajax in 2005 and 2006. First, many users began to experience the rapid browser–server interactions provided by Google Maps and Gmail, which were among the early Web applications to use Ajax. For example, Google Maps can use asynchronous requests to the server to quickly replace small parts of the displayed map called tiles. This allows the user to scroll in any direction and have the map grow in that direction by adding new small rectangles on the growing side, without ever requiring the browser to re-render the whole screen. Most users had never used a Web application with such powerful interactive capabilities. Second, Jesse James Garrett named this technology Ajax in early 2005. It may appear odd to some, including me, that the acquisition of a name was an important part of the motivation for the huge growth in interest in the new approach to building Web applications, but it clearly was.

10.1.2 Ajax Technology

A typical traditional (non-Ajax) session of Web use begins with the user requesting an initial document, either by typing a URL or clicking a link on his or her browser. At that point, the browser is blocked from activity while it waits for the server to provide the new document. When the document arrives, the browser replaces the former display with a rendering of the new document. This cycle takes some time, both in network latency and in rendering time. Nothing can be done to speed this process of fetching and rendering a complete document. However, user interactions with the displayed document may require that only relatively small parts of the document be modified or updated. In a non-Ajax Web application, even the smallest change in the displayed document, if it needs data from the server, requires the same process that produced the initial display. The request must go to the server, the server must construct and send back a complete document, and the whole display must be re-rendered. During this time, the browser is locked and the user can do nothing but wait. If a Web application requires many such interactions, the workflow of the user can be seriously disrupted. Clearly, this mode of operation is utterly unable to support RIAs.

As previously stated, Ajax is meant to significantly increase the speed of user interactions with Web applications. For those user requests that update only a small part of the displayed document, Ajax technology shortens the required time for both transmitting and rendering the document. It does this by having the server provide only a relatively small part of the document—the part that must change. This shortens the transmission time because the document being transmitted is much smaller, and it shortens the rendering time because, once again, only a small part of the display must be re-rendered. This is a simple idea, but one that can provide great improvements in the richness of the Web user experience, at least with applications that have frequent browser–server interactions.

Another key feature of Ajax is that requests from the browser to the server are asynchronous (the *A* in *A*jax). This means that when the browser requests a new part of its displayed document from the server, it does not need to lock while it waits for the response. Both the user and the browser can continue to do something useful during the time it takes to fetch and render the new document part.

Ajax is especially important in the use of mobile devices. Cell phones, for example, have limited capabilities relative to notebook and desktop computers. In particular, they have slower processors, smaller memories, smaller screens, and less communications bandwidth. Because Ajax requires less processing and data communication, it relieves the strain on those capabilities and makes the devices more effective for Web use.

Traditional (non-Ajax) browser interactions with a server and Ajax interactions with a server are shown in Figure 10.1.

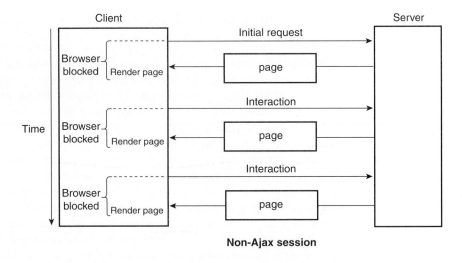

Non-Ajax session

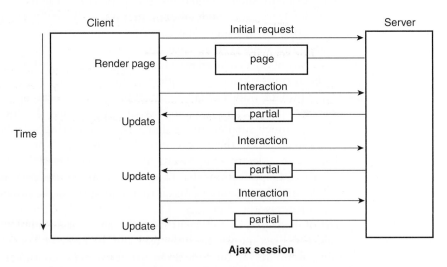

Ajax session

Figure 10.1 Traditional and Ajax browser–server interactions

10.1.3 Implementing Ajax

Ajax is not a new programming language or even a new API. In fact, one of the most attractive characteristics of Ajax is that it does not require Web programmers to learn new programming languages or markup languages in order to build Web sites that use Ajax. True to its name, Ajax uses JavaScript as its primary programming language. Most Web programmers—certainly including those who have studied this book—already know JavaScript. The *x* in Ajax represents XML. An Ajax request results in the server returning the requested data, perhaps in the form of an XML document, although other forms of data also are often returned. Again, most Web programmers also already know XML. The other technologies used in Ajax are the DOM and CSS, both well known to Web programmers (and readers of this book). So, Ajax is very attractive in the sense that no new technologies must be acquired or learned in order to use it. Furthermore, the technologies it uses are already present on the vast majority of Web browsers.

While Ajax uses JavaScript on the client side, it can work with virtually any server-side language or technology—for example, PHP, Java servlets, and ASP.NET.

Ajax can be implemented in several different ways. First, it can be implemented with just the basic tools, including JavaScript on the client (browser), the XMLHttpRequest object, and virtually any server-side software, using text, XHTML, or XML to transmit data.

Another way to implement Ajax is with the help of a client-side toolkit, such as Dojo or Prototype. There are also server-side tools, such as DWR and GWT. Dojo is discussed and used in an example in Section 10.4; the others are briefly introduced in that same section.

There also are frameworks for implementing applications that use Ajax, such as Adobe Flex, ASP.NET Ajax, JavaServer Faces, and Rails. JavaServer Faces is discussed in Chapter 11; ASP.NET Ajax is discussed in Chapter 12; and Rails is discussed in Chapter 15.

For security reasons, Ajax requests using XMLHttpRequest can be made only to the server and site that provided the document in which the request originated. However, an application can make requests to other sites by using alternative techniques, such as making requests through a proxy in the server. This is one approach used to building mashups, which are Web sites that use data from two or more sites to provide a service.

10.2 The Basics of Ajax

In this section, a Web application is developed and used to illustrate the basics of Ajax. Such an application includes four parts: an HTML document to produce the initial display, a JavaScript script to produce the Ajax request of the server, a server-side program to receive the request and produce the requested data, and a JavaScript script to receive the new data and integrate it into the original document being displayed.

10.2.1   The Application

The application used in this section, which has been used previously for the same purpose,[1] is as devoid of complexity as possible, but is still able to illustrate the fundamentals of the Ajax technology. The example initially displays the first part of the popcorn sales form used in Chapters 2 and 9. Only the first part of the form, which gathers the name and address information from the user, is included. In a

---

1. A similar example appears in D. Crane, et al., *Ajax in Action*, Manning Publications (2006).

feeble attempt to make it more attractive, a small picture of popcorn has been added. The concept of this application is that it uses Ajax to help the user enter his or her address information. Specifically, a form displays the text box for the user's zip code above the text boxes for the city and state of residence. When the zip code has been entered, signaled by the DOM as the `blur` event on the zip code's text box, a JavaScript event handler function that constructs an asynchronous request to the server is called. The zip code is then sent to the server mentioned in the request, which uses it to look up the city and state, which are then returned to the browser. When the JavaScript code receives the names of the city and state, it inserts them into the city and state text boxes on the form.

10.2.2 The Form Document

The first thing needed for this application is the document to present the initial form. One requirement of the document is that the zip code text box register a JavaScript function handler for its `blur` event. The call to the handler must pass the value in the zip code text box. In the call to the handler within the text box element, this value can be referenced as `this.value`. The handler is named `getPlace`. Another requirement is that both the city and state text boxes have id attributes, so that they can be addressed conveniently by the code that must insert the values returned from the server. Finally, the document must reference the JavaScript code file in a script element in its head. The complete document, named `popcornA.html`, is as follows:

```
<!DOCTYPE html>
<!-- popcornA.html
     This describes popcorn sales form page which uses
     Ajax and the zip code to fill in the city and state
     of the customer's address
     -->
<html lang = "en">
  <head>
    <title> Popcorn Sales Form (Ajax) </title>
    <meta charset = "utf-8" />
    <style type = "text/css">
      input.name {position: absolute; left: 120px;}
      input.address {position: absolute; left: 120px;}
      input.zip {position: absolute; left: 120px;}
      input.city {position: absolute; left: 120px;}
      input.state {position: absolute; left: 120px;}
      img {position: absolute; left: 400px;  top: 50px;}
    </style>
    <script type = "text/JavaScript" src = "popcornA.js">
    </script>
```

```
  </head>
  <body>
    <h2> Welcome to Millennium Gymnastics Booster Club Popcorn
        Sales
    </h2>
    <form action = "">
      <p>

<!-- The text widgets for name and address -->
        Buyer's Name:
        <input class = "name"  type = "text"  name = "name"
            size = "30" />
      </p>
      <p>
        Street Address:
          <input class = "address"  type = "text"  name = "street"
              size = "30" />
      </p>
      <p>
        Zip code:
        <input class = "zip"  type = "text"  name = "zip"
            size = "10"
            onblur = "getPlace(this.value)" />
      </p>
      <p>
        City:
        <input class = "city"  type = "text"  name = "city"
            id = "city"  size = "30" />
      </p>
      <p>
        State:
        <input class = "state"  type = "text"  name = "state"
            id = "state"  size = "30" />
      </p>
      <img src = "../images/popcorn.png" alt = "picture of popcorn"
          width = "150" height = "150"/>

<!-- The submit and reset buttons -->
      <p>
        <input type = "submit"  value = "Submit Order" />
        <input type = "reset"  value = "Clear Order Form" />
      </p>
    </form>
  </body>
</html>
```

A display of the `popcornA.html` document is shown in Figure 10.2.

Welcome to Millennium Gymnastics Booster Club Popcorn Sales

Buyer's Name:

Street Address:

Zip code:

City:

State:

[Submit Order] [Clear Order Form]

Figure 10.2 A display of the `popcornA.html` document

10.2.3   The Request Phase

The application requires two functions: the `blur` event handler and a function to receive the response from the server. The receiver function is called a *callback function* because the server calls the receiver function of the requestor back in order to return the requested data. Such a response is required for asynchronous calls. This section discusses the request phase—the `blur` handler. The receiver phase is discussed in Section 10.2.5.

The request phase of the application is focused entirely on `XMLHttpRequest`, the object used to communicate asynchronously with the server. The first step is to create an object by using the `new` operator and call the `XMLHttpRequest` constructor, as in the following statement:

```
var xhr = new XMLHttpRequest();
```

For the remainder of this chapter, we will refer to the `XMLHttpRequest` object as the XHR object. This object has six properties and six methods. However, for now only two properties and two methods will be discussed.

When the server receives a request through an XHR object, it notifies the sender several times while it is servicing the request. Like the function being called, these notifications are called *callbacks*. They are meant to inform the sender of the progress being made by the server regarding the request. There are five different values returned by the server to indicate progress: `0 .. 4`. The only one of interest here is `4`, which indicates that the response is complete. This indicator will be used in the receiver phase. The callback function is named `receivePlace`.

The next part of the request is to register the callback function, which implements the receive phase of the application. This function is registered to the `onreadystatechange` property of the XHR object, as follows:

```
xhr.onreadystatechange = receivePlace;
```

Note that this statement does not include a call to receivePlace; it is an assignment of the address of the function to the onreadystatechange property. Therefore, there can be no parentheses following the name of the handler function. This handler registration causes receivePlace to be called several times while the server deals with the request, each time setting the readyState property of the XHR object to the progress value. Section 10.2.5 describes how the receivePlace handler deals with this situation.

The next step for the getPlace handler is to call the open method of the XHR object. The open method makes the necessary arrangements for the server request. The method takes two required parameters and three optional parameters. The first parameter, which is mandatory, is the HTTP method—GET or POST—to be used for the request message. For this application, GET will be used. Recall that GET is used when there is a relatively small amount of data to be retrieved and the data is not valuable to an intruder. POST is used when there are many widgets on the form, making the form data lengthy, or when it is important that the retrieved data be secure. The HTTP method is passed as a literal string, so it must be quoted.

The second parameter to open is the URL of the response document on the server, which will either be the response or produce it. In this application, the document will be the response, in the form of plain text. This URL is often just a file name without a path, because the file that produces the response is often in the same directory as the form document.

The third parameter specifies whether the request is to be asynchronous or synchronous, with true signifying asynchronous. Because the whole idea of Ajax is to use asynchronous requests, we will always send true as the third parameter to open, even though true is the default value if the parameter is omitted.

The last two optional parameters, when used, specify a user name and password. These two parameters were included to allow some authentication of requests on the server. However, because it is impossible to reliably prevent users from viewing JavaScript code, it is a poor practice to put user names and passwords in the call to open. Therefore, these two parameters are rarely used.

Because the request handler uses the GET method and the user-entered zip code must be sent to the server, that zip code must be attached with a question mark to the URL of the response document. Recall that the catenation operator in JavaScript is the plus sign (+). Following is the call to open for our application:

```
xhr.open("GET", "getCityState.php?zip=" + zip, true);
```

Notice that a PHP document, getCityState.php, will be used to generate the response document.

The final step in the request handler is to send the request to the server. This is done with the send method of the XHR object, which takes a single parameter. The parameter could be used to send a string or a DOM object to the server to be posted, but that rarely happens. Instead, null is used as the parameter for our application, as is seen in the following call to send:

```
xhr.send(null);
```

Following is the complete request handler function:

```
// function getPlace
//    parameter: zip code
//    action: create the XMLHttpRequest object, register the
//            handler for onreadystatechange, prepare to send
//            the request (with open), and send the request,
//            along with the zip code, to the server

function getPlace(zip) {
  var xhr = new XMLHttpRequest();
  xhr.onreadystatechange = receivePlace;
  xhr.open("GET", "getCityState.php?zip=" + zip, true);
  xhr.send(null);
}
```

10.2.4   The Response Document

The response document for this application is simple: It is a small PHP script. Rather than using a database that has zip codes, cities, and states, for the sake of simplicity only a hash with a few entries is used for testing. The actual response is produced with a PHP `print` statement. The HTTP header should have the content type set to the MIME type of the returned value, usually either `text/plain`, `text/html`, or `text/xml`. If the return document is XML, it is assigned to `responseXML`; otherwise it is assigned to `responseText`. If the content type is not set in the response, it defaults to `text/html`. If the MIME type is set to `text/xml`, but what is returned is not syntactically correct XML, the returned value is assigned to `responseText`, not `responseXML`.

The MIME type is set in PHP with the `header` function, as in the following call:

```
header("Content-Type: text/plain");
```

Any output produced by the response document will be returned to the requester browser. Because the zip code text box value was sent with GET, it can be retrieved from the predefined PHP array `$_GET`. Following is the complete response document:

```
<?php
// getCityState.php
//    Gets the form value from the "zip" widget, looks up the
//    city and state for that zip code, and prints it for the
//    form

  $cityState = array("81611" => "Aspen, Colorado",
                     "81411" => "Bedrock, Colorado",
```

```
                          "80908" => "Black Forest, Colorado",
                          "80301" => "Boulder, Colorado",
                          "81127" => "Chimney Rock, Colorado",
                          "80901" => "Colorado Springs, Colorado",
                          "81223" => "Cotopaxi, Colorado",
                          "80201" => "Denver, Colorado",
                          "81657" => "Vail, Colorado",
                          "80435" => "Keystone, Colorado",
                          "80536" => "Virginia Dale, Colorado",
                          );
    header("Content-Type: text/plain");
    $zip = $_GET["zip"];
    if (array_key_exists($zip, $cityState))
      print $cityState[$zip];
    else
      print " , ";
?>
```

Notice that the response data is a string consisting of a city name, followed by a comma, a space, and a state name. Also, getCityState checks to see if it "knows" the zip code. If it does, it returns the city and state; otherwise it returns blanks, which results in the form elements for city and state remaining blank if they also are not set by the user.

10.2.5   The Receiver Phase

The receiver phase is implemented as a JavaScript function with no parameters. The function's task is to receive the server response, which in this case is plain text, split it into a city name and a state name, and set the city and state text boxes to the results.

The receiver function obviously must be able to access the XHR object, which was created in the request phase function getPlace. If the XHR object is created as a global and both getPlace and the receiver function are placed in a file with the declaration of the XHR object, that would provide both with access. Unfortunately, that also would allow another problem to arise: More than one request could be made before the response occurs, meaning that the earlier XHR object could be overwritten by the creation of another one. One solution to this problem is to register the receiver function definition directly—that is, to place the definition of the receiver function in the request function. So, instead of registering the name of a function, whose definition is elsewhere, the function is not named and its definition is assigned directly to onreadystatechange. The unnamed receiver function was earlier named receivePlace (in getPlace). Note that such a nameless function is sometimes called a *closure*. It inherits the environment in which it is defined, which in our case gives it access to the XHR object.

The first action of the receiver function is to determine the value of the `readyState` property of the XHR object. Recall that a value of 4 means that the response has been completed. The XHR object also has a property that gets `status`, the status of the request. If the request was successfully completed, the `status` value will be 200. However, if the requested resource was not found, the `status` value will be 404. Also, a status value of 500 indicates that there was a server error while processing the request. Therefore, the receiver function encapsulates all of its actions in the then clause of an `if` construct, where the `if` condition is `xhr.readyState == 4 && status == 200`. The receiver function will be called several times when the value of `readyState` is less than 4. For these calls, the receiver function does nothing. So, it processes the returned value from the request only when `readyState` is 4 and `status` is 200. When this happens, the receiver function gets the response text, uses the `split` method to separate it into city and state (because the return data is a single string containing both the city and the state), and sets the text boxes for city and state to the values received. The assignments to the city and state text boxes are both placed in selection constructs to prevent the overwriting of user-input city and state names for the cases where the zip code was not found on the server or the data from the server was incorrect. The complete nameless receiver function is as follows:

```
function () {
  if (xhr.readyState == 4 && status == 200) {
    var result = xhr.responseText;
    var place = result.split(', ');
    if (document.getElementById("city").value == "")
      document.getElementById("city").value = place[0];

    if (document.getElementById("state").value == "")
      document.getElementById("state").value = place[1];
  }
}
```

The JavaScript file, `popcornA.js`, includes the request function, `getPlace`, with its embedded receiver functions:

```
// popcornA.js
// Ajax JavaScript code for the popcornA.html document

/***********************************************************/
// function getPlace
//   parameter: zip code
//   action:    create the XMLHttpRequest object, register the
```

```
//             handler for onreadystatechange, prepare to send
//             the request (with open), and send the request,
//             along with the zip code, to the server
//    includes: the anonymous handler for onreadystatechange,
//             which is the receiver function, which gets the
//             response text, splits it into city and state,
//             and puts them into the document

function getPlace(zip) {
  var xhr = new XMLHttpRequest();

// Register the embedded receiver function as the handler
  xhr.onreadystatechange = function () {
    if (xhr.readyState == 4 && xhr.status == 200) {
      var result = xhr.responseText;
      var place = result.split(', ');
      if (document.getElementById("city").value == "")
        document.getElementById("city").value = place[0];
      if (document.getElementById("state").value == "")
        document.getElementById("state").value = place[1];
    }
  }
  xhr.open("GET", "getCityState.php?zip=" + zip);
  xhr.send(null);
}
```

Figure 10.3 shows the displayed form after the zip code has been entered, but the zip code text box still has focus. Figure 10.4 shows the displayed form after the zip code text box has lost focus and the city and state have been provided by the response.

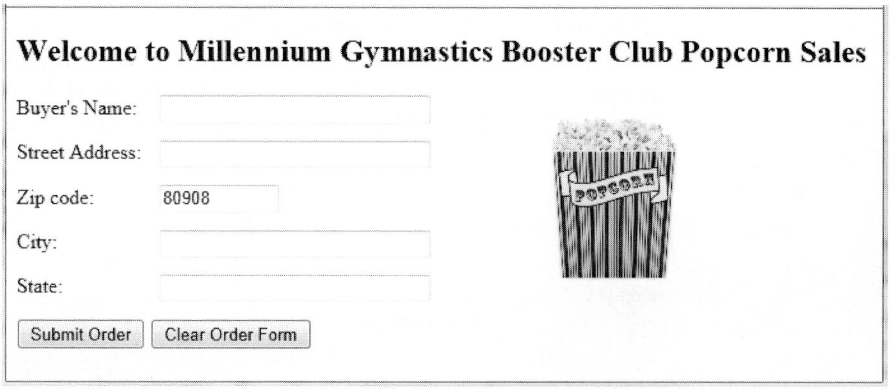

Figure 10.3 Display of the form after the zip code has been entered

Welcome to Millennium Gymnastics Booster Club Popcorn Sales

Buyer's Name: [   ]

Street Address: [   ]

Zip code: [80908   ]

City: [Black Forest   ]

State: [Colorado   ]

[Submit Order] [Clear Order Form]

Figure 10.4 Display of the form after the city and state have been provided

10.2.6   Cross-Browser Support

The application discussed in Section 10.2.5 works correctly with FX3 and IE9 browsers. However, it does not work with IE browsers before IE7. Because there are still some people who use IE6 or IE5, making Ajax work with those browsers must be considered.

The problem with IE5 and IE6 is that they do not support the XHR object named `XMLHttpRequest`. They do, however, support a similar object with a different name. So, to make Ajax applications operate correctly on both of these earlier browsers and also all contemporary browsers, these differences must be taken into account. The name of the IE5 and IE6 object is `Microsoft.XMLHTTP`, and it is an `ActiveXObject`.

Actually, `XMLHTTP` is the name of the original object used for asynchronous requests, invented by Microsoft. When Netscape adopted this idea, the company named its object `XMLHttpRequest`, and other browser makers followed. Finally, in IE7, Microsoft changed to the name used by the others.

The code to create the original object (used in IE5 and IE6) is as follows:

```
xhr = new ActiveXObject("Microsoft.XMLHTTP");
```

This code can determine whether `XMLHttpRequest` is supported by testing `window.XMLHttpRequest`. If this is `null` (which would evaluate to `false`), it is safe to assume that the browser is either IE5 or IE6 and, accordingly, create the `XMLHTTP` object. The cross-browser version of the `getPlace` function is as follows:

```
// function getPlace
//    parameter: zip code
//    action: create the SMLHttpRequest object, register the
//            handler for onreadystatechange, prepare to send
```

```
//            the request (with open), and send the request,
//            along with the zip code, to the server

function getPlace(zip) {

// Get the object for all browsers except IE5 and IE6
  if (window.XMLHttpRequest)
    xhr = new XMLHttpRequest();

// Otherwise get the object for IE5 and IE6
  else
    xhr = new ActiveXObject("Microsoft.XMLHTTP");

// Register the embedded receiver function as the handler
  xhr.onreadystatechange = function () {
    if (xhr.readyState == 4 && xhr.status == 200) {
      var result = xhr.responseText;
      var place = result.split(', ');
      if (document.getElementById("city").value == "")
        document.getElementById("city").value = place[0];
      if (document.getElementById("state").value == "")
        document.getElementById("state").value = place[1];
    }
  }
  xhr.open("GET", "getCityState.php?zip=" + zip);
  xhr.send(null);
}
```

10.3 Return Document Forms

Several different forms of data can be returned from an Ajax request to the server. Among the most common are plain text, as used in Section 10.2, HTML, XML, JavaScript code, and JavaScript Object Notation. Plain text is usually used for unstructured data, while the others are used for structured data. This section briefly discusses these alternatives.

10.3.1   HTML

HTML can, and often is, used as the form of structured data returned from the server. To use HTML, an empty `div` element is included in the original document (the one to be updated) and the returned HTML is placed in the `div` with the `innerHTML` property. For example, to replace a complete table element, the table element is placed in a `div` element, as in the following original document fragment:

```
<div id = "replaceable_list">
  <h2> 2010 US Champion/Runnerup - baseball </h2>
  <ul>
    <li> San Francisco Giants </li>
    <li> Texas Rangers </li>
  </ul>
</div>
```

Now suppose there were a menu in the initial document that allowed the user to choose alternative sports, such as football, basketball, or hockey. If the user chooses football, the response document fragment would look like the following:

```
<h2> 2010 US Champion/Runnerup - football </h2>
<ul>
  <li> Green Bay Packers </li>
  <li> Pittsburgh Steelers </li>
</ul>
```

Now, if the Ajax call returns this document fragment in `responseText`, the `div` can be replaced by interpreting the following JavaScript code:

```
var divDom = document.getElementById("replaceable_list");
divDom.innerHTML = xhr.responseText;
```

The disadvantage of HTML is that they are essentially markup languages for describing documents to be displayed, usually by a browser. What is often returned from the server after an Ajax request is data of some form. If that data must be processed, the markup document fragment must be parsed to extract the data. Also, if the markup is complicated, say, with extensive CSS, it would be a complex task for the server to generate it.

10.3.2   XML

The name *Ajax* implies that XML is an integral part of the technology. Because XML is the de facto standard way of storing and transmitting structured data on the Web, this is natural. In our example, the XML document fragment would appear as follows:

```
<header> 2010 US Champion/Runnerup - football </header>
<list_item> Green Bay Packers </list_item>
<list_item> Pittsburgh Steelers </list_item>
```

When XML is used as the form of document returned from an Ajax request, the response is returned in the `responseXML` property of the XHR object. This property has the DOM address of the DOM tree of the XML document. To extract the data from the XML document, its representation must be parsed. The DOM binding provides the tools for this parsing. (Some of these methods

were introduced in Chapter 5.) The data extracted from the XML could be
used to construct a new HTML document by means of DOM methods such as
`createElement` and `appendChild`. If the structure of the original HTML
document need not be changed, the `innerHTML` property can be employed
to change the content of any element, using the data parsed from the XML
document.

The process of parsing XML with DOM methods has two disadvantages:
Writing the parsing code is tedious and the resulting code is complex and error
prone. Also, support for the DOM parsing methods varies somewhat among
browsers.

An alternative to parsing the returned XML document in this manner is to use
XSLT style sheets to convert it to HTML, as illustrated in Chapter 7. This approach
is often easier and more likely to lead to reliable conversion. The converted document can then be inserted into the displayed document as in Section 10.2.

The XSLT document to convert the XML return document for our example
is as follows:

```
<xsl:stylesheet version = "1.0"
    xmlns:xsl = "http://www.w3.org/1999/XSL/Transform"
    xmlns = "http://www.w3.org/1999/xhtml" >
  <xsl:template match = "/">
    <h2> <xsl:value-of select = "header" /> </h2> <br /><br />
    <ul>
      <xsl:for-each select = "list_item">
        <li> <xsl:value-of select = "list_item" />
            <br />
        </li>
      </xsl:for-each>
    </ul>
  </xsl:template>
</xsl:stylesheet>
```

10.3.3 JavaScript Object Notation

JavaScript Object Notation (JSON) is based on a subset of standard JavaScript
(ECMA-262, 3rd edition). It is a textual way to represent objects by using two
structures: collections of name–value pairs and arrays of values. Our interest here
in JSON is that it can be used as a simpler alternative to XML for returning data
from the server in response to an Ajax request. The primary reason to use JSON
instead of XML is to eliminate the complexity of parsing. JSON is easy for people
to read and write, and it is easy for machines to parse and generate.

JSON is a way to represent JavaScript objects as strings. Objects are unordered sets of property–value pairs. Each object is delimited by braces. Each

property–value pair consists of a property name, represented as a literal string, a colon, and a value. The property–value pairs in an object are separated by commas. The values can be literal strings, numeric literals, arrays or other objects, `true`, `false`, or `null`. Arrays are delimited by brackets. The values in an array are separated by commas, as shown in the following example:

```
{"employees" :
    [
        {"name" : "Dew, Dawn", "address" : "1222 Wet Lane"},
        {"name" : "Do, Dick", "address" : "332 Doer Road"},
        {"name" : "Deau, Donna", "address" : "222 Donne Street"}
    ]
}
```

This object consists of one property–value pair, where the property value is `employees`, whose value is an array of three objects, each with two property–value pairs.

The individual data values in such an object can be retrieved with the usual syntax for array elements and object properties. For example, the following statement puts `"332 Doer Road"` into `address2`:

```
var address2 = myObj.employees[1].address;
```

Because JSON objects are represented as strings, they can be returned from the server as the `responseText` property of the XHR object. The JavaScript eval function could be used to convert JSON strings to JavaScript objects. However, this is a dangerous practice, because `eval` interprets any JavaScript code. The returned JSON could have been modified by some malicious person to be destructive JavaScript code. Therefore, the returned JSON string must be checked to determine whether it is just JSON data and not a script. This can be done with a JSON parser. One such parser is `parse`, a method of the `JSON` object, which is available from `http://www.JSON.org/json2.js`.

The `parse` function takes a `JSON` object as its parameter and returns a JavaScript object with the structure and data of the `JSON` object, as in the following code:

```
var response = xhr.responseText;
var myObj = JSON.parse(response);
```

JSON has a number of general advantages over XML. First, JSON representations are smaller, resulting in quicker transmission from the server. Second, the `parse` function is fast—much faster than manual parsing or the use of XSLT to translate XML. Third, using `parse` is far simpler than either manual parsing or using XSLT on XML documents.

XML is clearly superior to JSON if the data being fetched with Ajax is going to be integrated, more or less intact, into the displayed document. In this situation, it is easiest to use XSLT to translate the fetched XML into HTML: Using JSON would require the construction of the HTML document fragment manually, by using the JavaScript functions for building documents.

Of course, if the fetched data must be processed before it is integrated into some existing HTML element, then JSON may be the better choice, because if the data is in the form of HTML, it will need to be parsed before any processing can be done.

Rest assured that the choice between JSON and XML is controversial and that there are legions of rabid supporters of each who would not dream of using the other.

Our example return document in JSON would appear as follows:

```
{"top_two":
  [
    {"sport": "football", "team": "Green Bay Packers"},
    {"sport": "football", "team": "Pittsburgh Steelers"},
  ]
}
```

The processing of this data to place it in the HTML document is as follows:

```
var myObj = JSON.parse(response);
document.write("<h2> 2007 US Champion/Runnerup" +
               myObj.top_two[0].sport + "</h2>");
document.write("<ul> <li>" + myObj.top_two[0].team +
               "</li>");
document.write("<li>" + myObj.top_two[1].team +
               "</li></ul>");
```

Recent versions of the Ajax toolkit Prototype (see Section 10.4.2) allow data to be returned from the server through a special HTTP message header called X-JSON.

10.4 Ajax Toolkits

There are a large and growing number of toolkits for developing Ajax applications. Any survey of all of them would require an entire chapter of a book, and it would be obsolete long before it found the shelves of any bookstore. This section briefly introduces only two of the more commonly used toolkits, Dojo and Prototype, both of which assist in the development of client-side Ajax software.

There are also server-side Ajax development tools. Among the most commonly used of these are Google Web Toolkit (GWT) and Direct Web Remoting (DWR). GWT allows the development of Ajax software, which is normally written in JavaScript, in Java. The system includes a compiler that translates Java to JavaScript. This feature allows a Java developer to build Ajax applications without learning or using JavaScript directly. Another benefit is that Java code is generally thought to be more reliable than JavaScript code.

DWR is a remote procedure call library that makes it possible and convenient for JavaScript to call Java functions and vice versa. DWR also supports the exchange of data in virtually any data structure between the two languages. The server side is supported by a Java servlet running on the server.

Neither GWT nor DWR is discussed further here.

10.4.1   Dojo

The Dojo Toolkit is a free JavaScript library of modules that support many aspects of Web applications, including Ajax requests, animation of visual effects, drag and drop of document elements, and event handling. Dojo makes these tasks easier by providing some of the commonly needed code, in the form of functions, and by taking care of some cross-browser issues. As a result, Ajax requests that work on all common browsers are greatly simplified with Dojo. Another example of this simplification is the functions for manipulating the DOM. Dojo includes a collection of widgets for creating RIAs, so it is actually a toolkit for many parts of the process used to create dynamic Web sites, which naturally includes Ajax interactions. Because our interest here is focused on Ajax, only a small part of Dojo is discussed.

The Dojo Toolkit can be downloaded from the Web site `http://dojotoolkit.org`. For development purposes, Dojo can also be used directly from an AOL Web site, thereby eliminating the bother of the download and installation. The Web site is `http://o.aolcdn.com/dojo/0.4.2/dojo.js`. For software that is to be deployed, however, one should download the Dojo software and install it on the server machine. This approach avoids the dependence on AOL's continued support, as well as the security risk of using a third party's server and software.

The only part of Dojo described here is one of the most used Dojo functions for Ajax: `bind`. This function is included in the `io` module of the Dojo collection of modules. The name that must be used for this function in a script is `dojo.io.bind`. The purpose of `bind` is to create an XHR object and build an Ajax request.

To use any part of Dojo in a script, after downloading and installing it, the Dojo JavaScript file, `dojo.js`, must be imported with an element similar to the following:

```
<script type = "text/javascript"
  src = "dojo/dojo.js">
</script>
```

This element assumes that `dojo.js` is stored in the `dojo` subdirectory of the directory in which public markup documents are stored. To illustrate the use of `dojo.io.bind`, we will use Dojo to rewrite the `getPlace` request function from Section 10.2.6. Following is a copy of the original `getPlace` function:

```
// getPlace.js
//   Ajax JavaScript code for the popcornA.html document
//   This version is written to support all browsers


/**********************************************************/
// function getPlace
//   parameter: zip code
//   action:    create the XMLHttpRequest object, register the
//              handler for onreadystatechange, prepare to send
//              the request (with open), and send the request,
//              along with the zip code, to the server
//   includes: the anonymous handler for onreadystatechange,
//              which is the receiver function, which gets the
//              response text, splits it into city and state,
//              and puts them into the document
function getPlace(zip) {
  var xhr;


// Get the object for all browsers except IE5 and IE6
  if (window.XMLHttpRequest)
    xhr = new XMLHttpRequest();


// Otherwise get the object for IE5 and IE6
  else
    xhr = new ActiveXObject("Microsoft.XMLHTTP");


// Register the embedded receiver function as the handler
  xhr.onreadystatechange = function () {
    if (xhr.readyState == 4) {
      var result = xhr.responseText;
      var place = result.split(', ');
      if (document.getElementById("city").value == "")
        document.getElementById("city").value = place[0];
      if (document.getElementById("state").value == "")
        document.getElementById("state").value = place[1];
    }
  }
  xhr.open("GET", "getCityState.php?zip=" + zip);
  xhr.send(null);
}
```

The `bind` function takes a single literal object parameter. Recall that an object literal is a list of property–value pairs, separated by commas and delimited by braces. Each property name is separated from its associated value with a colon. The values can be any expression, including anonymous function definitions. The parameter to `bind` must have the two properties `url` and `load`. In addition, it should have `method`, `error`, and `mimetype` properties. The value of the `url` property is the URL of the server to which the request is to be sent. The value of the `load` property is a function that uses the data returned by the server as a result of the request. For both the `load` and `error` functions, directly defined anonymous functions are used. The value of the `method` property is either `"GET"` or `"POST"`. The value of the `error` property is a function that is called if there is an error in processing the request. Finally, `mimetype` is the MIME type of the returned data.

The call to `bind` that does what the `getPlace` function does is as follows:

```
dojo.io.bind({
  url:  "getCityState.php?zip=" + zip,
  load: function (type, data, evt) {
              var place = data.split(', ');
              if (dojo.byId("city").value == "")
                dojo.byId("city").value = place[0];
              if (dojo.byId("state").value == "")
                dojo.byId("state").value = place[1];
            },
  error: function (type, data, evt) {
              alert("Error in request, returned data: " + data);
            },
  method: "GET",
  mimetype: "text/plain"
});
```

10.4.2   An Example

In this section, an example of using Dojo to create an Ajax application is developed. Many people now shop on the Web for practically every kind of product. One of the many small frustrations of shopping on the Web is the following: The shopper is trying to purchase an article of clothing. After choosing a particular item, a size is selected from a list. Next, a color is chosen. If the particular size and color of the item happens not to be in stock at the time, the server returns a new document to indicate that fact to the user. This takes time to transmit to the browser and still more time to render. The user, when informed, must start over again. This small frustration can be avoided by having the site present only the colors and sizes of the chosen item that are currently in stock. Then the user can choose among the available colors, rather than possibly choosing a color that is not in stock. With the use of Ajax, the time required to return the available colors will be short. Furthermore, only the list of colors need be returned and rendered as a menu by the browser.

The original document for the example will be a document for one specific shirt. It will include a brief description of the shirt and a menu of the sizes available. It will also include a title and an empty menu for the colors. The color menu will be constructed when the Ajax request returns the available colors. The original document, named `shirt.html`, is as follows:

```
<!DOCTYPE html>
<!-- shirt.html
     Use Ajax to get the available colors of shirts
     -->
<html lang = "en">
  <head>
    <title> Shirt orders </title>
    <meta charset = "utf-8" />
    <script type = "text/javascript"
            src = "dojo/dojo.js">
    </script>
    <script type = "text/javascript"  src = "shirt.js">
    </script>
    <link rel = "stylesheet"  type = "text/css"
          href = "shirtstyles.css" />
  </head>
  <body>
    <h3> Shirt Style 425 - broadcloth, short sleeve,
         button-down collar </h3>
    <form>
      Size selection:
      <select name = "sizes"  onchange = "getColors(this.value)" >
        <option value = ""> 00 </option>
        <option value = "14.5"> 14 &frac12; </option>
        <option value = "15"> 15 </option>
        <option value = "15.5"> 15 &frac12; </option>
        <option value = "16"> 16 </option>
        <option value = "16.5"> 16 &frac12; </option>
        <option value = "17"> 17 </option>
        <option value = "17.5"> 17 &frac12; </option>
        <option value = "18"> 18 </option>
      </select>
```

```
        <div class = "colors"
             id = "colorlist"> Colors available and in stock:
        <select id = "colorselect">
        </select>
      </div>
    </form>
  </body>
</html>
```

Notice that one script tag in this document references the `dojo.js` script and another references another JavaScript file, `shirt.js`. The `div` element at the bottom of the document will be the target of the data that will be returned by the Ajax request. This data will be placed in a select element that will be built by the Ajax callback function. The style sheet for this document is as follows:

```
/* shirtstyles.css - style sheet for shirt.html */
h3 {color: blue}
div.colors {position: absolute; left: 200px; top: 55px;}
```

The initial display of `shirt.html` is shown in Figure 10.5.

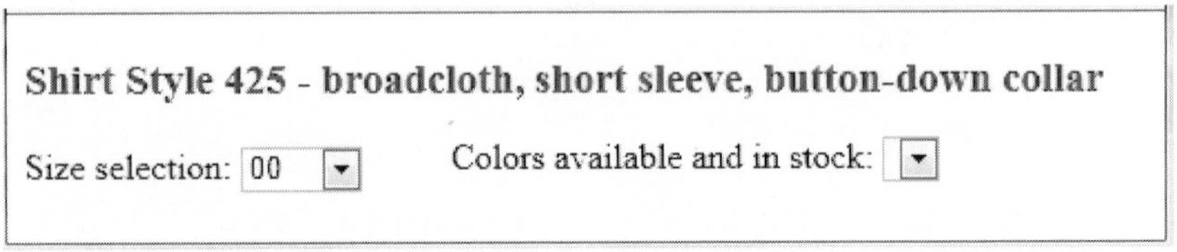

Shirt Style 425 - broadcloth, short sleeve, button-down collar

Size selection: 00 ▾   Colors available and in stock: ▾

Figure 10.5 The initial display of `shirt.html`

The JavaScript for the shirt application defines two functions: the callback function for the Ajax request, `buildMenu`, which builds the menu of colors, and a wrapper function, `getColors`, that includes the call to the actual request function, `dojo.io.bind`, which creates the request. The function `dojo.io.bind` comes from the `dojo.js` script.

First, the `buildMenu` function gets the DOM address of the initially empty select element. Then, in case this is not the first request, the `options` property of the select element is set to 0 (to empty the select). Next, `buildMenu` splits the value returned by the request, which is a string of color names separated by commas and spaces. This places the colors in the array `colors`. Then, `buildMenu` iterates through the colors array, building a new Options object for each element (color). The color is sent to the Options constructor and becomes the value of the option. Finally, the new Options object is added to the select object with the add method. Unfortunately, the second parameter to the add method is browser dependent. For the IE browsers, it must be set to –1 to indicate that the option is not initially set. For other browsers, it must be set to null. This problem is handled with a try-catch clause. If add is called with –1 as the second parameter and the browser is not IE, an exception is raised, which executes the catch clause that uses null as the second parameter.

The getColors callback function contains only the call to dojo.io.bind. The url is set to getColors.php with the size parameter attached (because the request is made with the GET method). The complete JavaScript file, shirt.js, is as follows:

```
// shirt.js
//  Ajax JavaScript code for the shirt.html document
//  Uses Dojo

// The function that builds the menu of colors
function buildMenu(type, data, evt) {
  var menuDOM = document.getElementById("colorselect");
  var nextColor, nextItem;

// Delete previous items in the color menu
  menuDOM.options.length = 0;

// Split the data into an array of colors
  var colors = data.split(', ');

// Go through the returned array of colors
  for (index = 0; index < colors.length; index++) {
    nextColor = colors[index];
    nextItem = new Option(nextColor);

// Add the new item to the menu
    try {
      menuDOM.add(nextItem, -1);
    }
    catch (e) {
      menuDOM.add(nextItem, null);
    }
  }
}
```

```
// The function that calls bind to request data
function getColors(size) {
  dojo.io.bind( {url: "getColors.php" + "?size=" + size,
             load: buildMenu,
             method: "GET",
             mimetype: "text/plain"
             } );
}
```

If `shirt.html` were a real application, the response document would be produced by a program that searched the company's inventory and produced a list of colors for the given size that were currently in stock. To test `shirt.html`, however, a PHP script that simply returns a string of color names was used.

Figure 10.6 shows the display after a size has been selected and the request has returned a list of colors, which have been used to build a select element.

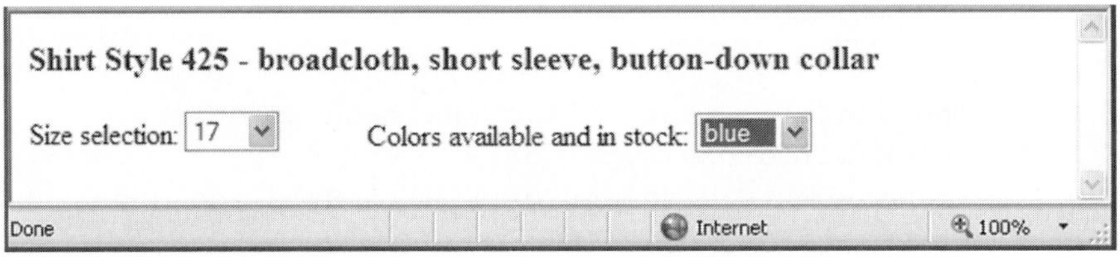

Figure 10.6 Display of `shirt.html` after a size has been selected

10.4.3   Prototype

Prototype is a toolkit for JavaScript. In addition to providing tools for Ajax, it extends the JavaScript language. For example, Prototype provides a more powerful way of supporting inheritance through its `Class` module. Prototype was written by Sam Stephenson, who works on the Rails team. Its original purpose was to provide the JavaScript tools needed to support the Rails framework for constructing Web software applications. In Chapter 15 the JavaScript tools in Prototype are used, although some of them are wrapped in Ruby methods. Prototype can be downloaded from `http://prototypejs.org`.

The Prototype toolkit includes a large number of functions that provide shortcuts to, and abbreviations of, commonly needed JavaScript code. The only one of these used here is the abbreviation for `document.getElementById`, which is simply a dollar sign ($). For example, the following two assignment statements are equivalent in Prototype:

```
document.getElementById("name").value = "Freddie";
$("name").value = "Freddie";
```

Although a description of Prototype is a long story, our discussion here is brief, because our interest is focused on Ajax. All of the Ajax functionality of

Prototype is encapsulated in the `Ajax` object. An Ajax request with Prototype is strikingly similar to one in Dojo. The request is made by creating an object of the `Ajax.Request` type, sending the relevant parameters to the constructor for the new object. Requests with `Ajax.Request` are asynchronous by default. The first parameter of the `Ajax.Request` constructor is the URL of the server to which the request is being made. The second parameter is a literal object with a list of relevant information.

The parameters, which are properties of the second parameter of `Ajax.Request`, are similar to those of the `bind` function of Dojo. The most commonly used parameters are the following: The value of the `method` parameter is either `"get"` or `"post"`, with the default being `"post"`. The value of the `parameters` property is the parameters that are to be attached to the URL of a `get` method. For example, for the zip code example, the value of the `parameters` property would be `"zip="` + `zip`. The value of the `onSuccess` property is the callback function to handle the data returned by the server in response to the request in those cases where the request succeeded. The value of the `onFailure` property is the callback function for those cases where the request failed. Following is an example of the creation of an `Ajax.Request` object:

```
new Ajax.request("getCityState.php", {
  method: "get",
  parameters: "zip=" + zip,
  onSuccess: function(request) {
            var place = request.responseText.split(', ');
            $("city").value = place[0];
            $("state").value = place[1];
          }
  onFailure: function(request) {
            alert("Error - request failed");
          }
} );
```

Prototype serves as the basis for several other toolkits, two of the most popular among them being Script.aculo.us and Rico.

10.5 **Security and Ajax**

Section 1.8 introduced the topic of security issues associated with the Web. Ajax-enabled Web applications create new opportunities for security breaches. They also require some new approaches to Web security testing. This section introduces some of the vulnerabilities of Ajax applications and suggests ways developers can guard against them in some cases.

An Ajax application requires client-side JavaScript code, and complex applications require a good deal of it. There is a temptation on the part of developers of this code to include security controls, in part because they formerly wrote server-side code, the natural home of security controls. However, security controls in client-side software are not effective, because intruders can change the code running on the client. Therefore, security controls must be designed into server-side software, even if they also appear in the client-side software.

Non-Ajax applications often have only one or a few server-side response programs, each of which produces significant content. Ajax applications frequently have a much larger number of response programs, each of which is small and handles only requests for changes in one small part of the initial document. This increase in the number of server response programs increases the attack surface of the whole application, providing more opportunities for intruders.

Cross-site scripting provides another opportunity for intruders. Ajax applications often return JavaScript code to the client. Such code could be modified by an intruder to include destructive operations. To protect against this possibility, any JavaScript code returned by the server must be scanned before it is interpreted. Another version of the problem may appear when text boxes are used to collect information returned from the server. The text box could include a script tag that includes malicious JavaScript code. Therefore, such received text should be scanned for script tags.

Summary

Ajax is a relatively new technology for building Web applications that can implement relatively quick updates to parts of documents. Asynchronous requests are made to the server, allowing users to continue to interact with the browser while the request is being handled. JavaScript code is used to create the Ajax request object. Any server software can be used to generate the response. JavaScript is again used to receive the new partial document and insert it into the currently displayed document.

Internet Explorer browsers prior to IE7 must be handled differently, because the object used to make asynchronous requests has a different name in the JavaScript supported by those browsers.

The request phase of an Ajax request for data has several tasks: It must create the object to be used for the request, register the callback function to handle the returned data, call the `open` method of the request object, and actually send the object to the server. The request object is browser dependent, so the request function must take this into account. The response document for an Ajax request can be a simple PHP script that creates the return data. It could be any program or script that returns data. The receiver phase of an Ajax communication, the callback function, is called several times by the server. When the `readyState` property of the request object is `4` and the `status` property is `200`, the callback function can process the returned data. Processing ultimately uses the data, either directly or indirectly, to update part of the displayed document.

The form of the returned document, or data, varies widely. It can be HTML or HTML, XML, pure text, or even JavaScript code to be interpreted on the browser. It could also be JSON, which is a compact data form that is part of JavaScript.

Many toolkits and frameworks support the production of Web sites that use Ajax. Dojo and Prototype are two of the most common of the toolkits. Both relieve the developer of cross-browser concerns and make writing Ajax requests much easier.

Ajax brings its own set of issues to the problem of security. One of these is the temptation of developers who formerly worked on the server side to place security controls in client-side code, where they are far less effective. Another is that Ajax applications have more server-side scripts, each of which can be a security risk. Also, cross-site scripting, which is used in some Ajax applications, creates new opportunities for intruders.

Review Questions

10.1   What is the goal of the use of Ajax in a Web application?

10.2   What does it mean for a request to be asynchronous?

10.3   What new languages are employed to program Web applications that use Ajax?

10.4   What new software must be installed on a browser or server to run Web applications that use Ajax?

10.5   What is required for an Ajax application to run on both IE6 and the latest versions of browsers?

10.6   What is stored in the `readyState` property of an XHR object?

10.7   What is a callback function in an Ajax application?

10.8   What is the purpose of the `onreadystatechange` property of the XHR object?

10.9   Under what circumstances would one use the `POST` method for an Ajax request?

10.10   How are parameters passed in a `GET` Ajax request?

10.11   Under what circumstances is HTML used for the return data for an Ajax request?

10.12   What is the disadvantage of using HTML for the return data for an Ajax request?

10.13   When XML is used for the return data for an Ajax request, where does the callback function find it?

10.14 What are the two ways XML is used in the callback function?

10.15 What two data types provide the forms of the data in a JSON string?

10.16 What property of the XHR object stores the JSON data from an Ajax request?

10.17 What is the danger of using `eval` to process a JSON string?

10.18 What are the two major advantages of JSON over XML for the response data from an Ajax request?

10.19 For simple Ajax applications, what is the advantage of using Dojo?

10.20 For what framework was Prototype developed?

10.21 Explain how Ajax applications have a larger attack surface than traditional Web applications.

10.22 What is cross-site scripting and why does it create security problems?

Exercises

10.1 Explain the two characteristics of Ajax that help it achieve its goals.

10.2 Explain why the callback function is written as an anonymous function in the request phase function.

10.3 Modify the example application of Section 10.2 to have it provide the addresses of repeat customers, using a hash of names and addresses.

10.4 Modify the example application of Section 10.2 to have it validate the zip code when it is entered, to ensure that it is a valid zip code for the given city and state. The response document can be a PHP script that looks up the zip code and the city and state in a small table of examples.

10.5 Modify the example application of Section 10.2 to use Dojo.

10.6 Modify the example application of Section 10.2 to use Prototype.

10.7 Modify the example application of Section 10.4 to use Prototype.

10.8 Modify the example application of Section 10.4 to allow the user to select a make and model of used cars. The make must be in a menu. When a make is chosen, a menu of models must be displayed. This menu is produced by hardwired data in the original document. When a model is chosen, an Ajax request must be made to get a list of the years and colors of the chosen make and model that are available. Make up a server-resident script to produce the data from an example array or hash.

Java Web Software

This chapter discusses Java server-based software, specifically servlets, JavaServer Pages, JavaBeans, and JavaServer Faces. First, we introduce servlets, including their general structure and common uses. We then discuss the servlet methods for handling GET and POST HTTP requests. Next, we use a simple example to illustrate the basics of servlets. Following this, we introduce the NetBeans IDE. We then illustrate the use of NetBeans by using it to redevelop the previously presented servlet example.

Next, we discuss cookies[1] and describe how they can be implemented with servlets. A complete application is developed to demonstrate the use of cookies in a servlet.

The last three sections of the chapter introduce technologies built on top of servlets: JavaServer Pages (JSP), the JSP Standard Tag Library (JSTL), the JSP Expression Language (EL), JavaBeans, and JavaServer Faces (JSF). The same application is repeated four times, once with two JSP documents using the EL,

---

1. Cookies are also discussed in Chapter 9.

once with one JSP document using the EL, once with a JavaBean class, and once with JSF, which also uses a JavaBean class.

11.1   Introduction to Servlets

This section describes the structure and use of servlets. Servlets were the first Java technology targeted to Web server-side software.

11.1.1   Overview

A servlet is a Java object that is executed on a Web server system that responds to HTTP requests. In this chapter such requests are created by browsers while they display markup documents, although HTTP requests can have several different origins. The servlet class normally is instantiated when the Web server receives an HTTP request for the URL that addresses the servlet. The execution of servlets is managed by a *servlet container*, sometimes called a *servlet engine*. The servlet container may run in the same process as the Web server, in a different process on the server host machine, or even on a different machine. The servlet request and response processes are supported with the HTTP protocol, so the servlet must respond to the HTTP GET or POST method, or both. A servlet container might also define and enforce security restrictions on the execution of its servlets. Section 11.1.3 briefly discusses a few of the currently popular servlet containers.

When an HTTP request is received by a Web server, the Web server examines the request. If a servlet must be called, the Web server passes the request to the servlet container. The container determines which servlet must be executed, ensures that it is loaded, and calls it. A call to a servlet passes two parameter objects: one for the request and one for the response. The servlet receives the input data associated with the request through the request object, which may include form data as well as the identity of the requesting client. As the servlet handles the request, it dynamically generates an HTTP response. In many cases, the response is a markup document that is returned to the server through the response object parameter. The process of handling the request (by the servlet) is accomplished in part by calling methods on the request and response objects. When finished, the servlet container returns control to the Web server.

Servlets are often used to generate responses to browser requests dynamically. They are also used as alternatives to server extensions, such as Apache modules, which users can write and add to an Apache server to extend its capabilities.

The use of a servlet to access a database is discussed in Chapter 13.

11.1.2   Details

All servlets either implement the Servlet interface or extend a class that implements it. The Servlet interface, which is defined in the javax.servlet package, declares the methods that manage servlets and their interactions with clients. The author of a servlet must provide definitions of these methods.

Most user-written servlets are extensions to the predefined class HttpServlet, which implements the Servlet interface.

In addition to the Servlet interface, the javax.servlet package contains several other interfaces required for implementing servlets. The ServletRequest and ServletResponse interfaces encapsulate the communication from the client to the servlet and from the servlet back to the client, respectively. The Servlet-Request interface provides servlet access to ServletInputStream, through which input from the client flows. The ServletResponse interface provides servlet access to ServletOutputStream, as well as a method for sending information, usually in the form of a markup document, back to the client.

Every subclass of HttpServlet must override at least one of the methods of HttpServlet, the most common of which are shown in Table 11.1.

Table 11.1 Commonly used methods of HttpServlet

Method	Purpose
doGet	To handle HTTP GET requests
doPost	To handle HTTP POST requests
doPut	To handle HTTP PUT requests
doDelete	To handle HTTP DELETE requests

The doGet, doPost, doPut, and doDelete methods are called by the server. The HTTP PUT request allows a client to send a file to be stored on the server. The HTTP DELETE request allows a client to delete a document or Web page from the server. In many cases, users are not allowed to add files to the server or delete files that are stored on the server. The doGet and doPost methods are the focus of this section because they are the most frequently used of the HttpServlet methods.

The protocol of the doGet method is as follows:

```
protected void doGet (HttpServletRequest request,
                      HttpServletResponse response)
    throws ServletException, IOException
```

ServletException is a subclass of Exception that serves as a wrapper for every kind of general servlet problem. IOException can be thrown for the usual reasons. In the preceding protocol model, request and response are the names we have chosen to be the reference variables for the request and response objects, respectively. The HttpServletRequest object parameter, request, contains the client request; the HttpServletResponse object parameter, response, provides the means to communicate the response that the servlet sends back to the client.

The protocol of the doPost method is the same as that of doGet.

Servlet output to the requesting client usually is created by defining a `Print-Writer` object, created by calling the `getWriter` method of the response object. The `PrintWriter` class provides a collection of methods, such as `println`, that sends response markup to the client through the response object. The `Print-Writer` object is created with the following declaration:

```
PrintWriter out = response.getWriter();
```

Before any output can be created with the `PrintWriter` methods, the content type of the return document must be set. This is done with the `set-ContentType` method of the `HttpServletResponse` object, as shown in the following call:

```
response.setContentType("text/html");
```

Now the `println` method of the `out` object can be used to generate the markup document to be returned to the requesting client.

We are now ready to look at a complete servlet example. This servlet simply responds to a call from a form that uses the GET HTTP method. The form sends no data and requires no processing, so the only action of the servlet is to produce a markup document with a message to indicate that the call was received. The call to the servlet, which appears in the form tag, specifies the servlet as the value of the form tag's `action` attribute. The following is the document that will call the servlet:

```html
<!DOCTYPE html>
<!-- tstGreet.html
     Used to test the servlet Greet
     -->
<html lang = "en">
  <head>
    <title> Test greeting </title>
    <meta charset = "utf-8" />
  </head>
  <body>
    <form action = "Greet"  method = "get">
      <p>
        Press the button to run the servlet
        <input type = "submit" value = "Run Servlet" />
      </p>
    </form>
  </body>
</html>
```

Figure 11.1 shows the display created by `tstGreet.html`.

Figure 11.1 Display of `tstGreet.html`

The `Greet` servlet class extends `HttpServlet` and implements the `doGet` method, which produces the markup response to the browser call. Following is a listing of the `Greet` servlet:

```java
/*  Greet.java
    A servlet to illustrate a simple GET request
    */
import java.io.IOException;
import java.io.PrintWriter;
import javax.servlet.ServletException;
import javax.servlet.http.HttpServlet;
import javax.servlet.http.HttpServletRequest;
import javax.servlet.http.HttpServletResponse;

public class Greet extends HttpServlet {
  public void doGet(HttpServletRequest request,
                    HttpServletResponse response)
  throws ServletException, IOException {
      response.setContentType("text/html");
      PrintWriter out = response.getWriter();
      out.println("<html><head><title>");
      out.println("A simple GET servlet");
      out.println("</title></head><body>");
      out.println(
          "<h2> This is your servlet answering - hi! </h2>");
      out.println("</body></html>");
  }
}
```

Figure 11.2 shows the response from the `Greet` servlet.

This is your servlet answering – hi!

Figure 11.2 Response from the Greet servlet

Notice that the markup document produced by this servlet is bare-bones HTML, without a DOCTYPE, the language attribute in the html element, and the meta element to specify the character coding.

The Greet servlet and the markup document that calls it are written with a Servlet specification that was in effect before 2003. To run the application, the two files would need to be placed in directories specified by the particular servlet container being used. Then a browser could be pointed to the markup document to run the application. The problem with this approach was that such an application could not be ported easily from one servlet container to another, because they all used different directory structures for the two files.

The problem was alleviated with the appearance of a new Servlet specification in late 2003, which is further discussed in Section 11.2.

So, the Greet servlet is presented here only for illustrative purposes, not as a servlet to be run on a servlet container, since we did not describe the other parts required to run it.

11.1.3   Servlet Containers

There are now a number of servlet containers available. One of the most popular is the Apache Tomcat (formerly Apache Jakarta Tomcat) servlet container, which is available free from the Apache Group at http://tomcat.apache .org/. Tomcat can run as a stand-alone servlet container or as part of a Web server.

There are also several application servers[2] that include servlet containers. Among these are GlassFish, which is an application server for Java EE. It is distributed as part of Java EE, but it can also be obtained from https:// glassfish.dev.java.net/public/downloadsindex.html. GlassFish, which includes a derivative of Tomcat as its servlet container, is a free open-source product.

BEA and IBM developed and now market commercial application servers for Java software that include servlet containers. The BEA WebLogic Server is an application server for Java EE (http://www.bea.com). IBM's WebSphere Application Server (http://www.ibm.com/websphere) supports all forms of Java applications and includes a servlet container.

The application server GlassFish was used to run the servlets in this chapter.

Figure 11.3 shows the processing flow of the use of a servlet.

---

2. An application server provides access to business logic to client application programs through several different protocols, including HTTP. So, an application server is a generalization of a Web server.

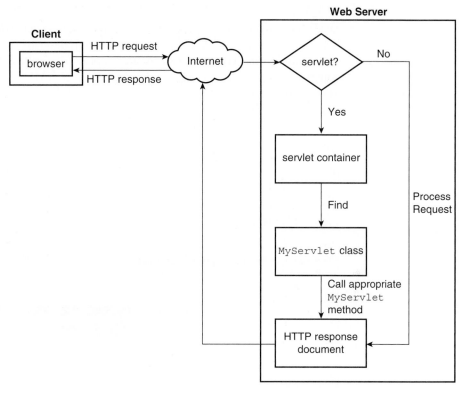

Figure 11.3 The processing flow of the use of the servlet `MyServlet`

11.2 The NetBeans Integrated Development Environment

During the first part of the evolution of servlet technology, it was relatively simple to deploy a servlet for a specific server that supported servlets. The most commonly used servlet container was Tomcat. For example, in the fourth edition of this book, the servlets were deployed for Tomcat by creating a subdirectory under the main directory of the document tree and placing the compiled servlet class in that directory. The servlet was referenced with its address relative to the main document directory. The `Greet` servlet example in Section 11.1 is written as though it would be run in this outdated way.

Deployment became far more complicated with the arrival and use of a collection of servlet containers. It became difficult to deploy a servlet that could be run by different servers. To alleviate this problem, a standard packaging scheme was developed with the release of the Servlet 2.2 specification in 2003. An application is now packaged as a WAR file. WAR files can be built and disassembled with tools that build and disassemble Zip files, because they have the same structure. The file structure that resides in a WAR file is complex. Partly because of this complexity, many people now avoid developing servlets without the assistance of development tools. We could describe the process of developing a complete WAR file for our `Greet` example of Section 11.1, but such a description would be lengthy and complicated. Therefore, this section describes how to use NetBeans, a commonly used IDE for creating and deploying servlets. NetBeans implicitly constructs the required WAR file structure and the XML deployment file, as well as skeletal versions of the calling markup file and the servlet file, for the application being built. Of course, a complete description of NetBeans is far beyond the scope of this book. Therefore, we will discuss only the subset of NetBeans necessary to develop a few simple examples.

NetBeans is available free from `http://www.netbeans.org`. The version illustrated in this section is version 7.0.

The narrative that follows describes building the application that implements the `Greet` servlet with NetBeans. After starting NetBeans, the screen shown in Figure 11.4 is displayed.

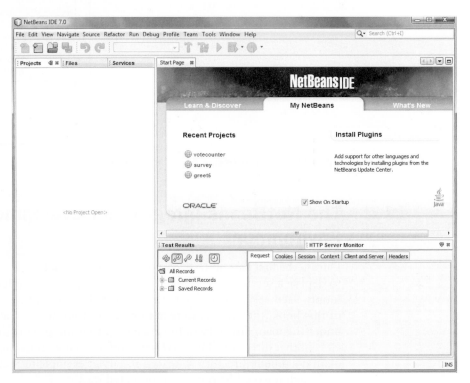

Figure 11.4 The initial screen upon starting NetBeans

The most useful part of this screen is the panel in the upper-left corner, which contains a list of the existing projects. Every project has its own directory, which is the same as the project name. Any of the existing projects can be opened by clicking its name in this list.

To create a new project, we select *File/New Project* from the screen shown in Figure 11.4. This brings up the screen shown in Figure 11.5.

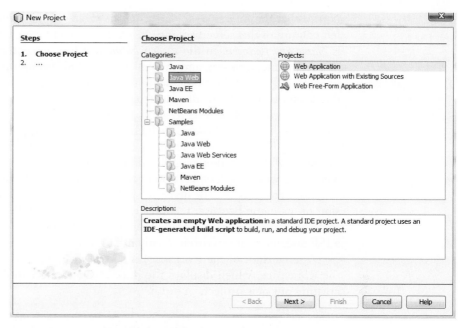

Figure 11.5 The *New Project* screen

From this screen, we select the *Java Web* category and the *Web Application* project. We then click *Next* to get to the next screen, as shown in Figure 11.6.

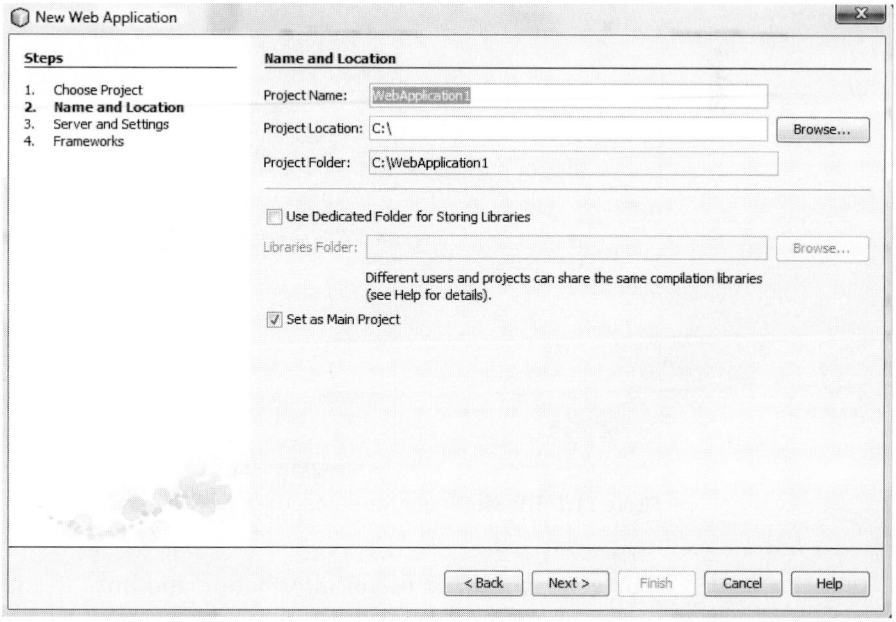

Figure 11.6 The *New Web Application* screen

Notice that the four steps for creating the skeleton of a project are listed in the left column of this screen (Figure 11.6). The current step, which is highlighted, is *Name and Location*. In the *Project Name* text box, we enter our choice for the project's name, `greetn`, and then click *Next*. This brings up the *Server and Settings* screen, which shows the default server, the default version of Java EE, and the default context path, all of which are appropriate for our example. From this screen, we could click *Next* to get to the screen for the fourth step, from which a framework can be chosen in which to develop the application—for example, *JavaServer Faces* or *Struts*. Because we will not use a framework (other than the NetBeans IDE) to build our application, we click *Finish*. This opens the NetBeans workspace with a skeletal version of the initial markup document of the project, which is named (by NetBeans) `index.jsp`. The document has the `.jsp` extension on its name because, technically, it is a JavaServer Page (JSP) document. JSP is discussed in Section 11.6. Although the document we are working with is a JSP document, it is written mostly in HTML.

A screenshot of the workspace is shown in Figure 11.7. This figure shows the workspace, which displays the initial skeletal markup document, just after creating our new project, `greetn`.

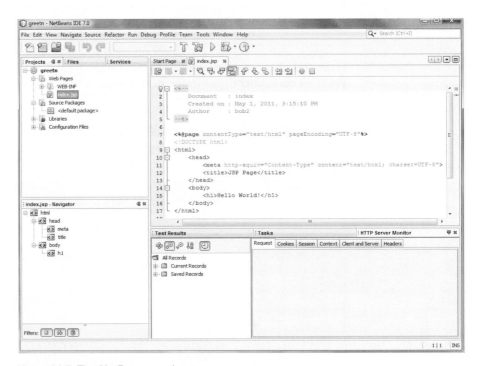

Figure 11.7 The NetBeans workspace

There is a wealth of useful information and links to tools on the workspace screen. Across the top is a list of menus, many of which are similar to those of other systems, such as *File*, *Edit*, *Tools*, and *Help*. Immediately below these menus is a toolbar of icons, some of which we will use to construct our example applications.

In the upper-left area of the screen is a window with the title *Projects*, which lists the names of projects that have been created with the installation of Net-Beans. The greetn item has been clicked, displaying a list of subdirectories for this project. The *Web Pages* directory has the markup file of the project, index .jsp, which will call the servlet; the *Source Packages* directory has a subdirectory, *<default package>*, which will contain the servlet class. Both have been expanded by clicking the plus signs to their left.

The center panel shows the skeletal markup document of the project. This document, created by NetBeans, is discussed shortly.

If we select *Tools/Palette/HTML/JSP Code Clips*, we open the *Palette Manager* window. Figure 11.8 shows this window after we have expanded the *HTML* and *HTMLForms* items.

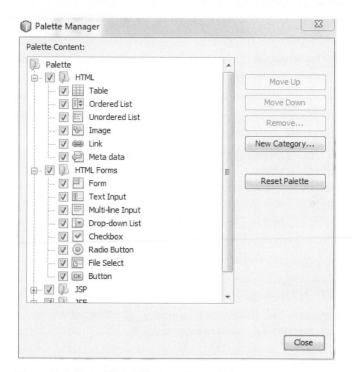

Figure 11.8 The *HTML/JSP Code Clips* window

The entries for JSP and JSF are described later in this chapter. Any of the elements in the palette can be dragged onto the document in the center panel. This feature is an aid to writing markup—it allows the author to avoid some typing. It also makes it easier to get the syntax correct. If you begin to type an element into the document, NetBeans attempts to help by supplying a menu of elements that you might want, based on the first one or two letters typed. This feature is another aid to markup creation.

The style of the document index.jsp generated by NetBeans does not match the style we have used for markup documents. It includes JSP comments and a JSP page directive, so it is not strictly an HTML document.

The next step in the construction of the application is to type the body of the document index.jsp (from tstGreet.html in Section 11.1) into the skeletal document provided by NetBeans. After the body has been entered, we save the document (by selecting *File/Save*). To verify that the document display is what was wanted, we build and run the project by selecting *Run/Run Main Project*.[3] This opens a browser window and displays the content of index.jsp, which is exactly as is shown in Figure 11.1.

The NetBeans template for servlets includes a number of statements that we choose not to have in our servlets. In this case, we modify the template so that all of our servlet examples begin with just the statements we want them to have. To modify the template, we select *Tools/Templates* and expand the *Web* directory entry, selecting *Servlet*, and then click *Open in Editor*. Just to see the servlet template provided by NetBeans, we created a servlet named junkx, which follows:

```
/*
 * To change this template, choose Tools | Templates
 * and open the template in the editor.
 */

import java.io.IOException;
import java.io.PrintWriter;
import javax.servlet.ServletException;
import javax.servlet.annotation.WebServlet;
import javax.servlet.http.HttpServlet;
import javax.servlet.http.HttpServletRequest;
import javax.servlet.http.HttpServletResponse;

/**
 *
 * @author bob7
 */
@WebServlet(name = "junkx", urlPatterns = {"/junkx"})
public class junkx extends HttpServlet {

    /**
     * Processes requests for both HTTP <code>GET</code> and
     *    <code>POST</code> methods.
     * @param request servlet request
     * @param response servlet response
     * @throws ServletException if a servlet-specific
     *    error occurs
     * @throws IOException if an I/O error occurs
```

---

3. In versions prior to 7.0 of NetBeans, it was necessary to first build a project before running it.

```
     */
    protected void processRequest(HttpServletRequest request,
                                  HttpServletResponse response)
        throws ServletException, IOException {
      response.setContentType("text/html;charset=UTF-8");
      PrintWriter out = response.getWriter();
      try {
          /* TODO output your page here
          out.println("<html>");
          out.println("<head>");
          out.println("<title>Servlet junkx</title>");
          out.println("</head>");
          out.println("<body>");
          out.println("<h1>Servlet junkx at " +
                       request.getContextPath () + "</h1>");
          out.println("</body>");
          out.println("</html>");
          */
      } finally {
          out.close();
      }
    }


    // <editor-fold defaultstate="collapsed"
    //    desc="HttpServlet methods.
    // Click on the + sign on the left to edit the code.">
    /**
     * Handles the HTTP <code>GET</code> method.
     * @param request servlet request
     * @param response servlet response
     * @throws ServletException if a servlet-specific
     *    error occurs
     * @throws IOException if an I/O error occurs
     */
    @Override
    protected void doGet(HttpServletRequest request,
                         HttpServletResponse response)
        throws ServletException, IOException {
      processRequest(request, response);
    }

    /**
     * Handles the HTTP <code>POST</code> method.
     * @param request servlet request
     * @param response servlet response
     * @throws ServletException if a servlet-specific
     *    error occurs
```

```
     * @throws IOException if an I/O error occurs
     */
    @Override
    protected void doPost(HttpServletRequest request,
                          HttpServletResponse response)
            throws ServletException, IOException {
        processRequest(request, response);
    }

    /**
     * Returns a short description of the servlet.
     * @return a String containing servlet description
     */
    @Override
    public String getServletInfo() {
        return "Short description";
    }// </editor-fold>
}
```

There are many parts of this template that we neither need nor want in our servlets. These include all of the comments, the try-finally construct in the processRequest method, and the whole getServletInfo method. After making the desired changes, we select *File/Save All* to save the new version of the servlet template:

```
/* Initial comments
   */

import java.io.IOException;
import java.io.PrintWriter;
import javax.servlet.ServletException;
import javax.servlet.http.HttpServlet;
import javax.servlet.http.HttpServletRequest;
import javax.servlet.http.HttpServletResponse;


public class ${name} extends HttpServlet {

    protected void processRequest(HttpServletRequest request,
                                  HttpServletResponse response)
        throws ServletException, IOException {
        response.setContentType("text/html;charset=UTF-8");
        PrintWriter out = response.getWriter();
        out.println("<html>");
        out.println("<head>");
        out.println("<title>Servlet ${name}</title>");
        out.println("</head>");
        out.println("<body>");
```

```
              out.println("<h1>Servlet ${name} at " +
                     request.getContextPath () + "</h1>");
          out.println("</body>");
          out.println("</html>");
      }

      protected void doGet(HttpServletRequest request,
                          HttpServletResponse response)
      throws ServletException, IOException {
          processRequest(request, response);
      }

      protected void doPost(HttpServletRequest request,
                           HttpServletResponse response)
      throws ServletException, IOException {
          processRequest(request, response);
      }
  }
```

Now we can create our example servlet from the new template. To begin this task, we right-click the project name (in the upper-left panel) and select *New/Servlet*, which produces the screen shown in Figure 11.9.

On this screen, we enter the name of the servlet, `Greet`, and click *Finish*. (The name of the servlet file is now `Greet.java`.) This produces the workspace with a template version of the servlet in the center panel.

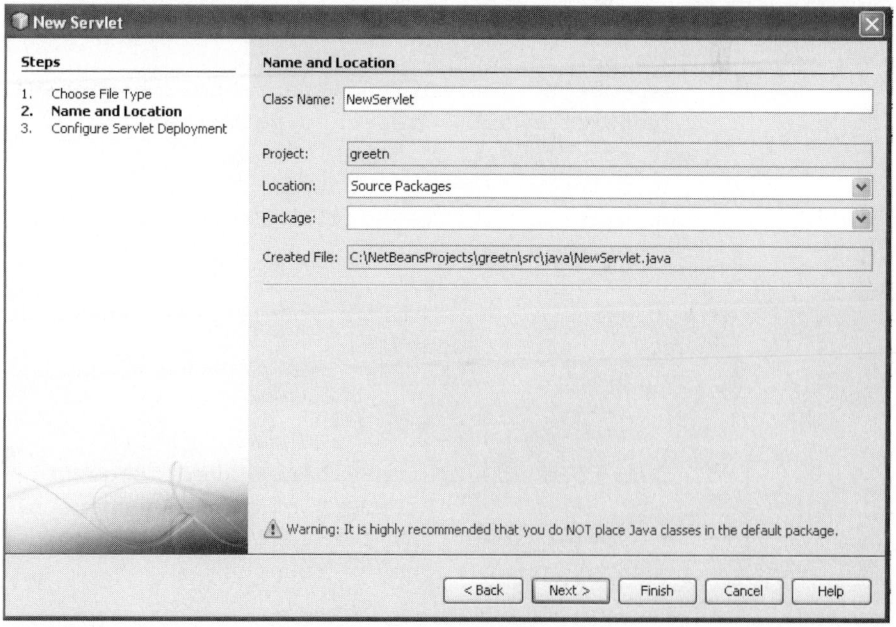

Figure 11.9 The *New Servlet* screen

This template servlet includes three methods: `processRequest`, `doGet`, and `doPost`. The `processRequest` method is called by both `doGet` and `doPost`, so it is where everything happens. Including both `doGet` and `doPost` allows the servlet to be called with either method. To build a servlet for a specific application, you modify the template's `processRequest` method to have it do what the application needs to do.

To build our greeting servlet, we can add the central parts of the original `Greet.java` from Section 11.1 to the `processRequest` method. When we type Java code into the workspace, the code is immediately checked for syntactic correctness. Lines with syntax errors are underlined in red.

Following is the listing of the `Greet` servlet created with NetBeans:

```java
/* Greet.java - a trivial servlet written with NetBeans that
               only returns a greeting
   */

import java.io.IOException;
import java.io.PrintWriter;
import javax.servlet.ServletException;
import javax.servlet.http.HttpServlet;
import javax.servlet.http.HttpServletRequest;
import javax.servlet.http.HttpServletResponse;

public class Greet extends HttpServlet {

    protected void processRequest(HttpServletRequest request,
                                  HttpServletResponse response)
        throws ServletException, IOException {
          response.setContentType("text/html;charset=UTF-8");
          PrintWriter out = response.getWriter();
          out.println("<html>");
          out.println("<head>");
          out.println("<title>Servlet Greet</title>");
          out.println("</head>");
          out.println("<body>");
          out.println("<h2>This is your servlet answering - hi!</h2>");
          out.println("</body>");
          out.println("</html>");
    }

    protected void doGet(HttpServletRequest request,
                         HttpServletResponse response)
    throws ServletException, IOException {
        processRequest(request, response);
    }
```

```
        protected void doPost(HttpServletRequest request,
                              HttpServletResponse response)
    throws ServletException, IOException {
        processRequest(request, response);
    }
}
```

Our project is run by selecting *Run/Run Project (greetn)*. This results in the opening of a browser and the display of the index.jsp document, as in Figure 11.1. The output of running the Greet servlet is the same as is shown in Figure 11.2.

To support our earlier contention that the project directory structure for a servlet application is complex, we counted the directories and files generated by NetBeans for the greetn application. There were 15 directories and 21 files. Note that most of these are neither needed nor used for the greetn application.

11.3 A Survey Example

The next servlet example is more complicated and interesting than the Greet servlet. The initial document of this example is a form used to gather responses for a survey of potential purchasers of consumer electronics products. The example uses a servlet to collect the responses and produce the cumulative results. The initial document for the survey project, which was built with NetBeans, is as follows:

```
<%--
    Document: index
    Creation: May 5, 2011, 10:21:15AM
    Author: bob2
    Purpose: Initial markup document for the Survey project
    --%>
<%@page contentType = "text/html" pageEncoding = "UTF-8"%>
<!DOCTYPE html>
<html>
    <head>
        <title> Survey </title>
        <meta http-equiv="Content-Type" content="text/html;
            charset=UTF-8">
    </head>
    <body>
        <form method="POST" action="Survey">
            <h2> Welcome to the Consumer Electronics Purchasing
```

```
                        Survey</h2>
            <p />
            <h4> Your Gender: </h4>
            <p>
                <label>
              <input type="radio" name="gender" value="female"
                             checked="checked" />
                    Female <br />
                </label>
                <label>
              <input type="radio" name="gender" value="male" />
                    Male <br /> <br /> <br />
                </label>
            </p>
            <p>
                <label>
                    <input type="radio" name="vote" value="0" />
                    TV <br />
                </label>
                <label>
                    <input type="radio" name="vote" value="1" />
                    Digital Camera <br />
                </label>
                <label>
                    <input type="radio" name="vote" value="2" />
                    MP3 player <br />
                </label>
                <label>
                    <input type="radio" name="vote" value="3" />
                    DVD player/recorder <br />
                </label>
                <label>
                    <input type="radio" name="vote" value="4" />
                    Camcorder <br />
                </label>
                <label>
                    <input type="radio" name="vote" value="5" />
                    PDA <br />
                </label>
                <label>
                    <input type="radio" name="vote" value="6"
                             checked="checked" />
                    Other <br /> <br />
                </label>
```

```
                     <input type = "submit" value = "Submit Vote" />
                     <input type = "reset" value = "Clear Vote Form" />
            </p>
        </form>
    </body>
</html>
```

Figure 11.10 shows the display of the initial form of the `survey` example.

Welcome to the Consumer Electronics Purchasing Survey

Your Gender:

⦿ Female
◯ Male

◯ TV
◯ Digital Camera
◯ MP3 player
◯ DVD player/recorder
◯ Camcorder
◯ PDA
⦿ Other

[Submit Vote] [Clear Vote Form]

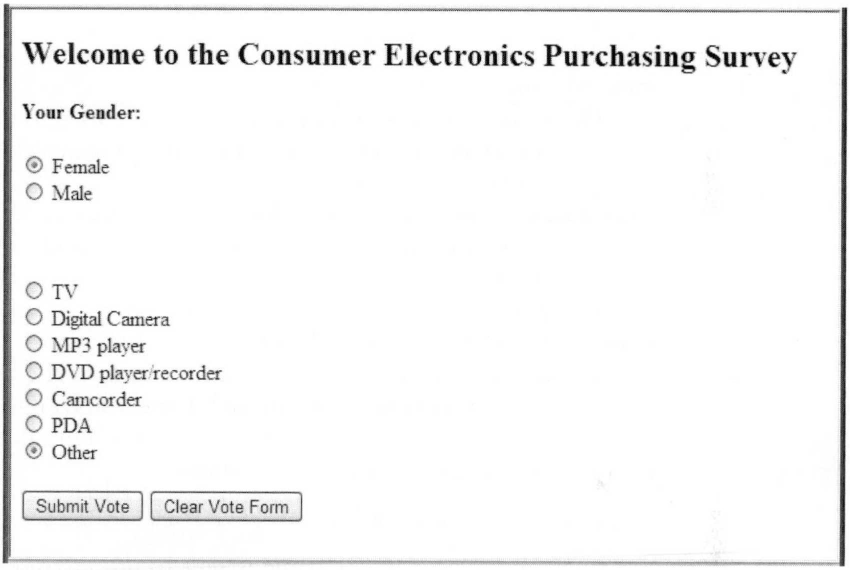

Figure 11.10 Display of the initial form of the `survey` example

Because the servlet that processes the form in this page must accumulate the results of the survey, it must create and use a file to store the survey results. The first time the form is submitted, the file must be created and written. For all subsequent submissions, the file is opened, read, and rewritten. The servlet will produce the cumulative vote totals for every client who submits a form. The survey results will be the two sets of totals, one for men and one for women.

The data stored in the vote totals file is an integer array of results.[4] The approach used is to read and write the file with the `ObjectInputStream` and `ObjectOutputStream` objects, respectively. This is a simple way to write any

---

4. We could have defined a class for the data, but chose an array for its simplicity, particularly for the reader who lacks expertise in Java.

object to a file. When input, the data object is cast to an integer array. For file output, the array object is written directly to the stream.

On all calls to the servlet except the first, the servlet must read the cumulative-vote array from the file, modify it, and write it back to the file. On the first call, there is no need to read the file first, because the call creates the first vote to be written to the file. The `ObjectInputStream` object used to read the file is created by a call to the `ObjectInputStream` constructor, passing an object of class `FileInputStream`, which is itself created by passing the file's program name to the `FileInputStream` constructor. All of this is specified with the following statement:

```
ObjectInputStream indat = new ObjectInputStream(
    new FileInputStream(File_variable_name));
```

In this statement, `indat` is defined as the program variable that references the input stream.

There can be concurrent accesses to the file used in this example, because a servlet container can support multiple simultaneous executions of a servlet. To prevent corruption caused by concurrent accesses to the file, a `synchronized` clause can be used to enclose the file accesses. Whatever code that is in such a clause executes completely before a different execution is allowed to enter the clause.

The servlet accesses the form data with the `getParameter` method of the request object that was passed to the `doPost` method. The `getParameter` method takes a string parameter, which is the name of the form component. The string value of the parameter is returned. For example, if the form has a component named `address`, the following statement will put the value of the address form component in the variable `newAddress`:

```
newAddress = request.getParameter("address");
```

If the component whose name is sent to `getParameter` does not have a form value, `getParameter` returns `null`. Note that `getParameter` also works for values passed through the GET HTTP method, so `getParameter` also can be used in `doGet` methods.

Form values do not all have the form of strings—for example, some are numbers. However, they are all collected from the user and passed as strings. So, if a form value is an integer number, it is passed as a string and must be converted to an integer value in the servlet. In Java, this is done with the `parseInt` method, which is defined in the wrapper class for integers, `Integer`. For example, to get the integer value of a parameter that is passed as the form value of a component named `price`, the following statement could be used:

```
price = Integer.parseInt(request.getParameter("price"));
```

Of course this approach is risky, because both `parseInt` and `getParameter` could fail. If no form parameter for a control was given, `getParameter` returns `null`, which should not be sent to `parseInt`. If the form parameter was not a valid string version of a number, `parseInt` would throw `NumberFormatException`. To detect these two problems and handle them, we could use the following code:

```
    str = request.getParameter("price");
    if (str != null)
      try {
        price = Integer.parseInt(str);
      }
      catch (NumberFormatException e) {
        out.println("Error - price is not a number");
      }
    else
      out.println("Error - price has no value");
```

We can now discuss the specifics of the servlet for processing the survey form data. In our example application, we ask the user to select one of seven different choices. The data file stores an array of 14 integers: seven votes for female voters and seven votes for male voters. The actions of the servlet are described in the following pseudocode algorithm:

> *If the votes data file exists*
> > *read the votes array from the data file*
> *else*
> > *create the votes array*
> *Get the gender form value*
> *Get the form value for the new vote*
> > *and convert it to an integer*
> *Add the vote to the votes array*
> *Write the votes array to the votes file*
> *Produce the return markup document that shows the*
> > *current results of the survey*

The servlet, Survey, that implements this process is as follows:

```
/* Survey.java
   Processes the consumer electronics survey form, updating the
   file that stores the survey data and producing the cumulative
   number of votes in the survey. The survey data file, survdat.ser,
   is stored on the Web server.
 */

import java.io.*;
import javax.servlet.ServletException;
import javax.servlet.http.HttpServlet;
import javax.servlet.http.HttpServletRequest;
import javax.servlet.http.HttpServletResponse;

public class Survey extends HttpServlet {

    protected void processRequest(HttpServletRequest request,
                                  HttpServletResponse response)
```

```
            throws ServletException, IOException {
    int[] votes = null;
    int index;
    int vote;
    File survdat = new File("survdat.ser");
    String gender;
    String[] products = {"TV", "Digital Camera", "MP3 player",
        "DVD player/recorder", "Camcorder", "PDA", "Other"};

// Set the content type for the response and get a writer
response.setContentType("text/html;charset=UTF-8");
PrintWriter out = response.getWriter();

// Create the initial part of the response document
    out.println("<html>");
    out.println("<head>");
    out.println("<title>Return message</title>");
    out.println("</head>");
    out.println("<body>");

    // Synchronize a block for the votes file access
    synchronized (this) {

        // If the file already exists, read in its data
      try {
            if (survdat.exists()) {
                ObjectInputStream indat = new
                 ObjectInputStream(new FileInputStream(
                    survdat));
                votes = (int[]) indat.readObject();
                indat.close();
            }

            // If the file does not exist (this is the first
            //  vote), create the votes array
            else {
                votes = new int[14];
            }
        } catch (Exception e) {
            e.printStackTrace();
        }

        // Get the gender of the survey respondent's
        gender = request.getParameter("gender");
```

```
    // Add the consumer electronics vote of the response
    //  to the votes array
  vote = Integer.parseInt(request.getParameter ("vote"));
    if (gender.equals("male")) {
        vote += votes.length / 2;
    }
    votes[vote]++;

    //Write updated votes array to disk
    ObjectOutputStream outdat = new ObjectOutputStream(
         new FileOutputStream(survdat));
    outdat.writeObject(votes);
    outdat.flush();
    outdat.close();

}  //** end of the synchronized block
// Create the initial response information
out.println(
       "<h3> Thank you for participating in the");
out.println(" Consumer Electronics Survey </h3>");
out.println("<h4> Current Survey Results: </h4>");

// Create the cumulative total votes return information
// for females
out.println("<h5> For Female Respondents </h5>");
for (index = 0; index < votes.length / 2; index++) {
    out.print(products[index]);
    out.print(": ");
    out.println(votes[index]);
    out.println("<br />");
}

// Create the cumulative total votes return information
// for males
out.println("<h5> For Male Respondents </h5>");
for (index = votes.length / 2; index < votes.length;
    index++) {
   out.print(products[index - (votes.length / 2)]);
                   out.print(": ");
   out.println(votes[index]);
   out.println("<br />");
}
out.close();
}
```

```
    protected void doGet(HttpServletRequest request,
                         HttpServletResponse response)
        throws ServletException, IOException {
      processRequest(request, response);
    }

    protected void doPost(HttpServletRequest request,
                          HttpServletResponse response)
        throws ServletException, IOException {
      processRequest(request, response);
    }
}
```

Notice that the servlet does not include code to detect errors with getPa-rameter and parseInt when the vote value is fetched from the form. The reason is that the form value has a low probability of being wrong; it is created in the calling document, rather than being input by a user.

This example illustrates the use of a servlet for form handling and data storage on the server. It shows that developing servlets is not very different from writing non-Web Java applications. Figure 11.11 shows the results of running the Survey servlet after some survey responses have been received.

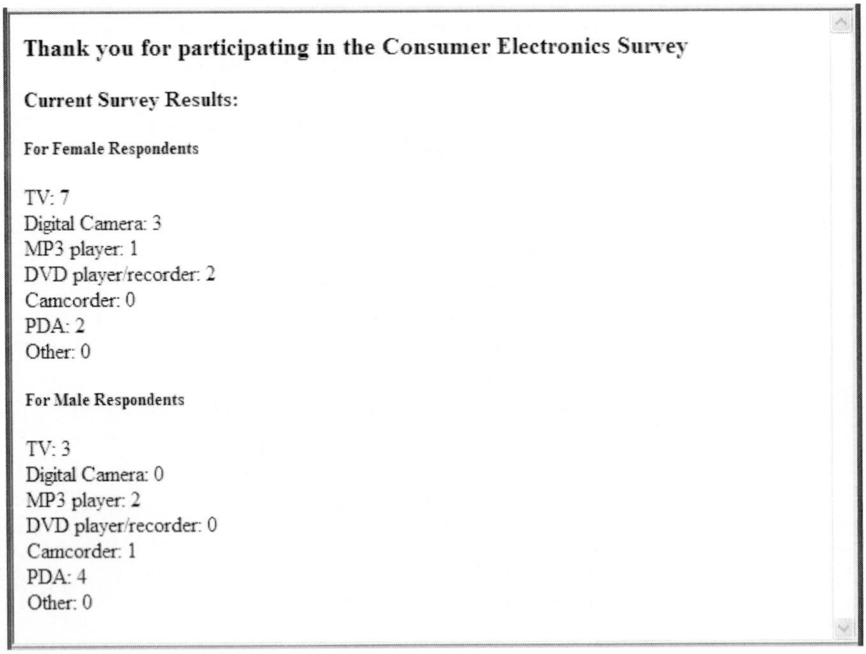

Thank you for participating in the Consumer Electronics Survey

Current Survey Results:

For Female Respondents

TV: 7
Digital Camera: 3
MP3 player: 1
DVD player/recorder: 2
Camcorder: 0
PDA: 2
Other: 0

For Male Respondents

TV: 3
Digital Camera: 0
MP3 player: 2
DVD player/recorder: 0
Camcorder: 1
PDA: 4
Other: 0

Figure 11.11 Results of the Survey servlet

11.4 **Storing Information on Clients**

Cookies provide a way to store information on a client machine about previous interactions with a specific server. The `javax.servlet` package provides the tools for creating and using cookies.

11.4.1 Cookies[5]

A *session* is the time span during which a browser interacts with a particular server. A session begins when a browser connects to a server. That session ends either when the browser is terminated or because the server terminated the session because of client inactivity. The length of time a server uses as the maximum time of inactivity is set in the configuration of the server. For example, the default maximum for some servers is 30 minutes.

The HTTP protocol is essentially stateless: It includes no means of storing information about a session that would be available to a subsequent session. However, there are a number of different reasons that it is useful for a server to be capable of relating a request made during a session to the other requests made by the same client during that session, as well as during previous and subsequent sessions.

One of the most common needs for session information is to implement shopping carts on Web sites. An e-commerce site can have any number of simultaneous online customers. At any time, any customer can add an item to or remove an item from his or her cart. Each user's shopping cart is identified by a session identifier, which could be implemented as a cookie. So, cookies can be used to identify each of the customers visiting the site at a given time.

Another common use of cookies is for a Web site to create profiles of visitors by remembering which parts of the site are perused by each visitor. Sometimes this is called *personalization*. If the server recognizes a request as being from a client who has made an earlier request from the same site, it can present a customized interface to that client. Also, later sessions can use such profiles to target advertising to the client in line with the client's past interests. These situations require that information about clients be accumulated and stored. Storing session information is becoming increasingly important as more and more Web sites make use of shopping carts, personalization, and targeted advertising.

Cookies provide a general approach to storing information about sessions on the browser system itself. The server is given this information when the browser makes subsequent requests for resources from the server. Note that some of the uses of cookies require them to be stored after the session in which they were created ends.

A *cookie* is a small object of information that includes a name and a textual value. A cookie is created by some software system on the server. Every HTTP communication between a browser and a server includes a header, which stores information about the message. The header part of an HTTP communication

---

5. The content of Section 11.4.1 also appears in Section 9.12.1.

can include cookies. So, every request sent from a browser to a server, and every response from a server to a browser, can include one or more cookies.

At the time it is created, a cookie is assigned a lifetime. When the time a cookie has existed reaches its lifetime, the cookie is deleted from the browser's host machine.

Every browser request includes all of the cookies its host machine has stored that are associated with the Web server to which the request is directed. Only the server that created a cookie can ever receive the cookie from the browser, so a particular cookie is information that is exchanged exclusively between one specific browser and one specific server. Because cookies are stored as text, the browser user can view them at any time.

Because cookies allow servers to record browser activities, some consider them to be privacy risks. Accordingly, browsers allow the client to change a browser setting to refuse to accept cookies from servers. This is clearly a drawback of using cookies—they are useless when clients reject them.

Cookies also can be deleted by the browser user, although the deletion process is different for different browsers. The help facility of a browser can be consulted to determine the cookie deletion process on any given browser.

It is a serious weakness of cookies that users can choose to set their browsers to reject them and also are able to delete them at any time. Because of this flaw, Java provides the Session Tracking API as a cookie alternative. This API provides classes, interfaces, and methods to support the storage and use of session objects for client sessions. These objects, which can store any set of Java objects, are stored on the server and are accessible by servlets. (Session tracking with Java is discussed no further in this book; details can be found in any book on servlets.)

11.4.2 Servlet Support for Cookies

On the server, a Java cookie associated with a servlet is an object of class `Cookie`; on a client, a cookie is just a text data value. It is important to keep these two uses of the term *cookie* distinct.

A Java cookie object has a collection of data members and methods. Among the most commonly used data members are those for storing the lifetime, or maximum age, of the cookie and for storing the cookie's name and value as strings, along with a comment, which is a string that can be used to explain the purpose of the cookie. The most commonly used `Cookie` methods are `setComment(String)`, `setMaxAge(int)`, `setValue(String)`, `getComment()`, `getMaxAge()`, `getName()`, and `getValue()`, all of whose purposes are obvious from their names.

A cookie object is created with the constructor of the `Cookie` class. This constructor takes two parameters: the cookie name and the cookie value. For example, consider the following statement:

```
Cookie newCookie = new Cookie(gender, vote);
```

By default, a cookie exists from the time it is created until the current session ends. If you want the cookie to exist past the end of the current session, you must use the `setMaxAge` method of `Cookie` to give the cookie a specific lifetime. The parameter to `setMaxAge` is the number of seconds, expressed as an integer expression. Because Java integers can have values up to a maximum of about two billion, cookies can have ages that range from 1 second to nearly 25,000 years. For example, the following method call gives `newCookie` a lifetime of 1 hour:

```
newCookie.setMaxAge(3600);
```

The browser can be forced to delete a cookie with a call to `setMaxAge` that sets its maximum age to zero.

A cookie is attached to a response from a server with the `addCookie` method of the `HttpServletResponse` class. For example, the cookie `newCookie` can be added to the response object `myResponse` with the following statement:

```
myResponse.addCookie(newCookie);
```

Because cookies are stored in the header of an HTTP communication, the cookie, like other header information, must be added to the response before any of the response body is created. Once again, remember that the cookie that a browser gets and stores is not a complete Java object—it has no methods; it is just some textual data.

The browser has little to do with cookies, at least directly. Browsers accept cookies, store them on the browser host system, and return them to the server that created them with each HTTP request to that server that occurs before the session ends or the cookie's lifetime ends. All of this is done implicitly by the browser.

A cookie that is sent from the browser to the server must be explicitly fetched by a servlet. This is done with the `getCookies` method of `HttpServletRequest`. The method returns an array of references to `Cookie` objects. The following code is an example of a cookie array declaration and a subsequent call to `getCookies`:

```
Cookie[] theCookies;
...
theCookies = request.getCookies();
```

Whatever cookie processing is required can be done before the cookies are attached to the response and sent back to the browser.

11.4.3   An Example

We now consider an example that presents a ballot form to the user and collects client votes in an election for the esteemed position of dogcatcher. The votes submitted through this form are recorded on the server by a servlet, which handles the form. This example uses a cookie to record, on the client, whether the voter has voted before, the objective being to prevent multiple votes from the same client. The ballot form is presented with the following document:

```
<%--
    Document: index (for the VoteCounter project)
    Creation: May 7, 2011, 3:01:19PM
    Author: bob2
    Purpose: The markup document for the vote counter project
             Presents a ballot to the user and calls the VoteCounter
             servlet for handling the form
    --%>
<%@page contentType = "text/html" pageEncoding = "UTF-8"%>
<!DOCTYPE html>
<html>
    <head>
        <title>Ballot</title>
        <meta http-equiv="Content-Type" content="text/html;
          charset=UTF-8">
    </head>
    <body>
        <form action="VoteCounter" method="POST">
            <h3> Please choose one candidate for dogcatcher </h3>
            <p>
                <input type="radio" name="vote" value="Dogman" />
                Daren Dogman <br />
                <input type="radio" name="vote" value="Taildragger" />
                Timmy Taildragger <br />
                <input type="radio" name="vote" value="Dogpile" />
                Don Dogpile <br />
            </p><p>
                <input type = "submit"  value = "Submit ballot" />
            </p>
        </form>
    </body>
</html>
```

Figure 11.12 shows the display of the initial document for the vote counter example.

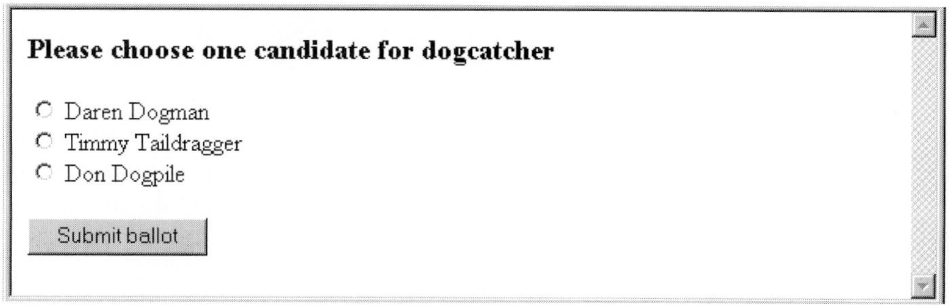

Figure 11.12 Display of the initial document

The users of the ballot form can vote for one of three persons for dogcatcher. The form presents the three choices as radio buttons and includes a *Submit bal-lot* button. The `action` attribute of the form specifies that it be handled by the servlet `VoteCounter`, using the `POST` method.

The vote-counting servlet has several processing responsibilities. For each ballot (request) the servlet receives, it must first determine whether a vote was actually cast (was a radio button clicked?). If no vote was cast, it must send a response document back to the client, asking the user to choose a candidate and click *Submit*. The servlet must also ensure that a voter has not previously voted, at least during some specified period. To do this, a cookie is returned to each voter. Each vote submission is checked to determine whether a cookie showing that the user has already voted came along with the ballot. If the ballot contains a vote—that is, if the form has one of its radio buttons pressed—and the voter has not voted previously, the vote must be processed. Processing a vote means reading the vote totals file, updating it, and writing it back to disk storage. Finally, the servlet must produce the current vote totals for each legitimate voter, in the form of a markup document. The actions of the `VoteCounter` servlet are outlined in the following pseudocode algorithm:

If the form does not have a vote
  return a message to the client—"no vote"
else
  If the client did not vote before
    If the votes data file exists
      read in the current votes array
    else
      create the votes array
    end if
    update the votes array with the new vote
    write the votes array to disk
    make an "iVoted" cookie and add it to the response
    return a message to the client, including the new vote totals

> *else*
> > *return a message to the client—"Illegal vote"*
> > *end if*
> *end if*

Two utility methods are used: a predicate method to determine whether the client has voted and a method to create the document header text. The servlet code is as follows:

```
/* VoteCounter.java
   This servlet processes the ballot form, returning a
   document asking for a new vote if no vote was made on the
   ballot. For legitimate ballots, the vote is added to
   the current totals, and those totals are presented to
   the user in a return document.
   A cookie is returned to the voter, recording the fact
   that a vote was received. The servlet examines all votes
   for cookies to ensure that there is no multiple voting.
   The voting data file, votesdat.ser, is stored on the Web
   server.
 */

import java.io.*;
import javax.servlet.ServletException;
import javax.servlet.http.Cookie;
import javax.servlet.http.HttpServlet;
import javax.servlet.http.HttpServletRequest;
import javax.servlet.http.HttpServletResponse;

public class VoteCounter extends HttpServlet {

    protected void processRequest(HttpServletRequest request,
                                  HttpServletResponse response)
        throws ServletException, IOException {
        Cookie[] cookies = null;
        int index;
        Cookie newCookie;
        int[] votes = null;
        String vote;
        File votesdat = new File("votesdat.ser");
        String[] candidates = {"Daren Dogman", "Timmy Taildragger",
            "Don Dogpile"
        };
```

```
// Set content type for response and get a writer
response.setContentType("text/html");
PrintWriter out = response.getWriter();

// Get cookies from the request
cookies = request.getCookies();

// Check to see if there was a vote on the form
vote = request.getParameter("vote");
if (vote == null) {  //** There was no vote
   // Create the return document
   makeHeader(response, out);
   out.println(
           "You submitted a ballot with no vote marked <br />");
   out.println(
           "Please mark the ballot and resubmit");
} //** end of if (vote == null) ...
else {  //** There was a vote

   // Check to see if this client voted before
   if (!votedBefore(cookies)) {

       // No previous vote, so get the contents of the file
       //  (if the file already exists)

       // Synchronize block for file input-output
       synchronized (this) {
           if (votesdat.exists()) {
               ObjectInputStream indat =
           new ObjectInputStream(new FileInputStream(votesdat));

               // We need the try-catch here because
               //  readObject can throw ClassNotFound
               try {
                   votes = (int[]) indat.readObject();
               } catch (ClassNotFoundException problem) {
                   problem.printStackTrace();
               }
           } //** end of if(votesdat.exists() ...

           // If the file does not exist (this is the first
           //  vote), create the votes array
           else {
               votes = new int[3];
```

```
                    // Add the new vote to the votes array
                    }
                    if (vote.equals("Dogman")) {
                        votes[0]++;
                    } else if (vote.equals("Taildragger")) {
                        votes[1]++;
                    } else {
                        votes[2]++;
                    }  //** end of if (vote.equals("Dogman"))

                    // Write updated votes array to disk
                    ObjectOutputStream outdat = new ObjectOutputStream(
                            new FileOutputStream(votesdat));
                    outdat.writeObject(votes);
                    outdat.flush();
                    outdat.close();
                }  //** end of synchronized block

                // Attach a cookie to the response
                newCookie = new Cookie("iVoted", "true");
                newCookie.setMaxAge(5);    //** Set to 5 for testing
                response.addCookie(newCookie);

                // Write a response message
                makeHeader(response, out);
                out.println("Your vote has been received");
                out.println(
                        "<br /><br /> Current Voting Totals: <br />");

                // Create the total votes return information
                for (index = 0; index < votes.length; index++) {
                    out.println("<br />");
                    out.print(candidates[index]);
                    out.print(": ");
                    out.println(votes[index]);
                }
            } //** end of if (!votedBefore(cookies) ...
            else {  // The client voted before

                // Write a response message
                makeHeader(response, out);
                out.println(
                        "Your vote is illegal - you have already voted!");
            }  // end of else clause - client voted before
        }  // end of else (there was a vote)
```

```java
            // Finish response document and close the stream
            out.println("</body> </html>");
            out.close();
        }   //** end of ProcessRequest


        //------------------------------------------------------------------
        // Method votedBefore - return true if the client voted before;
        //    false otherwise
        private boolean votedBefore(Cookie[] cookies) {
            if (cookies == null || cookies.length == 0) {
                return false;
            } else {

                // Check the cookies to see if this user voted before
                for (Cookie cookie: cookies) {
                    if (cookie.getName().equals("iVoted")) {
                        return true;
                    }
                }   // end of for (index = 0; ...
                return false;
            }   //** end of if (cookies == null ...
        }   //** end of votedBefore


        //------------------------------------------------------------------
        // Method makeHeader - get the writer and produce the
        //    response header
        private void makeHeader(HttpServletResponse response,
                                PrintWriter out)
                throws IOException {

            // Write the response document head and the message
            out.println("<html><head>");
            out.println(
              "<title> Return message </title></head><body>");
        }   //** end of makeHeader

        // Method doPost - just calls processRequest
        protected void doPost(HttpServletRequest request,
                HttpServletResponse response)
                throws ServletException, IOException {
            processRequest(request, response);
        }
    }
```

The outputs of the `VoteCounter` servlet for the three possibilities it handles— a nonvote ballot, a second ballot from the same client, and a ballot with a legal vote—are shown in Figures 11.13, 11.14, and 11.15, respectively.

You submitted a ballot with no vote marked
Please mark the ballot and resubmit

Figure 11.13 Output of the `VoteCounter` servlet for a form with no vote

Your vote is illegal - you have already voted!

Figure 11.14 Output of the `VoteCounter` for a form with a second vote from the same client

Your vote has been received

Current Voting Totals:

Daren Dogman: 3
Timmy Taildragger: 1
Don Dogpile: 0

Figure 11.15 Output of the `VoteCounter` for a form with legal vote

Notice that in several locations in the code of `VoteCounter.java` the specific data are hard coded—for example, in the following line:

```
if (vote.equals("Dogman")) {
```

While hard coding clarifies this program, in commercial applications it is a poor programming practice because any changes in the parameters (candidates in this example) require program modification and redeployment. Redeployment is a costly process in commercial applications and therefore must be avoided whenever possible. In this example, the problem can be avoided by reading candidates' names from a data file outside the program.

11.5   JavaServer Pages

JavaServer Pages (JSP), which are built on top of servlets, provide alternative ways of constructing dynamic Web documents. It is "ways," not "way," because JSP includes several different approaches to generate Web documents dynamically.

11.5.1   Motivations for JSP

A number of problems arise with the servlet approach, as well as some other related approaches, to providing dynamic Web documents. Among these problems is that of having the response document embedded in programming code. In the case of servlets, the entire response document is created by calls to the `print` and `println` methods of the `PrintWriter` class. This forces all maintenance of the user interface of the application to be done on program code.

A closely related problem is that development organizations often have two different kinds of personnel, with different skill sets, to work on the construction and maintenance of Web applications. On the one hand, Web designers focus on interface and presentation characteristics of Web documents. On the other, programmers design and maintain the code that processes form data, implements business logic, and handles interactions with databases. Most personnel belong in one or the other of these categories rather than both. Yet having markup code and programming code intermixed requires people from both categories to work on the same documents. Furthermore, these mixed-code documents are difficult for people from both categories to read.

JSP can be used to develop server-based dynamic documents in which there is a clean separation between presentation (markup) and business logic. Furthermore, in some cases server-based applications that produce dynamic documents can be developed in JSP by Web designers who are not hard-core Java programmers. The same cannot be said for servlet-based applications.

The basic capabilities of servlets and JSP are the same. The basis for deciding which to use is discussed in Section 11.5.2.

11.5.2   JSP Documents

There are two syntactic forms for writing JSP documents: the original way, now called *classic syntax*, and the alternative way, which uses XML syntax. The XML approach became possible in JSP 2.0, which was released in late 2003. XML syntax is useful if the JSP document will generate XML-compliant documents. However, XML syntax requires more effort and larger documents. The XML syntax of JSP documents is not further discussed in this chapter, and all of our JSP document examples in this book use classic syntax.[6]

JSP documents are processed by a software system called a *JSP container*. Normally, the JSP container translates a JSP document when the document is loaded onto the server; others translate them only when they are first requested by a client. The translation process converts a JSP document into a servlet and then compiles the servlet. So, JSP is actually a simplified approach to writing servlets.

Figure 11.16 shows the processing flow of a JSP document.

---

6. Some authors refer to JSP documents written in classic syntax as *JSP pages* and those written in XML as *JSP documents*. We will call ours JSP documents, although they are written in classical syntax.

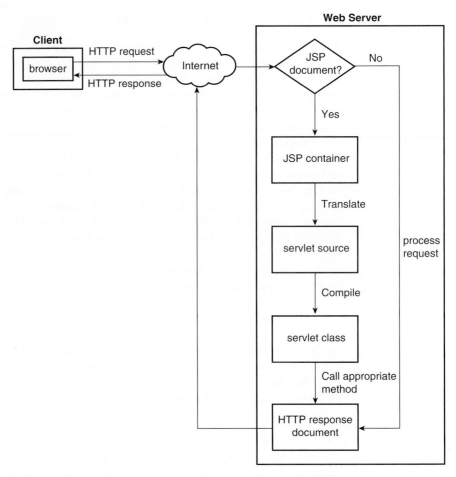

Figure 11.16 Processing flow of a JSP document

In early versions of JSP, snippets of Java code were embedded in documents, similar to the way PHP code appears in documents. These snippets were called *scriptlets*. This approach retains the problem of language mixing that is inherent with servlets. Later versions of JSP, however, have capabilities that eliminate the need for scriptlets, and the use of scriptlets is now discouraged.

Under the assumption that scriptlets are not used, a JSP document consists of three different kinds of elements: (1) traditional HTML, XHTML, or XML markup, (2) action elements, and (3) directives.

The markup in the document is used to produce the content that is fixed. This markup is called *template text*. It is the static part of the document. Everything in a JSP document that is not a JSP element is template text. Template text is not modified by the JSP container; it arrives at the browser exactly as it appears in the JSP document. The design choice between using a servlet and a JSP document is made on the basis of the proportion of the document that is template text. The more template text there is, the better it is to use JSP. If a document is mostly dynamically generated, then a servlet is the better choice. If both template text and dynamically generated text are needed, servlets and JSP can be used together in a Web application.

Action elements dynamically create content. The document that results from the execution of a servlet whose source is a JSP document is a combination of the template text and the output of the action elements. An action element has the form of a markup element: an opening tag, possibly including attributes; content, which is sometimes called the *action body*; and a closing tag. In fact, however, action elements represent program code that generates markup.

Action elements appear in three different categories: standard, custom, and JSP Standard Tag Library (JSTL). The standard action elements, defined by the JSP specification, include elements for dealing with JavaBeans,[7] including the response from a servlet or another JSP document, and elements for dynamically generating a markup element. For example, the action element `<jsp:element>` dynamically generates a markup element, possibly with attributes and content defined by nested actions. The `<jsp:include>` action element specifies a document file as the value of its `page` attribute. The document file is copied into the output document of the JSP document in which the `include` appears.

Custom action elements are designed for a specific category of JSP documents within an organization. Because of its complexity, the development of custom action elements is not discussed in this chapter.

The JSP standard action elements are highly limited in scope and utility, so there are many commonly needed tasks that cannot be done with them. These limitations led to a large number of different programmers defining their own custom action elements for these tasks, which was clearly a waste of effort. This situation was remedied by the development of the JSTL, which includes action elements for many commonly needed tasks. The JSTL consists of five libraries. The *Core* library includes elements for simple flow control—for example, selection and loop constructs. The *XML Processing* library includes elements for transformations of XML documents, including those specified by XSLT style-sheet documents. The *Internationalization and Formatting* library includes elements for formatting and parsing localized information. The *Relational Database Access* library includes elements for database access. The *Functions* library includes elements for Expression Language functions. (The Expression Language is described in Section 11.5.3.)

Action elements specify actions that are described with statements in a programming language. In fact, libraries of action elements form programming languages that can be used to write dynamic actions in the form of a markup language. The difference between using the action elements and using Java is twofold: First, the syntax is completely different; second, the special tags are simpler and easier to use than their Java equivalents, so they can be used by less experienced programmers.

A directive is a message to the JSP container, providing information about the document and the sources of predefined action elements of the document.

---

7. A JavaBean is a special Java class that defines a reusable component. JavaBeans are discussed in Section 11.6.

Directives can specify that content from other sources be included in a document. However, directives do not themselves produce content.

Syntactically, directives are tags that use `<%@` and `%>` delimiters. They use attributes to communicate to the container. The most commonly used directives are `page` and `taglib`. The `page` directive usually includes two attributes, `content-Type` and `pageEncoding`. `contentType` is usually set to `"text/html"` and `pageEncoding` is usually set to `"UTF-8"`. Following is a typical `page` directive:

```
<%@page contentType="text/html" pageEncoding="UTF-8"%>
```

The `taglib` directive specifies a library of action elements, or tags, that are used by the document. The library is specified in the directive by assigning the URI of the library to the `uri` attribute. The `taglib` directive can also define an abbreviation for the library by assigning the abbreviation to its `prefix` attribute. The abbreviation is then attached with a colon to the left end of any name from the library that is used in a document. This is exactly the syntax of the abbreviations used for XML namespaces. For example, a JSP document may contain the following directive:

```
<%@ taglib prefix = "c"
  uri = "http://java.sun.com/jsp/jstl/core" %>
```

This directive specifies the URI of the JSTL Core library and sets the prefix for its elements to `c`. Now a tag—for example, `if`—can be referenced as `<c:if>`. Examples of the use of Core library action elements appear in the JSP examples later in the chapter.[8]

11.5.3 The Expression Language

To use JSTL, one must be familiar with its two primary technologies: the tag set of JSTL and the JSP Expression Language.

The JSP Expression Language (EL) is similar to the expressions (but only the expressions) of a scripting language such as JavaScript, at least with regard to simplicity. This similarity is most evident in the type coercion rules, which obviate most of the explicit type conversions that are required in writing expressions involving strings and numbers in a strongly typed programming language such as Java. For example, if a string is added to a number in the EL, an attempt will be made by the JSP container to coerce the string to a number. This makes it convenient for dealing with form data, which is always in text form but often represents data of other types. It also makes the EL easier for Web designers, who often are not Java programmers.

The EL has no control statements such as selection or loop control.[9] The function of control statements is performed by action elements from the JSTL. The EL is true to its name: It is just a language for expressions.

---

8. The appearance of the `taglib` directive in a NetBeans 7.0 `jsp` file may cause an error message that indicates that the library cannot be found. This error can be eliminated by right-clicking the *Library* entry in the project, selecting *Add Library/JSTL 1.1* and clicking the *Add Library* button. It may be necessary to restart NetBeans to have this addition take effect.

9. This is not quite true; the EL includes the conditional expression that is part of C and many of its successors. In a strict sense, conditional expressions are control statements.

Syntactically, an EL expression is always introduced with a dollar sign ($) and is delimited by braces, as follows:

${ *expression* }

An EL expression can include literals, the usual arithmetic operators, implicit variables[10] that allow access to form data, and normal variables. The literals can be numeric, either in the form of floating-point or integer values; Boolean values (`true` or `false`); or strings delimited by either single or double quotes. The only variables we will use are those created by the JSTL action elements.

The reserved words of the EL are as follows:

```
and    div    empty    eq    false    ge     gt     instanceof
le     lt     mod      ne    not      null   or     true
```

Some of these words are synonyms for symbolic operators—for example, `le` for `<=` and `lt` for `<`. The use of these synonyms avoids any problems with having angle brackets in a markup document.

An EL expression can appear in two places in a JSP document: in template text or in the values of certain attributes of certain action elements. The EL often is used to set the attribute values of action elements. Because attributes take string values, the result of the evaluation of an EL expression is always coerced to a string.

The EL uses data that comes from several different sources. The most interesting data, for the purposes of our discussion, is the form data sent in a request form, which is made available through the implicit variable `param`. The `param` variable stores a collection of all of the form data values in much the same way JavaScript objects store their properties. To access a particular form data value, the name of the form element is used the way a property name is in JavaScript: catenated on the collection name with a period. For example, if there is a form component named `address`, it can be accessed with the following code:

${param.address}

If the form component name includes special characters, an alternative access form is used, which is to treat the component name, specified as a literal string, as a subscript into the `param` array, as follows:

{param['cust-address'] }

The EL defines a number of other implicit variables. Most of them are collections of values related to the request header, form values, cookies, and various scope variables. For example, the `pageContext` implicit variable is a reference to an object of class `javax.servlet.http.HttpServletRequest`, which has a long list of information about the request. Among this information are `content-Type`, `method`, which is the request method (`GET` or `POST`), `remoteAddr`, the IP of the client, and `contentLength`.

The value of an EL expression is implicitly placed in the result document when the expression is evaluated. However, if the text being inserted into the result document can include characters that could confuse the browser—for

---

10. Implicit variables are implicitly defined by the JSP container.

example, angle brackets or quotes—another approach is better. The value of the expression is assigned to the value attribute of the out action element defined in the JSTL Core library. The recommended prefix for this library is c. The form of the out action element is as follows:

```
<c:out value = "${EL expression}" />
```

The advantage of this approach to inserting values into the result document is that all potentially bothersome characters in the value of the value attribute are implicitly replaced with their corresponding character entities. In our examples, we use the out element only if there is a chance that the expression's value could include potentially confusing (to the browser) characters.

The example application that follows, whose project is named tempConvertEL, consists of an initial JSP document with a form that solicits a temperature in Celsius from the user. The initial document uses another JSP document to process the form, which computes the equivalent temperature in Fahrenheit and displays it. This application, like all others in this chapter, was developed with the use of NetBeans. The initial JSP document is as follows:

```
<%--
  Document: index (for the tempConvertEL project)
  Created on: May 2, 2011, 4:53:03 PM
  Author: bob2
  Purpose: initial document for tempConvertEL project.
           Displays a form to collect a Celsius temperature from
           the user to be converted to Fahrenheit
  --%>
<%@page contentType="text/html" pageEncoding="UTF-8"%>
<!DOCTYPE html>
<html>
    <head>
        <title>Initial document for the tempConvertEL project</title>
        <meta http-equiv="Content-Type" content="text/html;
          charset=UTF-8">
    </head>
    <body>
        <form action="tempConvertEL2.jsp" method="POST">
            <p>Celsius temperature:
                <input type="text" name="ctemp" value="" />
                <input type = "submit"
                      value = "Convert to Fahrenheit" />
            </p>
        </form>
    </body>
</html>
```

The JSP document for processing the form data for the `tempConvertEL` application, `tempConvertEL2.jsp`, is as follows:

```
<%--
  Document:tempConvertEL2.jsp (response document for the
    tempConvertEL project)
  Created on: May 12, 2011, 2:30:02 PM
  Author: bob2
  Purpose: Convert a given temperature in Celsius to Fahrenheit
--%>
<%@page contentType="text/html" pageEncoding="UTF-8"%>
<!DOCTYPE html)
<html>
    <head>
        <title>tempConvertEL2.jsp</title>
        <meta http-equiv="Content-Type" content="text/html;
          charset=UTF-8">
    </head>
    <body>
        <p>
            Given temperature in Celsius:
            ${param.ctemp}
            <br /> <br />
            Temperature in Fahrenheit:
            ${(1.8 * param.ctemp) + 32}
        </p>
    </body>
</html>
```

This document performs the simple arithmetic computations required to convert the form data value of the component named `ctemp` to Fahrenheit with an EL expression. Both the input data value and the computed value are displayed.

11.5.4   JSTL Control Action Elements

The Core library of JSTL includes a collection of action elements for flow control in a JSP document. The most commonly used of these elements are `if`, `forEach`, `when`, `choose`, and `otherwise`. The form of an `if` element is as follows:

```
<c:if test = "boolean expression">
   JSP elements and/or markup
</c:if>
```

An `if` element could be used to write a JSP document that served as both the requesting document and the responding document. It could determine whether the document was being processed (after being interacted with and sent to the server) by checking whether the `method` implicit variable had been set to `"POST"`, as in the element:

```
<c:if test = "pageContext.request.method == 'POST'}">
    JSP elements and/or markup
</c:if>
```

The example that follows is a JSP document for the temperature conversion previously done in the `tempConvertEL` application, which uses its `index.jsp` and `tempConvertEL2.jsp` documents. By contrast, the new project gets the input and performs the temperature conversion in a single document. This new document uses an `if` element to decide which JSP code to return: the initial document that accepts the input or the document that computes and displays the result.

```
<%--
  Document: index.jsp (for the tempConvertEL1 project)
  Created on: May 27, 2011, 10:29:11 AM
  Author: bob2
  Purpose: Convert a given temperature in Celsius to Fahrenheit. This
           is both the request and the response document
--%>
<%@page contentType = "text/html" pageEncoding="UTF-8"%>
<%@ taglib prefix = "c"
           uri = "http://java.sun.com/jsp/jstl/core" %>
<!DOCTYPE html>
<html>
    <head>
        <title> Temperature Converter </title>
        <meta http-equiv="Content-Type" content="text/html;
        charset=UTF-8">
    </head>
    <body>
        <c:if test = "${pageContext.request.method != 'POST'}">
            <form action="index.jsp"  method="POST">
                Celsius temperature:
                <input type="text" name="ctemp" value="" />
                <input type = "submit"
                        value = "Convert to Fahrenheit" />
            </form>
        </c:if>
        <c:if test = "${pageContext.request.method == 'POST'}">
```

```
              Given temperature in Celsius:
                ${param.ctemp} <br />
                The temperature in Fahrenheit:
                ${(1.8 * param.ctemp) + 32}
          </c:if>
      </body>
</html>
```

Through the browser's "view source," one can see the two versions of the body of the index.jsp document of the tempConvertEL1 project that come to the browser. The first listing is the body of the initial document; the second is the body of the document after its form has been submitted with the input Celsius value of 100:

```
<body>
  <form action="index.jsp"  method="POST">
    Celsius temperature:
    <input type="text" name="ctemp" value="" />
    <input type="submit" value="Convert to Fahrenheit" />
  </form>
</body>


<body>
  Given temperature in Celsius:
    100 <br />
    The temperature in Fahrenheit:
  212.0
</body>
```

Checkboxes and menus have multiple values. The param implicit variable cannot be used to determine which values are set in the document that handles forms with these components. For this purpose, there is the paramValues implicit variable, which is an array of values for each form element. The forEach JSTL action element can be used to iterate through the elements of a param-Values array. The forEach element is related to the Java "for each" statement: It iterates on the basis of the elements of a collection, an iterator, an enumeration, or an array. The items attribute is assigned the data structure on which the iteration is based. The var attribute is assigned the variable name to which the structure's elements are assigned. The following checkboxes are illustrative:

```
<form method = "post">
  <label>
    <input type = "checkbox" name = "topping"
           value = "extracheese"
           checked = "checked" />      Extra cheese <br />
  </label>
```

```
<label>
  <input type = "checkbox" name = "topping"
         value = "pepperoni" /> Pepperoni <br />
</label>
<label>
  <input type = "checkbox" name = "topping"
         value = "olives" /> Olives <br />
</label>
<label>
  <input type = "checkbox" name = "topping"
         value = "onions" /> Onions <br />
</label>
<label>
  <input type = "checkbox" name = "topping"
         value = "bacon" /> Bacon <br />
</label>
<input type = "submit"  value = "Submit" /> <br />
</form>
```

To list the checkboxes that were checked, the following code could be used:

```
Pizza Toppings:
<c:forEach items = "${paramValues.topping}"
           var = "top">
  ${top} <br />
</c:forEach>
```

The forEach element can also be used to control a loop body based on a counter. For this, it uses the begin, end, and step attributes. For example, the following forEach element could be used simply to repeat the enclosed code 10 times:

```
<c:forEach begin = "1" end = "10">
  ...
<c:/forEach>
```

Radio buttons must be handled differently than checkboxes. All radio buttons in a group have the same name. For this situation, JSTL has three action elements that allow the specification of a form of a switch construct. These three elements are choose, when, and otherwise. The choose element, which takes no attributes, encloses the whole construct. A when element specifies one of the selectable sequences of code. The when attribute, test, is set to an EL expression that describes the Boolean expression that controls entry into the body of the element. The otherwise element, which takes no attributes, specifies the code for the case when none of the Boolean expressions in the when elements is true. The first when element with a true test attribute is chosen, so if the test attributes of more than one of the when elements are true, only one is chosen. The following example JSP document only displays the radio button that is currently pressed:

```jsp
<%--
  Document: index (for the radioButton project)
  Created on: June 11, 2011, 8:47:18 AM
  Author: bob2
  Purpose: To illustrate radio buttons in JSP
--%>
<%@page contentType = "text/html" pageEncoding="UTF-8"%>
<%@taglib prefix="c" uri="http://java.sun.com/jsp/jstl/core" %>
<!DOCTYPE html>
<html>
    <head>
        <title> Illustrate radio buttons </title>
        <meta http-equiv="Content-Type" content="text/html;
            charset=UTF-8">
    </head>
    <body>
        <form method="POST">
            <p>
                <label>
                    <input type="radio" name="payment"
                            value="visa" checked="checked" />
                    Visa <br />
                </label>
                <label>
                    <input type="radio" name="payment" value="mc" />
                    Master Charge <br />
                </label>
                <label>
                    <input type="radio" name="payment"
                            value="discover" />
                    Discover <br />
                </label>
                <label>
                    <input type="radio" name="payment" value="check" />
                    Check <br />
                </label>
                <input type = "submit" value = "Submit" />
            </p>
        </form>

        <!-- If the form has been submitted, display the payment
            method -->
        <c:if test = "${pageContext.request.method == 'POST'}">
          You have chosen the following payment method:
        <c:choose>
```

```
            <c:when test = "${param.payment == 'visa'}">
              Visa
            </c:when>
            <c:when test = "${param.payment == 'mc'}">
              Master Charge
            </c:when>
            <c:when test = "${param.payment == 'discover'}">
              Discover
            </c:when>
            <c:otherwise>
              Check
            </c:otherwise>
          </c:choose>
        </c:if>
      </body>
    </html>
```

11.6   JavaBeans

The JavaBeans architecture provides a set of rules for building a special category of Java classes that are designed to be reusable standalone software components. These components are called *beans*. Beans were designed to be used with visual system builders tools, such as NetBeans. To allow builder tools to determine the methods and data of a bean class easily, rigid naming conventions are required. All bean data that are to be exposed must have getter and setter methods whose names begin with `get` and `set`, respectively.[11] It is conventional to have the remainder of the access method's names be the data's variable name, spelled with an initial uppercase letter. For example, if a bean has an integer variable named `celsius`, the convention is that its getter and setter methods are named `getCelsius` and `setCelsius`, respectively.

In JSP, beans often are used as containers for data used in a Web application. They are frequently built with JSP IDEs, such as NetBeans. Beans are designed by programmers, but are often used by Web designers who do not have expertise in Java programming. When servlets and JSP are both used to build a Web application, beans are used to transmit data between the servlet and the JSP document. The EL can also use the data in a bean directly.

The data stored in a bean are called *properties*. Property names are like variable names in Java, in that they are case sensitive. However, property names must always begin with lowercase letters. Properties are always private. To make them accessible to JSP documents, properties have either getter, setter, or getter and setter methods. All of these are public. The setter methods can include validation code, as well as any useful computation code. Setter methods return nothing, so their return type is `void`. Getter methods have the same return type

---

11. If the data happens to be Boolean type, `is` is used instead of `get`.

as the property. A property that is both read and write accessible has both getter and setter methods. A read-only property has only a getter method; a write-only property has only a setter method.

Every bean class must have a parameterless constuctor. If the developer of a class does not include a constructor, a parameterless constructor is implicitly provided. The parameterless constructor allows tools to create bean instances, while knowing only the bean's class name.

The `<jsp:useBean>` JSP standard element is used to create an instance of a bean class and name it. This element requires two attributes: id and `class`. The id attribute is assigned a name, which will be used in the document to reference the bean instance. The package name and class name of the bean class are assigned to the `class` attribute. For example, to create an instance of the bean class whose name is `Converter` and is defined in the `org.mypackage.convert` package, the following statement could be used:

```
<jsp:useBean id = "myBean"
             class = "org.mypackage.convert.Converter" />
```

At the time a new bean instance is created with `<jsp:useBean>`, its properties have values only if they are assigned in the constructor of the bean class.

There are two other standard action elements for dealing with beans: `<jsp:setProperty>`, which sets a property value in a bean, and `<jsp:getProperty>`, which fetches a property value from a bean. The `<jsp:setProperty>` element takes three attributes: `name`, `property`, and `value`. The name of the bean instance (as given in the `<jsp:useBean>` id attribute) is assigned to the `name` attribute, the name of the property is assigned to the `property` attribute, and the value to be given to the property is assigned to the `value` attribute. For example, to set the `sum` property of the `myBean` bean instance to the value `100`, the following element could be used:

```
<jsp:setProperty name = "myBean" property = "sum"
                 value = "100" />
```

It is perhaps more common to set a property value to a value that is input into a form component by the user. In this case, the `value` attribute is not set in the `<jsp:setProperty>` element. If the property and the form component have the same name, no other attributes are required (beyond `name` and `property`). If the form component has a different name than the bean property, then the `param` attribute must be set to the name of the component. For example, to set the `zip` property of the `myBean` bean instance to the value of the component named `zipcode`, the following element could be used:

```
<jsp:setProperty name = "myBean" property = "zip"
                 param = "zipcode" />
```

All values in JSP documents are strings, as are all values input by a user into a form. If a value from a form or the value of a `value` attribute of `<jsp:setProperty>` is set to a property in a bean that has a type other than `String`, the value is implicitly converted to the type of the property.

When a `<jsp:getProperty>` element is processed by the JSP container, the value of the specified bean property is fetched, converted to a string, and inserted into the document that contains the `<jsp:getProperty>` element, effectively replacing that element. The `<jsp:getProperty>` element takes two attributes, `name` and `property`, which are the same as those of the `<jsp:setProperty>` element. For example, to get the `sum` property from the `myBean` bean instance, use the following element:

```
<jsp:getProperty name = "myBean" property = "sum" />
```

The EL can also be used to fetch a property from a bean. In fact, this is a simpler way to do it. To get the `sum` property of the `myBean` bean instance, simply use the following code:

```
${myBean.sum}
```

We now use the temperature conversion application to illustrate beans. The bean stores the Celsius and Fahrenheit versions of the input temperature. The getter method of the bean property that stores the Fahrenheit temperature includes the code to convert the current Celsius temperature to Fahrenheit.

After creating the project and naming it `tempConvertB`, we build the initial document, `index.jsp`. This document includes a form with a text box to collect the Celsius temperature from the user. The form also has a *Submit* button to use the bean to compute the equivalent Fahrenheit temperature. The computation will be part of the getter for the Fahrenheit temperature. The `index.jsp` file for the `tempConvertB` project is as follows:

```
<%--
    Document: index (for the tempConvertB project)
    Created on: June 13, 2011, 7:19:01 PM
    Author: bob2
    Purpose: The initial document for an application that uses a bean
             in the conversion of a given Celsius temperature to an
             equivalent Fahrenheit temperature
--%>
<%@page contentType="text/html" pageDEncoding="UTF-8"%>
<!DOCTYPE html>
<html>
    <head>
        <title>index.jsp for tempConvertB</title>
        <meta http-equiv="Content-Type" content="text/html;
            charset=UTF-8">
    </head>
    <body>
        <h2> Welcome to the temperature converter service </h2>
        <form name="Temperature input form" action="response.jsp"
```

```
                method="POST">
            Enter a temperature in Celsius:
            <input type="text" name="celsius" value="" size="4" />
            <p></p>
                <input type = "submit" value = "Convert to Fahrenheit" />
        </form>
    </body>
</html>
```

Next, we build the response JSP document. This document begins with a `<jsp:useBean>` element to create an instance of the bean. We name the bean `myBean` and give it the package name of `org.mypackage.convert` and the class name `Converter`. (We need to use these names when we create the bean class.) The next step is to include a `<jsp:setProperty>` element to move the value of the text box named `celsius` in the `index.jsp` document to the property named `celsius` of the bean. Because the text box and the property have the same name, the `value` attribute is not needed. Next, we insert a `<jsp:getProperty>` element to place the value of the `celsius` property of the bean into the document. Finally, we add a `<jsp:getProperty>` element to compute the `fahrenheit` property in the bean, as well as insert its value into the document. The complete response document, named `response.jsp`, is as follows:

```
<%--
  Document: response.jsp (for the tempConvertB project)
  Created on: June 14, 2011, 9:27:12 AM
  Author: bob2
  Purpose: This is the response document for the tempConvertB project.
           Uses a bean to convert a given Celsius temperature to the
           equivalent temperature in Fahrenheit
--%>
<%@page contentType="text/html" pageEncoding="UTF-8"%>
<!DOCTYPE html>
<html>
    <head>
        <title> Response document </title>
        <meta http-equiv="Content-Type" content="text/html;
          charset=UTF-8">

    </head>
    <body>
        <jsp:useBean id="myBean" scope="session"
                class="org.mypackage.convert.Converter" />
```

```
            <!-- Move the form value of celsius to the bean property -->
            <jsp:setProperty name="myBean" property="celsius" />
            Given Celsius temperature is:

            <!-- Move the value of the property celsius to the doc -->
            <jsp:getProperty name="myBean" property="celsius" />
            <br /> Equivalent temperature in Fahrenheit is:

            <!-- Compute the Fahrenheit value and place it in the doc -->
            <jsp:getProperty name="myBean" property="fahrenheit" />
    </body>
</html>
```

The last step in developing the application is to write the bean class. A right click on the project (in the *Projects* list) produces a long menu. Selecting *New/Java class* switches to a new screen on which the bean class and its package can be named. We name them `Converter` and `org.mypackage.convert`, respectively, as in the response JSP document. We then type the bean into the center panel in the workspace. Following is a listing of the `Converter` bean class:

```
// Converter - a bean for the tempConvertB application that
//             converts Celsius temperatures to Fahrenheit.

package org.mypackage.convert;

public class Converter {

    private String celsius;
    private String fahrenheit;

    public void setCelsius(String temperature) {
        this.celsius = temperature;
    }

    public String getCelsius() {
        return celsius;
    }
    public String getFahrenheit() {
        String temp;
        try {
            temp = Float.toString(
                        1.8f * Integer.parseInt(celsius) + 32.0f);
```

```
    } catch (NumberFormatException e) {
        temp = "Illegal Celsius Temperature";
    }
    return temp;
}
}
```

Our `Converter` bean has no need for a setter for its `fahrenheit` property, so it does not include one.

This completes the `tempConvertB` application. We have discussed only one very simple use of beans, but the reader can gain a basic understanding of the fundamentals of beans from this application.

11.7 Model–View–Controller Application Architecture

The Model–View–Controller (MVC) architecture was developed by Trygve Reenskaug, a Norwegian, in 1978–1979 while he was a visiting scientist at XeroxPARC working in the Smalltalk group. The original intent of MVC was to model graphical user interfaces, which were then being developed for Smalltalk. The MVC architecture clearly separates applications, both logically and physically, into three parts. The *model* is not only the data, but any enforced constraints on the data. For example, if a part of the data is the age of people, the model might ensure that no age value outside the usual range of human ages can be entered into the data storage. The *view* is the part of an application that prepares and presents results to the user. The *controller*, true to its name, controls the interaction between the user and the application. In addition, the controller performs many of the required computations. The intent of MVC is to reduce the coupling among the three parts of an application, making the application easier to develop and maintain.

As stated in the previous paragraph, MVC originally was developed for graphical user interfaces, but it has since been discovered that it is a valuable architecture for other applications, specifically Web applications. In fact, several IDEs developed for Web applications were designed around the concepts of MVC. One of these, Rails, is discussed in Chapter 15.

In an MVC Web application, a browser submits requests to the controller, which consults the model (which in turn consults its database). Next, the model reports results to the controller and, indirectly, to the view. The controller then instructs the view to produce a result document, which is transmitted to the client for display.

Web applications using Java server software can be designed and implemented with the MVC architecture. There are three general approaches to designing Web applications with the MVC architecture and Java server software. The first of these is the pure JSP approach. Separate JSP pages are used for the controller and the view parts of the application, with beans being used for the model part.

This is a good approach when the development organization is heavy in graphic designers and light in Java programmers. Relatively complex applications can be constructed with the use of only JSP and JSTL. The Java programmers can develop the beans to represent and manipulate the data. The JSP-only approach is also well suited for prototyping Web applications.

The second approach to MVC with Java server software is to use a combination of servlets, JSP, and beans. A servlet is used to accept requests and implement business logic. Beans are used to store and perform basic data manipulation. JSP, naturally, is used to implement the user views of results of requests, with some views displaying computed results and others returning failure notices. The servlet that receives requests can use other servlets to handle various kinds of requests.

The third approach to MVC with Java server software is to use servlets to implement the controller, JSP to implement the view, and Enterprise JavaBeans (EJBs)[12] for the model. This is clearly the most complex of the three approaches and is usually used only for the more sophisticated and complex Web applications.

Starting with version 6.9, NetBeans includes an elaborate framework for creating MVC architecture Web applications. This framework is named *Spring Web MVC*. Spring makes it relatively easy to develop MVC Web applications, though of course one must learn yet another framework. A discussion of Spring is beyond the scope of this chapter.

11.8 JavaServer Faces

The first version of JavaServer Faces (JSF), JSF 1.0, was released in 2004. JSF 1.2 was released in 2006, and JSF 2.0 was released in 2009. JSF 2.0 is discussed in this section. There were two major changes to JSF in its 2.0 version. First, a facility was added for creating template documents that consisted of parts of existing documents. Second, because of problems with using JSP for the template documents in a JSF Web application, the designers made it possible and encouraged the use of a different kind of view files. Rather than JSP, which is translated into a servlet, HTML is used, which results in a tree-structured document model—a tree of components. This view structure fits much better with Faces.

The JSF system adds another layer to the JSP technology. The primary contribution of JSF is an event-driven user interface programming model, for which JSP by itself has no capability. This model provides the ability to build interactive interfaces for Java Web applications. JSF is included in Java EE.

JSF includes the following specific capabilities:

- Client-generated events can be connected to server-side application code.
- User interface components can be bound to server-side data.
- User interfaces can be constructed with reusable and extensible components.
- The user interface state can be saved and restored beyond the life of the server request.

---

12. EJBs are the Java approach to components for distributed systems.

These capabilities allow JSF to provide an effective architecture for managing the state of components, processing component values, validating user input (through components), and handling user interface events.

As with JSP applications, JSF applications require an elaborate directory structure and two XML documents to support their deployment. And as with JSP, development IDEs relieve the developer from needing to deal with much of this complexity. NetBeans has excellent support for JSF and is used to develop the example application in this section.

JSF documents define user interfaces with components. The values of these components are stored and manipulated with beans, which are often called *managed beans* or *backing beans* in JSF applications.

11.8.1   The Tag Libraries

There are several tag libraries that are used in JSF view documents, most commonly XHTML, JSF Core, and JSF HTML. In some documents, the JSF Core tags are not used. These libraries are made available to a view document by including `xmlns` attributes for them in the `html` tag. If all these libraries are needed, the following `html` tag would be used:

```
<html xmlns = "http://www.w3.org/1999/xhtml"
      xmlns:c = "http://java.sun.com/jsf/core"
      xmlns:h = "http://java.sun.com/jsf/html">
```

There are more than 25 tags in the HTML library, but only a few of them are discussed in any detail here: `form`, `inputText`, and `outputText`. Other HTML library tags are identical to their corresponding tags in HTML, so no discussion is necessary. The `form` tag does nothing more than provide a container for the user interface component elements. It has many optional attributes, but none are required. The other two HTML tags discussed here are not as simple as `form`.

The `outputText` tag typically is used to display text or bean properties, using its `value` attribute. If the text is literal (which is not the norm), it is assigned as a quoted string to the `value` attribute. If a bean property is to be displayed, it is specified with a JSF expression. JSF expressions have a form that is similar to that of JSP EL. Rather than using the EL's $, JSF expressions use a pound sign (#). For example, to display the `sum` property of the bean whose name is `myBean`,[13] the following element could be used:

```
<h:outputText value = "#{myBean.sum}" />
```

The form of JSP ELs and the JSF expressions themselves (what appears between the braces) are exactly the same, although they are not interpreted at the same time.

The `inputText` tag is used to specify a text box for user input, like the HTML `input` tag with its `type` attribute set to `text`. The `inputText` tag has a long list of optional attributes, although none is required. The `size` attribute of `inputText` is the same as that of the HTML `input` tag. The `value` attribute is used to bind the value of the tag to a bean property. The property is referenced

---

13. The names of managed beans are discussed in Section 11.8.3.

just as with `outputText`. In most applications, component values are bound to bean properties.

Among the other JSF HTML tags are the following: `selectOneMenu` for single-item select menus, `selectManyMenu` for multi-item select menus, `selectOneRadio` for radio buttons, `selectBooleanCheckbox` for a single checkbox, `selectManyCheckbox` for a collection of checkboxes, and `panel-Grid` for HTML tables.

The Core library includes 18 tags and is less complicated than the HTML library. Some of the tags are discussed later in this section.

11.8.2 JSF Event Handling

JSF event handling is similar to the event handling that is used for graphical user interfaces to Java applications. Events are defined by classes, and event listeners are defined by classes that implement listener interfaces or by bean methods. Methods that are registered on a component as listeners are notified when an event occurs on that component.

There are three categories of events in JSF: value-change events, action events, and data-model events. Value-change events occur when the value of a component is changed. Action events occur when a button or hyperlink is activated. The topic of data-model events is complex and is not discussed here.

There are two ways an application can handle action or value-change events raised by a standard component. One option is to implement an event listener interface and register it on the component by nesting a `valueChangeListener` element or an `actionListener` element inside the component. These elements are in the JSF Core library. The alternative is to implement a method in the bean of the document that contains the component to handle the event. Such a method is referenced with a method-binding expression in an attribute of the component's tag. The latter approach is the focus of this section.

11.8.3 An Example Application

The example application of this section has the same purpose as the application presented in Section 11.6: to convert a given Celsius temperature to its equivalent Fahrenheit temperature. Once again, a button click is used to request the conversion. However, rather than the button being a *Submit* button, it is a Faces HTML `commandButton`. Furthermore, clicking this button does not transfer control to a secondary document; rather, it calls a method in the project's bean to perform the conversion. This application is named `tempConvertF2`.

To create a JSF application with NetBeans, we select *File/New Project* and then *Java Web* and *Web Application* on the resulting screen. Clicking *Next* produces the *New Web Application* screen with Step 2 *Name and Location* in boldface, into which we enter the project name, `tempConvertF2`, and again click *Next*. On the resulting screen, in which Step 3 *Server and Settings* is in boldface, we again click *Next*. On the resulting screen, in which Step 4, *Framework*, is in boldface, we click the *JavaServer Faces* checkbox and the *Finish* button. This produces the initial XHTML document, `index.xhtml`, furnished by NetBeans, which follows:

```
<?xml version='1.0' encoding='UTF-8' ?>
<!DOCTYPE html PUBLIC "-//W3C//DTD XHTML 1.0 Transitional//EN"
    "http://www.w3.org/TR/xhtml1/DTD/xhtml1-transitional.dtd">

<html xmlns="http://www.w3.org/1999/xhtml"
      xmlns:h="http://java.sun.com/jsf/html">
    <h:head>
        <title> Facelet Title </title>
    </h:head>
    <h:body>
        Hello from Facelets
    </h:body>
</html>
```

For the example application, the user interface is added to this document. The user interface consists of a form with an inputText component to collect the Celsius temperature from the user and to bind the value of the component to a bean property using the value attribute. The next component of the form is the commandButton element, which, when clicked, calls the conversion method in the bean. The form also includes an outputText element to display the Fahrenheit equivalent, which it fetches from the corresponding bean property. Following is the fleshed-out document:

```
<?xml version='1.0' encoding='UTF-8' ?>
<!DOCTYPE html PUBLIC "-//W3C//DTD XHTML 1.0 Transitional//EN"
    "http://www.w3.org/TR/xhtml1/DTD/xhtml1-transitional.dtd">

<!-- welcome.xhtml - the initial document for the tempConvertF2 project.
                Displays a text box to collect a temperature in
                Celsius from the user, which it then converts to
                Fahrenheit with the UserBean method called when the
                Convert button is clicked.
    -->
<html xmlns="http://www.w3.org/1999/xhtml"
      xmlns:h="http://java.sun.com/jsf/html">
    <h:head>
        <title> Initial document for tempConvertF2 </title>
    </h:head>
    <h:body>
        <h2> Welcome to the Faces temperature converter </h2>
        <h:form>
            <p>
```

```
        Enter a temperature in Celsius:
        <h:inputText size = "4"  value = "#{userBean.celsius}" />
        <br /><br />
        <h:commandButton value ="Convert to Fahrenheit"
                       action ="#{userBean.convert}" />
        <br /><br />
        The equivalent temperature in Fahrenheit is:
        <h:outputText value ="#{userBean.fahrenheit}" />
        </p>
    </h:form>
  </h:body>
</html>
```

The managed bean for this application, with the class name `UserBean`, is simple—it provides the storage for the Celsius and Fahrenheit temperatures, along with their getter and setter methods and the converter method, `convert`. Managed beans are special classes. The JSF container instantiates them, but only when they are needed. The class name of a managed bean begins with an upper-case letter. A managed bean object is referenced by its name, which is its class name with the first letter converted to lowercase.

To create the managed bean, we select *File/New File*, which brings up the screen shown in Figure 11.17.

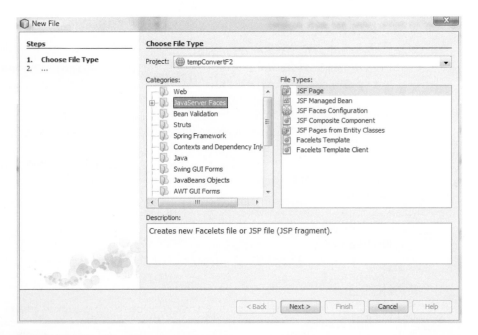

Figure 11.17 The *New File* screen

From the *New File* screen, we choose *Java Server Faces* and *JSF Managed Bean*. This produces the *New JSF Managed Bean* screen, as shown in Figure 11.18.

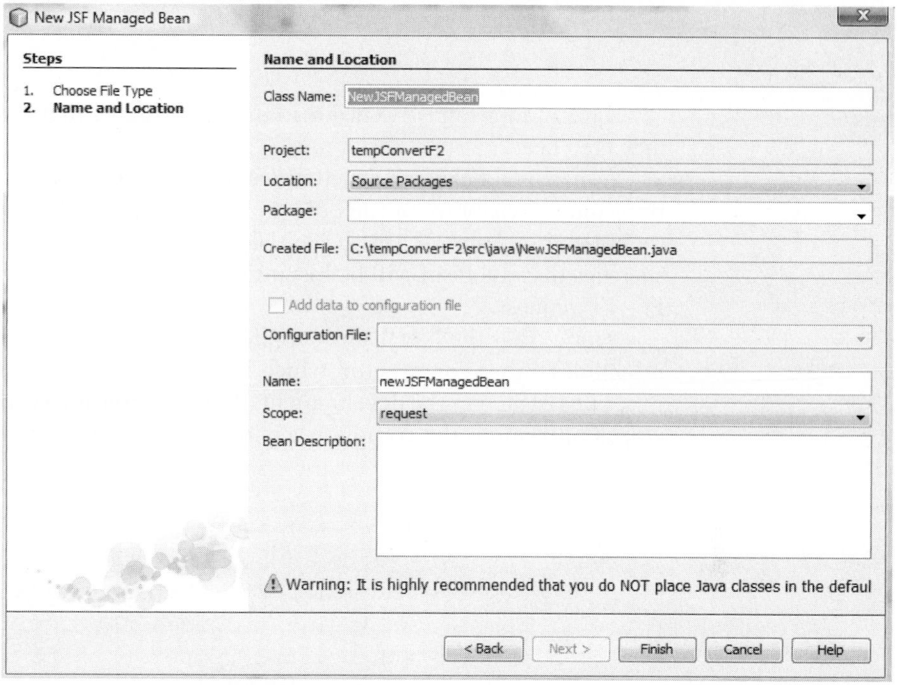

Figure 11.18 The *New JSF Managed Bean* screen

Following is the listing of the initial version of the `UserBean` bean:

```
/*
 * To change this template, choose Tools | Templates
 * and open the template in the editor.
 */
import javax.faces.bean.ManagedBean;
import javax.faces.bean.RequestScoped;

/**
 *
 * @author bob2
 */

@ManagedBean
@RequestScoped

public class UserBean {
```

```
/** Creates a new instance of UserBean */
public UserBean() {
}
```

The annotation @ManagedBean simply states that the following class is a managed bean.

A managed bean can specify several different scopes, which specify the lifetime and the visibility of the bean to the other parts of the project. The annotation @RequestScoped in the initial bean version will suffice for our needs. It specifies that the bean will be instantiated and stay available throughout a single HTTP request.

Notice that the NetBeans-supplied version of UserBean is of little value, as it includes only a constructor, which is not needed in this example.

The last step in the development of the example is to complete the UserBean class. Following is the complete version of the UserBean class:

```
/* UserBean.java - the managed bean for the tempConvertF2 project
                   Provides storage for the Celsius and Fahrenheit
                   temperatures and provides the action method to
                   convert the Celsius temperature to its equivale..
                   Fahrenheit temperature
   */
import javax.faces.bean.ManagedBean;
import javax.faces.bean.RequestScoped;

@ManagedBean
@RequestScoped

public class UserBean {
  private String celsius;
  private String fahrenheit;

  public void setCelsius(String temperature) {
      this.celsius = temperature;
  }

  public String getCelsius() {
      return celsius;
  }

  public String getFahrenheit(){
      return fahrenheit;
  }
```

```
    public void setFahrenheit(String temperature) {
        this.fahrenheit = temperature;
    }

    public String convert() {
        fahrenheit = Float.toString(1.8f *
                    Integer.parseInt(celsius) + 32.0f);
        return fahrenheit;
    }
}
```

Figure 11.19 shows a display of the initial document of the tempConvertF2 application, index.xhtml.

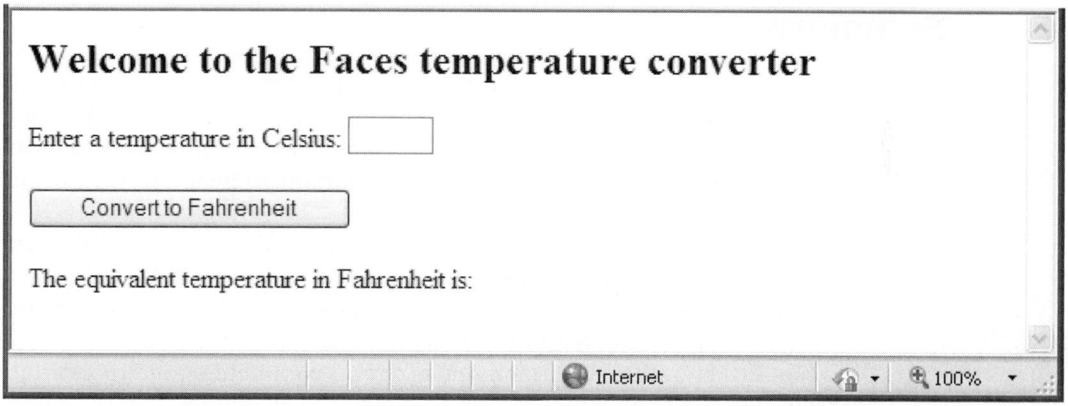

Figure 11.19 Display of index.xhtml for the tempConvertF2 project

Figure 11.20 shows a display of the tempConvertF2 application after a Celsius temperature has been entered and the focus has been shifted from the text box.

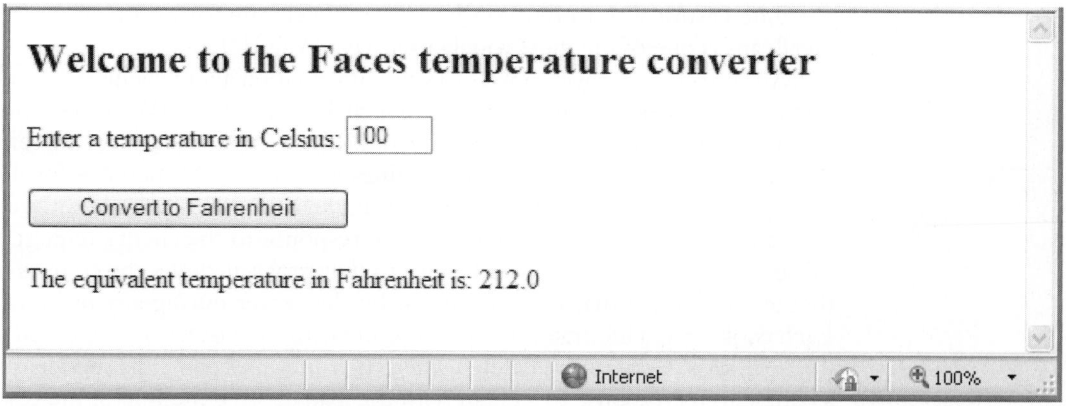

Figure 11.20 Display of tempConvertF2 after a temperature has been entered

Using the first version of JSF to build an application required the developer to edit an XML configuration file, `faces-config.xml`. If the application had more than a single JSP document, the `faces-config.xml` file would have to indicate the navigation path among them. This configuration file was also required to list any beans that were used to store the state of the application's forms. The NetBeans system took care of the beans entries, but even the developer who used NetBeans was required to enter the navigation information. Most of the need for changing the configuration file ended with JSP 2.0, with which only applications that use JSF and include many JSP documents with complex navigation paths among them require the developer to enter the navigation information in the configuration file. Our example included only a single JSP document, so even though it was developed with JSF 1.2, we were not required to enter any navigation information into `faces-config.xml`.

Summary

A servlet is a Java program that resides on the Web server and is enacted when requests are received from Web clients. A program called a servlet container, which runs on the Web server, controls the execution of servlets. The most common uses of servlets are as server-side programs to generate Web documents dynamically.

Most user-written servlets are extensions to the predefined abstract class `HttpServlet`, which is a predefined descendant of `GenericServlet`, which implements the `Servlet` interface. Any class that is derived from `HttpServlet` must override at least one of its methods—most often, `doGet` or `doPost`. The `doGet` and `doPost` methods take two parameters: one to get the input from the client and one to return results to the client. The `setContentType` method sets the MIME type for the return document. The `println` method of a `PrintWriter` object is used to create this document. The `getParameter` method is used to get the form values from the inquiry string of a form submission from the client. The method is called through the request object parameter.

The easiest way to develop Java-based Web applications is with an IDE. NetBeans is one of the most widely used Java Web IDEs.

A Web server can use cookies to store information about clients on the clients themselves. A session begins with the first client request to a Web server and ends when the client's browser is stopped. Cookies are implemented on the server as objects of the `Cookie` class, which defines a collection of methods for dealing with cookie objects. Each cookie stores a single name–value pair. The server may send a cookie to the client along with the response to the client's request. Each subsequent request made by that client to that server includes the cookies (those that are still alive) that have been sent by the server during any prior session. Each cookie has a lifetime, which is assigned with the `setMaxAge` method of the `Cookie` class. Cookies are deleted when their lifetimes end. The servlet attaches a cookie to its response to a client with the `addCookie` method of the response object. Cookies are obtained from a client request with the getCookies method of the request object.

JSP is a collection of several approaches to support dynamic documents on the server. It is an alternative to servlets, putting some form of code in markup, rather than adopting the servlet approach of producing markup with Java code. JSTL provides a set of action elements that form a programming language that has the form of markup. The EL is a simple expression language used with JSP. The if JSTL element provides a selection construct; the forEach element a loop construct; and choose, when, and otherwise a multiple selection construct.

Servlets should be used when there is little static content in the return document; JSP should be used when there is little dynamic content.

JavaBeans are Java classes that incorporate special conventions. In Web applications, JavaBean objects, called beans, are often used as containers for the data of the application. This data is exposed to JSP documents through getter and setter methods defined in the bean class. The data defined in a bean are called properties. The <jsp:useBean> JSP element is used to create an instance of a bean and give it a name that is accessible in the document. The <jsp:setProperty> element is used to set the value of a bean property. The <jsp:getProperty> element is used to fetch a property value from a bean. String values being set to properties that are not String type are coerced to their proper types. Non-String property values fetched from a bean are coerced to String type.

JSF adds to JSP the capabilities for building event-driven user interfaces to Web applications. There are two primary tag libraries used with JSF: the Core and HTML libraries. The form of a JSF document contains the JSF components that describe the user interface. Users create events by interacting with the components. The two most commonly used events are value-change events and action events. Events can be handled with classes that implement listener interfaces or with methods in the bean associated with the document that contains the components. JSF applications are usually developed with an IDE, such as NetBeans.

Review Questions

11.1   What is a servlet container?

11.2   Most user-written servlets extend what predefined class?

11.3   What are the purposes of the doGet, doPost, and doPut methods of the HttpServlet class?

11.4   Describe the two parameters to doGet and doPost.

11.5   What must the first markup output of a servlet to a client be?

11.6   What class of object is used to create markup output of a servlet to a client?

11.7   How does a servlet read form data values sent by a client to a servlet?

11.8   What are the primary benefits of using an IDE for building servlet applications?

11.9   What is a session?

11.10   Why would a Web server need to store information on a client about the client's previous requests?

11.11   What is a cookie?

11.12   What do the methods `setMaxAge`, `setValue`, and `getComment` do?

11.13   How is a cookie added to a response by a servlet?

11.14   How does a servlet get a cookie that is coming from a client?

11.15   What are the two kinds of people who develop and maintain dynamic documents?

11.16   What happens during the translation process for JSP documents?

11.17   What is template text?

11.18   What are the five parts of the JSTL?

11.19   What is the purpose of the `taglib` directive?

11.20   What is the syntactic form of an EL expression?

11.21   What are the two ways the `param` implicit variable can be used to access form values?

11.22   Describe the syntax and semantics of the `forEach` element when it is used to iterate through a collection.

11.23   Describe the semantics of a `choose` element that includes several `when` elements.

11.24   What is a JavaBean?

11.25   How are beans used by JSP applications?

11.26   What exactly does the `<jsp:useBean>` JSP element do?

11.27   What exactly does the `<jsp:setProperty>` JSP element do?

11.28   What exactly does the `<jsp:getProperty>` JSP element do?

11.29   How can a bean property be referenced in the EL?

11.30   What form of constructor is required in a bean class?

11.31   What role do beans play in the design of an MVC-based Web application?

11.32   What is the primary contribution of JSF?

11.33   What are the two standard tag libraries of JSF?

11.34   What is the form of a JSF expression?

11.35   What are the two most commonly used events in JSF?

11.36   How is the value of an `inputText` component associated with a bean property?

Exercises

11.1   Write a servlet that uses `doGet` to return a markup document that provides your name, e-mail address, and mailing address, along with a brief autobiography. Test your servlet with a simple markup document.

11.2   Write a servlet that returns a randomly chosen greeting from a list of five different greetings. The greetings must be stored as constant strings in the program.

11.3   Revise the survey sample servlet `Survey.java` to display the results of the survey in a table, with female responses in one column and male responses in another.

11.4   Revise the survey sample servlet `Survey.java` to record the number of votes so far in the data file and then display that count every time a vote is submitted or a survey result is requested. Also, change the output table so that its data is a percentage of the total votes for the particular gender category.

11.5   Write the markup document to create a form that collects favorite popular songs, including the name of the song, the composer, and the performing artist or group. This document must call a servlet when the form is submitted and another servlet to request a current list of survey results.

11.6   Modify the servlet for Exercise 11.5 to count the number of visitors and then display that number for each visitor.

11.7   Modify the HTML form for the election and the servlet `Vote-Counter` to allow voters to vote for one additional office. The new office is named catcatcher. Candidates for catcatcher are Kitty Catland, Al El Gato, Kitten Katnip, Tommie Cat, and Fred Feline. The election results must be in terms of the percentage of the total vote for an office. Votes are not counted if the client did not vote for both offices.

11.8   Write the markup document to create a form with the following capabilities:
       a.   A text widget to collect the user's name

      b. Four checkboxes, one each for the following items:

          i. Four 25-watt light bulbs for $2.39

          ii. Eight 25-watt light bulbs for $4.29

          iii. Four 25-watt long-life light bulbs for $3.95

          iv. Eight 25-watt long-life light bulbs for $7.49

      c. A collection of three radio buttons that are labeled as follows:

          i. Visa

          ii. MasterCard

          iii. Discover

11.9 Write a servlet that computes the total cost of the ordered light bulbs from Exercise 11.8 after adding 6.2 percent sales tax. The servlet must inform the buyer of exactly what was ordered, in a table.

11.10 Write a markup document to provide a form that collects names and telephone numbers. The phone numbers must be in the format ddd-ddd-dddd. Write a servlet that (1) checks the submitted telephone number to be sure that it conforms to the required format and then (2) returns a response that indicates whether the number was correct.

11.11 Revise the survey example so that it displays the result as a horizontal bar, similar to a progress bar, ranging from 0 to 100.

11.12 Write and test a JSP document that displays the form of Exercise 11.8 and produces the same response document as Exercise 11.9.

11.13 Write a markup document that displays a form that collects three numbers from the client and calls a JSP document that computes the value of multiplying the three numbers together. The JSP document must use a bean.

11.14 Explain the structure of a Web application that uses the MVC architecture.

11.15 Explain briefly the three approaches to using Java server software in an MVC architecture Web application.

11.16 Explain the two approaches to handling events in JSF.

11.17 Write a JSF application that accepts two numbers in text boxes and produces the sum, product, quotient, and difference of the first and second numbers when the second text box loses focus.

Introduction to ASP.NET

This chapter introduces ASP.NET and discusses its use for developing Web applications on Microsoft's .NET computing platform. Before describing ASP. NET, it is necessary to describe the .NET Framework, of which it is a part, and provide a few key features of the programming language C#, used in this chapter to discuss ASP.NET. Because of the similarity of C# to Java, this discussion is brief. After these preliminaries, ASP.NET is introduced, including the structure of ASP.NET documents and code-behind files. Next, the basic server-side Web controls of ASP.NET are described. To describe the processing of ASP.NET pages, the whole life cycle of that processing is presented. We then introduce Visual Studio and use it to reproduce one of the previous examples. Then page-level and control events are covered. Following this, the list Web controls are discussed. Then the Web controls that are used to validate form data are described. The next topic of the chapter is the use of ASP.NET AJAX to build Ajax-enabled Web applications. The last section of the chapter introduces Web services that use ASP.NET. Eight complete examples illustrate the concepts discussed.

The reader must keep in mind that many whole books have been devoted to describing ASP.NET. So, this one chapter can provide just a brief overview of what is a complex and powerful technology. Also, the chapter devotes less than five full pages to introduce a bit of C#. This coverage is wholly inadequate to a reader who is not familiar with Java. Such readers are advised to study Appendix A before tackling this chapter. However, because of the similarity of C# to Java, Java programmers should be able to begin to use C# for ASP.NET documents after studying the chapter. One final caveat: The fundamentals of Visual Studio, which is also the topic of many whole books (large ones, at that), are introduced in this chapter in only about six pages.

12.1   Overview of the .NET Framework

.NET is an umbrella term for a collection of technologies that was announced by Microsoft in early 2000. In January 2002, the software to support .NET was released. It was quickly adopted by a significant part of the Web software industry and will undoubtedly continue to be a major player in this industry in the future.

12.1.1   Background

.NET was developed in recognition that the future of a significant part of the computing business lies in Web-based software services, in which components of a software system may reside on different computers in different places on the Internet. Prior to .NET, Microsoft's technology for distributed component-based systems was named COM. The COM architecture suffered from several serious deficiencies. Although it allowed systems to be developed that included components written in different programming languages, it did not support inheritance among those languages. So, a Visual Basic program could not drive a new class from a C++ class. Another deficiency of COM was that mapping types between languages was complex.

A *component* is an encapsulation of software that can stand by itself and be used by other components, without those components being aware of how the functionality of the component is implemented. Components can also be created with technologies other than .NET. JavaBeans, which is introduced in Chapter 11, is a technology developed by Sun Microsystems to support distributed component-based computing using Java. The primary difference between JavaBeans and .NET components is that .NET components can be written in a variety of different programming languages; they are all language neutral.

The .NET Framework is exactly that—a framework for the development and deployment of .NET software. In .NET, the central concept is that a software system or service consists of a collection of components that can be written in different languages and reside on different computers in different locations. Also, because of the diversity of the languages employed, the collection of tools for development and deployment must be language neutral. These ideas permeate all of the parts of the .NET Framework.

12.1.2 .NET Languages

Initially, .NET included five languages: Visual Basic .NET (VB.NET), Managed C++ .NET, JScript .NET, J# .NET, and a new language, C#. J# .NET, a dialect of Java, has since been dropped, and F# has been added to the Microsoft-supported .NET languages. F# is a functional language based on OCaml. Also, Managed C++.NET has been replaced by C++/CLI, which is a garbage-collected language based on C++. JScript .NET is based on JavaScript but also provides full support for object-oriented programming. C# is briefly introduced in Section 12.2. There are now dozens of languages that run under .NET, including COBOL, Eiffel, Fortran, Perl, Python, and Ruby.

The multilanguage aspect of .NET sets it apart from similar systems. The advantage of supporting a variety of programming languages is that there is an easy migration path from software in many different languages to .NET. Organizations that use any of the .NET languages can easily transition to .NET. Programmers who are experienced and skilled in almost any common language can quickly become productive in a .NET environment. Still, although it makes reuse much more feasible, having a system composed of components written in different languages is not all good. One important disadvantage is that it complicates maintenance.

A disadvantage that .NET suffers relative to JavaBeans is that, although .NET has been ported to several non-Windows platforms, such systems have seen only limited use. So, whereas JavaBeans is now supported on a wide variety of systems, including Windows, .NET is still used almost exclusively on Windows.

12.1.3 The Common Language Runtime

The code execution technology for .NET is the Common Language Runtime (CLR), which provides language-neutral services for processing and executing .NET software. Among the most important services of the CLR are garbage collection, type checking, debugging, and exception handling. These services are used for all of the .NET languages.

For every .NET language, the CLR has a compiler to translate source programs to a common intermediate language, which was originally named Microsoft Intermediate Language (MSIL) but now is usually referred to by the name used in the ECMA standard for .NET, Common Intermediate Language (CIL). After compilation, all CIL programs have the same form, regardless of the original source language. Before execution, CIL programs are incrementally compiled to machine code for the host machine by a Just-In-Time (JIT) compiler, which is part of the CLR. A JIT compiler translates a method to machine code only when the method is called. Once compiled, the machine code version of the method is kept for the duration of execution of the program so that subsequent calls do not require recompilation. Because some executions of some programs do not cause all of the program's methods to be called, this is an efficient approach to compilation. In .NET, it is also possible to compile a whole program into machine code before execution begins. JIT compilers are commonly used for Java program execution. One major difference between Java's approach to program execution and that of the .NET languages is that CIL programs are never interpreted in the .NET Framework, as bytecode (the Java intermediate language) programs sometimes are. In fact, the .NET Framework does not include a CIL interpreter, which would be similar in purpose to the Java Virtual Machine.

12.1.4   The Common Language Infrastructure

To allow the CLR to be used for multiple languages, those languages must adhere to a set of common characteristics. These characteristics are specified by the Common Language Infrastructure (CLI), which consists of two specifications: the Common Type System (CTS) and the Common Language Specification (CLS).

The CTS defines a set of types that are supported by .NET languages. It also provides a mapping from every type in each language to its corresponding common type. For example, the CTS defines a type named Int32, which is a 32-bit signed integer type. The C# type int corresponds to Int32. The concept of common base types is analogous to what is done with the Common Object Request Broker Architecture (CORBA) (http://www.corba.org), which defines a similar set of types and gives a mapping from various languages to these common types. In CTS, types occur in two natural categories: value types and reference types. *Value types* refer directly to values in memory cells; that is, the value of a value type object is a value. *Reference types* refer to, or address, a memory cell that has a value. So, the value of a reference type is not a value; it is an address.

Having common types among languages is, of course, necessary if components in those languages are expected to interoperate correctly. All types of all .NET languages derive from a single type: System.Object.

The CLS defines the language features that must be supported by all .NET languages. .NET languages can, however, include features beyond what is specified in CLS. Of course, the use of such features in a program jeopardizes the possibility of interoperation of that program with programs in languages that do not support those features. Following are some examples of CLS restrictions:

1. There is no operator overloading.

2. There are no pointers.

3. Identifiers are not case sensitive.

Interestingly, C#, the language introduced with .NET, includes overloading, pointers, and case-sensitive identifiers. However, they should not be used in C# programs that will interoperate with components written in other .NET languages that do not include them. For example, VB.NET identifiers are not case sensitive. If a C# component must interoperate with a VB.NET component, the C# component must not use two different identifiers whose only difference is case (e.g., Sum and sum) in the interface to the VB.NET component. To design a language that can be a .NET language, the designer must ensure that all of the CLI features are supported.

The .NET Framework includes a large collection of class libraries called the Framework Class Libraries (FCL). The initial release of FCL included more than 4,000 classes that support a wide array of application areas. For example, there are APIs for networking, reflection, Web forms, database access, and file system access. Also included are APIs for access to Windows features such as the registry, as well as other Win32 functions. These functions are called through FCL classes and are executed in the CLR.

The most important result of having the CLI and the CLR may be that components written in any of the .NET languages can use any class in the FCL. More striking, perhaps, is the result that a component in any .NET language can use classes defined in any other component written in any other .NET language. This capability enables a program to call the methods of a class written in any other .NET language. It also allows a program in any .NET language to subclass classes written in any other .NET language. For example, a C# program can subclass a class written in VB.NET. It can also call the methods of a class written in C++/CLI.

12.2   A Bit of C#

This section provides a brief introduction to a few parts of C#, primarily features that are often used in ASP.NET and that differ from their Java counterparts. It is written with the assumption that the reader is familiar with Java. C# is used for the examples in this chapter, but little of the language used will be unfamiliar to Java programmers.

12.2.1   Origins

C# was designed to address the needs of .NET programming. As with most other "new" programming languages, most of C# is not in fact new, but is borrowed from existing languages. C# can be thought of as a recent iteration of the chronological sequence of C-based languages. C++ was derived from C (and SIMULA 67), and Java was derived, at least partially, from C++. C# was derived from both C++ and Java, having been based on Java, but including some features that are part of C++ but not Java. From Java, C# gets single inheritance, interfaces, garbage collection, the absence of global types or variables, and its level of assignment type coercion. From C++, C# gets pointers, operator overloading, a preprocessor, structs, and enumerations (although its structs and enumerations differ significantly from those of C++). From Delphi and VB, C# inherits properties. Finally, from J++ (Microsoft's early version of Java), C# gets delegates. Among the new C# features are indexes, attributes, and events. Overall, C# is less complex than C++ without giving up much of the expressivity of that language, which is also the case with Java. Although C# is more complex than Java, it is also more expressive.

12.2.2   Primitive Types and Expressions

C# has two categories of data: primitives and objects. C# includes a long list of primitive types, ranging from `byte`, which is an unsigned 1-byte integer, and `char`, which is a 2-byte Unicode character, to `int`, `float`, `double`, and `decimal`, which is a 16-byte decimal type that can store up to 28 decimal digits.

Symbolic constants are defined by preceding the type name in a declaration with the `const` reserved word. Every symbolic constant declaration must include an initial value—for example,

```
const float pi = 3.14159265;
```

C# has the same collection of arithmetic operators as Java, so its expressions are like those of Java.

The `Math` class provides static methods for commonly needed mathematical calculations, such as `Abs` for absolute value, `Cos` for cosine, `Sqrt` for square root, and `Pow`, which raises its first parameter to the power of its second parameter. For example,

```
X = Math.Pow(y, 3);
```

This sets x to the value of the y cubed.

12.2.3   Data Structures

The C# `String` type is similar to that of Java. Its `StringBuilder` class is the same as Java's `StringBuffer` class. The `String` class provides methods for operations on strings. One such method, `Split`, which is related to Java's `StringTokenizer` class, separates a string value into substrings, which are placed in the returned array. The parameter to `Split` is an array of characters, where any of the characters that are found in the string object on which `Split` is called specify the places to split the string. For example, consider the following code:

```
string str = "apples,prunes carrots,grapes";
char[] delimiters = new char[] {' ', ','};
String[] substrings;
substrings = str.Split(delimiters);
```

After executing this code, the value of `substrings` is `["apples"`, `"prunes"`, `"carrots"`, `"grapes"]`.

C# also supports regular expressions, like those of JavaScript, that can be used to specify the boundaries among substrings of a string in a `split` operation. In that case, the `Split` method of the regular expression class, `Regex`, is used.

The .NET FCL defines an extensive variety of collection classes, including `Array`, `ArrayList` (dynamic length arrays), `Queue`, `Stack`, and `Hashtable`. All of these store objects of any type.

Although `Array` is a class, the syntax of array references is exactly like that of C. Because it is a class, array access is through reference variables. The following is an example of a declaration of a reference to an `int` array:

```
int[] myIntArray;
```

The variable `myIntArray` can reference any one-dimensional array of `int` elements. An array object is created with the `new` operator, as in the following statement:

```
myIntArray = new int[100];
```

After execution, `myIntArray` references an array of 100 integers on the heap.

The `Array` class provides a large collection of methods and properties. Among the methods are `BinarySearch`, `Copy`, and `Sort`. One of the most frequently used properties is `Length`. For example, the following assignment statement sets `len` to `100`:

```
len = myIntArray.Length;
```

12.2.4   Control Statements

The control statements of C# are nearly identical to those of Java (as well as the other C-based languages). Two differences are the `foreach` and `switch` statements. The `foreach` statement is a data-structure-controlled iterator that has a syntax different from that of its counterpart in Java. It can be used on arrays and other collections. The syntax of `foreach` is as follows:

```
foreach (type identifier in collection) { ... }
```

An example is

```
foreach (int myInt in myIntArray) { ... }
```

The `switch` statement of C# is similar to that of Java but with one important restriction. The `switch` statements of C, C++, and Java all suffer the same problem: Although in the vast majority of cases control should exit the construct after a selected segment has executed, the default semantics is that control flows to the next segment after the selected segment has executed. Therefore, most segments in `switch` constructs must include a `break` statement. Leaving out the `break` is a common error in `switch` constructs. To avoid these errors, the C# `switch` requires that every selectable segment in a `switch` construct end with an unconditional branch instruction—either a `break` or a `goto`. To force control to continue to the next segment, a `goto` is used. For example, consider the following `switch` construct:

```
switch (value) {
  case -1:
    Negatives++;
    break;
```

```
case 0:
  Zeros++;
   goto case 1;
case 1:
  Positives++;
default:
  Console.WriteLine("Error in switch \n");
}
```

Note that `WriteLine` is a method of the `Console` class that is used to produce output to the screen.

12.2.5   Classes, Methods, and Structures

C# is a pure object-oriented programming language in the same sense as Java. There are no subprograms other than methods, which can be defined only in classes (and structs) and can be called only through objects or classes. Most of the syntax and semantics of C# classes and methods are the same as those of Java. In the paragraphs that follow, the most important differences are discussed.

Parameters to methods can be passed by value, passed by reference, or passed by result. These three implement, respectively, in mode, which is the default mode (one-way communication to the method), inout mode (two-way communication between the caller and the called method), and out mode (one-way communication from the called method to the calling method) parameter semantics. Reference variables implicitly have pass-by-reference semantics. Pass by reference is specified for value types by preceding the formal parameter with the `ref` reserved word. Pass by result is specified for value types by preceding the formal parameter with the `out` reserved word.

In some object-oriented languages, such as Java, it is relatively easy to write methods that accidentally override inherited methods.[1] This happens because the author of the new method either forgets or is unaware that a method with the same name already exists in the class ancestry. To avoid that kind of error, C# requires methods that are allowed to be overridden to be marked `virtual`. Furthermore, any method that is meant to override an inherited method must be marked `override`. If a method is defined that has the same protocol as an inherited method, but is not meant to override it, it must be marked `new`. Such a method hides the inherited version.

The `private`, `public`, and `protected` access modifiers in C# have the same semantics as those in Java.

A struct in C++ is similar to a class. In C#, however, a struct is quite different from the classes of the language. A C# struct is a lightweight class that does not support inheritance or subclassing. However, C# structs can implement interfaces

---

1. This would happen only if the author of the inherited method wants to allow it to be overridden somewhere among the class descendants. If the method should never be overridden, it is marked `final`, which prevents all descendant classes from overriding it.

and have constructors. Structs are value types, which means that they are allocated on the runtime stack. The syntactic form of a struct declaration is identical to that of a class, except that the reserved word `struct` is used in place of `class`. All C# primitive types are implemented as structs.

For some projects, one or more classes may become quite large. In C# such classes can span more than one file, which makes them more manageable. For example, all of the data members, constants, and constructors may be placed in one file and the remainder of the class in another. Each of the files appears syntactically to be a separate class definition, except that each includes the `partial` reserved word in the first line. The compiler puts the separate files together during compilation, so there is no logical difference between a class defined in one file and one defined in two. Another motivation for partial classes is when one part is generated by a tool, such as the .NET Framework, and other parts are written by developers. This can help developers focus on the parts they write, rather than the whole class.

In contemporary object-oriented programming languages, programs have access to large, comprehensive, and complex class libraries that provide services and commonly needed types. For .NET, this is the FCL. The most commonly used classes of the .NET FCL are included in the `System` namespace, which also includes classes for input and output, string manipulation, event handling, threading, and collections, among others.

12.2.6   Exception Handling

Exception handling in C# is similar to that of Java. All exception classes are descendants of `Exception`, which has two subclasses: `SystemException` and `ApplicationException`. Some common system exceptions are `IndexOutOfRangeException`, `NullReferenceException`, and `ArithmeticException`. The `try-catch-finally` structure of C# is the same as that of Java, except that C# `catch` blocks do not require a parameter. Such a `catch` catches any exception.

12.2.7   Output

The root class for all C# classes is `Object`, which is in the `System` namespace. Variables can be declared with the type name `object`, which is an alias for `System.Object`. A value of any type can be assigned to an `object` variable. When a primitive type value is assigned to an `object` variable, it is implicitly converted to an `object` object through a process called *boxing*.

Output from an ASP.NET document, which becomes part of the markup document returned to the browser, is generated through a `Response` object. The `Response` class, which is included in the `System` namespace, defines the `Write` method, whose string parameter is markup. The following statement is illustrative:

```
System.Response.Write("<h1> Today's Report </h1>");
```

If the output must be formatted—for instance, to include the values of variables—the `Format` method of the `string` type (`string` is an alias for the `System.String` class) is used, as in the following example:

```
string msg = string.Format("The answer is: {0} <br />",
                            answer);
System.Response.Write(msg);
```

The notation `{0}` specifies the position in the string for the value of the variable named after the string.

The `using` statement can be used to abbreviate the names of classes in a namespace. For example,

```
using System;
```

allows the program to access the classes defined in `System` without including the prefix `System` in the names of those classes.

In place of the packages of Java, C# uses namespaces. A namespace is specified with the `namespace` reserved word—for example,

```
namespace myStuff {
  ...
}
```

This concludes our quick tour of C#.

12.3   Introduction to ASP.NET

ASP.NET is a large and complex topic. This section provides a brief introduction to its fundamentals. Additional features of ASP.NET are discussed in subsequent sections.

12.3.1   The Basics

ASP.NET is a Microsoft technology for building dynamic Web documents. (ASP is an abbreviation for *Active Server Pages*.) Dynamic ASP.NET documents are supported by programming code executed on the Web server. Although ASP.NET documents can also include client-side scripts, we focus on the server side. ASP.NET is based on its predecessor, ASP, which allowed embedded server-side scripts written in either JScript (Microsoft's JavaScript) or VBScript (a scripting dialect of VB). Both of these languages were purely interpreted, making programs written in them execute much more slowly than semantically equivalent programs written in compiled languages. There are a few other problems with using purely interpreted code to provide server-side dynamic documents. First, documents that include both scripting code and markup are complex, especially if they are large. Mixing markup and programming code, which mixes presentation and business logic, creates confusing documents. Furthermore, Web markup designers and programmers must deal with the same document. Second, purely interpreting scripts before delivering documents is inefficient. Third, there is the problem of the reliability of code written in scripting languages, in part because they use either dynamic typing or relaxed typing rules. Also, in many scripting languages array index ranges are not checked.

As we saw in Chapter 11, JSP offers one solution to these problems: Use Java to describe the computation associated with user interactions with Web documents. The Java language is much more reliable than the scripting languages, largely because of the strict type checking and array index range checking. Furthermore, compiled Java code is faster than interpreted scripting code. Finally, although Java can be directly embedded in markup documents with JSP, it is entirely separate when JavaBeans are used. An alternative to JSP, ASP.NET allows the server-side programming code to be written in any of the .NET languages, although most is written in either VB.NET or C#.

Programming code that is part of a Web application but resides outside the ASP.NET document (the markup document file) is placed in a separate file called the *code-behind* file. It is good to keep all program code separate from the ASP.NET document, for the same reasons that it is good to keep JavaScript in separate files rather than embedded in a markup document.

Every ASP.NET document is compiled into a class in a specific .NET programming language, which resides in an assembly—the unit in which compiled classes are stored in .NET. An assembly is also the unit of deployment for .NET. Compiling a markup document, which may or may not include embedded programming code, into a class is precisely what happens to JSP documents: They are compiled into servlets, which are classes. From a programmer's point of view, developing dynamic Web documents (and the supporting code) in ASP.NET is similar to developing non-Web applications. Both involve defining classes based on library classes, implementing interfaces from a library, and calling methods defined in library classes. An application class uses and interacts with existing classes. In ASP.NET, this is exactly the same for Web applications.

The class to which an ASP.NET document is compiled is a descendant of the `System.Web.UI.Page` class, from which it inherits a collection of members. Among the most commonly used are the `Request` and `Response` objects, the `WebControls` class, and the `IsPostBack` property. As we saw previously, the `Write` method of the `Response` object is used to create output from an ASP.NET document. The Web `Controls` class defines a large collection of server-side controls that are available to ASP.NET documents. Sample documents that use the Web controls appear in Section 12.4. The `IsPostBack` property is used to determine whether the current request is a result of a user interaction with a form (as opposed to an initial request for a document). Its use is illustrated in an example document in Section 12.4.2.

An ASP.NET document that does not use a code-behind file is compiled[2] into a direct subclass of `Page`. Code-behind files also are compiled into subclasses of `System.Web.UI.Page`. We call the class that results from compiling

---

2. This is technically a misuse of the term "compile," although ASP.NET documents are translated from their original form to C# programs.

the ASP.NET document the *document class*. Note that a document class is pure C# source code rather than an intermediate code version. Document classes that use a code-behind file are subclasses of the code-behind class, an intermediate class between the document class and `System.Web.UI.Page`. So, programming code in an ASP.NET document inherits from both `Page` and the class of the code-behind file. Inheritance diagrams for ASP.NET documents with and without code-behind files are shown in Figure 12.1.

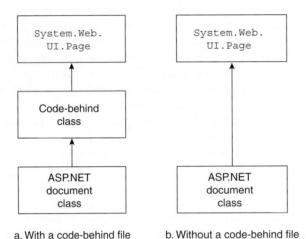

a. With a code-behind file   b. Without a code-behind file

Figure 12.1 Inheritance diagrams for ASP.NET documents with and without code-behind files

12.3.2   **ASP.NET Documents**

ASP.NET documents can include a number of different kinds of text. First, they can contain HTML or XHTML markup, including comments, as well as non-standard ASP.NET-specific markup elements. The markup can include static elements, elements made dynamic by client-side scripts, and elements made dynamic by server-side code.

Second, an ASP.NET document can include one or more directives, the most common of which is `Page`, which can have any of a large number of different attributes.

Third, documents can have *render blocks*, which use the `<%` opening tag and `%>` closing tag and have programming code as content. This code, which cannot include subprogram definitions, is placed (by the document compiler) into a function of the class of the document when the document is translated to a class. The function's body typically consists of method calls and output statements to create the static markup of the document. The function is executed when the document class is executed (producing the markup document that is returned to the requesting browser).

Fourth, documents can contain programming code as the content of script elements that include the attribute `runat`, set to `"server"`. Such code is called a *declaration block*, because it is not implicitly executed. Subprograms, including event handlers, are defined in declaration blocks. The code in declaration blocks is inserted directly into the class created for the document.

Finally, documents can include server-side comments, which appear in elements that use the opening tag `<%--` and the closing tag `--%>`.

A directive appears in an element whose opening tag is `<%@` and closing tag is `$>`. So, the general form of a directive is as follows:

```
<%@ directive-name attributes %>
```

The only directive required in every ASP.NET document that includes embedded programming code is `Page`. For these documents, the `Page` directive must minimally include a `Language` attribute, which is assigned the name of the .NET language that is used for embedded programming code in the document. This name, of course, is necessary to inform the CLR which compiler is to be used to compile the document.

At this point, an example application is in order. The simple ASP.NET document that follows uses C# code in a render block to compute and display the number of days, hours, and minutes left in the year.[3] The `Now` method of the .NET `DateTime` class is used to get the current date and time in a `DateTime` object. The constructor for this class is then used to create the second `DateTime` object, with the date January 1, 2013. The time between the two objects is computed with the `Subtract` method of the `DateTime` object for New Year's Day. Then the values returned by the `Days`, `Hours`, and `Minutes` methods of that object are converted to strings to produce the output.

Following is the ASP.NET document, which has the `.aspx` suffix. Such ASP.NET documents are often referred to as *source documents*.

```
<!-- timeLeft.aspx
     A simple example of an ASP.NET document
     It displays the number of days, hours, and minutes
     left this year (2012)
     -->
<%@ Page language="c#" %>

<html xmlns = "http://www.w3.org/1999/xhtml">
  <head> <title> timeLeft </title>
  </head>
  <body>
    <h3> Days, hours, and minutes left this year </h3>
    <%
      string msg, days, hours, minutes;
      DateTime rightnow, newYears;
      TimeSpan timeSpan;
```

---

3. For simplicity, our example assumes that the current year is 2012.

```
        // Set date/time of right now and new years day
        rightnow = DateTime.Now;
        newYears = new DateTime(2013, 1, 1);

        // Compute the difference in time/dates
        timeSpan = newYears.Subtract(rightnow);

        // Compute and display the differences in days, hours, and
        // minutes
        days = timeSpan.Days.ToString();
        msg = string.Format("Days: {0},   ", days);
        Response.Write(msg);
        hours = timeSpan.Hours.ToString();
        msg = string.Format("Hours: {0},   ", hours);
        Response.Write(msg);
        minutes = timeSpan.Minutes.ToString();
        msg = string.Format("Minutes: {0} <br />", minutes);
        Response.Write(msg);
    %>
  </body>
</html>
```

All of the examples in this chapter were developed with ASP.NET 4.0.

12.3.3   Code-Behind Files

As stated in Section 12.3.1, it is better to keep programming code separate from markup documents, thereby also separating program logic from presentation. In ASP.NET, this is done by storing programming code in code-behind files.

To illustrate the difference between declaration blocks and code-behind files, timeLeft.aspx is rewritten here as timeLeft2.aspx and the code-behind file timeLeft2.aspx.cs, both of which are shown next. The process of timeLeft.aspx is written as a method, and only the call to it is left in the new source document, timeLeft2.aspx. The code-behind file defines the class TimeLeft and its method, timer. Here are the two documents:

```
<!-- timeLeft2.aspx
     A simple example of an ASP.NET document with a code-behind
     file. It has the same functionality as timeLeft.aspx
     -->
<%@ Page language="C#"  Inherits = "TimeLeft"
        Src = "timeLeft2.aspx.cs" %>

<html xmlns = "http://www.w3.org/1999/xhtml">
  <head> <title> timeLeft2 </title>
```

```
    </head>
    <body>
      <h3> Days, hours, and minutes left this year </h3>
      <%
        timer();
      %>
    </body>
  </html>
```

```csharp
// timeLeft2.aspx.cs
//   The code-behind file for timeLeft2.aspx
//   Defines a class with a method to compute and
//   display the days, hours, and minutes left
//   this year

using System;
using System.Web;
using System.Web.UI;

public class TimeLeft2 : Page {

  string msg, days, hours, minutes;
  TimeSpan timeSpan;

  public void timer() {

    // Set date/time of New Years Day and right now
    DateTime rightnow = DateTime.Now;
    DateTime newYears = new DateTime(2013, 1, 1);

    // Compute the difference in time/dates
    timeSpan = newYears.Subtract(rightnow);

    // Compute and display the differences in days, hours, and
    // minutes
    days = timeSpan.Days.ToString();
    msg = string.Format("Days: {0},   ", days);
    Response.Write(msg);
    hours = timeSpan.Hours.ToString();
    msg = string.Format("Hours: {0},   ", hours);
    Response.Write(msg);
    minutes = timeSpan.Minutes.ToString();
    msg = string.Format("Minutes: {0} <br />", minutes);
    Response.Write(msg);
  }
}
```

Notice that the `Page` directive in the source document includes two new attributes. The `Inherits` attribute specifies that the document inherits from its code-behind file's class. The name used for this attribute is the same as the base name of the file. Also included is the `Src` attribute, which gives the full name of the code-behind file. When the `Src` attribute is included, the code-behind file is implicitly compiled the first time its associated source document is requested. If the code-behind file is changed, the next request for the associated source document implicitly causes its recompilation.

If the `Src` attribute is absent, the code-behind file must be explicitly compiled and placed in the `bin` subdirectory of the directory in which the source document is stored, before the associated source document is requested. This approach has the advantage of allowing the detection and repair of syntax errors in the code-behind file before deployment.

The reason the `using` directives are included in the code-behind file but not in the source document is that the compiled source file is a subclass of the class defined in the code-behind file.

Figure 12.2 displays the output of `timeLeft2.aspx`.

Days, hours, and minutes left this year

Days: 92, Hours: 14, Minutes: 31

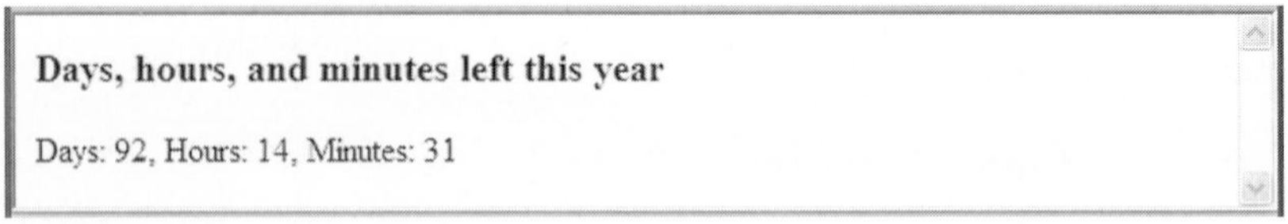

Figure 12.2 Display of the output of `timeLeft2.aspx`

12.4 ASP.NET Controls

ASP.NET controls are related to HTML form components, but they have associated program code that is executed on the server. Therefore, they are called *server controls*. There are two categories of ASP.NET server controls: HTML controls and Web controls. Because HTML controls are less used than Web controls, HTML controls are not covered in this book.

The conversion, or compilation, process translates all Web controls into HTML elements. This is, of course, necessary to allow all browsers to display the ASP.NET documents.

12.4.1 Web Controls

Some Web controls correspond to the ordinary HTML form elements. For example, there are controls for checkboxes, radio buttons, and tables. There are also controls that do not have corresponding HTML elements, such as checkbox lists and radio button lists. In addition, there are special controls for form data validation and data binding. The validation controls are discussed in Section 12.4.8, the data-binding controls in Chapter 13. The most commonly used non–special Web controls are shown in Table 12.1.

All of the Web controls are in the namespace with the prefix `asp`, so the tag names are all qualified with `asp:`. For example, a text box control is specified with `asp:TextBox`.

All Web controls are server controls. This relationship is indicated by including the runat attribute set to "server", as in the following control:

```
<asp:TextBox ID="phone"  runat="server" />
```

The ListControl class has four subclass controls. Two of them—DropDownList and ListBox—are converted to HTML select elements. The ListBox control can display one or more of its items. The number of display items defaults to four but can be set to any number. A vertical scrollbar is implicitly included if the control has more items than the number it can display. More than one item in a ListBox can be selected. The DropDownList control remains hidden until the user clicks its button. The browser chooses the number of items displayed when the drop-down button is clicked. DropDownList controls do not allow multiselection mode. (Only one item can be selected at a time, as in a radio button group.)

Table 12.1   Commonly used Web controls and related HTML elements

Web Control Type	Corresponding HTML Element
AdRotator	`<img>` and `<link>`

Button	`<input type = "button" />`
	`<input type = "submit" />`
	`<input type = "reset" />`

Calendar	None
Checkbox	`<input type = "checkbox" />`
CheckBoxList	None
DropDownList	`<select>`
Image	`<img>`
ImageButton	None
ImageMap	None
Label	None
Panel	`<div>`
RadioButton	`<input type = "radio" />`
RadioButtonList	None
Table	`<table>`
TableCell	`<th>,<td>`
TableRow	`<tr>`
TextBox	`<input type = "text" />`

The two other `ListControl` subclass controls are `CheckBoxList` and `RadioButtonList`, both of which are normally translated to table HTML elements. In both cases, the purpose is to allow programming code access to the items in the lists. Such access supports the possibility of adding or deleting list items dynamically as the result of user interaction. It also makes it possible for list items to be fetched from a database or other external source. `CheckBoxList` and `RadioButtonList` controls are discussed further in Section 12.4.7.

Some of the Web controls do not correspond to HTML components and are translated to combinations of components. Among these are `Xml`, `Panel`, and `AdRotator`. The `Xml` control provides the ability to include XSL transformations on XML input as part of the output HTML document. The `Panel` control provides a container for other controls, for those situations in which one wants to control the position or visibility of the contained controls as a unit. The `AdRotator` provides a way to produce different content on different requests implicitly. An `AdRotator` control is translated to an HTML image and a link.

12.4.2   Life Cycle of a Simple ASP.NET Document

A source document that includes a form serves both to describe the initial content of a markup document for browser display and to provide the event handling to process user interactions with the form in the document. So, for all source documents that include forms, there are two kinds of requests. First, there is an initial request, which results in the requested document and its form being displayed for the client. Second, there is a request made after the form has been changed by the client. This kind of request is called a *postback*, because the form values are posted back to the document on the server. Programming code in a document or the code-behind file can determine whether a request is a postback request by testing the `IsPostBack` property of the `Page` class, which is true if it is a postback request.

Programming code can access the values of controls through the `Value` property of the associated object. The object associated with a control has the same name as the control's id attribute. So, if a form has a text box with the id phone, its value can be accessed as `phone.Value`.

To clarify the sequence of events that takes place for a source document that includes a form, consider the following simple document:

```
<!-- hello.aspx
     A simple example of an ASP.NET document with controls.
     It uses textboxes to get the name and age of the client,
     which are then displayed.
     -->
<%@ Page language="c#" %>

<html>
  <head> <title> Hello </title>
  </head>
```

```
<body>
  <form runat = "server">
    <p>
      Your name:
      <asp:textbox id = "name"  runat = "server" />
      <br />
      Your age:
      <asp:textbox id = "age"  runat = "server" />
      <br />
      <asp:button id = "submit" runat = "server"
                  text = "Submit" />
    <br />
    <% if (IsPostBack) { %>
      Hello <%= name.Text %> <br />
      You are <%= age.Text %> years old <br />
      <% } %>
    </p>
  </form>
</body>
</html>
```

Notice that both the form and the controls in the form must include the runat attribute, set to "server". In this example, the markup in the first part of the body is displayed when the document is first delivered to the browser. On subsequent postback requests for the document, the C# code at the end of the form is executed on the server and the resulting markup is sent to the browser and is displayed.

ASP.NET implicitly stores the control state of a document class instance before the server returns the output of the instance to the client. This information is stored in a hidden control named ViewState, which is a property of the Page class. ViewState is a reference to a StateBag object, which is a data structure similar to a hash. StateBag objects are valid only while the page is active. If the browser is pointed at a different document, the StateBag object is discarded. When the document is posted back to the server, the ViewState data is used to initialize the new instance implicitly. Of course, ViewState will not have form data on the first postback. After initialization with ViewState, the client input from the form is used for a second initialization of the instance. Therefore, any control whose value is not input by the client retains its previous value. ViewState provides implicit form state preservation between requests. So, it does what the HTTP protocol cannot do: save the state across the round trips to the server.

Of course, saving the state with ViewState is not free. For a large form with many controls, the resulting ViewState will require more time for browser–server communications, as well as storage space on the client machine.

The flowchart in Figure 12.3 shows the list of the things that happen when the `hello.aspx` document is requested, delivered to the browser, has its text boxes filled in by the user, is posted back to the server, and, finally, is returned to the browser. Note that several events are raised during this processing, although none is described in the flowchart.

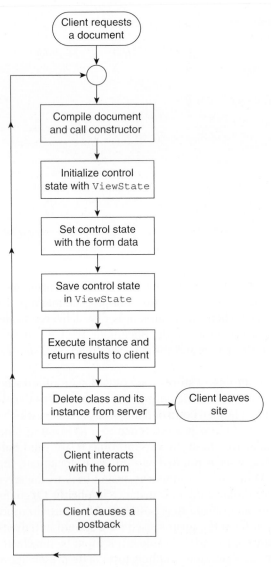

Figure 12.3 A flowchart indicating the life cycle of an ASP.NET document

`ViewState` is user accessible, so it can be used to store state information other than form data. All controls inherit `ViewState` from the `Controls` class. Any textual data can be placed in `ViewState` with a simple assignment statement—for example,

```
ViewState["myName"] = "Freddie";
```

Accessing the values in `ViewState` is slightly complicated by the necessity of casting the value to the proper type. For example, to fetch the `myName` value in the preceding statement, the following assignment could be used:

```
name = (string)ViewState["myName"];
```

To use `ViewState` for nonform data, that data must be assigned to `ViewState` before `ViewState` gets the form data, because it is then that `ViewState` is finalized. In Section 12.4.4, the `PreRender` event is introduced, which is the perfect time to record nonform data in `ViewState`.

The document created by the document class that was compiled from the `hello.aspx` document, after it has had its form filled by the client, is as follows:

```
<!-- hello.aspx
     A simple example of an ASP.NET document with controls.
     It uses textboxes to get the name and age of the client,
     which are then displayed.
     -->
<html>
  <head> <title> Hello </title>
  </head>
  <body>
    <form name="ct100" method="post" action="hello.aspx" id="ct100">
      <div>
        <input type="hidden" name="__VIEWSTATE" id="__VIEWSTATE"
               value="/wEPDwUKMTQyOTM4OTczNmRkgGqzeOWp5+
                  9PqFirn31TKZMNYGc=" />
      </div>
      <div>
        <input type="hidden" name="_EVENTVALIDATION"
               id="_EVENTVALIDATION"
               value="wEWBALDWau5BAL7uPQdAtCCr60GAty7hLYE4ZUNQF1+
                  GAAuhXGhNipCLhmIuSIiqpwctzFQUu54peg="
      </div>
      <p>
        Your name:
        <input name="name" type="text" value="Mike" id="name" />
        <br />
        Your age:
        <input name="age" type="text" value="47" id="age" />
        <br />
```

```
            <input type="submit" name="submit" value="Submit"
                 id="submit" />
            <br />

            Hello Mike <br />
            You are 47 years old <br />

         </p>
      </form>
   </body>
</html>
```

This document differs from the original version of `hello.aspx` in three particulars. First, it includes the `ViewState` hidden control, which has a coded version of the form data. The code used is in base 64. Second, the form has an internal name and `id` (`ct100`). Third, the render block to produce the return markup has been replaced by its output.

Figure 12.4 displays `hello.aspx` after the postback.

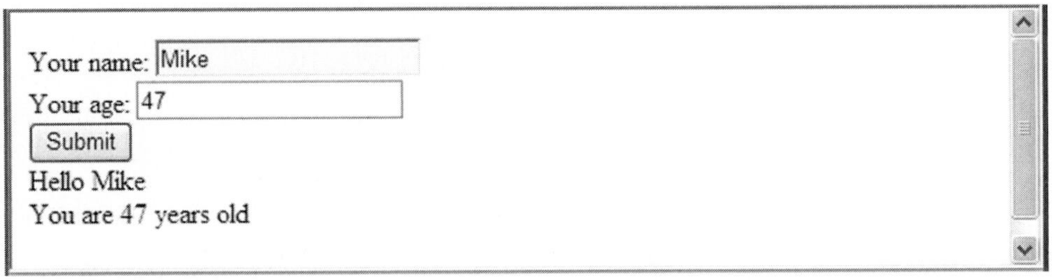

Figure 12.4 Display of `hello.aspx` after the postback

A postback can be initiated by a user in more than one way. Of course, a postback occurs if the user clicks the *Submit* button of a form. It also happens when any button is clicked. The user has the option of having a postback happen when a checkbox is clicked or a select item is selected. This option is controlled by the `AutoPostBack` property of the control. If `AutoPostBack` is set to `"true"`, then a change in the control's value causes a postback.

12.4.3   Visual Studio

Microsoft's Visual Studio is an integrated development environment (IDE) for building both Web and non-Web applications for .NET. It has matured into a powerful tool that simplifies and eases the workload of creating .NET software systems. Although it is possible to build Web applications for .NET without it, as seen in Section 12.3, using Visual Studio is in most cases easier and faster.

Visual Studio is an immense software system that requires a lengthy study to master all of its capabilities. However, learning to use it on relatively small and simple systems does not require a great deal of time or effort. Although the complete Visual Studio is expensive, Microsoft has available a less powerful version, currently named Visual Web Developer 2010 Express, for free. Visual Studio 2010 is introduced in this section and used in the remainder of the chapter. Henceforth, we refer to it as VS. In part because NetBeans, the related IDE, was introduced and used in Chapter 11, it should be relatively easy to get started with VS.

VS offers a long list of capabilities. The following are a few of the most useful:

1. VS includes a built-in Web server that allows the development and testing of Web applications without using an external Web server.
2. VS includes an integrated debugger for all .NET languages.
3. Toolbars and information windows in VS can be customized and moved and docked to any side of the main development window.
4. VS supports the ability to show two parallel windows, one with a graphical representation of a form and its controls and the other with the code that supports the form's controls.

When VS is opened, its *Start Page* is displayed, as shown in Figure 12.5.

The layout of the *Start Page* is typical: The top line is its title, the second line is a menu bar, and the third is a toolbar. The main part of the display shows several windows, the largest of which is the news window, which is labeled with *Latest News*. This window contains a list of links to articles discussing developments of the topic. At the left-center of the start page is the *Recent Projects* window, which invites the user to choose to open an existing project or create a new project. At the bottom of the screen is the *Error List* window, which is not used until a project is opened or created.

The *Solution Explorer* window appears on the right side of the *Start Page*. It can be locked open with the button whose icon is a pin. A locked-open window is said to be "pinned." Once pinned, a window can be dragged to a different location on the edge of the main window. When a window is open and attached to an edge of the main window, it is said to be "docked" there. The contents of the *Solution Explorer* will be discussed after a project has been opened.

An application built with VS consists of a collection of files, all of which are stored in a directory. The default location of this directory depends on the operating system. On XP, it is `C:\Documents and Settings\your username\My Documents\Visual Studio 2008\Projects`. On Vista and Windows 7, it is `C:\users\your username\Documents\Visual Studio 2010\Websites`. On either system, the default directory for a project can be changed on the *Start Page* by selecting *Tools/Options/Projects and Solutions*. For the projects in this book, we have changed the default destination to `C:\vStudio 2010`.

Figure 12.5 The VS *Start Page*

As always, the most effective way to discuss the VS IDE is by explaining the steps involved in creating an example project. In this section, we use VS to build the example application `hello.aspx` discussed in Section 12.4.2. We will name this new application `helloVS`.

The process of creating a new Web application is begun by selecting *File/New/Web Site* on the *Start Page*. This opens the *New Web Site* window shown in Figure 12.6.

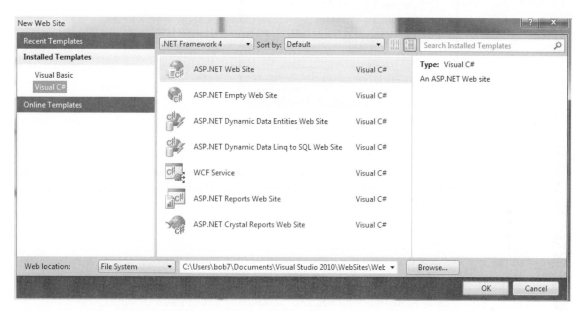

Figure 12.6 The *New Web Site* window

The central window of the *New Web Site* screen displays a list of seven installed templates, the first of which, *ASP.NET Web Site*, is selected initially. When used, these templates produce skeletal versions of the source document and the code-behind file. Above the list of templates is a menu showing the item *.NET Framework 4*. The other items of this menu are *.NET Framework 2.0* and *.NET Framework 3.0*, and *.NET Framework 3.5*.

The *Location* menu near the bottom of the screen has the displayed item *File System*. The other two possible items in this menu are *HTTP* and *FTP*. The *File System* option specifies that the new Web site will be stored on the machine's file system, and when it is run, it will use the internal test Web server, rather than IIS. When *File System* is chosen, a menu to the right of the *Location* menu displays a directory location and file name for the new Web site. If *HTTP* is chosen, the application will be served by IIS and therefore must be stored in an IIS virtual directory, which is automatically created by VS. The *FTP* option allows the creation of the Web site at a remote location.

VS applications are called *solutions*. Every solution has its own directory, which may contain one or more projects. The solution directory includes source documents (`.aspx`), code files, data sources, and a configuration file.

The next step is to select *ASP.NET Empty Web Site*, type in the address (at the bottom of the window) `C:\vStudio2010\helloVS`, and click *OK*. This produces a screen with the *Solution Explorer* on its right side. This is shown in Figure 12.7.

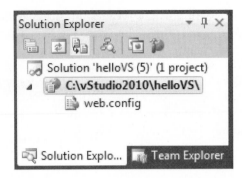

Figure 12.7 *Solution Explorer* window

Next, right click the second line shown in the *Solution Explorer*, select *Add New Item*, select *Web Form*, and click *Add* on the resulting window. This produces the following document:

```
<%@ Page Language="C#" AutoEventWireup="true" CodeFile="Default.aspx.cs"
        Inherits="_Default" %>
<!DOCTYPE html PUBLIC "-//W3C//DTD XHTML 1.0 Transitional//EN"
                "http://www.w3.org/TR/xhtml1/DTD/xhtml1-
                    transitional.dtd">

<html xmlns="http://www.w3.org/1999/xhtml">
<head runat="server">
    <title></title>
</head>
<body>
    <form id="form1" runat="server">
    <div>

    </div>
    </form>
</body>
</html>
```

Note that web.config. is one of the file names shown in the *Solution Explorer*. This XML file is related to the deployment descriptor file, web.xml, required by all Java servlet, JSP, and Faces applications. It contains configuration information for the application. Although web.config is a necessary part of every ASP.NET application, because VS builds it implicitly, the developer rarely needs to create or modify it.

The name of the ASP.NET document shown in the *Solution Explorer*, which is `Default.aspx` initially, can be changed by right-clicking it. We change this one to `helloVS.aspx`.

Before adding functionality to the application, we added initial documentation, changed the title element content, and deleted the unnecessary `div` element. Next, we click the *Split* button at the bottom of the workspace, which divides the center window horizontally, with the source window, which displays the markup, in the top half and an empty window in the bottom that is used for visually designing the document. We then open the toolbox by selecting *View/Toolbox*. The *Toolbox* window opens on the left edge of the screen. To prevent the overlap of the toolbox and source windows, we pin the toolbox. The toolbox contains a long list of names of controls, beginning with the *Standard* controls. Farther down the list are a number of elided sublists, for example *Validation* and *AJAX Extensions*, which are discussed later in this chapter.

The next step is to add the controls, which we do by dragging two text boxes and a button from the toolbox to the design window. Notice that the markup for the controls is implicitly placed in the source window. Of course, the controls have generic ids, so we change them to the more meaningful identifiers used in the previous document `hello.aspx`. We also add the labels *Your name* and *Your age* and change the text of the button to *Submit*. The last step is to add the response code from `hello.aspx`.

The resulting document is as follows:

```
<!-- helloVS.aspx
     A simple example of an ASP.NET document with controls, built
     with VS. It uses textboxes to get the name and age of the
     client, which are then displayed.
     -->
<%@ Page Language="C#" AutoEventWireup="true"
        CodeFile="helloVS.aspx.cs" Inherits="_Default" %>

<!DOCTYPE html PUBLIC
        "-//W3C//DTD XHTML 1.0 Transitional//EN"
        "http://www.w3.org/TR/xhtml1/DTD/xhtml1-transitional.dtd">

<html xmlns="http://www.w3.org/1999/xhtml">
<head runat="server">
    <title> helloVS </title>
</head>
<body>
    <form id="form1" runat="server">
    <p>
        Your name:
        <asp:TextBox ID="name" runat="server"></asp:TextBox>
        <br />
```

```
      Your age:
      <asp:TextBox ID="age" runat="server"> </asp:TextBox>
      <br />
      <asp:Button ID="submit" runat="server" Text="Submit" />
      <br />
      <% if (IsPostBack){ %>
        Hello <%= name.Text%> <br />
        You are <%= age.Text%> years old <br />
      <% } %>
    </p>
  </form>
</body>
</html>
```

We test the new document by clicking the *Debug* menu at the top of the screen and selecting *Start without Debugging*. This runs the internal Web server of VS and produces the same display as shown in Figure 12.4.

VS will be used to produce all of the subsequent applications in this chapter.

12.4.4 ASP.NET Events

There are a large number of events that can be raised while an ASP.NET document is being processed and displayed. Applications, sessions, the page itself, and controls can all raise events. Application and session events are not discussed in this chapter. A discussion of page-level events and control events follows.

Page-Level Events

Page-level events are created by the Page class at specific times in the life cycle of a source document. The page-level events are Init, which is raised immediately after a document class is instantiated; Load, which is raised just after the instance has its state set from form data and ViewState; PreRender, which is raised just before the instance is executed to construct the client response document; and Unload, which is raised just before the instance is discarded.

There are two ways to design and register handlers for the page-level events. The first is to write the handlers by using predefined names that are implicitly registered when the document class is created. This implicit handler registration is called *auto event wireup*. It is controlled by the Page directive attribute, AutoEventWireup, which has the default value of true. If this attribute is set to false, the implicit registration is not done and registration must be done manually. The names of the handlers that are implicitly registered are Page_Load, Page_Unload, Page_PreRender, and Page_Init. All return void and take two parameters, the first of object type and the second of System.EventArgs type. The Page_Load handler is illustrated in an example in Section 12.4.7.

The second way to design and register event handlers for page-level events is to override the virtual handler methods defined in the Page class. Such handlers must be manually registered in the document. This approach is not further discussed here.

Control Events

Many ASP.NET control events are handled on the server, although many are raised on the client. The HTML events discussed in Chapter 5 are both raised and handled on the client. When some ASP.NET control events occur, they cause an immediate postback to the server. In other cases, the notification is delayed until the next postback. In the case of the Click event, there is an immediate postback (using HTTP POST) with the event message. When such a postback is received, the server searches for a handler for Click, and if one is found, it executes it.

Not all events can be handled on the server, because of the time required to do them. For example, because of the frequency with which it may occur, the MouseOver event cannot be handled on the server: It would simply take too much time for the postback and handling each time it was raised. So, MouseOver is one of the events that is still handled on the client.

As stated previously, control events are either postback or nonpostback; either they cause an immediate postback when raised or they are saved until the next postback. For some controls, all events are postback; for example, Button and Menu. CheckBox, TextBox, and RadioButton are nonpostback controls.

Event handlers for controls are registered the way JavaScript client-side event handlers are registered through HTML attributes. Different controls have attributes with different names for event handler registration. TextBox controls use the OnTextChanged attribute; Button controls use OnClick; CheckBox and RadioButton controls use OnCheckedChanged. The CheckBoxList and RadioButtonList controls use SelectedIndexChanged. The handlers all return void and take the same two parameters as the page-level event handlers. The following event handler for a text box control, along with the control, is illustrative:

```
protected void TextBoxHandler(object src,
                             System.EventArgs e) {
  ...
}
...
<asp:TextBox ID="Name" OnTextChanged="TextBoxHandler"
            runat="server" />
```

12.4.5   Creating Control Elements with Code

Server-side controls can be specified for a source document in two different ways: with markup or with programming code. For example, a button can be created with the following markup:

```
<asp:Button ID="helpButton"  Text="help"
            OnClick="OnClickHandler"
            runat="server" />
```

The same button could be created with C# code, as follows:

```
protected Button helpButton = new Button();
helpButton.Text = "help";
helpButton.id = "helpButton";
helpButton.OnClick = "OnClickHandler";
helpButton.runat = "server";
```

There are two problems with creating controls with program code: First, it requires more typing, and as we all know, every time the keyboard is touched, there is a small, but real, possibility that the wrong key will be pressed; second, the placement of the control on the document display is problematic. It has to be added to something already in the document. To control the placement, a placeholder element can be defined in the markup. Then the control can be added by using the id attribute of the placeholder. This gives the exact position within the document for the control. For example, the placeholder could be specified with the following element:

```
<asp:PlaceHolder ID="buttonPlace"  runat="server" />
```

The following statement places the button at the position where the placeholder element appeared:

```
buttonPlace.Controls.Add(helpButton);
```

More than one control can be put in a placeholder. They are maintained in a property of the placeholder element, `Controls`. So, the `Controls` property is a collection of control elements. The order in which controls are added to the placeholder's `Controls` property determines the order in which the controls will appear in the display.

Although it is easier to create elements with markup, modifying elements is a good use of program code. For example, the list items of a select element could be added with program code, after the select element had been specified in markup. This approach is especially useful if the list items have come from some other data source. Program code is also useful for modifying the attributes of a markup-created element. Dynamic construction of the items of a list control will be illustrated in an example project in Section 12.4.7.

12.4.6   Response Output for Controls

The first two sample source documents of this chapter (`timeLeft.aspx` and `timeLeft2.aspx`) used the `Response.Write` method to place text in the response buffer. This is not a viable approach when there are controls in the document, because the output from `Response.Write` goes to the beginning of the buffer rather than to the position among the controls of the call to `Response.Write` (assuming that the code is embedded in a source document). As a more effective alternative, the text can be placed in a label control, which produces the text at the position of the label control in the response buffer. The text is assigned to the `Text` property of the label control. For example, suppose the document includes the following element (at the position where the output text should be):

```
<asp:Label ID="output"  runat="server" />
```

Then the following code places the given text at that position of the label in the response buffer:

```
<% string msg = string.Format(
               "The result is {0} <br />", result);
output.Text = msg; %>
```

In this example, the `string.Format` method is used to create a formatted string that consists of literal text and the value of the variable, `result`, which has been converted to text by `Format`. Of course, the program code could also appear in a code-behind file.

12.4.7   List Controls

This section provides information about the most commonly used ASP.NET Web list controls: `DropDownList`, `CheckBoxList`, and `RadioButtonList`.

The list controls share some common characteristics. The items in the lists (individual menu items, checkboxes, or radio buttons) are modeled with `ListItem` objects, which have the `Value` and `Text` properties. The collection of items of a control are modeled with the `Item` object. The `ListItem` objects can be defined statically or added dynamically with the `Add` method. The `SelectedIndex` and `SelectedItem` properties of the control reference the index and value of the selected item with the lowest index. In the case of checkboxes and menus, other checked items can be determined by iteration through the `Items` collection of the control, testing the `Selected` property of each `ListItem`. The value of the selected item can be accessed through the `SelectedValue` property of the control. Finally, all of the list controls raise the `SelectedIndexChanged` event.

As discussed in Section 12.4.1, the set of ASP.NET Web controls includes controls for single checkboxes (`CheckBox`) and single radio buttons (`RadioButton`), a control for collections of checkboxes (`CheckBoxList`), and one for collections of radio buttons (`RadioButtonList`). If checkboxes or radio buttons are needed and they can be statically constructed, `CheckBox` or `RadioButton` controls should be used. However, if checkboxes or radio buttons are to be filled from a data source or, for some other reason, dynamically constructed, then `CheckBoxList` or `RadioButtonList` controls should be used.

The next example creates a text box, a drop-down list, and a label in an ASP. NET source document. It uses code in a code-behind file to create the list items of the drop-down list. The document also includes a label control to provide a place for the return message from the code-behind file. We built this source document with VS, dragging all of the controls onto the skeletal document furnished by VS. We added some initial documentation, changed the ids of the controls to meaningful words, and renamed the document `controls.aspx`. The completed source document is as follows:

```
<!-- controls.aspx
     An example of an ASP.NET document that creates a text box,
     a drop-down list, and a label.
     A code-behind file is used to populate the drop-down list
     and display a message when an item from the drop-down list
     is selected. The label is used for the message
     -->
<%@ Page Language="C#" AutoEventWireup="true"
        CodeFile="controls.aspx.cs" Inherits="_Default" %>

<!DOCTYPE html PUBLIC "-//W3C//DTD XHTML 1.0 Transitional//EN"
        "http://www.w3.org/TR/xhtml1/DTD/xhtml1-transitional.dtd">

<html xmlns="http://www.w3.org/1999/xhtml">
<head runat="server">
    <title>Controls</title>
</head>
<body>
    <form id="form1" runat="server">
    <div>
        Name: <asp:TextBox ID="name" runat="server"></asp:TextBox>
        <br /><br />
        Favorite color:
          <asp:DropDownList ID="color" runat="server"
                            AutoPostBack="true"
                            OnSelectedIndexChanged="itemSelected">
          </asp:DropDownList>
        <br /><br />
        <asp:Label ID="message" runat="server" > </asp:Label>
    </div>
    </form>
</body>
</html>
```

The code-behind file, which was implicitly created by VS, is brought to the workspace by selecting it in the *Solution Explorer* (you must click the triangle in front of the `.aspx` file's name to see it). Its name is `controls.aspx.cs`. The initial version of this file is as follows:

```
using System;
using System.Collections;
using System.Configuration;
using System.Data;
using System.Linq;
using System.Web;
using System.Web.Security;
using System.Web.UI;
using System.Web.UI.HtmlControls;
using System.Web.UI.WebControls;
using System.Web.UI.WebControls.WebParts;
using System.Xml.Linq;

namespace controls
{
    public partial class _Default : System.Web.UI.Page
    {
        protected void Page_Load(object sender, EventArgs e)
        {

        }
    }
}
```

The first task is to remove the `using` statements for classes we do not need, which are all except `System`, `System.Web`, `System.Web.UI`, and `System.Web.UI.WebControls`.

Notice that the initial code-behind file includes a skeletal handler, `Page_Load`, for the `Load` event. We fleshed out this handler with the code to build the drop-down list. The list items were added to the select element with the `Add` method of the `Items` property of the select. Each new item was created with a call to the list item constructor, `ListItem`, passing the value of the new item. For example, to add a list item with the value `"red"` to the select control with the id `mySelect`, the following statement could be used:

```
mySelect.Items.Add(new ListItem("red"));
```

The handler for `SelectedIndexChanged` returns a message to the client, giving his or her name and the chosen select item, which in this case is a color. The client name is retrieved from the `name` text box of the document, by means of the Text property of the text box. The chosen color is retrieved from the form with the SelectedItem property of the drop-down list.

Just above the main code window on the right side is a menu of events that could be handled by the code-behind file. From this menu, we selected the OnSelectedIndexChanged item. The handler for the OnSelectedIndexChanged event was created by double-clicking the drop-down list in the *Design* view. This handler was initially empty; it included only the skeletal handler with the correct name, itemSelected. We added the required two statements to the handler, one to create the string of the output and one to put the string into the Text of the message label element.

The completed ASP.NET document and its code-behind file is as follows:

```
<!-- controls.aspx
     An example of an ASP.NET document that creates a text box,
     a drop-down list, and a label.
     A code-behind file is used to populate the drop-down list
     and display a message when an item from the drop-down list
     is selected. The label is used for the message
     -->
<%@ Page Language="C#" AutoEventWireup="true"
         CodeFile="controls.aspx.cs" Inherits="_Default" %>
<!DOCTYPE html PUBLIC "-//W3C//DTD XHTML 1.0 Transitional//EN"
        "http://www.w3.org/TR/xhtml1/DTD/xhtml1-transitional.dtd">
<html xmlns="http://www.w3.org/1999/xhtml">
<head runat="server">
    <title>Controls</title>
</head>
<body>
    <form id="form1" runat="server">
    <div>
        Name: <asp:TextBox ID="name" runat="server"></asp:TextBox>
        <br /><br />
        Favorite color:
          <asp:DropDownList ID="color" runat="server"
                            AutoPostBack="true"
                            OnSelectedIndexChanged="itemSelected">
          </asp:DropDownList>
        <br /><br />
        <asp:Label ID="message" runat="server" Text=""></asp:Label>
    </div>
    </form>
</body>
</html>
```

```
// controls.aspx.cs
//   The code-behind file for controls.aspx
//   In a Page_Load handler, it populates the drop-down
//   list created in the associated source document.
//   It also includes a handler for the button, which
//   produces a message to the client, including the
//   client's name and the chosen item from the drop-down
//   list

using System;
using System.Web;
using System.Web.UI;
using System.Web.UI.WebControls;

public partial class _Default : System.Web.UI.Page
{
    protected void Page_Load(object sender, EventArgs e)
    {
        if (!IsPostBack)
        {
            color.Items.Add(new ListItem("blue"));
            color.Items.Add(new ListItem("red"));
            color.Items.Add(new ListItem("green"));
            color.Items.Add(new ListItem("yellow"));
        }
    }

    protected void itemSelected(object sender, EventArgs e)
    {
        string newMsg = string.Format(
            "Hi {0}; your favorite color is {1}",
            name.Text, color.SelectedItem);
        message.Text = newMsg;
    }
}
```

This example illustrates how the items of a list control can be created dynamically with code. The example also shows a simple event handler for a text box and how dynamic output can be directed to the user without replacing the display. Figure 12.8 shows a display of the result of running `controls.aspx` after a name has been entered and a color chosen.

Figure 12.8 Display of `controls.aspx`

12.4.8 Validation Controls

Client-side form data validation with JavaScript was discussed in Chapter 5. Although there are important reasons for doing form data validation on the client, there are also important reasons to do it again on the server. First among these is that client-side validation can be subverted by a devious client. Also, in some cases form data goes directly into a database, which could be corrupted by bad data. So, it is often necessary to do form data validation on both the client and the server side. In the paragraphs that follow, we introduce the ASP.NET Web controls designed to make server-side form data validation relatively easy.

There are six validation controls defined in the ASP.NET Web controls collection. These controls, along with their attributes and values, are shown in Table 12.2.

Some of the most commonly used attributes for the validation controls that are not control specific are `runat`, `ControlToValidate`, `Text`, and `ErrorMessage`.

Validation controls often are placed immediately after the controls whose values they are to validate, although that is not necessary. This placement is preferred because then the error messages produced by the validation controls appear next to the controls being validated. The actual error message is specified in the `ErrorMessage` attribute of the validation control. The validation control is connected to the control it is to validate with the `ControlToValidate` attribute, which is set to the id of the control. The `Display` attribute is used to specify how the error message will be displayed. The value `"Static"` means that space for the message is reserved on the displayed document. The value `"Dynamic"` means that space for the message is not reserved. The value `"None"` means that no error message will be displayed, although the error is still recorded in a log. Validation controls must also include the `runat` attribute, set, of course, to `"server"`.

Table 12.2 Validation controls and their attributes

Control	Control-Specific Attributes	Values
`RequiredFieldValidator`	None	None
`CompareValidator`	`Operator`	`Equal`, `NotEqual`, `GreaterThan`, `GreaterThanEqual`, `LessThan`, `LessThanEqual`, `DataTypeCheck`
	`Type`	`String`, `Currency`, `Date`, `Double`, `Integer`
	`ValueToCompare`	Constant
	`ControlToCompare`	Another control
`RangeValidator`	`MaximumValue`	Constant
	`MinimumValue`	Constant
	`Type`	`String`, `Currency`, `Date`, `Double`, `Integer`
`RegularExpressionVali-dator`	`ValidationExpression`	Regular expression
`CustomValidator`	`ClientValidationFunction`	Name of a client function
	`OnServerValidate`	Name of a server function
`ValidationSummary`	`DisplayMode`, `HeaderText`, `ShowSummary`	

The following example, `validate.aspx`, illustrates three of the validation controls:

```
<!-- validate.aspx
    An example of an ASP.NET document to illustrate server-side
    validation controls. Uses text boxes to get the name, phone
    number, and age of the client. These three controls are
    validated on the server.
    -->
<%@ Page Language="C#" %>

<!DOCTYPE html PUBLIC "-//W3C//DTD XHTML 1.0 Transitional//EN"
        "http://www.w3.org/TR/xhtml1/DTD/xhtml1-transitional.dtd">

<html xmlns="http://www.w3.org/1999/xhtml">
<head runat="server">
    <title> validate </title>
```

```
</head>
<body>
    <form id="form1" runat="server">
      <p>
        Your name:
        <asp:TextBox ID="name" runat="server"
                     style="margin-left: 56px">
        </asp:TextBox>
        <asp:RequiredFieldValidator
          ID="nameValidator"
          ControlToValidate="name"
          Display="Static"
          runat="server"
          ErrorMessage="Please enter your name">
        </asp:RequiredFieldValidator>
        <br />

        Your phone number:
        <asp:TextBox ID="phone" runat="server"></asp:TextBox>
        <asp:RegularExpressionValidator
          ID="phoneValidator"
          ControlToValidate="phone"
          Display="Static"
          runat="server"
          ErrorMessage="Phone number form must be ddd-ddd-dddd"
          ValidationExpression="\d{3}-\d{3}-\d{4}">
        </asp:RegularExpressionValidator>
        <br />

        Your age:
        <asp:TextBox ID="age" runat="server" style="margin-left: 68px"
                     Width="40px">
        </asp:TextBox>
        <asp:RangeValidator
          ID="RangeValidator1"
          ControlToValidate="age"
          Display="Static"
          runat="server"
          ErrorMessage="Age must be in the range of 10 to 110"
          MinimumValue="10"
          MaximumValue="110"
          Type="Integer">
        </asp:RangeValidator>
        <br />
```

```
            <asp:Button runat="server" Text="Submit" />
        </p>
      </form>
   </body>
</html>
```

The name text box is validated to ensure that a name is given. The phone number text box is validated to ensure that its format matches the given regular expression. (Regular expressions are described in Chapter 4.) The age text box is validated to ensure that the given age is at least 10 but not greater than 110.

Figure 12.9 shows the display of the validate.aspx document after its fields have been filled incorrectly, which results in the appearance of error messages to the right of the text boxes.

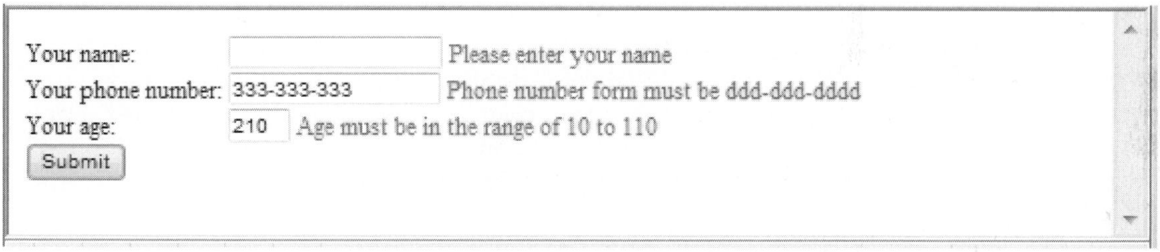

Your name:		Please enter your name
Your phone number:	333-333-333	Phone number form must be ddd-ddd-dddd
Your age:	210	Age must be in the range of 10 to 110
Submit		

Figure 12.9 Display of validate.aspx after being filled

Custom validation controls can be designed for special validation. These controls are used when the validation cannot be done with one of the other validation controls. Such a custom validation can be defined with a CustomValidator control. The actual validation can be done either with client code (e.g., with a JavaScript function), server code (e.g., with a C# method), or both. Following is an example of a CustomValidator control, which in this case is to validate some characteristic of the text entered into the text box with the id "name" that immediately precedes the validator control:

```
<asp:CustomValidator runat = "server"
   id = "CustomValidator1"
   ControlToValidate = "name"
   ValidateEmptyText = "false"
   Display = "Static"
   ErrorMessage = "The text entered is not valid..."
   ClientValidationFunction = "clientValidator"
   OnServerValidate = "serverValidator">
</asp:CustomValidator>
```

For this validator control, a JavaScript validator function, `clientValida-tor`, and a C# server validator function, `serverValidator`, are both defined. Both of the validation subprograms take two parameters. For the C# method, the first is an `object` and the second is a `ServerValidateEventArgs` type. The `Value` property of the second parameter object has the value the user typed into the text box. The same two parameters are used for the JavaScript function, although in that case the types are not needed in the function definition.

Setting the `ValidateEmptyText` attribute of `CustomValidator` to `false` specifies that an empty text box is considered invalid. The default value of this attribute is `true`.

Following is an example of a document that illustrates the use of a `Custom-Validator` control. The example presents a text box into which the user is asked to enter an even number.[4] It includes a JavaScript function in the document to test, on the client, whether the input was even, as well as a C# method in a code-behind file to perform the same test on the server:

```
<!-- customValid.aspx
    Illustrates a CustomValidator control that presents a text box
    to the user and requests the input of an even number. Uses both
    a JavaScript client-side function and a C# server-side method
    to ensure that the input was even.
    -->
<%@ Page Language="C#" AutoEventWireup="true"
    CodeBehind="customValid.aspx.cs" Inherits="customValid._Default" %>

<!DOCTYPE html PUBLIC "-//W3C//DTD XHTML 1.0 Transitional//EN"
        "http://www.w3.org/TR/xhtml1/DTD/xhtml1-transitional.dtd">

<html xmlns="http://www.w3.org/1999/xhtml" >
<head runat="server">
    <title>Example of a CustomValidator control</title>
    <script type="text/javascript" language="javascript">
      function testEvenNumberClient(sender, e) {
        if (e.Value % 2 == 0)
          e.IsValid = true;
        else
          e.IsValid = false;
      }
    </script>
</head>
<body>
```

---

4. Such an input is a simple way to test whether the user is a human being (rather than a poten-tially malicious program). This kind of test is now most often done by presenting a sequence of stylized characters that the user must identify.

```
    <form id="form1" runat="server">
    Please enter an even number:
      <asp:TextBox ID="even" runat="server" Width="40px" />
      <asp:CustomValidator
        ID="CustomValidator1"
        runat="server"
        ControlToValidate="even"
        ErrorMessage="Number must be even"
        ClientValidationFunction="testEvenNumberClient"
        OnServerValidate="evenNumberTest" >
      </asp:CustomValidator>
      <br />
      <asp:Button runat="server" Text="Submit" />
      <br />
      <asp:Label ID="output" runat="server" />
    </form>
</body>
</html>
```

```
// customValid.aspx.cs
//    The code-behind file for customValid.aspx.
//    Defines the server-side method to test the text box input
//    to determine whether it is even.
//    The method's output is only for testing.

using System;
using System.Web;
using System.Web.UI;
using System.Web.UI.WebControls;

namespace customValid
{
    public partial class _Default : System.Web.UI.Page
    {
        protected void evenNumberTest(object sender,
                                    ServerValidateEventArgs e)
        {
            int number = Convert.ToInt32(e.Value);
            if (number % 2 == 0) {
                e.IsValid = true;
                output.Text = "Good, the number is even";
            }
```

```
            else {
                e.IsValid = false;
                output.Text = "The number is odd!!!";
            }
        }
    }
}
```

The conversion of the value of the text box from string to integer is performed with a call to the `ToInt32` method of the `Convert` class, which is defined in `System`. There are `Convert` methods for a long list of source-target types.

If the input value is odd, the client-side test detects that and produces the error message from the `ErrorMessage` attribute of the `CustomValidator` control. In this case, the server-side test is not executed, because the form is not submitted to the server. If the input is even, both client-side and server-side tests are run. To prove that the server-side test was run, we include a trace message in it (`"Good, the number is even"`). Figures 12.10 and 12.11 show, respectively, the resulting displays when odd and even numbers are entered.

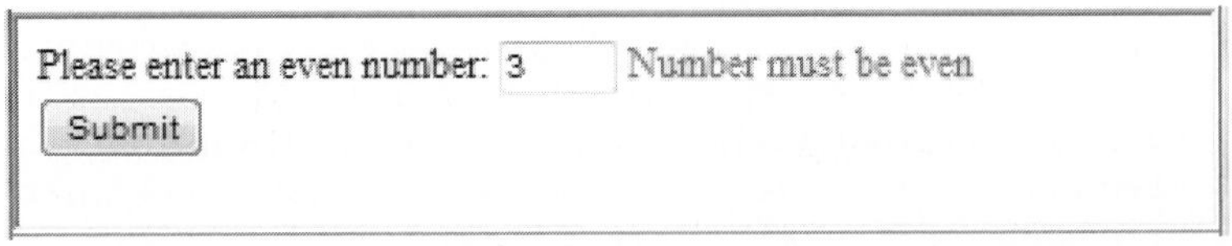

Figure 12.10 Display of running `customValid.aspx` after entering an odd number

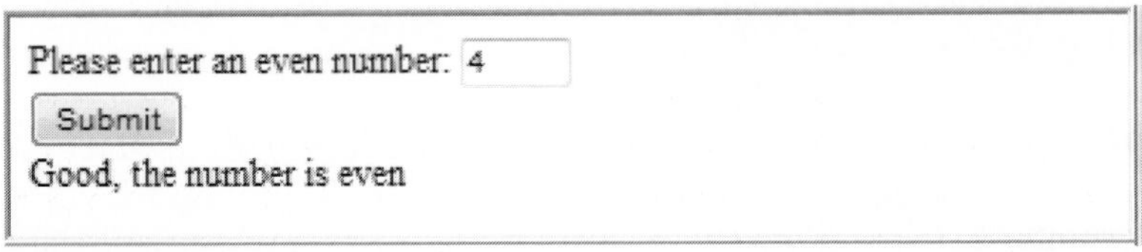

Figure 12.11 Display of running `customValid.aspx` after entering an even number

The `ValidationSummary` control provides a convenient way to produce a summary of all of the validation errors found on a form. The summary appears at the bottom of the form. The most commonly used format of the summary is that of an unordered list, with each error message displayed after a bullet. Following is an example of a typical `ValidationSummary` control:

```
<asp:ValidationSummary
    ID="ValidationSummary1"
    runat="server"
    DisplayMode="BulletList"
```

```
HeaderText="The following errors were found"
ShowSummary="true" />
```

The `HeaderText` value is displayed only if errors were detected. To avoid having error messages appearing both in the form and in the summary, the `Text` attribute of the control can be set to `"*"`, which suppresses the display of the error message in the form, but still allows it to appear in the summary.

12.4.9 Master Documents

External style sheets are used to give each document on a site a consistent look and feel. In many cases, there is some content—for example, a header or a footer—that should be on each document of the site. Also, there may some standard layout of information that controls the appearance of each document. With ASP.NET, these concepts can be implemented easily. A *master document* is defined, into which the content of other documents, called *content documents*, can be implicitly merged. So, if we want a particular header, perhaps consisting of one or more images and the name of the site, to appear on every one of the content documents, we define that header in a master document. Then, the site consists of the master document and a collection of content documents. The browser user never sees the two different kinds of documents. When the user requests one of the content documents, that document is merged into the master document, on the server, and the result is sent to the browser.

A simple example will demonstrate the process of building a master document and a content document. The master document will have no active controls and no code, although these features could be included. The example master document simply produces a standard header consisting of the company's name and two small images of airplanes. The ASP.NET Web control for images is `<asp:Image>`. The attribute for the image file is `imageUrl`, rather than the HTML attribute, `src`. All master documents need to begin with a `Master` directive. Other than that, there is little difference between conventional source documents and master documents.

To create a master document with VS, first create a new Web site. Then right-click the project in the *Solution Explorer*, which opens a lengthy menu. Select *Add New Item* from this menu, whereupon a window will open that shows a long list of template buttons, one of which is *Master Page*. Click this button and rename the new page `airad.master`. Then click the *Add* button. This produces the following skeletal document:

```
<%@ Master Language="C#" AutoEventWireup="true"
        CodeFile="airad.master.cs" Inherits="airad" %>

<!DOCTYPE html PUBLIC "-//W3C//DTD XHTML 1.0 Transitional//EN"
    "http://www.w3.org/TR/xhtml1/DTD/xhtml1-transitional.dtd">
<html xmlns="http://www.w3.org/1999/xhtml">
<head runat="server">
```

```
        <title>Untitled Page</title>
        <asp:ContentPlaceHolder id="head" runat="server">
        </asp:ContentPlaceHolder>
        </head>
<body>
        <form id="form1" runat="server">
        <div>
            <asp:ContentPlaceHolder id="ContentPlaceHolder1"
                                    runat="server">
            </asp:ContentPlaceHolder>
        </div>
        </form>
</body>
</html>
```

Notice that the initial document has two `ContentPlaceHolder` controls, one in the head and one in the body of the document. These are where the content files can be inserted into the master document. For this example, only the `ContentPlaceHolder` in the body will be used.

We now add the content and styles for the master document, as well as initial documentation. The completed document is as follows:

```
<!-- airad.master
     A simple example of an ASP.NET master document.
     airadContent.aspx is a content document for this document
     -->
<%@ Master Language="C#" AutoEventWireup="true"
        CodeFile="airad.master.cs" Inherits="airad" %>

<!DOCTYPE html PUBLIC "-//W3C//DTD XHTML 1.0 Transitional//EN"
    "http://www.w3.org/TR/xhtml1/DTD/xhtml1-transitional.dtd">

<html xmlns="http://www.w3.org/1999/xhtml">
<head runat="server">
    <title>airad master</title>
    <asp:ContentPlaceHolder id="head" runat="server">
    </asp:ContentPlaceHolder>
    <style type="text/css">
      span {font-style: italic; font-size: 30;
            font-weight: bold; color: Blue;}
    </style>

</head>
<body>
```

```
<form id="form1" runat="server">
<div>

    <asp:Image ID="plane1" runat="server"
               imageUrl="images\plane1.png"
               height="70px" width="70px" />
    <span>   Aidan's Used Airplanes    
    </span>
    <asp:Image ID="plane2" runat="server"
               imageUrl="images/plane2.png" />
    <br /><br /><br />
    <asp:ContentPlaceHolder id="TopPageContent"
                                runat="server">
    </asp:ContentPlaceHolder>
</div>
</form>
</body>
</html>
```

Content documents must begin with a Page directive that includes the attribute masterpagefile, to which must be assigned the file name of the master document. The whole document, after the Page directive, is an <asp:Content> element. This element must have its runat attribute set to "server". Also, it must include the id of the ContentPlaceHolder element in the master document. This id must be assigned to the ContentPlaceHolderID attribute. For example, the opening asp:Content tag could be as follows:

```
<asp:Content runat="server"
             ContentPlaceHolderID="TopPageContent" >
```

To create a content document, select the *Solution Explorer*, right-click on the project, and select *Add New Item*. Then select *Web Form* from the resulting list, change its name to airadContent.aspx, select *Select Master Page*, and click the *Add* button. This opens a *Select a Master Page* window. Select the master page, airad.master, from the window, and click the *OK* button. This produces the following document:

```
<%@ Page Language="C#" MasterPageFile="~/airad.master"
         AutoEventWireup="true" CodeFile="airadContent.aspx.cs"
         Inherits="airadContent" Title="Untitled Page" %>

<asp:Content ID="Content1" ContentPlaceHolderID="head"
             Runat="Server">
</asp:Content>
<asp:Content ID="Content2" ContentPlaceHolderID="TopPageContent"
             Runat="Server">
</asp:Content>
```

The remainder of the content document is a `div` element that contains whatever we want to be merged into the master document. For our example, the complete content document, named `airadContent.aspx`, is as follows:

```
<!-- airadContent.aspx
     A content document for the airad application. Uses the master
     document, airad.master.
     -->

<%@ Page Language="C#" MasterPageFile="~/airad.master"
        AutoEventWireup="true" CodeFile="airadContent.aspx.cs"
        Inherits="airadContent" Title="Untitled Page" %>

<asp:Content ID="Content2" ContentPlaceHolderID="TopPageContent"
           Runat="Server">
<!-- airadContent.aspx
     A content file for the airad master document
     -->
  <div>
    <h3> Today's Special </h3>
    1975 Cessna 172, light blue & grey, 850 hours SMOH <br />
    Great condition! Price reduced! Call us! <br />
    719-444-6999
  </div>
</asp:Content>
```

A display of the master document, `airad.master`, with the content document, `airadContent.aspx` merged, is shown in Figure 12.12.

Aidan's Used Airplanes

Today's Special

1975 Cessna 172, light blue & grey, 850 hours SMOH
Great condition! Price reduced! Call us!
719-444-6999

Figure 12.12 Display of the master document, `airad.master`, with `airadContent.aspx` merged

Note that the URL of a master–content document is the name of the content document.

A master document can have any number of `contentplaceholder` elements, each of which must have content documents that reference its id. There is, of course, much more to master documents, but those additional details are not covered here.

12.5 ASP.NET AJAX

In response to the widespread interest in and positive effects of Ajax, Microsoft developed the software to make the use of Ajax simple in ASP.NET. Implementing Ajax in ASP.NET is especially easy when the application is constructed with one of the Microsoft IDEs for ASP.NET development: VS or Visual Web Developer. Though it sounds rather remarkable, Ajax can be implemented with these systems without the developer writing a single line of JavaScript—Ajax without writing the "j"!

Ajax-enabled Web applications are written with VS by using ASP.NET AJAX server controls, which are included in the toolbox under the heading *AJAX Extensions*. The AJAX server controls differ from the standard server controls in that AJAX server controls add script to documents that is run on the client system, whereas all standard server control processing is done on the server.

The `ScriptManager` control loads the required JavaScript libraries for ASP .NET AJAX. Every document that uses any part of ASP.NET AJAX must have a `ScriptManager` control, which has the following form:

```
<asp:ScriptManager ID="whatever"
                   runat="server" />
```

The `UpdatePanel` control defines the area of a document that can be updated with the returned value from an asynchronous request to the server. This results in the re-rendering of part of the document—the very definition of Ajax interactions. The part of the document that is to be updateable through Ajax interactions is placed in the content of an `UpdatePanel` control, and VS makes the arrangements necessary to make it happen, including ensuring that the required client-side code is cross-browser compatible. This approach obviates much of the code written in the Ajax applications of Chapter 10.

The general form of the `UpdatePanel` control is as follows:

```
<asp:UpdatePanel runat="server"  ID="whatever" />
  <ContentTemplate>
     (whatever is to be Ajax-updateable)
  </ContentTemplate>
</asp:UpdatePanel>
```

Once again, a simple example is the best way to illustrate the implementation of an Ajax application with ASP.NET AJAX. The example application is a familiar one: using Ajax to provide the values for the city and state text boxes of a form, given the zip code. With VS, only the source file with the form and the C# code to provide the city and state names need be written. In VS, we begin by creating a new Web site, as before, and naming it CityState.

Next, we drag a ScriptManager element onto the document and place it just after the opening form tag. We begin building the form by adding Text-Box controls for the name and address of the user. Because these elements are static, we could use either HTML text box elements or TextBox ASP.NET controls. The third element added is the TextBox for the zip code, which gets id, columns, and runat attributes, but also needs two special attributes. First, it needs an AutoPostBack attribute, set to "true". This is necessary because we want this text box to trigger the Ajax request for the city and state names and, by default, changes to text boxes do not cause postbacks. So, when the text box is changed and the cursor is positioned outside the text box, an automatic postback is done. The other required attribute is OnTextChanged, to which is assigned the name of the C# method in the code-behind file that is to be called when the text box is changed. We chose the name Zip_OnTextChanged for this method.

An UpdatePanel control follows the zip code text box. The only thing in the UpdatePanel control is a ContentTemplate control, in which are nested text boxes for city and state. The city and state text boxes are the ones to be filled in by the data returned as the result of an Ajax request. Just to make clear that the implicit filling in of the city and state text boxes is a result of only a partial re-rendering of the form, two labels are included as placeholders for time stamps provided by the code-behind file, one for the initial rendering of the form and one for each Ajax update. These labels have the following form:

```
<asp:Label ID="whatever"  runat="server" > </asp:Label>
```

The ids of the labels are used to reference them in the C# code. The complete source document for the application is as follows:

```
<!-- CityState.aspx
     This document presents a form to the user, requesting
     the user's name, address, and zip code. When the zip
     code is entered, the document uses an Ajax request to
     get the names of the city and state that correspond to
     the given zip code. Time stamps are used to indicate
     that the initial display and the Ajax updated display
     were at different times.
     -->
<%@ Page Language="C#" AutoEventWireup="true"
        CodeFile="CityState.aspx.cs" Inherits="_Default" %>
<!DOCTYPE html PUBLIC "-//W3C//DTD XHTML 1.0 Transitional//EN"
     "http://www.w3.org/TR/xhtml1/DTD/xhtml1-transitional.dtd">
<html xmlns="http://www.w3.org/1999/xhtml">
<head runat="server">
    <title>Untitled Page</title>
</head>
```

```
<body>
    <form ID="form1" runat="server">

        <asp:ScriptManager ID="ScriptManager1" runat="server">
        </asp:ScriptManager>
        <asp:Label ID="Label1" runat="server" >
        </asp:Label>
        <br /><br />
        <asp:TextBox ID="name" columns="30" runat="server"/>
        Name <br />
        <asp:TextBox ID="address" columns="30" runat="server"/>
        Address <br />
        <asp:TextBox ID="zip" columns="30" runat="server"
                 AutoPostBack="true"
                 OnTextChanged="Zip_OnTextChanged"/>
        Zip code
        <asp:UpdatePanel ID="UpdatePanel1" runat="server">
            <ContentTemplate>
                <asp:TextBox ID="city" columns="30" runat="server"/>
                City <br />
                <asp:TextBox ID="state" columns="30" runat="server"/>
                State <br /><br />
                <asp:Label ID="Label2" runat="server" >
                </asp:Label>
            </ContentTemplate>
        </asp:UpdatePanel>
    </form>
</body>
</html>
```

Next, we build the code-behind file. We begin by selecting *File/Open/File* and then selecting `CityState.aspx.cs`. This opens the skeletal C# code-behind file generated by VS. To this skeletal partial class definition, we add the handler method for the zip code text box. In this method, we include a `HashTable` object that we initialize to a collection of zip codes and their corresponding cities and states. The code of the method is simple: It checks to see if the hash object includes the zip code given in the form, whose name is `zip.Text`. This checking is done with the `Contains` method of the hash table. If the zip code is in the hash table, the city and state names are split from the value part of the correct hash table element and assigned to `city.Text` and `state.Text`, which represent the contents of the city and state text boxes.

This code is followed by the code to insert a time stamp on the document every time an Ajax request is made. The code to do so is as follows:

```
Label2.Text = "(Refreshed at " + DateTime.Now.ToString() +
              ")";
```

The `Page_Load` method is completed by adding another time stamp, this time placed at the top of the form at page load time. This time stamp must be placed in a selector, which ensures that it is executed only during the initial display of the document. If the selector is not included, the time stamp will be repeated for each Ajax update, because each such update raises a `Page_Load` event. The complete code-behind file is as follows:

```
// CityState.aspx.cs
// The C# code-behind file for the CityState project.
// Includes a method, Zip_OnTextChanged, to create a hash of
// zip codes and city-state strings. When the zip code is
// changed on the form, the method looks for the zip code in
// the hash, setting the city and state text boxes to the
// values found. If the zip code is not in the hash, it places empty
// strings in those text boxes

using System;
using System.Web;
using System.Web.UI;
using System.Web.UI.WebControls;
public partial class _Default : System.Web.UI.Page
{
    protected void Zip_OnTextChanged(object sender, EventArgs e)
    {
        Hashtable zipCityState = new Hashtable();
        char[] delimiter = new char[] { ',' };
        zipCityState.Add("81611", "Aspen,Colorado");
        zipCityState.Add("81411", "Bedrock,Colorado");
        zipCityState.Add("80908", "Black Forest,Colorado");
        zipCityState.Add("80301", "Boulder,Colorado");
        zipCityState.Add("81127", "Chimney Rock,Colorado");
        zipCityState.Add("80901", "Colorado Springs,Colorado");
        zipCityState.Add("81223", "Cotopaxi,Colorado");
        zipCityState.Add("80201", "Denver,Colorado");
        zipCityState.Add("81657", "Vail,Colorado");
        zipCityState.Add("80435", "Keystone,Colorado");
        zipCityState.Add("80536", "Virginia Dale,Colorado");

        if (zipCityState.Contains(zip.Text))
        {
            city.Text =
                ((String)zipCityState[zip.Text]).Split(delimiter)[0];
            state.Text =
                ((String)zipCityState[zip.Text]).Split(delimiter)[1];
        }
        else
```

```
        {
            city.Text = "";
            state.Text = "";
        }
        Label2.Text = "(Refreshed at " + DateTime.Now.ToString() +
            ")";
    }

    protected void Page_Load(object sender, EventArgs e) {
        if (!Page.IsPostBack)
            Label1.Text = "(Initially loaded at " +
                DateTime.Now.ToString() + ")";
    }
}
```

Figure 12.13 shows the browser display of the initial screen of the `CityState` Web site.

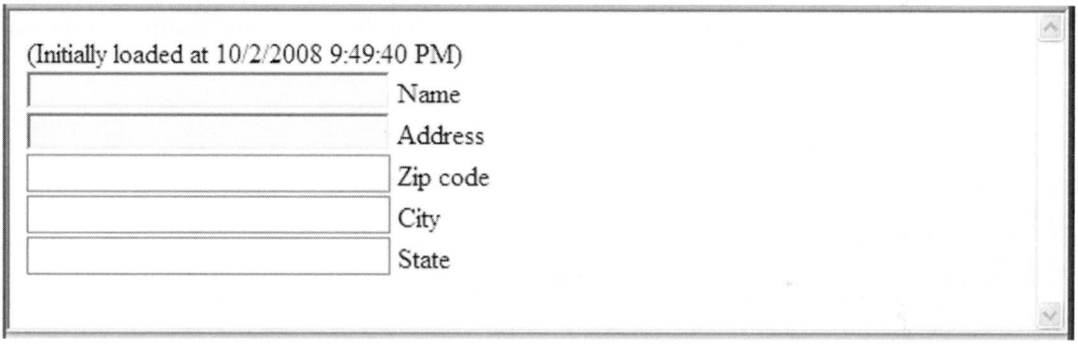

Figure 12.13 Initial screen of the `CityState` Web site

Figure 12.14 shows the browser display after entering a name, address, and zip code.

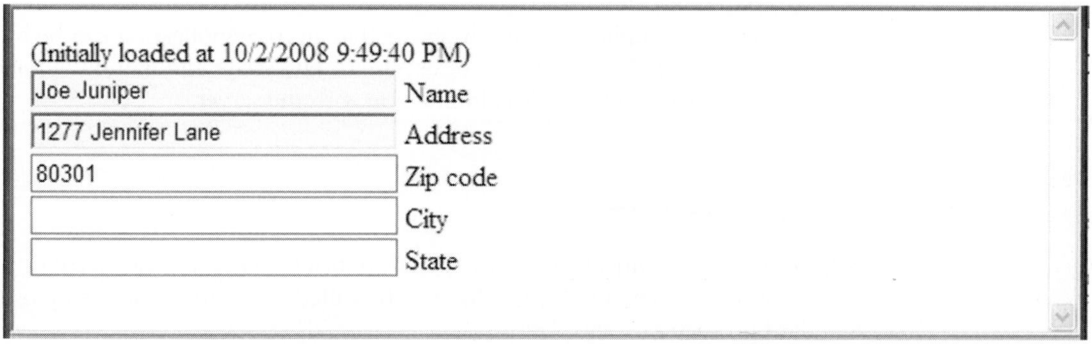

Figure 12.14 Screen after entering a name, address, and zip code

Figure 12.15 shows the browser display after moving the cursor out of the zip code text box.

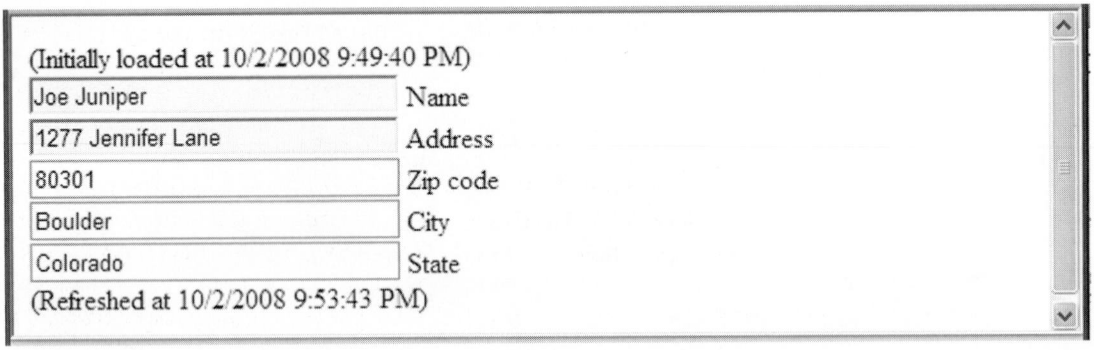

Figure 12.15 Screen after the Ajax entry of the city and state

Figure 12.16 shows the browser display after entering a new zip code and moving the cursor out of the zip code text box. Notice that the refreshed time stamp differs from the earlier update, but the initial time stamp stays the same.

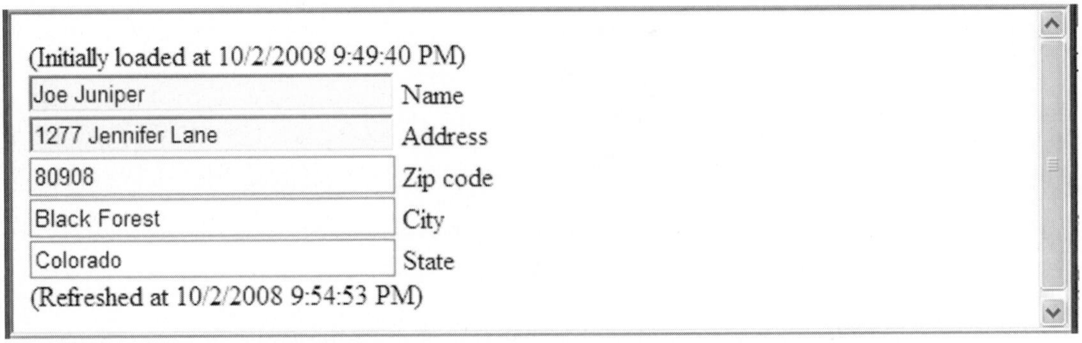

Figure 12.16 Screen after a second Ajax entry

The example application clearly shows that an Ajax application can be built with ASP.NET AJAX without any direct use of JavaScript and without actually coding, in any language, the Ajax interaction with the server.

12.6 Web Services

Web services were introduced in Chapter 7. In brief, a Web service is a collection of one or more related methods that can be called by remote systems by using standard protocols on the Web.

The .NET Framework provides two different ways to construct and advertise Web services. The traditional way, since 2002, is to use ASP.NET. The alternative, since the appearance of .NET 3.0 in late 2006, is the Windows Communication Foundation (WCF). The WCF approach to building Web services differs from that of ASP.NET in that the resulting services are not restricted to use with the Web. In this book, we have chosen to describe the ASP.NET approach, because it is simpler.

12.6.1 Constructing Web Services

We use a simple example to illustrate the construction of a Web service using VS. The example is a service to compute the payment on a loan. The parameters of the loan, which will be the parameters of the service, are the loan amount, the annual interest rate, and the length of the loan in months. The service will consist of a single method.

We begin by starting VS and selecting *File/New Website/ASP.NET Web Service*. We choose *File System* for the location, `c:\vStudio2010\PaymentService` for the name, and C# as the language, and click *OK*. We then change the names of the `.asmx` and `.cs` files to `PaymentService`. This is done by going to the *Solution Explorer*, right-clicking the file names, and selecting *Rename*. Because of these name changes, we must also change `PaymentService.asmx`, which refers to the code-behind file and the inherited class name of the service. The code-behind file is now `PaymentService.cs` and the inherited class is `PaymentService`. The new version of `PaymentService.asmx` is as follows:

```
<%@ WebService Language="C#"
               CodeBehind="~/App_Code/PaymentService.cs"
               Class="PaymentService" %>
```

Next, we open `PaymentService.cs`, whose initial file is as follows:

```
using System;
using System.Linq;
using System.Web;
using System.Web.Services;
using System.Web.Services.Protocols;
using System.Xml.Linq;

[WebService(Namespace = "http://tempuri.org/")]
[WebServiceBinding(ConformsTo = WsiProfiles.BasicProfile1_1)]
// To allow this Web Service to be called from script,
// using ASP.NET AJAX, uncomment the following line:
```

```
// [System.Web.Script.Services.ScriptService]
public class Service : System.Web.Services.WebService
{
    Public Service () {

        //Uncomment the following line if using designed components
        //InitializeComponent();
    }


    [WebMethod]
    public string HelloWorld() {
        return "Hello World";
    }

}
```

The class `PaymentService` is preceded by three attributes, although the third is commented out. The first, `WebService`, sets an XML namespace that is used in Web service messages. The second, `WebServiceBinding`, specifies the level of conformance to standards of the Web service. The third, `System.Web .Script.Services.ScriptService`, which takes no parameters, specifies that the Web service allows JSON calls from JavaScript clients.

Now we modify `PaymentService.cs` to perform the calculation of the loan payment. First, we delete all `using` statements except `using System` and `using System.Web.Services`. Then we rename the class `PaymentService` and delete the constructor. We then replace the `HelloWorld` method with the following method:

```
public double CalculatePayment(double loanAmt,
                               double intRate,
                               int months)
{
    double monthRate, payment;
    monthRate = intRate / 12.0d;
    payment = (monthRate * loanAmt) /
        (1.0d - Math.Pow(1.0d + monthRate, -months));
    return payment;
}
```

The `d` suffix on the numeric literals in the method specify that they are `double` type.
The complete modified version of `PaymentService.cs` is as follows:

```
// PaymentService.cs
// The PaymentService class definition, which includes the
// CalculatePayment method, which provides the actual Web service.
```

```
using System;
using System.Web;
using System.Web.Services;

[WebService(Namespace = "http://www.uccs.sebesta/services/")]
[WebServiceBinding(ConformsTo = WsiProfiles.BasicProfile1_1)]
// To allow this Web Service to be called from script,
// using ASP.NET AJAX, uncomment the following line:
// [System.Web.Script.Services.ScriptService]
public class PaymentService : System.Web.Services.WebService
{
    [WebMethod]
    public double CalculatePayment(double loanAmt, double intRate,
                                   int months)
    {
        double monthRate, payment;
        monthRate = intRate / 12.0d;
        payment = (monthRate * loanAmt) /
                     (1.0d - Math.Pow(1.0d + monthRate, -months));
        return payment;
    }
}
```

We can now test `PaymentService.cs` with a test harness provided by VS by selecting *Debug/Start Without Debugging*, which produces the screen shown in Figure 12.17.

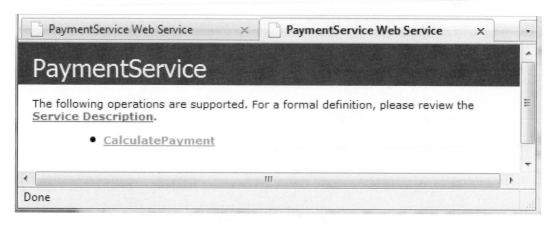

Figure 12.17 The test harness for `PaymentService.cs`

If the *Service Description* link in Figure 12.17 is clicked, the WSDL description of the service created by VS will be displayed.

To test the `CalculatePayment` method, we click its link, which produces the screen shown in Figure 12.18.

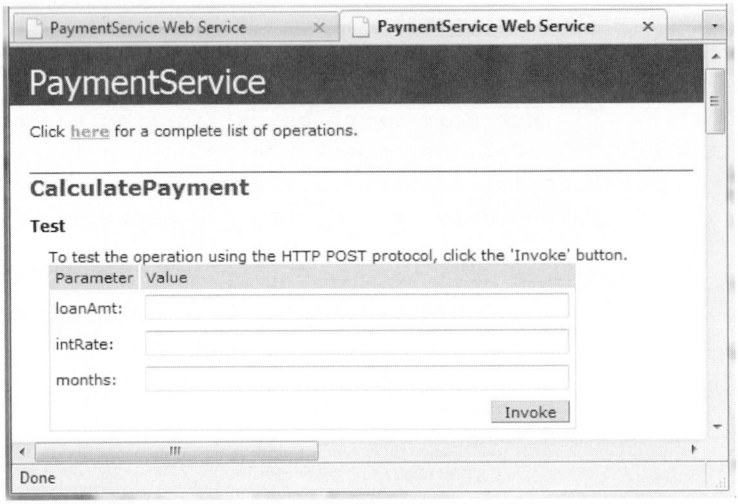

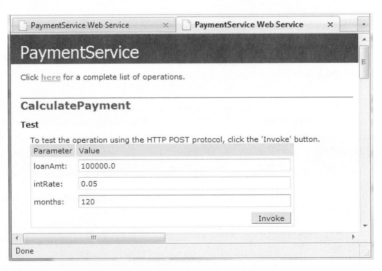

Figure 12.18 The input screen for `CalculatePayment`

Figure 12.19 shows the input screen after we have entered values.

Figure 12.19 The input screen after entering values

Figure 12.20 shows the result after clicking *Invoke*.

```
<?xml version="1.0" encoding="utf-8" ?>
<double xmlns="http://www.uccs.sebesta/services/">1060.6551523907554</double>
```

Figure 12.20 The result of invoking `CalculatePayment`

12.6.2   Consuming a Web Service

The purpose of a Web service is to provide operations that can be called remotely. Therefore, the normal use of the `PaymentService` service is through a client Web application. We will now create such a client application named `Payment-User` within the same solution as the service (although it could be anywhere on the Web). We begin by selecting *File/Add New Web Site/ASP.NET Web Site* (while the `PaymentService` project is open) and name it `PaymentUser`.

We now modify `Default.aspx` by renaming it `PaymentUser.aspx` and replacing `_Default` with `PaymentUser` in its `Page` directive. Next, we change `PaymentUser.aspx` by adding text boxes to collect the input parameters from the user and a button to call the service. This button uses an `onClick` attribute to call the handler that actually calls the service. We also include a `Label` element to provide a placeholder for the value returned from the service. The complete `PaymentUser.aspx` document is as follows:

```
<!-- PaymentUser.aspx
    A simple client to test the PaymentService Web service.
    Gets the loan amount, interest rate, and term of a loan
    from the user. It presents a button the user can click to
    enact the service. The button calls the code-behind code
    for the event handler that actually calls the service.
    -->
<%@ Page Language="C#" AutoEventWireup="true"
        CodeFile="PaymentUser.aspx.cs" Inherits="PaymentUser" %>

<!DOCTYPE html PUBLIC "-//W3C//DTD XHTML 1.0 Transitional//EN"
        "http://www.w3.org/TR/xhtml1/DTD/xhtml1-transitional.dtd">

<html xmlns="http://www.w3.org/1999/xhtml">
<head runat="server">
    <title>PaymentUser</title>
</head>
<body>
    <form id="form1" runat="server">
    <div>
        <p>
            Loan amount: <asp:TextBox ID="Loan"
                                      runat="server"
                                      columns="8" />
            Interest rate: <asp:TextBox ID="Interest"
                                        runat="server"
                                        columns="6" />
            Number of months: <asp:TextBox ID="Months"
                                           runat="server"
                                           columns="4" />
```

```
                          <br /> <br />
                          <asp:Button ID="callService" runat="server"
                                      Text="Call CalculatePayment Service"
                                      onClick="buttonClick" />
                          <br />
                          <asp:Label ID="Result" runat="server" />
                      </p>
                  </div>
              </form>
          </body>
          </html>
```

Next, we modify the code-behind file to perform the call to the service, which is done through a proxy that was provided by VS. First, we delete all `using` statement except `using System` and `using System.Web.UI`. Then, we add a `using localhost`, which will be the source of the service. Next, we rename the partial class `PaymentUser` and rename the `Page_Load` method `buttonClick`. Recall that Web services are called through proxy classes. In this case, the proxy class was implicitly created by VS. Now that class must be instantiated and used to call the method in the service class. The instantiation is accomplished with the following statement:

```
PaymentService proxy = new PaymentService();
```

The return value from the service must be inserted into a string and then set to the `Text` attribute of the `Label` element in the `PaymentUser.aspx` document. The `Format` method of `String` is used for this purpose. The placeholder in the `Format`, which is often just a number in braces, in this case will use a `C` formatting character. This character is used for money: It rounds the value to two digits to the right of the decimal point and attaches a dollar sign to the beginning of the value. The parameters passed to the service method, because they came from a form, are all in string form. In the call to the service, these values are converted to numeric values by the .NET conversion methods `ToDouble` and `ToInt32` of the `Convert` class. Following is the complete `PaymentUser.aspx.cs` code-behind file:

```
// PaymentUser.aspx.cs
// The code-behind file for the PaymentUser.aspx document. Defines
// the event handler that creates the proxy, and calls it to produce
// the results.

using System;
using System.Web.UI;
using localhost;
```

```
public partial class PaymentUser : System.Web.UI.Page
{
    protected void buttonClick(object sender, EventArgs e)
    {
        PaymentService proxy = new PaymentService();
        Result.Text = String.Format("<br />Payment is: {0:C}",
            proxy.CalculatePayment(
              Convert.ToDouble(Loan.Text),
              Convert.ToDouble(Interest.Text),
              Convert.ToInt32(Months.Text)));
    }
}
```

The last step of the process of creating the client Web application is to create a Web reference in the client to the Web service. This is another task that is made simple with VS. The process is as follows: First, we right-click the *PaymentUser* entry in the *Solution Explorer*, and select *Add Web Reference*, which produces the screen shown in Figure 12.21.

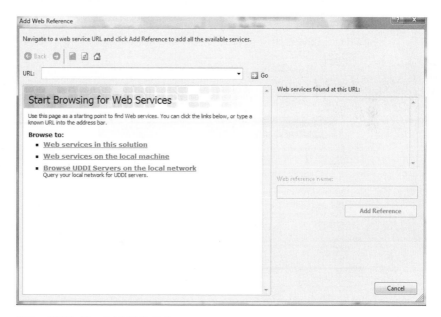

Figure 12.21 The *Add Web Reference* screen

From this screen, we select *Web Services in this Solution*, because the service is part of the same solution as the client. This produces the screen shown in Figure 12.22.

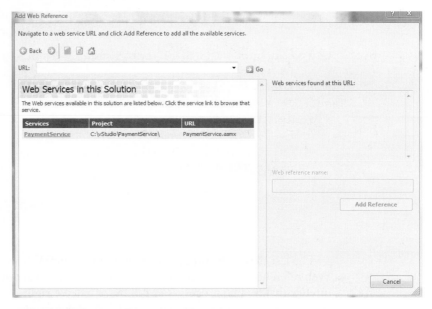

Figure 12.22 The *Web Services in this Solution* screen

In this screen, we select the only service shown, *PaymentService*, which produces the screen shown in Figure 12.23.

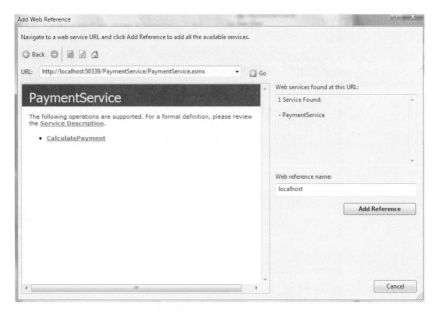

Figure 12.23 The *PaymentService* screen

Now we click the *Add Web Reference* button. This produces the Web reference, which appears in the *Solution Explorer* in the client.

Finally, we can test the service by running the client. This is done by right-clicking `PaymentUser.aspx` and selecting *View in Browser*. The screen shown in Figure 12.24 then appears.

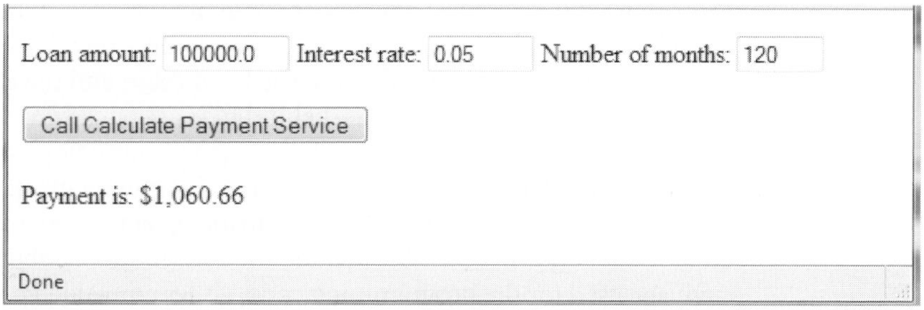

Loan amount: 100000.0   Interest rate: 0.05   Number of months: 120

[Call Calculate Payment Service]

Payment is: $1,060.66

Done

Figure 12.24 The interface to the *PaymentService* Web service

12.6.3   Advertising Web Services

It is common that a potential client does not know the URL of a possibly useful Web service. There are two approaches used with .NET to make Web services available to clients: with a Web services discovery document and with a Web services directory written with the Universal Description, Discovery, and Integration (UDDI) language (introduced in Section 7.11). In both cases, a directory of all Web services provided by a Web site can be made available to potential clients through a single URL on the site.

UDDI is part of Windows in the .NET Server release. It can be used to set up a UDDI server for inside an enterprise, as well as to register electronic services to make them available to the outside world. These activities are supported by the .NET UDDI SDK, which includes documentation, the `Microsoft.Uddi` assembly for the .NET Framework, and several example applications.

Summary

NET is a collection of technologies that supports the development and deployment of distributed component-based software systems written in variety of languages. The .NET Framework is a generic support structure for the .NET family of languages. The CLR is a runtime system, which includes JIT compilers that support the execution of .NET software. The CTS defines a set of types that must be supported by .NET languages. The CLS defines a minimal set of language features that must be supported by .NET languages. Software in any .NET language can interact in a variety of ways with software written in any of the other .NET languages.

C# was designed specifically for the .NET system. C# is based on Java but includes some features of other languages—notably, C++, VB, and Delphi—as well as some new language features. Among its features are an improved `switch` construct, a `foreach` statement, some new controls on method inheritance, a value type struct, and properties.

ASP.NET is an approach to server-side support of dynamic documents. It is similar to JSP but is language neutral. Programming code can reside in an ASP.NET document or in a separate file called a code-behind file. In either case, the code is compiled before it is executed. Every ASP.NET document is compiled into a class before it is used, regardless of whether it contains programming code. All such classes are subclasses of the predefined class `Page`, unless they have code-behind files, in which case the code-behind file inherits from `Page` and the class for the ASP.NET document inherits from the code-behind file.

ASP.NET documents consist of markup, programming code (either in script elements or in render blocks), directives, server-side comments, and server-side controls. Server-side controls include the `runat` attribute, set to `"server"`. The only required directive is `Page`, which must include the `Language` attribute, which specifies the language used for the programming code, either embedded or in a code-behind file. Just as JavaBeans is the best way to use Java in a dynamic document, code-behind files are the best way to use a .NET language to support dynamic documents.

ASP.NET includes a large collection of controls that result in objects in the compiled `Page`-derived class. By contrast, the static markup code of a document is simply emitted by the execution of the `Page`-derived class. Different controls can raise different events, most of which can be handled by server-side code. The id attribute value of a control becomes the associated variable's name in the compiled version of the document.

The state of an ASP.NET document is implicitly maintained between requests with the `ViewState` hidden field.

Visual Studio is a powerful IDE for building .NET software applications. It provides skeletal ASP.NET documents and code-behind files. It also provides drag-and-drop ASP.NET elements and a built-in Web server for development and testing.

There are four page-level events defined in the `Page` class: `Init`, `Load`, `Unload`, and `PreRender`. These events can be handled in server-side code. The handlers can be implicitly registered by naming them with predefined names and using the proper protocol. Alternatively, they can be subscribed to the event handler delegate, `EventHandler`.

ASP.NET elements can be created as markup or with programming code. Response output for controls is created with the `Format` method of the `String` class. The position of output is specified with `Label` elements.

List controls provide a way of dealing with collections of checkboxes, radio buttons, and the items of drop-down lists. Control event handlers are registered by referencing them in an attribute on the control. ASP.NET includes several kinds of validation controls, which make common kinds of input validation simple.

ASP.NET defines a collection of validation controls that assist in performing either client-side or server-side validation of form input, or both.

Master documents are ASP.NET documents that are used to avoid duplication of common content on a collection of documents.

ASP.NET AJAX provides the tools to build Ajax capabilities into an ASP.NET application. The `ScriptManager` control loads the required libraries of JavaScript code to support Ajax in ASP.NET. The `UpdatePanel` is a control that encapsulates the part of a document that can be Ajax updateable. The actual code to specify the

Ajax communication is furnished by Visual Studio, so an Ajax application can be written without writing a single line of JavaScript.

Visual Studio provides significant assistance for all phases of the process of building Web services, from constructing the service itself to consuming the service.

Review Questions

12.1 What is a component?

12.2 What is the difference between a JavaBean and a .NET component?

12.3 When does a JIT compiler perform its translation of a method?

12.4 What is the primary benefit of the multilanguage aspect of .NET?

12.5 What part of the .NET system controls the execution of programs?

12.6 Explain how a JIT compiler works.

12.7 Describe briefly the two parts of the CLI.

12.8 On what languages is C# based?

12.9 Explain how the `switch` statement of C# is safer than that of Java.

12.10 What parameter-passing methods are available in C# that are not available in Java?

12.11 What characteristic is specified by attaching `virtual` to a C# method?

12.12 What does it mean when a C# method includes the `new` modifier?

12.13 Where are C# `struct` objects allocated?

12.14 What are the two kinds of disadvantages of scripting languages when used for supporting dynamic documents?

12.15 What exactly is a code-behind file?

12.16 From what class does an ASP.NET document class that does not use a code-behind file inherit?

12.17 From what class does an ASP.NET document class that does use a code-behind file inherit?

12.18 What kind of code is placed in a render block?

12.19 What kind of code is placed in a script element?

12.20 Describe what is specified by the `Page` attribute `Src`.

12.21 What is the syntactic difference between an XHTML widget and its corresponding ASP.NET control?

12.22 Why do ASP.NET server-side forms not require an `action` attribute?

12.23 What is a postback?

12.24   What is the purpose of the hidden control `ViewState`?

12.25   How can an ASP.NET checkbox control be forced to cause a postback when it is checked?

12.26   What are the four page-level events?

12.27   Explain auto event wireup.

12.28   Explain how event handlers for controls are registered.

12.29   What is the purpose of the `Xml` control?

12.30   Why should form data validation be done on the server as well as the client?

12.31   What is the difference between a control that includes the `runat` attribute set to `"server"` and one that does not?

12.32   What method is used to produce output from an ASP.NET document?

12.33   What event is raised by a drop-down list?

12.34   What are the values of the `Display` attribute of a validation control?

12.35   Under what circumstances is a `CustomValidator` control used?

12.36   What is a master document and how is one used?

12.37   What is the purpose of the `ScriptManager` control?

12.38   What is the purpose of the `UpdatePanel` control?

12.39   What is the purpose of the time stamps in the zip code ASP.NET AJAX application?

12.40   What part of a simple ASP.NET AJAX application must the developer write in JavaScript?

12.41   What is the suffix of a file that contains a Web service?

12.42   What attribute precedes a method that defines part or all of a Web service?

12.43   How does one run a Web service client if it co-resides with the service in a solution?

Exercises

12.1   Modify the ASP.NET document `hello.aspx` to use radio buttons to get the marital status of the user (single, married, divorced, widowed) and display the result.

12.2   Modify the ASP.NET document `helloVS.aspx`, as with `hello.aspx` in Exercise 12.1.

12.3   Modify the ASP.NET document `controls.aspx` and its accompanying code-behind file, `controls.aspx.cs`, to add the following: a text box for the user's address and a drop-down list for favorite category of music (rock, rap, country, classical, jazz), which must be populated in the code-behind file. The values of the new controls must be output when a postback is done.

12.4   Modify the ASP.NET document `validate.aspx` to add the following: a text box for address, which the document must validate to ensure that the address begins with a number, which is followed by a space and a text string that includes only letters; and a text box to collect a Social Security number, which must be validated to ensure that it is in the form ddd-dd-dddd, with no other characters in the text box.

12.5   Modify the ASP.NET AJAX zip code application to provide the address, zip code, city, and state of old customers. Use a hash whose keys are last names and first names, catenated. The information about the customer can be a single string with the address, zip code, city, and state, all catenated together.

12.6   Build a Web service that computes a temperature in Celsius, given one in Fahrenheit. Also, build a client to use the service.

Database Access through the Web

We begin this chapter with a brief introduction to relational databases and the Structured Query Language. Then we discuss several different architectures for database access. Next, we introduce the primary commands of the MySQL relational database system. This is followed by three sections, each of which describes a different approach to accessing MySQL databases through the Web. First, we discuss the use of server-side scripting for building systems for Web access to a database, using PHP as the scripting language. Next, we describe Java's JDBC API, which provides classes to support database access from Java servlets. Finally, we cover the use of ASP.NET and ADO.NET to construct Web sites that access MySQL databases. We include complete examples of all three different approaches.

13.1   Relational Databases

A database is a collection of data organized to allow relatively easy access for retrievals, additions, modifications, and deletions. A number of different approaches to structuring data have been developed and used for databases. The most widely used of these is called *relational database system*. The original design for relational databases, developed by E. F. Codd in the late 1960s, was based on Codd's mathematical theory of data. A significant number of books have been written to describe the structure and use of relational databases, so the topic is clearly a large and complex one. Because just one section of one chapter of this book is devoted to it, that section can provide only a brief overview. However, it is sufficient for our discussion of database access through the Web.

A relational database is a collection of tables of data. Each table can have any number of rows and columns of data, and the data itself can have a variety of different forms and types. The columns of a table are named. Each row usually contains a value for each column. The rows of a table are often referred to as *entities*. The collection of values in a row represents the *attributes* of the entity. Most tables have one column for special data values that uniquely identify the rows of the table. The values in this special column are called the *primary keys* of the table. Mathematically, the entities of a table are elements of a set, so they must be unique. Both data values and primary key values in a table are sometimes called *fields*.

One way to introduce the basic ideas of a relational database is to develop a simple example. Suppose we need a database that stores information about used Corvettes for sale.[1] We could just make a table named `Corvettes` with a column for the primary key of an entity, which could simply be a sequence of numbers. The table could have a column for the body style of the car, one for the year of manufacture, and one for the state where the car is for sale. It would also be useful to include information about the optional equipment of the cars. If six different kinds of equipment were interesting, that would require six more columns in the table.

The use of six columns of the `Corvettes` table for equipment is wasteful of memory. A better design is to use a second table—say, `Equipment`—to store the various kinds of equipment of interest, such as CD players and automatic transmissions. This table could have just two columns: a primary key and the specific equipment. It would need one row for each kind of equipment.

To make the separate table for equipment work, we need a way to relate cars to equipment. This need can be met with a cross-reference table, which has just two columns: one with primary keys from the `Corvettes` table and one with primary keys from the `Equipment` table. We could name this table `Corvettes_Equipment`. Each car in the `Corvettes` table could have several rows in `Equipment`, one for each specific option with which the car is equipped. This table does not need a primary key column and therefore does not have one.

Another way to conserve memory is not to store state names in the main table. The state names could be moved to a new table—say, `States`—and have references to it in the `Corvettes` table. A primary key to the `States` table,

---

1. A Corvette is a sports car built by Chevrolet.

which could be just an integer, would require far less space than a typical state name. A logical data model of the database could be that shown in Figure 13.1.

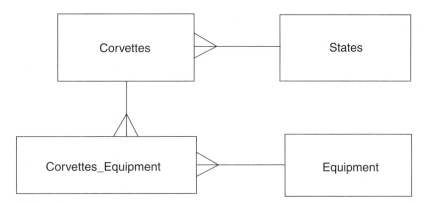

Figure 13.1 A logical data model for a database

The lines between the tables indicate the relationships between the connected tables. For example, the relationship between Corvettes and States is many-to-one: There may be many cars for sale in one state, but each car is in just one state. All of the relationships in our model are either one-to-many or many-to-one, depending on your point of view. Note that if we had not used the cross-reference table for this database, the relationship between Corvettes and Equipment would have been many-to-many.

The implementation of the database is illustrated with short examples of the required tables in Figures 13.2 to 13.5. This database will be used in the remainder of the chapter.

Vette_id	Body_style	Miles	Year	State
1	coupe	18.0	1997	4
2	hatchback	58.0	1996	7
3	convertible	13.5	2001	1
4	hatchback	19.0	1995	2
5	hatchback	25.0	1991	5
6	hardtop	15.0	2000	2
7	coupe	55.0	1979	10
8	convertible	17.0	1999	5
9	hardtop	17.0	2000	5
10	hatchback	50.0	1995	7

Equip_id	Equip
1	Automatic
2	4-speed
3	5-speed
4	6-speed
5	CD
6	Leather

Figure 13.2 The Equipment table

Figure 13.3 The Corvettes table

Vette_id	Equip
1	1
1	5
1	6
2	1
2	5
2	6
3	1
3	6
4	2
4	6
5	1
5	6
6	2
7	4
7	6
8	4
8	5
8	6
9	4
9	5
9	6
10	1
10	5

State_id	State
1	Alabama
2	Alaska
3	Arizona
4	Arkansas
5	California
6	Colorado
7	Connecticut
8	Delaware
9	Florida
10	Georgia

Figure 13.4 The `States` table

Figure 13.5 The `Corvettes_Equipment` cross-reference table

13.2   An Introduction to the Structured Query Language

The Structured Query Language (SQL) is a standard language for specifying accesses and modifications to relational databases. SQL was originally standardized by the American National Standards Institute (ANSI) and the International

Standards Organization (ISO) in 1986. SQL was significantly expanded and modified in its early years, the result of which was standardized in 1992. This version is often called SQL-2.[2] "SQL" can be pronounced as either "S-Q-L" or "sequel."

SQL is supported by the database management systems provided by all major database vendors. It is a standard that has truly become *the* standard. It is used to create, query, and modify relational databases, regardless of the particular database vendor.

SQL reserved words are not case sensitive, which means that `SELECT`, `select`, and `Select` are equivalent. However, the names of tables and table columns may or may not be case sensitive, depending on the particular database vendor. The white space separating reserved words and clauses is ignored, so commands can be spread across several lines if that is more readable. Apostrophes (') are used to delimit character strings.

SQL is quite different from most programming languages; it is actually more like a structured form of English. It was designed to be easily understood and useful for any vendor's database. This section describes some of the basic SQL commands.

13.2.1   The `SELECT` SQL Command

`SELECT` commands are used to specify queries of a database, which is how specific information is requested. The `SELECT` command has three clauses: `SELECT`, `FROM`, and `WHERE`. The general form is as follows:

`SELECT` *column names* `FROM` *table names* [`WHERE` *condition*]`;`

The brackets here indicate that the `WHERE` clause is optional.[3] The `SELECT` clause specifies the columns, or attributes, of a table. The `FROM` clause specifies the table or tables to be searched.[4] For example, the following query produces a list of all the values from the `Body_style` column of the `Corvettes` table:

`SELECT Body_style FROM Corvettes;`

The `WHERE` clause is used to specify constraints on the rows of the specified tables that are of interest. The following query produces a list of all the values from the `Body_style` column of the `Corvettes` table that have a `Year` column value greater than `1994`:

`SELECT Body_style FROM Corvettes WHERE Year > 1994;`

An asterisk (*) as the `SELECT` clause value indicates the selection of all the columns of the specified table of the rows that meet the condition specified in the

---

2. The current version of the SQL standard is SQL-3. It has not yet become widely used.

3. Actually, although the `WHERE` clause is often used, several other clauses can also appear in a `SELECT` command.

4. A `SELECT` command that specifies more than one table produces a join of the tables. Join operations are discussed in Section 13.2.2.

WHERE clause. For example, the following SELECT produces all of the columns of all rows of the Corvettes table in which the Year is greater than 1994.

```
SELECT * FROM Corvettes WHERE Year > 1994;
```

13.2.2 Joins

Suppose you want to produce a list of all Corvettes in the database that have CD players. To do this, you need information from two tables: Corvettes and Equipment. The connection between these two tables is through the cross-reference table Corvettes_Equipment. The SELECT command allows the temporary construction of a virtual table that includes information from the Corvettes and Equipment tables, using the Corvettes_Equipment table as the basis for producing the desired result. Such a virtual table is built with a *join* of the two tables. A join is specified with a SELECT command that has two tables named in the FROM clause and that uses a compound WHERE clause. The WHERE clause for our example must have three conditions. First, the Vette_id column from the Corvettes table must match the Vette_id column from the Corvettes_Equipment table. This restricts the rows of the Corvettes_ Equipment table to those associated with the row of interest in the Corvettes table. Second, the Equip column from the Corvettes_Equipment table mustmatch the Equip_id column of the Equipment table. This restricts the rows of the Equipment table to those associated with the row of interest of the Corvettes_Equipment table. Finally, the value of the Equip column from the Equipment table must be CD. The complete SELECT command to extract the cars with CD players follows:

```
SELECT Corvettes.Vette_id, Corvettes.Body_style,
       Corvettes.Miles, Corvettes.Year, Corvettes.State,
       Equipment.Equip
FROM Corvettes, Equipment, Corvettes_Equipment
WHERE Corvettes.Vette_id = Corvettes_Equipment.Vette_id
   AND Corvettes_Equipment.Equip = Equipment.Equip_id
   AND Equipment.Equip = 'CD';
```

This query produces the following result:

VETTE_ID	BODY_STYLE	MILES	YEAR	STATE	EQUIP
1	coupe	18.0	1997	4	CD
2	hatchback	58.0	1996	7	CD
8	convertible	17.0	1999	5	CD
9	hardtop	17.0	2000	5	CD
10	hatchback	50.0	1995	7	CD

Notice that all references to columns in this query are prefixed with the table names. This is necessary only when the column names are not unique to one table, as is the case for the Vette_id column, which appears in both the Corvettes and the Corvettes_Equipment tables. However, even if the column names are unique, including the table names makes the query more readable.

Recall that the `State` column of the `Corvettes` table does not store state names. Instead, it stores row references to the `States` table, which stores state names. Any user who submits a query on the `Corvettes` table would likely prefer that the states' names be returned, rather than the reference to the `States` table. This preference can be easily accommodated in SQL. First, we replace `Corvettes.State` with `States.State` in the `SELECT` clause. Next, we add `States` to the `FROM` clause. Finally, we add `AND Corvettes.State_id = States.State_id` to the `WHERE` clause. Following is the revised version of the previous `SELECT` command that produces states' names, rather than primary keys of states in the `States` table:

```
SELECT Corvettes.Vette_id, Corvettes.Body_style,
       Corvettes.Year, States.State, Equipment.Equip
FROM Corvettes, Equipment, Corvettes_Equipment, States
WHERE Corvettes.Vette_id = Corvettes_Equipment.Vette_id AND
      Corvettes.State = States.State_id AND
      Corvettes_Equipment.Equip = Equipment.Equip_id AND
      Equipment.Equip = 'CD' AND
      Corvettes.State = States.State_id;
```

13.2.3   The `INSERT` SQL Command

The `INSERT` command is used to add a row of data to a table. Its general form is

```
INSERT INTO table_name (column_name_1, column_name_2, ...,
    column_name_n)
VALUES (value_1, value_2, ..., value_n);
```

The correspondence between the column names and the values is positional: The first value goes into the column that is named first, and so forth. If `INSERT` is used on a table that has a column with the constraint `NOT NULL`, and that column is not named in the `INSERT`, an error will be detected and reported. Following is an example of an `INSERT` command:

```
INSERT INTO Corvettes(Vette_id, Body_style, Miles, Year,
                      State)
VALUES (37, 'convertible', 25.5, 1986, 17);
```

13.2.4   The `UPDATE` SQL Command

The `UPDATE` command is used to change one or more of the values of a row of a table. Its general form is as follows:

```
UPDATE table_name
SET column_name_1 = value_1,
    column_name_2 = value_2,
    ...
    column_name_n = value_n
WHERE primary_key = value;
```

The WHERE clause in an UPDATE command specifies the primary key of the row to be updated. Any subset of the columns of the table can appear in a SET clause. For example, to correct an error, you could change the year of the row with Vette_id = 17 in the Corvettes table to 1996 with the following command:

```
UPDATE Corvettes
SET Year = 1996
WHERE Vette_id = 17;
```

13.2.5   The DELETE SQL Command

One or more rows of a table can be deleted with the DELETE command, whose general form is as follows:

```
DELETE FROM table_name
WHERE primary_key = value;
```

The WHERE clause specifies the primary key of the row to be deleted. For example, if the car with the Vette_id value 27 is sold and should no longer be in the database, it could be removed from the Corvettes table with the following command:

```
DELETE FROM Corvettes
WHERE Vette_id = 27;
```

The WHERE clause of a DELETE command can specify more than one row of the table, in which case all rows that satisfy the WHERE clause are deleted.

13.2.6   The DROP SQL Command

The DROP command can be used to delete either whole databases or complete tables. The general form is as follows:

```
DROP (TABLE | DATABASE) [IF EXISTS] name;
```

In this line, the parentheses and brackets are metasymbols. DROP is used with either TABLE or DATABASE. The IF EXISTS clause is included to avoid errors if the named table or database may not exist:

```
DROP TABLE IF EXISTS States;
```

13.2.7   The CREATE TABLE SQL Command

A table in a database can be created with the CREATE command, whose general form is as follows:

```
CREATE TABLE table_name (
    column_name_1    data_type constraints,
```

column_name_2   data_type constraints ,

. . .

column_name_n   data_type constraints) ;

A large number of data types exist for table data, including INTEGER, REAL, DOUBLE, and CHAR (*length*) .[5] There are also several constraints, which can be somewhat different among various database vendors. Constraints are restrictions on the values that can appear in a column of a table. One common constraint is NOT NULL, which means that every row in the table must have a value in a column that has this constraint. Another common one is PRIMARY KEY, which means the column that has this constraint has a unique value for each row in the table. For example, you could have the following command:

```
CREATE TABLE States(
    State_id INTEGER PRIMARY KEY NOT NULL,
    State CHAR(20));
```

In some situations, table columns are referenced by position number rather than by name. The columns of a table are numbered starting with 1; that is, the first column is column 1.

We have now introduced enough SQL to make the topics in the remainder of this chapter understandable.

13.3   Architectures for Database Access

Web access to a database is provided by a client–server architecture. There are several different approaches to implementing this architecture. Client–server architectures and several of the most common of the implementation methods for Web access to databases are briefly introduced in the sections that follow.

13.3.1   Client–Server Architectures

The basic client–server architecture of the Web was discussed earlier in this book. In any client–server configuration, part of the work is done by the client and part is done by the server. For a database access architecture, the client machines provide a way for users to input requests to a database that is resident on a computer that runs a database server. Results of requests to the server are returned to the client, which may use them in subsequent computations or simply display them for the user. A database server implements a data manipulation language that presents an interface to clients. This language can directly access and update the database. In its simplest form, a client–server database configuration has only two components: the client and the server. Such systems are called *two-tier* systems.

---

5. More SQL data types and their corresponding Java data types are shown in Table 13.1 in Section 13.6.

In some cases, two-tier systems are adequate. For example, in simple uses of the Web, the server provides HTML documents and the client displays them. There is little computation to be divided between the two. However, some other applications require a great deal more complexity than browser requests for documents. In recent years, large database servers have been replaced by multiple smaller servers, thus lessening the capabilities of the individual servers to deal with the increasing complexity of applications. At the same time, client systems have grown in power and sophistication. It would thus seem natural for the computational load in client–server systems to gravitate toward the clients. Unfortunately, there are other problems with this solution—specifically, if any part of the application is moved to the clients, there is the problem of keeping the clients current with changes in the applications that use the database. This is clearly a serious problem if there are a large number of clients.

The most common solution to the problems of two-tier systems is to add a third component, thereby hatching a three-tier architecture. The first tier has the Web browser, which provides the user interface. The middle tier of such a system usually has the Web server and the applications that require database access. The third tier in the system has the database server and the database itself. The architecture of a three-tier Web-based database access system has the form shown in Figure 13.6.

Figure 13.6 Three-tier architecture of a Web site supported by databases

13.3.2   The Microsoft Open Database Connectivity

Open Database Connectivity (ODBC) specifies an API for a set of objects and methods that serves as an interface to different databases. Each database must have a driver, which is an implementation of these objects and methods. Vendors of most common databases provide ODBC drivers. By using ODBC, an application can include SQL statements (through the ODBC API) that work with any database for which a driver has been installed. A system called the *ODBC driver manager*, which runs on the client computer, chooses the proper driver for a request on a specific database. An example of the use of ODBC appears in Section 13.7.

13.3.3   PHP and Database Access

PHP includes support for a wide variety of database systems. For each database system supported, there is an associated API. These APIs provide the interface to the specific systems. For example, the MySQL API includes functions to connect to a database and apply SQL commands against the database. Web access to a database with the use of PHP is a natural architecture because PHP scripts are called through HTML documents from browsers. Using PHP and MySQL for database access is discussed in Section 13.5.

13.3.4   The Java JDBC Architecture

The Java JDBC architecture is a Java API for database access.[6] JDBC is similar to ODBC, at least in terms of purpose. Both have the X/OPEN SQL Call Level Interface (SQL CLI) in their heritages.

JDBC provides a standard set of interfaces between applications that use databases and the low-level access software that actually manipulates the databases, which is supplied by the database vendor and is dependent on the particular brand of database being used. JDBC allows applications to be independent of the database system being used, as long as a JDBC driver is installed on the platform on which the application is run.

The advantages of JDBC are basically those of Java: The language is expressive and relatively safe, and programs are highly portable among platforms. The disadvantage of JDBC is that Java–JDBC programs are more complex than programs that accomplish the same things but are written in PHP.

JDBC is described in Section 13.6.

Figure 13.7 shows the most common database access architecture.

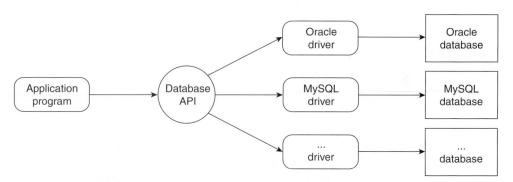

Figure 13.7 Common database access architecture

13.4   The MySQL Database System

MySQL is a free, efficient, widely used database system that implements SQL. It is available for all popular computing platforms. MySQL software and documentation can be downloaded from `http://www.mysql.org`. Some Linux system distributions, such as those from Red Hat, include MySQL. This section

---

6. JDBC sounds like an acronym for Java Database Connectivity, but Sun Microsystems has denied this. In fact, Sun has registered JDBC as a trademark, but has not done the same for Java Database Connectivity.

describes a small part of MySQL. As with other software systems illustrated in this book, we do not discuss how to install or manage MySQL. These are usually system administration tasks. MySQL 5.1.59 was used for the examples in this chapter.

The first step in using MySQL is logging into the MySQL system, which is done with the following command (at the command line of the operating system):

```
mysql [-h host] [-u username] [database_name] [-p]
```

The parts of this command that are in square brackets are optional. The *host* is the name of the server running MySQL; if *host* is absent, MySQL assumes that it denotes the user's machine. If *username* is absent, MySQL assumes that the name you used to log onto the machine is the correct username. If *database_name* is given, that database is selected as the focus of MySQL, making it the object of subsequent commands. If –p is included, a password is required, and MySQL will ask for it.

Once you have successfully logged into MySQL, it is ready to receive commands. Although it is called "logging on," what you are actually doing is starting execution of the MySQL system.

If the database to be accessed already exists, but its name was not included in the logon to MySQL, the use command can be used to focus on the database of interest. For example, if we want to access a database named cars, the following command would be used:

```
use cars;
```

This is sometimes called making a specific database the "current" database for the MySQL server. The MySQL response to this command is as follows:

```
Database changed
```

This response seems odd because no change has been made to a database. Note the semicolon at the end of the use command; it is essential here, as it is for all MySQL commands. If a command is given without a semicolon, MySQL will wait indefinitely for one. Until a semicolon is found, MySQL behaves as if the remainder of the command is yet to be typed.

If a database is not specified in the logon to MySQL and a database command is given before use is used to focus on a database, the following error message will be issued:

```
ERROR 1046: No Database Selected
```

If a new database is to be created, the database itself must be created first and then the tables that will make up the database. A new database is created with the SQL CREATE DATABASE command:

```
CREATE DATABASE cars;
```

This command also elicits an odd response from MySQL:

```
Query ok, 1 row affected (0.05 sec)
```

The time given varies with the speed of the host machine and its current load.

The tables of a database are created with the CREATE TABLE command, whose syntax is that of SQL. For example, in

```
CREATE TABLE Equipment
    (Equip_id   INT   UNSIGNED   NOT NULL   AUTO_INCREMENT
                PRIMARY KEY,
     Equip   CHAR(10)
     );
```

the INT and UNSIGNED parts of the Equip_id column indicate the data type. The AUTO_INCREMENT is a MySQL convenience. It specifies that the values of this column need not be given in populating the table. The values 1, 2, 3, and so forth will be implicitly assigned. The value NULL is given in place of a value for a column so specified in populating the table with INSERT. A large number of different data types are possible for field values. The most common of these are CHAR(*length*), INT, and FLOAT(*total, fractional*), where *total* specifies the total number of characters, including both digits and the decimal point, and *fractional* gives the number of digits to the right of the decimal point.

The SHOW command can be used to display the tables of the database:

```
SHOW TABLES;
```

If our sample database, cars, is the database of current focus, the preceding command produces the following output:

```
- - - - - - - - - - - - -
show
- - - - - - - - - - - - -
+---------------------+
|                     |
| Tables_in_cars      |
|                     |
+---------------------+
| Corvettes           |
| Corvettes_Equipment |
| Equipment           |
| States              |
+---------------------+
```

The DESCRIBE command can be used to display the description of the structure of a table. For example,

```
DESCRIBE Corvettes;
```

produces the following table:

```
+----------+----------------+-----+----+--------+--------------+
|Field     |Type            |Null |Key |Default |Extra         |
+----------+----------------+-----+----+--------+--------------+
|Vette_id  |int(10) unsigned|     |PRI |NULL    |auto_increment|
+----------+----------------+-----+----+--------+--------------+
|Body_style|char(12)        |     |    |        |              |
+----------+----------------+-----+----+--------+--------------+
|Miles     |float(4,1)      |     |    |0.0     |              |
+----------+----------------+-----+----+--------+--------------+
|Year      |int(10) unsigned|     |    |0       |              |
+----------+----------------+-----+----+--------+--------------+
|State     |int(10) unsigned|     |    |0       |              |
+----------+----------------+-----+----+--------+--------------+
```

The other MySQL commands that are needed here—INSERT, SELECT, DROP, UPDATE, and DELETE—are all implementations of their corresponding SQL commands. Therefore, their descriptions need not be repeated in this section.

There are many tools available to aid in database administration (e.g., from http://dev.mysql.com). One of these, MySQL Administrator, is a program that configures, monitors, and starts and stops a MySQL server; manages users and connections; performs backups; and carries out several other administrative tasks.

13.5 Database Access with PHP and MySQL

PHP access to a database is often done with two HTML documents: one to collect a user request for a database access and one to host the PHP code to process the request and generate the return HTML document. The user request collector is a simple HTML document. Therefore, this section is primarily about the database connection and processing.

13.5.1 Potential Problems with Special Characters

When a query is made on a database through a browser, the result of the query must be returned to the browser as HTML. Putting database field data into an HTML document creates a potential problem. A field retrieved from the database may contain characters that are special in HTML, namely >, <, ", or &. PHP includes a function, htmlspecialchars, that replaces all occurrences of these four special characters in its parameter with their corresponding entities. For example, consider the following code:

```
$str = "Apples & grapes <raisins, too>";
$str = htmlspecialchars($str);
```

After the interpretation of this code, the value of $str is as follows:

```
"Apples &amp; grapes &lt;raisins, too&gt;"
```

This string is now ready to be made the content of an HTML tag without causing any browser confusion.

Another problem with special characters can occur with PHP scripts that get values through GET or POST or from a cookie. Strings from these sources could include single quotes, double quotes, backslashes, and null characters, all of which could cause problems if they are used in other strings in a script. To avoid these problems, the PHP system has an implicit backslashing function named magic_quotes_gpc, which can be turned on or off in the PHP.ini file. When this function is enabled, which is the default, all values received in a script from $_POST, $_GET, and $_COOKIE have backslashes implicitly inserted in front of all single quotes, double quotes, backslashes, and null characters. This strategy avoids any problems that could be caused by those characters. For example, if the string O'Reilly is fetched from $_POST, it would be converted by magic_quotes_gpc to O\'Reilly. Unfortunately, this causes other problems. If the script compares the name with a nonslashed version, the comparison will fail. Furthermore, even displaying the name will show the backslash.

This problem is relevant here because we want to have a PHP script get SQL commands from a text box in an HTML document. For example, suppose magic_quotes_gpc is on and the value for a query obtained from a text box on a form is as follows:

```
SELECT * FROM Corvettes WHERE Body_style = 'coupe'
```

If the name of the text box is query, its value is put in $query with the following statement:

```
$query = $_POST['query'];
```

The value of $query is converted to the following by magic_quotes_gpc:

```
SELECT * FROM Corvettes WHERE Body_style = \'coupe\'
```

Unfortunately, this string is not a valid SQL command (because of the backslashes). If it is sent to MySQL as a command, MySQL will reject it and report an error. Therefore, if complete SQL commands are to be collected from a form, magic_quotes_gpc must be disabled in PHP.ini to avoid the extra backslashes. The alternative to changing the value of magic_quotes_gpc is to remove the extra slashes in the PHP script with the predefined function stripslashes, as in the following statement:

```
$query = stripslashes($query);
```

13.5.2   Connecting to MySQL and Selecting a Database

The PHP function `mysqli_connect` connects a script to a MySQL server and selects a database. This function takes four parameters. The first is the host that is running MySQL; the default is localhost (the machine on which the script is running). The second parameter is the username for MySQL; the default is the username in which the PHP process runs. The third parameter is the password for the database; the default is blank (which works if the database does not require a password). The fourth is the name of the selected database. If left out, the script must call `mysqli_select_db` to set the default database. For example, the following statement connects to MySQL and selects the `cars` database, assuming it has no password:

```
$db = mysqli_connect("localhost", "root", "", "cars");
```

Of course, the connect operation could fail. One way to test this is to call `mysqli_connect_errno`, which returns zero if the connection succeeded. If it returns a value greater than zero, the script can call `mysqli_connect_error` and display its returned value, which is an error message. For example, the following code is often placed just after the call to `mysqli_connect`:

```
if (mysqli_connect_errno()) {
  printf("Connect failed: %s <br />",
          mysqli_connect_error());
  exit();
}
```

The connection to a database is terminated with the `mysqli_close` function. This function is not necessary when MySQL is used through a PHP script, because the connection will be closed implicitly when the script terminates.

If we want to display the query, it is best to send it to `htmlspecialcharacters` first, because the display process is done by the browser.

13.5.3   Requesting MySQL Operations

MySQL select and insert operations are requested through the `mysqli_query` function. This function takes two parameters, the return value from the `mysqli_connect` and the MySQL command. Typically, the command, in the form of a string literal, is assigned to a variable. Then `mysqli_query` is called with that variable as its second parameter, as in the following code:

```
$query = "SELECT * from Corvettes";
$result = mysqli_query($db, $query);
```

The return value from `mysqli_query` is the data that resulted from the operation. In most cases, the first thing to do with the result of a SELECT command is to determine the number of rows in the result. This is obtained with the `mysqli_num_rows` function, which is passed the result returned by `mysqli_query`:

```
$num_rows = mysqli_num_rows($result);
```

The number of fields in the result rows can be determined with `mysqli_num_fields`, as in the following statement:

```
$num_fields = mysqli_num_fields($result);
```

The rows of the result can be retrieved in several different forms. We will use `mysqli_fetch_assoc`, which returns an associative array of the next row of the result. The keys are the column names and the values are the values of those column fields. This function is an iterator—it returns the next row of the result of a query, if there is one. If there are no more rows, `mysqli_fetch_assoc` returns `false`.

The field values can be obtained by subscripting the return array from `mysqli_fetch_assoc` with the column names. For example, the following code displays the results of a given query that are in `$result`:

```
// Get the numbers of rows and fields
$num_rows = mysqli_num_rows($result);
$num_fields = mysqli_num_fields($result);

// Get first row
$row = mysqli_fetch_assoc($result);

// Display the column names
$keys = array_keys($row);
for ($index = 0; $index < $num_fields; $index++)
  print $keys[$index] . "   ";
print "<br />";

// Display the values of the fields in the rows
for ($row_num = 0; $row_num < $num_rows; $row_num++) {
  $values = array_values($row);
  for ($index = 0; $index < $num_fields; $index++) {
    $value = htmlspecialchars($values[$index]);
    print $value . "   ";
  }
  print "<br />";
  $row = mysqli_fetch_assoc($result);
}
```

13.5.4   A PHP–MySQL Example

One simple example of Web access to a database is to use an HTML form to collect a query from a user, apply the query to the database, and return a document that shows the results of the query. Following is the HTML document `carsdata.html`, which collects queries on the `cars` database from the user:

```
<!-- carsdata.html
     Uses a form to collect a query against the cars
     database.
     Calls the PHP script access_cars.php to perform
     the given query and display the results
     -->
<!DOCTYPE html>
<html lang = "en">
  <head>
    <title> Access to the cars database </title>
    <meta charset = "utf-8" />
  </head>
  <body>
    <p>
      Please enter your query:
      <br />
      <form action  = "access_cars.php" method = "post">
        <textarea  rows = "2"  cols = "80" name = "query" >
        </textarea>
        <br /><br />
        <input type = "reset"  value = "Reset" />
        <input type = "submit"  value = "Submit request" />
      </form>
    </p>
  </body>
</html>
```

The following HTML/PHP document, `access_cars.php`, processes a query and places the results in an HTML table:

```
<!-- access_cars.php
     A PHP script to access the cars database
     through MySQL
     -->
```

```
<!DOCTYPE html>
<html lang = "en">
  <head>
    <title> Access the cars database with MySQL </title>
    <meta charset = "utf-8" />
  </head>
  <body>
    <?php

// Connect to MySQL
    $db = mysqli_connect("localhost", "root", "", "cars");
    if (mysqli_connect_errno()) {
      print "Connect failed: " . mysqli_connect_error();
      exit();
    }


// Get the query and clean it up (delete leading and trailing
// whitespace and remove backslashes from magic_quotes_gpc)

    $query = $_POST['query'];
    trim($query);
    $query = stripslashes($query);

// Display the query, after fixing html characters
    $query_html = htmlspecialchars($query);
    print "<p> The query is: " . $query_html . "</p>";

// Execute the query
    $result = mysqli_query($db, $query);
    if (!$result) {
      print "Error - the query could not be executed" .
        mysqli_error();
      exit;
    }

// Display the results in a table
    print "<table><caption> <h2> Query Results </h2> </caption>";
    print "<tr align = 'center'>";

// Get the number of rows in the result
    $num_rows = mysqli_num_rows($result);

// If there are rows in the result, put them in an HTML table
    if ($num_rows > 0) {
```

```
        $row = mysqli_fetch_assoc($result);
        $num_fields = mysqli_num_fields($result);

// Produce the column labels
        $keys = array_keys($row);
        for ($index = 0; $index < $num_fields; $index++)
          print "<th>" . $keys[$index] . "</th>";

        print "</tr>";

// Output the values of the fields in the rows
        for ($row_num = 0; $row_num < $num_rows; $row_num++) {
          print "<tr>";
          $values = array_values($row);
          for ($index = 0; $index < $num_fields; $index++) {
            $value = htmlspecialchars($values[$index]);
            print "<td>" . $value . "</td>";
          }

        print "</tr>";
        $row = mysqli_fetch_assoc($result);
        }
      }
      else {
        print "There were no such rows in the table <br />";
      }
      print "</table>";
    ?>
  </body>
</html>
```

Figure 13.8 displays the results of access_cars.php on the given query.

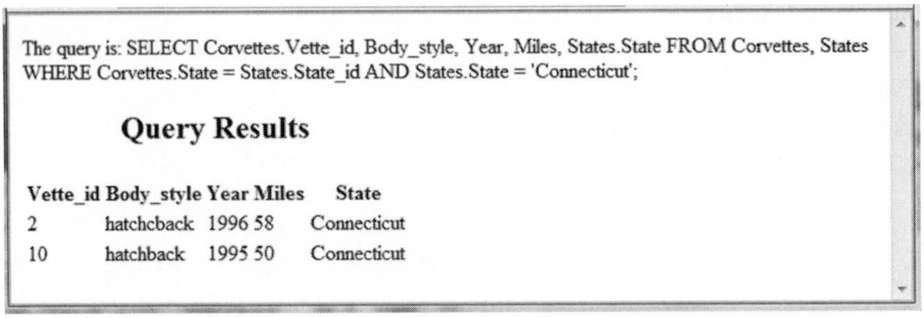

The query is: SELECT Corvettes.Vette_id, Body_style, Year, Miles, States.State FROM Corvettes, States WHERE Corvettes.State = States.State_id AND States.State = 'Connecticut';

Query Results

Vette_id	Body_style	Year	Miles	State
2	hatchcback	1996	58	Connecticut
10	hatchback	1995	50	Connecticut

Figure 13.8 Display of the results of access_cars.php

The two documents, `carsdata.html` and `access_cars.php`, which together collect a query from a user, apply it to the database, and return the results, can be combined. After inserting the HTML markup from `carsdata.html` into `access_cars.php`, we must make several modifications and additions to the resulting document. First, the `action` attribute of the form must be changed to be self-referential. This is done by changing the value to the name of the combined file. Next, there is the issue of how to get the PHP processor to produce the query collection markup the first time the document is requested and to interpret the query processing code on the next request. The commonly used approach is to create a hidden input element that sets its value when the document is first displayed. The PHP code in the document checks the value of the hidden element to determine whether the action is to display a text area to collect a query or to apply the query to the database and display the result. The hidden element is defined with markup as shown here:

```
<input type = "hidden"  name = "stage"  value = "1" />
```

The PHP code to test the value of the hidden element has the following form:

```
$stage = $_POST["stage"];
if (!IsSet($stage)) { ... }
```

The then clause of this selector would contain the display of the form to collect the query. The else clause would contain the query processing and result display code. The combination of `carsdata.html` and `access_cars.php`, named `access_cars2.php`, follows:

```
<!-- access_cars2.php
     A PHP script to both get a query from the user and
     access the cars database through MySQL to get and
     display the result of the query.
     -->
<!DOCTYPE html>
<html lang = "en">
  <head>
    <title> Access the cars database with MySQL </title>
    <meta charset = "utf-8" />
  </head>
  <body>
    <?php
      $stage = $_POST["stage"];
      if (!IsSet($stage)) {
    ?>
        <p>
          Please enter your query:
          <br />
```

```
                     <form  method = "POST"  action = "access_cars2.php" >
                        <textarea  rows = "2"  cols = "80"  name = "query">
                        </textarea>
                        <br /><br />
                        <input type = "hidden"  name = "stage"  value = "1" />
                        <input type = "submit"  value = "Submit request" />
                     </form>
                  </p>
                  <?php
               } else {  // $stage was set, so process the query

// Connect to MySQL
            $db = mysqli_connect("localhost", "root", "", "cars");
            if (mysqli_connect_errno()) {
              print "Connect failed: " . mysqli_connect_error();
              exit();
            }

// Get the query and clean it up (delete leading and trailing
// whitespace and remove backslashes from magic_quotes_gpc)

            $query = $_POST['query'];
            trim($query);
            $query = stripslashes($query);

// Display the query, after fixing html characters
            $query_html = htmlspecialchars($query);
            print "<p> The query is: " . $query_html . "</p>";

// Execute the query
            $result = mysqli_query($db, $query);
            if (!$result) {
              print "Error - the query could not be executed" .
                mysqli_error();
              exit;
            }

// Display the results in a table
            print "<table><caption> <h2> Query Results </h2> </caption>";
            print "<tr align = 'center'>";

// Get the number of rows in the result
            $num_rows = mysqli_num_rows($result);
```

```php
// If there are rows in the result, put them in an HTML table
    if ($num_rows > 0) {
        $row = mysqli_fetch_assoc($result);
        $num_fields = mysqli_num_fields($result);

// Produce the column labels
        $keys = array_keys($row);
        for ($index = 0; $index < $num_fields; $index++)
          print "<th>" . $keys[$index] . "</th>";

        print "</tr>";

// Output the values of the fields in the rows
        for ($row_num = 0; $row_num < $num_rows; $row_num++) {
          print "<tr>";
          $values = array_values($row);
          for ($index = 0; $index < $num_fields; $index++) {
            $value = htmlspecialchars($values[$index]);
            print "<td>" . $value . "</td>";
          } //* end of for ($index ...

          print "</tr>";
          $row = mysqli_fetch_assoc($result);
        }  //* end of for ($row_num ...
      }  //* end of if ($num_rows ...
      else {
        print "There were no such rows in the table <br />";
      }
    print "</table>";
    } //  end of the else clause for if (!IsSet($stage...
    ?>
  </body>
</html>
```

13.6 Database Access with JDBC and MySQL

JDBC is a Java API for database access. A servlet can use JDBC to connect to a database and send SQL commands to the database as the parameter of a JDBC method. The Java interfaces that define JDBC are included in the `java.sql` package, which is part of the standard Java distribution. For the example in this section, we used NetBeans 7.0, MySQL Server 5.1.59, and GlassFish 3.

13.6.1   JDBC and MySQL

This section describes the mechanisms for using JDBC in a servlet to perform simple SQL operations on an existing database. The first step is to establish a connection between the application and the database. A database driver for MySQL, as well as some other database systems, is included with recent versions of NetBeans, so it is not necessary to download or register a driver to use MySQL with JDBC on NetBeans.

The connection to a database from a servlet is made by creating a `Connection` object with the `getConnection` method of the `DriverManager` class. This method takes three parameters, the first of which is a reference to the host and the database in the form of a string literal. For the sample database `cars` and the MySQL database system, this is `"jdbc:mysql://localhost/cars"`. This assumes that we will access this database through JDBC and MySQL using the Web server on our machine (`localhost`). The second parameter is the user, for which we will use `"root"`. The third parameter is the password for the database, which in our case will be the empty string, because the `cars` database has no password. So, the `Connection` object for our example can be created with the following statement:

```
myCon = DriverManager.getConnection(

    "jdbc:mysql://localhost/cars", "root", "");
```

The `Connection` object is used to specify all database operations from the servlet.

After the connection to the database is established, a servlet can access the database by using SQL commands. The first step in using SQL from a servlet is to create a `Statement` object through which one of the `Statement` methods can actually issue the command. The `Statement` object is created with the `createStatement` method of the `Connection` class. If `myCon` is the `Connection` object, the following statement can be used:

```
Statement myStmt = myCon.createStatement();
```

SQL commands can be created as `String` objects, as shown in the following example:

```
final String sql_com =
    "UPDATE Corvettes SET Year = 1991 WHERE Vette_id = 7";
```

For JDBC, there are two categories of SQL commands: the action commands, which include `INSERT`, `UPDATE`, `DELETE`, `CREATE TABLE`, and `DROP TABLE`; and the query command, `SELECT`. The action commands are executed through the `executeUpdate` method of the `Statement` object. For example, the previous SQL command, `sql_com`, can be executed with the following statement:

```
myStmt.executeUpdate(sql_com);
```

The `executeUpdate` method returns the number of rows that were affected by the command that it sent to the database.

A `SELECT` SQL command can be executed by passing it as the parameter to the `executeQuery` method of the `Statement` object. Executing a `SELECT` command differs from executing an action command in that the `SELECT` command is expected to return a part of the data found in the database. So, a call to `executeQuery` must be assigned to a program variable. The class of this variable must be `ResultSet`, which is structured to store such results and which has methods to provide access to the data of the result. The following code is illustrative:

```
ResultSet result;
final String sql_com =
    "SELECT * FROM Corvettes WHERE Year <= 1990"
result = myStmt.executeQuery(sql_com);
```

Objects of the `ResultSet` class are similar to objects of classes that implement the related interface `Enumeration`. In both cases, the elements of the object are accessed through an iterator method. In the case of `Enumeration`, the iterator method is named `nextElement`; in the case of `ResultSet`, it is named `next`. The `next` method is a predicate; it returns a Boolean value, depending on whether there is another element in the `ResultSet` object. Its action is to make the next element of the `ResultSet` object the current one—that is, the one that can be accessed through one of the access methods provided by `ResultSet`. Initially, there is no current element of a `ResultSet` object. Therefore, `next` must be called to make the first element current. The elements of a `ResultSet` object are typically accessed in a loop such as the following:

```
while(result.next()) {
    access and process the current element
}
```

Here, `result` is the object returned by `executeQuery`.

The actual structure of a `ResultSet` object is not visible to the application, so it is irrelevant. The information in a `ResultSet` object is extracted through a collection of access methods. Each element of a `ResultSet` object represents the information in a row of the result of the query operation. Field values in the rows can be extracted by the access methods, whose names are in the following general form:

get *Type_name*

Here, the *Type_name* part is one of the Java data types, either a primitive type such as `int` or `float` or a class such as `String`.

There are actually two of each of the named access methods: one that takes an `int` parameter, which specifies the column number, starting at 1; and one that takes a `String` parameter, which specifies the column name. For example, suppose the first row of the `ResultSet` object for the `SELECT` specified previously happened to be

```
3, "convertible", 13.5, 2001, 1
```

Then, if the variable `style` is defined to be a `String` object, the value of the `Body_style` column `"convertible"` could be obtained with either of the following two method calls:

```
style = result.getString("Body_style");
style = result.getString(2);
```

The SQL data types do not perfectly match the Java data types. Some of the most commonly used SQL data types and their Java counterparts are shown in Table 13.1.

The get*Type_name* methods attempt to convert SQL data types to equivalent Java data types. For example, if `getString` is used to fetch an `INTEGER` value, the number will be converted to a `String` object.

Table 13.1   Common SQL data types and their Java counterparts

SQL Data Type	Java Data Type
`INTEGER` or `INT`	`int`
`SMALLINT`	`short`
`FLOAT` (*n*)	`double`
`REAL`	`float`
`DOUBLE`	`double`
`CHARACTER` (*n*) or `CHAR` (*n*)	`String`
`VARCHAR` (*n*)	`String`
`BOOLEAN`	`boolean`

13.6.2   Metadata

If a servlet is being developed that must work with any database—that is, the exact structure of the database is not known—the code must be able to get table names and column names from the database. Also, the types of the data in the result rows must be known. Information that describes the database itself or some part of the database is called *metadata*. There are two kinds of metadata: metadata that describes the database and metadata that describes a `ResultSet` object that is returned by the execution of a query.

The method `getMetaData` of the `Connection` object creates an object of `DatabaseMetaData` type, which can be used to get information about a database, as in the statement

```
DatabaseMetaData dbmd = myCon.getMetaData();
```

To deal with the many different database configurations, many different methods are defined in the `DatabaseMetaData` class. Fortunately, most of them are used infrequently, and we can illustrate the use of metadata through just one that is commonly used: `getTables`. Although `getTables` returns a variety of information, here we are interested only in table names.

The `getTables` method takes four parameters, only the last of which interests us. The last actual parameter to `getTables` specifies an array of `String` objects with just one element, which is set to the value `"TABLE"`. The other three actual parameters can be `null`. The `getTables` method returns a `ResultSet` object that has information about the tables of the database, the third row of which has the table names. Assuming that the `Connection` object for a database is `myCon`, the code to produce a list of the names of the tables in the database is as follows:

```
String tbl[] = {"TABLE"};
DatabaseMetaData dbmd = myCon.getMetaData();
result = dbmd.getTables(null, null, null, tbl);
System.out.println("The tables in the database are: \n\n");
while (result.next()) {
  System.out.println(result.getString(3));
}
```

Adding this code to a program with access to the `cars` database would produce the following output:

```
The tables in this database are:
CORVETTES
CORVETTES_EQUIPMENT
EQUIPMENT
STATES
```

Fetching metadata about the result of a query on a database is more complicated than getting the table names. The metadata for a query result has a different structure than that for the general database information. For the query result, the metadata is stored in an object of the `ResultSetMetaData` class. An object of this class is returned from the `ResultSet` object when the `getMetaData` method is called, as with the following statement:

```
ResultSetMetaData resultMd = result.getMetaData();
```

The number of columns and their names, types, and sizes can be determined with the `resultMd` object through the methods of `ResultSetMetaData`. The number of columns is returned by `getColumnCount`. The name of the ith column is returned by `getColumnLabel(i)`.

Using these objects and methods, the following code creates a display of the column names of the result produced by a query:

```
// Create an object for the metadata
ResultSetMetaData resultMd = result.getMetaData();
```

```
// Loop to fetch and display the column names
for (int i = 1; i <= resultMd.getColumnCount(); i++) {
  String columnName = resultMd.getColumnLabel(i);
  System.out.print(columnName + "\t");
}

System.out.println("\n");
```

The display produced by this code is as follows:

```
Vette_id       Body_style       Miles    Year    State
```

The problem of not knowing the types of the data in the result rows has a simple solution: The data can be converted to strings with `getString`, a method of the result object. This solution is illustrated in Section 13.6.3.

13.6.3   An Example

As an example we use an HTML document that collects a database query in a text box. This document is similar to `carsdata.html`, which was used in Section 13.5.4 as the user interface to the PHP–MySQL example. The document calls a servlet to perform the query. The servlet uses its `init` method to establish the database connection and create the `Statement` object for the query method, `executeQuery`. These operations could be specified in the `doPost` method, but that would require reconnection to the database with every query. In the `init` method, reconnection happens only once.

The `doPost` method performs the query operations and builds the return document of the results of the query. The query results are placed in an HTML table so that the output has a presentable appearance.

```
// JDBCServlet.java
//  This servlet receives an SQL query from its HTML document,
//   connects to the cars database, performs the query on the
//   database, and returns an HTML table of the results of the
//   query

import java.io.IOException;
import java.io.PrintWriter;
import javax.servlet.ServletException;
import javax.servlet.annotation.WebServlet;
import javax.servlet.http.HttpServlet;
import javax.servlet.http.HttpServletRequest;
import javax.servlet.http.HttpServletResponse;
import java.sql.*;

@WebServlet(name = "JDBCServlet", urlPatterns =
    {"/JDBCServlet"})
```

```
public class JDBCServlet extends HttpServlet {
  private Connection myCon;
  private Statement myStmt;
  private PrintWriter out;

  // The processRequest method - does it all for this project
  protected void processRequest(HttpServletRequest request,
                                HttpServletResponse response)
         throws ServletException, IOException {
     ResultSet result;
     String query, colName, dat;
     int numCols, index;
     ResultSetMetaData resultMd;

  // Set the MIME type and get a writer
     response.setContentType("text/html;charset=UTF-8");
     out = response.getWriter();

// Create the document head and body opening
     out.println("<html>");
     out.println("<head><title>JDBCServlet</title></head>");
     out.println("<body>");

// Create the connection to the cars db
     try {
         myCon = DriverManager.getConnection (
                   "jdbc:mysql://localhost/cars", "root", "");
     }
     catch (SQLException e) {
         out.println("getConnection failed");
     }

// Create the statement for SQL queries
     try {
       myStmt = myCon.createStatement();
     }
     catch (Exception e) {
         out.println("createStatement failed");
     }

// Get the SQL request command
     query = request.getParameter("query");
     out.print("<p><b>The query is: </b>" + query + "</p>");

// Perform the query
     try {
         result = myStmt.executeQuery(query);
```

```java
          // Get the result's metadata and the number of result rows
             resultMd = result.getMetaData();
             numCols = resultMd.getColumnCount();

          // Produce the table header and caption
             out.println("<table border>");
             out.println("<caption> <b> Query Results </b>
                </caption>");
             out.println("<tr>");

          // Loop to produce the column headings
             for (index = 1; index <= numCols; index++) {
                colName = resultMd.getColumnLabel(index);
                out.print("<th>" + colName + "</th>");
             }
             out.println("</tr>");

          // Loop to produce the rows of the result
             while (result.next()) {
                out.println("<tr>");

          // Loop to produce the data of a row of the result
                for (index = 1; index <= numCols; index++) {
                   dat = result.getString(index);
                   out.println("<td>" + dat + "</td>");
                }  //** end of for (index = 0; ...
                out.println("</tr>");
             }  //** end of while (result.next()) ...
             out.println("</table>");
          }  //** end of try

          catch (Exception e) {
             out.println("executeQuery failed </br>");
          }  //** end of catch
          out.println("</body></html>");
       }  //** end of processRequest method

       @Override
       protected void doGet(HttpServletRequest request,
                            HttpServletResponse response)
            throws ServletException, IOException {
          processRequest(request, response);
       }
```

```
        @Override
        protected void doPost(HttpServletRequest request,
                              HttpServletResponse response)
             throws ServletException, IOException {
          processRequest(request, response);
        }
}
```

Figure 13.9 diplays the results of JDBCServlet on the given query.

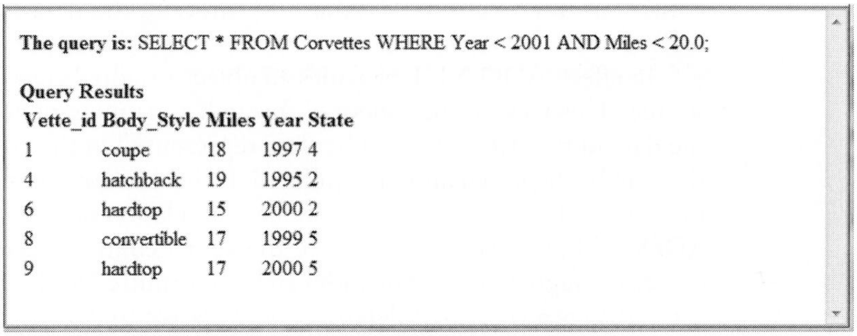

The query is: SELECT * FROM Corvettes WHERE Year < 2001 AND Miles < 20.0;

Query Results

Vette_id	Body_Style	Miles	Year	State
1	coupe	18	1997	4
4	hatchback	19	1995	2
6	hardtop	15	2000	2
8	convertible	17	1999	5
9	hardtop	17	2000	5

Figure 13.9 Display of the results of JDBCServlet

13.7 Database Access with ASP.NET and MySQL

Microsoft provides support for data management with its Access database management system, primarily for smaller applications; its more elaborate and scalable SQL Server database management system; its ADO.NET library of classes for data management; and its Open Database Connectivity (ODBC) API for connections to various databases. Support for database applications in ASP.NET is provided by a part of ADO.NET. Of course, only a small part of ADO.NET is covered here—specifically, that part defined by what is necessary to allow us to replicate the example Web document that accepts an SQL command in a text box, executes it against a database, and displays the resulting table.

13.7.1 MySQL and ADO.NET

Perhaps the most common database system that is used with ASP.NET Web sites is Microsoft's SQL Server. There are several reasons that SQL Server is not covered in this section. First, SQL Server, like other commercial database systems, is a large and complex software product. If we used it here, we would need to describe at least a part of it, but that would be a diversion from the chapter's task of describing database access through the Web. The second reason SQL Server is not covered here is that MySQL has been used for the other Web technologies discussed in this chapter: PHP and JDBC. Because MySQL already has been described, it is both practical and reasonable to use it again. The third reason we use MySQL is that commercial database systems, such as SQL Server, are expensive, while MySQL is free. This is an important consideration for a book written primarily for students. Finally, the approach to using MySQL is not very different from that to using SQL Server, so porting our discussion from MySQL to SQL Server is not difficult.

The fundamental aim of ADO.NET is to provide a relationship between markup controls and some data source, either in the program or external to it. If the data is in an external file, it could be hierarchical, such as XML, or tabular, as in a relational database. If internal, the data could be an array or a collection.

In effect, ADO.NET provides an object-oriented view of the data in the data source. This view is implemented through a mapping of controls to the form of the data in the data source. The data represented in the controls in the application can be displayed and manipulated. If the data source is a relational database, the control-based view is a set of table and relation objects. To support this view, ADO.NET has classes that create the actual connection to the data, as well as classes through which commands can be transmitted to the data (SQL commands if the data is a relational database), and classes to move data from the database to the application. This is the *connected* part of ADO.NET. The *disconnected* part of ADO.NET provides the classes that represent the data that is visible in the application. In the example in this section, the part of the data that is visible in the application will be the table returned from an SQL SELECT command executed against the database. For the remainder of the section, we deal only with data sources that are relational databases.

There are three kinds of classes that support the connected part of ADO .NET that will be discussed in this section: those for connections, those for commands, and those for data readers. A connection class object is the actual interface to the database. This corresponds to the connections made in previous sections in PHP and JDBC. For each database vendor that is supported, there is a connection class—for example, `OracleConnection` and `OdbcConnection`. An object of the command classes stores the commands that can be executed against the database. Like the connection classes, there are the `OracleCommand` and `OdbcCommand` classes, for Oracle and ODBC database systems, respectively. For executing SQL commands against a database, ADO.NET includes three methods: `ExecuteReader` for SELECT commands that return tables, `ExecuteNonQuery` for non-SELECT SQL commands, and `ExecuteScalar` for SELECT commands that return single values. These methods are from the specific `Command` class being used. They are called through an object of that class—for instance, for an application that accesses a database through ODBC, an object of the `OdbcCommand` class.

As just described, the approach of ADO.NET that allows a database application to be used on different database systems is to support a data provider class for each such system. This approach ties an application to a particular database system. As a result of this design, it requires more effort to switch database systems in an ADO.NET application than if it were a JDBC application.[7]

The approach used to access a MySQL database in this section is through Open Database Connectivity (ODBC, introduced in Section 13.3.2), using a MySQL driver. Thus, the application is written against ODBC, which allows it to be easily modified to be used against databases other than MySQL. Note that, although ODBC provides a relatively simple way to access the MySQL database from an ASP.NET application, it is also a relatively inefficient way of doing so. A commercial ASP.NET application would more likely use a dedicated MySQL provider.[8]

The general namespace for ADO.NET classes and interfaces is `System .Data`. The specific namespace for ODBC is `System.Data.Odbc`.

13.7.2   Data Binding

The ADO.NET data-binding model fetches data from a data source and dynamically associates that data with the properties of server controls. Such controls are called *data-bound controls*. The actual binding process is requested with the `DataBind` method of the object that represents the data-bound control. When executed, the `DataBind` method moves data from the data source to populate the control.

The `DataSource` property of a data-bound control specifies the data source object to which the control is bound. A data source control is directly connected to a data-bound control and interacts directly with the database. This data-binding process is often specified with code similar to the following two statements:

```
myControl.DataSource = data from some data reader method ;
myControl.DataBind();
```

There are six primary data-bound controls: `DataList`, `Repeater`, `Form-View`, `DetailsView`, `DataGrid`, and `GridView`.[9] We discuss only `GridView` in this section. `DataGrid` appeared in ASP.NET 1.1. `GridView`, which was introduced in ASP.NET 2.0, is a greatly enhanced version of `DataGrid`. `DataGrid` should not be used in new applications, but will continue to be used in legacy applications for some time.

`GridView` is a complex and powerful column-based data-bound control. A column-based control supports columns of data. If the data source is a relational database, the columns are the columns of a database table. There are several categories of `GridView` properties: behavior, such as `AllowSorting` and `AutoGenerateColumns`; style properties, such as `AlternatingRowStyle` and `HeaderStyle`; appearance, such as `BackImageUrl` and `GridLines`; and state properties, such as `Columns` and `PageCount`. Most of the large numbers

---

7. PHP's approach is similar to that of ADO.NET.

8. For example, see `http://www.devart.com/dotconnect/mysql/`.

9. In addition, because all form controls inherit the `DataBind` method, any of them can have its properties set to data values from a data source.

of properties have reasonable default values and need not be specified for a specific `GridView` control. Naturally, we cannot get into the specifics of most of the `GridView` properties in this section. A `GridView` control can be specified in an ASP.NET source document with no more than `ID` and `runat` properties. However, the large collection of properties gives the user extensive detailed control over the behavior and appearance of the data. A `GridView` control can raise 15 different events—another testament to the richness and complexity of this control.

The concept of binding data to markup controls, as used in ADO.NET, is a significant difference between the ADO.NET approach to data handling and that of JDBC.

13.7.3   Connection Strings

The connection to a database from an ASP.NET source document is made by passing a string of information about the connection to a connection object constructor. The string includes information about the driver to use, the server, the specific database, the user id, and, possibly, a database password. For the example application of this section, a MySQL ODBC driver is needed. One source of such a driver is `http://dev.mysql.com/downloads/connector/odbc/3.51 .html`. The name of the driver from this source is `MySQL ODBC 3.51 Driver`. After the driver has been downloaded, it must be installed. The connection string for our `cars` MySQL database, served locally, is as follows:

```
"Driver={MySQL ODBC 3.51 Driver}; server=localhost;" +
"Database=cars;uid=root"
```

The ASP.NET source document for our application will include a text box to collect a `SELECT` SQL command from the user, a button to submit the command to the code-behind file, a label element for displaying an error message that could come from the C# code in the code-behind file, and the `GridView` control to store and display the result of the `SELECT` command. The `GridView` control will be created with markup, but one of its attributes, `DataSource`, will be set dynamically with programming code. The programming code will need the `ID` of the control element, which is available through the variable whose name is the same as the ID of the control.

The programming code in the code-behind file defines a string constant as the connection string.[10] The file defines two methods: one that is a handler for the `Load` event and one that executes the SQL `SELECT` command. The `Page_ Load` handler method tests `IsPostBack` and, if it is true, calls the other method (which executes the `SELECT` command).

The second method first creates the `OdbcConnection` object, sending the connection string to the constructor. It then creates the `OdbcCommand` object by sending the text of the command and the connection object to the constructor.

---

10. Note that using a constant string for the connection string would not be the best of choices in a production environment, because such environments often change. One potentially better choice would be to store the connection string outside the application code, in the `web.config` XML file.

The following two statements exemplify the creation of these two objects, assuming that the variable `sqlCommand` has been set to a SQL `SELECT` command:

```
OdbcConnection con new OdbcConnection(ConnStr)
OdbcCommand cmd = new OdbcCommand(sqlCommand,con);
```

The next task of this method is to call the `Open` method on the connection. Then it calls the `ExecuteReader` method of the command object. This method takes a variable number of parameters, only one of which is used in the example and, hence, discussed here. This parameter is from the `System.Data` `.CommandBehavior` enumeration. In most cases, the `CloseConnection` value is used, which causes the connection to be closed after the read operation. The return value of `ExecuteReader` is an `OdbcDataReader` object, which contains the data, along with a collection of properties that have information about the data and a large set of methods that can be used to get information out of the `OdbcDataReader` object. The `OdbcDataReader` object is assigned to the `DataSource` property of the `GridView` control object, which corresponds to the `DataSource` attribute of the control. After the data to fill the control has been fetched and assigned to the control, the `DataBind` method of the object associated with the `GridView` control is called, binding the data to the control. This code is as follows:

```
con.Open();
results.DataSource =
        cmd.ExecuteReader(CommandBehavior.CloseConnection);
results.DataBind();
```

In this code, `results` is a reference to the `GridView` object.

Recall that the result of executing a `SELECT` SQL command using JDBC is a `ResultSet` object and that, to display the data in such an object, the application programmer must write code to iterate through the object and produce output based on it. Because the data-bound controls of ADO.NET handle both of these tasks implicitly, the ADO.NET application programmer need not develop such code.

A `finally` clause is included to ensure that a `Close` method is executed on the `GridView` control.

The complete source document, `sqlcars.aspx`, is as follows:

```
<!-- sqlcars.aspx
    Presents a form that includes a text box to collect an SQL
    command, a submit button to call a method to execute the command,
    a label element to provide a place for error messages, and a
    GridView control to present the results of the SELECT command
    -->

<%@ Page Language="C#" AutoEventWireup="true"
    CodeFile="sqlcars.aspx.cs" Inherits="sqlcars.MyClass" %>
```

```
<!DOCTYPE html PUBLIC "-//W3C//DTD XHTML 1.0 Transitional//EN"
           "http://www.w3.org/TR/xhtml1/DTD/xhtml1-transitional.dtd">

<html xmlns="http://www.w3.org/1999/xhtml" >
<head runat="server">
    <title>Display results for SQL commands on cars db </title>
    <style type = "text/css">
      .titles {font-style: italic; font-weight: bold;}
    </style>
</head>
<body>
    <p>
      <span class ="titles"> Please enter your command: </span>
    <form id="myForm" runat="server">
      <asp:TextBox ID="command" size="80" runat="server" />
      <br /><br />
      <asp:Button type="submit" value="Submit" Text="Submit command"
               runat="server" />
      <br /><br />
      <span class ="titles"> Results of your command: </span>
      <br /><br />
      <asp:Label ID="errors" runat="server" />
      <asp:GridView ID="results" runat="server" />
    </form>
</body>
</html>
```

The code-behind file is as follows:

```
// sqlcars.aspx.cs
// The code-behind file for sqlcars.aspx.
// Defines two methods in its class, MyClass.
using System.Web;
using System.Web.UI;
using System.Web.UI.WebControls;
using System.Data;
using System.Data.Odbc;

namespace sqlcars
{
    public partial class MyClass : System.Web.UI.Page
```

```
    {
        const string ConnStr = "Driver={MySQL ODBC 3.51 Driver};" +
            "Server=localhost;Database=cars;uid=root;options=3";

// The Page_Load method executes when the Page_Load event occurs
//  If IsPostBack, it calls the other method, DoCommand
        protected void Page_Load()
        {
            if (IsPostBack)
            {
                DoCommand(command.Text);
            }
        }

// The DoCommand method, which takes a string that has an SQL
//  SELECT command, creates the connection and command
//  objects, opens the connection, and calls ExecuteReader to
//  execute the SELECT command. It then assigns the results to the
//  data source of the GridView control in the ASP.NET document
        protected void DoCommand(string command)
        {
            OdbcConnection con = new OdbcConnection(ConnStr);
            OdbcCommand cmd = new OdbcCommand(command, con);
            try
            {
                con.Open();
                OdbcDataReader reader = cmd.ExecuteReader(
                            CommandBehavior.CloseConnection);
                results.DataSource = reader;
                results.DataBind();
            }
            catch (Exception ex)
            {
                errorLabel.Text = ex.Message;
            }
            finally
            {
                reader.Close();
            }
        }
    }
}
```

Figure 13.10 shows the display of `sqlcars.aspx` after an SQL SELECT command has been entered and the *Submit* button has been clicked.

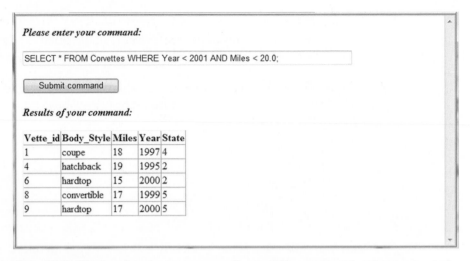

Figure 13.10 Display of `sqlcars.aspx` after an SQL command has been executed

One final note about binding data to controls: In addition to being able to specify the binding programmatically, as in the `sqlcars` application, the binding can be specified declaratively in ASP.NET markup. The following (incomplete) elements illustrate declarative data binding:

```
<asp:OdbcDataSource ID="mySource"
                    runat="server"
                    ConnectionString="..."
                    SelectCommand="..." />
<asp:GridView ID="results"
              DataSourceID="mySource"
              runat="server" />
```

Summary

A relational database consists of a collection of related tables of data. Most tables include a column of primary keys, which uniquely identify the rows. A cross-reference table contains no data; instead, it contains the primary keys of two data tables, providing a many-to-many relationship between the data in the two tables.

SQL is a standard language for specifying accesses and modifications to relational databases. All commonly used relational database systems support SQL. The most frequently used SQL commands are CREATE, SELECT, INSERT, UPDATE, and DELETE.

The CREATE command specifies a table name and a list of column names and their associated constraints. The SELECT command specifies one or more columns of one or more tables, along with a Boolean expression that provides a constraint on the data in the specified columns. SELECT is a complex and powerful tool. The INSERT command specifies a table name, a list of column names, and a list of values that correspond to the column names. The UPDATE command specifies a table name and a list of column name–value pairs, along with a particular primary key value. The DELETE command specifies a table name and the primary key of a particular column.

A join operation, which can be specified by a SELECT command, creates a new table by joining part of the data of one table with part of the data of another table. The objective of a join is to make information available to the user that is not stored in a single table.

A two-tier client–server architecture, in which a client machine communicates directly with a server machine, is common. The Web is an example of a two-tier client–server configuration. A third tier is used in a client–server architecture when it is better for one or both of the client and the server to communicate only indirectly with the other.

One approach to building database applications is to extend a general-purpose programming language so that it can specify SQL commands and interact with a database through those commands. The disadvantage of this approach is that such applications are not likely to be portable among the databases of different vendors. Microsoft's Access system provides a way to access the databases of most common vendors through an interface called ODBC. Because ODBC has been implemented by most vendors for their databases, the Microsoft approach provides a way to develop portable applications.

MySQL is a relational database server that implements SQL. There are drivers for MySQL for most common database APIs, including PHP and JDBC. The MySQL API for PHP includes functions for connecting to a database (mysql_connect), executing SQL commands (mysql_query), and retrieving rows from query results (e.g., mysql_fetch_array). Getting the column names for query results is a bit confusing but not difficult.

The goal of JDBC is related to that of ODBC, except that JDBC is part of one general-purpose programming language: Java. There are drivers for JDBC for all common database systems. A servlet must create a connection to a database for which a JDBC driver is available. Then it creates a Statement object into which an SQL command can be stored as a string. The command can be executed by passing it as a parameter to a method through the Statement object. The return value from the execution of a SELECT command is an object of Result-Set type, which stores the rows that were extracted from the database. Actual data values are obtained from the returned object by a collection of methods called through the object.

Metadata is data about the database, rather than data stored in the database. It is common to need information about the result object returned from the execution of a SELECT command. This information is obtained by a method called through the result object. Specific information is obtained by methods called through the metadata object.

ADO.NET is the part of .NET that supports data storage and access. Our focus in this text is on database systems, although ADO.NET can also deal with other data sources. ASP.NET's use of ADO.NET for database interactions is unique in that part of the database is read into storage in the application and then manipulated with no continued connection to the database. For storage and display of the part of the database of interest, ASP.NET uses elaborate server-side controls, the most common of which is `GridView`. Display of the part of a database table to which it is bound is implicit in the control, so the results of a database operation are displayed in tabular form without the writing of any code by the developer.

Review Questions

13.1   What is the purpose of the primary keys of a table in a relational database?

13.2   What is the purpose of a cross-reference table?

13.3   How are string literals delimited in SQL?

13.4   What does the `NOT NULL` constraint specify in a column of a `CREATE TABLE` SQL command?

13.5   What does an asterisk specify when it appears as the value of a `SELECT` clause?

13.6   What is specified by the `WHERE` clause of a `SELECT` command?

13.7   How are the column names associated with the values in an `INSERT` command?

13.8   What is the purpose of an `UPDATE` command?

13.9   What exactly is a table join, and how is one specified in SQL?

13.10   What is the purpose of a third tier in a client–server configuration for Web access to a database?

13.11   Why are two-tier client–server configurations sometimes inadequate?

13.12   Explain how SQL database access can be provided by extending a programming language.

13.13   What is the disadvantage of embedding SQL in a programming language?

13.14   What is ODBC, and why is it useful?

13.15   What is the relationship between ODBC and JDBC?

13.16   What is MySQL?

13.17   What does the MySQL constraint `auto_increment` do?

13.18 What is the problem with quotes in an SQL command obtained from a form element in an HTML document?

13.19 What is the purpose of the PHP `mysql_select_db` function?

13.20 How can a PHP program determine the number of rows in a query result?

13.21 What does the PHP function `mysql_fetch_array` do?

13.22 Explain the exact form of the value returned by `mysql_fetch_array`.

13.23 Explain the two ways of using JDBC.

13.24 What advantage does a third-tier computer provide when JDBC is used?

13.25 What method of what class is used to connect to a database when JDBC is used?

13.26 Explain the two ways to register a JDBC driver.

13.27 What purpose does a `Statement` object serve when SQL is used through JDBC?

13.28 What method of what class is used to execute an SQL action command?

13.29 What method of what class is used to execute a `SELECT` command?

13.30 What class of object is returned from the `executeQuery` method?

13.31 How can a program iterate through the object returned by `executeQuery`?

13.32 What is the form of the methods used to extract values from the object returned by `executeQuery`?

13.33 What is metadata?

13.34 How is the collection of metadata extracted from a database?

13.35 What are the two ways column labels can be obtained from an object of metadata?

13.36 What is SQL Server?

13.37 What is the design philosophy of ADO.NET?

13.38 What are the three kinds of classes that support the connected part of ADO.NET?

13.39 What is an ASP.NET data-bound control?

13.40 What information is in a connection string?

13.41 What does the `DataBind` method of the `GridView` control class do?

Exercises

13.1   Use MySQL to create a database of information about used trucks for sale, similar to the cars database used in this chapter. Make up equipment that characterizes trucks. Get the raw data from the ad section of your local newspaper. Instead of using the states in the cars database, divide your town into four sections and use them.

13.2   Modify and test the program access_cars.php to handle UPDATE and INSERT SQL commands, as well as SELECT.

13.3   Modify and test the program JDBCServlet.java to handle UPDATE and INSERT SQL commands, as well as SELECT.

13.4   Modify and test the program JDBCServlet.java to work with some other database management system to which you have access.

13.5   Modify and test the ASP.NET source document and code-behind file to work with some other database management system to which you have access.

13.6   Write and test a PHP program that requests the name of a table in a database from the user and returns the number of rows in the table.

13.7   Write and test a servlet that requests the name of a table in a database from the user and returns the number of rows in the table.

13.8   Write and test an ASP.NET source document and code-behind file that together request a name of a table in a database from the user and return the number of rows in the table.

Introduction to Ruby

Our primary interest in Ruby in this book is its use with the Web software development framework Rails. However, Ruby is an interesting and useful language outside its use in Rails. This chapter takes you on a quick tour of Ruby, introducing most of the important concepts and constructs but leaving out many details of the language. In spite of its brevity, if you are an experienced programmer, particularly one well versed in object-oriented programming, you can learn to write useful Ruby programs by studying the chapter. In particular, after studying this chapter and the next, you will be in a position to become an effective Rails developer. However, be warned that Ruby fundamentally differs from conventional languages, such as C++, Java, and C#, both in its syntax and because it is an interpreted scripting language. If you need more details than can be found in this chapter, you can consult one of the books dedicated solely to Ruby, as well as visit `www.ruby-lang.org`, which includes a wide variety of information about the language.

The chapter begins with some background information about Ruby and a description of its scalar data types and their use in expressions and assignment statements. Next, it covers control expressions and the collection of control constructs available in Ruby. Then, it discusses Ruby's two built-in data structures: arrays and hashes. This discussion is followed by a description of methods and how they are defined and called. Next, some of the details of classes are introduced. Finally, code blocks, iterators, and pattern matching are described. Although we attempt to introduce a significant subset of Ruby in a single chapter, do not be misled into thinking that Ruby is a small or simple language—it is neither.

14.1 Origins and Uses of Ruby

As stated in Chapter 1, Ruby was designed in Japan by Yukihiro Matsumoto (a.k.a. Matz) and was released in 1996. It started as a replacement for Perl and Python, languages that Matz found inadequate for his purposes. The use of Ruby grew rapidly in Japan and spread to the rest of the world a few years later. The quick growth of the use of Rails, the Web application development framework that both is written in Ruby and uses Ruby, has accelerated the expansion of the language. Rails is probably the most common use of Ruby.

Learning Ruby is made easier by its implementation method: pure interpretation. Rather than needing to learn about and write a layer of boilerplate code around some simple logic, in Ruby one can write just that simple logic and request its interpretation. For example, consider the difference between a complete "Hello, World" program in a language like C++ or Java and the Ruby "Hello, World" program:

```
puts "Hello, World"
```

From Perl, Ruby gets regular expressions and implicit variables. From JavaScript, it gets objects that can change during execution. However, Ruby has many more differences with those languages than it has similarities. For example, as in pure object-oriented languages, every data value in Ruby is an object, whether it is a simple integer literal or a complete file system.

Ruby is available for every common computing platform. Furthermore, as is the case with PHP, the Ruby implementation is free.

14.2 Scalar Types and Their Operations

Ruby has three categories of data types: scalars, arrays, and hashes. This section discusses the important characteristics of the most commonly used type: scalars. There are two categories of scalar types: numerics and character strings.

As stated earlier, everything in Ruby is an object—numeric literals, arrays, and even classes. Although this design is much more elegant than the mixed-type design of Java and C++, it takes a bit of getting used to.

14.2.1   Numeric and String Literals

All numeric data types in Ruby are descendants of the Numeric class. The immediate child classes of Numeric are Float and Integer. The Integer class has two child classes: Fixnum and Bignum.

An integer literal that fits into the range of a machine word, which is often 32 bits, is a Fixnum object. An integer literal that is outside the Fixnum range is a Bignum object. Though it is odd among programming languages, there is no length limitation (other than your computer's memory size) on integer literals. If a Fixnum integer grows beyond the size limitation of Fixnum objects, it is coerced to a Bignum object. Likewise, if an operation on a Bignum object results in a value that fits into a Fixnum object, it is coerced to a Fixnum type.

Underscore characters can appear embedded in integer literals. Ruby ignores such underscores, allowing large numbers to be slightly more readable. For example, instead of 124761325, 124_761_325 can be used.

A numeric literal that has either an embedded decimal point or a following exponent is a Float object, which is stored as the underlying machine's double-precision floating-point type. The decimal point must be embedded; that is, it must be both preceded and followed by at least one digit. Therefore, .435 is not a legal literal in Ruby.

All string literals are String objects, which are sequences of bytes that represent characters. There are two categories of string literals: single quoted and double quoted. Single-quoted string literals cannot include characters specified with escape sequences, such as newline characters specified with \n. If an actual single-quote character is needed in a string literal that is delimited by single quotes, the embedded single quote is preceded by a backslash, as in the following example:

```
'I\'ll meet you at O\'Malleys'
```

If an escape sequence is embedded in a single-quoted string literal, each character in the sequence is taken literally as itself. For example, the sequence \n in the following string literal will be treated as two characters—a backslash and an n:

```
'Some apples are red, \n some are green'
```

If a string literal with the same characteristics as a single-quoted string is needed, but you want to use a different delimiter, precede the delimiter with q, as in the following example:

```
q$Don't you think she's pretty?$
```

If the new delimiter is a parenthesis, a brace, a bracket, or an angle bracket, the left element of the pair must be used on the left and the right element must be used on the right, as in

```
q<Don't you think she's pretty?>
```

Double-quoted string literals differ from single-quoted string literals in two ways: First, they can include special characters specified with escape sequences; second, the values of variable names can be interpolated into the string, which means that their values are substituted for their names. The first of these differences is discussed here; the other will be discussed in Section 14.2.2.

In many situations, special characters that are specified with escape sequences must be included in string literals. For example, if the words on a line must be spaced by tabs, a double-quoted literal with embedded escape sequences for the tab character can be used as in the following string:

```
"Runs \t Hits \t Errors"
```

A double quote can be embedded in a double-quoted string literal by preceding it with a backslash.

A different delimiter can be specified for string literals with the characteristics of double-quoted strings by preceding the new delimiter with Q as follows:

```
Q@"Why not learn Ruby?", he asked.@
```

The null string (the string with no characters) can be denoted with either `''` or `""`.

14.2.2   Variables and Assignment Statements

Naming conventions in Ruby help identify different categories of variables. For now, we will deal with local variables only.[1] Other naming conventions will be explained as needed.

The form of variable names is a lowercase letter or an underscore, followed by any number of uppercase or lowercase letters, digits, or underscores. The letters in a variable name are case sensitive, meaning that `fRIZZY`, `frizzy`, `frIzZy`, and `friZZy` are all distinct names. However, by convention, programmer-defined variable names do not include uppercase letters.

As mentioned earlier, double-quoted string literals can include the values of variables. In fact, the result of executing any Ruby code can be included. This is specified by placing the code in braces and preceding the left brace with a pound sign (#). For example, if the value of `tue_high` is 83, then the string

```
"Tuesday's high temperature was #{tue_high}"
```

has the following value:

```
"Tuesday's high temperature was 83"
```

Similarly, if the value of price is `1.65` and that of quantity is 6, then the value of the string

```
"The cost of our apple order is $#{price * quantity}"
```

is

```
"The cost of our apple order is $9.90"
```

Because Ruby is a pure object-oriented programming language, all of its variables are references to objects. This is in contrast to more conventional

---

1. A local variable is neither a class nor an instance variable. Its scope is the closest enclosing block, method definition, class definition, module definition, or the top-level program.

languages, such as C++ and Java, which have two categories of variables: those for primitives and those that reference objects. In Ruby, every data value is an object, so it needs references only. Because references are typeless, there is no point in declaring them. In fact, there is no way explicitly to declare a variable in Ruby. All variables are implicitly declared when they first appear in a program.

A scalar variable that has not been assigned a value by the program has the value `nil`.

Ruby has constants, which are distinguished from variables by their names, which always begin with uppercase letters. A constant is created when it is assigned a value, which can be any constant expression. In Ruby, a constant can be assigned a new value, although it causes a warning message to the user.

Ruby includes some predefined, or *implicit*, variables. The name of an implicit scalar variable begins with a dollar sign. The rest of the name is often just one more special character, such as an underscore (_), a circumflex (^), or a backslash (\\). This chapter and the next include some uses of these implicit variables.

The assignment statements of Ruby are exactly like those of the programming languages derived from C. The only thing to remember is that the variables of Ruby are all typeless references. All that is ever assigned in an assignment statement is the address of an object.

14.2.3 Numeric Operators

Most of Ruby's numeric operators are similar to those in other common programming languages, so they should be familiar to most readers. There are the binary operators: + for addition, - for subtraction, * for multiplication, / for division, ** for exponentiation, and % for modulus. The modulus operator is defined as follows: x % y produces the remainder of the value of x after division by y. If an integer is divided by an integer, integer division is done. Therefore, 3 / 2 produces 1.

The precedence rules of a language specify which operator is evaluated first when two operators that have different levels of precedence appear in an expression and are separated only by an operand. The associativity rules of a language specify which operator is evaluated first when two operators with the same precedence level appear in an expression and are separated only by an operand. The precedence and associativity of the numeric operators are given in Table 14.1.

Table 14.1 Precedence and associativity of the numeric operators

Operator*	Associativity
**	Right
unary +, -	Right
*, /, %	Left
binary +, -	Left

*The operators listed first have the highest precedence.

Note that Ruby does not include the increment (++) and decrement (--) operators found in all of the C-based languages.

Ruby includes the `Math` module, which has methods for basic trigonometric and transcendental functions. Among these methods are `cos` (cosine), `sin` (sine), `log` (logarithm), and `sqrt` (square root). The methods of the `Math` module are referenced by prefixing their names with `Math.`, as in `Math.sin(x)`. All of these take any numeric type as a parameter and return a `Float` value.

Included with the Ruby implementation is an interactive interpreter, which is very useful to the student of Ruby. It allows one to type any Ruby expression and get an immediate response from the interpreter. The interactive interpreter's name is *Interactive Ruby*, whose acronym, IRB, in lowercase form is the name of the program that supports it. One enters `irb` simply by typing `irb` at the command prompt in the directory that contains the Ruby interpreter. For example, if the command prompt is a percent sign (`%`), one can type

```
% irb
```

after which `irb` will respond with its own prompt, which is

```
irb(main):001:0>
```

At this prompt, any Ruby expression or statement can be typed, whereupon `irb` interprets the expression or statement and returns the value after an implication symbol (`=>`), as in the following example:

```
irb(main):001:0> 17 * 3
=> 51
irb(main):002:0>
```

The lengthy default prompt can be easily changed. We prefer the simple ">>" prompt. The default prompt can be changed to this with the following command:

```
irb(main):002:0> conf.prompt_i = ">>"
```

From here on, we will use this simple prompt.

14.2.4 String Methods

The Ruby `String` class has more than 75 methods, a few of which are described in this section. Many of these methods can be used as if they were operators. In fact, we sometimes call them operators, even though underneath they are all methods.

The `String` method for catenation is specified by plus (+), which can be used as a binary operator. This method creates a new string from its operands:

```
>> "Happy" + " " + "Holidays!"
=> "Happy Holidays!"
```

The << method appends a string to the right end of another string, which, of course, makes sense only if the left operand is a variable. Like +, the << method can be used as a binary operator. For example, in the interactions

```
>> mystr = "G'day,"
=> "G'day,"
>> mystr << "mate"
=> "G'day, mate"
```

the first assignment creates the specified string literal and sets the variable mystr to reference that memory location. If mystr is assigned to another variable, that variable will reference the same memory location as mystr:

```
>> mystr = "Wow!"
=> "Wow!"
>> yourstr = mystr
=> "Wow!"
>> yourstr
=> "Wow!"
```

Now both mystr and yourstr reference the same memory location: the place that has the string "Wow!". If a different string literal is assigned to mystr, Ruby will build a memory location with the value of the new string literal and mystr will reference that location. But yourstr will still reference the location with "Wow!":

```
>> mystr = "Wow!"
=> "Wow!"
>> yourstr = mystr
=> "Wow!"
>> mystr = "What?"
=> "What?"
>> yourstr
=> "Wow!"
```

If you want to change the value of the location that mystr references, but let mystr reference the same memory location, the replace method is used, as in the following interactions:

```
>> mystr = "Wow!"
=> "Wow!"
>> yourstr = mystr
=> "Wow!"
>> mystr.replace("Golly!")
=> "Golly!"
>> mystr
=> "Golly!"
>> yourstr
=> "Golly!"
```

Now `mystr` and `yourstr` still reference the same memory location.

The append operation can also be done with the `+=` assignment operator. So, instead of `mystr << "mate"`, `mystr += "mate"` could be used.

In the paragraphs that follow, other string functions will be introduced that also change a string value but leave the affected variable referencing the same memory location.

The other most commonly used `String` methods of Ruby are similar to those of other programming languages. Among these are the ones shown in Table 14.2; all of them create new strings.

Table 14.2   Some commonly used string methods

Method	Action
`capitalize`	Converts the first letter to uppercase and the rest of the letters to lowercase
`chop`	Removes the last character
`chomp`	Removes a newline from the right end if there is one
`upcase`	Converts all of the lowercase letters in the object to uppercase
`downcase`	Converts all of the uppercase letters in the object to lowercase
`strip`	Removes the spaces on both ends
`lstrip`	Removes the spaces on the left end
`rstrip`	Removes the spaces on the right end
`reverse`	Reverses the characters of the string
`swapcase`	Converts all uppercase letters to lowercase and all lowercase letters to uppercase

As stated previously, all of these methods produce new strings, rather than modify the given string in place. However, all of the methods also have versions that modify their objects in place. These methods are called *bang* or *mutator* methods and are specified by following their names with an exclamation point (`!`). To illustrate the difference between a string method and its bang counterpart, consider the following interactions:

```
>> str = "Frank"
=> "Frank"
>> str.upcase
=> "FRANK"
>> str
=> "Frank"
>> str.upcase!
=> "FRANK"
```

```
>> str
=> "FRANK"
```

Note that, after upcase is executed, the value of str is unchanged (it is still "Frank"), but after upcase! is executed, it is changed (it is "FRANK").

Ruby strings can be indexed, somewhat as if they were arrays. As one would expect, the indices begin at zero. The brackets of this method specify a getter method. The catch is that the getter method returns the ASCII code (as a Fixnum object), rather than the character. To get the character, the chr method must be called, as in the following interactions:

```
>> str = "Shelley"
=> "Shelley"
>> str[1]
=> 104
>> str[1].chr
=> "h"
```

If a negative subscript is used as an index, the position is counted from the right.

A multicharacter substring of a string can be accessed by including two numbers in the brackets, in which case the first is the position of the first character of the substring and the second is the number of characters in the substring. Unlike the single-character reference, however, in this case the value is a string, not a number:

```
>> str = "Shelley"
=> "Shelley"
>> str[2,4]
=> "elle"
```

The substring getter can be used on individual characters to get one character without calling the chr method.

Specific characters of a string can be set with the setter method, []=, as in the following interactions:

```
>> str = "Donald"
=> "Donald"
>> str[3,3] = "nie"
=> "nie"
>> str
=> "Donnie"
```

The usual way to compare strings for equality is to use the == method as an operator:

```
>> "snowstorm" == "snowstorm"
=> true
>> "snowie" == "snowy"
=> false
```

A different sense of equality is tested with the `equal?` method, which determines whether its parameter references the same object as the one to which it is sent. For example, the interactions

```
>> "snowstorm".equal?("snowstorm")
=> false
```

produces `false` because, although the contents of the two string literals are the same, they are different objects.

Yet another sense of equality is tested with the `eql?` method, which returns `true` if its receiver object and its parameter have the same types and the same values. The following interactions illustrate an instance of equality and an instance of inequality:

```
>> 7 == 7.0
=> true
>> 7.eql?(7.0)
=> false
```

To facilitate ordering, Ruby includes the "spaceship" operator, `<=>`, which returns `-1` if the second operand is greater than the first, `0` if the two operands are equal, and `1` if the first operand is greater than the second. "Greater" in this case means that the text in question belongs later alphabetically. The following interactions illustrate all three cases:

```
>> "apple" <=> "prune"
=> -1
>> "grape" <=> "grape"
=> 0
>> "grape" <=> "apple"
=> 1
```

The repetition operator is specified with an asterisk (`*`). It takes a string as its left operand and an expression that evaluates to a number as its right operand. The left operand is replicated the number of times equal to the value of the right operand:

```
>> "More! " * 3
=> "More! More! More! "
```

14.3   Simple Input and Output

Among the most fundamental constructs in most programming languages are the statements or functions that provide screen output and keyboard input. This section introduces these constructs as they appear in Ruby.

14.3.1   Screen Output

Output is directed to the screen with the `puts` method (or operator). We prefer to treat it as an operator. The operand for `puts` is a string literal. A newline character is implicitly appended to the string operand. If the value of a variable is to be part of a line of output, the #{...} notation can be used to insert it into a double-quoted string literal, as in the following interactions:

```
>> name = "Fudgy"
=> "Fudgy"
>> puts "My name is #{name}"
My name is Fudgy
=> nil
```

The value returned by puts is nil, and that is the value returned after the string has been displayed.

The print method is used if you do not want the implied newline that puts adds to the end of your literal string.

The way to convert a floating-point value to a formatted string is with a variation of the C language function sprintf. This function, which also is named sprintf, takes a string parameter that contains a format code followed by the name of a variable whose value is to be converted. The string version is returned by the function. The format codes most commonly used are f and d. The form of a format code is a percent sign (%), followed by a field width, followed by the code letter (f or d). The field width for the f code appears in two parts, separated by a decimal point. For example, %f7.2 means a total field width of seven spaces, with two digits to the right of the decimal point—a perfect format for money. The d code field width is just a number of spaces—for example, %5d. So, to convert a floating-point value referenced by the variable total to a string with two digits to the right of the decimal point, the following statement could be used:

```
str = sprintf("%5.2f", total)
```

14.3.2   Keyboard Input

Because Ruby is used primarily for Rails in this book, there is little need for keyboard input. However, keyboard input is certainly useful for other applications, so it is briefly introduced here.

The gets method gets a line of input from the keyboard. The retrieved line includes the newline character. If the newline is not needed, it can be discarded with chomp:

```
>> name = gets
apples
=> "apples\n"
>> name = name.chomp
=> "apples"
```

This code could be shortened by applying chomp directly to the value returned by gets:

```
>> name = gets.chomp
apples
=> "apples"
```

If a number is to be input from the keyboard, the string from `gets` must be converted to an integer with the `to_i` method, as in the following interactions:

```
>> age = gets.to_i
27
=> 27
```

If the number is a floating-point value, the conversion method is `to_f`:

```
>> age = gets.to_f
27.5
=> 27.5
```

In this same vein, we must mention that there is a similar method, `to_s`, to which every object responds. The method converts the value of the object to which it is sent to a string. However, because `puts` implicitly converts its operand to a string, `to_s` is not often explicitly called.

The following listing is of a trivial program created with a text editor and stored in a file:

```
# quadeval.rb — A simple Ruby program
# Input:  Four numbers, representing the values of
#         a, b, c, and x
# Output: The value of the expression
#         a*x**2 + b*x + c
# Get input
puts "Please input the value of a "
a = gets.to_i
puts "Please input the value of b "
b = gets.to_i
puts "Please input the value of c "
c = gets.to_i
puts "Please input the value of x "
x = gets/to_i
# Compute and display the result
result = a * x ** 2 + b * x + c
puts "The value of the expression is: #{result}"
```

A program stored in a file can be run by the command

```
>ruby filename
```

So, our example program can be run (interpreted) with

```
>ruby quadeval.rb
```

To compile, but not interpret, a program, just to check the syntactic correctness of the program, the `-c` flag is included after the `ruby` command. It is also a good idea to include the -w flag, which causes `ruby` to produce warning messages for a variety of suspicious things it may find in a program. For example, to check the syntax of our example program, the following statement could be used:

```
>ruby -cw quadeval.rb
```

If the program is found to be syntactically correct, the response to this command is as follows:

```
Syntax OK
```

14.4 Control Statements

Ruby includes a complete collection of statements for controlling the flow of execution through programs. This section introduces the control expressions and control statements of Ruby.

14.4.1 Control Expressions

The expressions upon which statement control flow is based are Boolean expressions. They can be either of the constants `true` or `false`, variables, relational expressions, or compound expressions. A control expression that is a simple variable is true if its value is anything except `nil` (in other words, if it references some object). If its value is `nil`, it is false.

A relational expression has two operands and a relational operator. Relational operators can have any scalar-valued expression as operands. The relational operators of Ruby are shown in Table 14.3.

Table 14.3   Relational operators

Operator	Operation
==	Is equal to
!=	Is not equal to
<	Is less than
>	Is greater than
<=	Is less than or equal to
>=	Is greater than or equal to
<=>	Compare, returning -1, 0, or +1
eql?	True if the receiver object and the parameter have the same type and equal values
equal?	True if the receiver object and the parameter have the same object ID

Recall that the `<=>` operator is often used for comparing strings. Also, `equal?` is used to determine whether two variables are aliases (i.e., whether they reference the same object).

Ruby has two sets of operators for the AND, OR, and NOT Boolean operations. The two sets have the same semantics but different precedence levels. The operators with the higher precedence are `&&` (AND), `||` (OR), and `!` (NOT). Those with the lower precedence are `and`, `or`, and `not`. The precedence of these latter operators is lower than that of any other operators in Ruby, so, regardless of what operators appear in their operands, these operators will be evaluated last.

All of the relational operators are methods, but all except `eql?` and `equal?` can be used as operators.

The precedence and associativity of all operators discussed so far in this chapter are shown in Table 14.4.

Table 14.4 Operator precedence and associativity

Operator	Associativity
`**`	Right
`!`, unary `+` and `-`	Right
`*`, `/`, `%`	Left
`+`, `-`	Left
`&`	Left
`+`, `-`	Left
`>`, `<`, `>=`, `<=`	Nonassociative
`==`, `!=`, `<=>`	Nonassociative
`&&`	Left
`||`	Left
`=`, `+=`, `-=`, `*=`, `**=`, `/=`, `%=`, `&=`, `&&=`, `||=`	Right
`not`	Right
`or`, `and`	Left

Operators of highest precedence are listed first.
The method names for unary minus and plus are -@ and +@, respectively.

Because assignment statements have values (the value of an assignment is the value assigned to the left-side variable), they can be used as control expressions. One common application that uses this form is a loop that uses an assignment statement that reads a line of input as its control expression. The `gets` method returns `nil` when it gets the end-of-file (EOF) character, so this character can be conveniently used to terminate loops. Following is a typical example:

```
while (next = gets) { ... }
```

The keyboard EOF character is Control-D in UNIX, Control-Z in Windows, and CMD+. (period) in Macintosh systems.

14.4.2 Selection and Loop Statements

Control statements require some syntactic container for sequences of statements whose execution they are meant to control. The Ruby form of such containers is to use a simple sequence of statements terminated with `else` (if the sequence is a then clause) or `end` (if the sequence is either an else clause or a then clause, in which case there is no else clause). A *control construct* is a control statement together with the segment of code whose execution it controls.

Ruby's `if` statement is similar to that of other languages. One syntactic difference is that there are no parentheses around the control expression, as is the case with most of the languages based directly or even loosely on C. The following construct is illustrative:

```
if a > 10
  b = a * 2
end
```

An `if` construct can include `elsif` (note that it is *not* spelled "elseif") clauses, which provide a way of having a more readable sequence of nested `if` constructs. The following `if` construct is typical:

```
if snowrate < 1
  puts "Light snow"
elsif snowrate < 2
  puts "Moderate snow"
else
  puts "Heavy snow"
end
```

Ruby has an `unless` statement, which is the same as its `if` statement, except that the inverse of the value of the control expression is used. This is convenient if you want a selection construct with an else clause but no then clause. The following construct illustrates an `unless` statement:

```
unless sum > 1000
  puts "We are not finished yet!"
end
```

Ruby includes two kinds of multiple selection constructs, both named case. One Ruby case construct, which is similar to a switch, has the following form:

```
case expression
when value then
```

```
   - statement sequence
. . .
when value then
   - statement sequence
[else
   - statement sequence]
end
```

The value of the case expression is compared with the values of the when clauses, one at a time, from top to bottom, until a match is found, at which time the sequence of statements that follow is interpreted. The comparison is done with the === relational operator, which is defined for all built-in classes. If the when value is a range, such as (1..100), === is defined as an inclusive test, yielding true if the value of the case expression is in the given range. If the when value is a class name, === is defined to yield true if the case value is an object of the case expression class or one of its superclasses. If the when value is a regular expression, === is defined to be a simple pattern match. Note that the === operator is used only for the comparisons in case constructs.

Consider the following example:

```
case in_val
when -1 then
   neg_count += 1
when 0 then
   zero_count += 1
when 1 then
   pos_count += 1
else
   puts "Error - in_val is out of range"
end
```

Note that no break statements are needed at the ends of the sequences of selectable statements in this construct: There are implied branches at the end of each when clause that cause execution to exit the construct.

The second form of case constructs uses a Boolean expression to choose a value to be produced by the construct. The general form of this case is as follows:

```
case
when Boolean expression then expression
. . .
when Boolean expression then expression
else expression
end
```

The semantics of the construct is straightforward. The Boolean expressions are evaluated one at a time, until one evaluates to true. The value of the whole construct is the value of the expression that corresponds to the true Boolean expression. If none of the Boolean expressions is true, the else expression is evaluated and its value is the value of the construct. For example, consider the following assignment statement:[2]

```
leap = case
       when year % 400 == 0 then true
       when year % 100 == 0 then false
       else year % 4 == 0
       end
```

This case expression evaluates to true if the value of `year` is a leap year.

The Ruby `while` and `for` statements are similar to those of C and its descendants. The bodies of both are sequences of statements that end with `end`. The general form of the `while` statement is as follows:

```
while control expression
     loop body statement(s)
end
```

The control expression could be followed by the do reserved word.

The `until` statement is similar to the `while` statement, except that the inverse of the value of the control expression is used.

For those situations in which a loop is needed in which the conditional termination is at some position in the loop other than the top, Ruby has an infinite loop construct and loop exit statements. The body of the infinite loop construct is like that of `while`: a sequence of statements that optionally begins with do and always ends with `end`.

There are two ways to control an infinite loop: with the `break` and `next` statements. These statements can be made conditional by putting them in the then clause of an if construct. The `break` statement causes control to go to the first statement following the loop body. The `next` statement causes control to go to the first statement in the loop body. For example, consider the following two infinite loop constructs:

```
sum = 0
loop do
  dat = gets.to_i
  if dat < 0 break
  sum += dat
  end

sum = 0
loop do
  dat = gets.to_i
  if dat < 0 next
  sum += dat
  end
```

---

2. This example is from Dave Thomas, C. Fowler, and A. Hunt, *Programming Ruby*, Pragmatic Bookshelf (2005).

In the first construct, the loop is terminated when a negative value is input. In the second, negative values are not added to sum, but the loop continues.

Ruby does not have a general `for` statement, which is ubiquitous among languages with C in their ancestry. However, Ruby includes convenient ways to construct the counting loops implemented with `for` statements in other common languages. These loops are built with iterator methods, which we postpone discussing until methods and arrays have been introduced. Also, there are the `for` and `for-in` constructs in Ruby, which are used for iterating through arrays and hashes (associative arrays).

14.5 Fundamentals of Arrays

Ruby includes two structured classes or types: arrays and hashes. Arrays are introduced in this section; hashes are introduced in Section 14.6.

Arrays in Ruby are more flexible than those of most of the other common languages. This flexibility is a result of two fundamental differences between Ruby arrays and those of other common languages such as C, C++, and Java. First, the length of a Ruby array is dynamic: It can grow or shrink anytime during program execution. Second, a Ruby array can store different types of data. For example, an array may have some numeric elements, some string elements, and even some array elements. So, in these cases, Ruby arrays are similar to those of PHP.

Ruby arrays can be created in two different ways. First, an array can be created by sending the `new` message to the predefined `Array` class, including a parameter for the size of the array. The second way is simply to assign a list literal to a variable, where a list, literal is a list of literals delimited by brackets. For example, in the following interactions, the first array is created with `new` and the second is created by assignment:

```
>> list1 = Array.new(5)
=> [nil, nil, nil, nil, nil]
>> list2 = [2, 4, 3.14159, "Fred", [] ]
=> [2, 4, 3.14159, "Fred", []]
```

An array created with the `new` method can also be initialized by including a second parameter, but every element is given the same value (that of the second parameter). Thus, we may have the following interactions:

```
>> list1 = Array.new(5, "Ho")
=> ["Ho", "Ho", "Ho", "Ho", "Ho"]
```

Actually, this form of initialization is rarely useful, because not only is each element given the same value, but also each is given the same reference. Thus, all of the elements reference the same object. So, if one is changed, all are changed.

All Ruby array elements use integers as subscripts, and the lower bound subscript of every array is zero. Array elements are referenced through subscripts delimited by brackets (`[]`), which actually constitutes a getter method that is allowed to be used as a unary operator. Likewise, `[]=` is a setter method. A subscript can be any numeric-valued expression. If an expression with a floating-point value is used as a subscript, the fractional part is truncated. The following interactions illustrate the use of subscripts to reference array elements:

```
>> list = [2, 4, 6, 8]
=> [2, 4, 6, 8]
>> second = list[1]
=> 4
>> list[3] = 9
=> 9
>> list
=> [2, 4, 6, 9]
>> list[2.999999]
=> 6
```

The length of an array is dynamic; elements can be added to or removed from an array by using the methods subsequently described in Section 14.5.2. The length of an array can be retrieved with the `length` method, as illustrated in the following interactions:

```
>> len = list.length
=> 4
```

14.5.1   The `for-in` Statement

The `for-in` statement is used to process the elements of an array. For example, the following code computes the sum of all of the values in `list`:

```
>> sum = 0
=> 0
>> list = [2, 4, 6, 8]
=> [2, 4, 6, 8]
>> for value in list
>>    sum += value
>> end
=> [2, 4, 6, 8]
>> sum
=> 20
```

Notice that the interpreter's response to the `for-in` construct is to display the list of values assumed by the scalar variable.

The scalar variable in a `for-in` takes on the values of the `list` array, one at a time. Notice that the scalar *does not* get references to array elements; it gets the values. Therefore, operations on the scalar variable have no affect on the array, as illustrated in the following interactions:

```
>> list = [1, 3, 5, 7]
=> [1, 3, 5, 7]
>> for value in list
```

```
>>    value += 2
>> end
=> [1, 3, 5, 7]
>> list
=> [1, 3, 5, 7]
```

A literal array value can be used in the `for-in` construct:

```
>> list = [2, 4, 6]
=> [2, 4, 6]
>> for index in [0, 1, 2]
>> puts "For index = #{index}, the value is #{list[index]}"
>> end
For index = 0, the element is 2
For index = 1, the element is 4
For index = 2, the element is 6
```

14.5.2   Built-In Methods for Arrays and Lists

This section introduces a few of the many built-in methods that are part of Ruby.

Frequently, it is necessary to place new elements on one end or the other of an array. Ruby has four methods for this purpose: `unshift` and `shift`, which deal with the left end of arrays; and `pop` and `push`, which deal with the right end of arrays.

The `shift` method removes and returns the first element (the one with lowest subscript) of the array object to which it is sent. For example, the following statement removes the first element of `list` and places it in `first`:

```
>> list = [3, 7, 13, 17]
=> [3, 7, 13, 17]
>> first = list.shift
=> 3
>> list
=> [7, 13, 17]
```

The subscripts of all of the other elements in the array are reduced by 1 as a result of the `shift` operation.

The `pop` method removes and returns the last element from the array object to which it is sent. In this case, there is no change in the subscripts of the array's other elements.

The `unshift` method takes a scalar or an array literal as a parameter and appends it to the beginning of the array. This requires an increase in the subscripts of all other array elements to create space in the array for the new elements. The `push` method takes a scalar or an array literal and adds it to the high end of the array:

```
>> list = [2, 4, 6]
=> [2, 4, 6]
>> list.push(8, 10)
=> {2, 4, 6, 8, 10]
```

Either `pop` and `unshift` or `push` and `shift` can be used to implement a queue in an array, depending on the direction in which the queue should grow.

Although `push` is a convenient way to add literal elements to an array, if an array is to be catenated to the end of another array, another method, `concat`, is used:

```
>> list1 = [1, 3, 5, 7]
=> [1, 3, 5, 7]
>> list2 = [2, 4, 6, 8]
=> [2, 4, 6, 8]
>> list1.concat(list2)
=> [1, 3, 5, 7, 2, 4, 6, 8]
```

If two arrays need to be catenated and the result saved as a new array, the plus (+) method can be used as a binary operator, as in the following interactions:

```
>> list1 = [0.1, 2.4, 5.6, 7.9]
=> [0.1, 2.4, 5.6, 7.9]
>> list2 = [3.4, 2.1, 7.5]
=> [3.4, 2.1, 7.5]
>> list3 = list1 + list2
=> [0.1, 2.4, 5.6, 7.9, 3.4, 2.1, 7.5]
```

Note that neither `list1` nor `list2` is affected by the plus method.

The `reverse` method does what its name implies:

```
>> list = [2, 4, 8, 16]
=> [2, 4, 8, 16]
>> list.reverse
=> [16, 8, 4, 2]
>> list
=> [2, 4, 8, 16]
```

Note that `reverse` returns a new array and does not affect the array to which it is sent. The mutator version of `reverse`, `reverse!`, does what `reverse` does, but changes the object to which it is sent:

```
>> list = [2, 4, 8, 16]
=> [2, 4, 8, 16]
>> list.reverse!
=> [16, 8, 4, 2]
>> list
=> [16, 8, 4, 2]
```

The `include?` predicate method searches an array for a specific object:

```
>> list = [2, 4, 8, 16]
=> [2, 4, 8, 16]
>> list.include?(4)
=> true
>> list.include?(10)
=> false
```

The `sort` method sorts the elements of an array, as long as Ruby is able to compare those elements. The most commonly sorted elements are either numbers or strings, and Ruby can compare numbers with numbers and strings with strings. So, `sort` works well on arrays of elements of either of these two types:

```
>> list = [16, 8, 4, 2]
=> [16, 8, 4, 2]
>> list.sort
=> [2, 4, 8, 16]
>> list2 = ["jo", "fred", "mike", "larry"]
=> ["jo", "fred", "mike", "larry"]
>> list2.sort
=> ["fred", "jo", "larry", "mike"]
```

If the `sort` method is sent to an array that has mixed types, Ruby produces an error message indicating that the comparison failed:

```
>> list = [2, "jo", 8, "fred"]
=> [2, "jo", 8, "fred"]
>> list.sort
ArgumentError: comparison of Fixnum with String failed
        from (irb):13:in 'sort'
        from (irb):13
        from :0
```

Note that `sort` returns a new array and does not change the array to which it is sent. By contrast, the mutator method, `sort!`, sorts the array to which it is sent, in place.

There are a number of other interesting and useful methods that operate on arrays that use blocks. Some of these methods will be discussed after subprograms and blocks have been introduced.

14.5.3   An Example

The example that follows illustrates a simple use of an array. A list of names is read from the keyboard. Each name is converted to all uppercase letters and placed in an array. The array is then sorted and displayed. Here is the document:

```
# process_names.rb — A simple Ruby program to
#   illustrate the use of arrays
#   Input: A list of lines of text, where each line
#          is a person's name
# Output: The input names, after all letters are
#          converted to uppercase, in alphabetical order

index = 0
names = Array.new
```

```
# Loop to read the names and process them
while (name = gets)

# Convert the name's letters to uppercase and put it
# in the names array
  names[index] = name.chomp.upcase
  index += 1
end

# Sort the array in place and display it
names.sort!
puts "The sorted array"
for name in names
  puts name
end
```

14.6 Hashes

Associative arrays are arrays in which each data element is paired with a key, which is used to identify the data element. Because hash functions are used both to create and to find specific elements in an associative array, associative arrays often are called *hashes*. There are two fundamental differences between arrays and hashes in Ruby: First, arrays use numeric subscripts to address specific elements, whereas hashes use string values (the keys) to address elements; second, the elements in arrays are ordered by subscript, but the elements in hashes are not. In a sense, elements of an array are like those in a list, whereas elements of a hash are like those in a set, where order is irrelevant. The actual arrangement of the elements of a hash in memory is determined by the hash function used to insert and access them.

Like arrays, hashes can be created in two ways, with the new method or by assigning a literal to a variable. In the latter case, the literal is a hash literal, in which each element is specified by a key–value pair, separated by the symbol =>. Hash literals are delimited with braces, as in the following interactions:

```
>> kids_ages = {"John" => 41, "Genny" => 39, "Jake" => 25,
"Darcie" => 24}
=> {"Darcie"=>24, "John"=>41, "Genny"=>39, "Jake"=>25}
```

Notice that the order of the hash returned by Ruby is not the same as the order in the hash literal used to create the hash. This is because the actual order of the hash in memory is unpredicatable (at least for the user program).

If the new method is sent to the Hash class without a parameter, it creates an empty hash, denoted by { }:

```
>> my_hash = Hash.new
=> {}
```

An individual value element of a hash can be referenced by "subscripting" the hash name with a key. The same brackets used for array element access are used to specify the subscripting operation:

```
>> kids_ages["Genny"]
=> 39
```

A new value is added to a hash by assigning the value of the new element to a reference to the key of the new element, as in the following example:

```
>> kids_ages["Aidan"] = 10;
=> {"Aidan"=>10, "Darcie"=>24, "John"=>41, "Genny"=>39,
"Jake"=>25}
```

An element is removed from a hash with the `delete` method, which takes an element key as a parameter:

```
>> kids_ages.delete("Genny")
=> 39
>> kids_ages
=> {"Aidan"=>10, "Darcie"=>24, "John"=>41, "Jake"=>25}
```

A hash can be set to empty in one of two ways: either an empty hash literal can be assigned to the hash, or the `clear` method can be used on the hash. These two approaches are illustrated with the following statements:

```
>> hi_temps = {"mon" => 74, "tue" => 78}
=> {"mon"=>74, "tue"=>78}
>> hi_temps = {}
=> {}
>> salaries = {"Fred" => 47400, "Mike" => 45250}
=> {"Fred" => 47400, "Mike" => 45250}
>> salaries.clear
=> {}
```

The `has_key?` predicate method is used to determine whether an element with a specific key is in a hash. The following interactions are illustrative, assuming that the `kids_ages` hash previously defined is still around:

```
>> kids_ages.has_key?("John")
=> true
>> kids_ages.has_key?("Henry")
=> false
```

The keys and values of a hash can be extracted into arrays with the methods `keys` and `values`, respectively:

```
>> kids_ages.keys
=> ["Aidan", "Darcie", "John", "Jake"]
>> kids_ages.values
=> [10, 24, 41, 25]
```

14.7 Methods

Subprograms are central to the usefulness of most programming languages. Ruby's subprograms are all methods because it is an object-oriented language. However, Ruby's methods can be defined outside user-defined classes, so they are like functions, both in appearance and in behavior, when defined outside a class. When a method that is defined in a class is called from outside that class, the call must begin with a reference to an object of that class. When a method is called without an object reference, the default object on which it is called is `self`, which is a reference to the current object. Therefore, whenever a method is defined outside a user-defined class, it is called without an object reference. This section describes the basics of Ruby's methods. Classes are introduced in Section 14.8.

14.7.1 Fundamentals

A *method definition* includes the method's header and a sequence of statements, ending with the `end` reserved word, which describes its actions. A *method header* is the reserved word `def`, the method's name, and optionally a parenthesized list of formal parameters. Method names must begin with lowercase letters. If the method has no parameters, the parentheses are omitted. In fact, the parentheses are optional in all cases, but it is common practice to include them when there are parameters and omit them when there are no parameters. The types of the parameters are not specified in the parameter list, because Ruby variables do not have types—they are all references to objects. The type of the return object is also not specified in a method definition.

A method that returns an object that is to be used immediately is called in the position of an operand in an expression (or as the whole expression). A method that does not return an object that is to be used can be called by a stand-alone statement.

A method can specify the value it returns in two ways: explicitly and implicitly. The `return` statement takes an expression as its parameter. The value of the expression is returned when the `return` is executed. A method can have any number of `return` statements, including none. If there are no `return` statements in a method or if execution arrives at the end of the method without encountering a `return`, the object that is implicitly returned is the value of the last expression evaluated in the method.

The `Time` object is used to obtain various aspects of time from the system clock. The `now` method of `Time` returns the current time and date as a string. This method is used in the following example methods, one with a `return` and one without a `return`:

```
def date_time1
  return Time.now
end
def date_time2
  Time.now
end
```

The following calls to `date_time1` and `date_time2` yield the returned values shown:

```
>> date_time1
=> Thu Jun 07 16:00:06 Mountain Daylight Time 2007
>> date_time2
=> Thu Jun 07 16:00:08 Mountain Daylight Time 2007
```

14.7.2   Local Variables in Methods

Local variables in methods either are formal parameters or are variables created in a method. A variable is created in a method by assigning an object to it. The scope of a local variable in a method is from the header of the method to the end of the method. If the name of a local variable conflicts with that of a global variable, the local variable is used. This is the advantage of local variables: When you make up their names, you need not be concerned that a global variable with the same name may exist in the program.

The name of a local variable must begin with either a lowercase letter or an underscore (_). Beyond the first character, local variable names can have any number of letters, digits, or underscores.

The lifetime of a variable is the period over which it exists and can be referenced. The lifetime of a local variable is from the time it is created until the end of the execution of the method. So, the local variables of a method cannot be used to store data between calls to the method.

14.7.3   Parameters

The parameter values that appear in a call to a method are called *actual parameters*. The parameter names used in the method, which correspond to the actual parameters, are called *formal parameters*. In effect, scalar actual parameters specify the *values* of objects, not their addresses. So, in Ruby, the transmission of scalar parameters is strictly one way into the method. The values of the scalar actual parameters are available to the method through its formal parameters. The formal parameters that correspond to scalar actual parameters are local variables that are initialized to reference new objects that have the values of the corresponding actual parameters. Whatever a method does to its formal parameters, it has no effect on the actual parameters in the calling program unit. The following example illustrates a method that does not change its parameters:

```
def side3(side1, side2)
   return Math.sqrt(side1 ** 2 + side2 ** 2)
end
```

Now, we illustrate a method that attempts to change its parameters. The intent of the following method was to interchange its parameters:

```
>> def  swap(x, y)
>>   t = x
```

```
>>   x = y
>>   y = t
>> end
=> nil
>> a = 1
>> b = 2
>> swap(a, b)
=> 1
>> a
=> 1
>> b
=> 2
```

So, you see that, although swap changes its formal parameters, the actual parameters a and b sent to it are unchanged. The return value from the call to swap is 1, because that is the value assigned in the last assignment statement in the method (y = t).

Actual parameters that are arrays or hashes are, in effect, passed by reference, so it is a two-way communication between the calling program unit and the called method. For example, if an array is passed to a method and the method changes the array, the changes are reflected in the corresponding actual parameter in the caller.

Following is a method that computes the median of a given array of numbers:

```ruby
# median - a method
#   Parameter: An array of numbers
#   Return value: The median of the parameter array
#
def median(list)

# Sort the array
  list2 = list.sort

# Get the length of the array
  len = list2.length

# Compute the median
  if(len % 2 == 1)   # length is odd
    return list2[len / 2]
  else               # length is even
    return (list2[len / 2] + list2[len / 2 - 1]) / 2
  end
end   # end of the median method
```

Note that the sorted value of the array passed to this method is stored in a local array (list2). This is done to prevent changes to the actual parameter array.

Normally, a call to a method must have the same number of actual parameters as the number of formal parameters in the method's definition. A mismatch of these two numbers results in a run-time error. However, a method can be defined to take a variable number of parameters by defining it with a parameter that is preceded by an asterisk (*). Such a parameter is called an *asterisk parameter*. For example, the following method can take any number of parameters, including none.

```
def fun1(*params)
. . .
end
```

The actual parameters that are passed are placed in the array named `params` (in this example). The asterisk parameter can be preceded by other parameters, in which case only those actual parameters that do not correspond to named formal parameters are placed in the array of parameters. For example, suppose `fun2` is defined as follows:

```
def fun2(sum, list, length, *params)
. . .
end
```

Now, suppose `fun2` is called with the following statement:

```
fun2(new_sum, my_list, len, speed, time, alpha)
```

Then the actual parameters `speed`, `time`, and `alpha` will be passed into the array `params`. Of course, the asterisk parameter must always appear at the end of the list of formal parameters. Any normal parameters that follow an asterisk parameter will always be ignored, because the asterisk parameter receives all remaining actual parameters.

Formal parameters can have default values, making their corresponding actual parameters optional. For example, consider the following skeletal method definition:

```
def lister(list, len = 100)
. . .
end
```

If this method is called with the following statement, the formal parameter `len` gets the value `50`:

```
lister(my_list, 50)
```

But if it is called with the following statement, `len` will default to `100`:

```
lister(my_list)
```

Some programming languages (e.g., Ada and Python) support keyword parameters. In a *keyword parameter*, the actual parameter specifies the name of its associated formal parameter, as in the following statement:

```
lister(list => my_list, len => 50)
```

The advantage of keyword parameters is that they eliminate the possibility of making mistakes in the association of actual parameters with formal parameters. This property is particularly useful when there are more than a few parameters.

Ruby does not support keyword parameters, but there is a way to achieve the same benefit with hashes. A hash literal has an appearance that is similar to keyword parameters. For example, if a hash literal is passed as the second parameter to a method named `find`, the call could appear as follows:

```
find(age, {'first' => 'Davy', 'last' => 'Jones'})
```

Whenever such a hash literal is passed as an actual parameter and it follows all normal scalar parameters and precedes all array and block parameters, the braces can be omitted. So, in the preceding example, the braces are unnecessary.

Ruby includes a category of objects that appears in no other widely used programming language:[3] symbols. Symbols are created by preceding an unquoted string with a colon (:).[4] A symbol made from a variable name can be thought of as that variable's name. Such a symbol does not refer to the value of the variable, nor is it related to a particular instance of a variable—so symbols are context independent. All symbols are instances of the `Symbol` class. Symbols can be used to specify parameters in method calls and as the keys of elements of hash literals. It has become a Ruby idiom, and even a convention in Rails, to use symbols, rather than literal strings, for the keys in hash literals when they are used as parameters. The following method call is illustrative:

```
find(age, :first => 'Davy', :last => 'Jones')
```

14.8 Classes

Classes in Ruby are like those of other object-oriented programming languages, at least in purpose. A class defines the template for a category of objects, of which any number can be created.

14.8.1 The Basics of Classes

The methods and variables of a class are defined in the syntactic container that has the following form:

```
class class_name
...
end
```

Class names, like constant names, must begin with uppercase letters.

---

3. Common Lisp is the only other language of which we are aware that has a symbol data type.

4. Actually, many different things, including operators, constants, class names, and method names, can be prefixed with a colon to create a symbol.

As stated previously, instance variables are used to store the state of an object. They are defined in the class definition, and every object of the class gets its own copy of the instance variables. The name of an instance variable must begin with an at sign (@), which distinguishes instance variables from other variables.

Each class implicitly has a constructor method named new. This method is called on the class name (new is a class method) to create an instance of the class. new allocates space for the object and then calls the initializer method of the class, which the class designer usually overrides with one that assigns initial values to some of the instance variables of the class. The initializer method is always named initialize. Obviously, a class can have just one initialize method. Parameters to initialize are passed to new.

Following is an example of a class, named Stack2_class, that defines a stacklike data structure implemented in an array. The difference between this structure and a stack is that both the top element and the element that is second from the top are accessible. The latter element is fetched with the top2 method. Here is the class:

```ruby
# Stack2_class.rb - a class to implement a stacklike
#                   structure in an array
class Stack2_class

# Constructor - parameter is the size of the stack - default is 100
  def initialize(len = 100)
    @stack_ref = Array.new(len)
    @max_len = len
    @top_index = -1
  end

# push method
  def push(number)
    if @top_index == @max_len
      puts "Error in push - stack is full"
    else
      @top_index += 1
      @stack_ref[@top_index] = number
    end
  end

# pop method
  def pop()
    if @top_index == -1
      puts "Error in pop - stack is empty"
    else
      @top_index -= 1
    end
  end
```

```
# top method
  def top()
    if @top_index > -1
      return @stack_ref[@top_index]
    else
      puts "Error in top - no elements"
    end
  end

# top2 method
  def top2
    if @top_index > 0
      return @stack_ref[@top_index - 1]
    else
      puts "Error in top2 - there are not 2 elements"
    end
  end

# empty method
  def empty()
    @topIndex == -1
  end
end
```

Following is simple code to illustrate the use of the `Stack2_class` class:

```
# Test code for Stack2_class
  mystack = Stack2_class.new(50)
  mystack.push(42)
  mystack.push(29)
  puts "Top element is (should be 29): #{mystack.top}"
  puts "Second from the top is (should be 42): #{mystack.top2}"
  mystack.pop
  mystack.pop
  mystack.pop  # Produces an error message - empty stack
```

Classes in Ruby are dynamic in the sense that members can be added at any time, simply by including additional class definitions that specify the new members. Methods can also be removed from a class, by providing another class definition in which the method to be removed is sent to the method remove_method as a parameter. The dynamic classes of Ruby are another example of a language designer trading readability (and, as a consequence, reliability) for flexibility. Allowing dynamic changes to classes clearly adds flexibility to the language, but harms readability. To determine the current definition of a class, one must find and consider all of its definitions in the program.

14.8.2   Access Control

In a clear departure from the other common programming languages, access control in Ruby is different for access to data than it is for access to methods. All instance data has private access by default, and it cannot be changed. If external access to an instance variable is required, access methods must be defined. For example, consider the following skeletal class definition:

```ruby
class My_class
# Constructor
  def initialize
    @one = 1
    @two = 2
  end

# A getter for @one
  def one
    @one
  end

# A setter for @one
  def one=(my_one)
    @one = my_one
  end

end  # of class My_class
```

The equal sign (=) attached to the name of the setter method means that the method is assignable. So, all setter methods have equal signs attached to their names. The body of the one method illustrates the Ruby design whereby methods return the value of the last expression evaluated when there is no return statement. In this case, the value of @one is returned. When an instance variable that has a getter or setter is referenced outside the class, the at sign (@) part of the name is not included, because it is the method that is being referenced, not the instance variable. The following code that uses My_class (which obviously is outside the class) is illustrative:

```ruby
mc = My_class.new
puts "The value of one is #{mc.one}"
```

Because getter and setter methods are frequently needed, Ruby provides shortcuts for both. If one wants a class to have getter methods for two instance variables, @one and @two, those getters can be specified with the single statement in the class as follows:

```
attr_reader :one, :two
```

Note that attr_reader is actually a method call, using the symbols :one and :two as the actual parameters.

The function that similarly creates setters is called attr_writer. This function has the same parameter profile as attr_reader.

The functions for creating getter and setter methods are so named because they provide the protocol for some of the instance variables of the class, which are called *attributes* in Ruby. So, the attributes of a class constitute the data interface (the public data) to objects of the class.

The three levels of access control for methods are defined as follows: "Public access" means that the method can be called by any code. This is the default access method. "Protected access" means that only objects of the defining class and its subclasses may call the method. "Private access" means that the method cannot be called with an explicit receiver object. Because the default receiver object is self, a private method can be called only in the context of the current object. So, no code can ever call the private methods of another class. Note that private access in Ruby is quite different from private access in other programming languages, such as C++, Java, and C#.

Access control for methods in Ruby is dynamic, so access violations are detected only during execution. There are two ways to specify the access control, both of which use functions with the same names as the access levels: private, protected, and public. One way is to call the appropriate function without parameters. This resets the default access for all subsequent defined methods in the class, until a call to a different access control method appears. The following class illustrates the first way:

```
class My_class
  def meth1
  ...
  end
  ...
private
  def meth7
  ...
  end
  ...
protected
  def meth11
  ...
  end
  ...
end  # of class My_class
```

The alternative is to call the access control functions with the names of the specific methods as parameters. For example, the following is semantically equivalent to the previous class definition:

```ruby
class My_class
  def meth1
  ...
  end
  ...
  def meth7
  ...
  end
  ...
  def meth11
  ...
  end
  ...
  private :meth7, ...
  protected :meth11, ...
  end  # of class My_class
```

The default access control for `initialize` is private. Class variables are private to the class and its instances. That cannot be changed. Also, unlike global and instance variables, class variables must be initialized before they are used.

14.8.3   Inheritance

Subclasses are defined in Ruby with the left angle bracket (<):

```ruby
class My_Subclass < Base_class
```

One distinctive feature of Ruby's method access controls is that they can be changed in a subclass simply by calling the access control functions. This means that two subclasses of a base class can be defined so that objects of one of the subclasses can access a method defined in the base class, but objects of the other subclass cannot. Also, it allows one to change the access of a publically accessible method in the base class to a privately accessible method in the subclass.

Ruby modules provide a naming encapsulation that is often used to define libraries of methods. Perhaps the most interesting aspect of modules, however, is that their methods can be accessed directly from classes. Access to a module in a class is specified with an `include` statement, such as the following:

```ruby
include Math
```

The effect of including a module is that the class gains a pointer to the module and effectively inherits the functions defined in the module. In fact, when a module is included in a class, the module becomes a proxy superclass of the class. Such a module is called a *mixin*, because its functions get mixed into the methods defined in the class. Mixins provide a way to include the functionality of a module in any class that needs it—and, of course, the class still has a normal superclass from which it inherits members. So, mixins provide the benefits of multiple inheritance, without the naming collisions that could occur if modules did not require module names on their functions.

14.9 Blocks and Iterators

A *block* is a sequence of code, delimited by either braces or the do and end reserved words. Blocks can be used with specially written methods to create many useful constructs, including simple iterators for arrays and hashes. This construct consists of a method call followed by a block. We begin our discussion of iterators by introducing a few of the built-in iterator methods that are designed to use blocks.

The times iterator method provides a way to build simple counting loops. Typically, times is sent to a number object. It repeats the attached block the number of times that is the value of the object. Consider the following example:

```
>> 4.times {puts "Hey!"}
Hey!
Hey!
Hey!
Hey!
=> 4
```

In this example, the times method repeatedly executes the block. This is a different approach to subprogram control. (A block is clearly a form of a subprogram.)

The most common iterator is each, which is often used to go through arrays and apply a block to each element. For this purpose, it is convenient to allow blocks to have parameters, which, if present, appear at the beginning of the block, delimited by vertical bars (| |). The following example, which uses a block parameter, illustrates the use of each:

```
>> list = [2, 4, 6, 8]
=> [2, 4, 6, 8]
>> list.each {|value| puts value}
2
4
6
8
=> [2, 4, 6, 8]
```

The each iterator works equally well on array literals, as in the following interactions:

```
>> ["Joe", "Jo", "Joanne"].each {|name| puts name}
Joe
Jo
Joanne
=> ["Joe", "Jo", "Joanne"]
```

If each is called on a hash, two block parameters must be included, one for the key and one for the value:

```
>> high_temps = {"Mon"=>72, "Tue"=>84, "Wed"=>80}
=> {"Wed"=>80, "Mon"=>72, "Tue"=>84}
>> high_temps.each
        {|day, temp| puts "The high on #{day} was #{temp}"
The high on Wed was 80
The high on Mon was 72
The high on Tue was 84
=> {"Wed"=>80, "Mon"=>72, "Tue"=>84}
```

The upto iterator method is used like times, except that the last value of the counter is given as a parameter:

```
>> 5.upto(8) {|value| puts value}
5
6
7
8
=> 5
```

The step iterator method takes a terminal value and a step size as parameters and generates the values from that of the object to which it is sent and the terminal value:

```
>> 0.step(6, 2) {|value| puts value}
0
2
4
6
=> 0
```

Like each, the collect iterator method takes the elements from an array, one at a time, and puts the values generated by the given block into a new array:

```
>> list = [5, 10, 15, 20]
=> [5, 10, 15, 20]
>> list.collect {|value| value = value - 5}
=> [0, 5, 10, 15]
>> list
=> [5, 10, 15, 20]
>> list.collect! {|value| value = value - 5}
=> [0, 5, 10, 15]
>> list
=> [0, 5, 10, 15]
```

As can be seen from this example, the mutator version of `collect` is probably more often useful than the nonmutator version, which does not save its result.

Now we consider user-defined methods and blocks. There must be some statement in the method that "calls" the block. This statement is `yield`. The `yield` statement is similar to a method call, except that there is no receiver object and the call is a request to execute the block attached to the method call, rather than a call to a usual method. If the block has parameters, they are specified in parentheses in the `yield` statement. The value returned by a block is that of the last expression evaluated in the block. A method can include any number of `yield` statements, so it can cause the block to be "called" any number of times. It is this process that is used to implement the built-in iterators illustrated earlier in this section.

When a block is used in a call to a method, part of the effect of the call is provided by the code in the method and part is provided by the block. This separation of functionality allows a method to have different effects on different calls, with the different effects provided by the block attached to the call. The following example is illustrative:

```
>> def get_name
>>   puts "Your name:"
>>   name = gets
>>   yield(name)
>> end
=> nil
>> get_name {|name| puts "Hello, " + name}
Your name:
Freddie
Hello, Freddie
=> nil
```

One final fact about blocks is that they can be passed as parameters to methods. For example, the `create_table` method of Rails, which is illustrated in Chapter 15, sometimes takes an object and a block as its parameters.

14.10 Pattern Matching

Regular expressions in JavaScript were discussed in Chapter 4. Because the regular expressions of both JavaScript and Ruby are based directly on those of Perl, readers who are not familiar with regular expressions are referred to Sections 4.12.1 to 4.12.3. The pattern-matching operations of Ruby are different from those of JavaScript, so they are discussed here.

14.10.1 The Basics of Pattern Matching

In Ruby, the pattern-matching operation is specified with the matching operators `=~`, for positive matches, and `!~`, for negative matches. Patterns are placed between slashes (/). For example, in the following interactions the right operand pattern is matched against the left operand string:

```
>> street = "Hammel"
=> "Hammel"
>> street =~ /mm/
=> 2
```

The result of evaluating a pattern-matching expression is the position in the string where the pattern matched.

The `split` method is frequently used in string processing. The method uses its parameter, which is a pattern, to determine how to split the string object to which it is sent into substrings. For example, the interactions

```
>> str = "Jake used to be a small child, but now is not."
=> "Jake used to be a small child, but now is not."
>> words = str.split(/[ .,]\s*/)
=> ["Jake", "used", "to", "be", "a", "small", "child",
"but", "now", "is", "not"]
```

puts the words from `str` into the `words` array, where the words in `str` are defined to be terminated with either a space, a period, or a comma, any of which could be followed by more white-space characters.

The example program that follows illustrates a simple use of pattern matching and hashes. The program reads lines of text in which the words are separated by whitespace or some common kinds of punctuation, such as commas, periods, semicolons, and so forth. The objective of the program is to produce a frequency table of the words found in the input. A hash is an ideal way to build the word-frequency table. The keys can be the words, and the values can be the number of times they have appeared. The `split` method provides a convenient way to split each line of the input file into its component words. For each word, the program uses `has_key?` on the hash to determine whether the word has occurred before. If so, its count is incremented; if not, the word is entered into the hash with a count of `1`. Here is the code:

```
# word_table.rb
# Input: Text from the keyboard. All words in the input are
#   separated by whitespace or punctuation, possibly followed
#   by whitespace, where the punctuation can be a comma, a
#   semicolon, a question mark, an exclamation point, a period,
#   or a colon.
# Output: A list of all unique words in the input, in alphabetical
#   order, along with their frequencies of occurrence

freq = Hash.new
line_words = Array.new
```

```
# Main loop to get and process lines of input text
while line = gets

   # Split the line into words
   line_words = line.chomp.split( /[ \.,;:!\?]\s*/)

   # Loop to count the words (either increment or initialize to 1)
   for word in line_words
      if freq.has_key?(word) then
         freq[word] = freq[word] + 1
      else
         freq[word] = 1
      end
   end
end
# Display the words and their frequencies
puts "\n Word \t\t Frequency \n\n"
for word in freq.keys.sort
   puts " #{word} \t\t #{freq[word]}"
end
```

Notice that the two normally special characters, . (period) and ? (question mark), are not backslashed in the pattern for split in this program. This is because the normally special characters for patterns (metacharacters) are not special in character classes.

14.10.2   Remembering Matches

The part of the string that matched a part of the pattern can be saved in an implicit variable for later use. The part of the pattern whose match you want to save is placed in parentheses. The substring that matched the first parenthesized part of the pattern is saved in $1, the second in $2, and so forth. The following interactions show how this is done:

```
>> str = "4 July 1776"
=> "4 July 1776"
>> str =~ /(\d+) (\w+) (\d+)/
=> 0
>> puts "#{$2} #{$1}, #{$3}"
=> July 4, 1776
```

In some situations, it is convenient to be able to reference the part of the string that preceded the match, the part that matched, or the part that followed the match. These three strings are available after a match through the implicit variables $`, $&, and $', respectively.

14.10.3   Substitutions

Sometimes the substring of a string that matched a pattern must be replaced by another string. Ruby's String class has four methods designed to do exactly that. The most basic of these, the substitute method, sub, takes two parameters: a pattern and a string (or an expression that evaluates to a string value). The sub method matches the pattern against the string object to which it is sent. If sub finds a match, the matched substring is replaced by its second parameter, as in the following interactions:

```
>> str = "The old car is great, but old"
=> "The old car is great, but old"
>> str.sub(/old/, "new")
=> "The new car is great, but old"
```

The gsub method is similar to sub, except that it finds *all* substring matches and replaces *all* of them with its second parameter:

```
>> str = "The old car is great, but old"
=> "The old car is great, but old"
>> str.gsub(/old/, "new")
=> "The new car is great, but new"
>> str
=> "The old car is great, but old"
```

Notice from the last line that gsub does not alter the string object on which it is called. The same is true for sub. However, sub and gsub have mutator versions, named sub! and gsub!. The following interactions illustrate how gsub! works:

```
>> str = "The old car is great, but old"
=> "The old car is great, but old"
>> str.gsub!(/old/, "new")
=> "The new car is great, but new"
>> str
=> "The new car is great, but new"
```

The i modifier, which tells the pattern matcher to ignore the case of letters, can also be used with the substitute method by attaching it to the right end of the pattern, as shown in the following code:

```
>> str = "Is it Rose, rose, or ROSE?"
=> "Is it Rose, rose, or ROSE?"
>> str.gsub(/rose/i, "rose")
=> "Is it rose, rose, or rose?"
```

Summary

Ruby is a pure object-oriented interpreted scripting language. One important motivation for its popularity is its use in the Rails framework for building Web applications.

Ruby has three categories of data types: scalars, arrays, and hashes. The scalar classes are `Float`, `Fixnum`, `Bignum`, and `String`. Ruby's arithmetic expressions and assignment statements are like those of other common languages. All Ruby variables are references to objects. Unlike C++, Java, and C#, Ruby has no primitive types. Although expressions appear in the same form as in other languages, underneath they are all executed by methods and message passing. The `String` class has a large number of methods.

Ruby includes the usual collection of control statements, including two different multiple-selection statements. Arrays in Ruby are different from arrays in the more conventional languages in that Ruby arrays can store any type objects and have dynamic length. The `Array` class provides a large collection of methods, including those for implementing stacks and queues in arrays. Ruby's hashes also have many methods.

Methods can be defined in classes, but also outside classes, in which case they are much like functions. Asterisk parameters provide the means of supporting a variable number of parameters. Objects are dynamic, in the sense that methods and variables can be added or deleted at any time. Access control is provided by calling the `public`, `private`, and `protected` methods. Ruby includes an implicit way to provide getters and setters.

One unique feature of Ruby is its code blocks and iterators. The `each` and `find` iterators are frequently used to deal with arrays. Ruby's pattern-matching operations use the same regular expressions as JavaScript.

Review Questions

14.1 What is one of the most common uses of Ruby?

14.2 What are the two integer classes of Ruby?

14.3 What is the length limit of a `Bignum` object?

14.4 Why is `10.` not a legal `Float` constant in Ruby?

14.5 What is the difference between the two kinds of string literals?

14.6 How can the value of a variable be embedded in a `String` literal?

14.7 What numeric operators in C and Java are not included in Ruby?

14.8 What is the name of Ruby's interactive interpreter?

14.9 What does the `String` method `replace` do?

14.10   What is the difference between the `downcase` and `downcase!` methods?

14.11   How can the substring consisting of the second and third characters of the string `str` be referenced?

14.12   What exactly is the operation of the spaceship operator?

14.13   What is the difference between the puts and print methods?

14.14   How can a `String` value be converted to a `Float` value?

14.15   What values of a variable are considered true?

14.16   What are the syntactic differences between the JavaScript `if` statement and that of Ruby?

14.17   In what two ways can an `Array` object be created?

14.18   Describe what the `for-in` statement does.

14.19   Describe how the catenation operator for arrays works.

14.20   What does the `include?` method do?

14.21   What is the form of a hash literal?

14.22   Do method headers require parentheses?

14.23   What is an asterisk parameter?

14.24   What is the form of an instance variable's name?

14.25   What is an attribute in Ruby?

14.26   What does it mean when we say Ruby classes are dynamic?

14.27   When are access control violations for methods detected?

14.28   What is the effect of including a module in a class?

14.29   How are blocks delimited?

14.30   Explain what the `each` method does.

Exercises

14.1   Write, test, and debug (if necessary) a Ruby program with the following specification:

Input: Three numbers, a, b, and c, each on its own line, from the keyboard.

Output: The value of the expression `10ab-((c-1)/17.44)`.

14.2   Write, test, and debug (if necessary) a Ruby program with the following specification:

Input: A list of numbers from the keyboard.

Output: The second-smallest number in the list, along with its position in the list, with 1 being the position of the first number.

14.3   Write, test, and debug (if necessary) a Ruby program with the following specification:

Input: Three names, on separate lines, from the keyboard.

Output: The input names in alphabetical order. Do not use arrays.

14.4   Write, test, and debug (if necessary) a Ruby program with the following specification:

Input: A list of lines of text from the keyboard.

Output: Every input line that has more than 10 characters (not counting the newline), but fewer than 20 characters (not counting the newline), and that contains the string "ed".

14.5   Write, test, and debug (if necessary) a Ruby program with the following specification:

Input: A list of numbers from the keyboard.

Output: Two lists of numbers, one with input numbers greater than zero and one with those less than zero (ignore the zero-valued numbers). You must first build two arrays with the required output numbers before you display any of them.

14.6   Write, test, and debug (if necessary) a Ruby program with the following specification:

Input: A list of numbers from the keyboard.

Output: The median of the input numbers.

Introduction to Rails

As stated in Chapter 14, our primary interest in Ruby in this book is its use with the Web software development framework Rails. This chapter introduces Rails, a complex system with a large array of powerful capabilities. Because this is but one chapter of a book, only a quick introduction to a few of the most fundamental features and straightforward uses of Rails will be examined. The chapter begins with an overview of Rails. The remainder of the chapter is a discussion of Rails through several example applications, beginning with the simplest of applications: Hello, World. This application is then modified to produce simple dynamic content. Next, a small application that accesses a database is developed. Because Rails was designed to be used in an incremental approach to application development, that approach is used in this example. The first version, which is generated entirely by Rails, builds a database, but only provides basic database maintenance operations. The next version adds a database search operation for users. The last version includes developer-written layouts and style sheets.

15.1   Overview of Rails

Rails[1] is a software development framework for Web-based applications—in particular, those that access databases. A framework is a system in which much of the more-or-less standard software parts are furnished by the framework, so they need not be written by the applications developer. Those parts are often skeletal classes, methods, or markup documents, but can also be complete utility methods. Rails was developed by David Heinemeier Hansson in the early 2000s and was released to the public in July 2004. Since then, it has rapidly gained widespread interest and usage.

Rails is a large and complex system: One book on Rails has 851 pages![2] Thus, by necessity, this chapter only briefly introduces some of the most fundamental capabilities of the system.

Rails, like some other Web development frameworks, such as Tapestry and Struts, is based on the Model–View–Controller (MVC) architecture for applications. The MVC architecture is described in Chapter 11.

Figure 15.1 shows the components and actions of a request and response in a Rails application that uses a database.

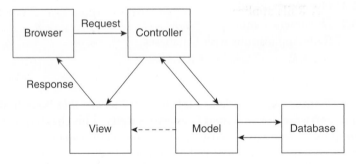

Figure 15.1 A request and response in a Rails application

The view part of a Rails application generates the user interface. Both data in the model and results of processing are made available to the user through view documents. View documents also provide the interface to add, modify, or delete data. View documents are markup documents that can have embedded Ruby code, which is interpreted on the server before the documents are sent to a browser, much like what happens with requested PHP documents.

The controller part of a Rails application, which is implemented as one or more Ruby classes, controls the interactions among the data model, the user, and the view. The controller receives user input, interacts with the model, and provides views of data and processing results back to the user. The developer must design and build the actions that are required by the application, implemented as methods in the controller classes.

---

1. The full name of Rails is "Ruby on Rails," but we will refer to it simply as Rails.

2. *The Rails Way*, Obie Fernandez, Addison-Wesley, 2008.

The model part of a Rails application maintains the state of the application, whether that state is internal and alive only during execution or is a permanent external database. The developer must design and build a model of the application's domain. The design of the model often includes a database that stores the data of the model. For example, if the application is an online bookstore, the model might include an inventory of books and a catalog of all books, among other things, that can be ordered through the store. The model also can include constraints on the data to be entered into the database.

So, what does Rails do for the developer of a Rails application? It does quite a lot, actually. Rails provides skeletal controller classes. It also implicitly connects the methods of a controller with the corresponding view documents. In addition, it provides the basic interface to a working database, as well as an empty version of the database itself. One of its most important contributions is a collection of conventions that implicitly connect the model, view, and controller. For example, the controller can fetch user-provided form data and place it in its instance variables, which are implicitly available to the Ruby code in view documents. Rails also provides partial view documents, known as layouts, and a simple way to include style sheets for documents. In addition, Rails provides a simple development and test environment, including Web servers. And Rails is free.

A Rails application is a program that provides a response when a client browser connects to a Rails-driven Web site. Because Rails uses an MVC architecture, building a Rails application consists of designing and building the three components of an MVC system. Rails offers a great deal of assistance in constructing an application, as will be evidenced in the example applications in this chapter.

There are two fundamental principles that guided the development of Rails, and it is valuable to be aware of them when learning and using Rails. The first principle has the acronym *DRY*, which stands for Do not Repeat Yourself. In Rails, DRY means that every element of information appears just once in the system. This minimizes the memory required by the system. In addition, changes to the system are highly localized, making them both easier and less error prone. The second principle is named *convention over configuration*. Web applications with JSP require elaborate and complicated XML configuration files to specify their structure. In Rails, the structure of an application is dictated by the MVC architecture. The connections between the different parts are established and maintained by convention, rather than being specified in a configuration document. For example, the names of database tables and their associated controller classes are intimately related by convention.

Rails is a product of a software development paradigm called *agile development*.[3] Some of this paradigm is related to the human interactions among development team members and between the team and the customer. However, part of it is the focus on the quick development of working software, rather than the creation of elaborate documentation and then software. Agile develop ment is an incremental approach to development that is facilitated by adherence to the principles used in creating Rails.

---

3. See http://agilemanifesto.org.

Rails differs from the other frameworks discussed in this book—Flash, NetBeans, and Visual Studio—in that it does not use a graphical user interface (GUI). Rather, Rails is a command-line-oriented system. Commands are issued by typing them at a prompt in a DOS-like or UNIX-like command window, rather than by clicking icons on a GUI.

Some of the innovations of Rails are described through examples presented later in the chapter, among the most interesting of which are the basic database operations furnished by Rails for a new database application and the use of migrations to manage version control of databases.

Rails 3.1.1 is discussed and used in this chapter.

15.2 Document Requests

Rails is a Web application development framework. The specific application area for Rails is Web applications that use relational databases, which are discussed in Chapter 13.

Before one can use Rails, the system must be downloaded and installed on one's computer. Rails is included in versions 1.8.7 or later of Ruby, as is RubyGems, a package manager for Ruby. If Ruby has been downloaded and installed, the next step is to download SQLite 3, which is the database management system used in this chapter. This can be downloaded from `http://www.sqlite.org`. The download includes two files, one for the command-line shell and one for the SQLite library. For Windows, after unzipping the two files, move the resulting files to `C:\Ruby\bin`. Then use the following commands to install SQLite 3 and Rails:

```
gem install sqlite3
gem install rails
```

The downloading and installation operations are similar for Linux and Mac OS X systems.

15.2.1 Static Documents: Hello, World in Rails

This section describes how to build a Hello, World application in Rails. The purpose of such an exercise is to demonstrate the directory structure of the simplest possible Rails application, showing what files must be created and where they must reside in the directory structure.

On our Windows system, Rails in installed in the `C:\Ruby192\bin`. Users usually create a new subdirectory for their Rails applications. We created a subdirectory named `examples` for the example applications of this chapter.

Next, we move to the `examples` directory and create a new Rails application named `greet` with the following command:

```
>rails new greet
```

Rails responds by creating a large number of files and directories. The most interesting of the new directories at this point is `app`. The `app` directory includes four subdirectories: `models`, `views`, and `controllers`—which correspond directly to the MVC architecture of a Rails application—and `helpers` (among others). The `helpers` subdirectory contains Rails-provided methods that aid in constructing applications. Most of the user code to support an application will reside in `models`, `views`, or `controllers`, or in subdirectories of those directories.

The Rails provided `generate` script is used to create part of an application controller. This script creates a file containing a class in the `controllers` directory, and also a subdirectory of the `views` directory where views documents will be stored. For our simple application, we pass three parameters to `generate`, the first of which is `controller`, which indicates that we want the controller class to be built. The second parameter is the name we chose for the controller. The third parameter is the name of a method in the controller class, which are called *action methods*. This will also be the name of the view markup file, usually called a *template*. If the controller has more than one action method, the others are also listed as parameters to the `generate` script. An important part of how Rails works is its focused use of names. Our first example of this feature is the name of the controller, which will also be part of the file name of the controller class and part of the name of the controller class itself. In addition, it will be the name of the subdirectory of the `views` directory and a part of the URL of the application. For our example, the following command is given in the `greet` directory to create the controller:

```
>rails generate controller say hello
```

With this command, we have chosen the name `say` for the controller and the name `hello` for the action method of our application. The response produced by the execution of the command indicates the files that were created, as well as the utility programs that were executed.

The `generate controller` command created a file named `say_controller.rb` in the `controller` directory. This file contains the `SayController` class. The `application.rb` file, which was created by the initial `rails` command, also resides in the `controller` directory. This file contains the `ApplicationController` class. The `SayController` class is a subclass of the `ApplicationController` class. As the parent class, `ApplicationController` provides the default behavior for `SayController`, the controller class of the application class. There may be other controllers and their corresponding controller classes in an application. Such classes also are subclasses of `ApplicationController`. The following is a listing of `say_controller.rb`:

```
class SayController < ApplicationController
  def hello
  end
end
```

Note the occurrence of `say` in both the name of the controller file and the name of the controller class. This is another example of the use of convention in Rails.

The class `SayController` is an empty class, other than the empty `hello` method and what it inherits from `ApplicationController`. The class

`ApplicationController` is a subclass of `ActionController`, which defines the basic functionality of a controller. Note that `SayController` produces, at least indirectly, the responses to requests. The `hello` method does not need to actually do anything, other than indicate a document that will describe the response.[4] The mere existence of the method specifies, by its name, the response document. So, the action will be nothing more than an empty method definition whose name will be the same as that of the response document in the `say` subdirectory of `views`.

Web sites, or applications, are specified in requests from browsers with URLs. Rails applications are no different. When Rails receives the URL of a request, it maps that URL to a specific controller name and action method. In simple situations, the mapping is trivial: the first domain following the hostname is interpreted as a controller name, and the next domain is interpreted as the name of an action method. There is no need to specify the application name, because, as we shall soon see, each application is served by its own server.

The host for our examples will be the machine on which the applications are resident. The default port for the server (chosen by Rails) is `3000`, so the host name will be `localhost:3000`. Thus, for the `greet` example, the request URL is as follows:

`http://localhost:3000/say/hello`

(Now it should be obvious why the base document is named `say`.)

Rails built a view document, which is often called a *template*, for us, but it is minimal:

```
<h1> say#hello</h1>
<p>Find me in app/views/say/hello.html.erb</p>
```

Following is our template file for the `hello` action method of the `greet` application:

```
<!DOCTYPE html>
<!-- hello.html.erb - the template for the greet application
    -->
<html lang = "en">
  <head>
    <title> greet </title>
    <meta charset = "utf-8" />
  </head>
  <body>
    <h1> Hello from Rails </h1>
  </body>
</html>
```

---

4. The action method could itself produce the output for this application, but then we could not also illustrate the view document.

The extension on this file's name is .html.erb because the file stores an HTML document, but it may include embedded Ruby code to be interpreted by the Ruby interpreter, ERb (an acronym for *Embedded Ruby*), before the template is returned to the requesting browser.

The template file for our application resides in the say subdirectory of the views subdirectory of the app subdirectory of the greet directory.

The structure of the examples directory is shown in Figure 15.2.

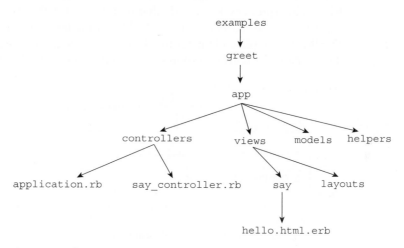

Figure 15.2 Directory structure for the greet application

Before the application can be tested, a Rails Web server must be started. A server is started with the server script from the script directory. The default server is WEBrick, although Rails could choose another server that is running on your system. To force the use of WEBrick, attach its name to the command to start the server, which is given at the application prompt, as in the following:

```
>rails server webrick
```

Note that the server is started by a command in the directory of the particular application—in our example, greet. This implies that no other application can be served by this server.

Figure 15.3 shows the output of the greet application when it is addressed by a browser.

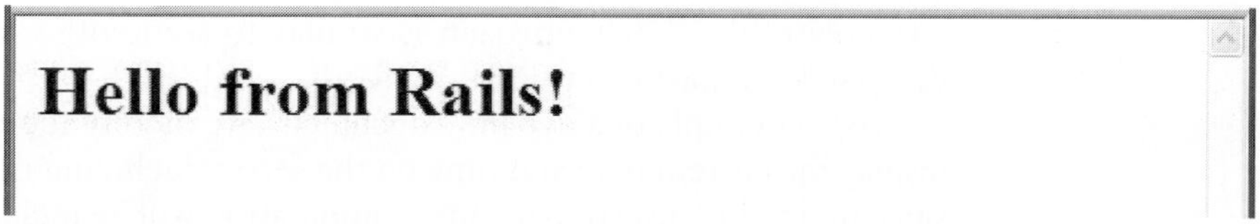

Hello from Rails!

Figure 15.3 The response from greet

The following summarizes how Rails reacts to a request for a static document: First, the name of the controller is extracted from the URL (it follows the hostname). Next, an instance of the controller class (found in the `app/controllers` subdirectory)—in our example, `SayController`—is created. The name of the action is then extracted from the URL—in our example, `hello`. This method is then called. In our example, this has no effect. Then Rails searches for a template with the same name as the action method in the subdirectory with the same name as the controller in the `app/views` directory. Next, the template file is given to ERb to interpret any Ruby code that is embedded in the template. In the case of `hello.html.erb`, there is no embedded Ruby code, so this step has no effect. Finally, the template file is returned to the requesting browser, which displays it. The activities of Rails in response to a simple request are shown in Figure 15.4.

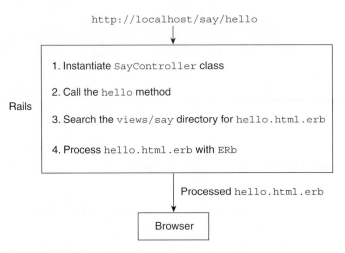

Figure 15.4 Rails actions for a simple request

The default method of a controller class is `index`. If the URL `http://localhost:3000/say/` was requested, Rails would search for an `index` method, which, in this example, does not exist. The result would be the following message on the display: `Unknown action - no action responded to index`.

15.2.2 Dynamic Documents

Dynamic documents can be constructed in Rails by embedding Ruby code in a template file. This approach is similar to some other approaches we have discussed—in particular, PHP, ASP.NET, and JSP.

As an example of a dynamic document, we modify the `greet` application to display the current date and time on the server, including the number of seconds since midnight (just so that some computation will be included). This modification will illustrate how Ruby code that is embedded in a template file can access instance variables that are created and assigned values in an action method of a controller.

Ruby code is embedded in a template file by placing it between the `<%` and `%>` markers. For example, we could insert the following in a template:

```
<% 3.times do %>
   I LOVE YOU MORE! <br />
<% end %>
```

If the Ruby code produces a result and the result is to be inserted into the template document, an equals sign (=) is attached to the opening marker. For example, consider the following element:

```
<p> The number of seconds in a day is: <%= 60 * 60 * 24 %>
</p>
```

When interpreted by ERb, the following is produced:

```
<p> The number of seconds in a day is: 86400 </p>
```

The date can be obtained by calling Ruby's `Time.now` method, which returns the current day of the week, the month, the day of the month, the time, the time zone,[5] and the year, as a string. So, we can put the date in the response template with

```
<p> It is now <%= Time.now %> </p>
```

The value returned by `Time.now` can be parsed with the methods of the `Time` class. For example, the `hour` method returns the hour of the day, the `min` method returns the minutes of the hour, and the `sec` method returns the seconds of the minute. These methods can be used to compute the number of seconds since midnight. Putting it all together results in the following template code:

```
It is now <%= t = Time.now %> <br />
Number of seconds since midnight:
<%= t.hour * 3600 + t.min * 60 + t.sec %>
```

It would be better to place the Ruby code for the time computation in the controller, because that would separate the program code from the markup. The modified `SayController` class is as follows:

```
class SayController < ApplicationController
  def hello
    @t = Time.now
    @tsec = @t.hour * 3600 + @t.min * 60 + @t.sec
  end
end
```

---

5. The time zone is represented as the number of hours from Coordinated Universal Time (UTC). For Mountain Daylight Time, this is –0600, for six hours after UTC.

The response template now needs to be able to access the instance variables in the `SayController` class. Rails makes this process trivial, for all instance variables in the controller class are visible to the template. The template code for displaying the time and number of seconds since midnight is as follows:

```
It is now <%= @t %> <br />
Number of seconds since midnight: <%= @tsec %>
```

Figure 15.5 shows the display of the modified `greet` application.

Hello from Rails

It is now 2011-10-19 21:00:22 -0600
Number of seconds since midnight: 75622

Figure 15.5 The output of the modified version of the `greet` application

15.3 Rails Applications with Databases

This section uses an example application to describe how a Rails application that uses a database is constructed. For the example database, a simple part of the `cars` database from Chapter 13 is used—just the main table. The operations that are implemented are simple: The user is presented with a welcome document that states the number of cars listed in the database. Also presented is a form that allows the user to specify the beginning and ending model years, as well as a specific body style, in which he or she is interested. The system searches the database for the entries that fit the given restrictions and displays them for the user.

A significant and characteristic part of Rails is its approach to connecting object-oriented software with a relational database. Each relational database table is implicitly mapped to a class. For example, if the database has a table named `employees`, the Rails application program that uses `employees` will have a class named `Employee`. Note that the class name is the singular form of the table name, with the first letter capitalized. Rows of the `employees` table will have corresponding objects of the `Employee` class, which will have methods to get and set the various state variables, which are Ruby attributes of objects of the class. In sum, Rails maps tables to classes, rows to objects, and columns to the fields of the objects. Furthermore, the `Employee` class will have methods for performing table-level operations, such as finding an object with a certain attribute value. The key aspect of the mapping is that it is implicit: The classes, objects, methods, and attributes that represent a database in Ruby are automatically built by Rails.

For this example, we create a new application named `cars` in the `examples` directory with the following command:

```
>rails new cars
```

15.3.1   Building the Basic Application

It takes but a few commands to coerce Rails into building a complete basic working Web application that uses a database. In this section, we begin building our application by instructing Rails to do just that.

The following command is used to create the model, the required database migration file,[6] and the table of the database, as well as a maintenance controller and testing support files for the application:

```
>rails generate scaffold corvette
       body_style:string miles:float year:integer
```

In this command we named the model `corvette`. The single table of the database, `corvettes`,[7] was specified by the command to have three columns: `body_style`, of `string` type; `miles`, of `float` type; and `year`, of `integer` type. Rails also supports `decimal`, `binary`, and `boolean` types, as well as four types related to time and date.

One of the innovations of Rails is a methodology that addresses the problem of version control for databases. Recall that Rails was designed to support agile software development, in which applications are built incrementally. In accordance with agile development, an initial system is built, tested, and presented to the customer. The customer's review and use of the system then leads to a variety of changes to the requirements and, ultimately, the software that implements the requirements. To manage this process with the physical files of code, a version control system is used. Version control supports the process of evolving the system, primarily in the forward direction, but occasionally in the reverse direction. As an application is incrementally built, a parallel evolution takes place with the application's database. New kinds of data are added, and sometimes one particular kind of data is removed. Unfortunately, database systems do not have integrated version control. What is needed is a methodology that allows a database to evolve in a way that is related to the evolution of the software.

Rails includes just such a methodology, which uses a sequence of migration programs, one for each set of changes to the database to evolve the database. Each migration, which is a Ruby source program, specifies how to add some part of the data or delete some part of the data, as well as how to undo the change specified in the migration. Therefore, the migration programs can be used to revise a database in either the forward direction, to a later version, or the backward direction, to some previous version.

Following is the migration class defined in the file named `20111016030420_create_corvettes.rb`,[8] which resides in the `cars/db/migrate` directory:

---

6. Migration files are discussed later in this section.

7. By convention, the name of the table is always the plural form of the name of the model.

8. The first part of this file's name is a time stamp.

```
class CreateCorvettes < ActiveRecord::Migration
  def change
    create_table :corvettes do |t|
      t.string :body_style
      t.float :miles
      t.integer :year

      t.timestamps
    end
  end
end
```

The `change` method updates the table to the next version. To create the initial version of the database table, the table description is included in the `change` method. To provide the columns of the table, the `t` object methods named after the data types are called, passing the column name in symbolic form as a parameter. For example, `t.float :miles` is a call to the `float` method of the `t` object, passing the column name `miles`, in the form of a symbol, as a parameter.[9] These calls appear in the body of the `create_table do` compound construct in `change`. In this example, the migration's `change` method creates a table named `corvettes`.

Some of the operations needed by most database applications perform basic maintenance on the records of the tables: create, read, update, and delete, which together have the catchy acronym CRUD. These operations are automatically generated for a table by Rails by including `scaffold` in the command to generate the table. The operations provide the scaffolding to make the table maintainable until more suitable operations are built—if, indeed, they are needed. In the majority of commercial applications, most, if not all, of the scaffolding is replaced before the application is deployed. However, it is often useful to have these operations provided before the developer writes any code. They allow the developer to get a basic application that uses a database working very quickly.

The actual creation of the database is a result of the following command:

```
>rake db:migrate
```

This command, which causes the execution of the `change` method of the `CreateCorvettes` class in `20111016030420_create_corvettes.rb`, produces the following response:

```
(in C:/Ruby192/bin/examples/cars)
== CreateCorvettes: migrating ============================
-- create_table(:corvettes)
   -> 0.0020s
== CreateCorvettes: migrated (0.0020s) ==================
```

---

9. Actually, `t.type_name` is a shorthand for `t.column :type_name`, so `column` is the method being called; there are no methods with the names of the data types.

Amazing as it seems, we now have a working application with a connected database, although the database is empty. And we have yet to write a single line of code! To see what we have, we point a browser at `http://localhost:3000/corvettes` and get the display shown in Figure 15.6.

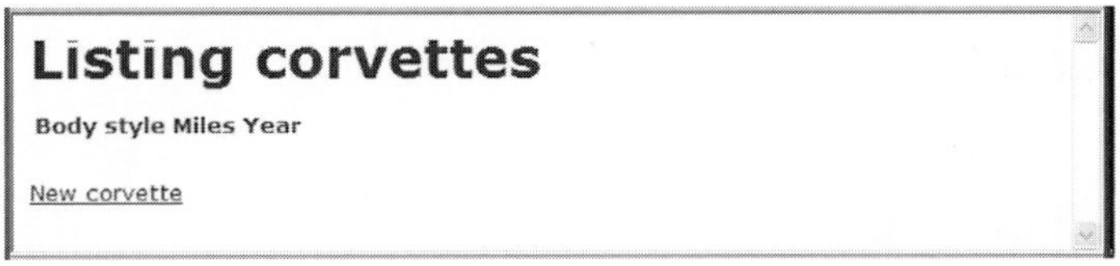

Figure 15.6 Display of the initial cars application

This document would provide a listing of the database if it contained data. The document also provides a link, *New corvette*, that takes the user to another document for entering a `corvettes` table row, as shown in Figure 15.7.

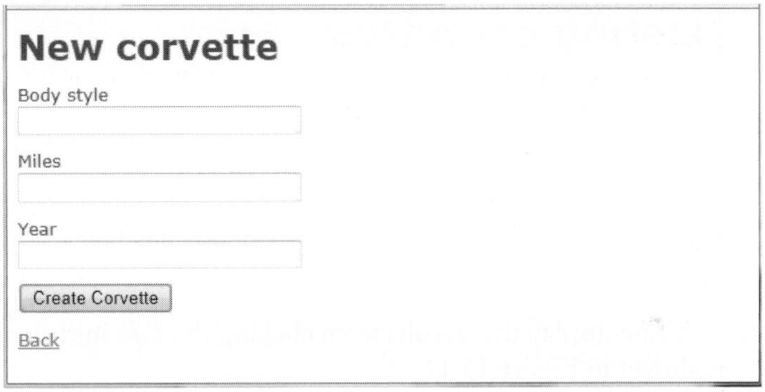

Figure 15.7 Display of the document to enter a row into the `corvettes` table

Figure 15.8 shows the document after a row of data has been entered.

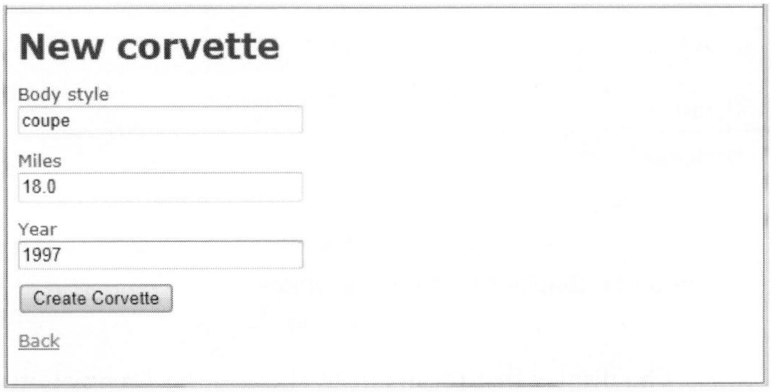

Figure 15.8 Display after a row of data has been entered

Figure 15.9 shows the result of clicking the *Create Corvette* button.

Corvette was successfully created.

Body style: coupe

Miles: 18.0

Year: 1997

Edit | Back

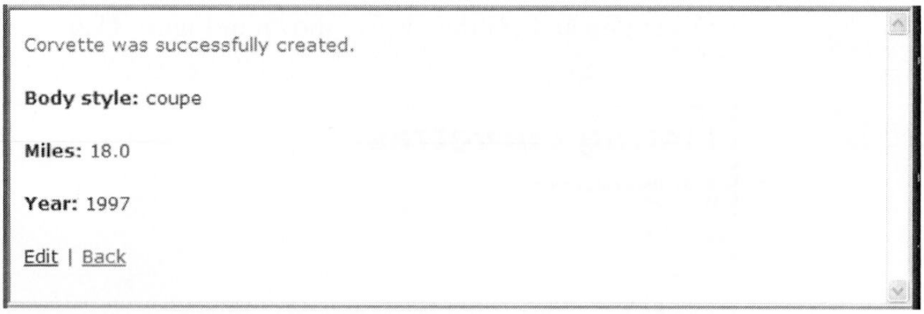

Figure 15.9 The result of clicking the *Create Corvette* button

Figure 15.10 shows the initial display after the *Back* button has been clicked.

Listing corvettes

Body style Miles Year
coupe   18.0   1997 Show Edit Destroy

New corvette

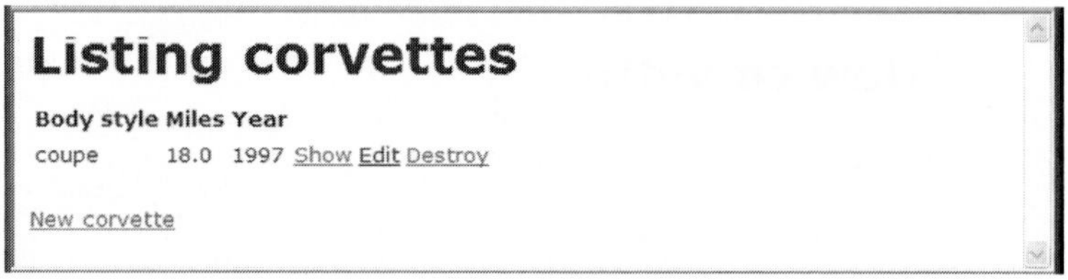

Figure 15.10 Initial display after the *Back* button has been clicked

The display that results from clicking the *Edit* button on the table's only row is shown in Figure 15.11.

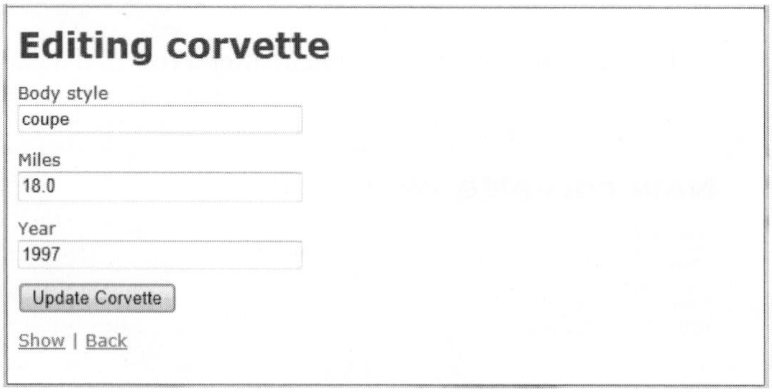

Editing corvette

Body style
coupe

Miles
18.0

Year
1997

Update Corvette

Show | Back

Figure 15.11 Display of the edit document

The display that results from clicking the *Destroy* button on the table's only row is shown in Figure 15.12.

Figure 15.12 Display of the destroy document

The model file that Rails built, which is named `corvette.rb`, resides in the `models` directory and defines the `Corvette` class as follows:

```
class Corvette < ActiveRecord::Base
end
```

It is common to add some kind of validation to data entered into a database table. This can be done by adding a call to the predefined `validates` method. One of the most fundamental things to validate is the presence of form values. To do this, we call `validates` with the symbolic names of the columns of the table as parameters. The final parameter is `:presence => true`. When a row is added to the table, this call to `validates` ensures that all of its columns have values. An error message is issued if any are left blank. For our example, the call would be as follows:

```
validates :body_style, :miles, :year, :presence => true
```

Another useful validation for our database would be to ensure that no year is entered that would be invalid. This validation can be done with the `validates` method, using the `numericality` parameter, which guarantees that the value of a field is a number and also enforces specified constraints on that number. The first parameter of this method is the field to be validated. The second parameter is `numericality`, which can be given a hash literal as a value. This hash literal can include elements with names such as `greater_than`, `greater_than_or_equal_to`, `less_than`, `less_than_or_equal_to`, and `equal_to`. For example, we could have the following call:

```
validates :year, numericality => {:greater_than => 1952,
        :less_than_or_equal_to => Time.now.year}
```

Calls to these validation methods would be placed in the `Corvette` class of the model files in our example.

The complete model class for our application, which is the file `car/app/models/corvette.rb`, is now as follows:

```
class Corvette < ActiveRecord::Base
    validates :body_style, :miles, :year, :presence => true
    validates :year, numericality => {:greater_than => 1952,
        :less_than_or_equal_to => Time.now.year}
end
```

The controller class is named `CorvetteController` by convention, from the name `Corvette` given in the command that created the application. The controller file, named `corvettes_controller.rb`, is stored in the controllers directory and defines the `CorvettesController` class. This class defines the support methods for the database table: `index`, which creates a list of the rows of the table; `show`, which creates the data for one row of the table; `new`, which creates a new row object; `edit`, which handles the editing of a row; `create`, which handles the creation of a new row; `update`, which handles the response to a *Create* button; and `delete`, which handles the deletion of a row.

There are four documents in the `views` directory. The `index.html.erb` document is as follows:

```
<h1>Listing corvettes</h1>

<table>
  <tr>
    <th>Body style</th>
    <th>Miles</th>
    <th>Year</th>
    <th></th>
    <th></th>
    <th></th>
  </tr>

<% @corvettes.each do |corvette| %>
  <tr>
    <td><%= corvette.body_style %></td>
    <td><%= corvette.miles %></td>
    <td><%= corvette.year %></td>
    <td><%= link_to 'Show', corvette %></td>
```

```
        <td><%= link_to 'Edit', edit_corvette_path(corvette) %></td>
        <td><%= link_to 'Destroy', corvette, confirm:
              'Are you sure?', method: :delete %></td>
    </tr>
<% end %>
</table>


<br />


<%= link_to 'New corvette', new_corvette_path %>
```

This document appears to be only a partial markup document; in fact, it is only the content of the body element of a complete HTML document. So, where is the rest of the document? The answer is that Rails includes a way to supply parts of documents in a separate document. The common parts of documents are factored out and merged back in when the document is about to be displayed. The document of these common parts is called a *layout*. Layouts are an example of the application of the DRY principle: If two or more documents have a common part, do not repeat it. All of the template documents associated with the `corvettes` controller appear only as the content of the body element; the common parts—in these cases, everything except the content of the body element—are in a document named `application.html.erb`, which is in the `cars/app/views/layout` directory. In this case, the layout document was provided by Rails through `scaffold`. However, such documents can also be supplied by the developer. The layout document is implicitly merged into the template documents by Rails. When a template document is to be sent to a browser for display, Rails first looks in the layout directory for a layout document. If it finds one, it is merged with the template document and the result is sent to a browser. User-defined layouts are discussed in Section 15.3.4.

The layout document, `application.html.erb`, built by Rails for `CorvetteController`, is as follows:

```
<!DOCTYPE html>
<html>
<head>
  <title>Cars</title>
  <%= stylesheet_link_tag "application" %>
  <%= javascript_include_tag "application" %>
  <%= csrf_meta_tags %>
</head>
<body>
```

```
<%= yield  %>

</body>
</html>
```

The call to `yield` tells Rails where the template file belongs in the layout. The call to `stylesheet_link_tag` specifies the style sheet to be used with the layout document. In this case, the style sheet, `application.css`, was furnished by `scaffold`. The `javascript_include_tag` method specifies the JavaScript libraries to be included. These are stored in `public/javascripts`. The third call is to `csrf_meta_tags`, which creates two `meta` elements that help prevent csrf attacks by defining an authenticity token.[10]

The documents for the `new` and `edit` operations both use the same form, which was factored out of them and placed in a separate document, `_form.html.erb`. The new document, `new.html.erb`, follows:

```
<h1> New corvette </h1>

<%= render 'form' %>

    <%= link_to 'Back', corvettes_path %>
```

The form document, `_form.html.erb`, follows:

```
<%= form_for(@corvette) do |f| %>
  <% if @corvette.errors.any? %>
    <div id="error_explanation">
      <h2><%= pluralize(@corvette.errors.count, "error") %>
        prohibited this corvette from being saved:</h2>

      <ul>
      <% @corvette.errors.full_messages.each do |msg| %>
        <li><%= msg %></li>
      <% end %>
      </ul>
    </div>
  <% end %>
```

---

10. Csrf is an abbreviation of cross-site request forgery. A csrf attack forces user code to execute unwanted actions (from an invader) on an application in which he or she is currently authenticated.

```
    <div class="field">
      <%= f.label :body_style %><br />
      <%= f.text_field :body_style %>
    </div>
    <div class="field">
      <%= f.label :miles %><br />
      <%= f.text_field :miles %>
    </div>
    <div class="field">
      <%= f.label :year %><br />
      <%= f.number_field :year %>
    </div>
    <div class="actions">
      <%= f.submit %>
    </div>
<% end %>
```

This document calls several helper methods that are defined in the `FormHelper` module: `form_for`, `label`, `text_field`, `number_field`, and `submit`, whose purposes are embodied in their names. When the form defined in this document is submitted, the values in its input fields are collected into the `params` object that is passed to the controller.[11]

The `show.html.erb` document is as follows:

```
<p id = "notice"> <%= notice %> </p>
<p>
  <b>Body style:</b>
  <%= @corvette.body_style %>
</p>
<p>
  <b>Miles:</b>
  <%= @corvette.miles %>
</p>
<p>
  <b>Year:</b>
  <%= @corvette.year %>
</p>

<%= link_to 'Edit', edit_corvette_path(@corvette) %> |
<%= link_to 'Back', corvettes_path %>
```

---

11. Use of the `params` object in a controller is illustrated in Section 15.3.2.

The embedded Ruby code—for example, `@corvette.body_style`—fetches the input from the corresponding text box.

Finally, the `edit.html.erb` document is as follows:

```
<h1>Editing corvette</h1>
<%= render 'form' %>
<%= link_to 'Show', @corvette %> |
<%= link_to 'Back', corvettes_path %>
```

The `edit.html.erb` document is similar to the `new.html.erb` document shown earlier.

15.3.2   Completing the Application

We must now expand the example so that it provides its user services: to present a form to the user in which he or she can specify queries, execute such queries against the database, and present the results to the user.

We need a new controller, which we name `main`, to implement the required actions for our application. The controller is created with the following command:

```
>rails generate controller main welcome
```

The template associated with the action method will provide the initial display to the user for the application. Recall that this display must include the current number of cars in the `corvettes` table of the database. Therefore, the `welcome` method must provide that number for the template. The number of rows in a table can be determined by calling the `count` method on the table's object. For example, the number of rows in the `corvettes` table is gotten with `Corvette.count`. We place the call to `Corvette.count` in the `welcome` action method and store the value returned in the instance variable `@num_cars`. The resulting controller is as follows:

```
# main_controller.rb - for the cars application
class MainController < ApplicationController

# welcome method - fetches values for the
#   initial view
  def welcome
    @num_cars = Corvette.count
  end
end
```

Every model class (and therefore, every database table) supports the `where` method, which searches its table for rows that satisfy given criteria. The simplest use of `where` is to pass it a specific value for one of the columns, as the following statement does:

```
mycar = Corvette.where(:body_style => "convertible")
```

A `RecordNotFound` exception is thrown if such a row cannot be found.

A qualifier, `first`, `last`, or `all`, can be attached with a period to the call to `where`, with `first` being the default. So, the above call finds the first row that that has a `body_style` value of `"convertible"`.

More than one condition can be specified, as shown in the following statement:

```
sixty_five_conv = Corvette.where([:year = 1965,
                      :body_style = 'convertible']).all
```

This form of call to `where` is adequate only if the conditions are all literals. In many cases, however, a condition is at least partially made up of user input, often form data. For example, the `year` condition value could be in the `@year` instance variable. To deal with this situation, Rails includes a different form of the `where`. In this form, the parameter value for `where` is placed in an array literal, question marks appear in place of the user-input values, and the condition is followed by a comma and the variables that have the values. The new form of the preceding example is as follows:

```
my_year_conv = Corvette.where(
    ["year = ? and body_style = 'convertible'", @year]).all
```

Now we can develop the `welcome` template, which is stored in the `welcome .html.erb` file in the `views` directory. This document must give the initial information and then display a form that the user can fill in and submit to learn about specific cars that are for sale. The `welcome` document uses `@num_cars`, the value produced by the `welcome` method of the main controller. The `welcome .html.erb` file is as follows:

```
<!-- welcome.html.erb - initial view for the cars application
    -->
<!-- The initial information -->
<p>
  <h1> Aidan's Used Car Lot </h1>
  <h2> Welcome to our home document </h2>
  We currently have <%= @num_cars %> used Corvettes listed <br />
  To request information on available cars, please fill out <br />
  the following form and submit it
</p>
```

```
<!-- The form to collect input from the user about their interests
  -->
<form action = "result"  method = "post" >
  From year: <input type = "text"  size = "4"  name = "year1" />
  To year: <input type = "text"  size = "4"  name = "year2" />
  Body style: <input type = "text"  size = "12"  name = "body" />
  <br />
  <input  type = "submit"  value = "Submit request" /> <br />
  <input type = "reset"  value = "Reset form" /> <br />
</form>
```

Note that the `action` attribute of the form element in `welcome.html.erb` is set to `"result"`, which will need to be an action method in the `main` controller. Note also that the method is `post`, which is required in Rails.

Like the template document produced by `scaffold`, this template is missing its first and last parts. That will also be the case for the other template developed in this section: `result`. The other parts of these templates will be added with a layout document in Section 15.3.4.

The display of the `welcome` template is shown in Figure 15.13.[12]

Figure 15.13 Display of `welcome.html.erb`

The next step in the construction of the application is to build the action method in the `MainController` class to process the form data when the form is submitted. In the initial template file, `welcome.html.erb`, this method is named `result` in the `action` attribute of the form tag. The `result` method has two tasks, the first of which is to fetch the form data. This data is used to display information back to the customer and to compute results. The form data is made available to the controller class through the Rails-defined object `params`, a hashlike object that contains all of the form data (as well as some other things). It is hash*like* because it is a hash that can be indexed with either Ruby symbols or

---

12. While you were reading, we sneaked four more rows into the `corvettes` table.

actual keys. (A hash object can be indexed only with keys.) The common Rails convention is to index params with symbols. For example, to fetch the value of the form element whose name is phone, we would use the following statement:[13]

```
@phone = params[:phone]
```

Recall that all form data is in string form. However, some of the values are integer numeric quantities, so they must be converted to integers with the to_i method of String. The form of the statements to fetch the form data is illustrated by the following statement:

```
@num_pizzas = params[:num_pizzas].to_i
```

Notice that the instance variable has the same name as the form element. In this case, the value is a quantity, which is converted to an integer.

Following is the complete MainController class:

```
# main_controller.rb - for the cars application
class MainController < ApplicationController

# welcome method - fetches values for the initial view
  def welcome
    @num_cars = Corvette.count
  end

# result method - fetches values for the result view
  def result
    @year1 = params[:year1].to_i
    @year2 = params[:year2].to_i
    @body = params[:body]
    @selected_cars = Corvette.where(
                ["year >= ? and year <= ? and body_style = ?",
                @year1, @year2, @body]).all
  end
end
```

The last step of the development of the application is to design the result template, which is stored in the result.html.erb file. To provide a pleasant appearance, the information about the specified cars is placed in a table. An each iterator is used to go through all of the cars in the @selected_cars array provided by the result method in the controller.

---

13. If a space appears between the word params and the left bracket ([) that follows it, Rails produces the error message wrong number of arguments (1 for 0), which could be difficult to understand.

The complete `result.html.erb` template document is as follows:

```
<!-- result.html.erb - the result of the user request for
                    information about cars
     -->
    <p>

<!-- Display what the user asked for -->
      Cars from <%= @year1 %> to <%= @year2 %>
      with the <%= @body %> body style
    </p>

<!-- Display the results of the request in a table -->
    <table border = "border">
      <tr>
        <th> Body Style </th>
        <th> Miles </th>
        <th> Year </th>
        <th> State </th>
      </tr>

<!-- Put the cars in @selected_cars in the table -->
      <% @selected_cars.each do |car| %>
        <tr>
          <td> <%= car.body_style %> </td>
          <td> <%= car.miles %> </td>
          <td> <%= car.year %> </td>
        </tr>
      <% end %> <!-- end of do loop -->
    </table>
```

Finally, the use of the cars application can be illustrated. Figure 15.14 shows a display of the welcome template after it has been filled in by a user.[14]

---

14. We tested this with an early version of Rails 3.1. It was necessary to add the line: post "main/result" to the config/routes.rb file to avoid a routing error.

Figure 15.14 A filled–in `welcome` template for `cars`

Figure 15.15 shows the `result` template after the `welcome` form shown in Figure 15.14 has been submitted.

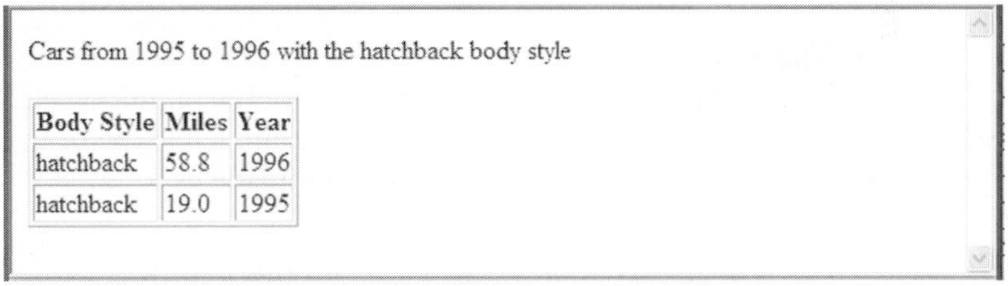

Figure 15.15 The `result` template for `cars`

15.3.3 Modifying a Database

The process of agile software development, for which Rails was designed, is one of creating a minimal initial version of the application quickly and presenting it to the customer. This allows the customer to see and evaluate the design and to interact with the designers early in the development process. In many cases, a customer wants some specific feature, but, when presented with an implementation of that feature, the customer changes his or her mind. Incremental development, coupled with frequent interactions with the customer, characterizes agile software development.

The design of the database for an application often changes during development, because the needs or desires of either the developer or the customer change. Therefore, Rails includes effective tools for database modification. In Section 15.3.1, the initial migration file was shown and discussed. It was created by Rails in response to information provided in the command that built the initial version of the `cars` application. Recall that the name of this file is `20111016030420_create_corvettes.rb` and that that file built the initial version of the `corvettes` table.

During both the development and use of an application, the database may change in various ways. In addition, it often happens that a database must change in the reverse direction; that is, some changes must be undone. Rails supports database changes in both directions through the use of migration classes. To change a database, one generates a new migration class. For example, the first changes to a database will have the migration class file name that begins with a later time stamp than the first migration file does. Recall that migration files reside in the `db/migrate` subdirectory of the application directory.

To illustrate a change to a database, we now create a new migration class for the `corvettes` table of the database for the `cars` application. It would be advantageous to include a state column in the `corvettes` table, to indicate the state where the car is available. We now make that change to the database, as well as the required changes to the `main` controller and its view template.

A new migration is created with a script. For our example, the command is as follows:

```
>rails generate migration AddStateToCorvette
        state:string
```

The `migration` parameter tells `generate` that a migration class is to be built. The next parameter specifies the name of the migration class, which we made up. The last parameter provides the name and data type of the column to be added to the table. Rails responds to this command as follows:

```
invoke active_record
create db/migrate/20111017205052_add_state_to_corvette.rb
```

The second line above tells the user that the `20111017205052_add_state_to_corvette.rb` file has been created and has the class name `AddStateToCorvette`.

The migration file created by the command `20111017205052_add_state_to_corvette.rb`, is as follows:

```
class AddStateToCorvette < ActiveRecord::Migration
  def change
    add_column :corvettes, :state, :string
  end
end
```

Now the `rake` command, given in the application directory, can be used to update the database:

```
>rake db:migrate
```

Rails's response to this command is as follows:

```
(in C:\Ruby192\bin\examples\cars)
== AddStateToCorvette: migrating ========================
-- add_column(:corvettes, :state, :string)
   -> 0.0010s
== AddStateToCorvette: migrated (0.0010s) ==============
```

Now the template documents for the revised table must be modified to take the new column into account. This is a relatively simple task.

After these changes are made, pointing the browser at the `corvettes` controller produces the display shown in Figure 15.16.

Listing corvettes

Body style	Miles	Year	State			
coupe	18.0	1997	Arkansas	Show	Edit	Destroy
hatchback	58.8	1996	Connecticut	Show	Edit	Destroy
convertible	13.5	2001	Alabama	Show	Edit	Destroy
hatchback	19.0	1995	Alaska	Show	Edit	Destroy
hatchback	25.0	1991	California	Show	Edit	Destroy

New corvette

Figure 15.16 The `cars_development` database after adding the `state` column

The latest changes to the database, made by means of the latest migration class, can be removed with the following command:

```
>rake db:rollback
```

If you want to roll back the database to an earlier migration, that can be done by using `migrate` and providing a version number to which you want to return. For example, to roll back a database to an earlier version, the following command could be used:

```
>rake db:migrate VERSION=20091016120032
```

15.3.4 Layouts and Style Sheets

Recall that the templates for the `cars` application `main` controller were only partial. In this section, we develop a layout document to complete those templates.

There are two views templates for `main`: one for the `welcome` action and one for the `result` action. Both of these could use the same header information. We can build a layout to specify the header for the templates associated with each of these actions. We then use the layout to include a copyright line at the bottom

of the view documents for both actions. This new layout, which is named `main`
`.html.erb`, is as follows:

```
<!DOCTYPE html>
<!-- main.html.erb - a layout for the main controller of cars -->
<html lang = "en">
  <head>
    <title> Main </title>
    <meta charset = UTF-8 />
  </head>
  <body>
    <h1> Aidan's Used Car Lot </h1>
    <h2> Welcome to our home document </h2>
    <%= yield  %>
    <hr/>
    <p> Copyright 2012, AUCL, Inc. </p>
  </body>
</html>
```

Now that the header is in the layout, it must be removed from `welcome`
`.html.erb` to prevent it from appearing twice.

We now add an external style sheet to the layout template, just to illustrate
how style sheets are used in Rails. The style sheet only sets the colors of the headings and the text box labels and the font style of the main title and the labels. The
style-sheet file, which is named `mainstyles.css`, is as follows:

```
/* mainstyles.css - a style sheet for the main controller */
h1 {font-style: italic; color: blue;}
h2 {color: blue;}
.labels {font-style: italic; color: red;}
```

External style sheets for template files for the `cars` application are stored in
the `cars/app/assets/stylesheets` directory.

The reference to the layout style sheet is placed in the layout for the
main controller, `main.html.erb`. The reference is Ruby code that calls the
`stylesheet_link_tag` method, passing the name of the style sheet, without
the file name extension, as a literal string. In this example, the following reference
is placed in the head of `main.html.erb`:

```
<%= stylesheet_link_tag "mainstyles" %>
```

The display of the welcome template, using main layout and the mainstyles style sheet, is shown in Figure 15.17.

Aidan's Used Car Lot

Welcome to our home document

We currently have 5 used Corvettes listed
To request information on available cars, please fill out
the following form and submit it

From year: [   ]   To year: [   ]   Body style: [   ]
[Submit request]
[Reset form]

Copyright 2012, AUCL, Inc.

http://localhost:3000/main/result

Figure 15.17 Display of the welcome template with the mainstyles style sheet

Notice that the document includes the javascript_include_tag to gain access to the Prototype library.

Summary

Rails is a Ruby software development framework for Web applications. Although it is applicable to all Web applications, it is particularly suited to Web applications that interact with relational databases. One characteristic aspect of Rails is its use of an object-relational mapping for connecting object-oriented Ruby to relational databases. Rails uses the Model–View–Controller model of software applications.

A Hello, World Rails application can be built easily. A basic skeletal application is built with the rails command, giving the application's name as a parameter. This creates the many directories and files that support the application. A controller class can be generated by running the script/generate script, providing a name for the controller as a parameter. Then an empty action method is added to the controller class. The last step in developing this application is to build the view, or template file, whose name must be the same as the action method in the controller. The template file in this case is a simple markup document whose content is Hello, World. After starting a Web server within Rails, this application is ready to be requested by a browser.

Dynamic documents in Rails are closely related to those constructed with PHP. Ruby code can be embedded in the template within the <% and %> delimiters. When requested by a browser, the Ruby code is interpreted and its output is placed in the template, which is then returned to the requesting browser. In most cases, data and computations are placed in the controller action method, rather than in the template. All instance variables in the action method are visible in the associated template file.

Form processing in Rails is relatively simple. Form values are available to the controller class through a hashlike object. The action method extracts the form values into instance variables.

Rails applications are cleanly integrated with database servers. SQLite 3, a database server, is used in this chapter, by default. The tables of the database are accessible to the controller through classes whose names are singular forms of the table names, with the first letter in uppercase. The rows of the tables are objects of the table classes. The items in a table row are available as fields of the table objects. A Web application, including a one-table database and the basic table maintenance operations, can be built with only a few commands. The `find` method of a table class provides a powerful way to extract data from the database.

Database tables are constructed with the `rake` command, which uses a migration file that provides the column names and types. A database is often the result of applying a sequence of migration files, all of which are saved. A table can also be reverted to any existing migration file.

Layouts provide a convenient way to include boilerplate markup in all of the templates of an application. Boilerplate markup is placed in a template file in the `layouts` subdirectory of the `views` directory.

Review Questions

15.1   For what is MVC an acronym?

15.2   For what is ORM an acronym?

15.3   What is the intent of MVC development?

15.4   Explain the DRY principle of software development.

15.5   Explain the principle of convention-over-configuration.

15.6   What is generated with the `generate controller` script?

15.7   What must be placed in an application's controller class?

15.8   In what directory are templates placed?

15.9   Why does a template file's name have the `.html.erb` extension?

15.10   How are form control data gotten by an action method?

15.11   How can a template access the instance variables defined in an action method?

15.12   In what directory are database files stored?

15.13   What kinds of operations are provided by the action methods generated by `scaffold`?

15.14   What is the basis for the acronym CRUD?

15.15 What Rails command actually builds a database?

15.16 What is described in a schema file?

15.17 Explain in detail the use of `validate_presence_of`.

15.18 Describe the command that is used to add a column to a table of a database.

15.19 In what directory are style sheets stored?

15.20 What is a layout?

Exercises

15.1 Describe briefly an MVC application.

15.2 Describe briefly the ORM used by Rails.

15.3 Explain how migration files help a developer manage a database.

15.4 Build a simple Rails application that returns a static document to a requesting browser, where the static document is a brief description of you.

15.5 Build a Rails application that accepts two integer values, produces the product of the two values, and returns the product to the client.

15.6 Build a Rails application that constructs a database with a single table listing well-known players from some specific team sport with which you or someone you know is familiar. The table must have columns for name, age, and team for which the person plays. The application must accept user requests for players of a specific team and age range and return a list of such people from the database.

15.7 Modify the example application of Exercise 15.6 to add a column for position played by the person. Also, modify the query form to include position played.

Introduction to Java

This appendix provides a quick introduction to Java for programmers who are familiar with C++ and object-oriented programming. It covers only a small part of Java, focusing on the features needed to understand Java programs similar to those discussed in this book. In some cases—for example, concurrency—the discussion of a topic can be found in the chapter of the book in which it is used, rather than in this appendix.

This appendix begins with a broad overview of the features and capabilities of Java. The data types and data structures of Java are then discussed, as well as the control statements. Next, it introduces the class definitions of Java, including some of the details of data and method definitions. Java interfaces, which provide a limited kind of multiple inheritance, are then discussed. This is followed by a description of Java exception handling.

A.1 Overview of Java

Java is based on C++, so it is closely related to that language. However, some parts of C++ were left out of the design of Java in an attempt to make it smaller and simpler. Other C++ features were redesigned in Java. Java also includes some constructs that are not part of C++. In comparison with C++, Java can be characterized by the following categories of differences: exclusive support for object-oriented programming, no user-defined overloading, implicit deallocation of heap objects, use of interfaces, lack of pointers, and far fewer type coercions.

C++ was designed originally as an extension to C to provide support for object-oriented programming. Because virtually nothing was left out of C, C++ supports procedure-oriented programming as well as object-oriented programming. Java does not support procedure-oriented programming. In practical terms, this means that subprograms in Java can only appear as methods defined in class definitions. The same is true for data definitions. Therefore, all data and functionality are associated with classes, and therefore with objects.

C++ allows users to define new operations that are specified by existing operator symbols. For example, if a user defines a class to support complex numbers, he or she can overload the definitions of + and – so that they can be used as binary operators for complex objects. For the sake of simplicity, Java does not allow user-defined operator overloading.

In C++, user programs can both allocate and deallocate storage from the heap. This leads to a number of different programming problems, including the possibility of dangling pointers. A dangling pointer is one that is pointing to a memory cell that has been explicitly deallocated from its previous use and possibly reallocated to a new use. Some of these problems are avoided by making heap storage deallocation a system responsibility rather than a user one. In Java, all heap storage deallocation is implicit and a technique named *garbage collection* is used to reclaim heap storage that has been implicitly deallocated.

In C++, a user program can define a class to extend two or more different classes, thereby making use of multiple inheritance. Although multiple inheritance is sometimes convenient, it has some disadvantages, among them the possibility of designing programs whose complexity makes them difficult to understand. For this reason, Java does not support multiple inheritance. In its place, Java has interfaces, which provide some of the functionality of multiple inheritance. Interfaces are discussed in Section A.4.

Pointers are notoriously risky, especially when pointer arithmetic is allowed. Java does not include pointers. Instead, Java provides references, which are also supported by C++, though in a somewhat different way. Reference variables in Java are used to reference objects, rather than memory cells, so they cannot be used as the operands of arithmetic operators. This, in conjunction with the lack of a deallocation operator for heap objects, makes references far safer than the pointers of C++.

In C++, as in many other programming languages, it is legal to assign a value of any numeric type to a variable of any other numeric type. This requires the compiler to build type conversion code, called *coercions*, into the program. Half of these conversions are narrowing conversions, in which it may not be possible to convert the value into even an approximation in the new type. For example, in C++ it is legal to assign a `float` value to an `int` variable, although this is a narrowing conversion. For example, `float` values such as `1.23E15` cannot be converted to anything close to that value as an `int` value. Java does not allow narrowing coercions in assignment statements. It is syntactically illegal to write such an assignment statement. This results in an increase in the overall safety of programs written in Java over those written in C++.

The control statements of Java are almost exactly like those in C++. One difference is that control expressions in control statements in Java must have Boolean values, whereas in C++ the control expression can be either Boolean or a numeric type. For example, in Java, the following statement is illegal:

```
if (2 * count) ...
```

Output to the screen from a Java application is through the object `System.out`, which represents the console window associated with the application. This object has two methods, `print` and `println`, which do something similar to what you would expect given their names. Both take a string parameter, but also permit variables as parameters. The values of non-`String` variables that appear in the parameter to `System.out.print` or `System.out.println` are implicitly converted to strings. The `print` method produces a string of output to the screen without attaching a newline character to the end. The `println` method does what `print` does, except that it attaches a newline character to the end. The string parameter to `print` and `println` is often specified as a catenation of several strings, using the + catenation operator. The following method calls illustrate the use of `print` and `println`:

```
System.out.println("Apples are good for you");
System.out.println("You should eat " + numApples +
                   " apples each week");
System.out.print("Grapes ");
System.out.println("are good, too");
```

If `numApples` is 7, these statements produce the following display:

```
Apples are good for you
You should eat 7 apples each week
Grapes are good, too
```

Naming conventions used in Java are as follows:

- Class and interface names begin with uppercase letters.
- Variable and method names begin with lowercase letters.
- Package names are all lowercase letters.
- Constant names are all uppercase letters, with underscores used as separators.

- Except for package and constant names, when a name consists of more than one word, the first letters of all embedded words are capitalized.
- Except for constant names, all but the first letters of embedded words are lowercase.

Java does not have an address-of operator (& in C++), a dereference operator (unary * in C++), or an operator to return the size of a type or object (sizeof in C++).

A.2 Data Types and Structures

In both C++ and Java, there are two kinds of data values: primitives and objects. This is a compromise design, for it provides efficiency in arithmetic operations on primitive values at the expense of complicating the object model of the language. Arithmetic operations can be done very quickly on primitive values, but are more costly when the operands are objects.

C++ has three different kinds of variables for objects: those whose value is a stack-allocated object, pointers that reference heap-allocated objects, and references that reference heap-allocated objects. In Java, there is only one way to reference an object, namely, through a reference variable. This simplicity is possible because all objects are allocated from the heap and there are no pointer variables in Java.

The Java primitive types are int, float, double, char, and boolean. Operations on primitive values are similar to those in other programming languages. Each of the primitive types has a corresponding *wrapper class*, which is used when it is convenient to treat a primitive value as an object.[1] The Java wrapper classes are named with the name of the associated primitive type, except that the first letter is capitalized. For example, the wrapper class for double is Double. An object of a wrapper class is created with the new operator and the class's constructor, as shown in the following example:

```
Integer wrapsum = new Integer(sum);
```

One of the purposes of wrapper classes is to provide methods that operate on primitive values. For example, a float value can be converted to a string by creating an object for it and using the toString method on that object. To convert the float value speed to a String object, the following could be used:

```
float speedObj = new Float(speed);
String speedStr = speedObj.toString();
```

As stated previously, all objects are referenced through reference variables. Reference variables are defined the same way as primitive variables. For example:

```
int sum;
String str1;
```

---

1. These classes are called wrapper classes because in effect they wrap a primitive value so it looks like an object.

In this example, sum is a primitive variable of type int, and str1 is a reference variable that can reference a String object, initially set to null.

Although an array of characters can be created and used in Java, it is more convenient to use the String and StringBuffer classes for character strings. String objects are immutable strings of characters. They can be created in two ways: either with the new operator or implicitly, as illustrated with the following declarations:

```
String greet1 = new String("Guten Morgen");
String greet2 = "Guten Morgen";
```

These two strings are equivalent. All Java String and StringBuffer objects use 2 bytes per character because they use the Unicode character codings, which are 16 bits wide.

String catenation, which is specified with the plus operator (+), can be used on String objects, as shown in the following example:

```
greet3 = greet3 + " New Year";
```

There are a number of methods that can be called through String objects to perform more or less standard string operations—for example, charAt, substring, concat, and indexOf. The equals method of String must be used to compare two strings for equality. Because strings are objects, the == operator is of no use between strings.

If a string must be manipulated, it cannot be a String object (because String objects cannot be changed). For this situation, a StringBuffer object can be used. StringBuffer objects are created with new, as shown in the following example:

```
StringBuffer greet3 = new StringBuffer("Happy");
```

The StringBuffer class has a collection of methods to manipulate its objects. Among them are append, which appends a given value to the end of the object; delete, which deletes one or more characters from the object; and insert, which inserts a value into its string object. In the cases of append and insert, if the given parameter is not a string, it is implicitly converted to a string.

In Java, arrays are objects of a class that has some special functionality. Array objects, like all other objects, are always referenced through reference variables and are always allocated on the heap. Array objects can be created with statements having the following form:

element_type array_name [] = new *element_type* [*length*] ;

For example:

```
int[] list1 = new int[100];
float[] list2 = new float[10];
```

If an array reference variable has been previously created, as with

```
int[] list3;
```

an object can be created with

```
list3 = new int[200];
```

As with other related languages, the subscript ranges of Java arrays always begin with zero. In a departure from C++, all references to array elements are checked to be sure the subscript values are within the defined subscript ranges of the array. Therefore, it is not possible to reference or assign an array element that does not exist. When a subscript that is out of range is detected, the exception `ArrayIndexOutOfBoundsException` is thrown. Java exception handling is discussed in Section A.5.

Java does not have the `struct` and `union` data structures that are part of C++. It also does not have the `unsigned` types or the `typedef` declaration.

A.3   Classes, Objects, and Methods

There are several important differences between C++ class definitions and those of Java. All Java classes have a parent class, whereas in C++ a class does not need to have a parent. The parent of a class is specified in the class definition with the `extends` reserved word. The general form of a class definition is

[*modifiers*] `class` *class_name* [`extends` *parent_class*] { . . . }

The square brackets here indicate that what they delimit is optional. Three different modifiers can appear at the beginning of a class definition: `public`, `abstract`, and `final`. The `public` modifier makes the class visible to classes that are not in the same package (packages are described later in this section). The `abstract` modifier specifies that the class cannot be instantiated. An abstract class is designed to be a class model that can be extended by nonabstract classes. The `final` modifier specifies that the class cannot be extended.

The root class of all Java classes is `Object`. A class definition that does not specify a parent is made a subclass of `Object`.

In C++, the visibility of variables and member functions (methods) defined in classes is specified by placing their declarations in `public`, `private`, or `protected` clauses. In Java, these same reserved words are used, but on individual declarations rather than on clauses. The meanings of these access modifiers are the same as in C++.

In addition to the access modifiers, a variable declaration can include the `final` modifier, which specifies that the variable is actually a constant, in which case it must be initialized. Java does not use C++'s `const` reserved word to specify constants.

In Java, all methods are defined in a class. Java class methods are specified by including the `static` modifier in their definitions. Any method without `static` is an instance method. Methods can also have several other modifiers. Among these are `abstract` and `final`. The `abstract` modifier specifies that the method is not defined in the class. The `final` modifier specifies that the method cannot be overridden.

Whereas C++ depends on classes as its only encapsulation construct, Java includes a second one at a level above classes, the *package*. Packages can contain more than one class definition, and the classes in a package are similar to the friend classes of C++. The entities defined in a class that are public or protected or have no access specifier are visible to all other classes in the package. This is an expansion of the definition of protected as used in C++, in which protected members are visible only in the class in which they are defined and in subclasses of that class. Entities without access modifiers are said to have *package scope*, because they are visible throughout the package. Therefore, Java has less need for explicit friend declarations and in fact does not include either the friend functions or friend classes of C++. Packages, which often contain libraries, can be defined in hierarchies. The standard class libraries of Java are defined in a hierarchy of packages.

A file whose class definitions are to be put in a named package includes a package declaration, as shown in the following example:

```
package cars;
```

The external visibility of entities in a class is controlled by the accessibility modifiers on the entities. Entities from other classes that are visible can be referenced through their complete name, which begins with the name of the package in which the class is defined and includes the name of the class in which the entity is defined. For example, if we have a package named `weatherpkg`, which includes a class named `WeatherData`, which defines a public variable named `avgTemp`, `avgTemp` can be referenced in any other class where it is visible with the following:

```
weatherpkg.WeatherData.avgTemp
```

An `import` statement provides a way to abbreviate such imported names. For example, suppose we include the following statement in our program:

```
import weatherpkg.WeatherData;
```

Now the variable `avgTemp` can be accessed directly (with just its name). The `import` statement can include an asterisk instead of a class name, in which case all classes in the package are imported. For example:

```
import weatherpkg.*;
```

A Java application program is a compiled class that includes a method named `main`. The `main` method of a Java application is where the Java interpreter begins. The following illustrates the simplest kind of Java application program:

```java
public class Trivial {
  public static void main (String[] args) {
    System.out.println("A maximally trivial Java
                        application");
  }
}
```

The modifiers on the `main` method are always the same. It must have public accessibility, and it cannot be extended. The `void` modifier indicates that `main` does not return a value. The only parameter to `main` is an array of strings that contains any command-line parameters from the user. In many cases, command-line parameters are not used. When they are used, the interpreter passes them to `main` as strings.

In C++, methods can be defined in a somewhat indirect way: The protocol is given in the class definition, but the definition of the method appears elsewhere. In Java, however, method definitions must appear in their associated classes.

As with C++, Java constructors have the same names as the classes in which they appear. C++ uses destructor methods to deallocate heap storage for instance data members, among other things. Because Java uses implicit heap deallocation, it does not have destructors.

In some object-oriented programming languages, including C++, method calls can be bound to methods either statically (at compile time) or dynamically (during runtime). In C++, the default binding of method calls to methods is static. Only methods defined to be virtual are dynamically bound. In Java, the default is dynamic.

Objects of user-defined classes are created with `new`. As with array objects, a reference variable is required to access an object, but both the reference variable and the object can be created in the same statement. For example:

```
MyClass myObject1;
myObject1 = new MyClass();
MyClass myObject2 = new MyClass();
```

The two reference variables, `myObject1` and `myObject2`, refer to new objects of class `MyClass`.

As is the case with C++, Java classes can have instance or class variables or both. There is a single version of a class variable per class; there is an instance variable for every instance of the class in which it is defined. Both instance and class variables that are not explicitly initialized in their declarations are implicitly initialized. Numeric variables are implicitly initialized to zero, Boolean variables are initialized to `false`, and reference variables are initialized to `null`.

Inside the methods of a class, instance variables are referenced directly. In other classes, instance variables are referenced through the reference variables that point at their associated objects. For example:

```
class MyClass extends Object {
    public int sum;
    . . .
}
MyClass myObject = new MyClass();
```

In other classes that either import `MyClass` or are defined in the same package, the instance variable `sum` can be referenced as follows:

```
myObject.sum
```

Similar to class methods, class variables are specified by preceding their declarations with the static reserved word.

The following is an example of a class definition that illustrates some of the aspects of Java we have discussed. It implements a stack in an array.

```java
import java.io.*;
class Stack_class {
  private int [] stack_ref;
  private int max_len,
              top_index;
  public Stack_class() {   // A constructor
    stack_ref = new int [100];
    max_len = 99;
    top_index = -1;
  }
  public void push(int number) {
    if (top_index == max_len)
      System.out.println("Error in push--stack is full");
    else stack_ref[++top_index] = number;
  }
  public void pop() {
    if (top_index == -1)
      System.out.println("Error in pop--stack is empty");
    else --top_index;
  }
  public int top() {return (stack_ref[top_index]);}
  public boolean empty() {return (top_index == -1);}
}
```

An example class that uses Stack_class follows:

```java
public class Tst_Stack {
  public static void main(String[] args) {
    Stack_class myStack = new Stack_class();
    myStack.push(42);
    myStack.push(29);
    System.out.println("29 is: " + myStack.top());
    myStack.pop();
    System.out.println("42 is: " + myStack.top());
    myStack.pop();
    myStack.pop();   // Produces an error message
  }
}
```

We must note here that a stack is a silly example for Java because the Java library includes a class definition for stacks.

A.4   Interfaces

Java directly supports only single inheritance. However, it includes a construct similar to a virtual class, called an *interface*, that provides something closely related to multiple inheritance. An interface definition is similar to a class definition except that it can contain only named constants and method declarations (not definitions). So, an interface is no more than what its name indicates, just the specification of a class. (Recall that a C++ abstract class can have instance variables, and all but one of the methods can be completely defined.) The typical use of an interface is to define a class that inherits some of the methods and variables from its parent class and implements an interface as well.

Applets are programs that are interpreted by a Web browser after being downloaded from a Web server. Calls to applets are embedded in the HTML code that describes an HTML document. These applets all need certain capabilities, which they can inherit from the predefined class `Applet`. When an applet is used to implement animation, it is often defined to run in its own thread of control. This concurrency is supported by a predefined class named `Thread`. However, an applet class being designed to use concurrency cannot inherit from both `Applet` and `Thread`. Therefore, Java includes a predefined interface named `Runnable` that supplies the interface (but not the implementation) to some of the methods of `Thread`. The syntax of the header of such an applet is exemplified by the following:

```
public class Clock extends Applet implements Runnable
```

Although this code appears to provide multiple inheritance, in this case it requires a further complication. For an object of the `Clock` class to run concurrently, a `Thread` object must be created and connected to the `Clock` object. The messages that control the concurrent execution of the `Clock` object must be sent to the corresponding `Thread` object. This is surely an inelegant and potentially confusing necessity.

A.5   Exception Handling

Java's exception handling is based on that of C++, but is designed to be more faithful to the object-oriented language paradigm.

A.5.1   Classes of Exceptions

All Java exceptions are objects of classes that are descendants of the `Throwable` class. The Java system includes two system-defined exception classes that are subclasses of `Throwable`: `Error` and `Exception`. The `Error` class and its descendants are related to errors that are thrown by the Java interpreter, such as running out of heap memory. These exceptions are never thrown by user programs, and they should never be handled there. The two system-defined direct descendants of `Exception` are `RuntimeException` and `IO-Exception`. As its name indicates,

`IOException` is thrown when an error has occurred in an input or output operation, all of which are defined as methods in the various classes defined in the package `java.io`.

System-defined classes that are descendants of `RuntimeException` exist. In most cases, `RuntimeException` is thrown when a user program causes an error. For example, `ArrayIndexOutOfBoundsException`, which is defined in `java.util`, is a commonly thrown exception that descends from `RuntimeException`. Another commonly thrown exception that descends from `RuntimeException` is `NullPointerException`.

User programs can define their own exception classes. The convention in Java is that user-defined exceptions are subclasses of `Exception`.

A.5.2   Exception Handlers

The exception handlers of Java have a form similar to those of C++, except that the parameter of every `catch` must be present and its class must be a descendant of the predefined class `Throwable`.

The syntax of the `try` construct in Java is exactly like that of C++.

A.5.3   Binding Exceptions to Handlers

Throwing an exception is quite simple. An instance of the exception class is given as the operand of the `throw` statement. For example, suppose we define an exception named `MyException` as follows:

```
class MyException extends Exception {
  public MyException() {}
  public MyException(String message) {
    super (message);
  }
}
```

The first constructor in this class does nothing. The second sends its parameter to the parent class (specified with `super`) constructor. This exception can be thrown with

```
throw new MyException();
```

The creation of the instance of the exception for the `throw` could be done separately from the `throw` statement, as shown in the following example:

```
MyException myExceptionObject = new MyException();
. . .
throw myExceptionObject;
```

Using the constructor with the parameter, our new exception could be thrown with

```
throw new MyException
    ("a message to specify the location of the error");
```

The binding of exceptions to handlers in Java is less complex than in C++. If an exception is thrown in the compound statement of a `try` construct, it is bound to the first handler (`catch` function) immediately following the `try` clause whose parameter is the same class as the thrown object or is an ancestor of it. If a matching handler is found, the `throw` is bound to it and is executed.

Exceptions can be handled and then rethrown by including a `throw` statement without an operand at the end of the handler. The newly thrown exception will not be handled in the same `try` where it was originally thrown, so looping is not a concern. This rethrowing is usually done when some local action is useful but further handling by an enclosing `try` clause or a caller is necessary. A `throw` statement in a handler could also throw some exception other than the one that transferred control to this handler; one particular exception could cause another to be thrown.

A.5.4   Exception Propagation

When a handler is found in the sequence of handlers in a `try` construct, that handler is executed and program execution continues with the statement following the `try` construct. If none is found, the handlers of enclosing `try` constructs are searched, innermost first. If no handler is found in this process, the exception is propagated to the caller of the method. If the method call was in a `try` clause, the search for a handler continues in the attached collection of handlers in the clause. Propagation continues until the original caller is found, which in the case of an application program is `main`. If no matching handler is found anywhere, the program is terminated. In many cases, exception handlers include a `return` statement to terminate the method in which the exception occurred.

To ensure that exceptions that can be thrown in a `try` clause are always handled in a method, a special handler can be written that matches all exceptions that are derived from `Exception`, simply by defining the handler with an `Exception` type parameter, as shown in the following example:

```
catch (Exception genericObject) {
. . .
}
```

Because a class name always matches itself or any ancestor class, any class derived from `Exception` matches `Exception`. Of course, such an exception handler should always be placed at the end of the list of handlers, because it will block the use of any handler that follows it in the `try` construct in which it appears. The search for a matching handler is sequential, and the search ends when a match is found.

The object parameter to an exception handler is not entirely useless, as it may have appeared to be so far in this discussion. During program execution, the Java runtime system stores the class name of every object in the program. The method `getClass` can be used to get an object that stores the class name, which itself can be gotten with the `getName` method. So, we can retrieve the name of the class of the actual parameter from the `throw` statement that caused the handler's execution. For the handler above, this is done with

```
genericObject.getClass().getName()
```

The message associated with the parameter object, which is created by the constructor, can be obtained with

```
genericObject.getMessage()
```

A.5.5   The `throws` Clause

The `throws` clause of Java has an appearance and placement (in a program) similar to that of the `throw` specification of C++. However, the semantics of `throws` is completely different from that of the C++ `throw` clause.

The appearance of an exception class name in the `throws` clause of a Java method specifies that that exception class or any of its descendant exception classes can be thrown by the method. For example, when a method specifies that it can throw `IOException`, it means it can throw an `IOException` object or an object of any of its descendant classes, such as `EOFException`.

Exceptions of class `Error` and `RuntimeException` and their descendants are called *unchecked exceptions*. All other exceptions are called *checked exceptions*. Unchecked exceptions are never a concern of the compiler. However, the compiler ensures that all checked exceptions a method can throw are either listed in its `throws` clause or handled in the method. The reason that exceptions of the classes `Error` and `RuntimeException` and their descendants are unchecked is that any method can throw them.

A method cannot declare more exceptions in its `throws` clause than the method it overrides, though it may declare fewer. So, if a method has no `throws` clause, neither can any method that overrides it. A method can throw any exception listed in its `throws` clause, along with any of the exceptions' descendant classes. A method that does not directly throw a particular exception but calls another method that could throw that exception must list the exception in its `throws` clause. This is the reason the `buildDist` method (in the example in Section A.5.6), which uses the `readLine` method, must specify `IOException` in the `throws` clause of its header.

A method that calls a method that lists a particular checked exception in its `throws` clause has three alternatives for dealing with that exception. First, it can catch the exception and handle it. Second, it can catch the exception and throw an exception that is listed in its own `throws` clause. Third, it can declare the exception in its own `throws` clause and not handle it, which effectively propagates the exception to an enclosing `try` clause, if there is one, or to the method's caller if there is no enclosing `try` clause.

Java has no default exception handlers, and it is not possible to disable exceptions.

A.5.6   An Example

The following example program illustrates two simple uses of exception handlers. The program computes and prints a distribution of input grades by using an array of counters. There are ten categories of grades (0–9, 10–19, ..., 90–100). The grades themselves are used to compute indexes into an array of counters, one for each grade category. Invalid input grades are detected by trapping indexing errors in the counter array. A grade of 100 is special in the computation of the grade distribution, because the categories all have ten possible grade values, except the highest, which has eleven (90, 91, ..., 100). (The fact that there are more possible A grades than Bs or Cs is conclusive evidence of the generosity of teachers.) The grade of 100 is also handled in the same exception handler that is used for invalid input data. Following is a Java class that implements this algorithm:

```java
import java.io.*;
// The exception definition to deal with the end of data
class NegativeInputException extends Exception {
  public NegativeInputException() {
    System.out.println("End of input data reached");
  } //** end of constructor
} //** end of NegativeInputException class
class GradeDist {
  int newGrade,
      index,
      limit_1,
      limit_2;
  int [] freq = {0, 0, 0, 0, 0, 0, 0, 0, 0, 0};
void buildDist() throws IOException {
//  Input: A list of integer values that represent
//         grades, followed by a negative number
// Output: A distribution of grades, as a percentage for
//         each of the categories 0-9, 10-19, ...,
//         90-100.
  DataInputStream in = new DataInputStream(System.in);
  try {
    while (true) {
      System.out.println("Please input a grade");
      newGrade = Integer.parseInt(in.readLine());
      if (newGrade < 0)
        throw new NegativeInputException();
      index = newGrade / 10;
      try {
        freq[index]++;
      } //** end of inner try clause
```

```
     catch(ArrayIndexOutOfBoundsException) {
        if (newGrade == 100)
          freq [9]++;
        else
          System.out.println("Error - new grade: " +
                             newGrade + " is out of range");
      } //** end of catch (ArrayIndex...
    } //** end of while (true) ...
  } //** end of outer try clause
  catch(NegativeInputException) {
    System.out.println ("\nLimits    Frequency\n");
    for (index = 0; index < 10; index++) {
      limit_1 = 10 * index;
      limit_2 = limit_1 + 9;
      if (index ==9)
        limit_2 = 100;
      System.out.println("" + limit_1 + " - " +
        limit_2 + "        " + freq [index]);
    } //** end of for (index = 0; ...
  } //** end of catch (NegativeInputException ...
} //** end of method buildDist
```

The exception for a negative input, `NegativeInputException`, is defined in the program. Its constructor displays a message when an object of the class is created. Its handler produces the output of the method. The `ArrayIndexOutOfBoundsException` is predefined and is thrown by the interpreter. In both cases, the handler does not include an object name in its parameter. In neither case would a name serve any purpose. Note that all handlers get objects as parameters, but they are often not useful.

Summary

Although Java is based on C++, it differs from that language in a variety of ways. The primary differences are Java's exclusive support for object-oriented programming, its lack of user-defined overloaded operators, its implicit deallocation and reclamation of heap objects, its interfaces, its lack of pointers, and its lower number of type coercions in assignment statements. Most of these differences were motivated by the perceived safety risks of C++.

Like C++, Java has primitive types and objects. Character strings can be stored as either `String` or `StringBuffer` objects, where `String` objects cannot be changed but `StringBuffer` objects can. Arrays are objects with special behavior. Array indices are always checked for range in Java.

Every Java class has a single parent class. Java does not have the public and private class derivations of C++. Java class derivation is always the same. Java has an additional encapsulation mechanism (besides the class)—the package. Entities defined in classes that do not specify a visibility have package scope, which makes them visible to all other classes in the package. Only one class in a package can be public. Rather than having public, private, and protected clauses in class definitions, the individual entities in Java classes can be defined to be public, private, or protected. All methods defined for a class are defined in the class. All binding of method calls to methods in Java is dynamic, unless the method is defined to be final, in which case it cannot be overridden and dynamic binding serves no purpose.

Class variables and class methods are specified to be static. In the absence of the `static` reserved word, variables are instance variables and methods are instance methods.

An interface defines the protocol of a class, but contains no variable definitions or method definitions. Interfaces are used to provide some of the benefits of multiple inheritance without all of the complexity of multiple inheritance. A class that implements an interface provides definitions for the methods of the interface.

Exception handling in Java is similar to that of C++, except that only objects of classes that descend from the predefined class `Throwable` can be exception objects. Propagation of exceptions is simpler in Java than it is in C++. The `throws` clause of Java is related to the `throw` clause of C++, but not closely. In Java, an exception class that appears in a `throws` clause means that the method in which `throws` appears can throw exceptions of that class or any of its descendants. A method cannot declare more exceptions in its `throws` clause than the method it overrides. A method that calls a method that can throw a particular exception must either catch and handle the exception, catch the exception and throw an exception that is declared in its `throws` clause, or declare the exception in its `throws` clause.

Named Colors and Their Hexadecimal Values

The actual colors can be viewed at the following address:

`http:/www.w3schools.com/html/html_colornames.asp`

Name	Hex Code	Name	Hex Code
aliceblue	F0FBFF	brown	A52A2A
antiquewhite	FAEBD7	burlywood	DEB887
aqua	00FFFF	cadetblue	5F9EA0
aquamarine	7FFFD4	chartreuse	7FFF00
azure	F0FFFF	chocolate	D2691E
beige	F5F5DC	coral	FF7F50
bisque	FFE4C4	cornflowerblue	6495ED
black	000000	cornsilk	FFF8DC
blanchedalmond	FFEBCD	crimson	DC143C
blue	0000FF	cyan	00FFFF
blueviolet	BA2BE2	darkblue	000088

Name	Hex Code
darkcyan	008B8B
darkgoldenrod	B8860B
darkgray	A9A9A9
darkgrey	A9A9A9
darkgreen	006400
darkkhaki	BDB76B
darkmagenta	8B008B
darkolivegreen	556B2F
darkorange	FF8C00
darkorchid	9932CC
darkred	8B0000
darksalmon	E9967A
darkseagreen	8FBCBF
darkslateblue	483D8B
darkslategray	2F4F4F
darkslategrey	2F4F4F
darkturquoise	00CED1
darkviolet	9400D3
darkpink	FF1493
darkskyblue	00BFFF
dimgray	696969
dimgrey	696969
dodgerblue	1E90FF
firebrick	B22222
floralwhite	FFFAF0
forestgreen	228B22
fuchsia	FF00FF
gainsboro	DCDCDC
ghostwhite	F8F8FF

Name	Hex Code
gold	FFD700
goldenrod	DAA520
gray	808080
grey	808080
green	008000
greenyellow	ADFF2F
honeydew	F0FFF0
hotpink	FF6984
indianred	CD5C5C
indigo	4G0082
ivory	FFFFF0
khaki	FDE68C
lavender	E6E6FA
lavenderblush	FFF0F5
lawngreen	7CFC00
lemonchiffon	FFFACD
lightblue	ADD8E6
lightcoral	F08080
lightcyan	E0FFFF
lightgoldenrodyellow	FAFAD2
lightgray	D3D3D3
lightgrey	D3D3D3
lightgreen	90EE90
lightpink	FFB6C1
lightsalmon	FFA07A
lightseagreen	20B2AA
lightskyblue	87CEFA
lightslategray	778899
lightslategrey	778899

Name	Hex Code
lightsteelblue	B0C4DE
lightyellow	FFFFE0
lime	00FF00
limegreen	32CD32
linen	FAF0E6
magenta	FF00FF
maroon	800000
mediumaquamarine	66CDAA
mediumblue	0000CD
mediumorchid	BA55D3
mediumpurple	9370D8
mediumseagreen	3CB371
mediumslateblue	7B68EE
mediumspringgreen	00FA9A
mediumturquoise	48D1CC
mediumvioletred	C71585
midnightblue	191970
mintcream	F5FFFA
mistyrose	FFE4E1
moccasin	FFE4B5
navajowhite	FFDEAD
navy	000080
oldlace	FDF5E6
olive	808000
olivedrab	6B8E23
orange	FFA500
orangered	FF4500
orchid	DA70D6
palegoldenrod	EEE8AA

Name	Hex Code
palegreen	98FB98
paleturquoise	AFEEEE
palevioletred	D87093
papayawhip	FFEFD5
peachpuff	FFDAB9
peru	CD853F
pink	FFC0CB
plum	DDA0DD
powderblue	B0E0E6
purple	800080
red	FF0000
rosybrown	BC8F8F
royalblue	4169E1
saddlebrown	8B4513
salmon	FA8072
sandybrown	F4A460
seagreen	2E8B57
seashell	FFF5EE
sienna	A0522D
silver	C0C0C0
skyblue	87CEEB
slateblue	6A5ACD
slategray	708090
slategrey	708090
snow	FFFAFA
springgreen	00FF7F
steelblue	4682B4
tan	D2B4BC
teal	008080

Name	Hex Code
thistle	D8BFD8
tomato	FF6347
turquoise	40E0D0
violet	EE82EE
wheat	F5DEB3

Name	Hex Code
white	FFFFFF
whitesmoke	F5F5F5
yellow	FFFF00
yellowgreen	9ACD32

Index